FINAL CRISIS

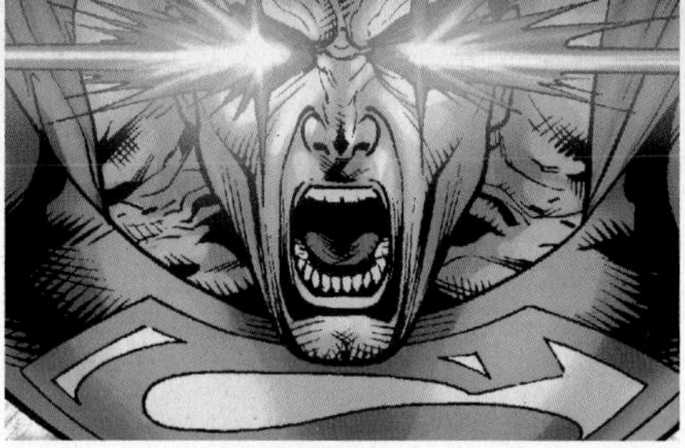

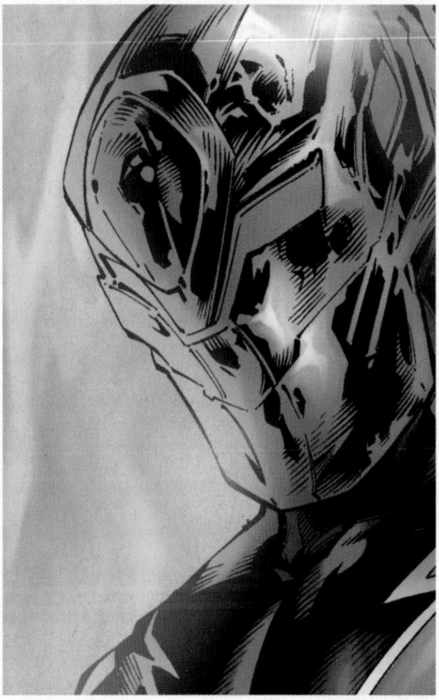

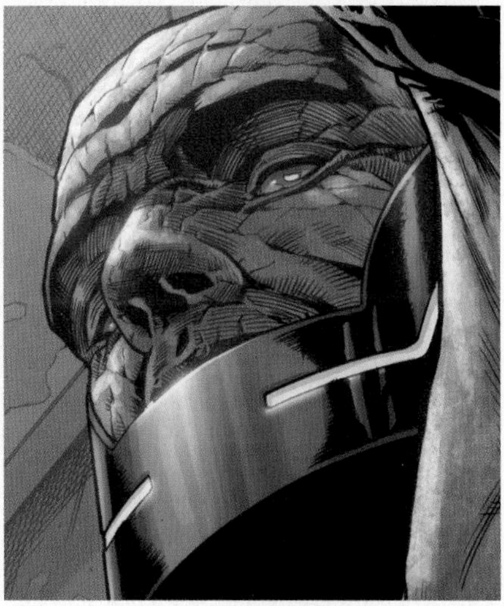

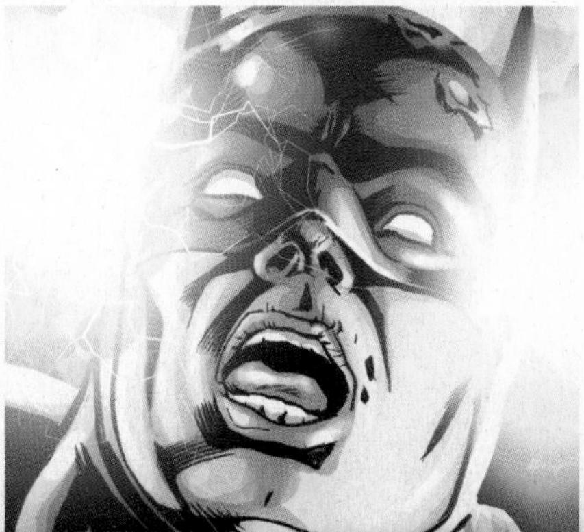

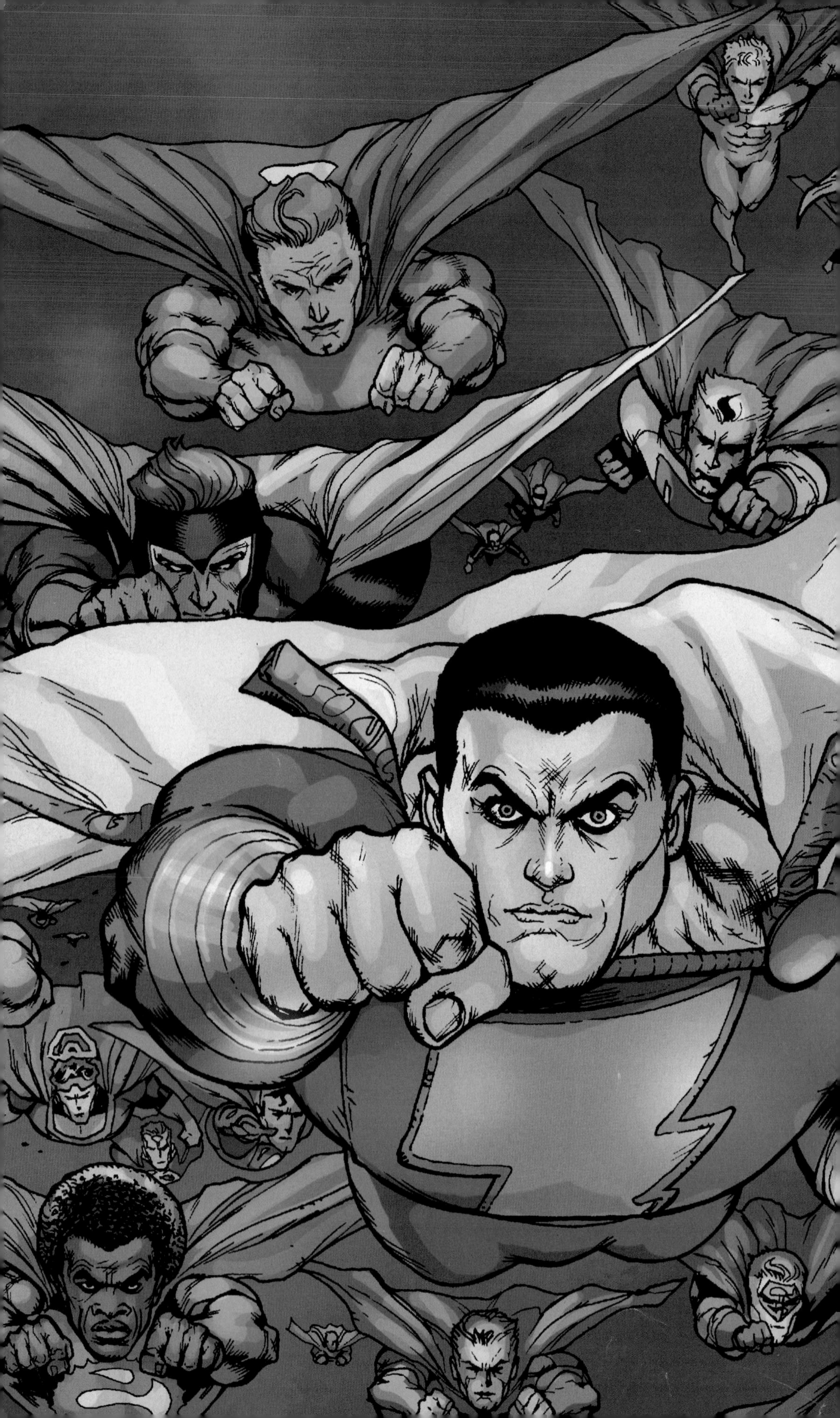

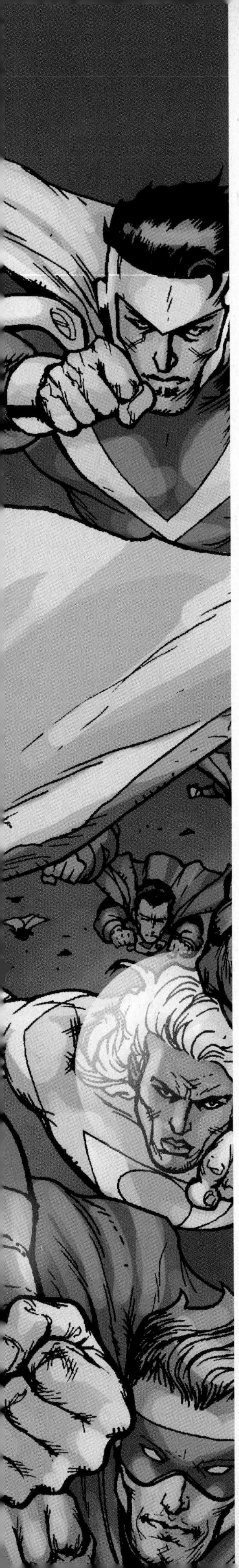

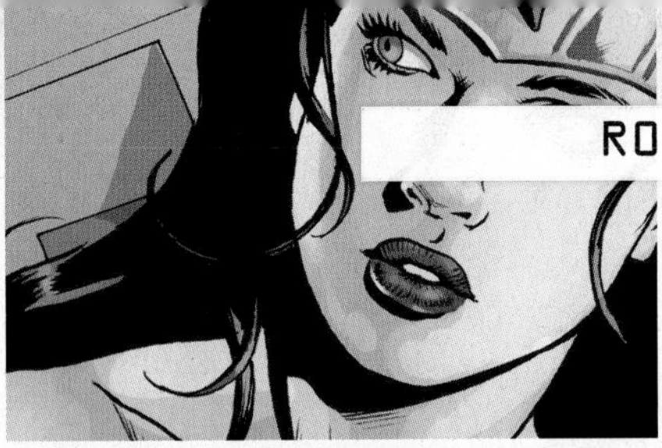

FINAL CRISIS

Grant Morrison
Script

J.G. Jones
Doug Mahnke
with
Carlos Pacheco
Matthew Clark
Jesus Merino
Marco Rudy
Christian Alamy
Tom Nguyen
Drew Geraci
Norm Rapmund
Rodney Ramos
Walden Wong
Derek Fridolfs
Rob Hunter
Don Ho
Art

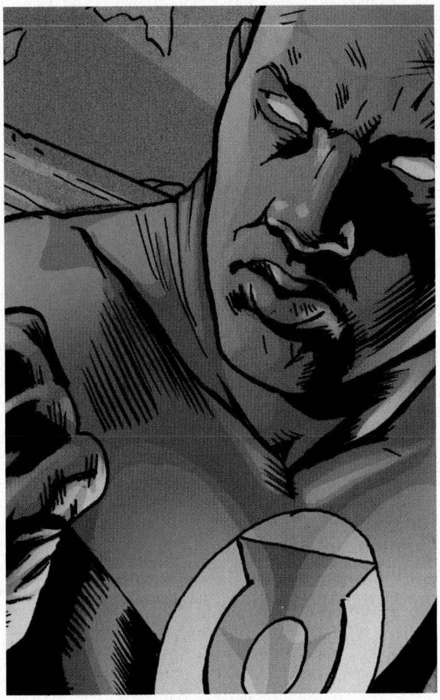

Alex Sinclair
Tony Avina
Pete Pantazis
David Baron
Richard & Tanya Horie
Color

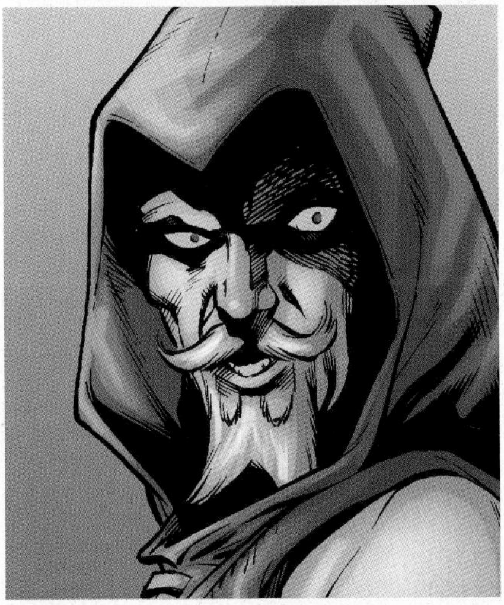

Rob Leigh
Rob Clark, Jr.
Travis Lanham
Steve Wands
Ken Lopez
Letters

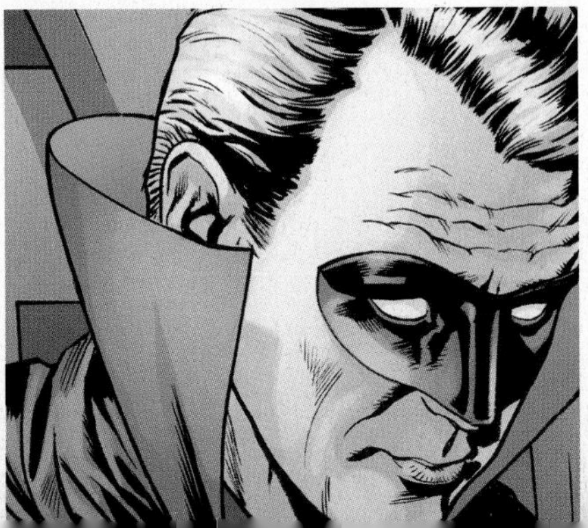

Dan DiDio   Senior VP-Executive Editor
Eddie Berganza   Editor-original series
Adam Schlagman   Associate Editor-original series
Bob Joy   Editor-collected edition
Robbin Brosterman   Senior Art Director
Paul Levitz   President & Publisher
Georg Brewer   VP-Design & DC Direct Creative
Richard Bruning   Senior VP-Creative Director
Patrick Caldon   Executive VP-Finance & Operations
Chris Caramalis   VP-Finance
John Cunningham   VP-Marketing
Terri Cunningham   VP-Managing Editor
Amy Genkins   Senior VP-Business & Legal Affairs
Alison Gill   VP-Manufacturing
David Hyde   VP-Publicity
Hank Kanalz   VP-General Manager, WildStorm
Jim Lee   Editorial Director-WildStorm
Gregory Noveck   Senior VP-Creative Affairs
Sue Pohja   VP-Book Trade Sales
Steve Rotterdam   Senior VP-Sales & Marketing
Cheryl Rubin   Senior VP-Brand Management
Alysse Soll   VP-Advertising & Custom Publishing
Jeff Trojan   VP-Business Development, DC Direct
Bob Wayne   VP-Sales

Cover by JG Jones

FINAL CRISIS

DC Comics, 1700 Broadway, New York, NY 10019
A Warner Bros. Entertainment Company
Printed in Canada. First Printing.
ISBN: 978-1-4012-2281-9
SC ISBN: 978-1-4012-2282-6

INTRODUCTION

It's another rainy Wednesday. We've been doing errands all afternoon in a borrowed car and we're on our way home after the last stop: Fat Jack's Comic Crypt in downtown Philadelphia. I'm in the passenger seat, giggling like a monkey.

"What are you laughing at?" my girlfriend asks in that way you do when you're concerned for someone's mental health.

In my best solemn narrator impression voice, I read aloud: "'As he speaks, the vast, slow motion **INVASION OF REALITY** begins. Machines bigger than **CITIES** arrive out of the **VOID** and **ANCHOR** themselves to the garbage heaps of **LIMBO**.'"

"It does not say that," she says with a breaking smile.

I turn the page and continue: "'Phantom armies clash on the battlefields of **LIMBO**. This strange, last outpost of **EXISTENCE**. The **FORGOTTEN** versus the **YET TO BE**. Like some half-remembered dream. All the rules of Existence are broken.'"

"It does not say that," she says, starting to chuckle.

"And then Superman yells, 'There are **52 WORLDS** in the multiversal super-structure! ...Warn everyone, like Paul Revere! Tell them Mandrakk is coming! **I'LL DO WHAT I CAN TO PLUG THE HOLE IN FOREVER!**'"

"Wow. And this is a Superman comic book? People are reading this?"

"It's SUPERMAN BEYOND 3D Number 2, which is part of the FINAL CRISIS miniseries, the number one title from DC right now."

We're stopped at a red light that never turns, so I show her the comic book. And she starts laughing, too. How old are we? We're both 38. But in this moment I feel like I'm 12 years old, reading aloud from CRISIS ON INFINITE EARTHS, riding home from an after-school trip to Comics Plus in Pomona, California with my eighth grade friends, courtesy of Kevin Kolodziej's endlessly benevolent supermom. Or, closer, I'm 28, reading aloud to a college friend on the phone some fantastic captions from a worn-out back issue of NEW GODS (or was it *Jimmy Olsen, Superman's Best Friend*? I can't remember) I'd just found at Another World Comics in Eagle Rock, California, where the excited narrator is describing the FOREVER PEOPLE, Jack Kirby's cosmic techno-hippies who live harmoniously in a psychedelic tree village somewhere outside Metropolis....

It's that laughter, that kind of involuntary-response joy/wonder/glee at your first awed, disbelieving encounter with an over-the-top-and-beyond idea/image in a comic book — something so **WEIRD** and **GREAT** and **TRUE** that you can't believe it actually got published — that is happening here, in this moment, as we wait for the accursed light to change, as we turn the pages and get to the part where Captain Adam demonstrates quantum super-position, and then Superman reaches his hand through… Well, you'll be finding out through what exactly soon enough. Let me just say this: I've been loving moments like this for as long as I've been reading comic books, which is a pretty long time, and no one has delivered more of them per issue during the last 20 years than writer Grant Morrison, from ANIMAL MAN, DOOM PATROL and (FINAL CRISIS overture) FLEX MENTALLO to New X-Men, JLA and ALL-STAR SUPERMAN. But FINAL CRISIS is his grandest-scale moment yet, a particularly harrowing section of the story that is the DC Universe, in which the ultimate conflict goes down—not who would win, Superman or Darkseid (although that's in here, too)—but the real biggie: existence versus non-existence! Is versus Isn't! **UNIVERSE VERSUS**   **!!!**

FINAL CRISIS is a major achievement of 21st century imagination and craft in mainstream media, works on countless levels, far too many for me to enumerate here. FINAL CRISIS is so good that although it's part of a continuing, decades-in-the-telling saga involving countless characters, you can follow the plot and dig on the ideas and the dialogue and the sheer spectacle of the events that spiral from the trash up into the transcendent, even if you're not familiar with all the backstory. (Rest assured that there are detailed annotations available online regarding previous references to Darkseid's hatred of music, which parallel earth Nubia and where her Wonder Horn comes from, and so on…) Of course, that's the way it's always been with DC Universe comic books: you don't always know everything about everyone, and sometimes you miss stuff, and sometimes you only suss out later what something was really all about. (Same is true for life in the real world, actually…) FINAL CRISIS continues in that tradition, but as you'll see, it's at a higher dose — a different pitch, a denser signal — than usual, one that mirrors the world we are living in, when too many things really are going terribly wrong all at the same time, when headlines really do scream about catastrophe, turmoil, doom, collapse and apocalypse.

And maybe that's this audacious work's genius, even more than its elegant architecture, its overwhelming dazzle, its virtuoso artwork by J. G. Jones and Doug Mahnke: the way that it shows us, sitting here in a car, a path *beyond* the current situation, out of economic cataclysm and endless horrible wars and ecological peril and unchanging red lights. We're being flat-out wowed into a very psychedelic, progressive, imaginative space by a superhero comic book. And that makes us laugh. We hum a brighter, richer tune. And then the light changes, and we go.

Plugging the hole in forever,

Jay Babcock
Philadelphia
February 2009

Jay Babcock is the editor and publisher of *Arthur*, the free bimonthly magazine of "homegrown counter-culture" and *Rolling Stone*'s "Hot Magazine" of 2005, whose contributors have included Alan Moore, Paul Pope, author Douglas Rushkoff, musicians Thurston Moore (Sonic Youth), David Byrne (Talking Heads), and many others. His writing on music, culture and ideas during the last 15 years has appeared in *Mojo*, *Vibe*, the *Washington Post*, the *Los Angeles Times*, and the *LAWeekly*.

ver to FINAL CRISIS #1 JG Jones

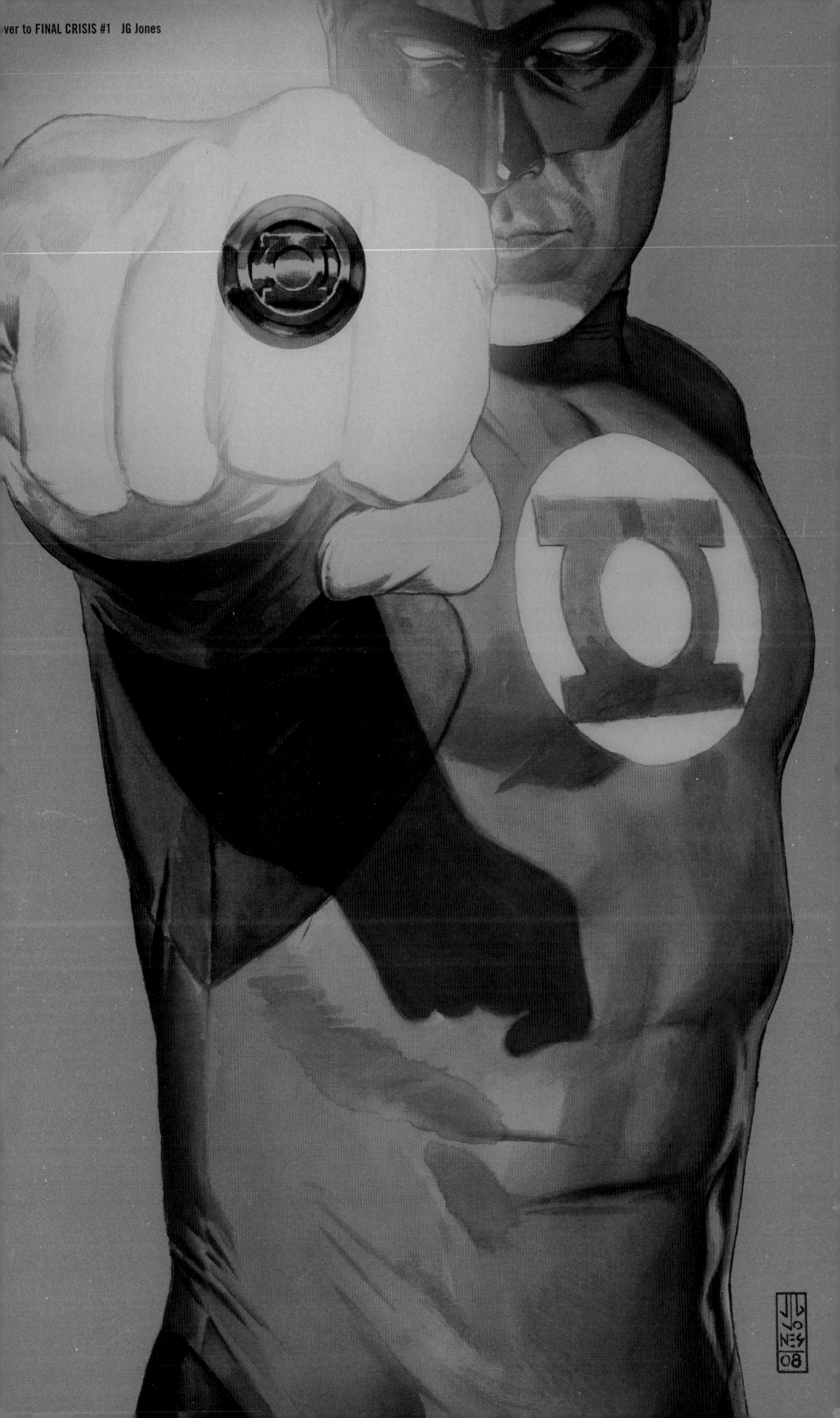
JG JONES
08

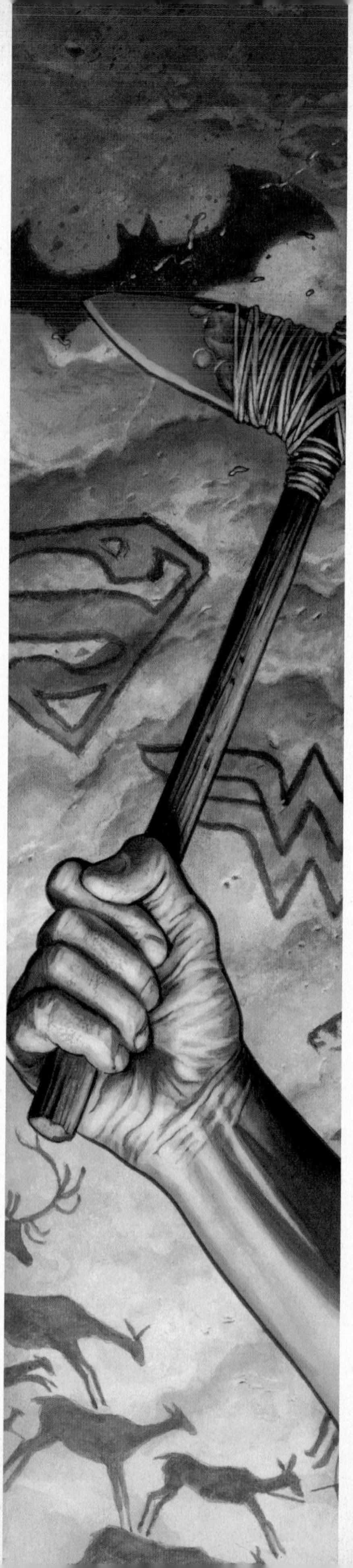

JG Jones

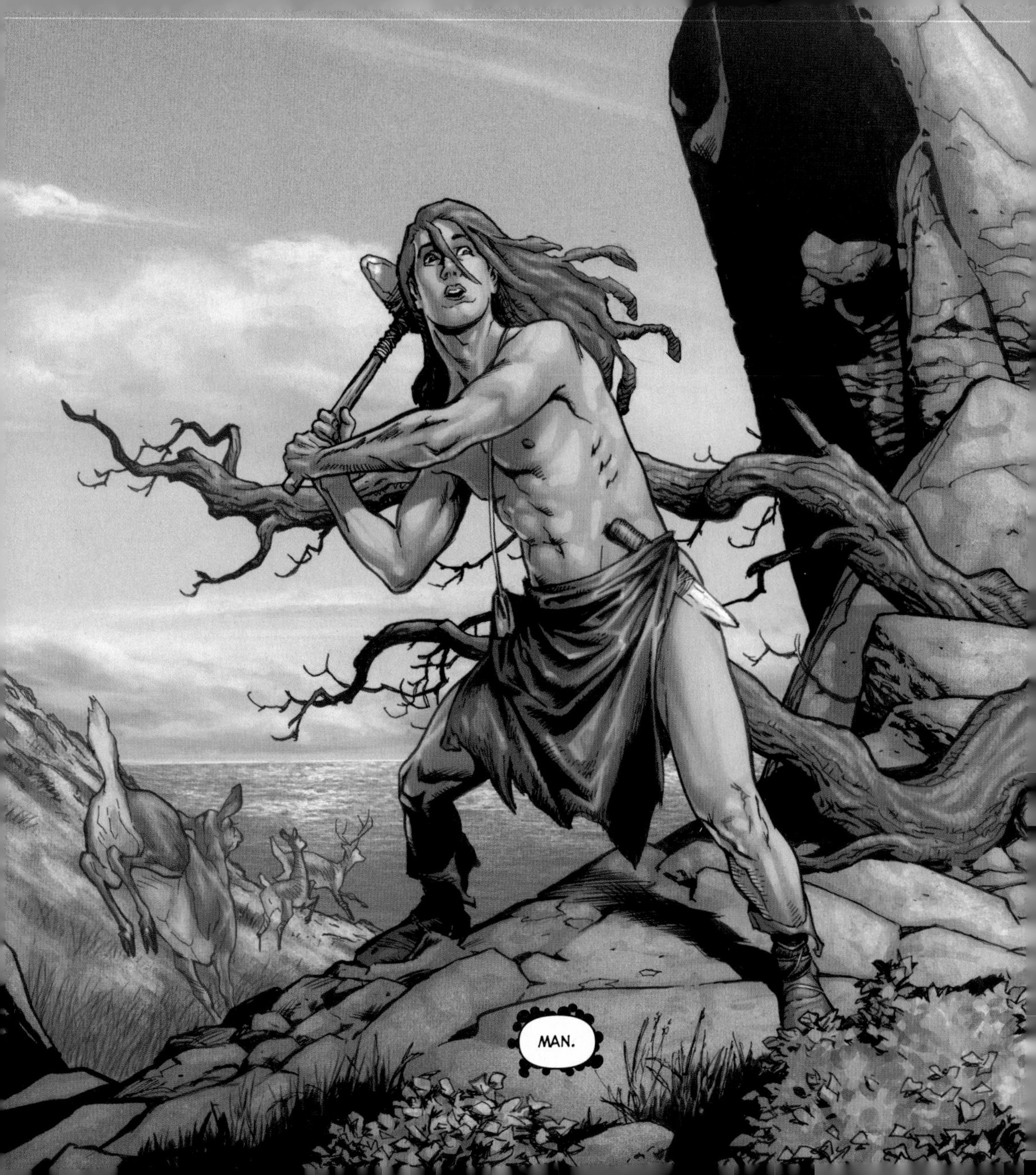
MAN.

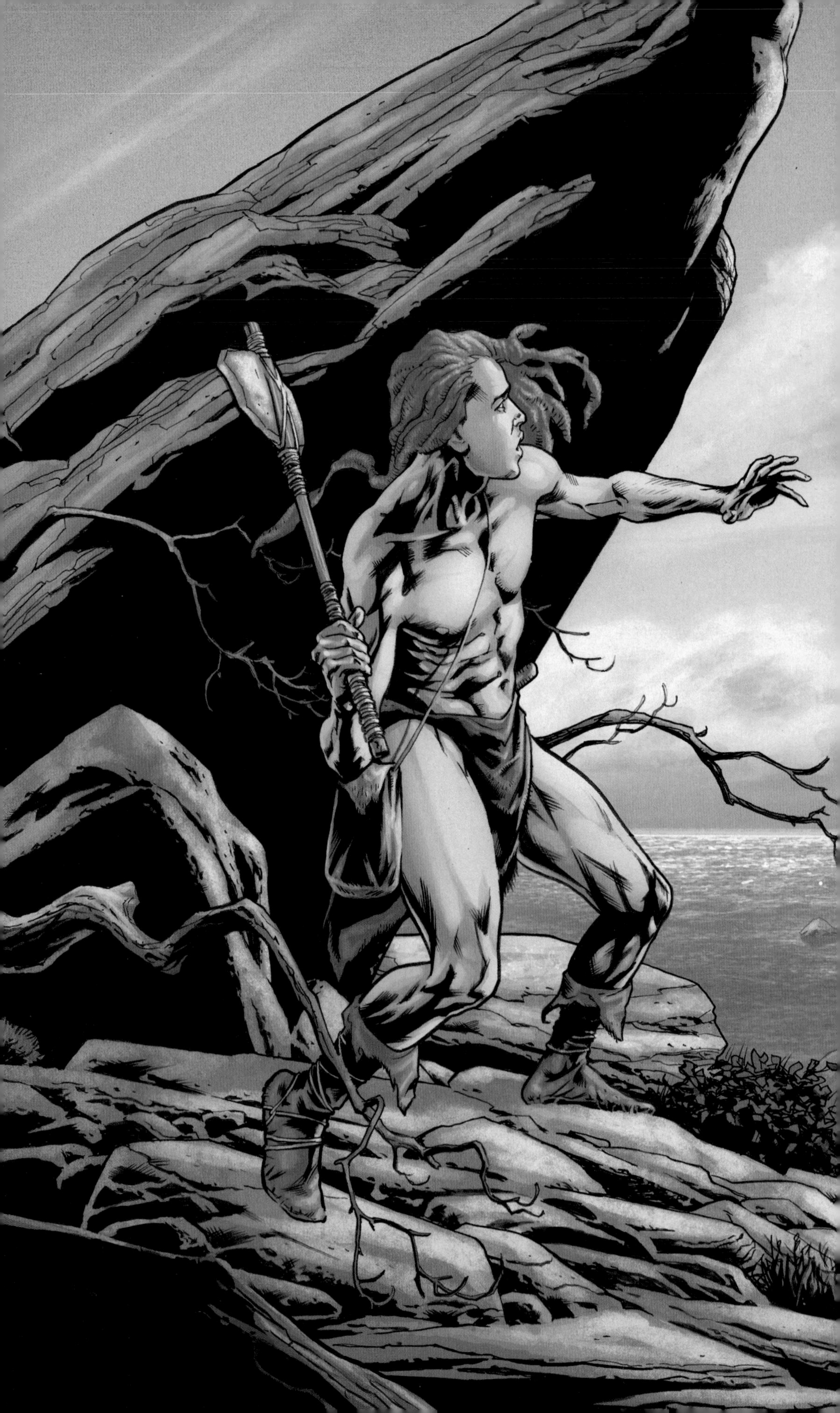

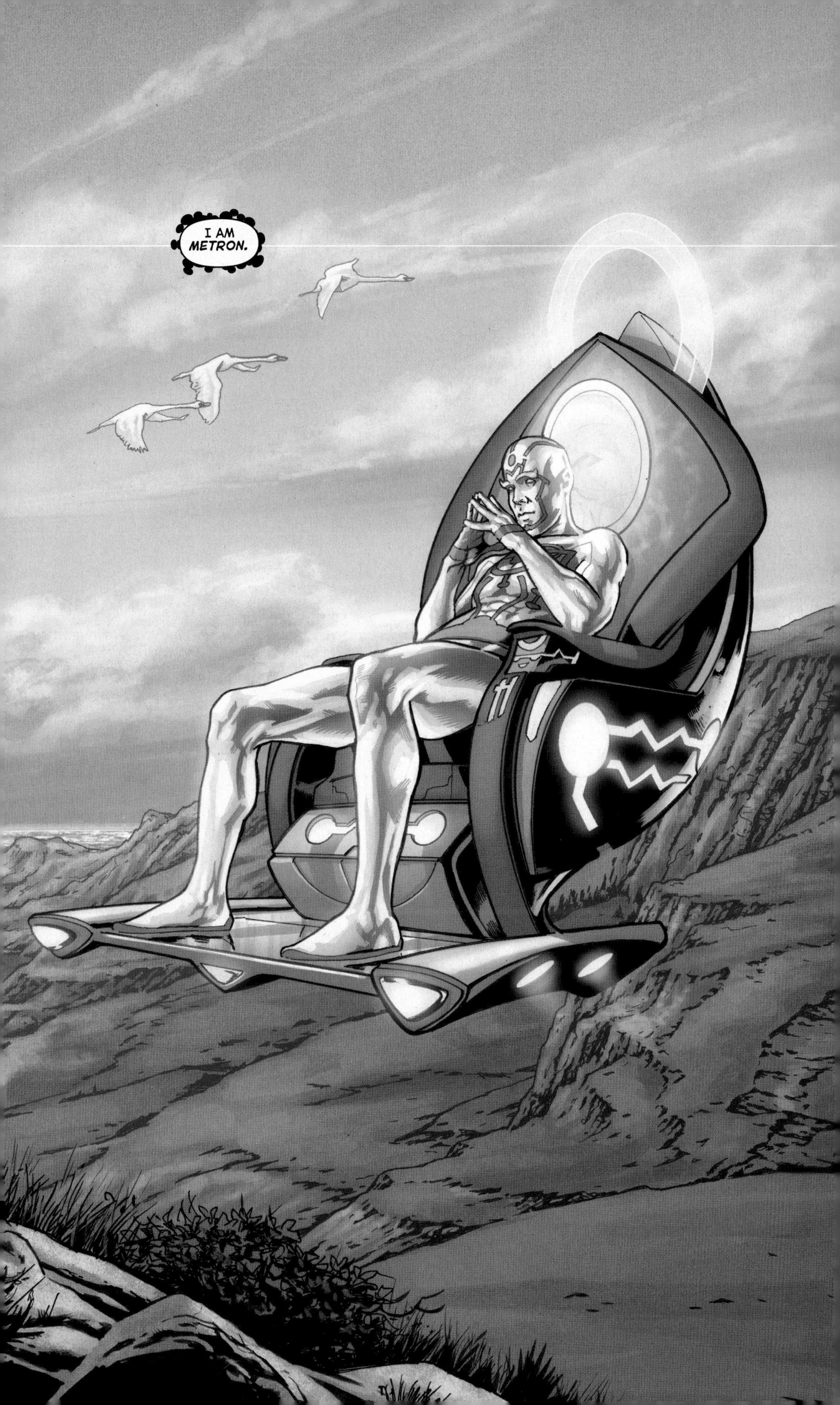
I AM METRON.

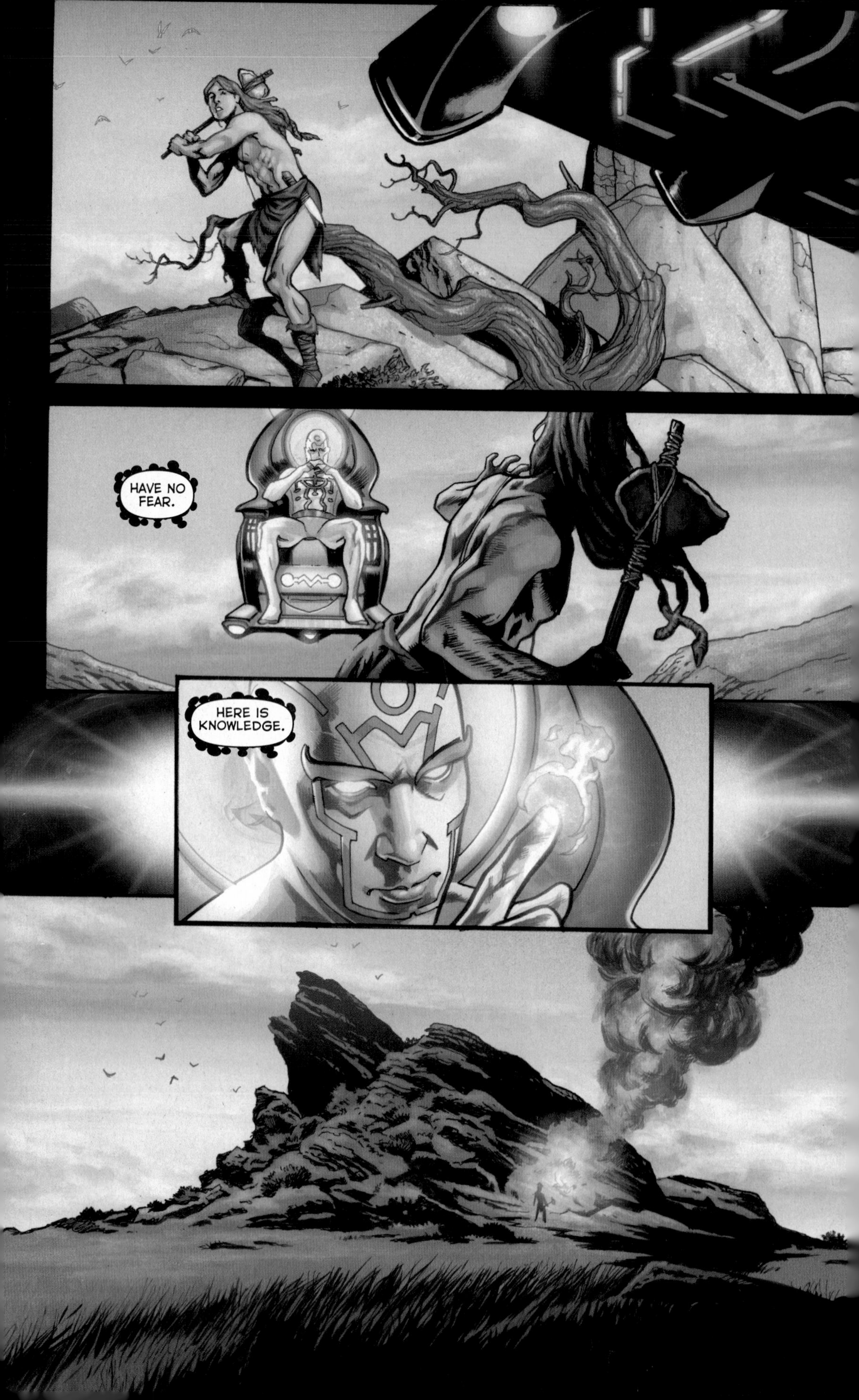
HAVE NO FEAR.
HERE IS KNOWLEDGE.

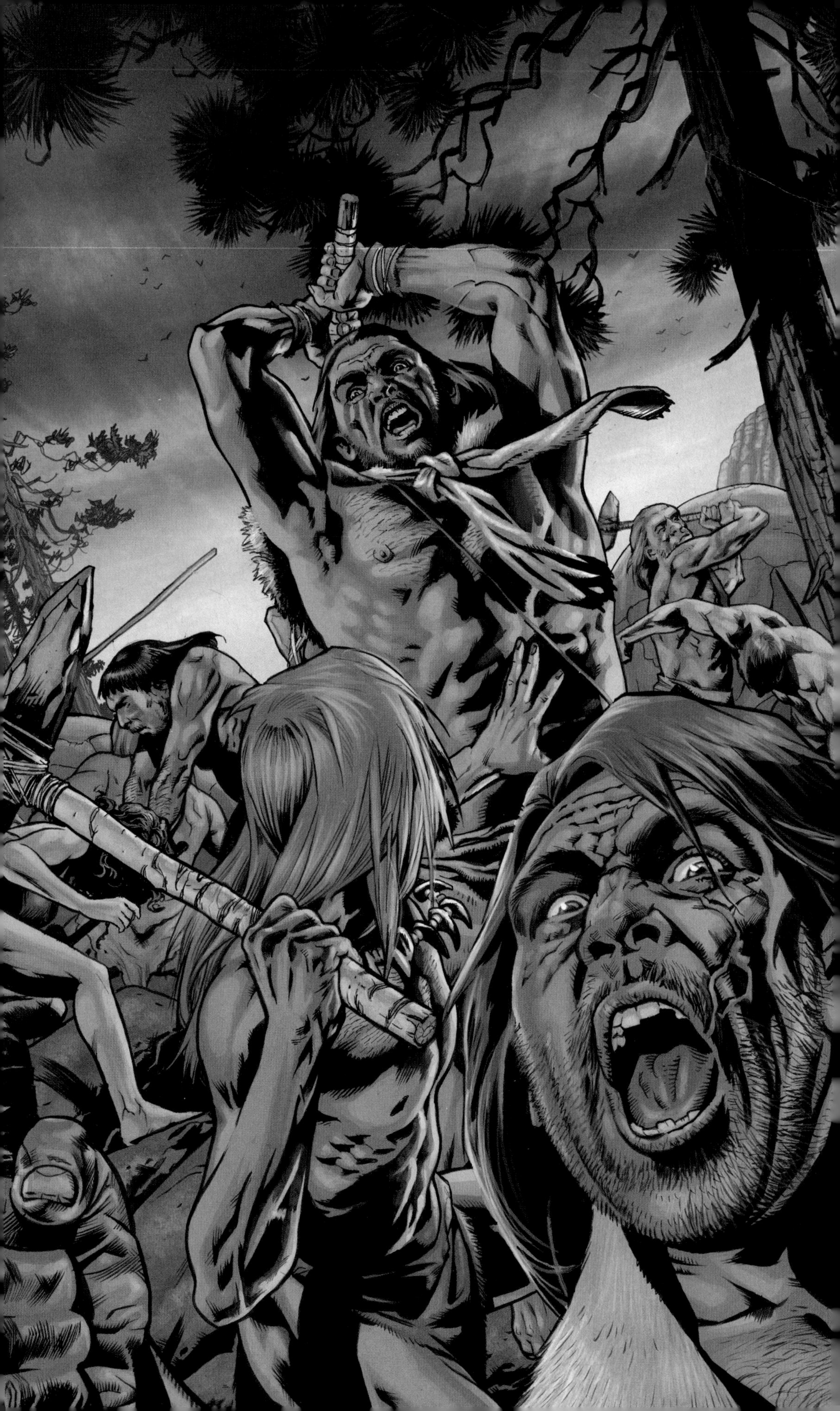

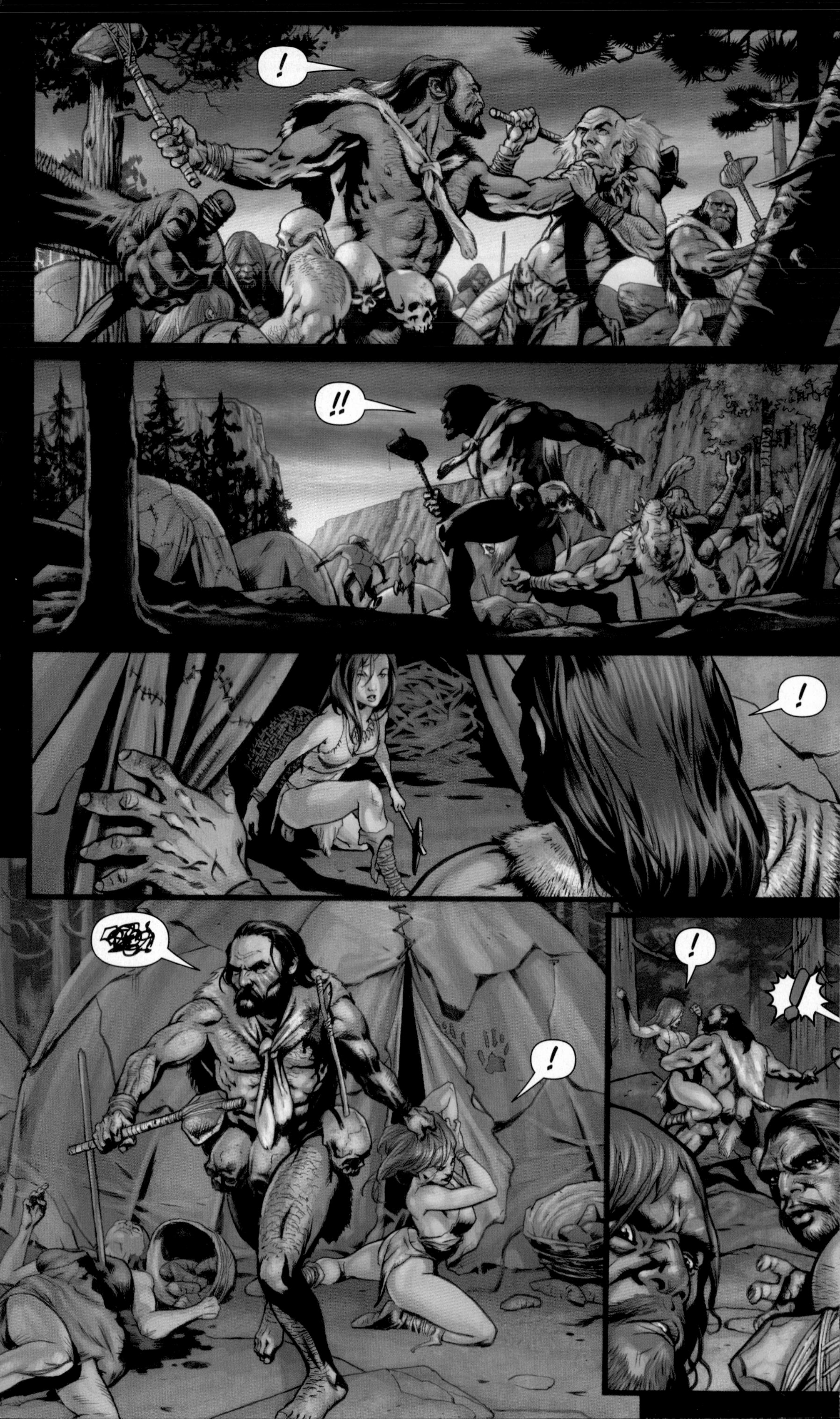
!
!!
!
!
!

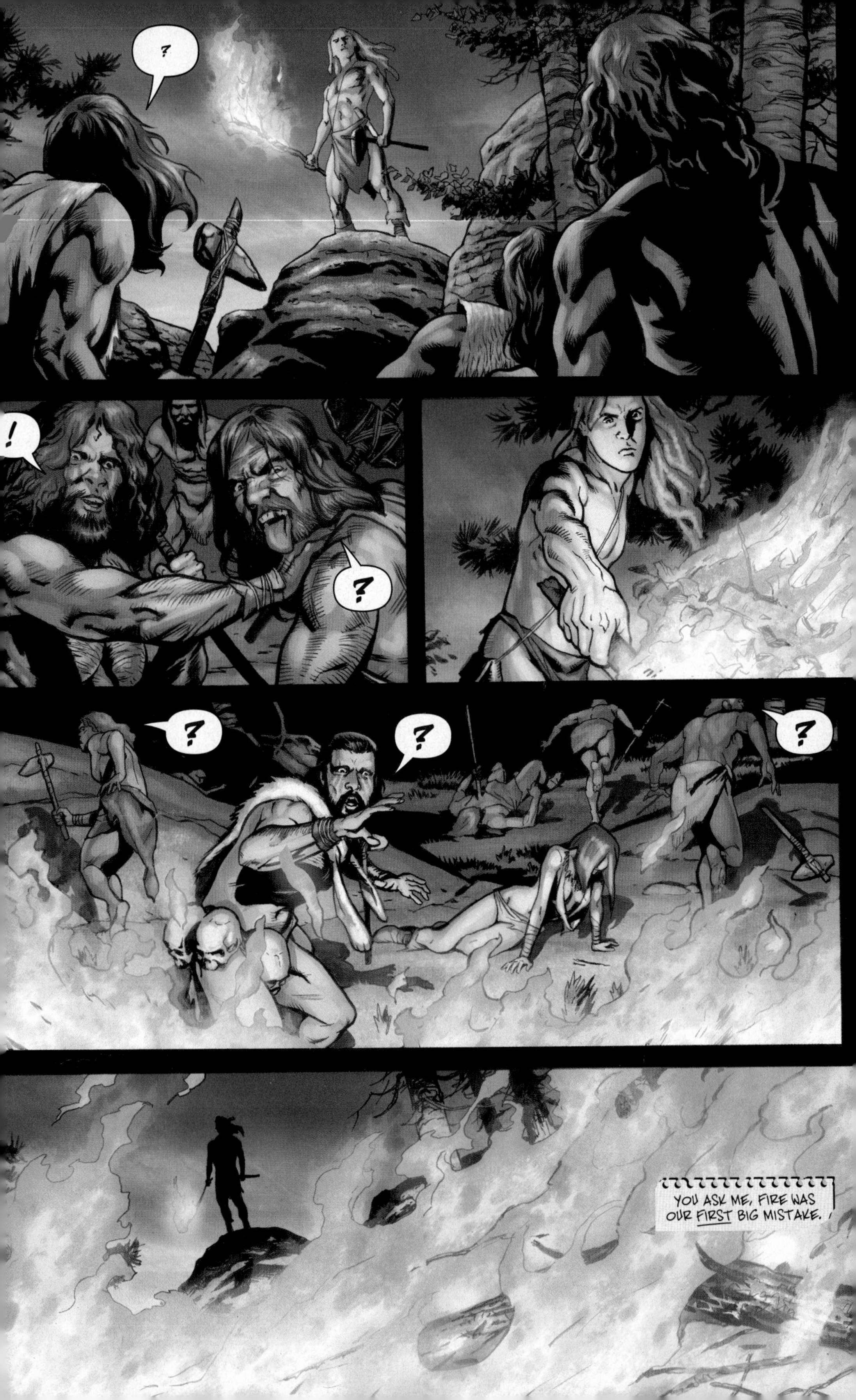
?
!
?
?
?
?
YOU ASK ME, FIRE WAS OUR FIRST BIG MISTAKE.

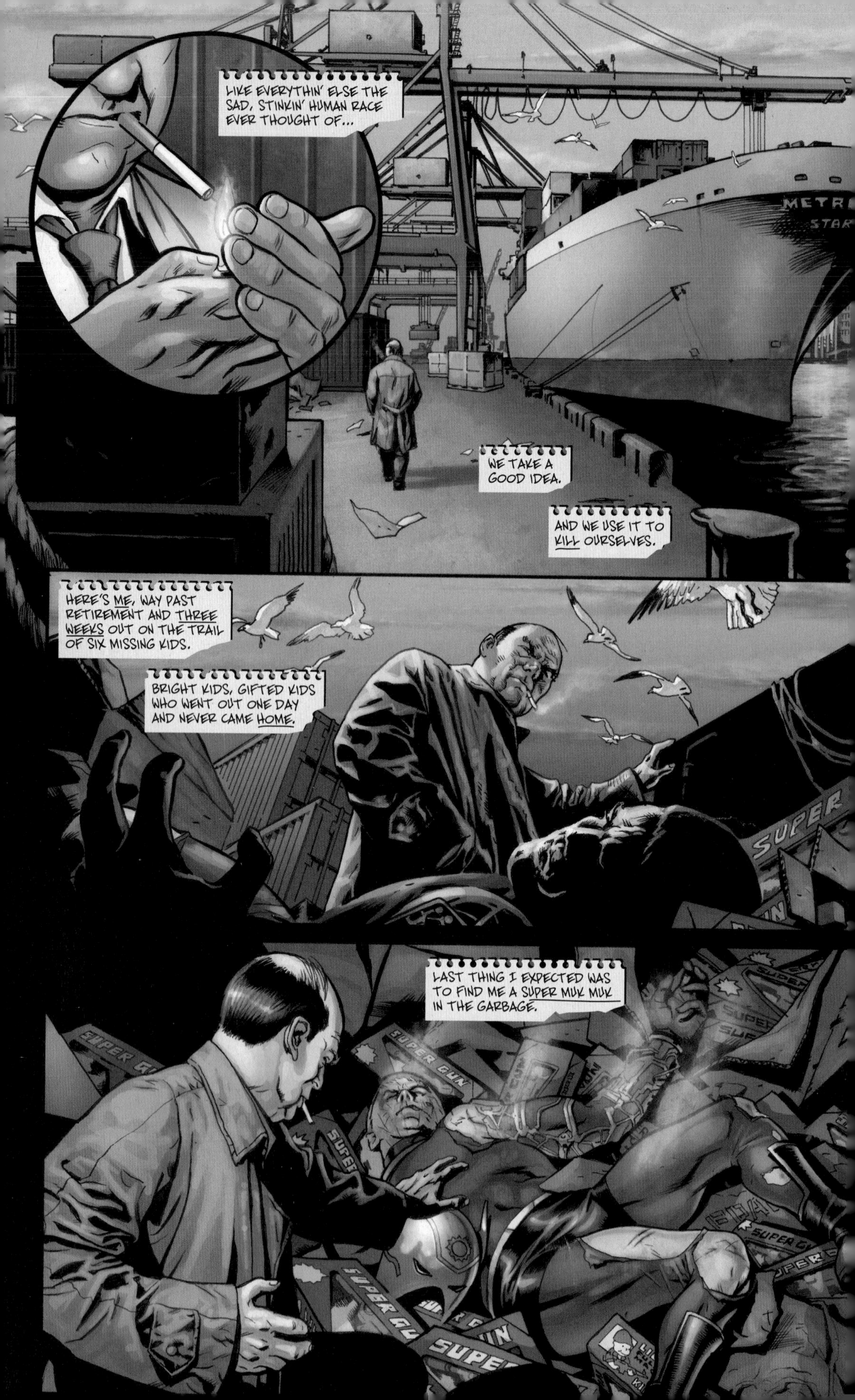
LIKE EVERYTHIN' ELSE THE SAD, STINKIN' HUMAN RACE EVER THOUGHT OF...
WE TAKE A GOOD IDEA.
AND WE USE IT TO KILL OURSELVES.
HERE'S ME, WAY PAST RETIREMENT AND THREE WEEKS OUT ON THE TRAIL OF SIX MISSING KIDS.
BRIGHT KIDS, GIFTED KIDS WHO WENT OUT ONE DAY AND NEVER CAME HOME.
LAST THING I EXPECTED WAS TO FIND ME A SUPER MUK MUK IN THE GARBAGE.

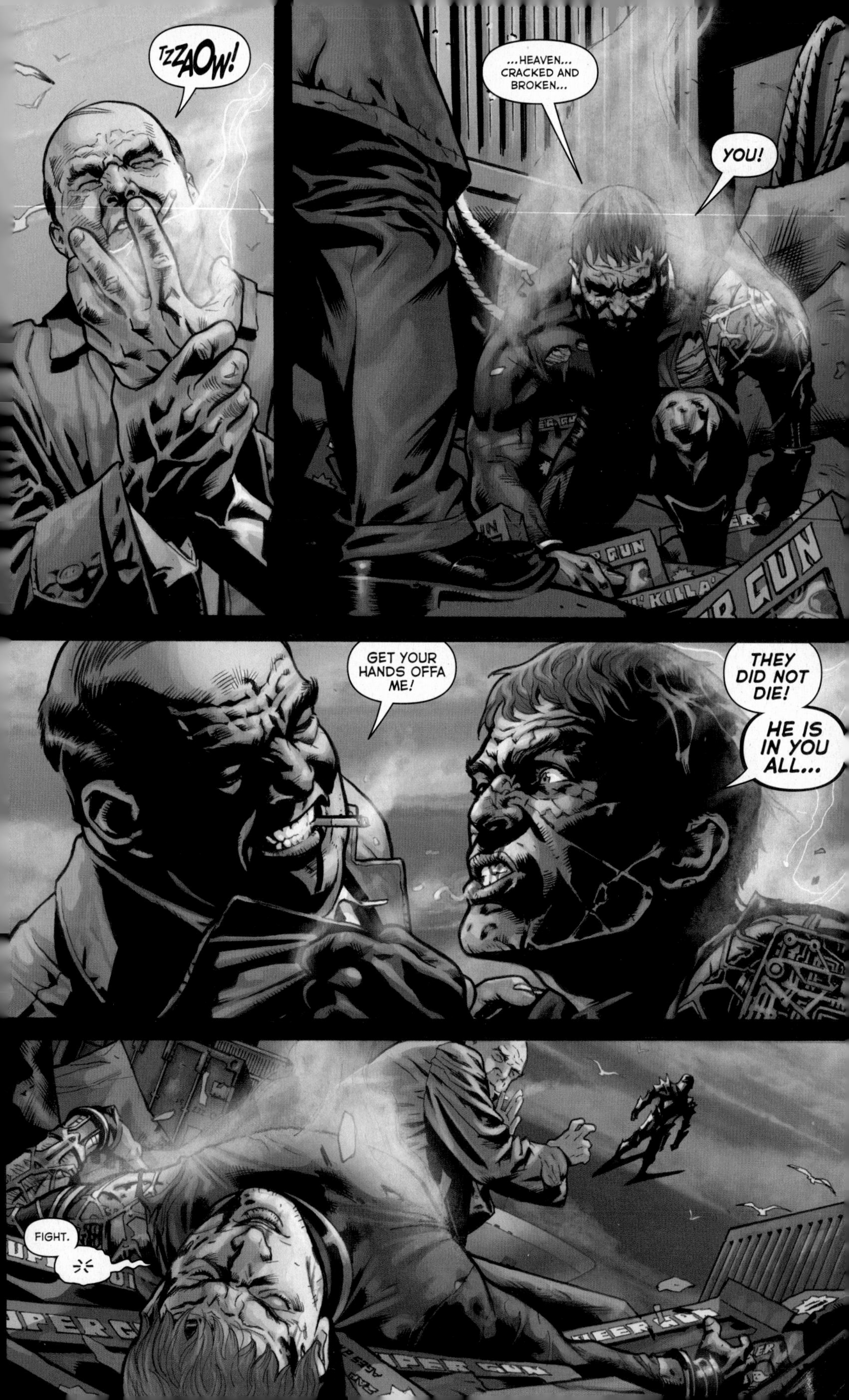
TZZAOW!
...HEAVEN... CRACKED AND BROKEN...
YOU!
GET YOUR HANDS OFFA ME!
THEY DID NOT DIE!
HE IS IN YOU ALL...
FIGHT.
SUPER GUN

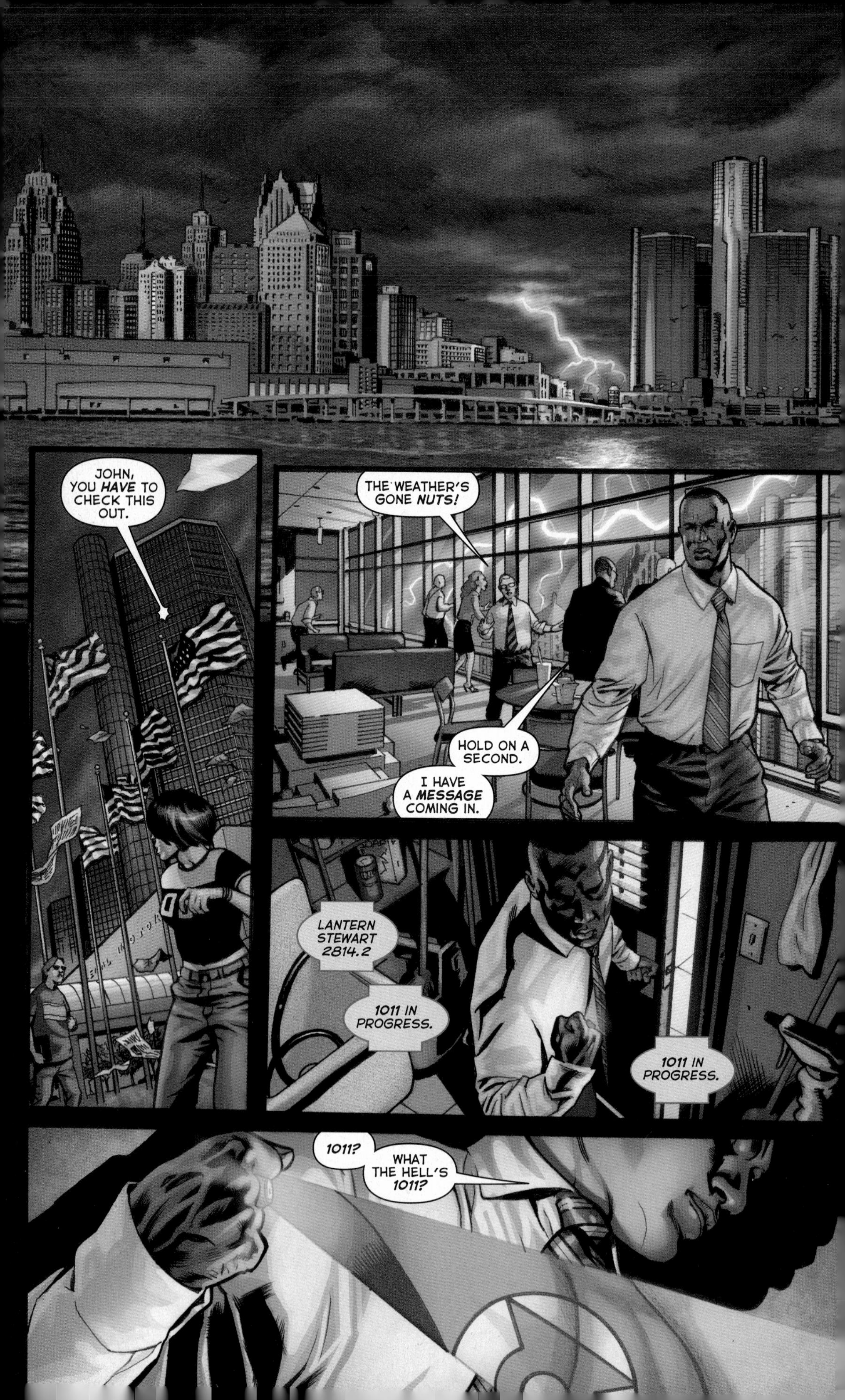
JOHN, YOU HAVE TO CHECK THIS OUT.
THE WEATHER'S GONE NUTS!
HOLD ON A SECOND.
I HAVE A MESSAGE COMING IN.
LANTERN STEWART 2814.2
1011 IN PROGRESS.
1011 IN PROGRESS.
1011?
WHAT THE HELL'S 1011?

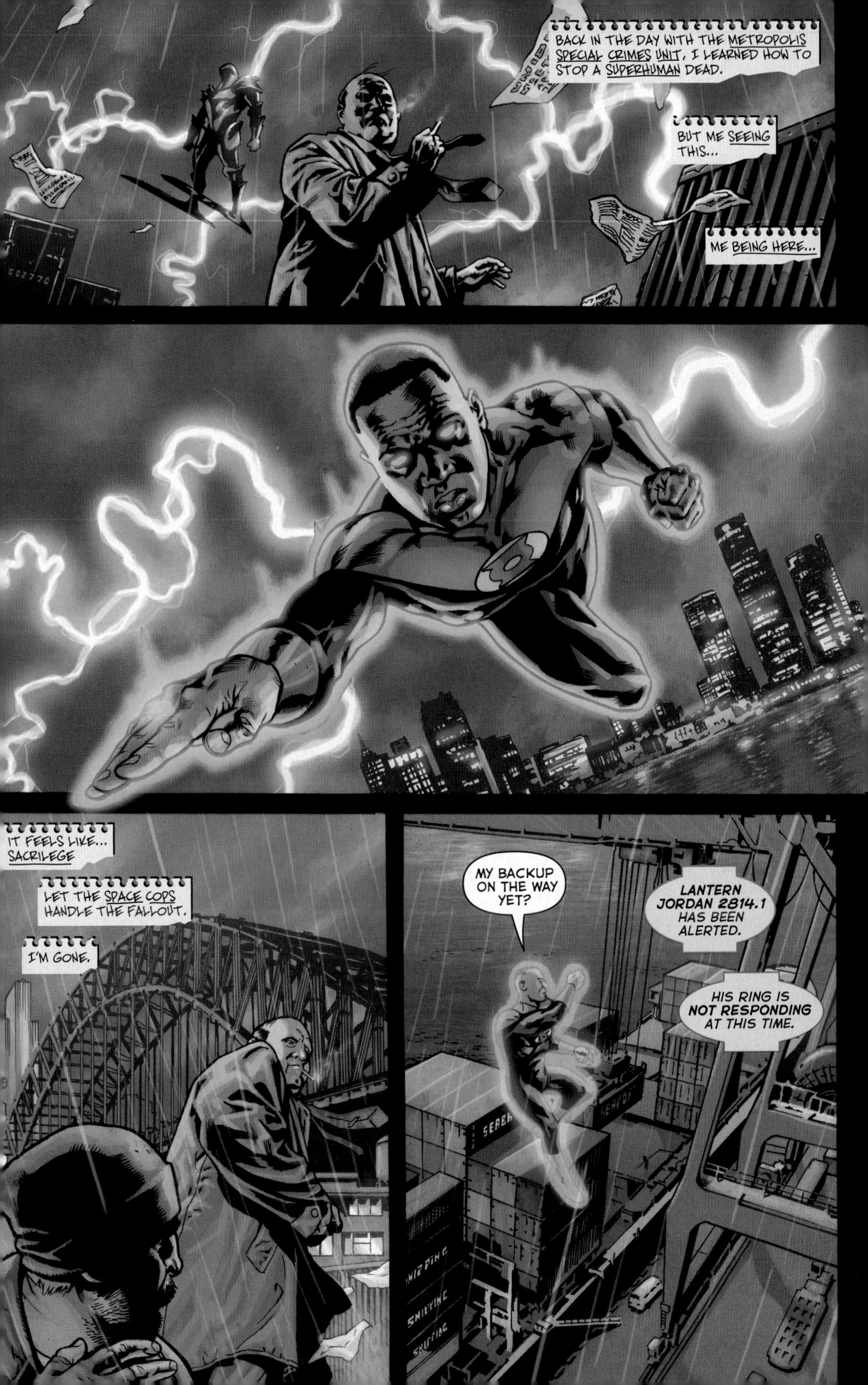
BACK IN THE DAY WITH THE METROPOLIS SPECIAL CRIMES UNIT, I LEARNED HOW TO STOP A SUPERHUMAN DEAD.
BUT ME SEEING THIS...
ME BEING HERE...
IT FEELS LIKE... SACRILEGE
LET THE SPACE COPS HANDLE THE FALLOUT.
I'M GONE.
MY BACKUP ON THE WAY YET?
LANTERN JORDAN 2814.1 HAS BEEN ALERTED.
HIS RING IS NOT RESPONDING AT THIS TIME.

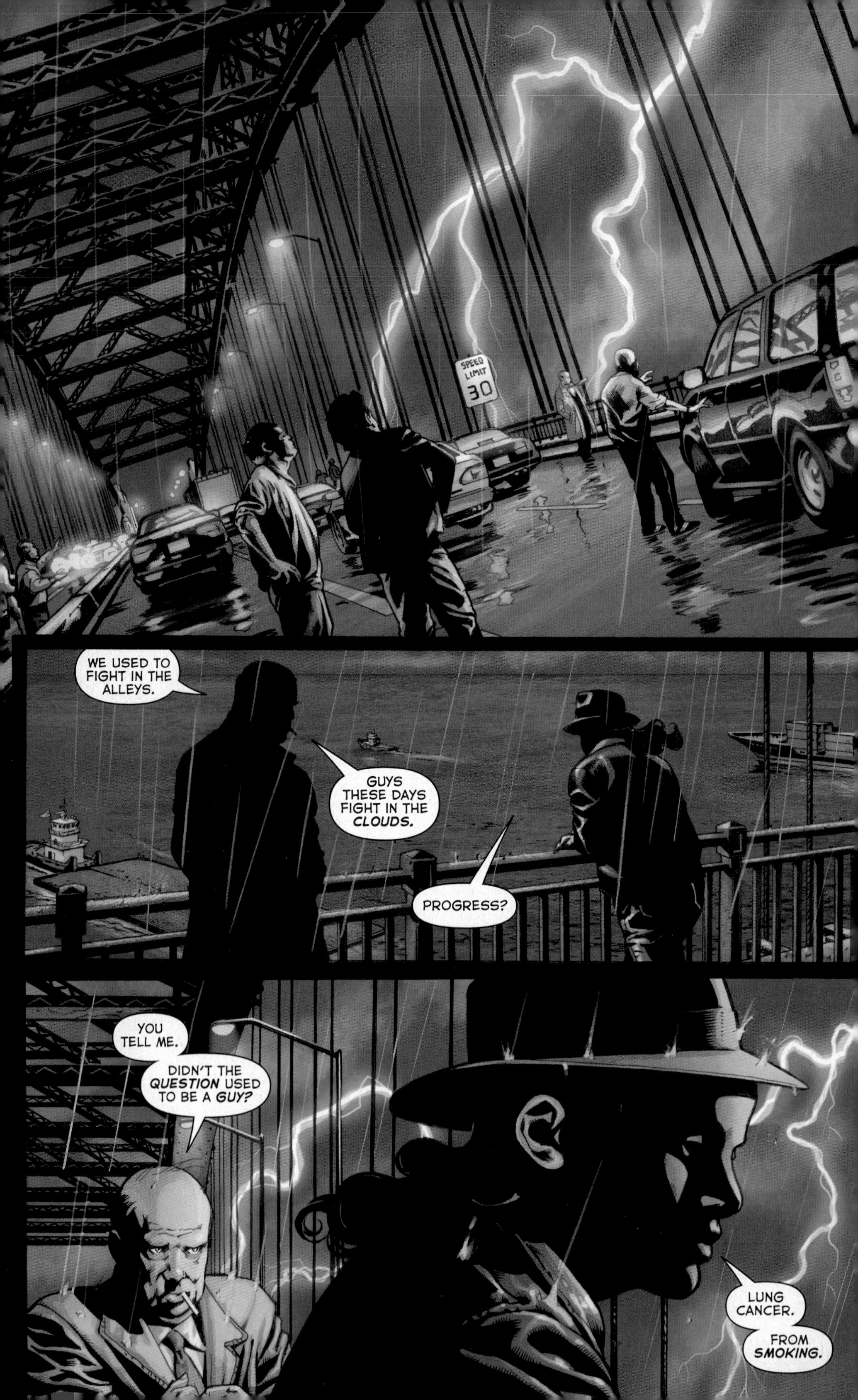
SPEED LIMIT 30
WE USED TO FIGHT IN THE ALLEYS.
GUYS THESE DAYS FIGHT IN THE *CLOUDS.*
PROGRESS?
YOU TELL ME.
DIDN'T THE *QUESTION* USED TO BE A *GUY?*
LUNG CANCER.
FROM *SMOKING.*

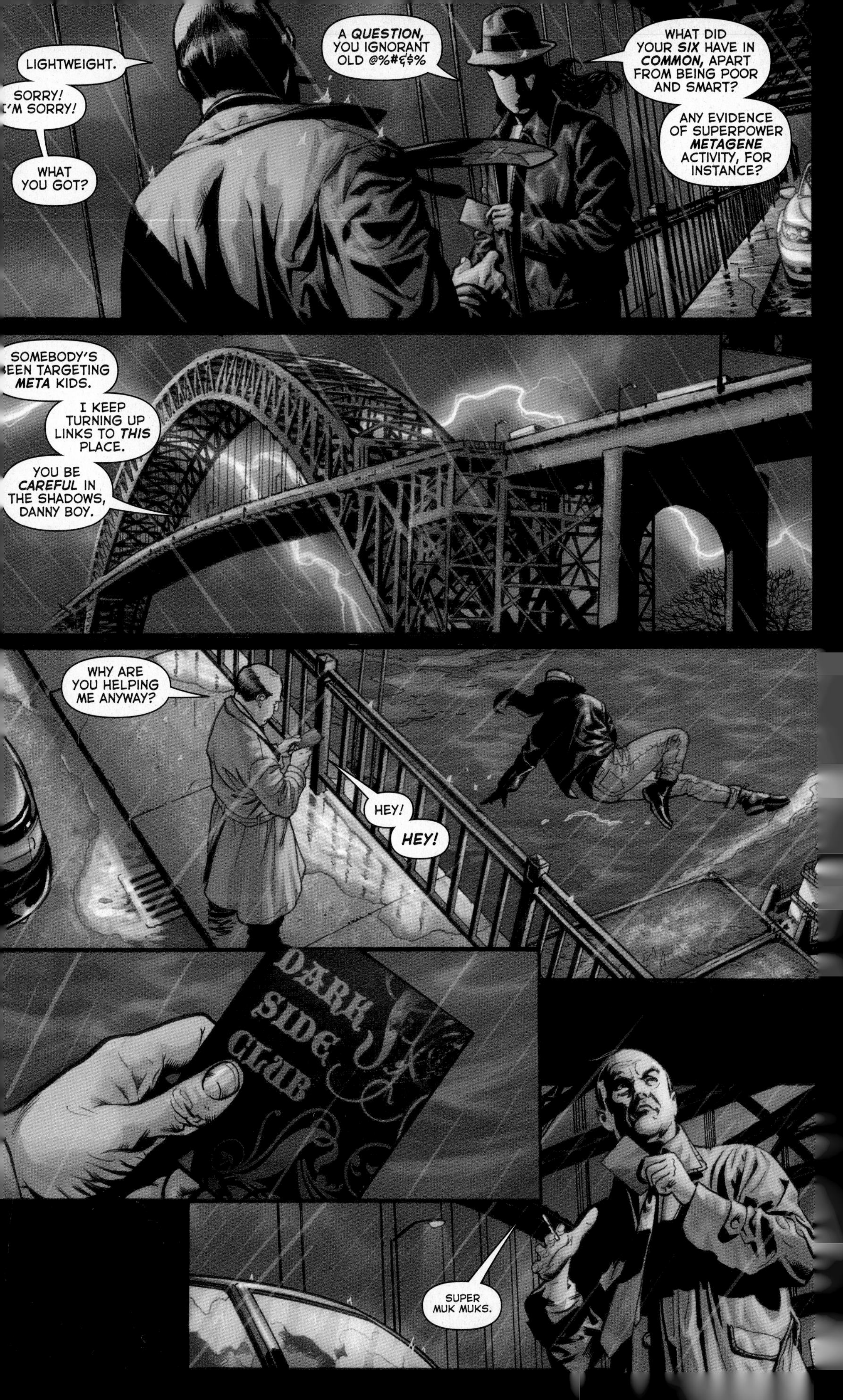
LIGHTWEIGHT.
SORRY! I'M SORRY!
WHAT YOU GOT?
A QUESTION, YOU IGNORANT OLD @%#&$%
WHAT DID YOUR SIX HAVE IN COMMON, APART FROM BEING POOR AND SMART?
ANY EVIDENCE OF SUPERPOWER METAGENE ACTIVITY, FOR INSTANCE?
SOMEBODY'S BEEN TARGETING META KIDS.
I KEEP TURNING UP LINKS TO THIS PLACE.
YOU BE CAREFUL IN THE SHADOWS, DANNY BOY.
WHY ARE YOU HELPING ME ANYWAY?
HEY!
HEY!
DARK SIDE CLUB
SUPER MUK MUKS.

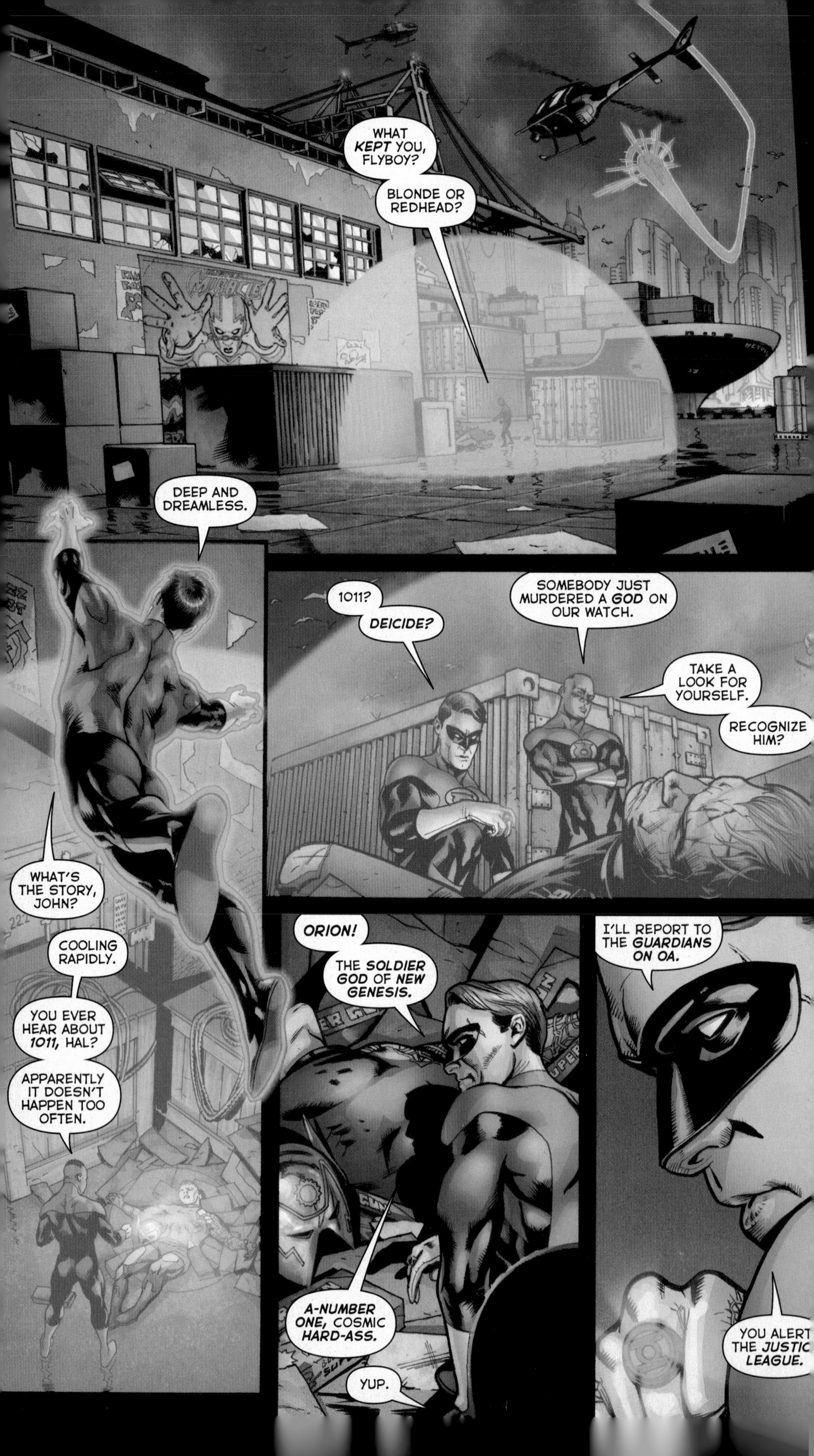
WHAT KEPT YOU, FLYBOY?
BLONDE OR REDHEAD?
DEEP AND DREAMLESS.
WHAT'S THE STORY, JOHN?
COOLING RAPIDLY.
YOU EVER HEAR ABOUT 1011, HAL?
APPARENTLY IT DOESN'T HAPPEN TOO OFTEN.
1011?
DEICIDE?
SOMEBODY JUST MURDERED A GOD ON OUR WATCH.
TAKE A LOOK FOR YOURSELF.
RECOGNIZE HIM?
ORION!
THE SOLDIER GOD OF NEW GENESIS.
A-NUMBER ONE, COSMIC HARD-ASS.
YUP.
I'LL REPORT TO THE GUARDIANS ON OA.
YOU ALERT THE JUSTIC LEAGUE.

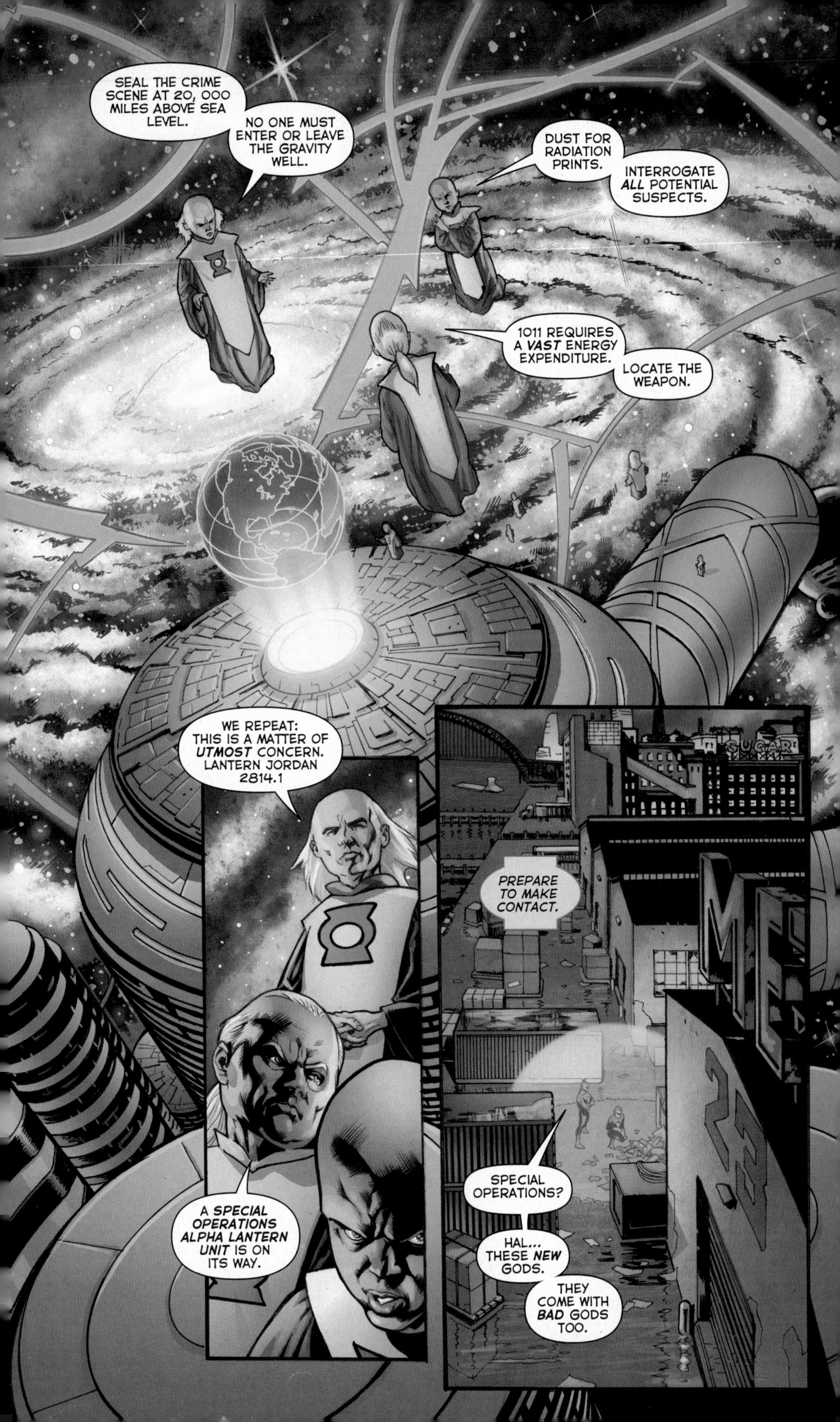

SEAL THE CRIME SCENE AT 20, 000 MILES ABOVE SEA LEVEL.
NO ONE MUST ENTER OR LEAVE THE GRAVITY WELL.
DUST FOR RADIATION PRINTS.
INTERROGATE *ALL* POTENTIAL SUSPECTS.
1011 REQUIRES A *VAST* ENERGY EXPENDITURE.
LOCATE THE WEAPON.
WE REPEAT: THIS IS A MATTER OF *UTMOST* CONCERN. LANTERN JORDAN 2814.1
PREPARE TO MAKE CONTACT.
SUGAR
A *SPECIAL OPERATIONS ALPHA LANTERN UNIT* IS ON ITS WAY.
SPECIAL OPERATIONS?
HAL... THESE *NEW* GODS.
THEY COME WITH *BAD* GODS TOO.

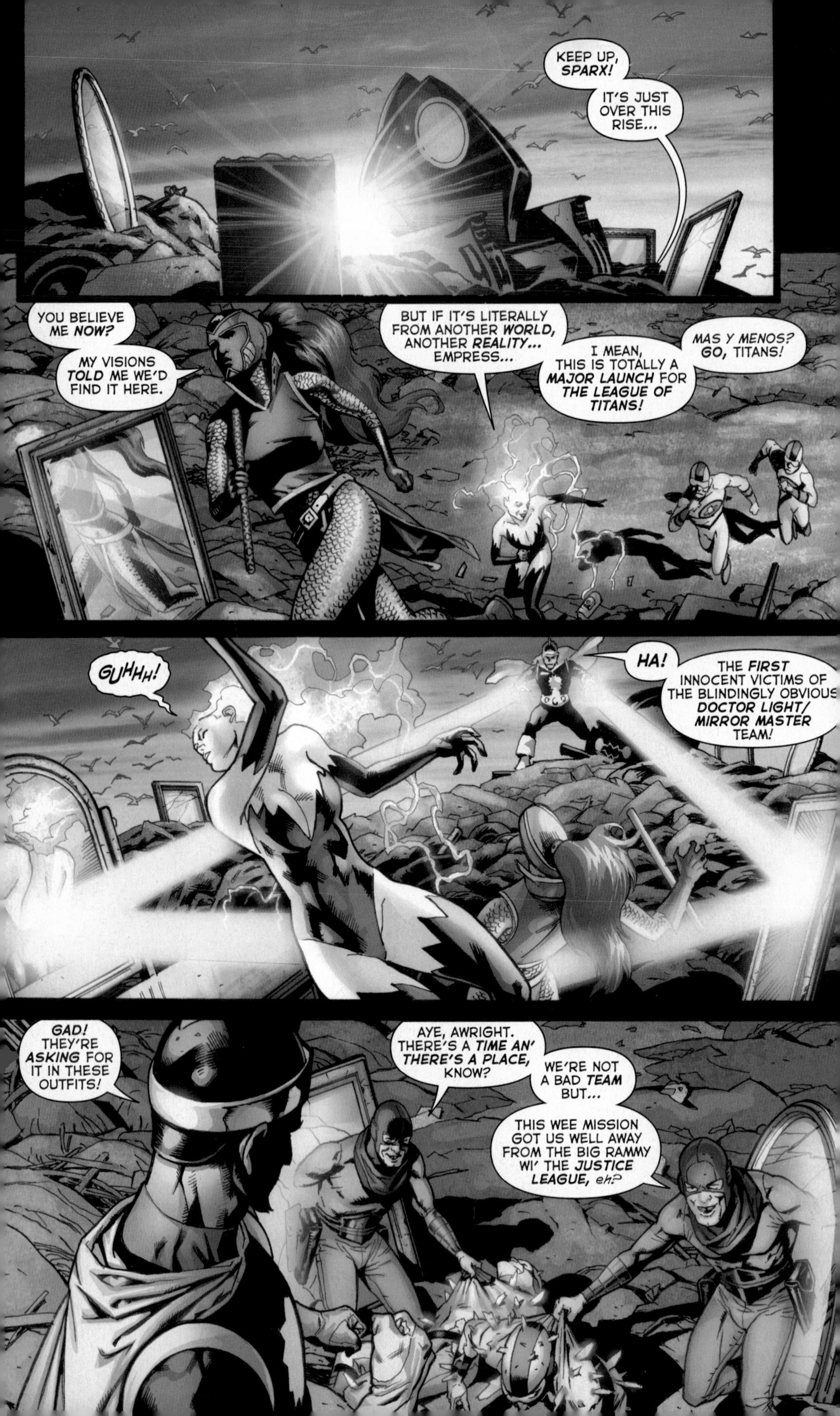
KEEP UP, SPARX!
IT'S JUST OVER THIS RISE...
YOU BELIEVE ME NOW?
MY VISIONS TOLD ME WE'D FIND IT HERE.
BUT IF IT'S LITERALLY FROM ANOTHER WORLD, ANOTHER REALITY... EMPRESS...
I MEAN, THIS IS TOTALLY A MAJOR LAUNCH FOR THE LEAGUE OF TITANS!
MAS Y MENOS? GO, TITANS!
GUHHH!
HA!
THE FIRST INNOCENT VICTIMS OF THE BLINDINGLY OBVIOUS DOCTOR LIGHT/ MIRROR MASTER TEAM!
GAD! THEY'RE ASKING FOR IT IN THESE OUTFITS!
AYE, AWRIGHT. THERE'S A TIME AN' THERE'S A PLACE, KNOW?
WE'RE NOT A BAD TEAM BUT...
THIS WEE MISSION GOT US WELL AWAY FROM THE BIG RAMMY WI' THE JUSTICE LEAGUE, eh?

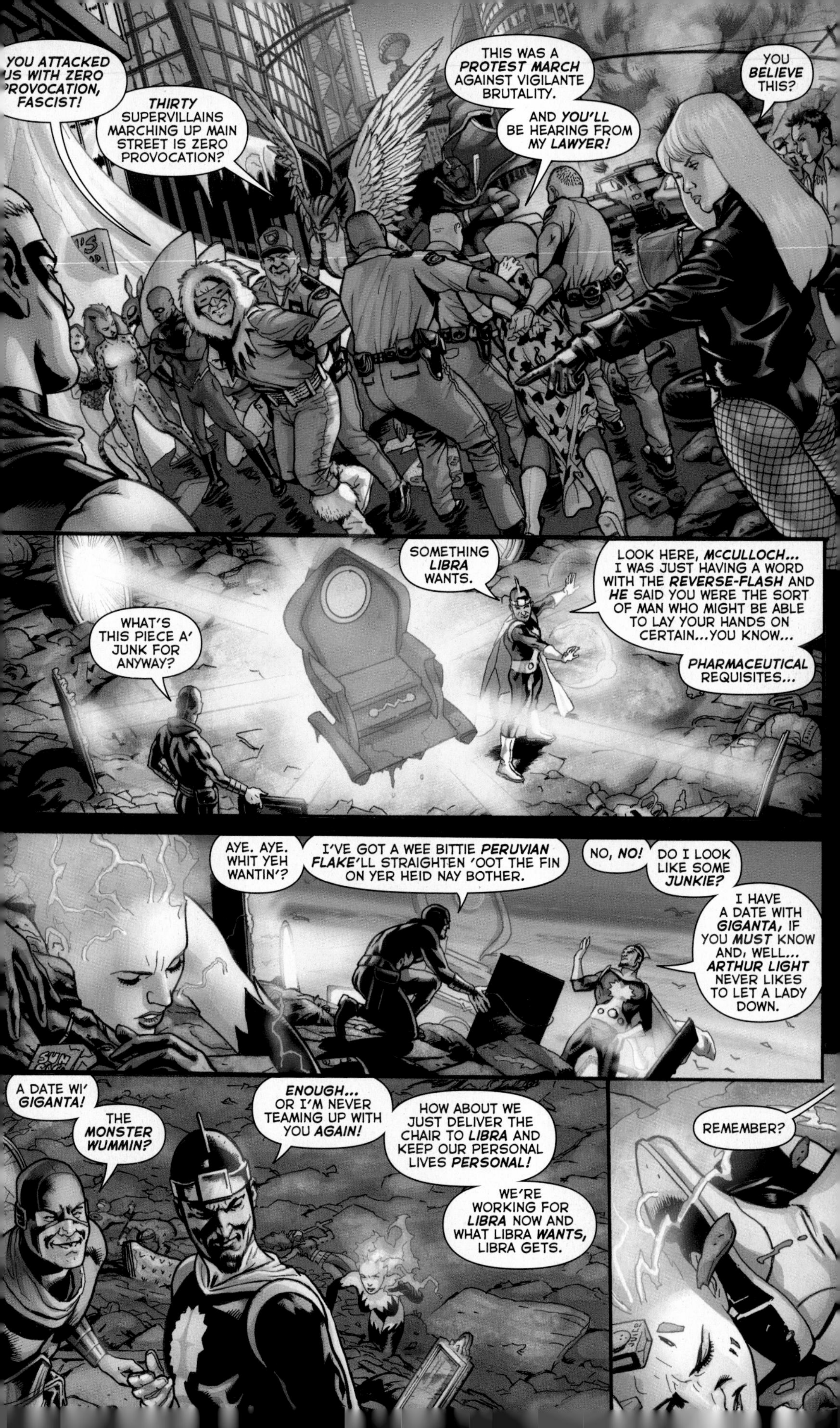
YOU ATTACKED US WITH ZERO PROVOCATION, FASCIST!
THIRTY SUPERVILLAINS MARCHING UP MAIN STREET IS ZERO PROVOCATION?
THIS WAS A PROTEST MARCH AGAINST VIGILANTE BRUTALITY.
AND YOU'LL BE HEARING FROM MY LAWYER!
YOU BELIEVE THIS?
SOMETHING LIBRA WANTS.
LOOK HERE, McCULLOCH... I WAS JUST HAVING A WORD WITH THE REVERSE-FLASH AND HE SAID YOU WERE THE SORT OF MAN WHO MIGHT BE ABLE TO LAY YOUR HANDS ON CERTAIN...YOU KNOW...
PHARMACEUTICAL REQUISITES...
WHAT'S THIS PIECE A' JUNK FOR ANYWAY?
AYE. AYE. WHIT YEH WANTIN'?
I'VE GOT A WEE BITTIE PERUVIAN FLAKE'LL STRAIGHTEN 'OOT THE FIN ON YER HEID NAY BOTHER.
NO, NO!
DO I LOOK LIKE SOME JUNKIE?
I HAVE A DATE WITH GIGANTA, IF YOU MUST KNOW AND, WELL... ARTHUR LIGHT NEVER LIKES TO LET A LADY DOWN.
A DATE WI' GIGANTA!
THE MONSTER WUMMIN?
ENOUGH... OR I'M NEVER TEAMING UP WITH YOU AGAIN!
HOW ABOUT WE JUST DELIVER THE CHAIR TO LIBRA AND KEEP OUR PERSONAL LIVES PERSONAL!
WE'RE WORKING FOR LIBRA NOW AND WHAT LIBRA WANTS, LIBRA GETS.
REMEMBER?

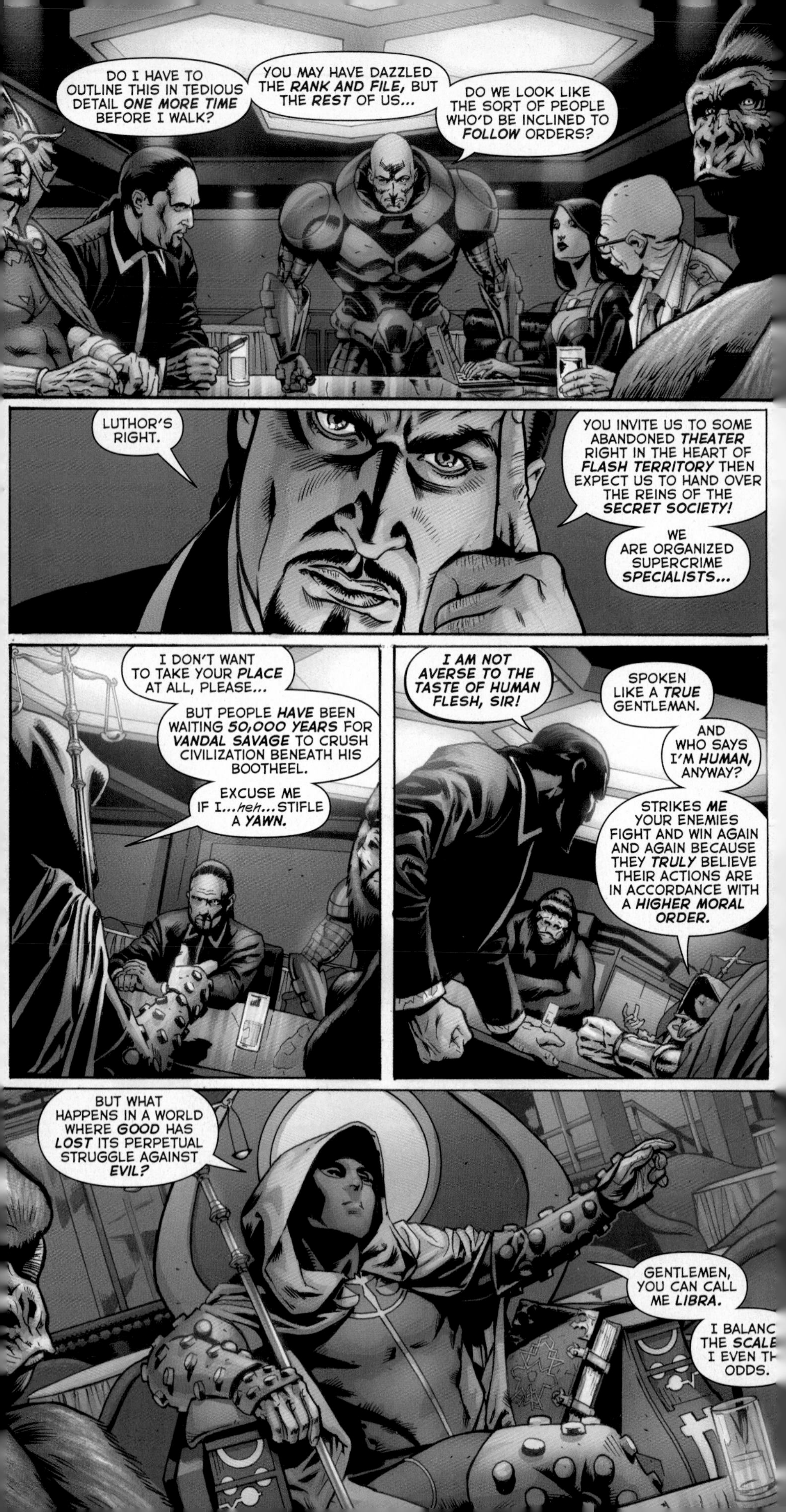
DO I HAVE TO OUTLINE THIS IN TEDIOUS DETAIL ONE MORE TIME BEFORE I WALK?
YOU MAY HAVE DAZZLED THE RANK AND FILE, BUT THE REST OF US...
DO WE LOOK LIKE THE SORT OF PEOPLE WHO'D BE INCLINED TO FOLLOW ORDERS?
LUTHOR'S RIGHT.
YOU INVITE US TO SOME ABANDONED THEATER RIGHT IN THE HEART OF FLASH TERRITORY THEN EXPECT US TO HAND OVER THE REINS OF THE SECRET SOCIETY!
WE ARE ORGANIZED SUPERCRIME SPECIALISTS...
I DON'T WANT TO TAKE YOUR PLACE AT ALL, PLEASE...
BUT PEOPLE HAVE BEEN WAITING 50,000 YEARS FOR VANDAL SAVAGE TO CRUSH CIVILIZATION BENEATH HIS BOOTHEEL.
EXCUSE ME IF I...heh...STIFLE A YAWN.
I AM NOT AVERSE TO THE TASTE OF HUMAN FLESH, SIR!
SPOKEN LIKE A TRUE GENTLEMAN.
AND WHO SAYS I'M HUMAN, ANYWAY?
STRIKES ME YOUR ENEMIES FIGHT AND WIN AGAIN AND AGAIN BECAUSE THEY TRULY BELIEVE THEIR ACTIONS ARE IN ACCORDANCE WITH A HIGHER MORAL ORDER.
BUT WHAT HAPPENS IN A WORLD WHERE GOOD HAS LOST ITS PERPETUAL STRUGGLE AGAINST EVIL?
GENTLEMEN, YOU CAN CALL ME LIBRA.
ODDS.

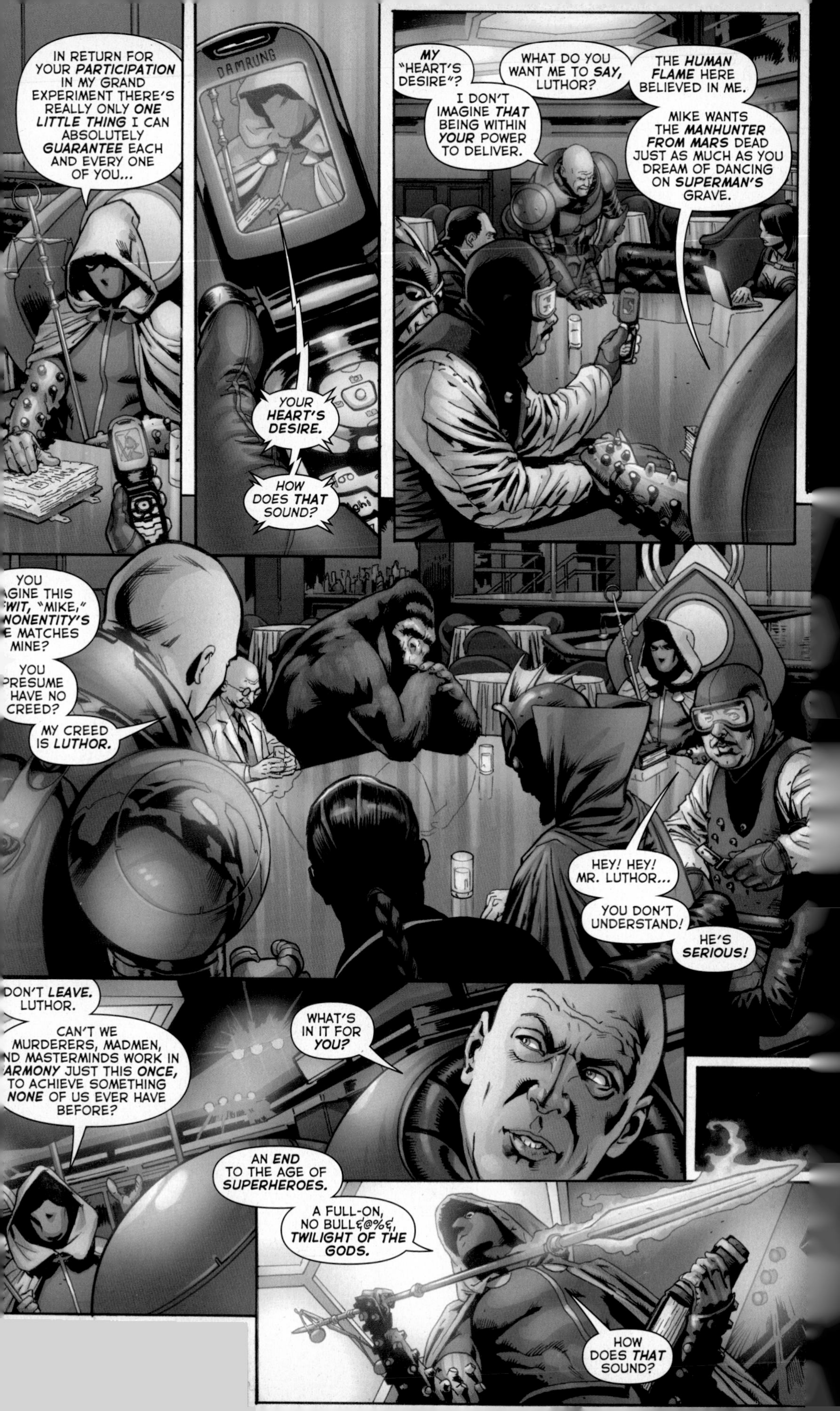

IN RETURN FOR YOUR PARTICIPATION IN MY GRAND EXPERIMENT THERE'S REALLY ONLY ONE LITTLE THING I CAN ABSOLUTELY GUARANTEE EACH AND EVERY ONE OF YOU...
DAMRUNG
YOUR HEART'S DESIRE.
HOW DOES THAT SOUND?
MY "HEART'S DESIRE"?
I DON'T IMAGINE THAT BEING WITHIN YOUR POWER TO DELIVER.
WHAT DO YOU WANT ME TO SAY, LUTHOR?
THE HUMAN FLAME HERE BELIEVED IN ME.
MIKE WANTS THE MANHUNTER FROM MARS DEAD JUST AS MUCH AS YOU DREAM OF DANCING ON SUPERMAN'S GRAVE.
YOU AGINE THIS TWIT, "MIKE," NONENTITY'S E MATCHES MINE?
YOU PRESUME HAVE NO CREED?
MY CREED IS LUTHOR.
HEY! HEY! MR. LUTHOR...
YOU DON'T UNDERSTAND!
HE'S SERIOUS!
DON'T LEAVE. LUTHOR.
CAN'T WE MURDERERS, MADMEN, ND MASTERMINDS WORK IN ARMONY JUST THIS ONCE, TO ACHIEVE SOMETHING NONE OF US EVER HAVE BEFORE?
WHAT'S IN IT FOR YOU?
AN END TO THE AGE OF SUPERHEROES.
A FULL-ON, NO BULL€@%€, TWILIGHT OF THE GODS.
HOW DOES THAT SOUND?

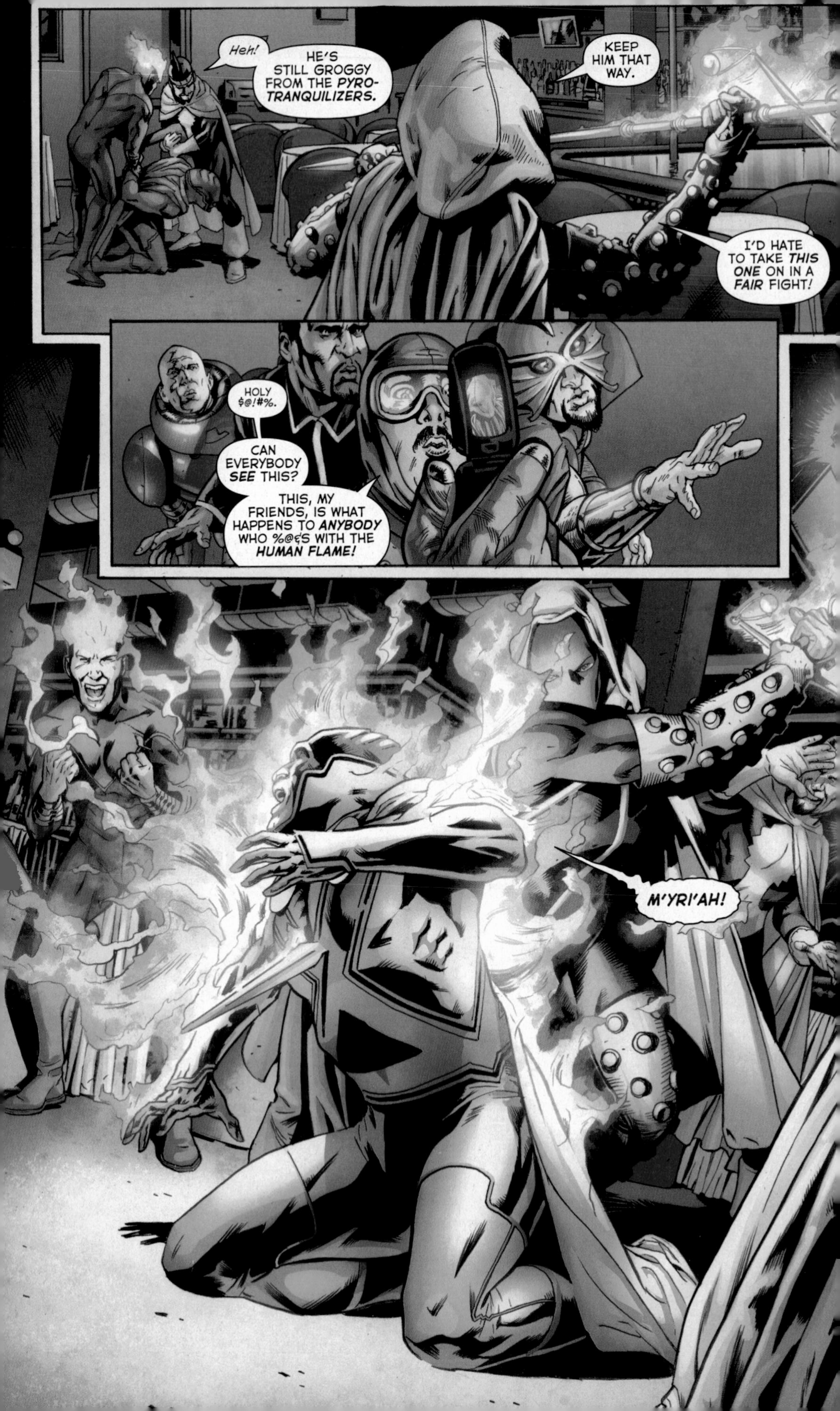
Heh!
HE'S STILL GROGGY FROM THE PYRO-TRANQUILIZERS.
KEEP HIM THAT WAY.
I'D HATE TO TAKE THIS ONE ON IN A FAIR FIGHT!
HOLY $@!#%.
CAN EVERYBODY SEE THIS?
THIS, MY FRIENDS, IS WHAT HAPPENS TO ANYBODY WHO %@¢S WITH THE HUMAN FLAME!
M'YRI'AH!

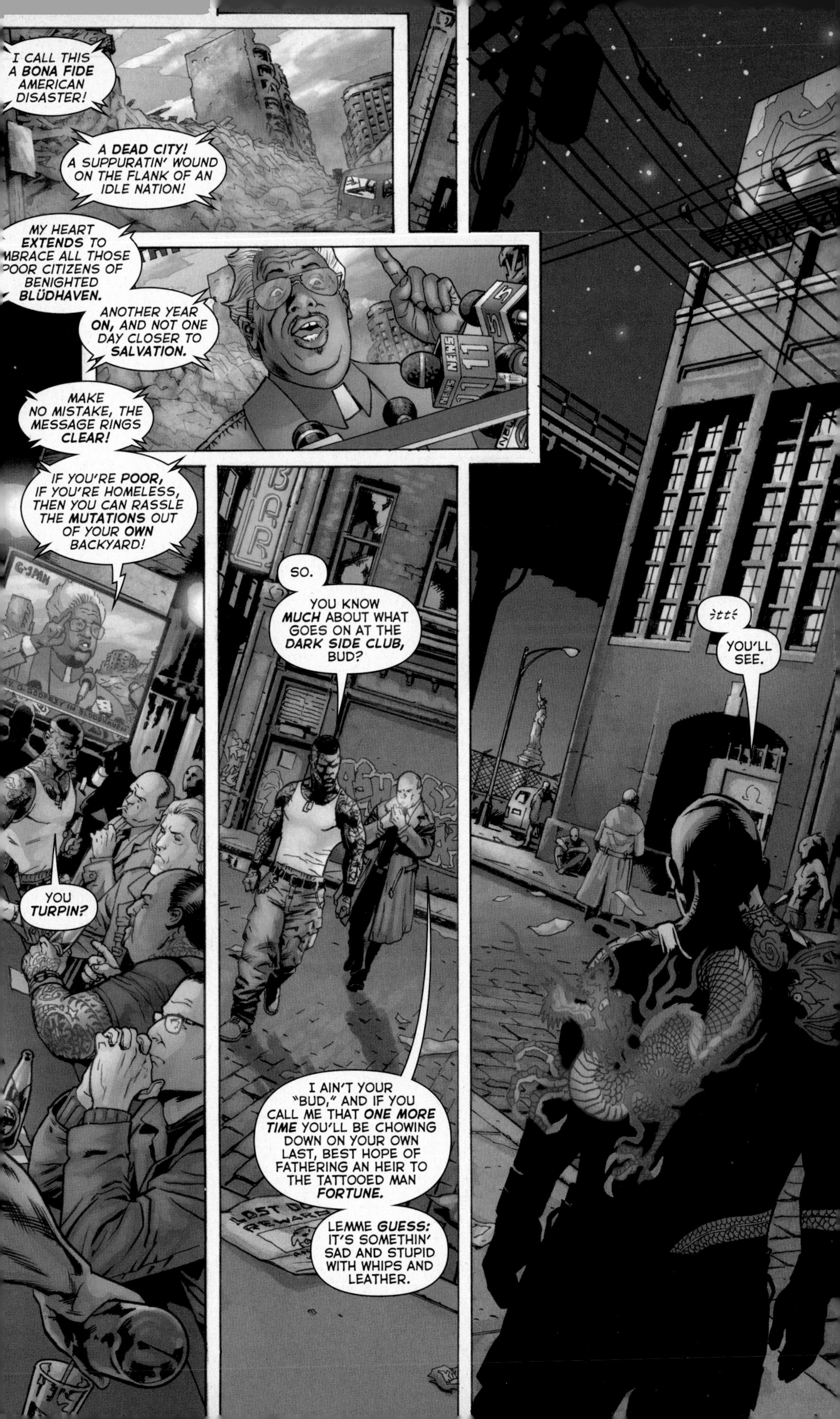
I CALL THIS A BONA FIDE AMERICAN DISASTER!
A DEAD CITY! A SUPPURATIN' WOUND ON THE FLANK OF AN IDLE NATION!
MY HEART EXTENDS TO EMBRACE ALL THOSE POOR CITIZENS OF BENIGHTED BLÜDHAVEN.
ANOTHER YEAR ON, AND NOT ONE DAY CLOSER TO SALVATION.
MAKE NO MISTAKE, THE MESSAGE RINGS CLEAR!
IF YOU'RE POOR, IF YOU'RE HOMELESS, THEN YOU CAN RASSLE THE MUTATIONS OUT OF YOUR OWN BACKYARD!
YOU TURPIN?
SO.
YOU KNOW MUCH ABOUT WHAT GOES ON AT THE DARK SIDE CLUB, BUD?
I AIN'T YOUR "BUD," AND IF YOU CALL ME THAT ONE MORE TIME YOU'LL BE CHOWING DOWN ON YOUR OWN LAST, BEST HOPE OF FATHERING AN HEIR TO THE TATTOOED MAN FORTUNE.
LEMME GUESS: IT'S SOMETHIN' SAD AND STUPID WITH WHIPS AND LEATHER.
tt
YOU'LL SEE.

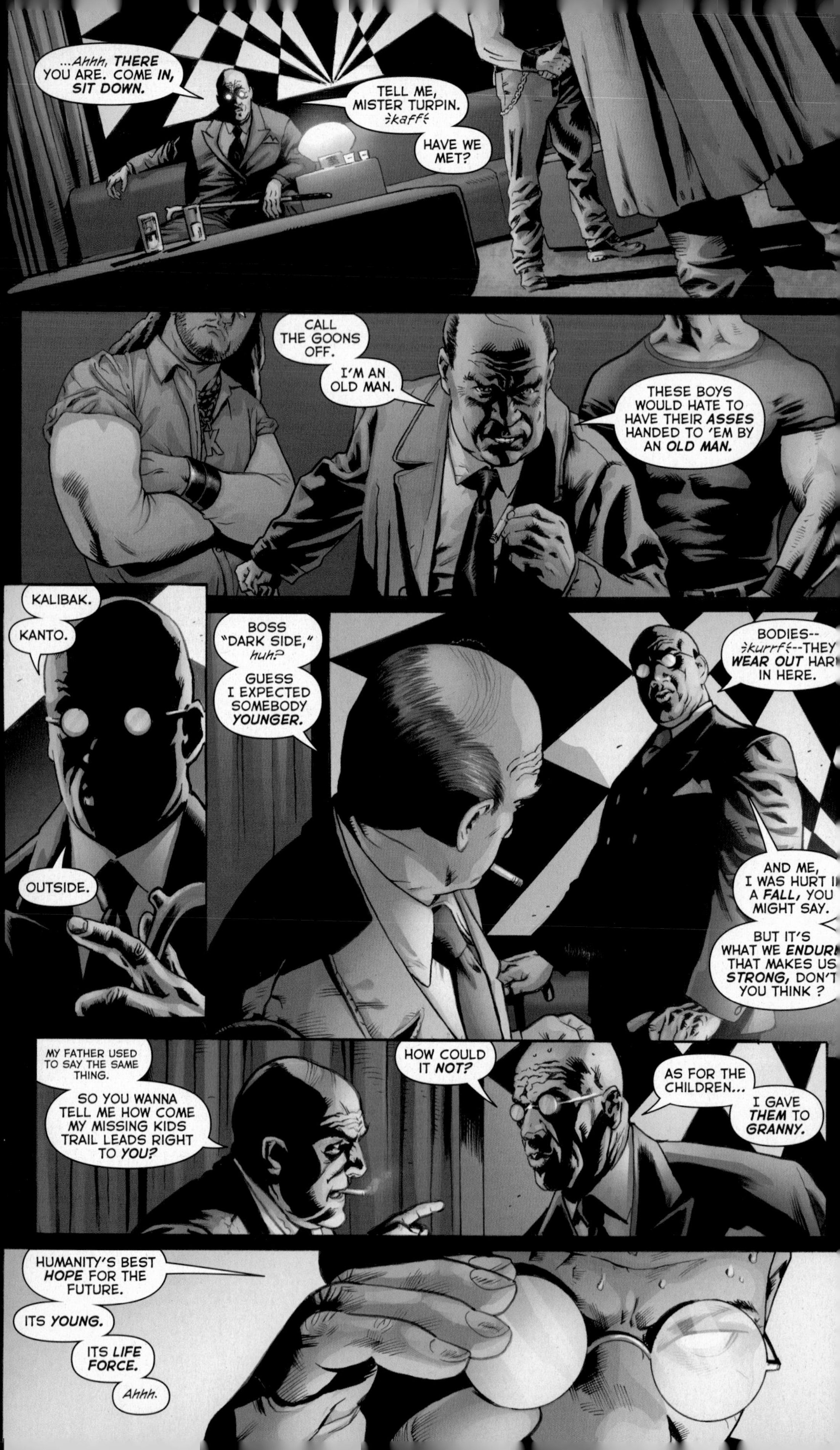
...Ahhh, THERE YOU ARE. COME IN, SIT DOWN.
TELL ME, MISTER TURPIN. kaff
HAVE WE MET?
CALL THE GOONS OFF.
I'M AN OLD MAN.
THESE BOYS WOULD HATE TO HAVE THEIR ASSES HANDED TO 'EM BY AN OLD MAN.
KALIBAK.
KANTO.
OUTSIDE.
BOSS "DARK SIDE," huh?
GUESS I EXPECTED SOMEBODY YOUNGER.
BODIES-- kurrf --THEY WEAR OUT HAR IN HERE.
AND ME, I WAS HURT I A FALL, YOU MIGHT SAY.
BUT IT'S WHAT WE ENDUR THAT MAKES US STRONG, DON'T YOU THINK ?
MY FATHER USED TO SAY THE SAME THING.
SO YOU WANNA TELL ME HOW COME MY MISSING KIDS TRAIL LEADS RIGHT TO YOU?
HOW COULD IT NOT?
AS FOR THE CHILDREN... I GAVE THEM TO GRANNY.
HUMANITY'S BEST HOPE FOR THE FUTURE.
ITS YOUNG.
ITS LIFE FORCE.
Ahhh.

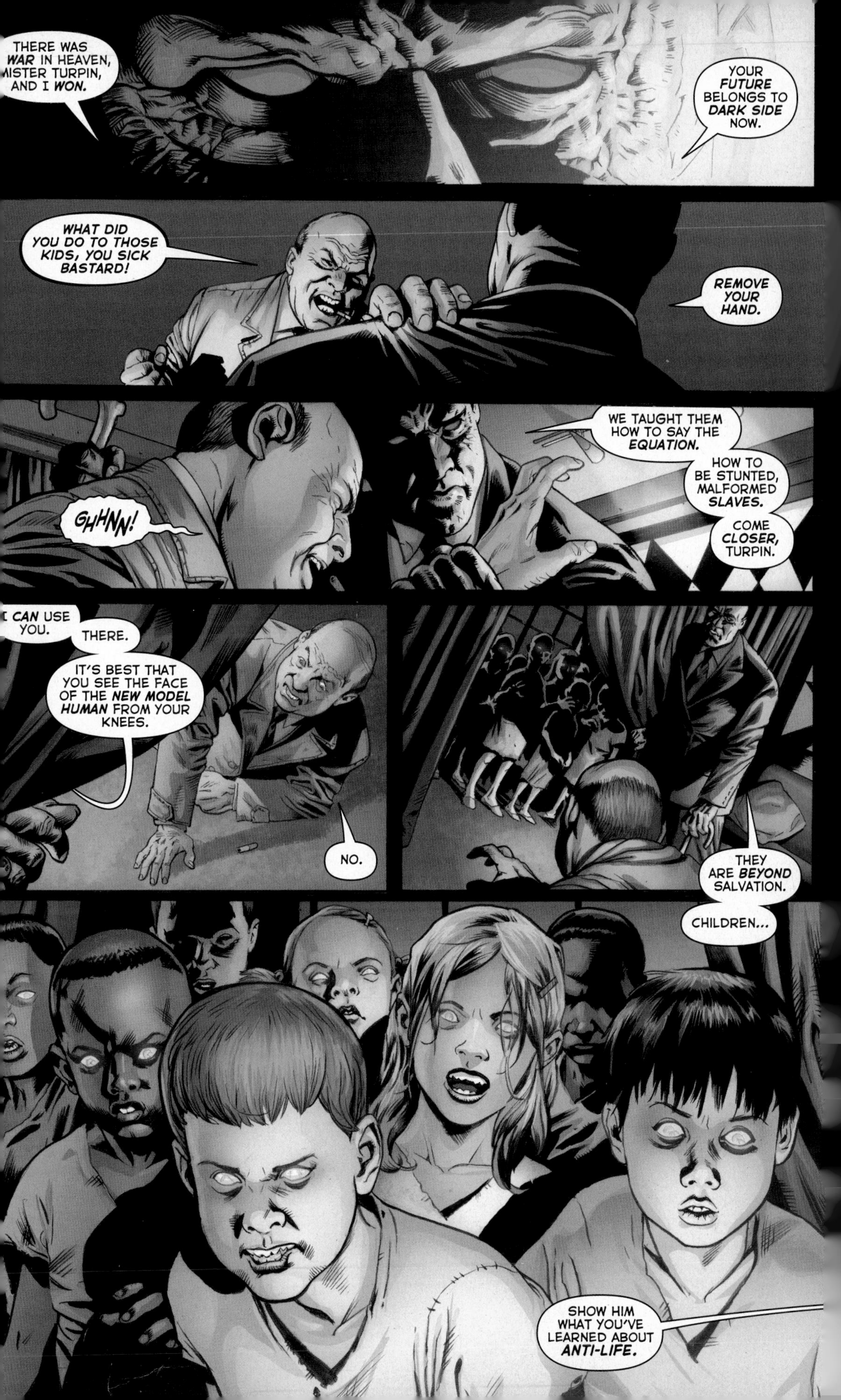

THERE WAS WAR IN HEAVEN, MISTER TURPIN, AND I WON.
YOUR FUTURE BELONGS TO DARK SIDE NOW.
WHAT DID YOU DO TO THOSE KIDS, YOU SICK BASTARD!
REMOVE YOUR HAND.
GHHNN!
WE TAUGHT THEM HOW TO SAY THE EQUATION.
HOW TO BE STUNTED, MALFORMED SLAVES.
COME CLOSER, TURPIN.
I CAN USE YOU.
THERE.
IT'S BEST THAT YOU SEE THE FACE OF THE NEW MODEL HUMAN FROM YOUR KNEES.
NO.
THEY ARE BEYOND SALVATION.
CHILDREN...
SHOW HIM WHAT YOU'VE LEARNED ABOUT ANTI-LIFE.

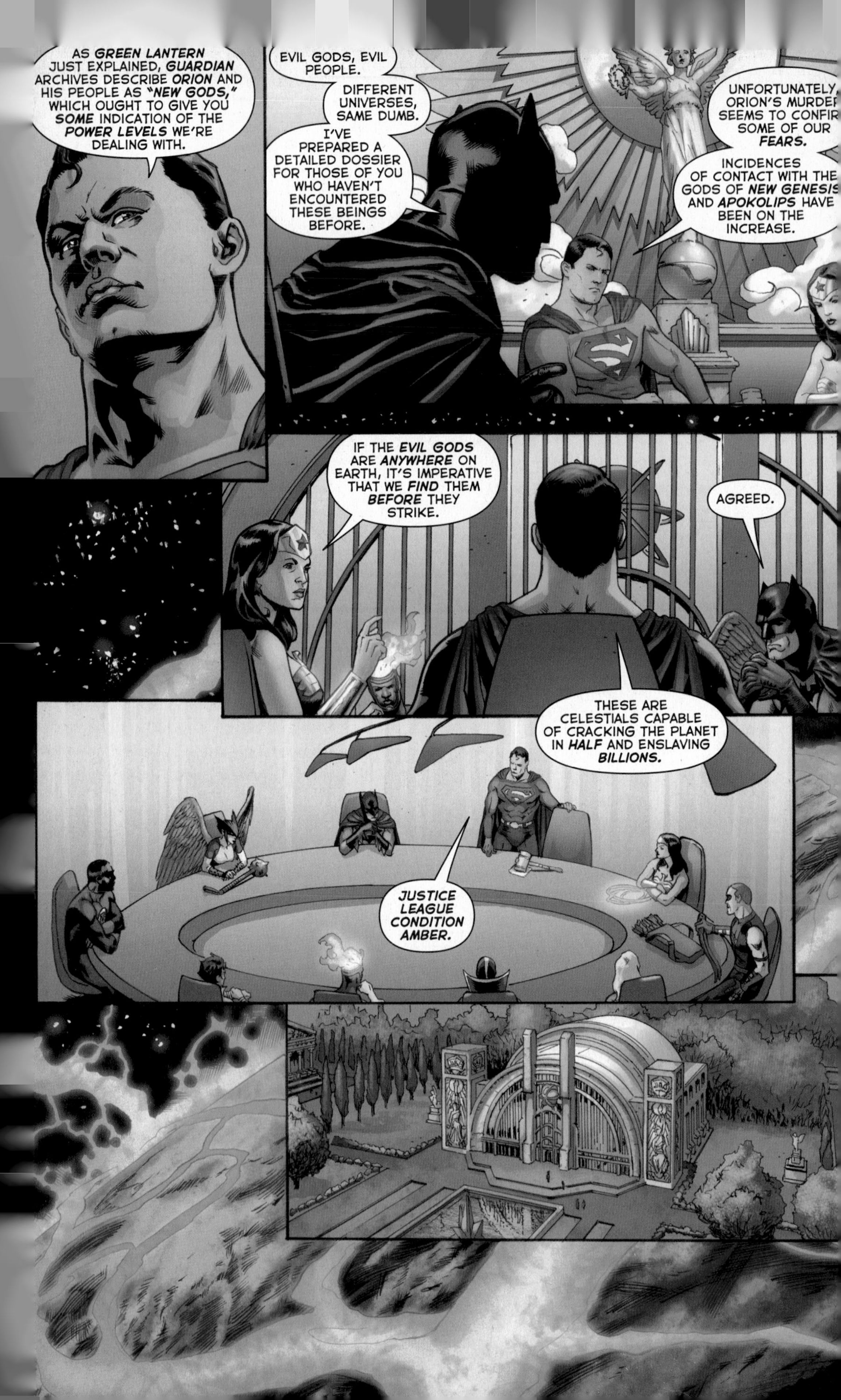

AS GREEN LANTERN JUST EXPLAINED, GUARDIAN ARCHIVES DESCRIBE ORION AND HIS PEOPLE AS "NEW GODS," WHICH OUGHT TO GIVE YOU SOME INDICATION OF THE POWER LEVELS WE'RE DEALING WITH.
EVIL GODS, EVIL PEOPLE.
DIFFERENT UNIVERSES, SAME DUMB.
I'VE PREPARED A DETAILED DOSSIER FOR THOSE OF YOU WHO HAVEN'T ENCOUNTERED THESE BEINGS BEFORE.
UNFORTUNATELY, ORION'S MURDER SEEMS TO CONFIR SOME OF OUR FEARS.
INCIDENCES OF CONTACT WITH THE GODS OF NEW GENESIS AND APOKOLIPS HAVE BEEN ON THE INCREASE.
IF THE EVIL GODS ARE ANYWHERE ON EARTH, IT'S IMPERATIVE THAT WE FIND THEM BEFORE THEY STRIKE.
AGREED.
THESE ARE CELESTIALS CAPABLE OF CRACKING THE PLANET IN HALF AND ENSLAVING BILLIONS.
JUSTICE LEAGUE CONDITION AMBER.

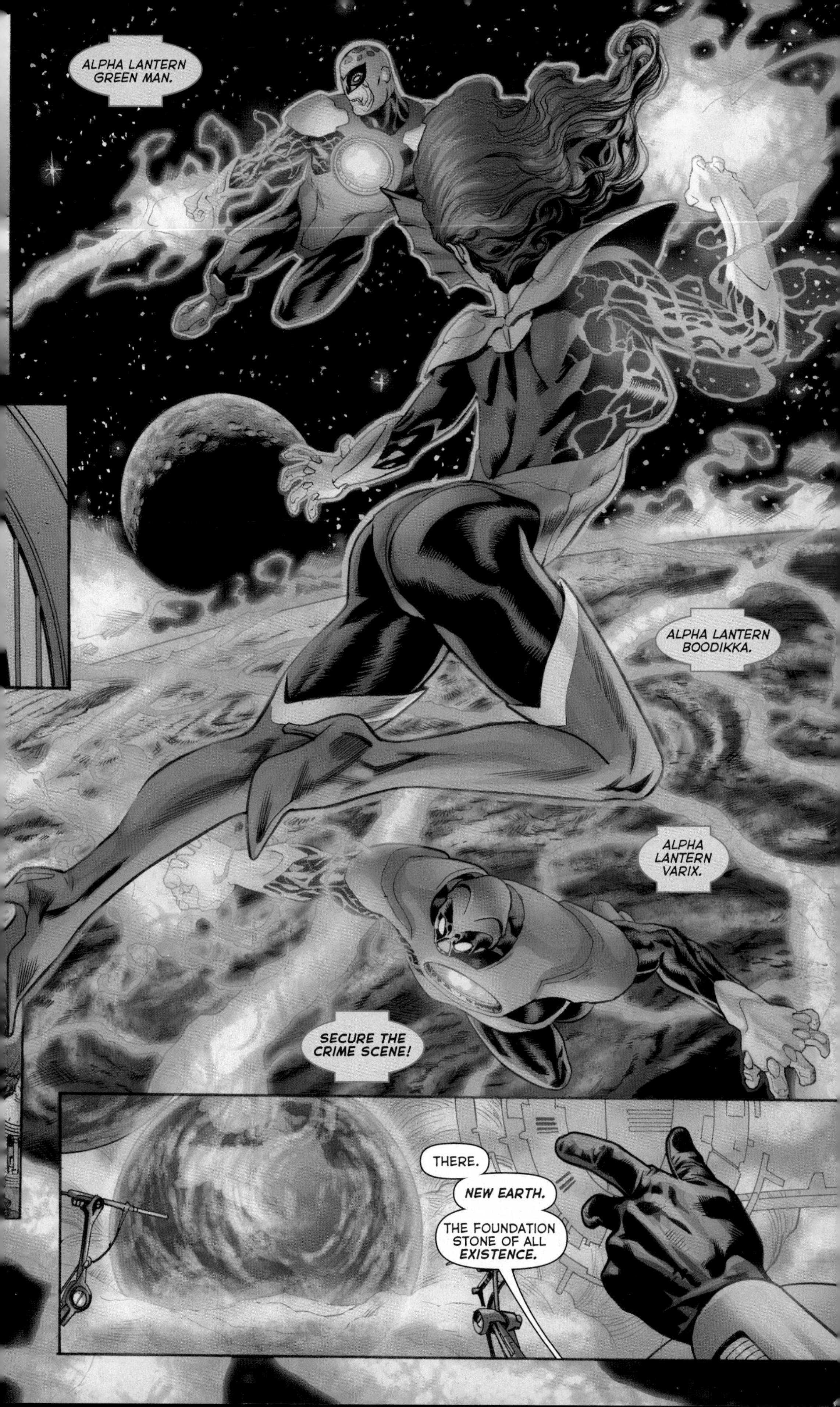
ALPHA LANTERN GREEN MAN.
ALPHA LANTERN BOODIKKA.
ALPHA LANTERN VARIX.
SECURE THE CRIME SCENE!
THERE.
NEW EARTH.
THE FOUNDATION STONE OF ALL EXISTENCE.

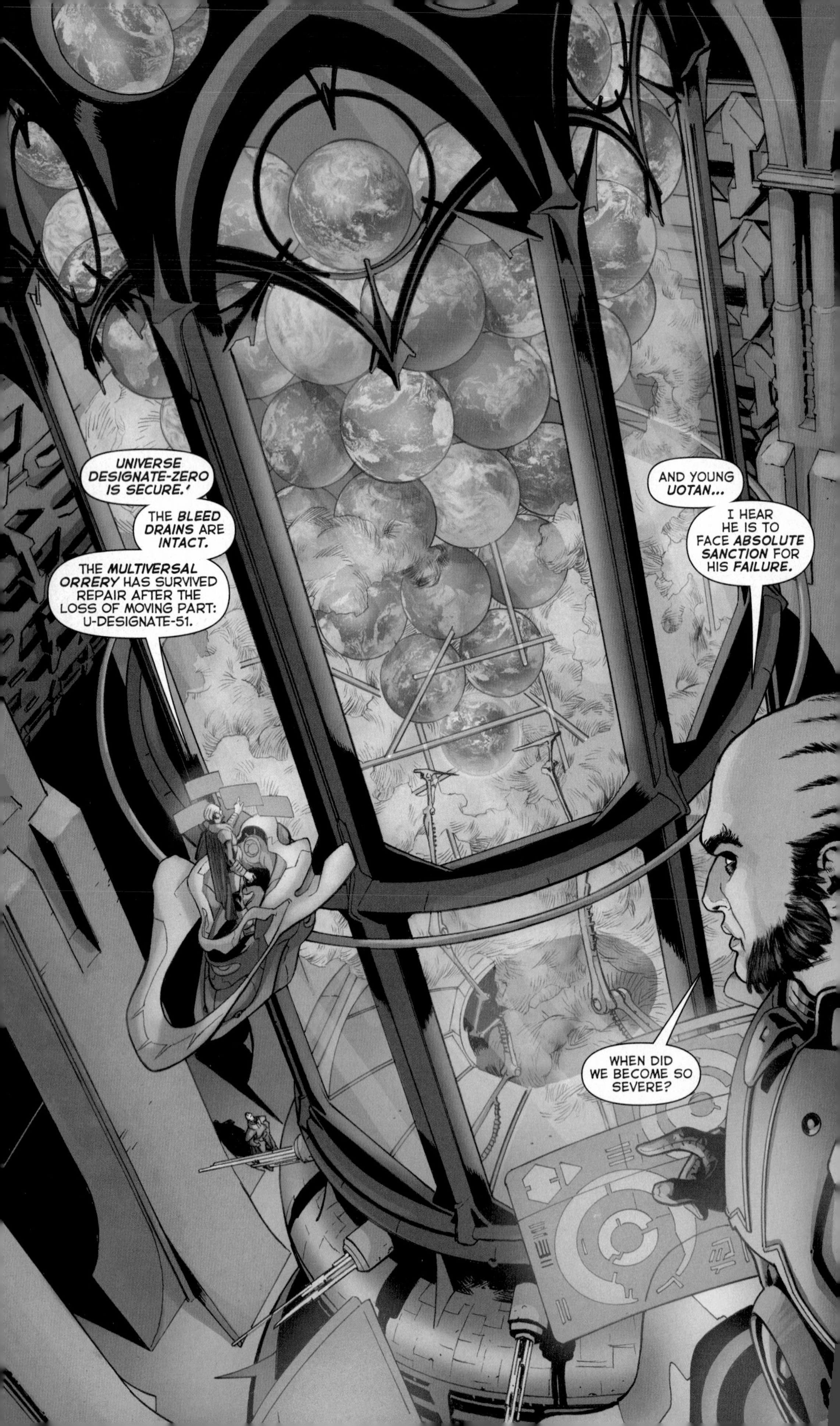

UNIVERSE DESIGNATE-ZERO IS SECURE.'
THE BLEED DRAINS ARE INTACT.
THE MULTIVERSAL ORRERY HAS SURVIVED REPAIR AFTER THE LOSS OF MOVING PART: U-DESIGNATE-51.
AND YOUNG UOTAN...
I HEAR HE IS TO FACE ABSOLUTE SANCTION FOR HIS FAILURE.
WHEN DID WE BECOME SO SEVERE?

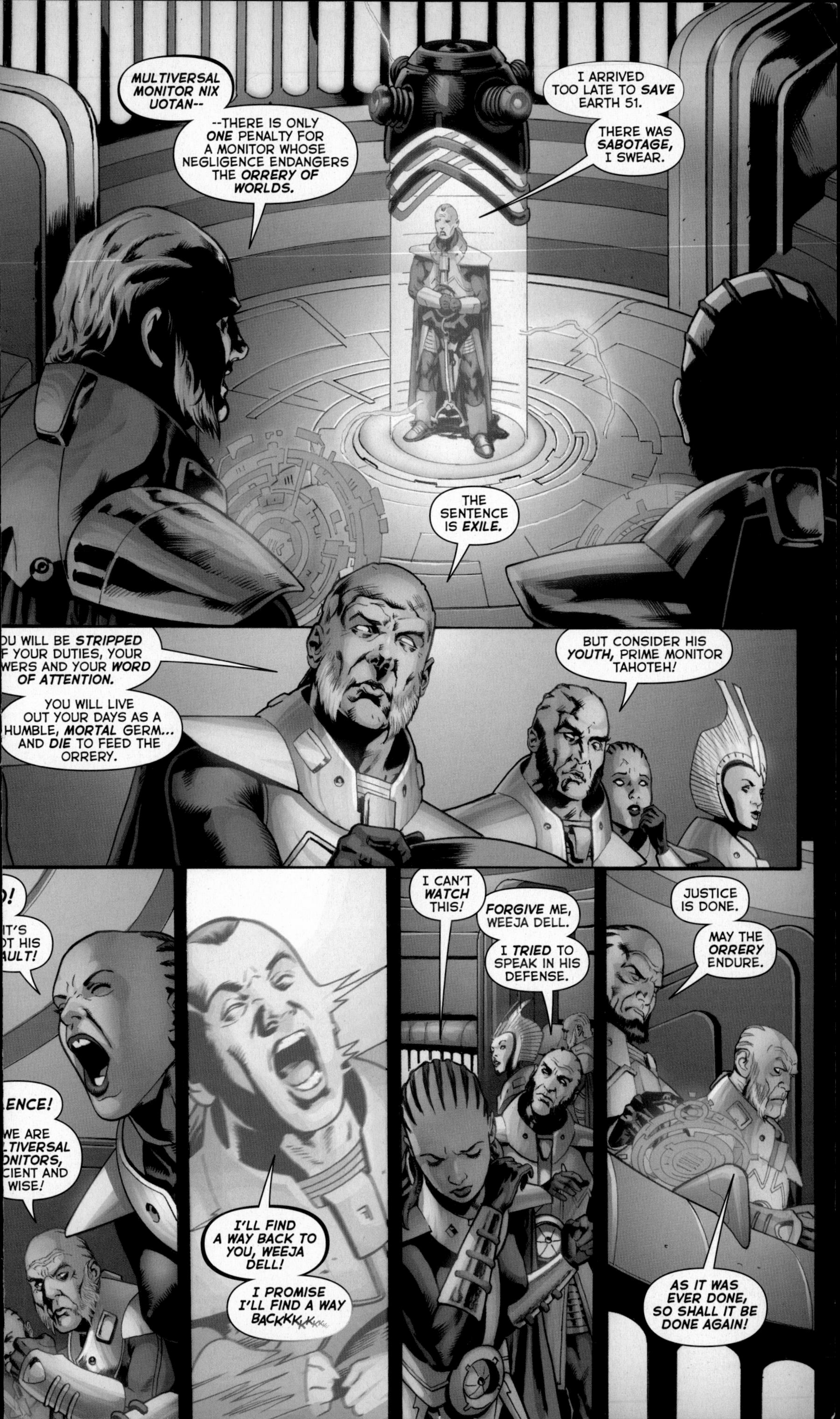

MULTIVERSAL MONITOR NIX UOTAN--
--THERE IS ONLY ONE PENALTY FOR A MONITOR WHOSE NEGLIGENCE ENDANGERS THE ORRERY OF WORLDS.
I ARRIVED TOO LATE TO SAVE EARTH 51.
THERE WAS SABOTAGE, I SWEAR.
THE SENTENCE IS EXILE.
OU WILL BE STRIPPED F YOUR DUTIES, YOUR WERS AND YOUR WORD OF ATTENTION.
YOU WILL LIVE OUT YOUR DAYS AS A HUMBLE, MORTAL GERM... AND DIE TO FEED THE ORRERY.
BUT CONSIDER HIS YOUTH, PRIME MONITOR TAHOTEH!
IT'S OT HIS AULT!
ENCE!
WE ARE LTIVERSAL ONITORS, CIENT AND WISE!
I'LL FIND A WAY BACK TO YOU, WEEJA DELL!
I PROMISE I'LL FIND A WAY BACKKKKKK
I CAN'T WATCH THIS!
FORGIVE ME, WEEJA DELL.
I TRIED TO SPEAK IN HIS DEFENSE.
JUSTICE IS DONE.
MAY THE ORRERY ENDURE.
AS IT WAS EVER DONE, SO SHALL IT BE DONE AGAIN!

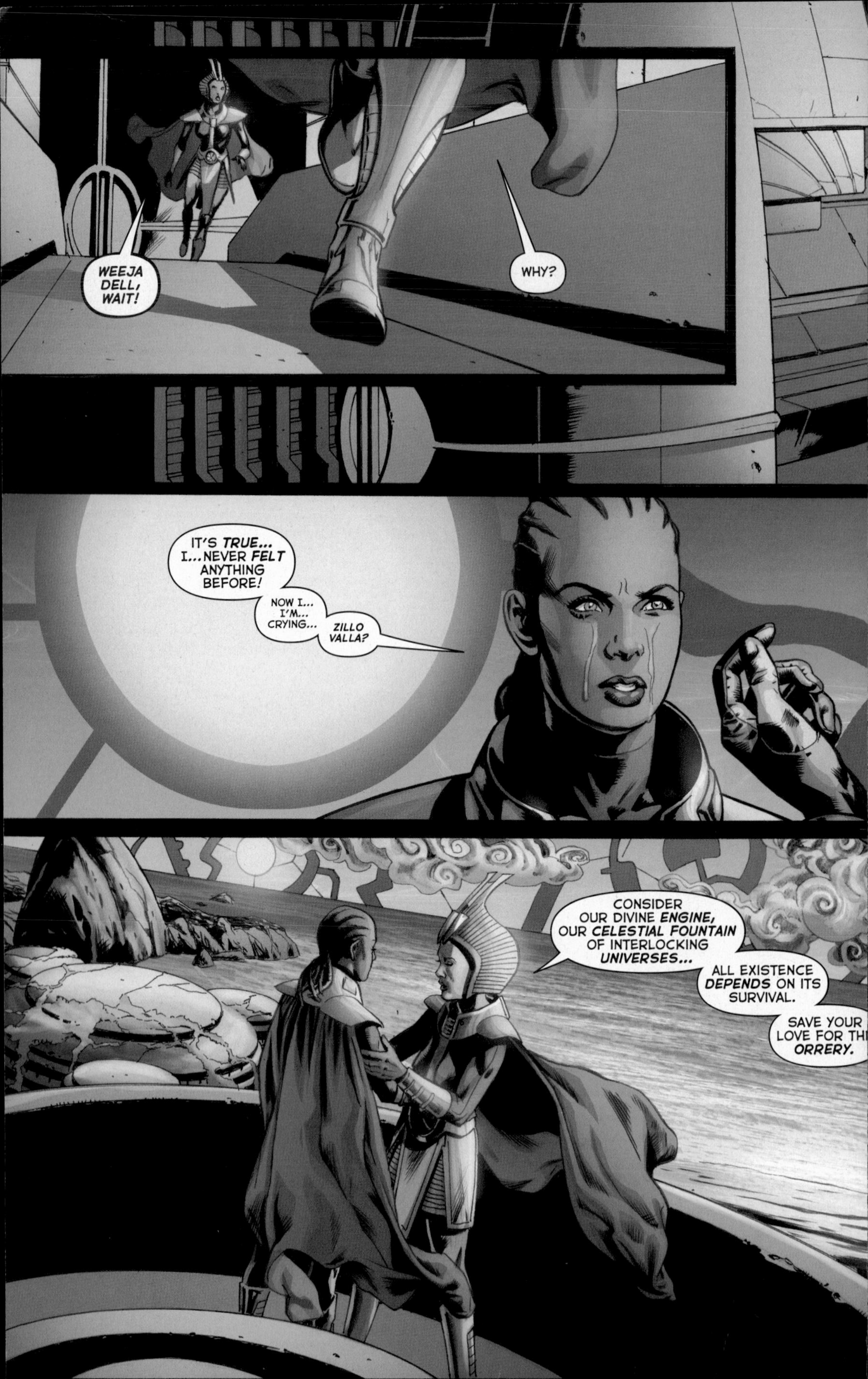
WEEJA DELL, WAIT!
WHY?
IT'S TRUE... I...NEVER FELT ANYTHING BEFORE!
NOW I... I'M... CRYING...
ZILLO VALLA?
CONSIDER OUR DIVINE ENGINE, OUR CELESTIAL FOUNTAIN OF INTERLOCKING UNIVERSES...
ALL EXISTENCE DEPENDS ON ITS SURVIVAL.
SAVE YOUR LOVE FOR THE ORRERY.

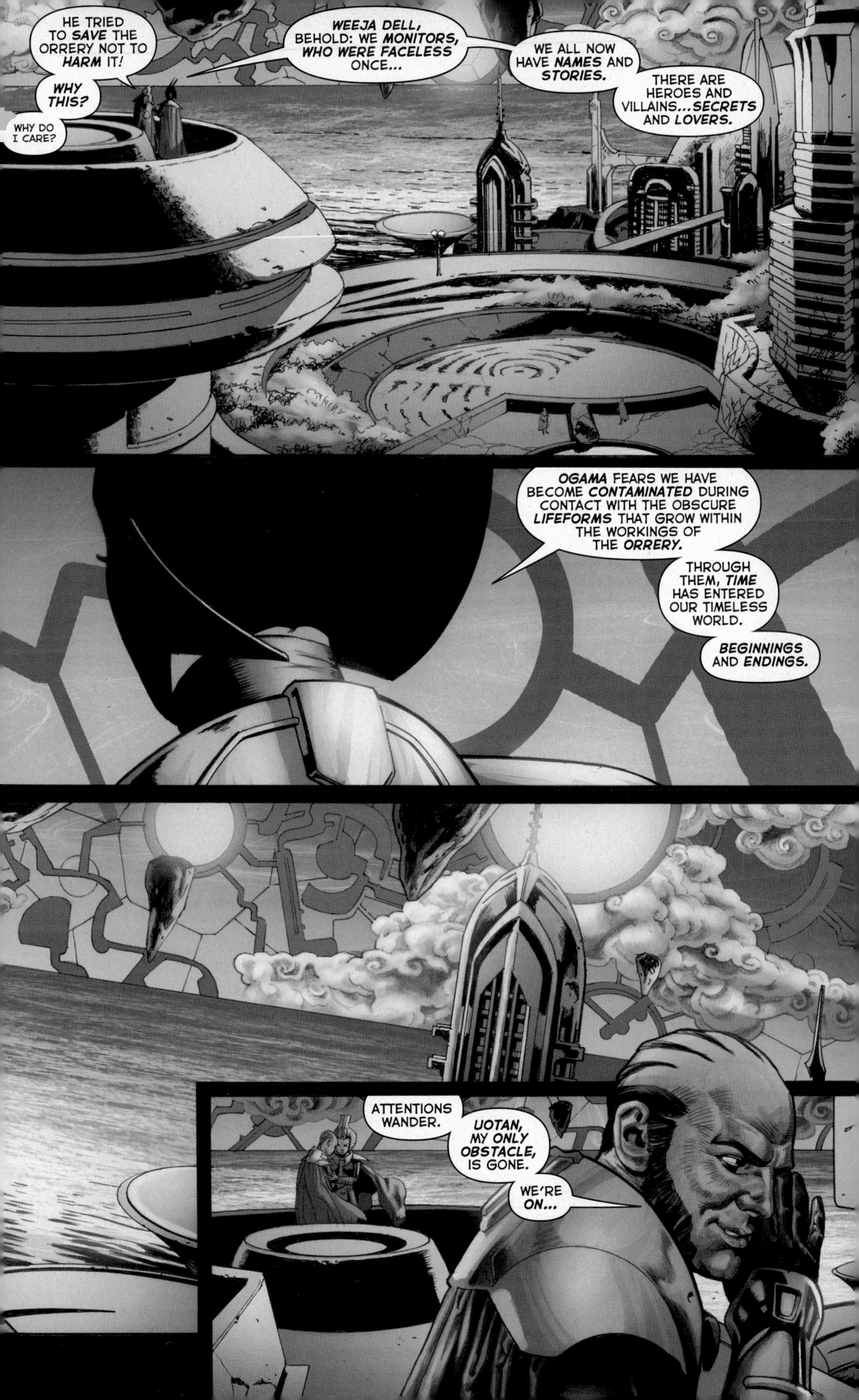
HE TRIED TO SAVE THE ORRERY NOT TO HARM IT!
WHY THIS?
WHY DO I CARE?
WEEJA DELL, BEHOLD: WE MONITORS, WHO WERE FACELESS ONCE...
WE ALL NOW HAVE NAMES AND STORIES.
THERE ARE HEROES AND VILLAINS...SECRETS AND LOVERS.
OGAMA FEARS WE HAVE BECOME CONTAMINATED DURING CONTACT WITH THE OBSCURE LIFEFORMS THAT GROW WITHIN THE WORKINGS OF THE ORRERY.
THROUGH THEM, TIME HAS ENTERED OUR TIMELESS WORLD.
BEGINNINGS AND ENDINGS.
ATTENTIONS WANDER.
UOTAN, MY ONLY OBSTACLE, IS GONE.
WE'RE ON...

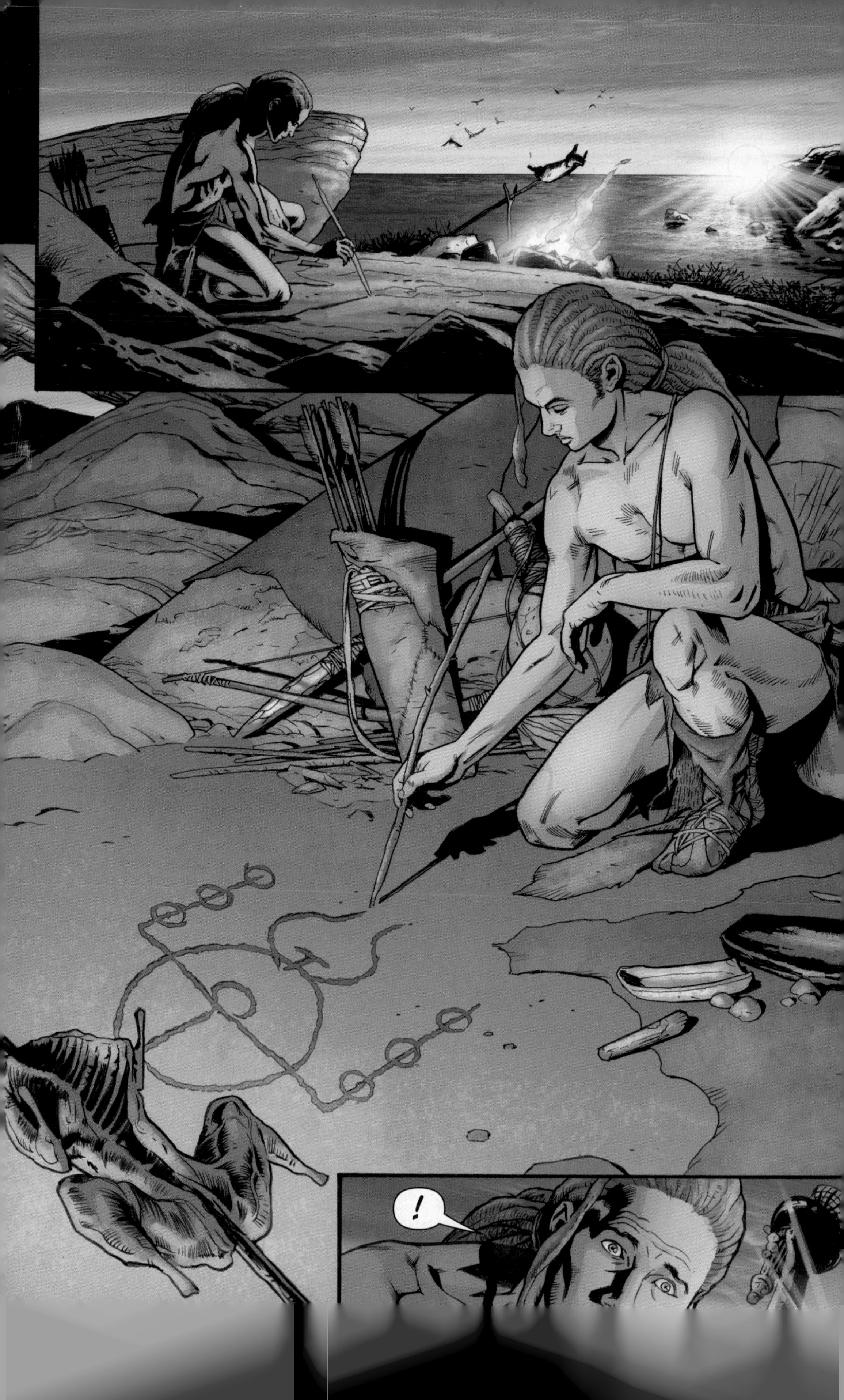
!

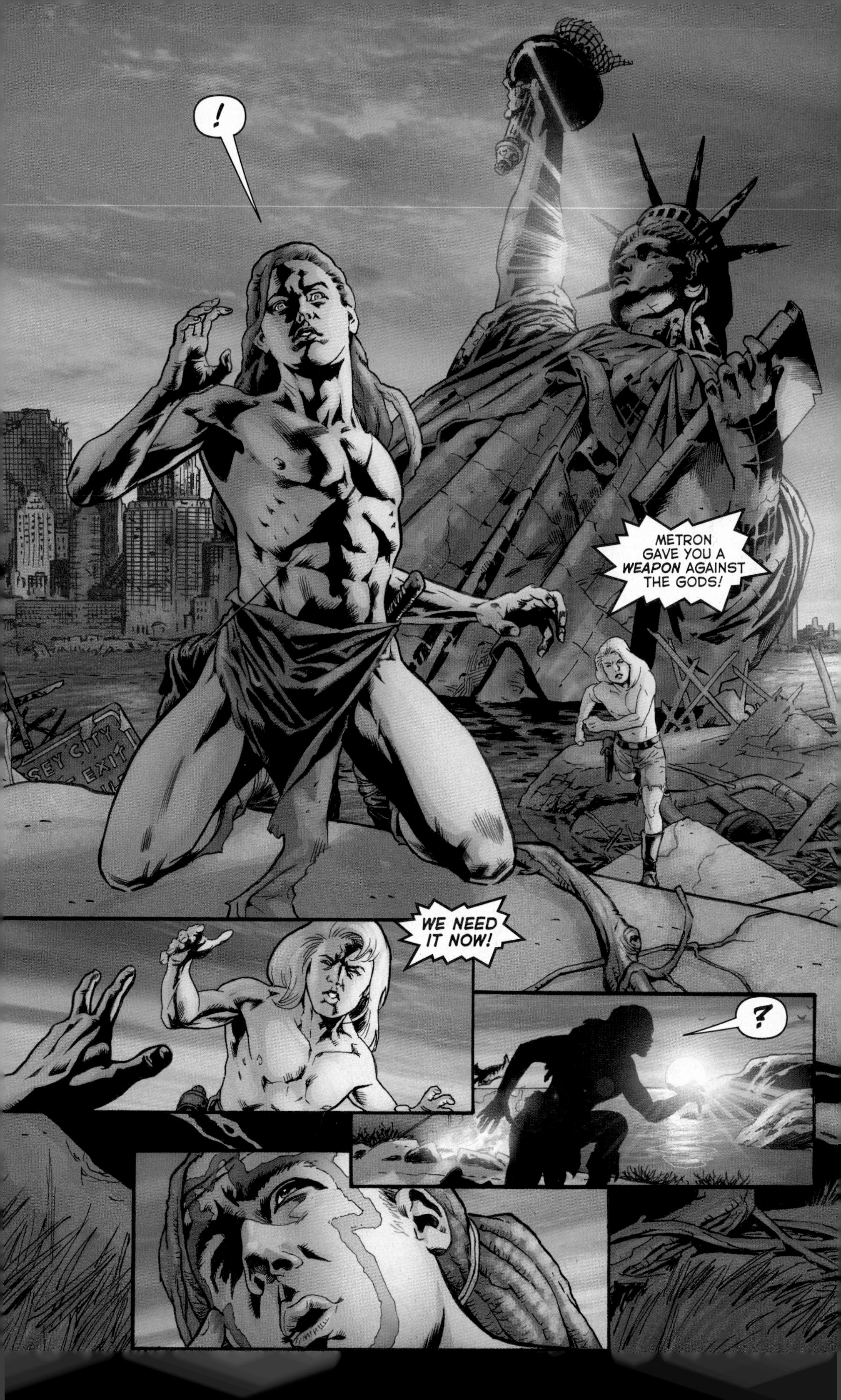
!
METRON GAVE YOU A WEAPON AGAINST THE GODS!
SEY CITY
EXIT
WE NEED IT NOW!
?

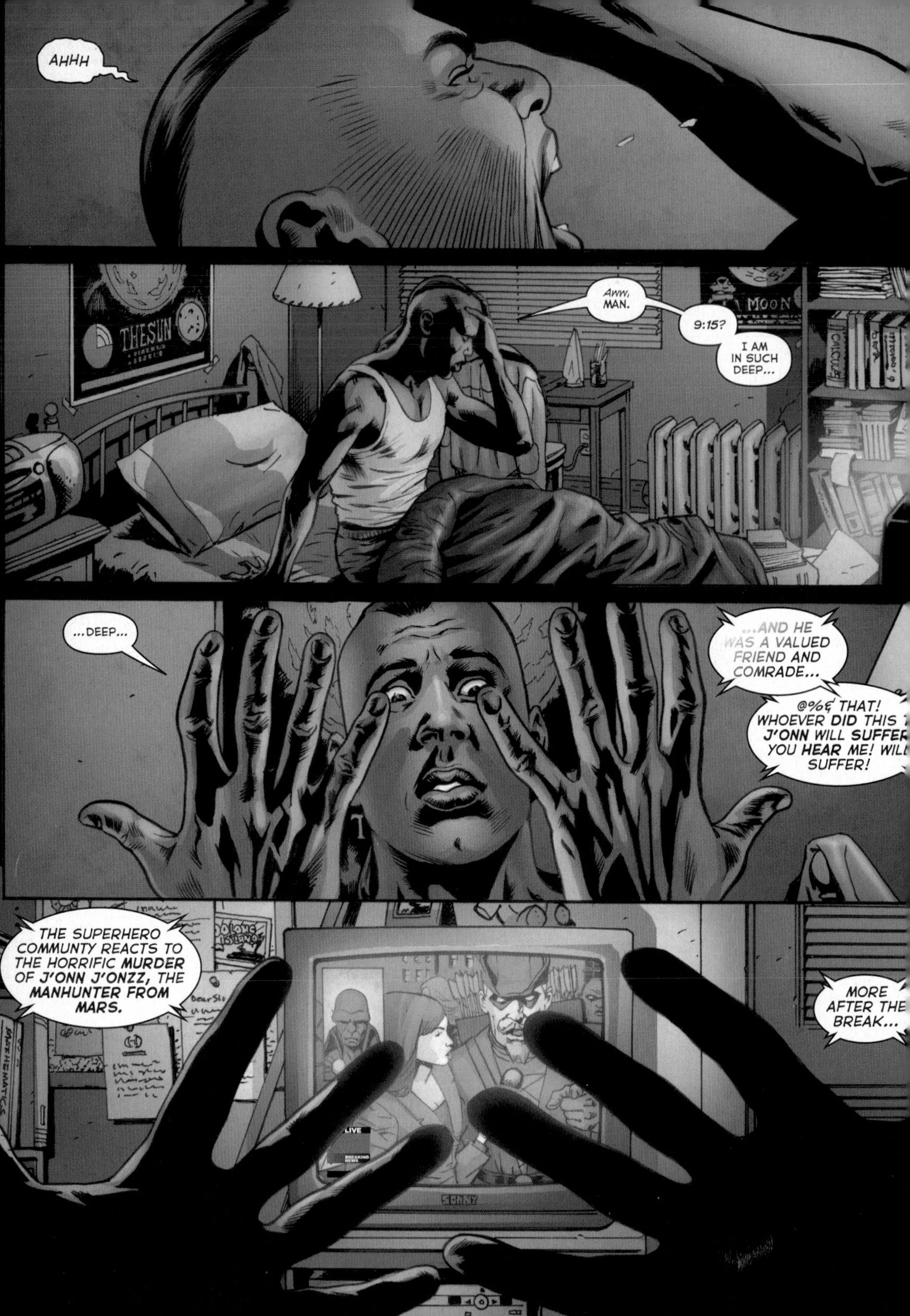
AHHH
AWW, MAN.
9:15?
I AM IN SUCH DEEP...
...DEEP...
...AND HE WAS A VALUED FRIEND AND COMRADE...
@%& THAT! WHOEVER DID THIS TO J'ONN WILL SUFFER, YOU HEAR ME! WILL SUFFER!
THE SUPERHERO COMMUNTY REACTS TO THE HORRIFIC MURDER OF J'ONN J'ONZZ, THE MANHUNTER FROM MARS.
MORE AFTER THE BREAK...
LIVE
BREAKING NEWS

YOU HAVE BEEN READING

D.O.A.: The GOD of WAR!

GRANT MORRISON SCRIPT JG JONES ART

ALEX SINCLAIR COLORS ROB LEIGH LETTERING

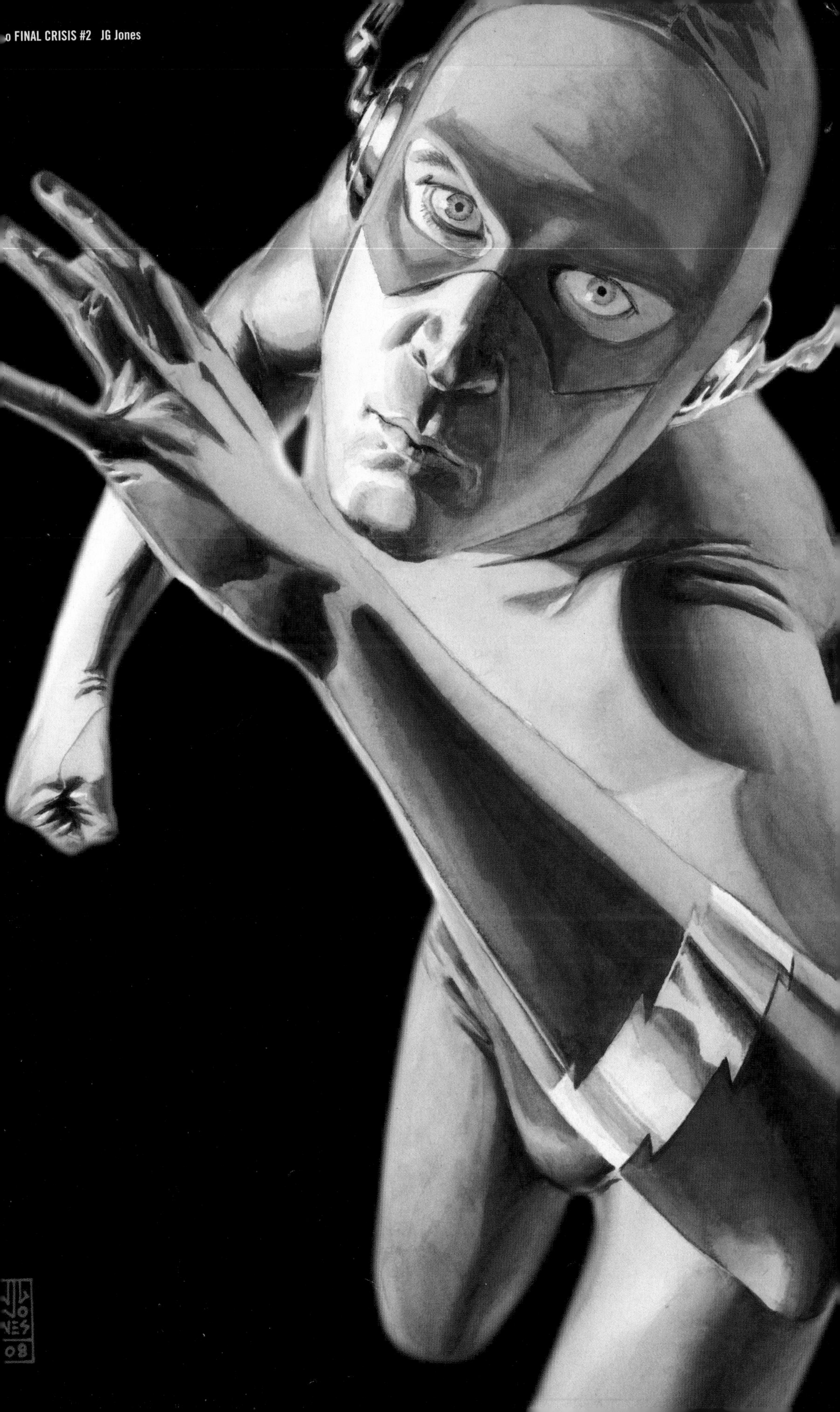

JG Jones with Alex Sinclair

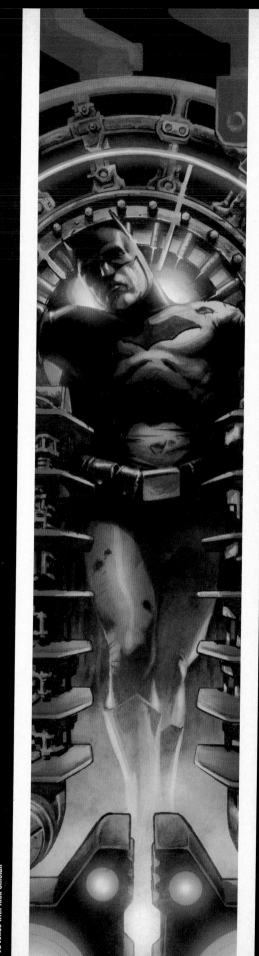

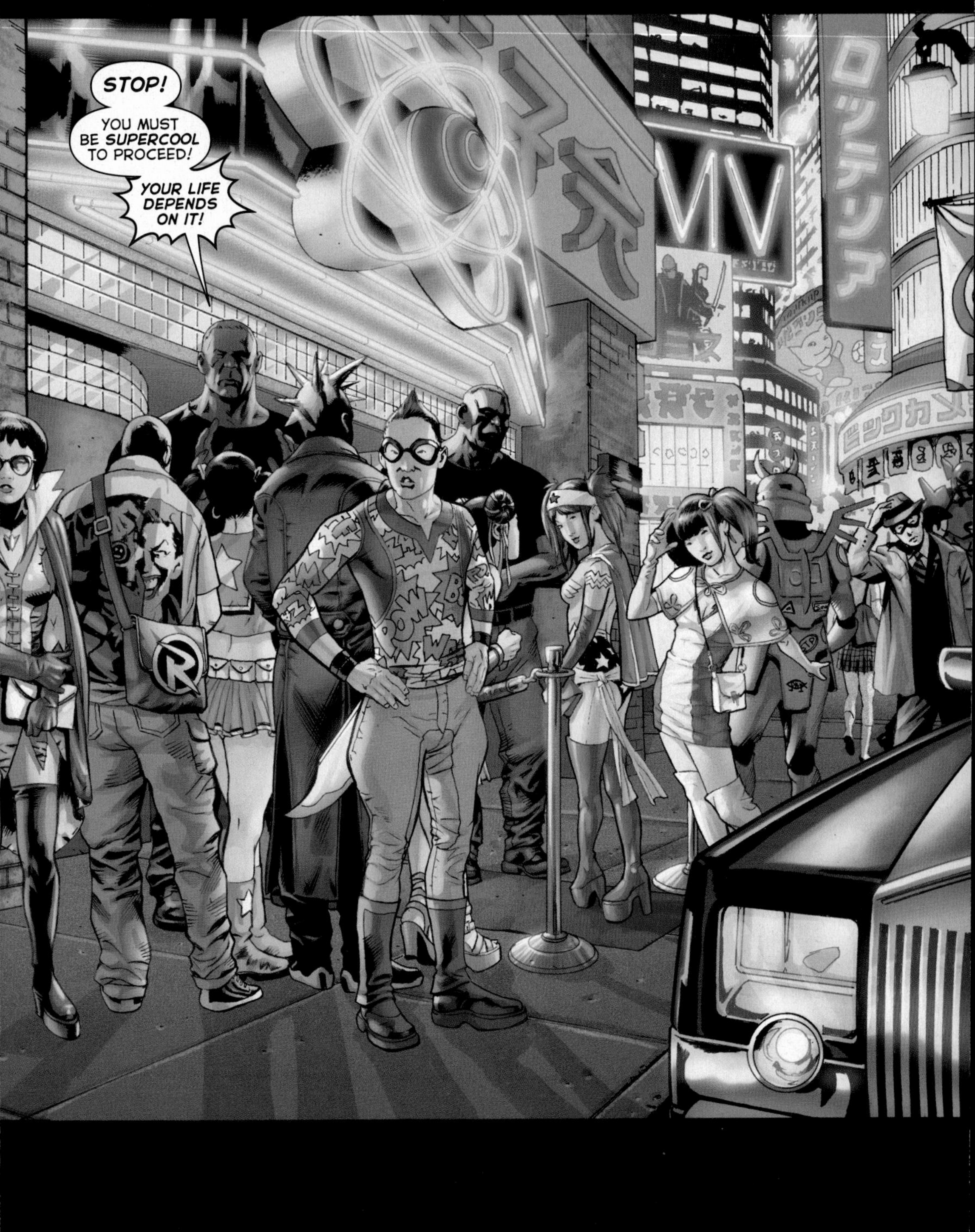
STOP!
YOU MUST BE SUPERCOOL TO PROCEED!
YOUR LIFE DEPENDS ON IT!

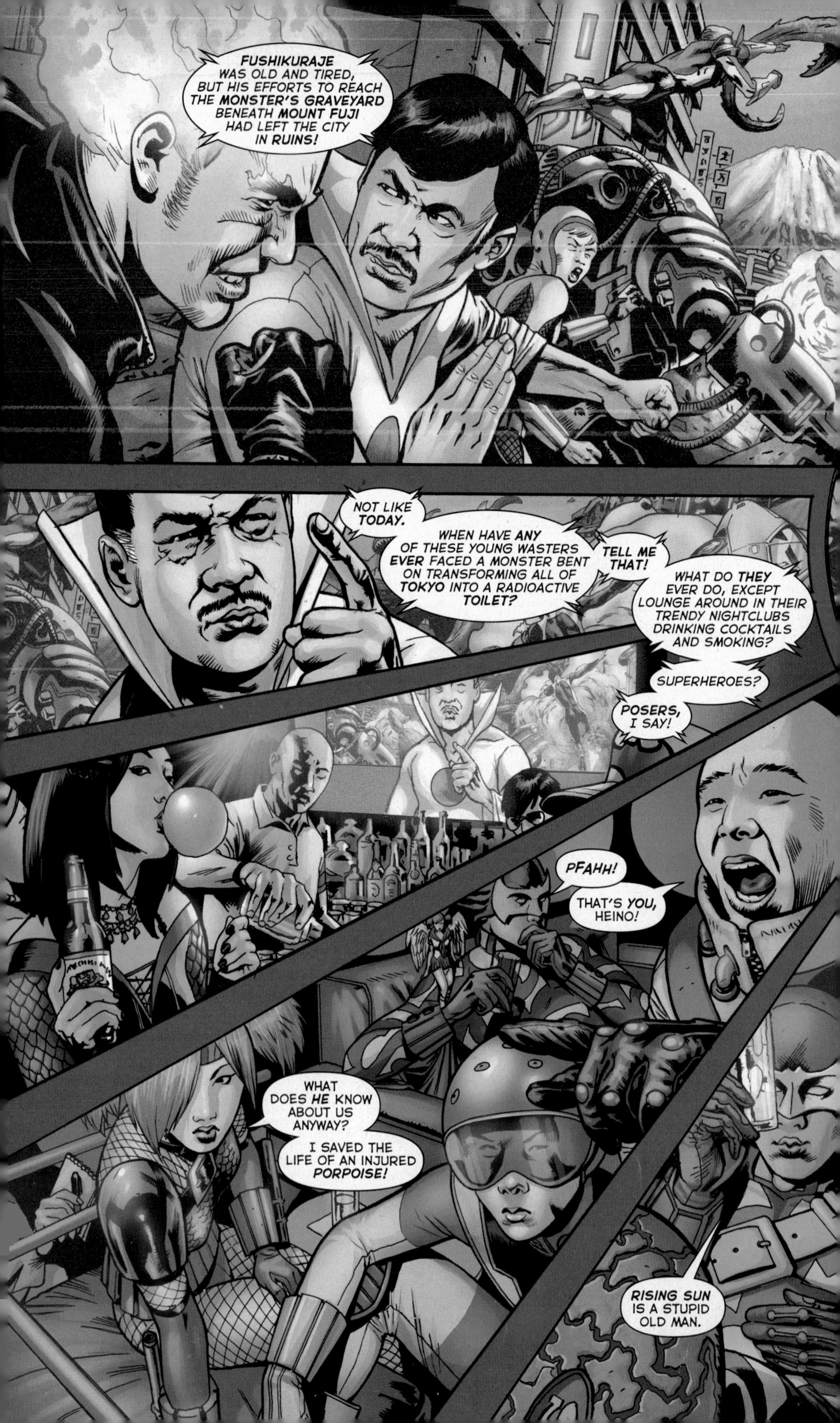

FUSHIKURAJE WAS OLD AND TIRED, BUT HIS EFFORTS TO REACH THE MONSTER'S GRAVEYARD BENEATH MOUNT FUJI HAD LEFT THE CITY IN RUINS!
NOT LIKE TODAY.
WHEN HAVE ANY OF THESE YOUNG WASTERS EVER FACED A MONSTER BENT ON TRANSFORMING ALL OF TOKYO INTO A RADIOACTIVE TOILET?
TELL ME THAT!
WHAT DO THEY EVER DO, EXCEPT LOUNGE AROUND IN THEIR TRENDY NIGHTCLUBS DRINKING COCKTAILS AND SMOKING?
SUPERHEROES?
POSERS, I SAY!
PFAHH!
THAT'S YOU, HEINO!
WHAT DOES HE KNOW ABOUT US ANYWAY?
I SAVED THE LIFE OF AN INJURED PORPOISE!
RISING SUN IS A STUPID OLD MAN.

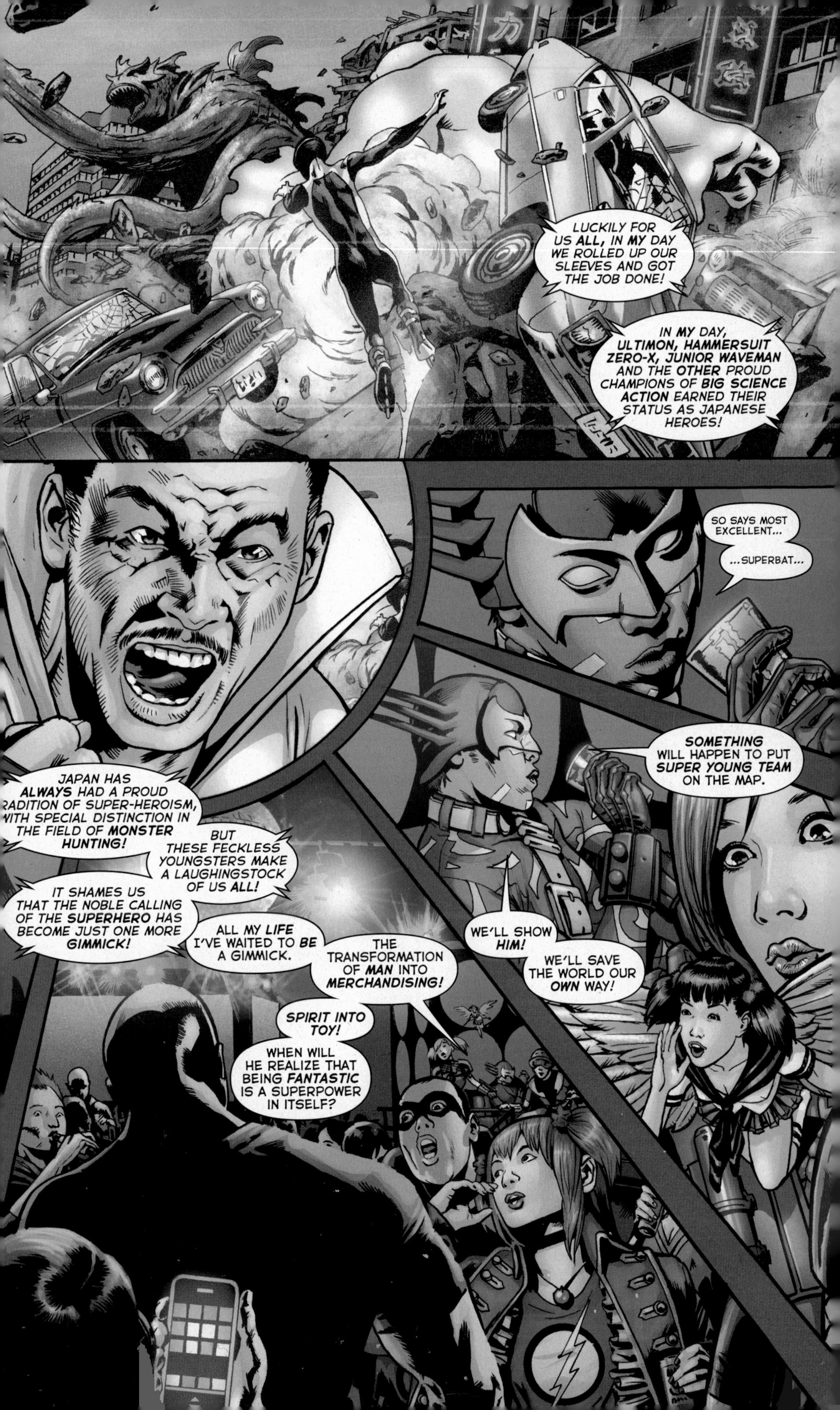

LUCKILY FOR US ALL, IN MY DAY WE ROLLED UP OUR SLEEVES AND GOT THE JOB DONE!
IN MY DAY, ULTIMON, HAMMERSUIT ZERO-X, JUNIOR WAVEMAN AND THE OTHER PROUD CHAMPIONS OF BIG SCIENCE ACTION EARNED THEIR STATUS AS JAPANESE HEROES!
JAPAN HAS ALWAYS HAD A PROUD RADITION OF SUPER-HEROISM, WITH SPECIAL DISTINCTION IN THE FIELD OF MONSTER HUNTING!
BUT THESE FECKLESS YOUNGSTERS MAKE A LAUGHINGSTOCK OF US ALL!
IT SHAMES US THAT THE NOBLE CALLING OF THE SUPERHERO HAS BECOME JUST ONE MORE GIMMICK!
ALL MY LIFE I'VE WAITED TO BE A GIMMICK.
THE TRANSFORMATION OF MAN INTO MERCHANDISING!
SPIRIT INTO TOY!
WHEN WILL HE REALIZE THAT BEING FANTASTIC IS A SUPERPOWER IN ITSELF?
SO SAYS MOST EXCELLENT...
...SUPERBAT...
SOMETHING WILL HAPPEN TO PUT SUPER YOUNG TEAM ON THE MAP.
WE'LL SHOW HIM!
WE'LL SAVE THE WORLD OUR OWN WAY!

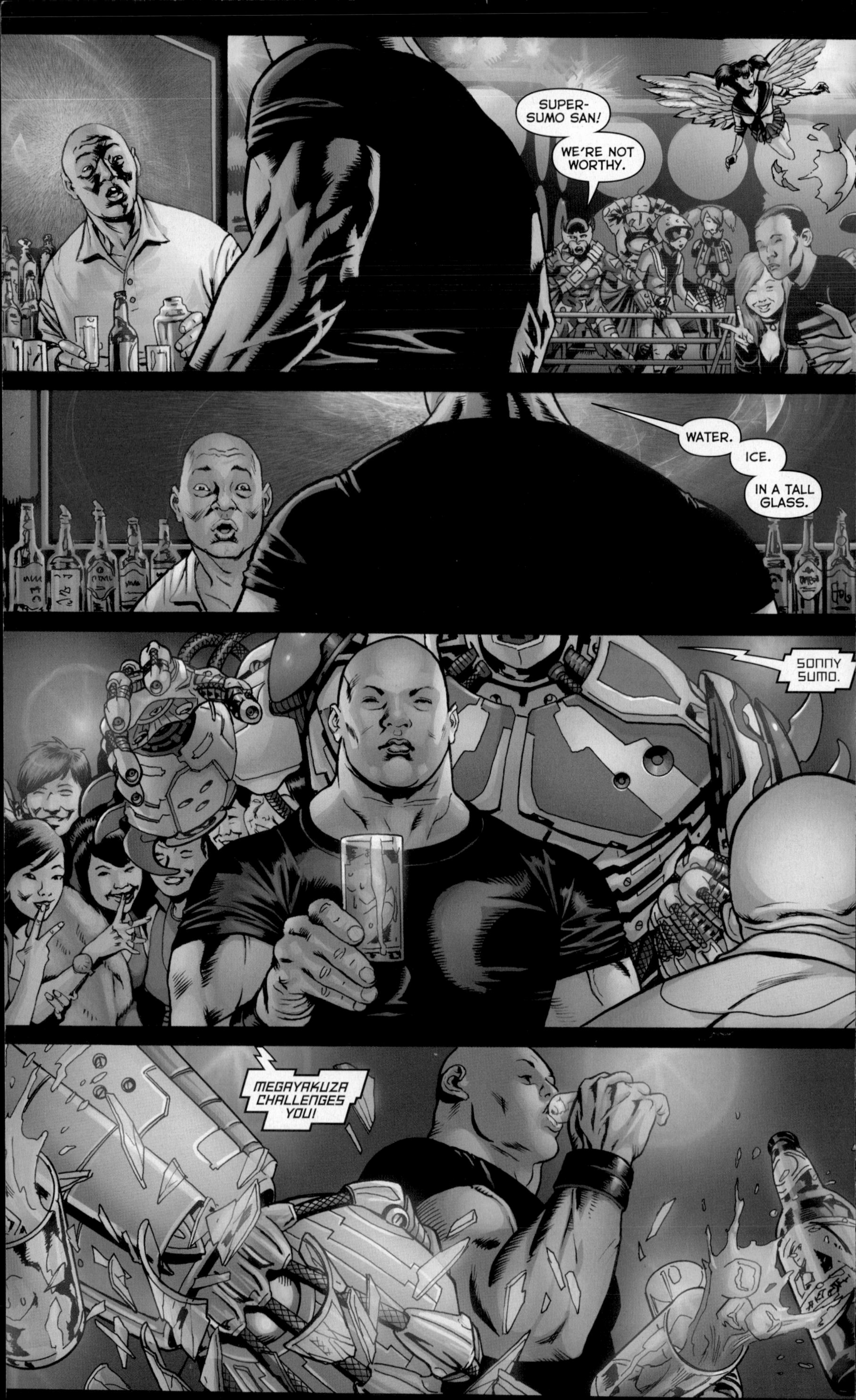
SUPER-SUMO SAN!
WE'RE NOT WORTHY.
WATER.
ICE.
IN A TALL GLASS.
SONNY SUMO.
MEGAYAKUZA CHALLENGES YOU!

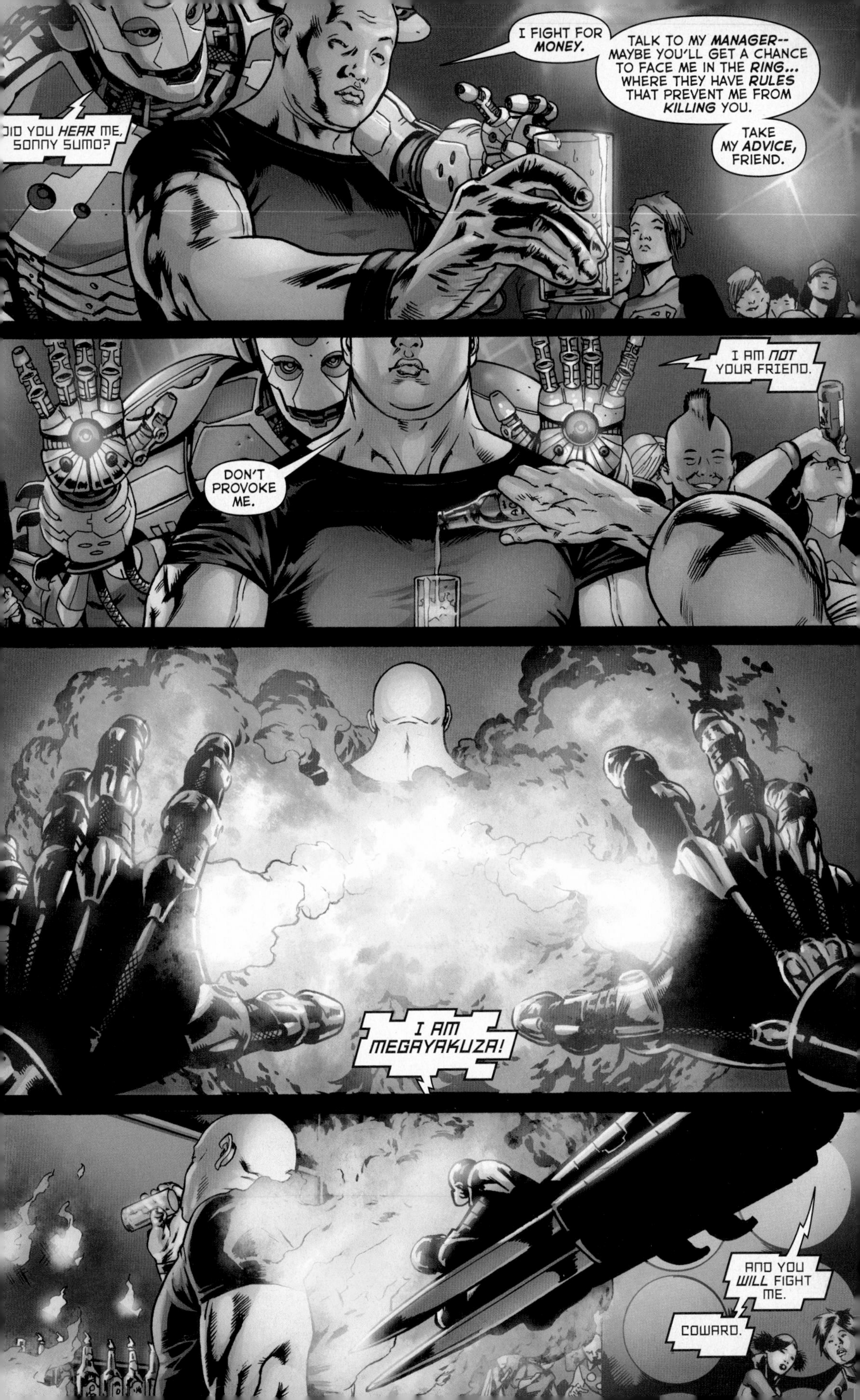

DID YOU *HEAR* ME, SONNY SUMO?
I FIGHT FOR *MONEY.*
TALK TO MY *MANAGER*-- MAYBE YOU'LL GET A CHANCE TO FACE ME IN THE *RING...* WHERE THEY HAVE *RULES* THAT PREVENT ME FROM *KILLING* YOU.
TAKE MY *ADVICE,* FRIEND.
I AM *NOT* YOUR FRIEND.
DON'T PROVOKE ME.
I AM MEGAYAKUZA!
AND YOU *WILL* FIGHT ME.
COWARD.

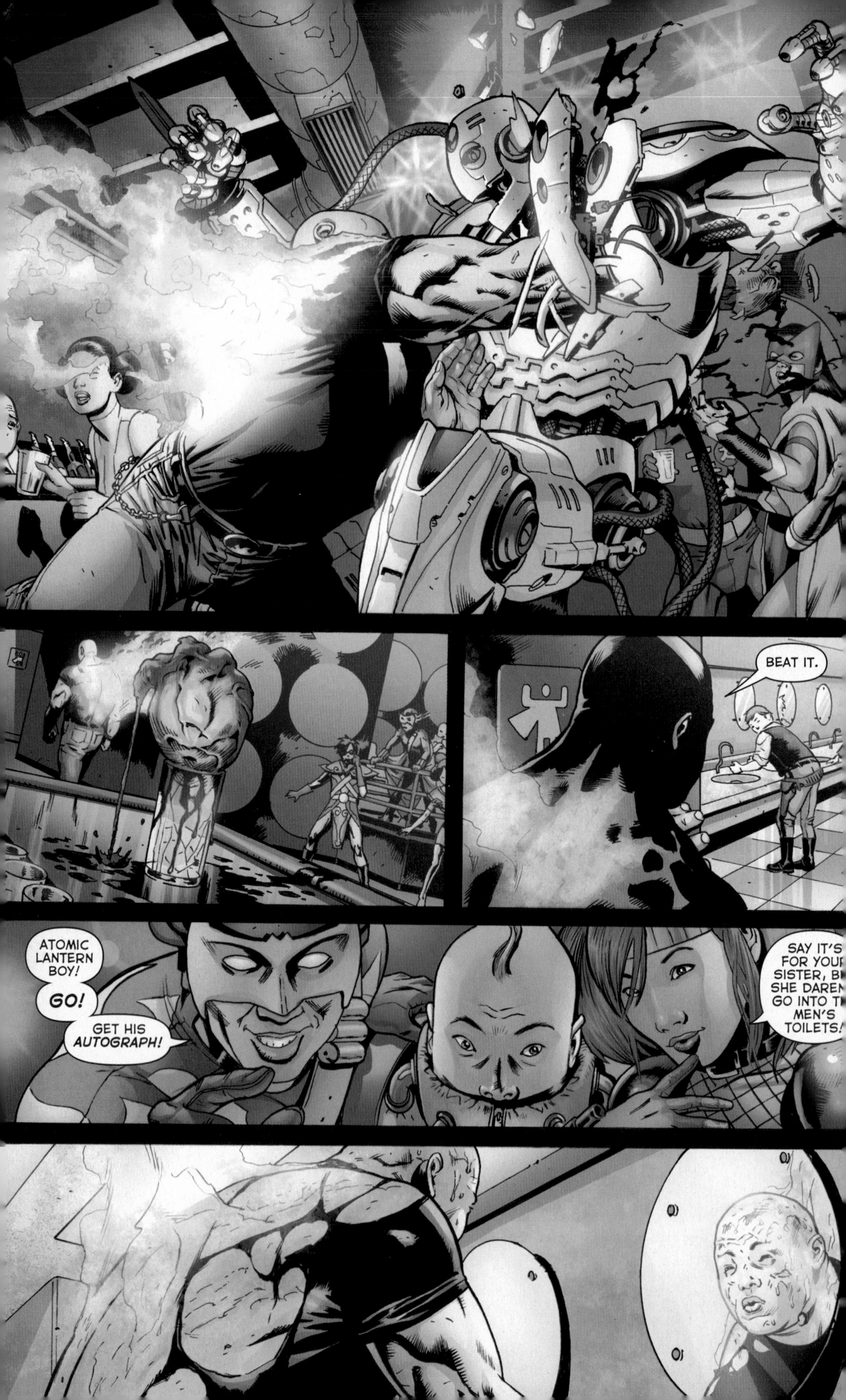
BEAT IT.
ATOMIC LANTERN BOY!
GO!
GET HIS AUTOGRAPH!
SAY IT'S FOR YOUR SISTER, B SHE DAREN GO INTO T MEN'S TOILETS!

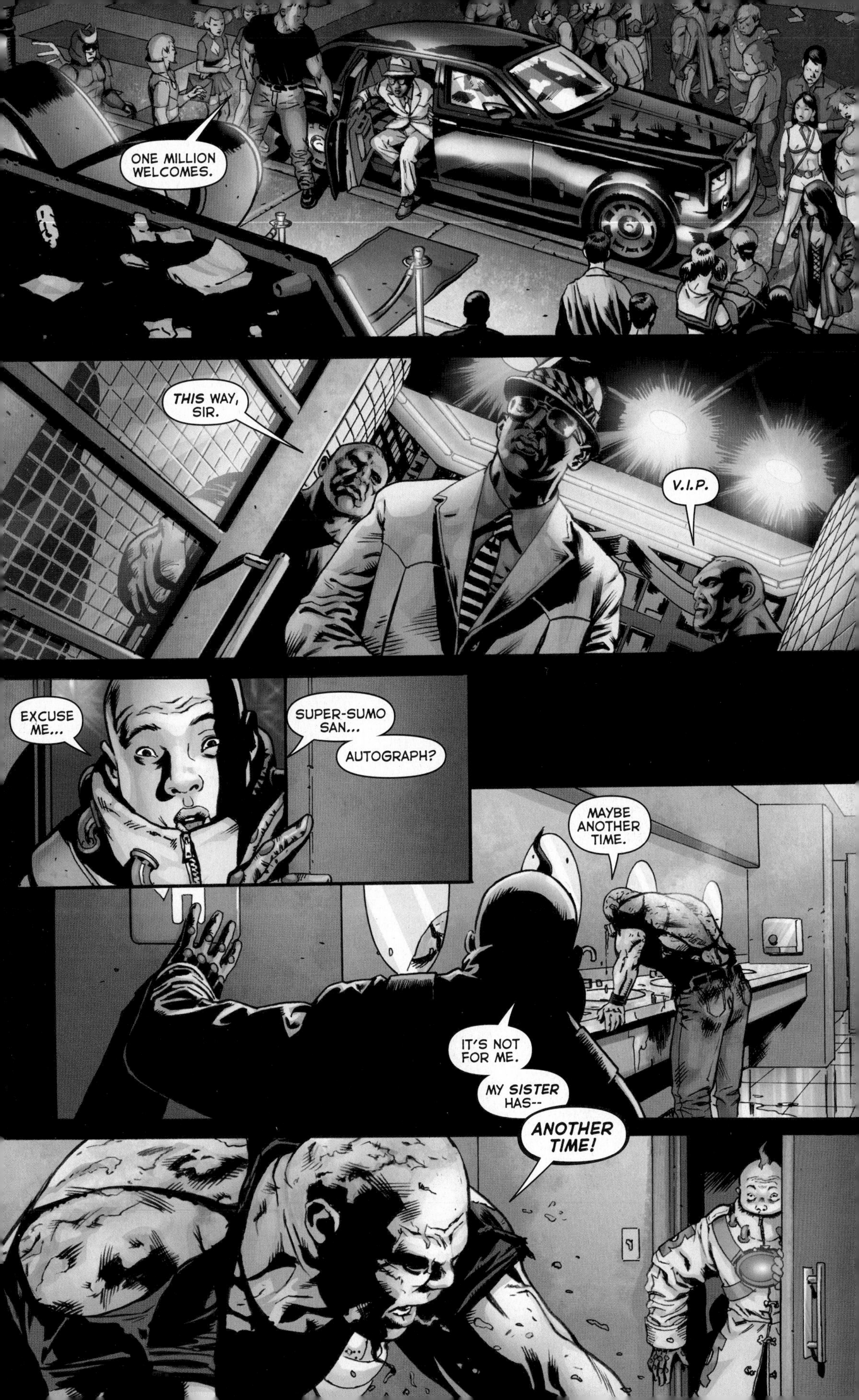
ONE MILLION WELCOMES.
THIS WAY, SIR.
V.I.P.
EXCUSE ME...
SUPER-SUMO SAN...
AUTOGRAPH?
MAYBE ANOTHER TIME.
IT'S NOT FOR ME.
MY SISTER HAS--
ANOTHER TIME!

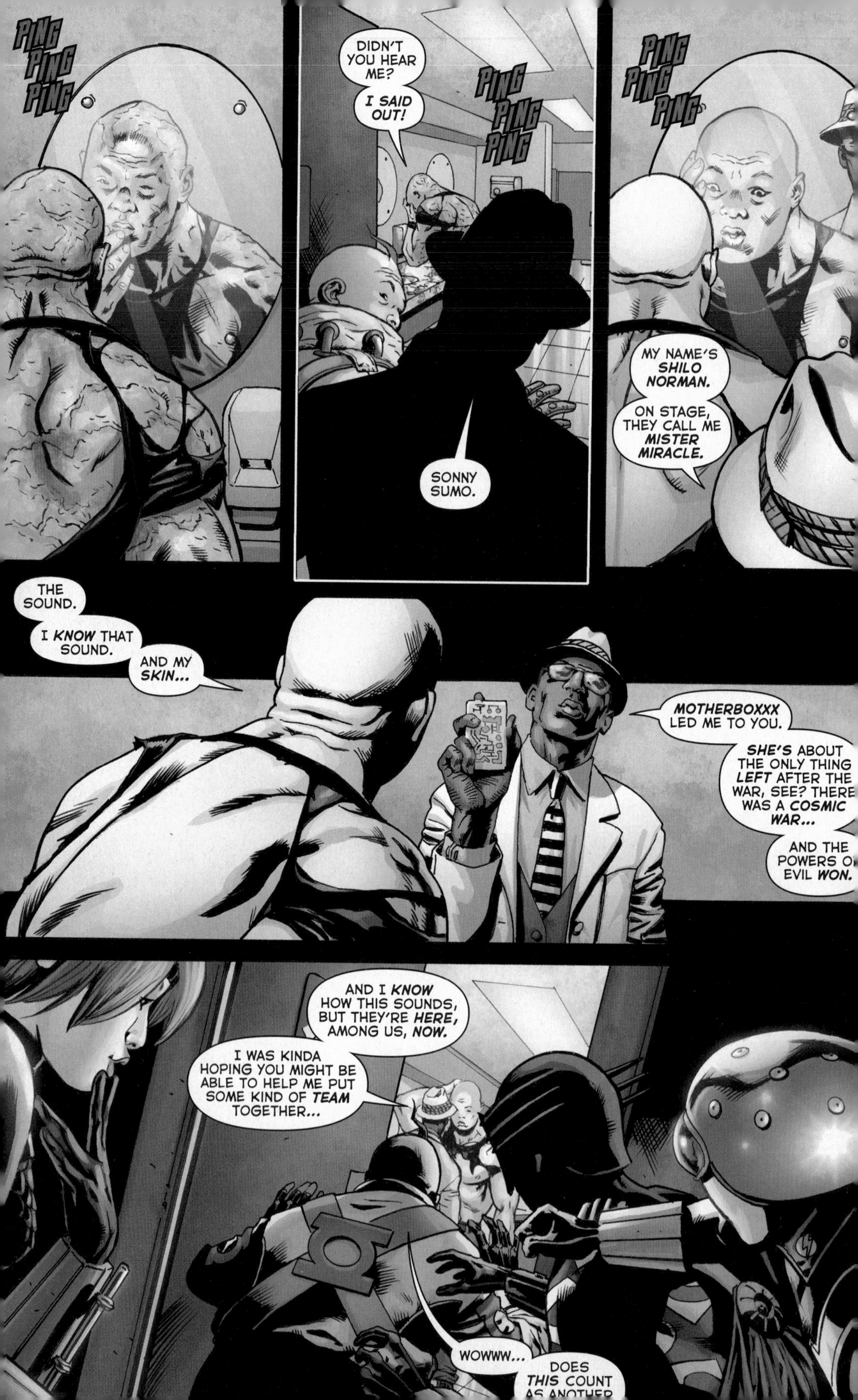
PING PING PING
DIDN'T YOU HEAR ME?
I SAID OUT!
PING PING PING
SONNY SUMO.
PING PING PING
MY NAME'S SHILO NORMAN.
ON STAGE, THEY CALL ME MISTER MIRACLE.
THE SOUND.
I KNOW THAT SOUND.
AND MY SKIN...
MOTHERBOXXX LED ME TO YOU.
SHE'S ABOUT THE ONLY THING LEFT AFTER THE WAR, SEE? THERE WAS A COSMIC WAR...
AND THE POWERS O EVIL WON.
AND I KNOW HOW THIS SOUNDS, BUT THEY'RE HERE, AMONG US, NOW.
I WAS KINDA HOPING YOU MIGHT BE ABLE TO HELP ME PUT SOME KIND OF TEAM TOGETHER...
WOWWW...
DOES THIS COUNT

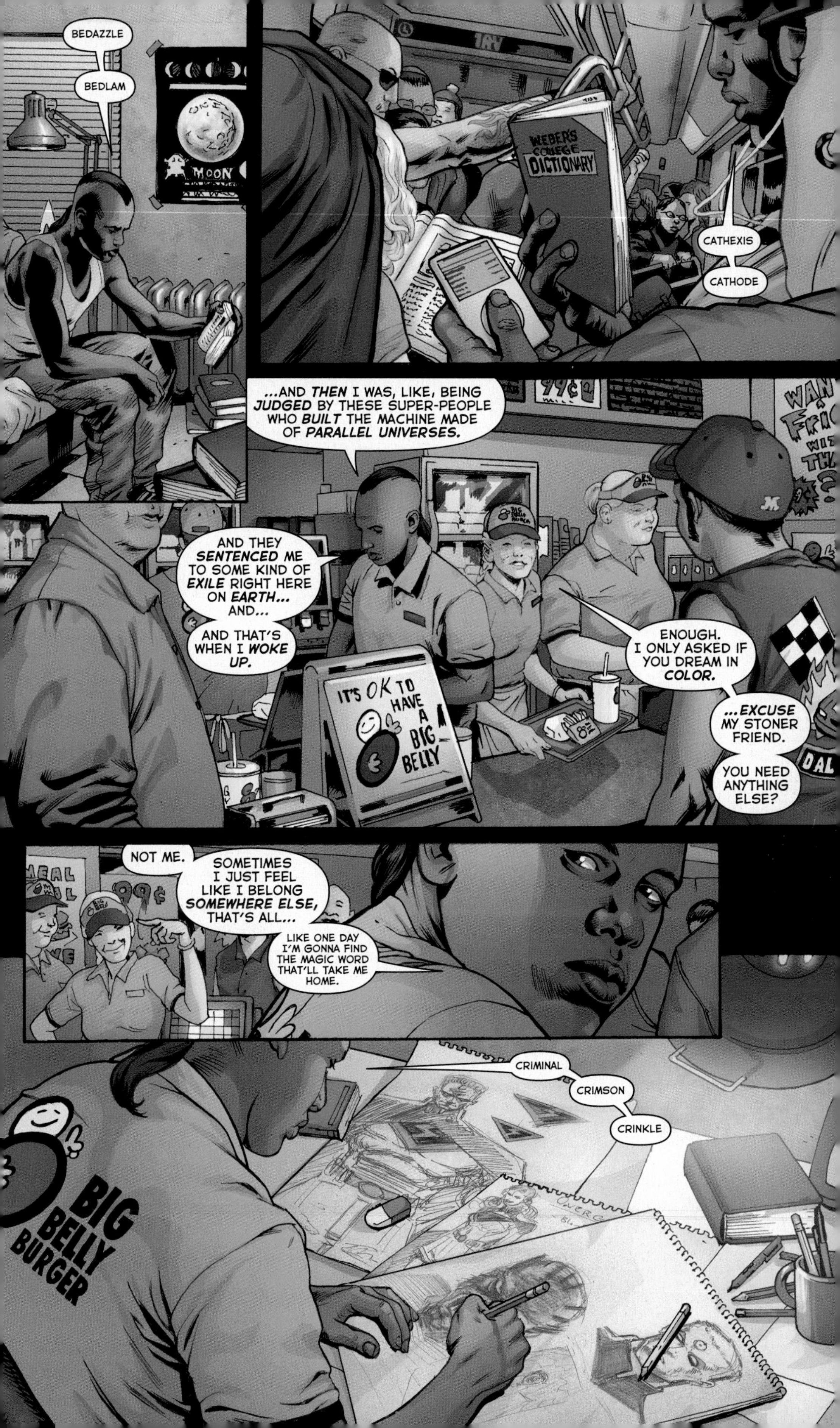
BEDAZZLE
BEDLAM
MOON
WEBER'S COLLEGE DICTIONARY
CATHEXIS
CATHODE
...AND THEN I WAS, LIKE, BEING JUDGED BY THESE SUPER-PEOPLE WHO BUILT THE MACHINE MADE OF PARALLEL UNIVERSES.
AND THEY SENTENCED ME TO SOME KIND OF EXILE RIGHT HERE ON EARTH... AND...
AND THAT'S WHEN I WOKE UP.
ENOUGH. I ONLY ASKED IF YOU DREAM IN COLOR.
...EXCUSE MY STONER FRIEND.
YOU NEED ANYTHING ELSE?
IT'S OK TO HAVE A BIG BELLY
NOT ME.
SOMETIMES I JUST FEEL LIKE I BELONG SOMEWHERE ELSE, THAT'S ALL...
LIKE ONE DAY I'M GONNA FIND THE MAGIC WORD THAT'LL TAKE ME HOME.
CRIMINAL
CRIMSON
CRINKLE
BIG BELLY BURGER

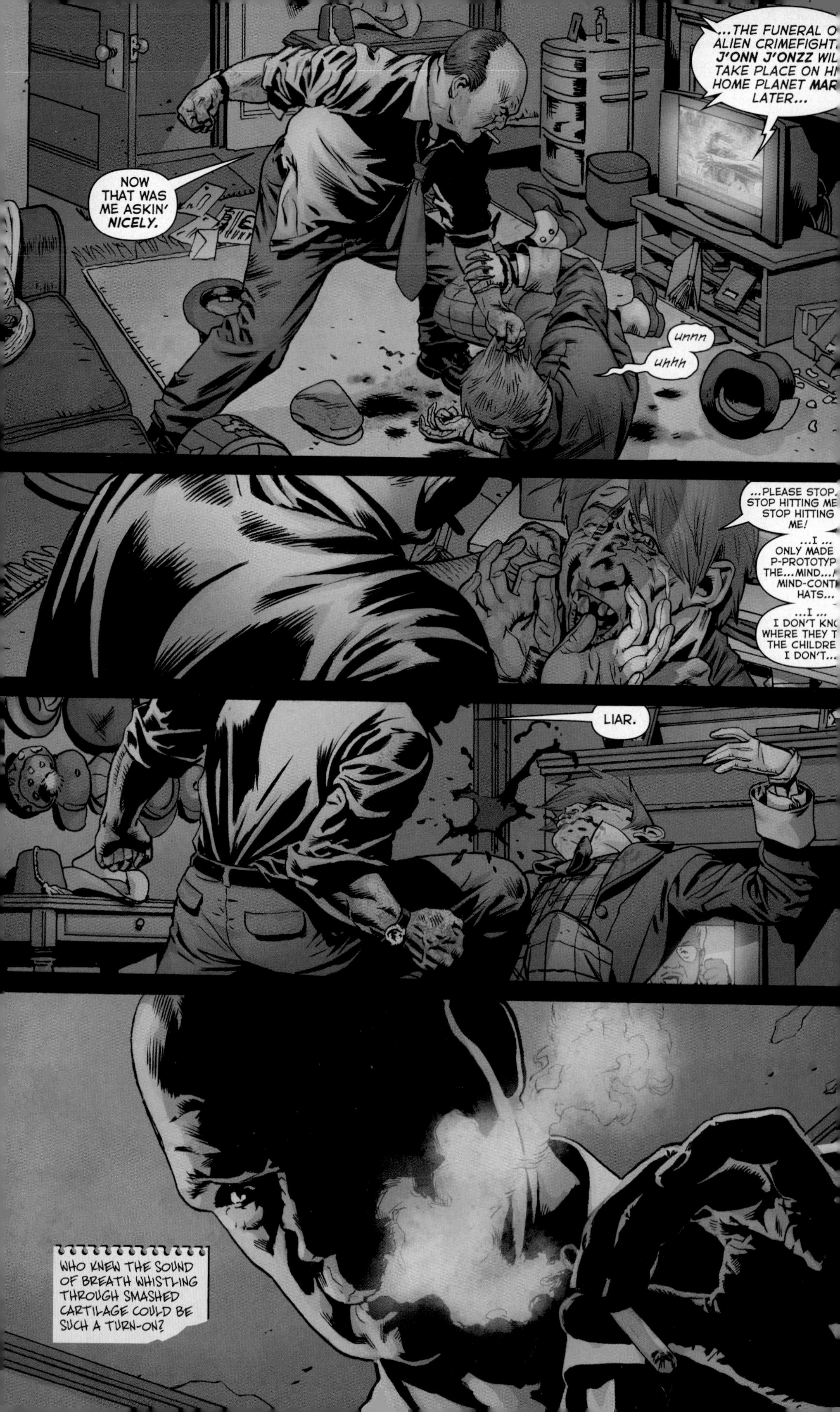
...THE FUNERAL O
ALIEN CRIMEFIGHT
J'ONN J'ONZZ WIL
TAKE PLACE ON HI
HOME PLANET MAR
LATER...
NOW THAT WAS ME ASKIN' NICELY.
unnn
uhhh
...PLEASE STOP.
STOP HITTING ME
STOP HITTING ME!
...I ... ONLY MADE P-PROTOTYP THE...MIND... MIND-CONT HATS...
...I ... I DON'T KN WHERE THEY T THE CHILDRE I DON'T...
LIAR.
WHO KNEW THE SOUND OF BREATH WHISTLING THROUGH SMASHED CARTILAGE COULD BE SUCH A TURN-ON?

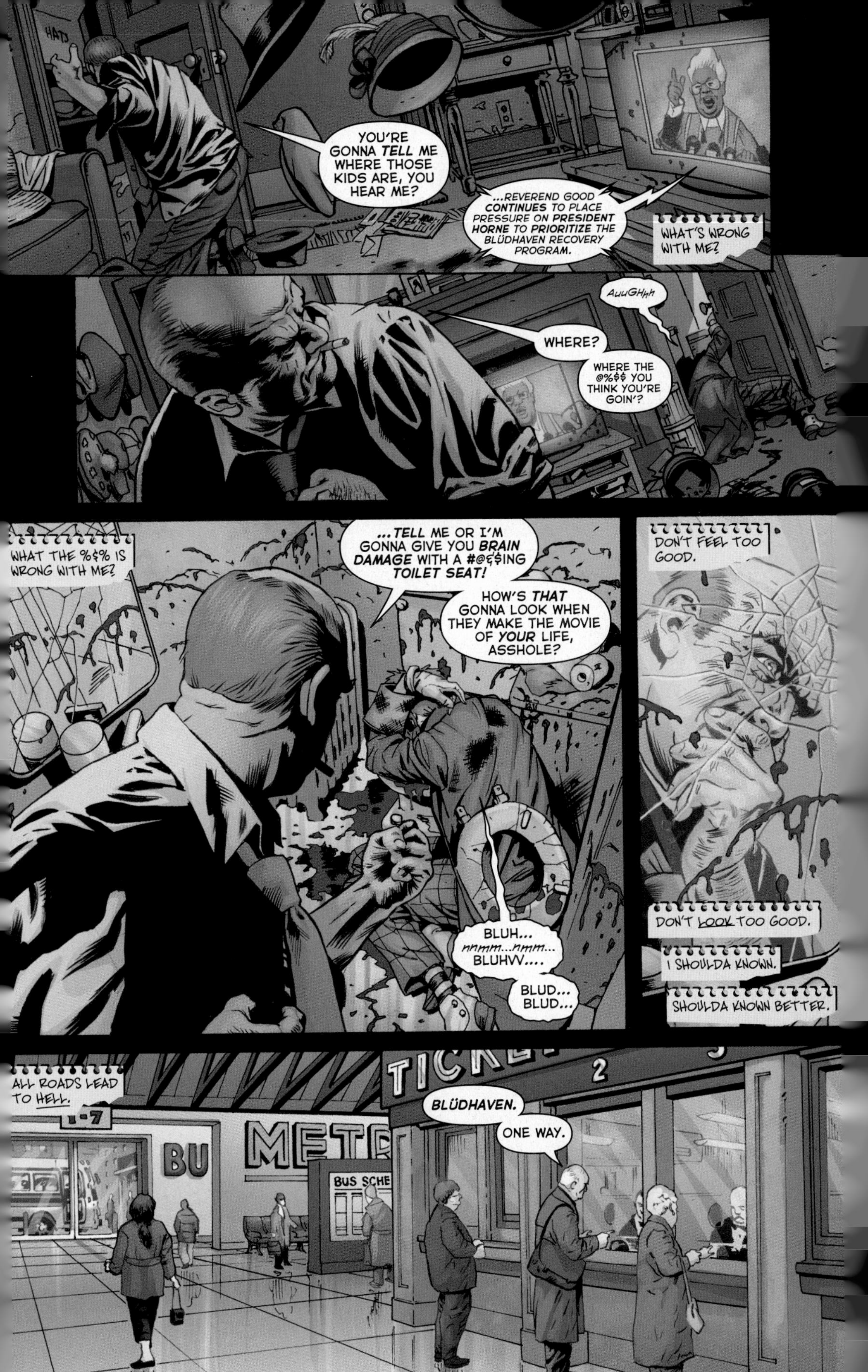
YOU'RE GONNA TELL ME WHERE THOSE KIDS ARE, YOU HEAR ME?
...REVEREND GOOD CONTINUES TO PLACE PRESSURE ON PRESIDENT HORNE TO PRIORITIZE THE BLÜDHAVEN RECOVERY PROGRAM.
WHAT'S WRONG WITH ME?
AuuGHhh
WHERE?
WHERE THE @%$$ YOU THINK YOU'RE GOIN'?
WHAT THE %$% IS WRONG WITH ME?
...TELL ME OR I'M GONNA GIVE YOU BRAIN DAMAGE WITH A #@¢$ING TOILET SEAT!
HOW'S THAT GONNA LOOK WHEN THEY MAKE THE MOVIE OF YOUR LIFE, ASSHOLE?
BLUH... nmmm...nmm... BLUHVV....
BLUD... BLUD...
DON'T FEEL TOO GOOD.
DON'T LOOK TOO GOOD.
I SHOULDA KNOWN.
SHOULDA KNOWN BETTER.
ALL ROADS LEAD TO HELL.
BLÜDHAVEN.
ONE WAY.

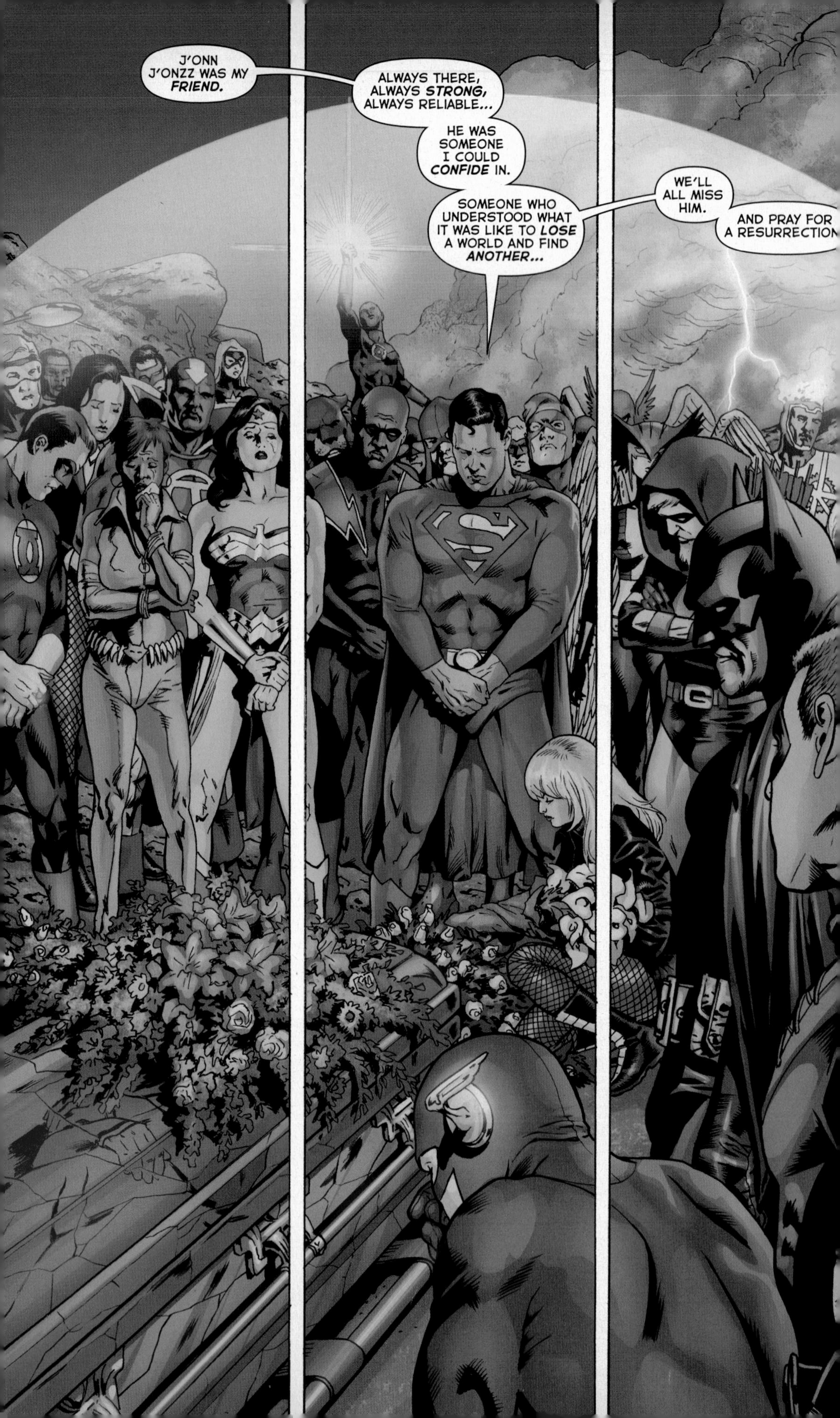
J'ONN J'ONZZ WAS MY FRIEND.
ALWAYS THERE, ALWAYS STRONG, ALWAYS RELIABLE...
HE WAS SOMEONE I COULD CONFIDE IN.
SOMEONE WHO UNDERSTOOD WHAT IT WAS LIKE TO LOSE A WORLD AND FIND ANOTHER...
WE'LL ALL MISS HIM.
AND PRAY FOR A RESURRECTION

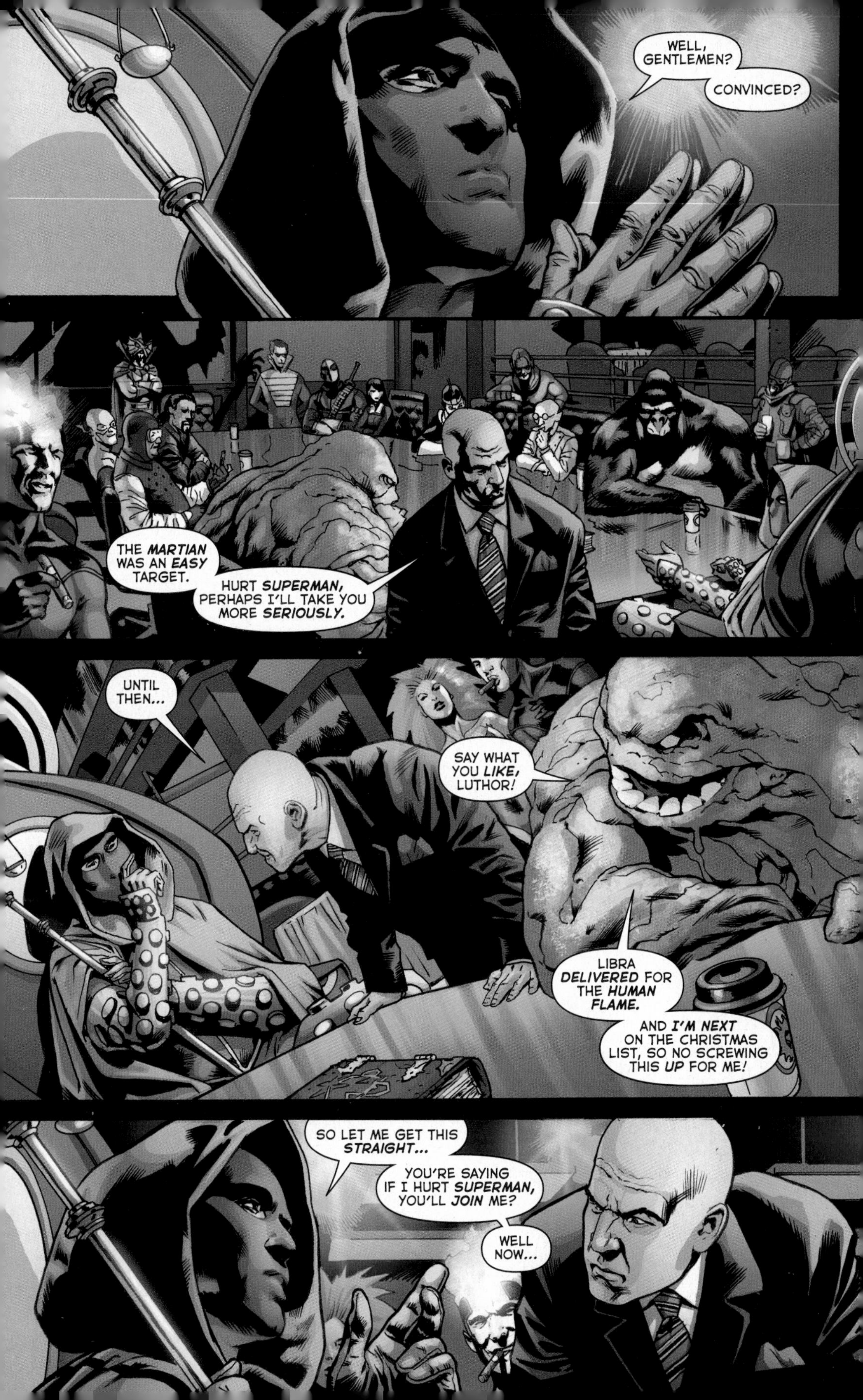
WELL, GENTLEMEN?
CONVINCED?
THE MARTIAN WAS AN EASY TARGET.
HURT SUPERMAN, PERHAPS I'LL TAKE YOU MORE SERIOUSLY.
UNTIL THEN...
SAY WHAT YOU LIKE, LUTHOR!
LIBRA DELIVERED FOR THE HUMAN FLAME.
AND I'M NEXT ON THE CHRISTMAS LIST, SO NO SCREWING THIS UP FOR ME!
SO LET ME GET THIS STRAIGHT...
YOU'RE SAYING IF I HURT SUPERMAN, YOU'LL JOIN ME?
WELL NOW...

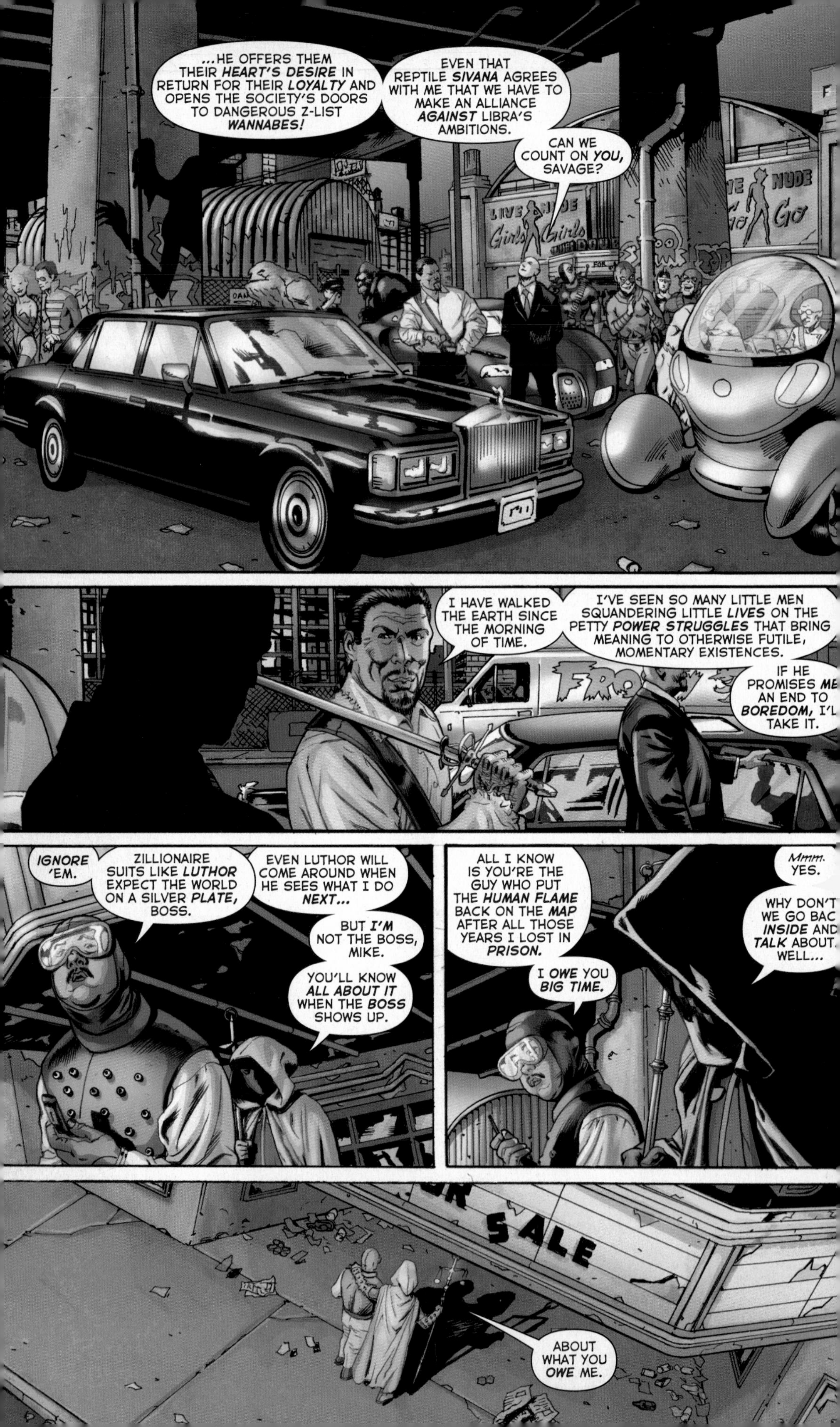
...HE OFFERS THEM THEIR HEART'S DESIRE IN RETURN FOR THEIR LOYALTY AND OPENS THE SOCIETY'S DOORS TO DANGEROUS Z-LIST WANNABES!
EVEN THAT REPTILE SIVANA AGREES WITH ME THAT WE HAVE TO MAKE AN ALLIANCE AGAINST LIBRA'S AMBITIONS.
CAN WE COUNT ON YOU, SAVAGE?
LIVE NUDE Girls Girls
NUDE Go
I HAVE WALKED THE EARTH SINCE THE MORNING OF TIME.
I'VE SEEN SO MANY LITTLE MEN SQUANDERING LITTLE LIVES ON THE PETTY POWER STRUGGLES THAT BRING MEANING TO OTHERWISE FUTILE, MOMENTARY EXISTENCES.
IF HE PROMISES ME AN END TO BOREDOM, I'L TAKE IT.
IGNORE 'EM.
ZILLIONAIRE SUITS LIKE LUTHOR EXPECT THE WORLD ON A SILVER PLATE, BOSS.
EVEN LUTHOR WILL COME AROUND WHEN HE SEES WHAT I DO NEXT...
BUT I'M NOT THE BOSS, MIKE.
YOU'LL KNOW ALL ABOUT IT WHEN THE BOSS SHOWS UP.
ALL I KNOW IS YOU'RE THE GUY WHO PUT THE HUMAN FLAME BACK ON THE MAP AFTER ALL THOSE YEARS I LOST IN PRISON.
I OWE YOU BIG TIME.
Mmm. YES.
WHY DON'T WE GO BAC INSIDE AND TALK ABOUT WELL...
SALE
ABOUT WHAT YOU OWE ME.

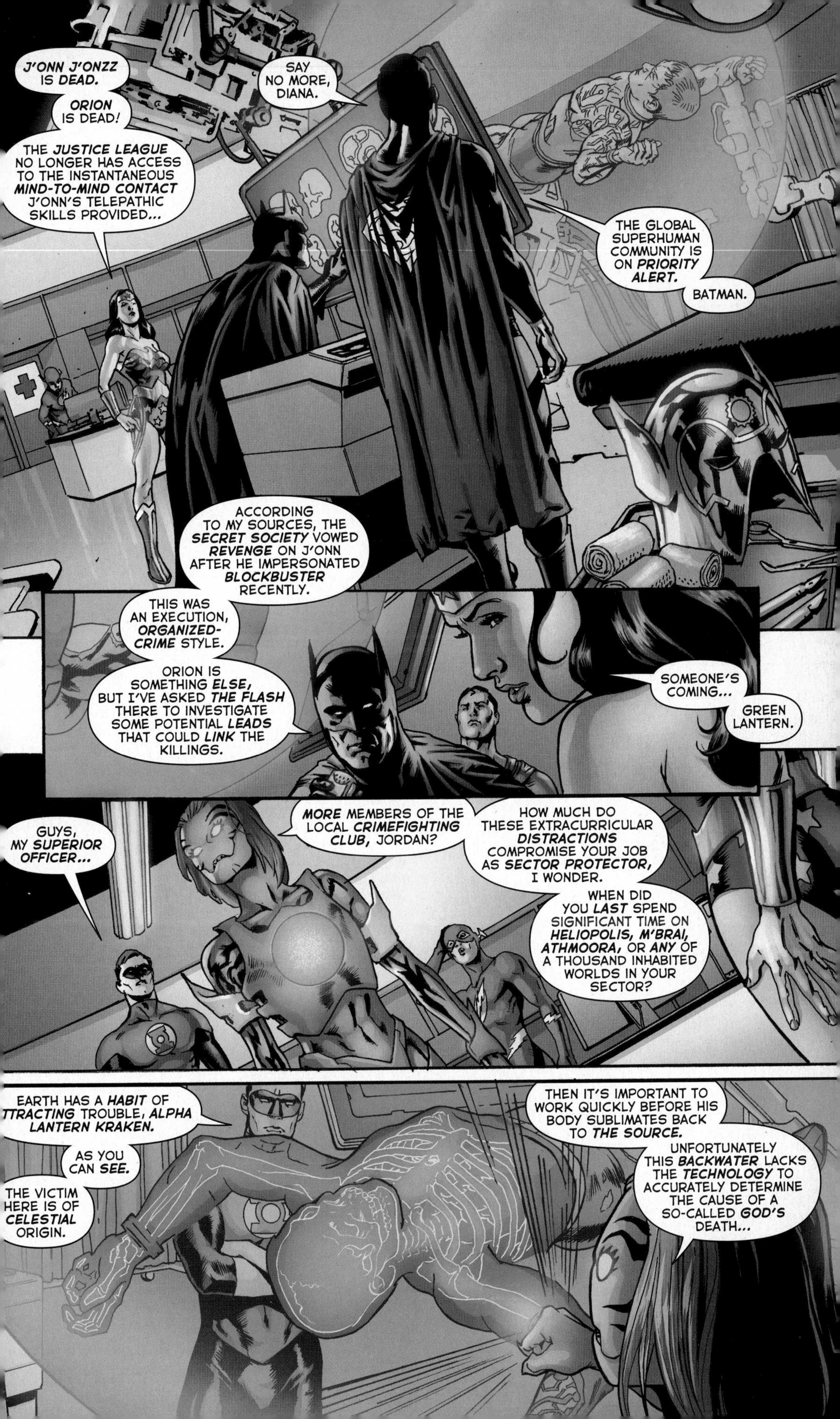
J'ONN J'ONZZ IS DEAD.
ORION IS DEAD!
THE JUSTICE LEAGUE NO LONGER HAS ACCESS TO THE INSTANTANEOUS MIND-TO-MIND CONTACT J'ONN'S TELEPATHIC SKILLS PROVIDED...
SAY NO MORE, DIANA.
THE GLOBAL SUPERHUMAN COMMUNITY IS ON PRIORITY ALERT.
BATMAN.
ACCORDING TO MY SOURCES, THE SECRET SOCIETY VOWED REVENGE ON J'ONN AFTER HE IMPERSONATED BLOCKBUSTER RECENTLY.
THIS WAS AN EXECUTION, ORGANIZED-CRIME STYLE.
ORION IS SOMETHING ELSE, BUT I'VE ASKED THE FLASH THERE TO INVESTIGATE SOME POTENTIAL LEADS THAT COULD LINK THE KILLINGS.
SOMEONE'S COMING...
GREEN LANTERN.
GUYS, MY SUPERIOR OFFICER...
MORE MEMBERS OF THE LOCAL CRIMEFIGHTING CLUB, JORDAN?
HOW MUCH DO THESE EXTRACURRICULAR DISTRACTIONS COMPROMISE YOUR JOB AS SECTOR PROTECTOR, I WONDER.
WHEN DID YOU LAST SPEND SIGNIFICANT TIME ON HELIOPOLIS, M'BRAI, ATHMOORA, OR ANY OF A THOUSAND INHABITED WORLDS IN YOUR SECTOR?
EARTH HAS A HABIT OF TTRACTING TROUBLE, ALPHA LANTERN KRAKEN.
AS YOU CAN SEE.
THE VICTIM HERE IS OF CELESTIAL ORIGIN.
THEN IT'S IMPORTANT TO WORK QUICKLY BEFORE HIS BODY SUBLIMATES BACK TO THE SOURCE.
UNFORTUNATELY THIS BACKWATER LACKS THE TECHNOLOGY TO ACCURATELY DETERMINE THE CAUSE OF A SO-CALLED GOD'S DEATH...

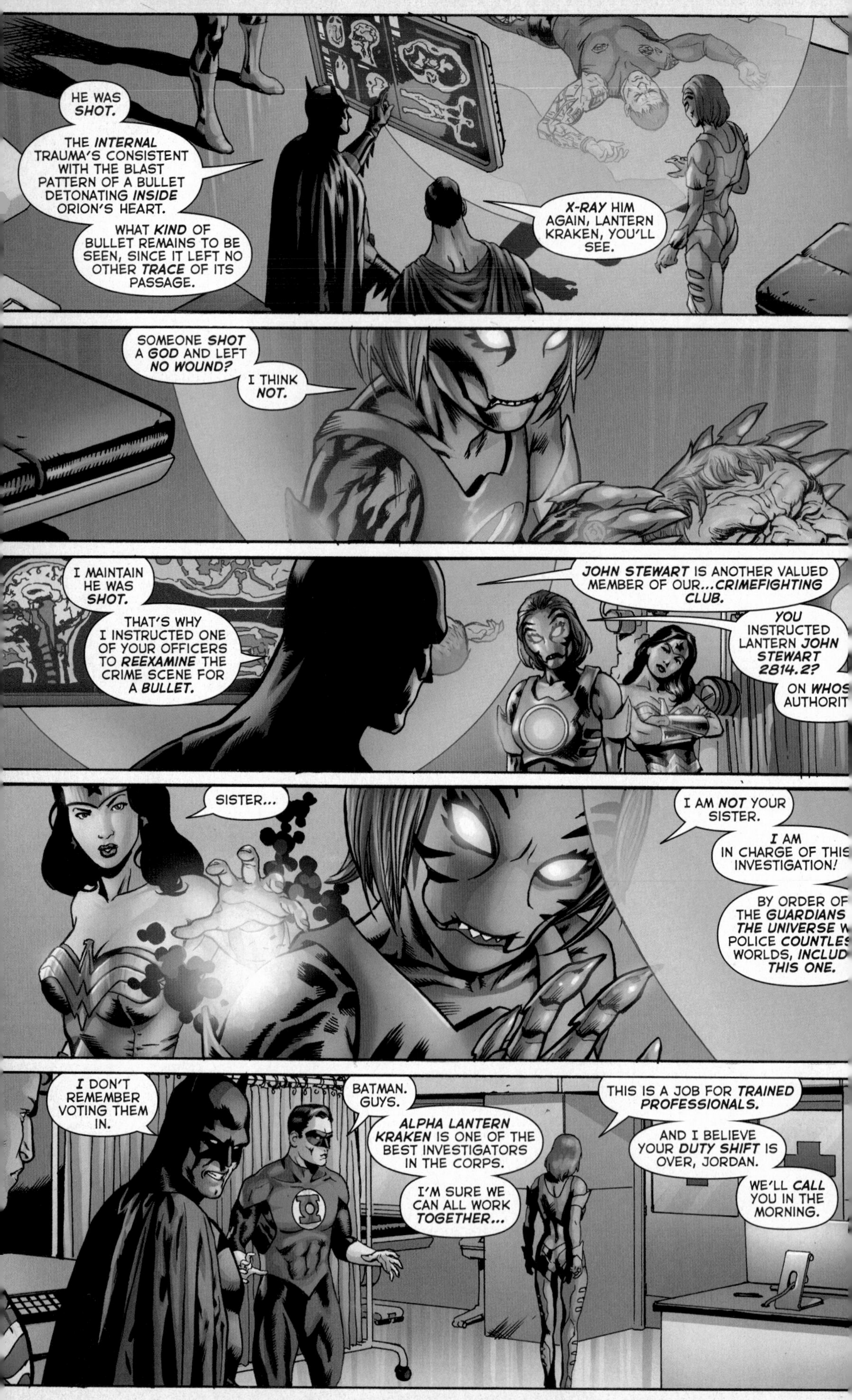

HE WAS SHOT.
THE INTERNAL TRAUMA'S CONSISTENT WITH THE BLAST PATTERN OF A BULLET DETONATING INSIDE ORION'S HEART.
WHAT KIND OF BULLET REMAINS TO BE SEEN, SINCE IT LEFT NO OTHER TRACE OF ITS PASSAGE.
X-RAY HIM AGAIN, LANTERN KRAKEN, YOU'LL SEE.
SOMEONE SHOT A GOD AND LEFT NO WOUND?
I THINK NOT.
I MAINTAIN HE WAS SHOT.
THAT'S WHY I INSTRUCTED ONE OF YOUR OFFICERS TO REEXAMINE THE CRIME SCENE FOR A BULLET.
JOHN STEWART IS ANOTHER VALUED MEMBER OF OUR...CRIMEFIGHTING CLUB.
YOU INSTRUCTED LANTERN JOHN STEWART 2814.2?
ON WHOS AUTHORIT
SISTER...
I AM NOT YOUR SISTER.
I AM IN CHARGE OF THIS INVESTIGATION!
BY ORDER OF THE GUARDIANS THE UNIVERSE W POLICE COUNTLES WORLDS, INCLUD THIS ONE.
I DON'T REMEMBER VOTING THEM IN.
BATMAN. GUYS.
ALPHA LANTERN KRAKEN IS ONE OF THE BEST INVESTIGATORS IN THE CORPS.
I'M SURE WE CAN ALL WORK TOGETHER...
THIS IS A JOB FOR TRAINED PROFESSIONALS.
AND I BELIEVE YOUR DUTY SHIFT IS OVER, JORDAN.
WE'LL CALL YOU IN THE MORNING.

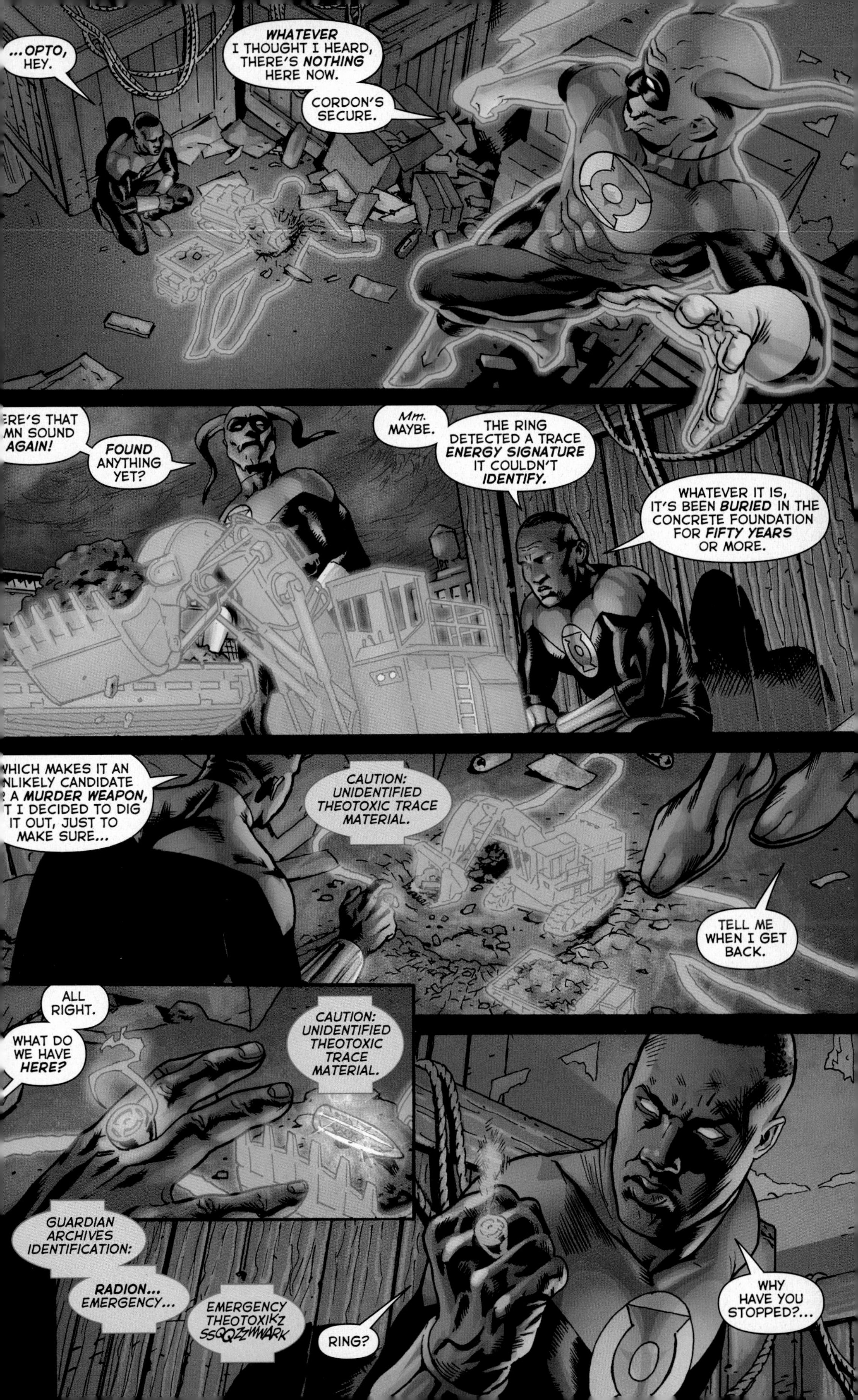

...OPTO, HEY.
WHATEVER I THOUGHT I HEARD, THERE'S NOTHING HERE NOW.
CORDON'S SECURE.
ERE'S THAT MN SOUND AGAIN!
FOUND ANYTHING YET?
Mm. MAYBE.
THE RING DETECTED A TRACE ENERGY SIGNATURE IT COULDN'T IDENTIFY.
WHATEVER IT IS, IT'S BEEN BURIED IN THE CONCRETE FOUNDATION FOR FIFTY YEARS OR MORE.
WHICH MAKES IT AN NLIKELY CANDIDATE A MURDER WEAPON, T I DECIDED TO DIG IT OUT, JUST TO MAKE SURE...
CAUTION: UNIDENTIFIED THEOTOXIC TRACE MATERIAL.
TELL ME WHEN I GET BACK.
ALL RIGHT.
WHAT DO WE HAVE HERE?
CAUTION: UNIDENTIFIED THEOTOXIC TRACE MATERIAL.
GUARDIAN ARCHIVES IDENTIFICATION:
RADION... EMERGENCY...
EMERGENCY THEOTOXIKZ SSQQZZWWARK
RING?
WHY HAVE YOU STOPPED?...

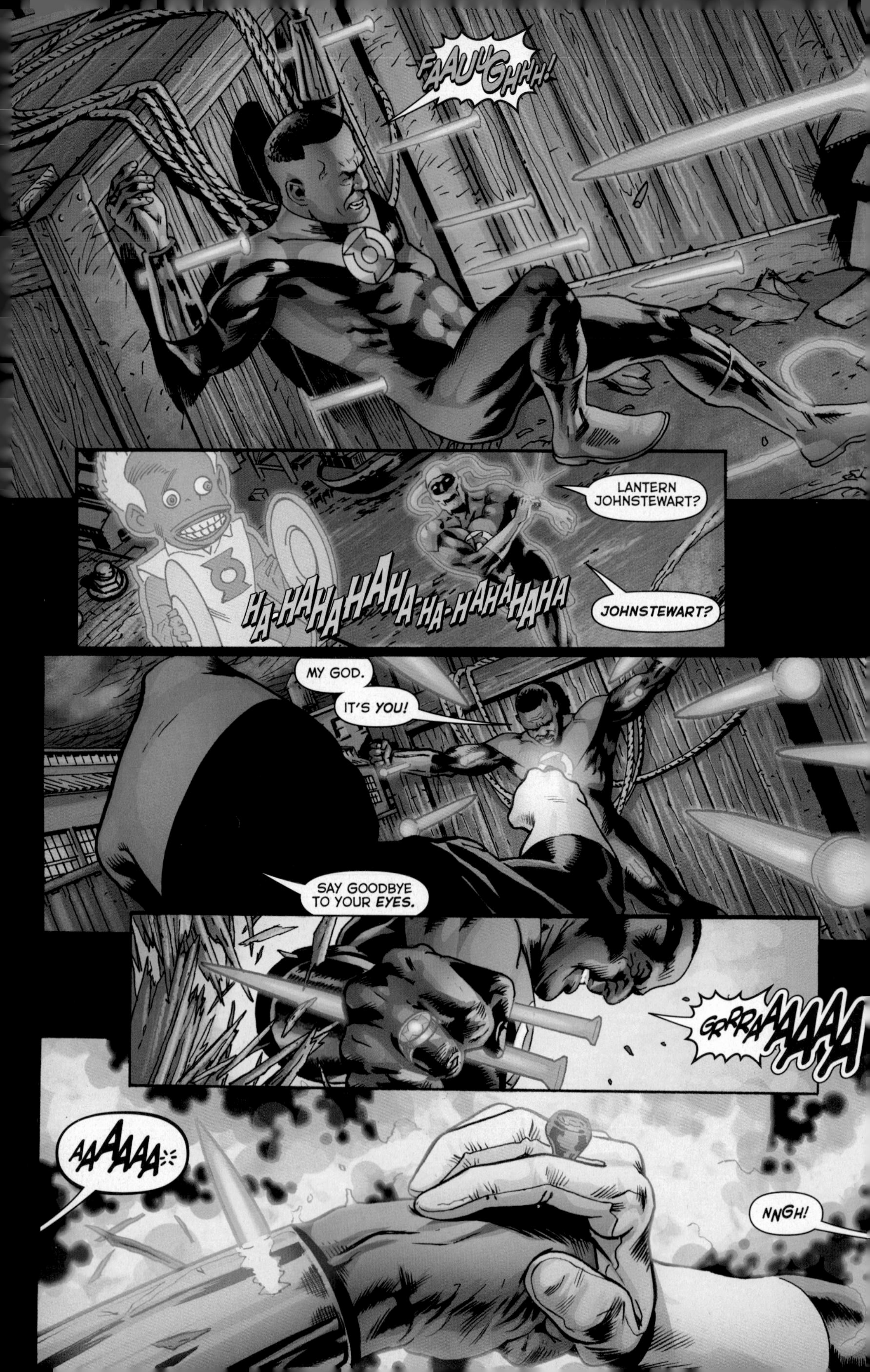

FAAUUGHHH!
LANTERN JOHNSTEWART?
HA-HAHAHAHAHA-HA-HAHAHAHA
JOHNSTEWART?
MY GOD.
IT'S *YOU!*
SAY GOODBYE TO YOUR *EYES.*
GRRRAAAAAAA
AAAAAA
NNGH!

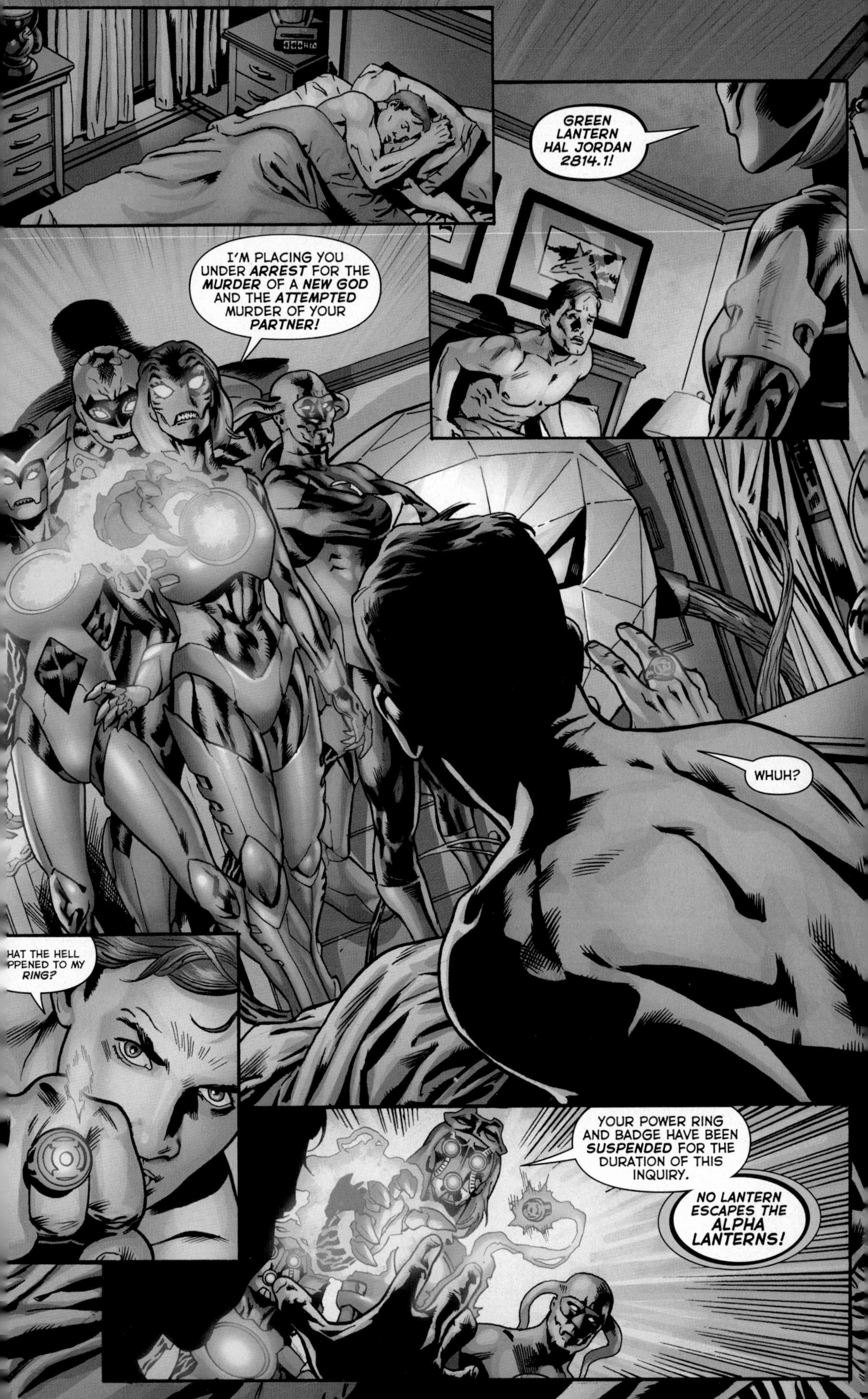
GREEN LANTERN HAL JORDAN 2814.1!
I'M PLACING YOU UNDER ARREST FOR THE MURDER OF A NEW GOD AND THE ATTEMPTED MURDER OF YOUR PARTNER!
WHUH?
HAT THE HELL PPENED TO MY RING?
YOUR POWER RING AND BADGE HAVE BEEN SUSPENDED FOR THE DURATION OF THIS INQUIRY.
NO LANTERN ESCAPES THE ALPHA LANTERNS!

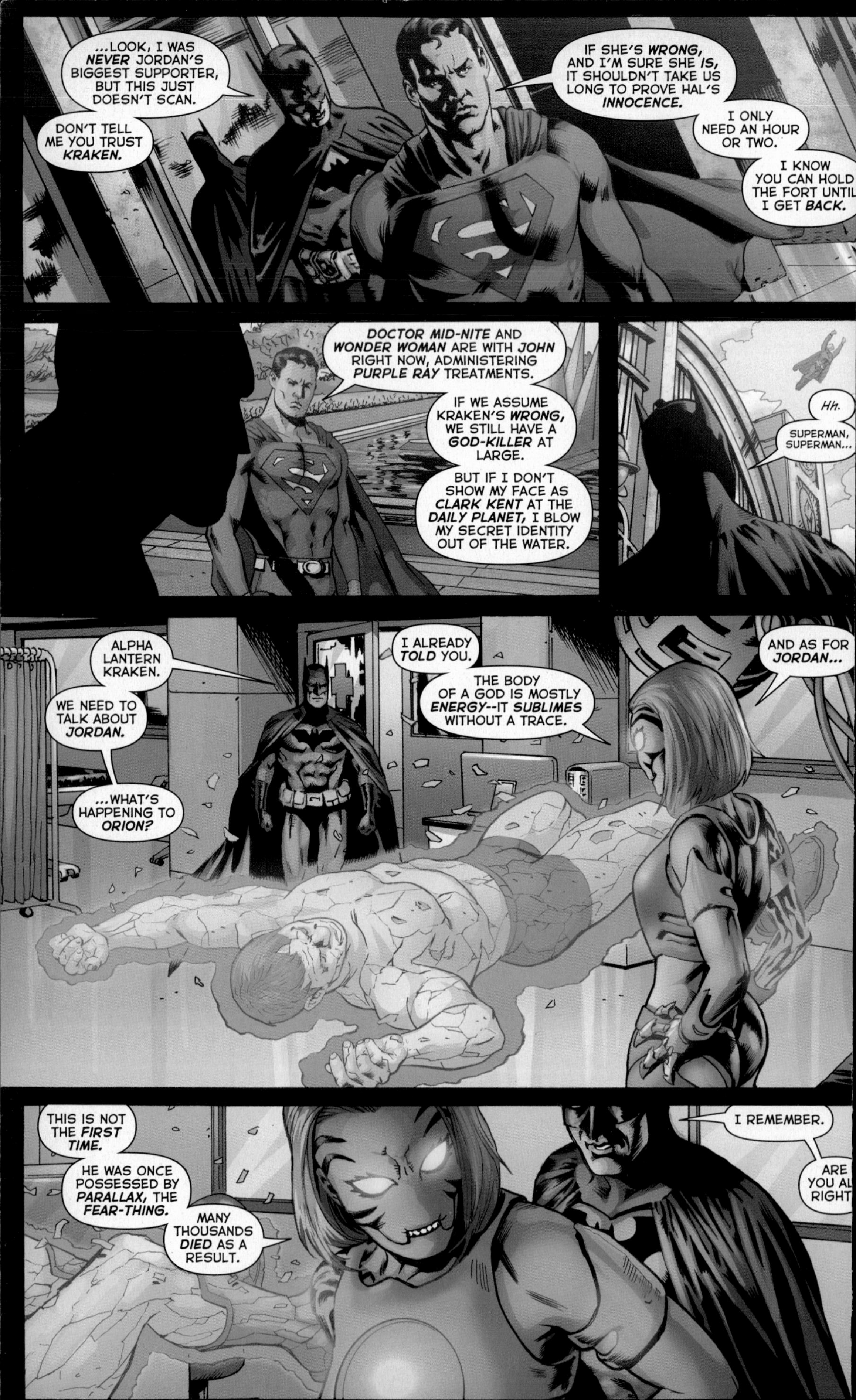
...LOOK, I WAS NEVER JORDAN'S BIGGEST SUPPORTER, BUT THIS JUST DOESN'T SCAN.
DON'T TELL ME YOU TRUST KRAKEN.
IF SHE'S WRONG, AND I'M SURE SHE IS, IT SHOULDN'T TAKE US LONG TO PROVE HAL'S INNOCENCE.
I ONLY NEED AN HOUR OR TWO.
I KNOW YOU CAN HOLD THE FORT UNTIL I GET BACK.
DOCTOR MID-NITE AND WONDER WOMAN ARE WITH JOHN RIGHT NOW, ADMINISTERING PURPLE RAY TREATMENTS.
IF WE ASSUME KRAKEN'S WRONG, WE STILL HAVE A GOD-KILLER AT LARGE.
BUT IF I DON'T SHOW MY FACE AS CLARK KENT AT THE DAILY PLANET, I BLOW MY SECRET IDENTITY OUT OF THE WATER.
Hh.
SUPERMAN, SUPERMAN...
ALPHA LANTERN KRAKEN.
WE NEED TO TALK ABOUT JORDAN.
...WHAT'S HAPPENING TO ORION?
I ALREADY TOLD YOU.
THE BODY OF A GOD IS MOSTLY ENERGY--IT SUBLIMES WITHOUT A TRACE.
AND AS FOR JORDAN...
THIS IS NOT THE FIRST TIME.
HE WAS ONCE POSSESSED BY PARALLAX, THE FEAR-THING.
MANY THOUSANDS DIED AS A RESULT.
I REMEMBER.
ARE YOU AL RIGHT

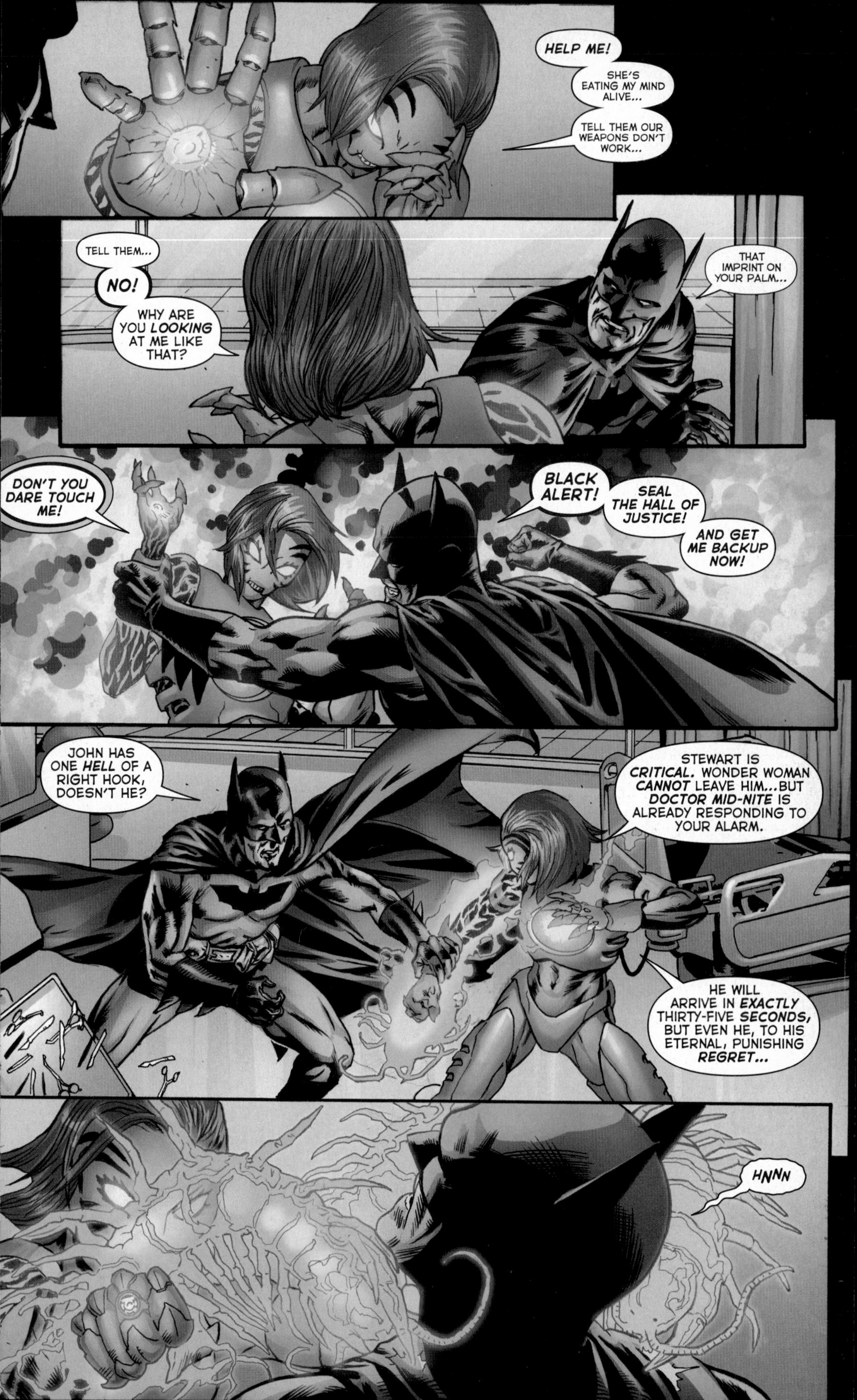
HELP ME!
SHE'S EATING MY MIND ALIVE...
TELL THEM OUR WEAPONS DON'T WORK...
TELL THEM...
NO!
WHY ARE YOU LOOKING AT ME LIKE THAT?
THAT IMPRINT ON YOUR PALM...
DON'T YOU DARE TOUCH ME!
BLACK ALERT!
SEAL THE HALL OF JUSTICE!
AND GET ME BACKUP NOW!
JOHN HAS ONE HELL OF A RIGHT HOOK, DOESN'T HE?
STEWART IS CRITICAL. WONDER WOMAN CANNOT LEAVE HIM...BUT DOCTOR MID-NITE IS ALREADY RESPONDING TO YOUR ALARM.
HE WILL ARRIVE IN EXACTLY THIRTY-FIVE SECONDS, BUT EVEN HE, TO HIS ETERNAL, PUNISHING REGRET...
HNNN

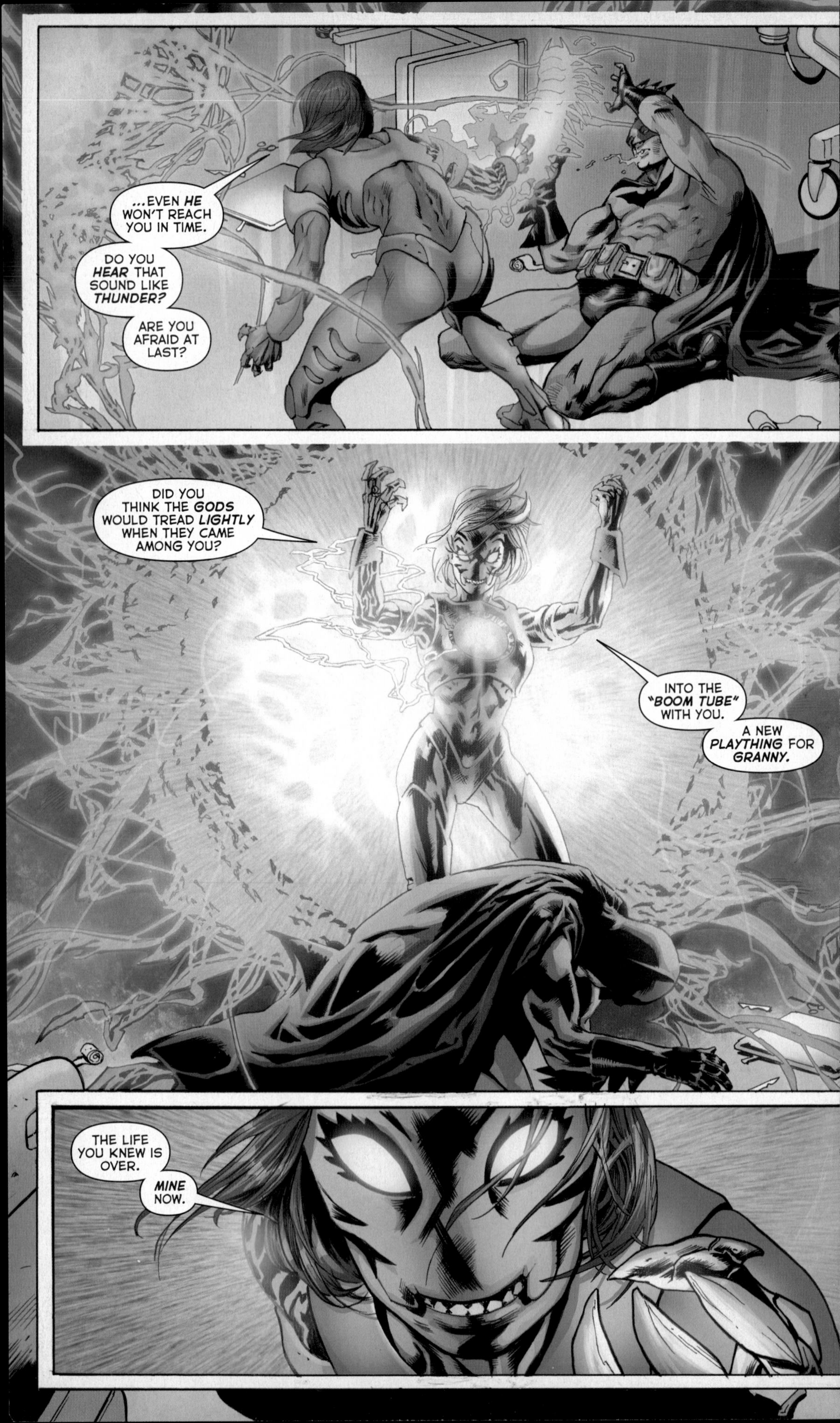

...EVEN HE WON'T REACH YOU IN TIME.
DO YOU HEAR THAT SOUND LIKE THUNDER?
ARE YOU AFRAID AT LAST?
DID YOU THINK THE GODS WOULD TREAD LIGHTLY WHEN THEY CAME AMONG YOU?
INTO THE "BOOM TUBE" WITH YOU.
A NEW PLAYTHING FOR GRANNY.
THE LIFE YOU KNEW IS OVER.
MINE NOW.

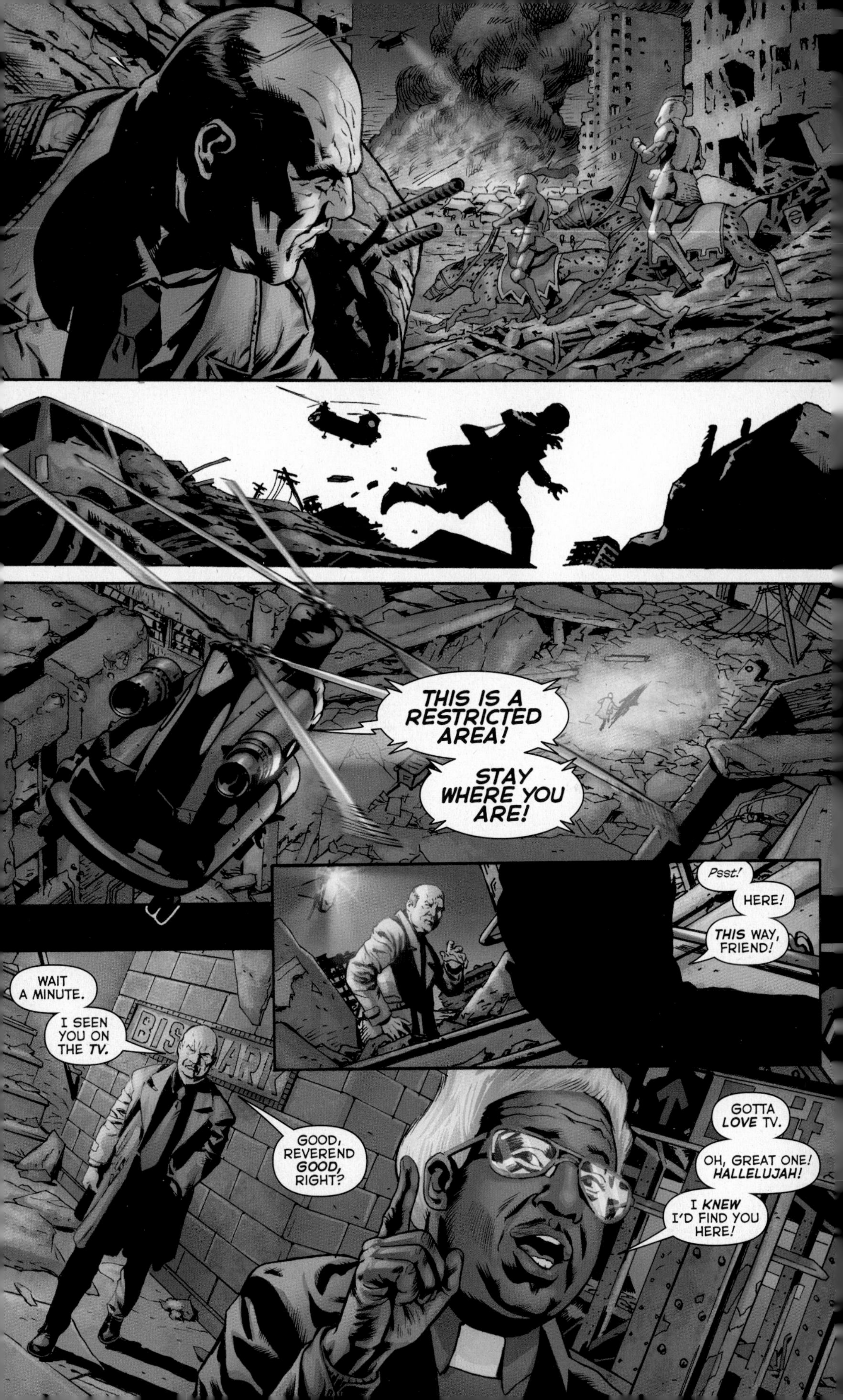
THIS IS A RESTRICTED AREA!
STAY WHERE YOU ARE!
Psst!
HERE!
THIS WAY, FRIEND!
WAIT A MINUTE.
I SEEN YOU ON THE TV.
GOOD, REVEREND GOOD, RIGHT?
GOTTA LOVE TV.
OH, GREAT ONE! HALLELUJAH!
I KNEW I'D FIND YOU HERE!
BISMARK

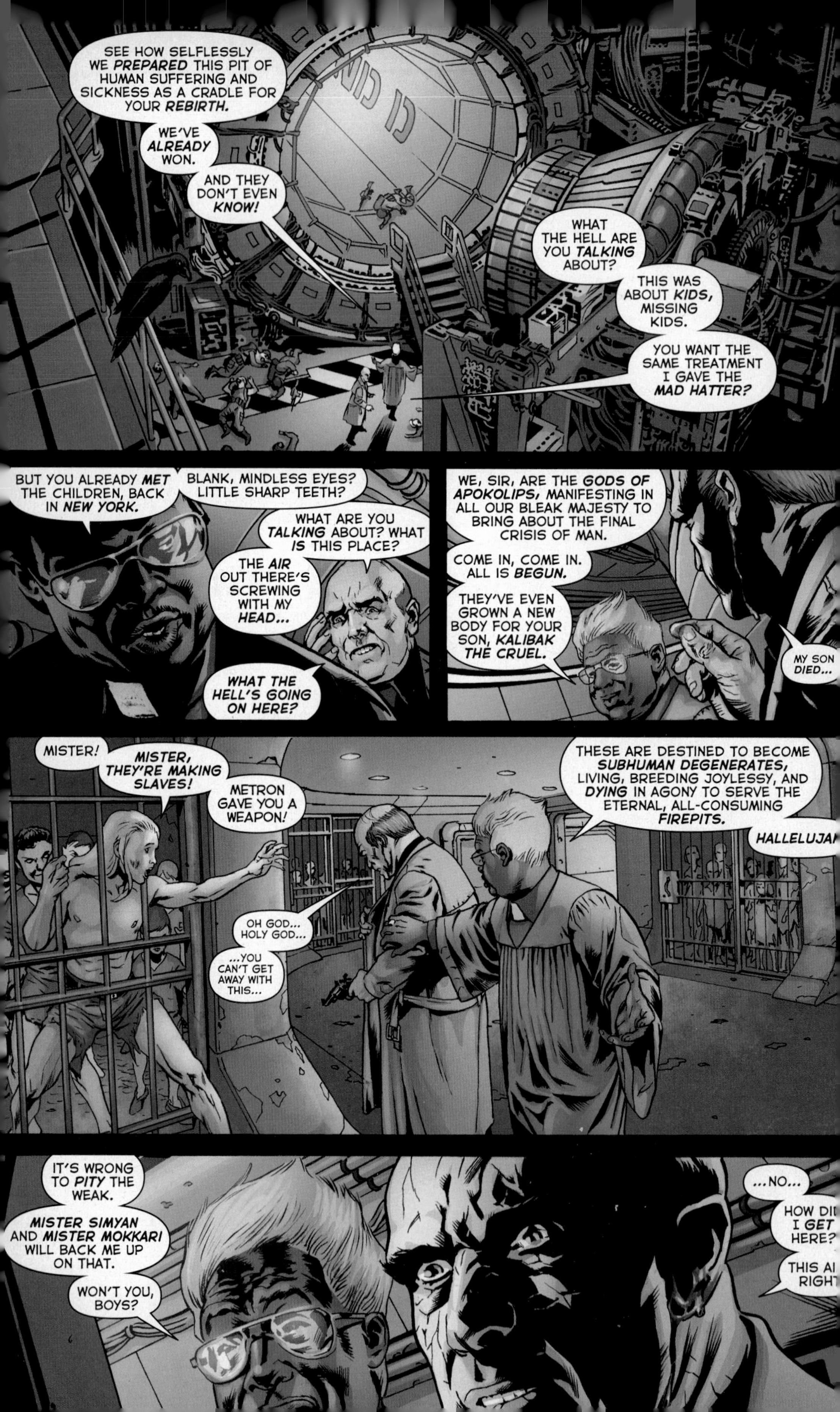
SEE HOW SELFLESSLY WE PREPARED THIS PIT OF HUMAN SUFFERING AND SICKNESS AS A CRADLE FOR YOUR REBIRTH.
WE'VE ALREADY WON.
AND THEY DON'T EVEN KNOW!
WHAT THE HELL ARE YOU TALKING ABOUT?
THIS WAS ABOUT KIDS, MISSING KIDS.
YOU WANT THE SAME TREATMENT I GAVE THE MAD HATTER?
BUT YOU ALREADY MET THE CHILDREN, BACK IN NEW YORK.
BLANK, MINDLESS EYES? LITTLE SHARP TEETH?
WHAT ARE YOU TALKING ABOUT? WHAT IS THIS PLACE?
THE AIR OUT THERE'S SCREWING WITH MY HEAD...
WHAT THE HELL'S GOING ON HERE?
WE, SIR, ARE THE GODS OF APOKOLIPS, MANIFESTING IN ALL OUR BLEAK MAJESTY TO BRING ABOUT THE FINAL CRISIS OF MAN.
COME IN, COME IN. ALL IS BEGUN.
THEY'VE EVEN GROWN A NEW BODY FOR YOUR SON, KALIBAK THE CRUEL.
MY SON DIED...
MISTER!
MISTER, THEY'RE MAKING SLAVES!
METRON GAVE YOU A WEAPON!
THESE ARE DESTINED TO BECOME SUBHUMAN DEGENERATES, LIVING, BREEDING JOYLESSY, AND DYING IN AGONY TO SERVE THE ETERNAL, ALL-CONSUMING FIREPITS.
HALLELUJA
OH GOD... HOLY GOD...
...YOU CAN'T GET AWAY WITH THIS...
IT'S WRONG TO PITY THE WEAK.
MISTER SIMYAN AND MISTER MOKKARI WILL BACK ME UP ON THAT.
WON'T YOU, BOYS?
...NO...
HOW DI I GET HERE?
THIS AI RIGHT

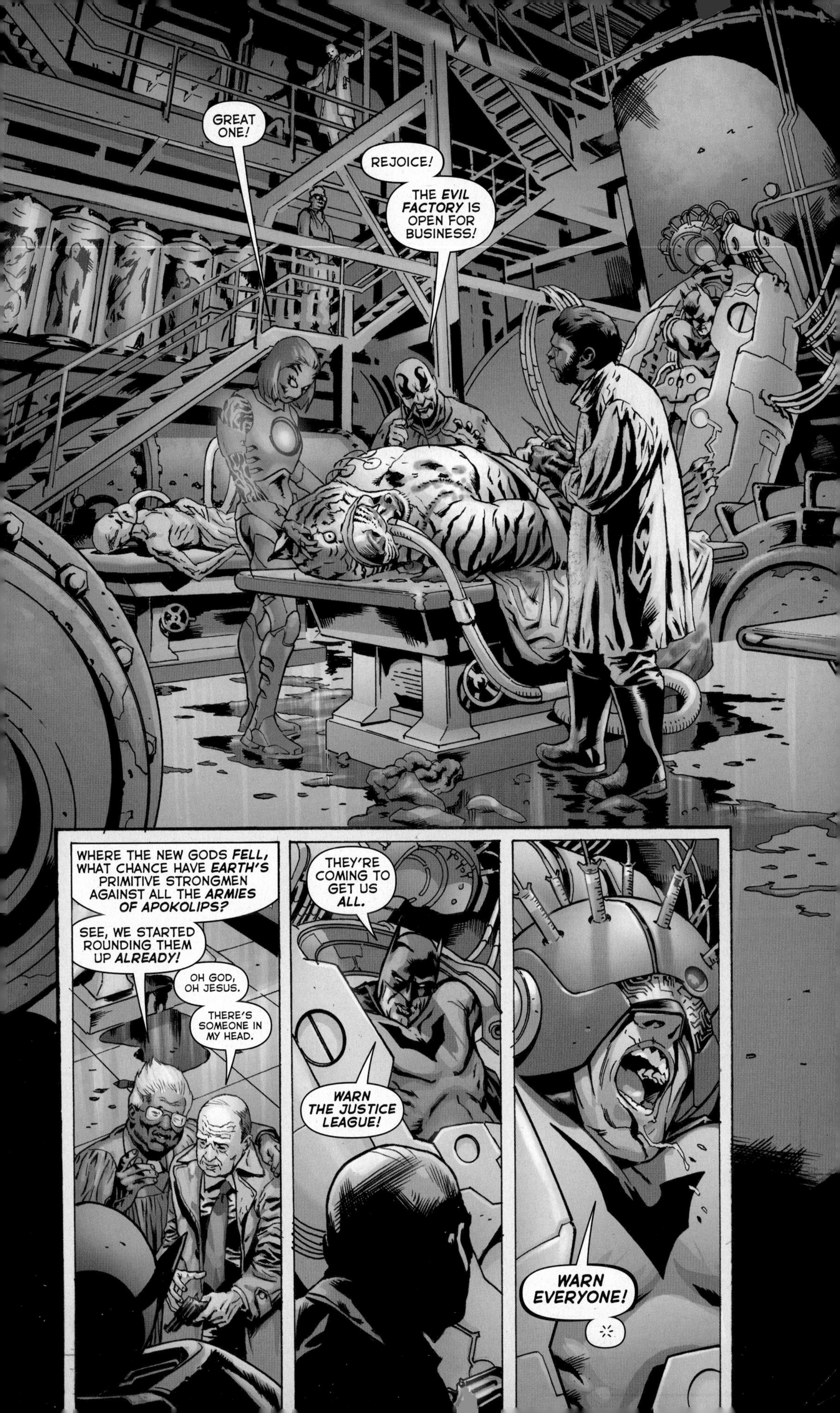
GREAT ONE!
REJOICE!
THE EVIL FACTORY IS OPEN FOR BUSINESS!
WHERE THE NEW GODS FELL, WHAT CHANCE HAVE EARTH'S PRIMITIVE STRONGMEN AGAINST ALL THE ARMIES OF APOKOLIPS?
SEE, WE STARTED ROUNDING THEM UP ALREADY!
OH GOD, OH JESUS.
THERE'S SOMEONE IN MY HEAD.
THEY'RE COMING TO GET US ALL.
WARN THE JUSTICE LEAGUE!
WARN EVERYONE!

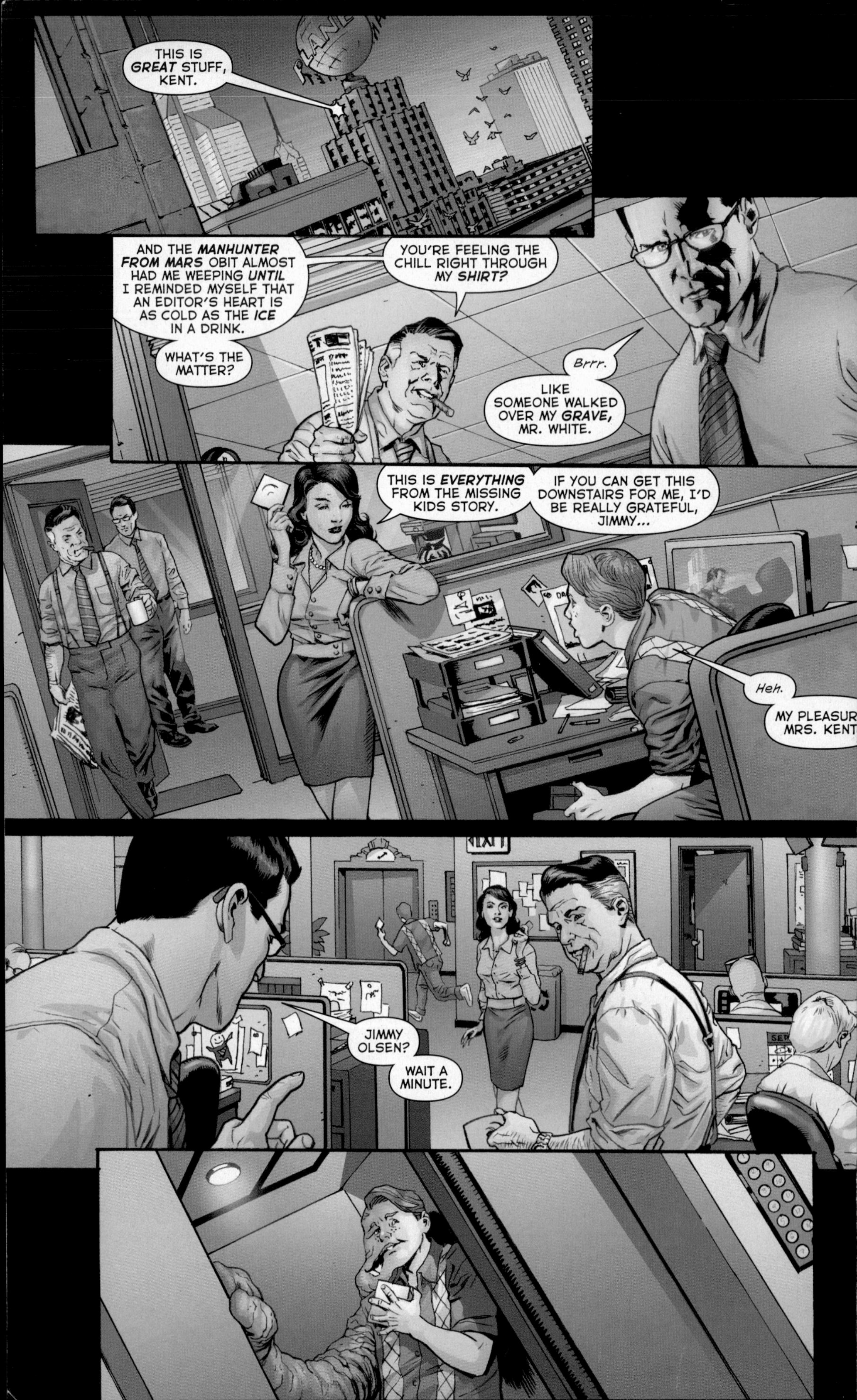
THIS IS GREAT STUFF, KENT.
AND THE MANHUNTER FROM MARS OBIT ALMOST HAD ME WEEPING UNTIL I REMINDED MYSELF THAT AN EDITOR'S HEART IS AS COLD AS THE ICE IN A DRINK.
WHAT'S THE MATTER?
YOU'RE FEELING THE CHILL RIGHT THROUGH MY SHIRT?
Brrr.
LIKE SOMEONE WALKED OVER MY GRAVE, MR. WHITE.
THIS IS EVERYTHING FROM THE MISSING KIDS STORY.
IF YOU CAN GET THIS DOWNSTAIRS FOR ME, I'D BE REALLY GRATEFUL, JIMMY...
Heh.
MY PLEASUR MRS. KENT
JIMMY OLSEN?
WAIT A MINUTE.

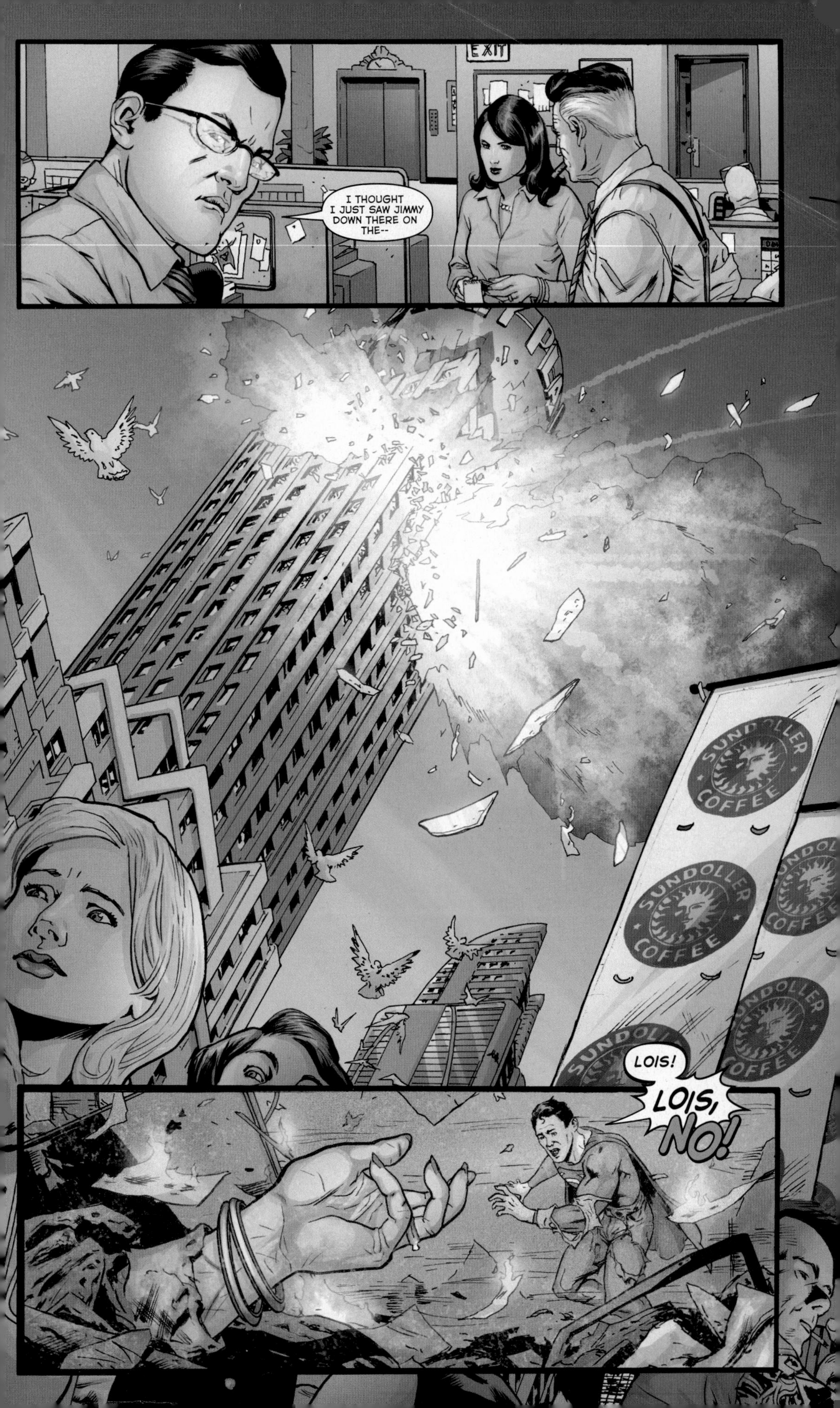
I THOUGHT I JUST SAW JIMMY DOWN THERE ON THE--
EXIT
SUNDOLLER COFFEE
LOIS!
LOIS, NO!

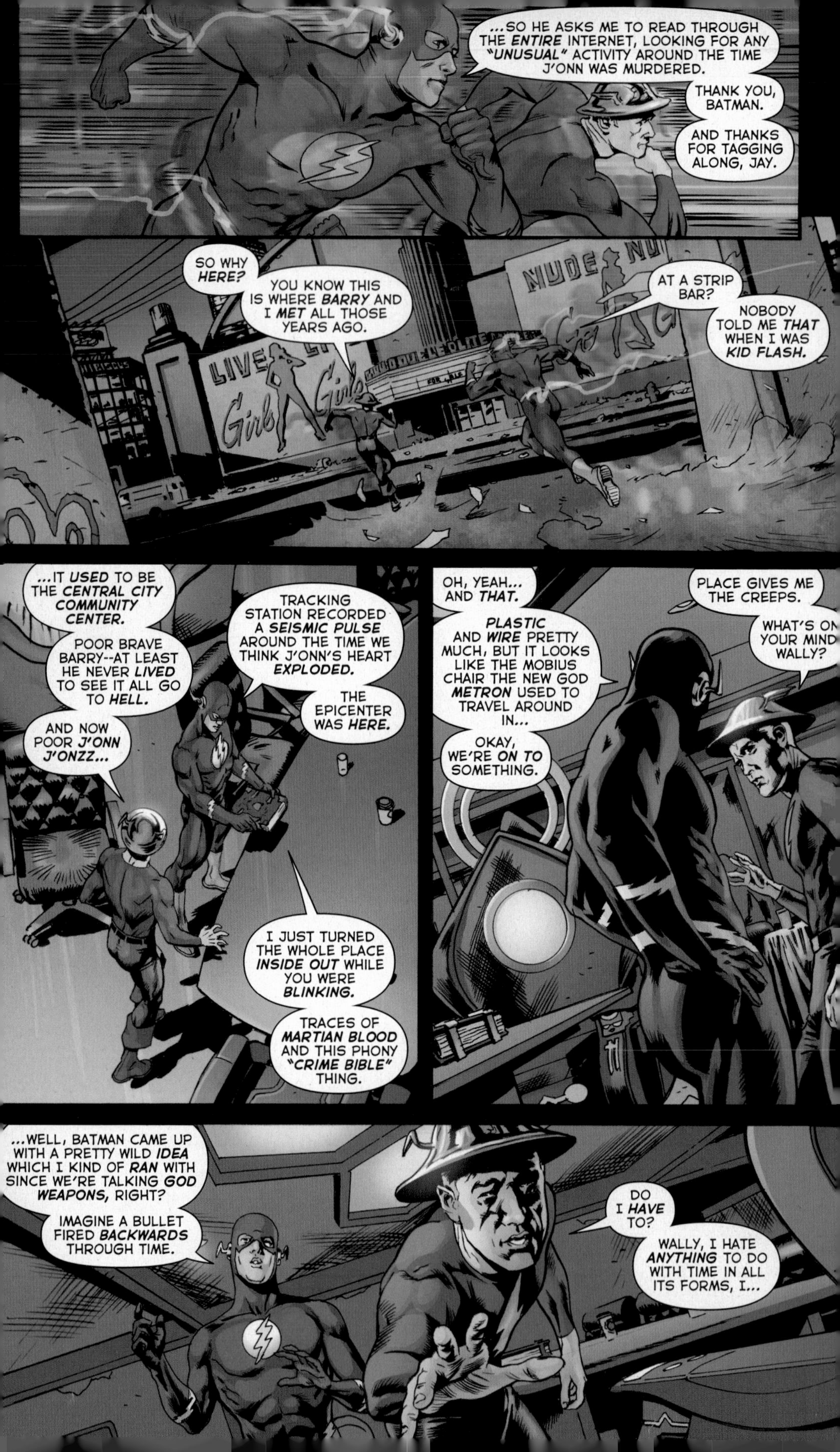
...SO HE ASKS ME TO READ THROUGH THE ENTIRE INTERNET, LOOKING FOR ANY "UNUSUAL" ACTIVITY AROUND THE TIME J'ONN WAS MURDERED.
THANK YOU, BATMAN.
AND THANKS FOR TAGGING ALONG, JAY.
SO WHY HERE?
YOU KNOW THIS IS WHERE BARRY AND I MET ALL THOSE YEARS AGO.
AT A STRIP BAR?
NOBODY TOLD ME THAT WHEN I WAS KID FLASH.
LIVE Girls
NUDE
...IT USED TO BE THE CENTRAL CITY COMMUNITY CENTER.
POOR BRAVE BARRY--AT LEAST HE NEVER LIVED TO SEE IT ALL GO TO HELL.
AND NOW POOR J'ONN J'ONZZ...
TRACKING STATION RECORDED A SEISMIC PULSE AROUND THE TIME WE THINK J'ONN'S HEART EXPLODED.
THE EPICENTER WAS HERE.
I JUST TURNED THE WHOLE PLACE INSIDE OUT WHILE YOU WERE BLINKING.
TRACES OF MARTIAN BLOOD AND THIS PHONY "CRIME BIBLE" THING.
OH, YEAH... AND THAT.
PLASTIC AND WIRE PRETTY MUCH, BUT IT LOOKS LIKE THE MOBIUS CHAIR THE NEW GOD METRON USED TO TRAVEL AROUND IN...
OKAY, WE'RE ON TO SOMETHING.
PLACE GIVES ME THE CREEPS.
WHAT'S ON YOUR MIND WALLY?
...WELL, BATMAN CAME UP WITH A PRETTY WILD IDEA WHICH I KIND OF RAN WITH SINCE WE'RE TALKING GOD WEAPONS, RIGHT?
IMAGINE A BULLET FIRED BACKWARDS THROUGH TIME.
DO I HAVE TO?
WALLY, I HATE ANYTHING TO DO WITH TIME IN ALL ITS FORMS, I...

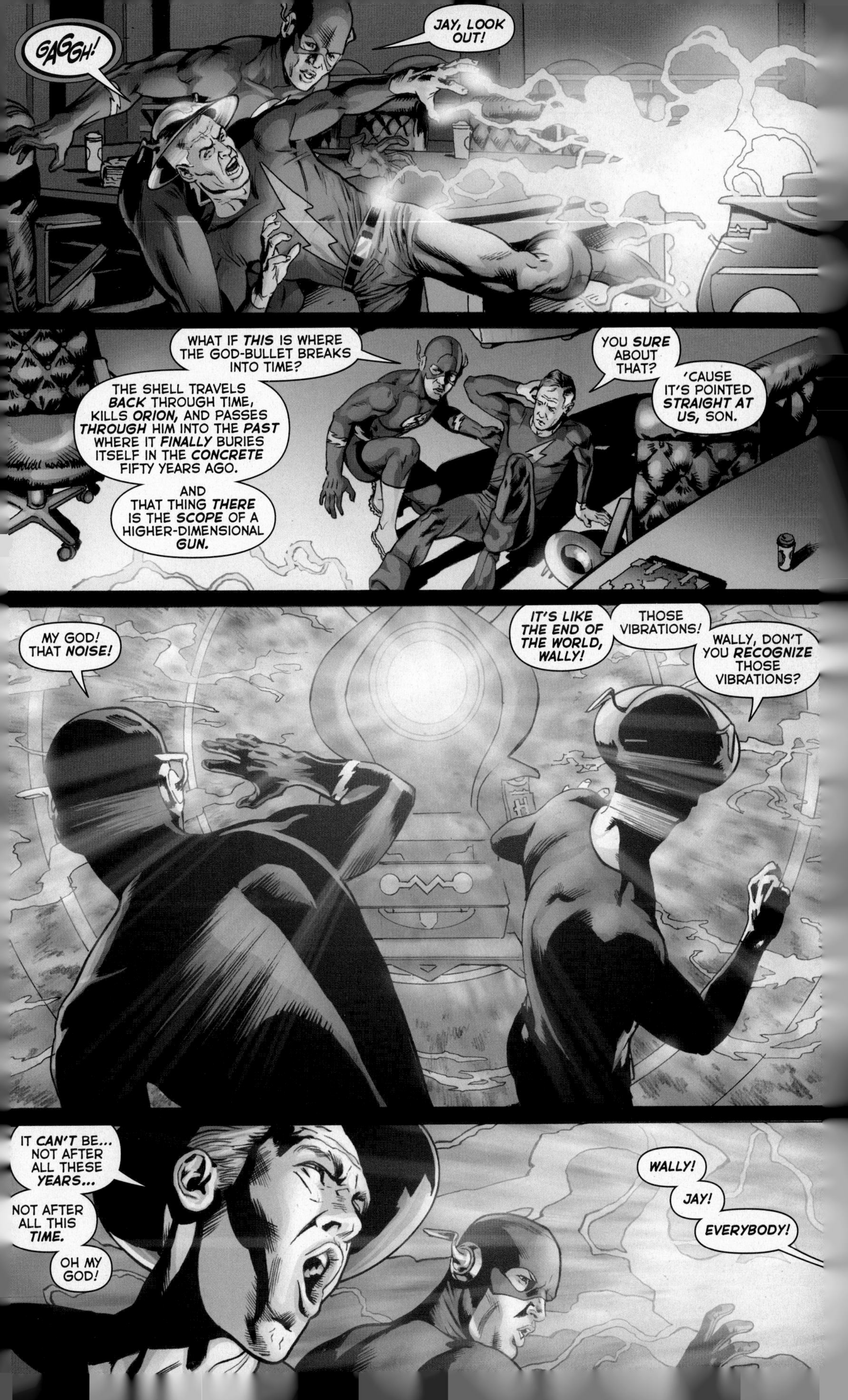
GAGGH!
JAY, LOOK OUT!
WHAT IF THIS IS WHERE THE GOD-BULLET BREAKS INTO TIME?
THE SHELL TRAVELS BACK THROUGH TIME, KILLS ORION, AND PASSES THROUGH HIM INTO THE PAST WHERE IT FINALLY BURIES ITSELF IN THE CONCRETE FIFTY YEARS AGO.
AND THAT THING THERE IS THE SCOPE OF A HIGHER-DIMENSIONAL GUN.
YOU SURE ABOUT THAT?
'CAUSE IT'S POINTED STRAIGHT AT US, SON.
MY GOD! THAT NOISE!
IT'S LIKE THE END OF THE WORLD, WALLY!
THOSE VIBRATIONS!
WALLY, DON'T YOU RECOGNIZE THOSE VIBRATIONS?
IT CAN'T BE... NOT AFTER ALL THESE YEARS...
NOT AFTER ALL THIS TIME.
OH MY GOD!
WALLY!
JAY!
EVERYBODY!

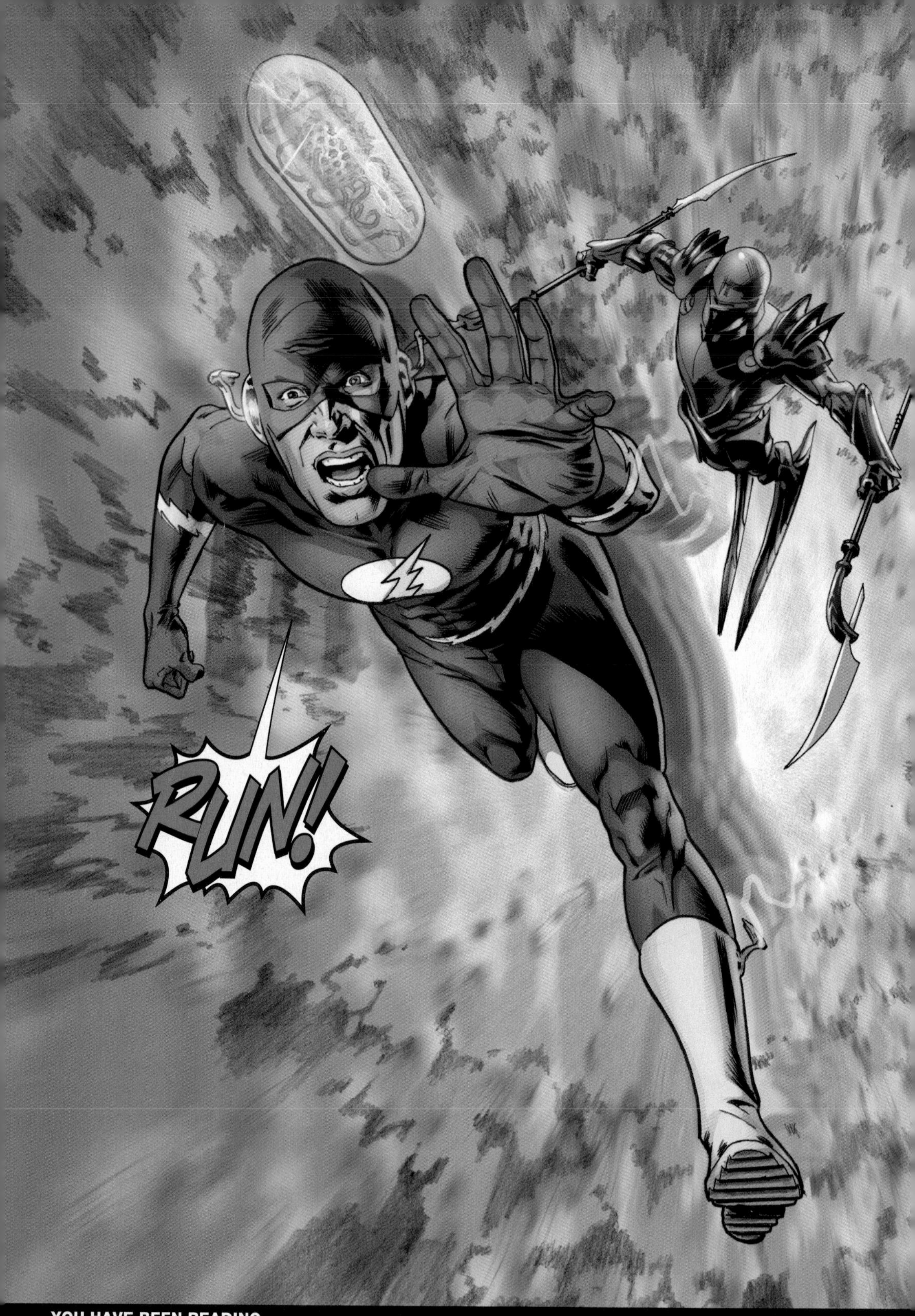

RUN!

YOU HAVE BEEN READING

TICKET to BLÜDHAVEN

GRANT MORRISON SCRIPT JG JONES ART

ALEX SINCLAIR COLORS ROB LEIGH LETTERING

er to FINAL CRISIS #3   JG Jones

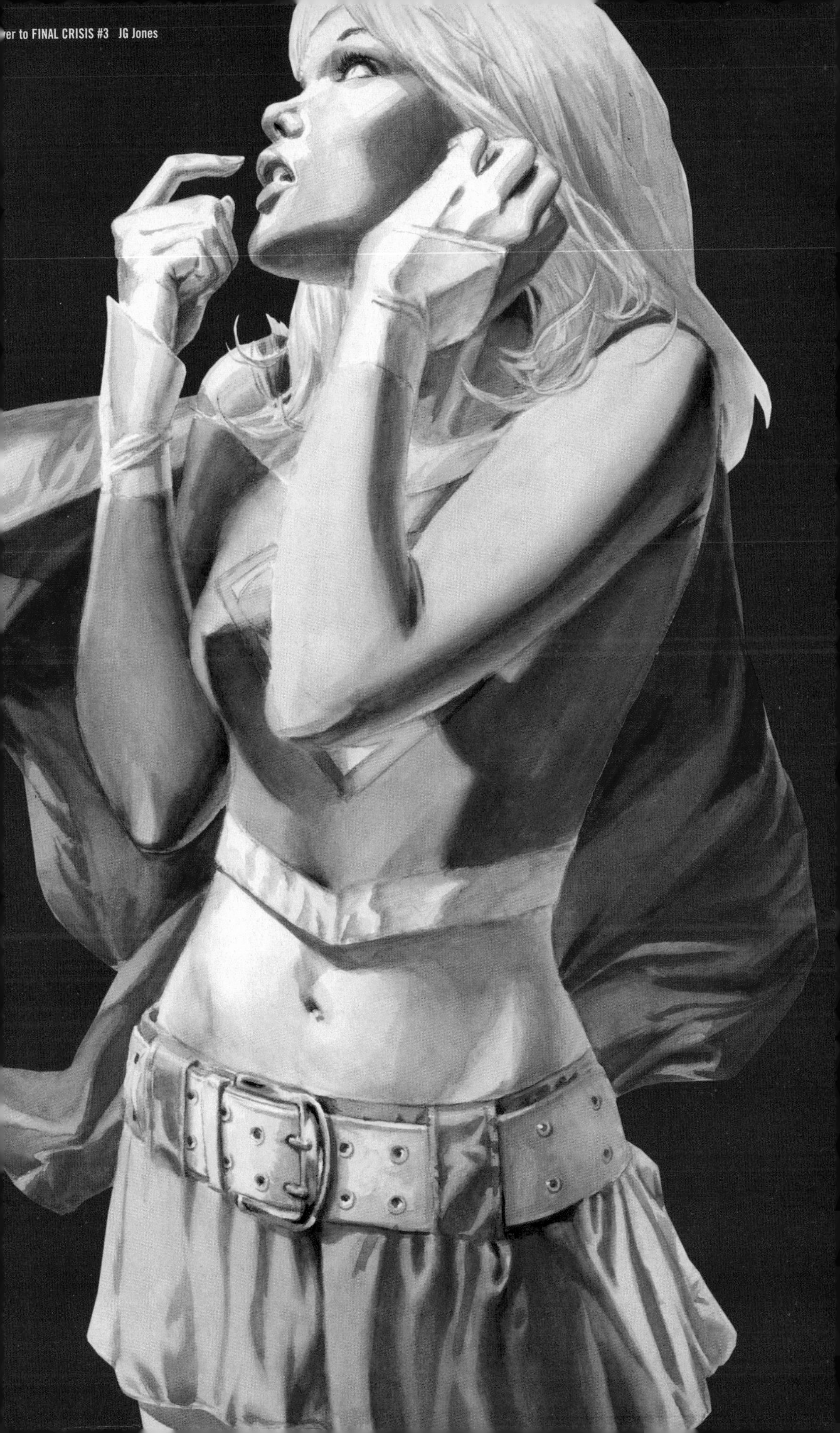

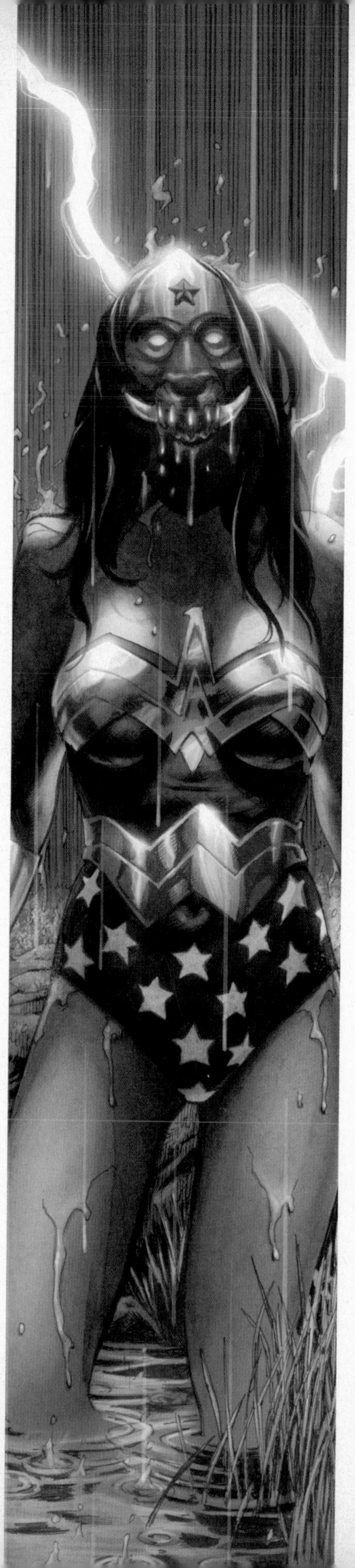

JG Jones with Alex Sinclair

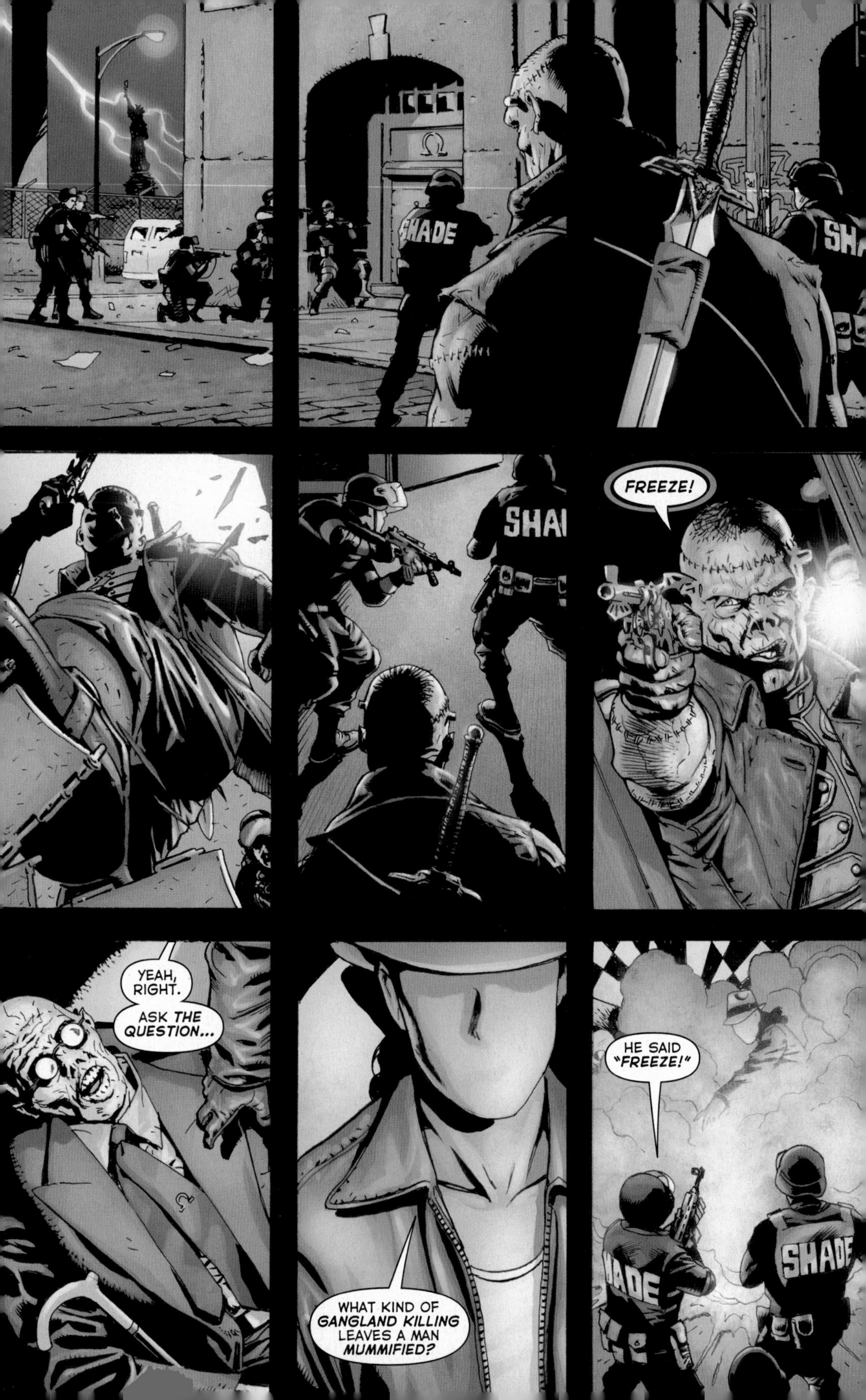
SHADE
SHADE
SHA
SHA
FREEZE!
YEAH, RIGHT.
ASK THE QUESTION...
WHAT KIND OF GANGLAND KILLING LEAVES A MAN MUMMIFIED?
HE SAID "FREEZE!"
SHADE
SHADE

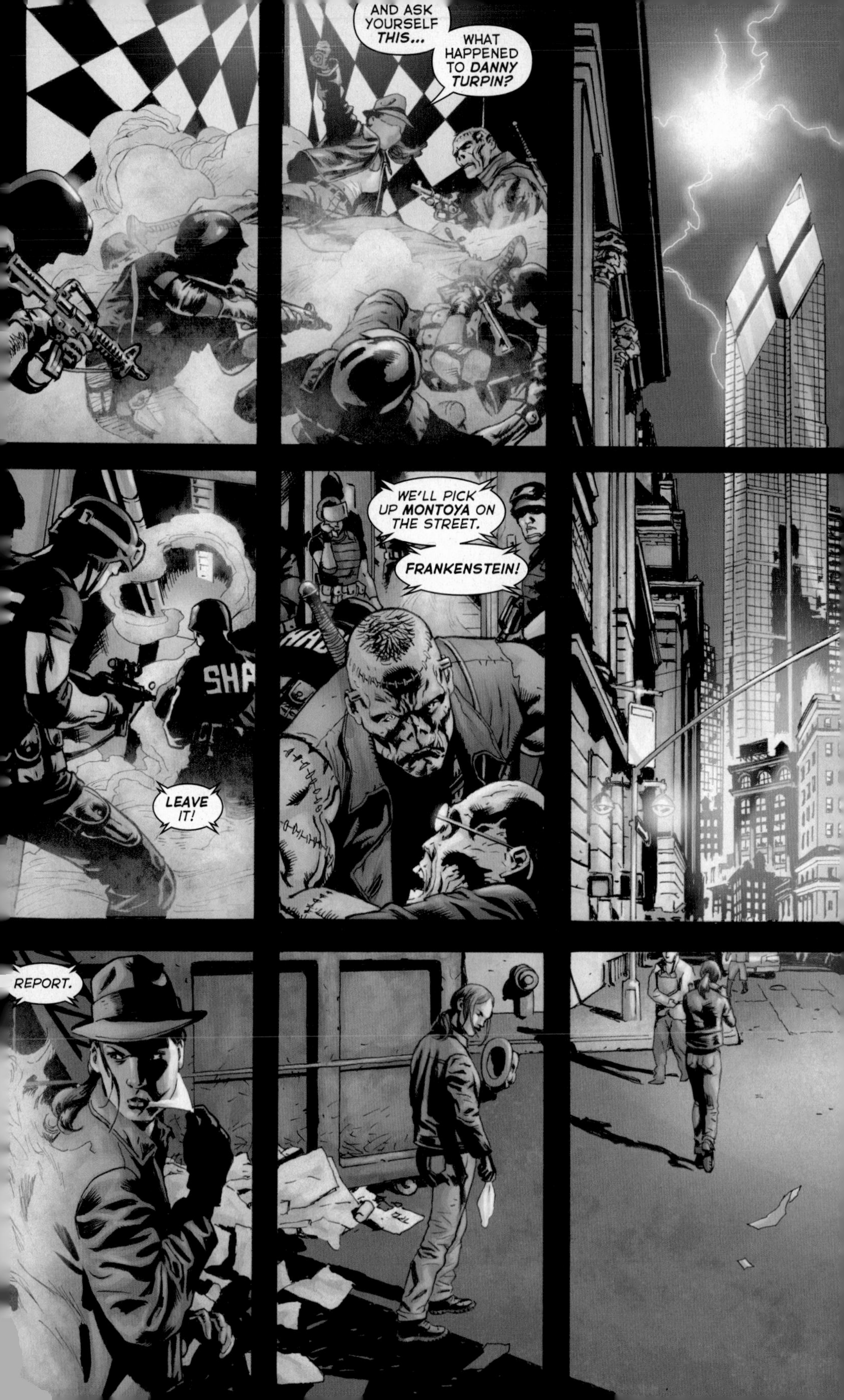
AND ASK YOURSELF THIS...
WHAT HAPPENED TO DANNY TURPIN?
WE'LL PICK UP MONTOYA ON THE STREET.
FRANKENSTEIN!
LEAVE IT!
REPORT.

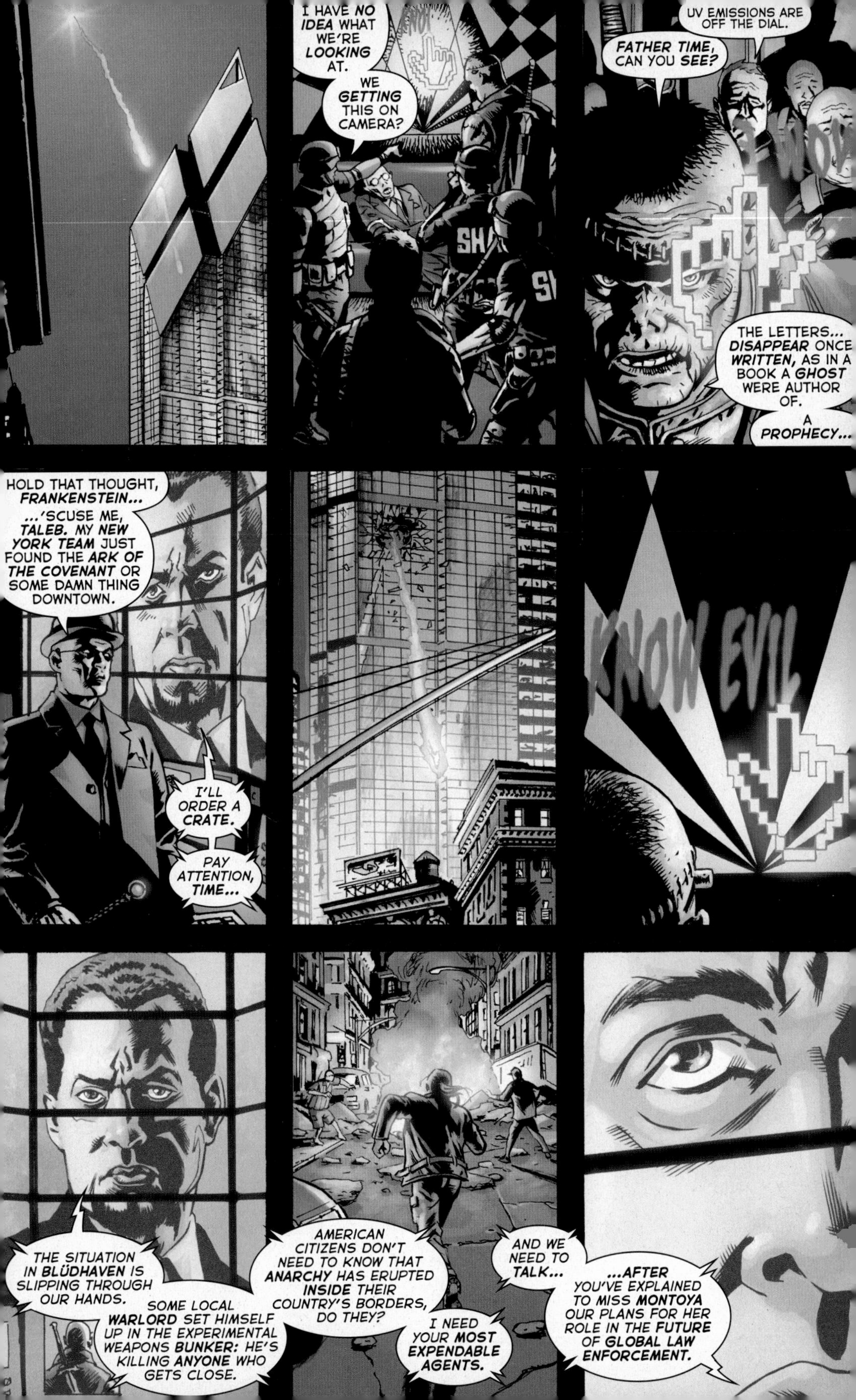
I HAVE NO IDEA WHAT WE'RE LOOKING AT.
WE GETTING THIS ON CAMERA?
UV EMISSIONS ARE OFF THE DIAL.
FATHER TIME, CAN YOU SEE?
THE LETTERS... DISAPPEAR ONCE WRITTEN, AS IN A BOOK A GHOST WERE AUTHOR OF.
A PROPHECY...
HOLD THAT THOUGHT, FRANKENSTEIN...
...'SCUSE ME, TALEB. MY NEW YORK TEAM JUST FOUND THE ARK OF THE COVENANT OR SOME DAMN THING DOWNTOWN.
I'LL ORDER A CRATE.
PAY ATTENTION, TIME...
KNOW EVIL
THE SITUATION IN BLÜDHAVEN IS SLIPPING THROUGH OUR HANDS.
SOME LOCAL WARLORD SET HIMSELF UP IN THE EXPERIMENTAL WEAPONS BUNKER: HE'S KILLING ANYONE WHO GETS CLOSE.
AMERICAN CITIZENS DON'T NEED TO KNOW THAT ANARCHY HAS ERUPTED INSIDE THEIR COUNTRY'S BORDERS, DO THEY?
I NEED YOUR MOST EXPENDABLE AGENTS.
AND WE NEED TO TALK...
...AFTER YOU'VE EXPLAINED TO MISS MONTOYA OUR PLANS FOR HER ROLE IN THE FUTURE OF GLOBAL LAW ENFORCEMENT.

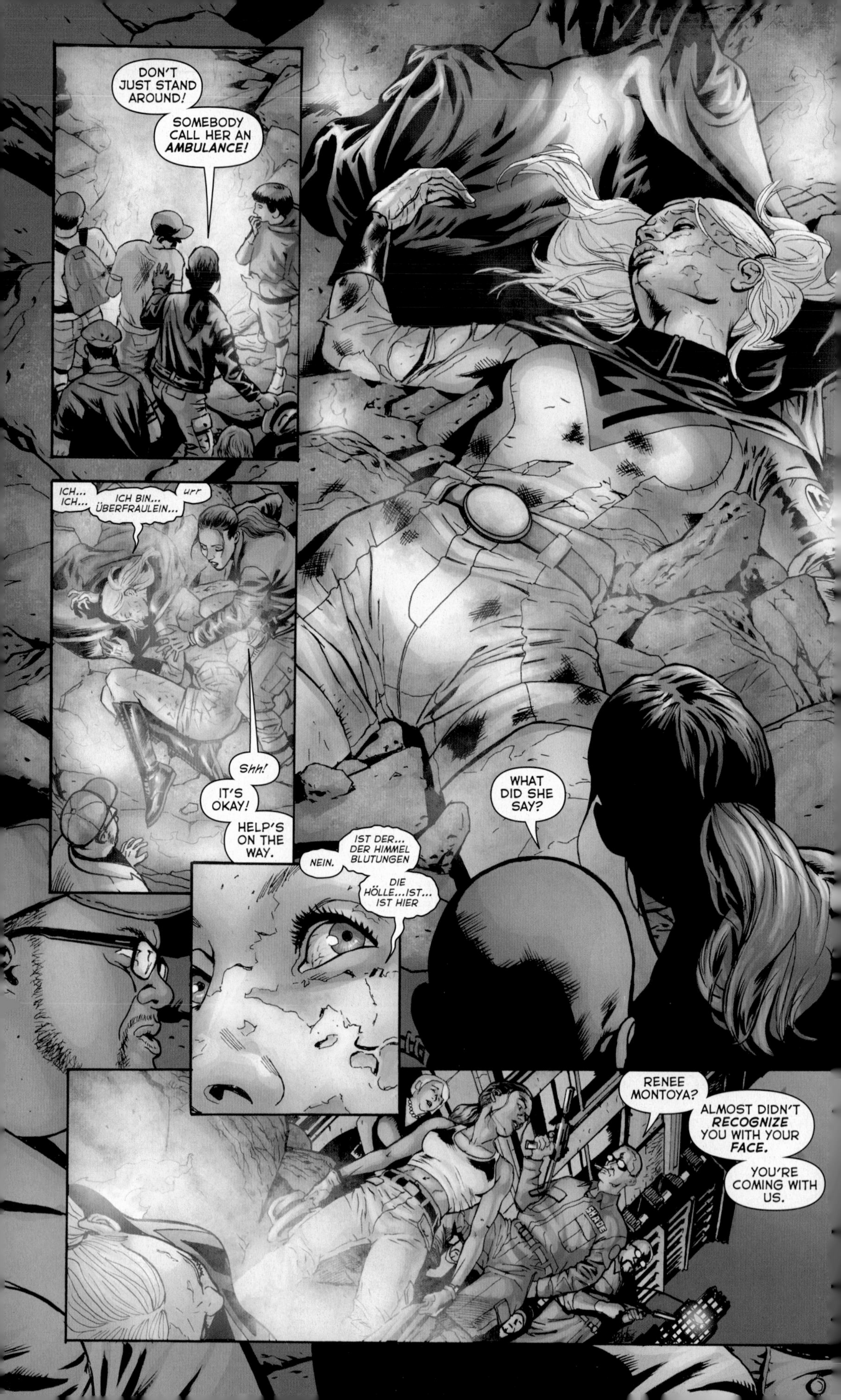

DON'T JUST STAND AROUND!
SOMEBODY CALL HER AN AMBULANCE!
ICH... ICH...
ICH BIN... ÜBERFRAULEIN...
urr
Shh!
IT'S OKAY!
HELP'S ON THE WAY.
WHAT DID SHE SAY?
NEIN.
IST DER... DER HIMMEL BLUTUNGEN
DIE HÖLLE...IST... IST HIER
RENEE MONTOYA?
ALMOST DIDN'T RECOGNIZE YOU WITH YOUR FACE.
YOU'RE COMING WITH US.

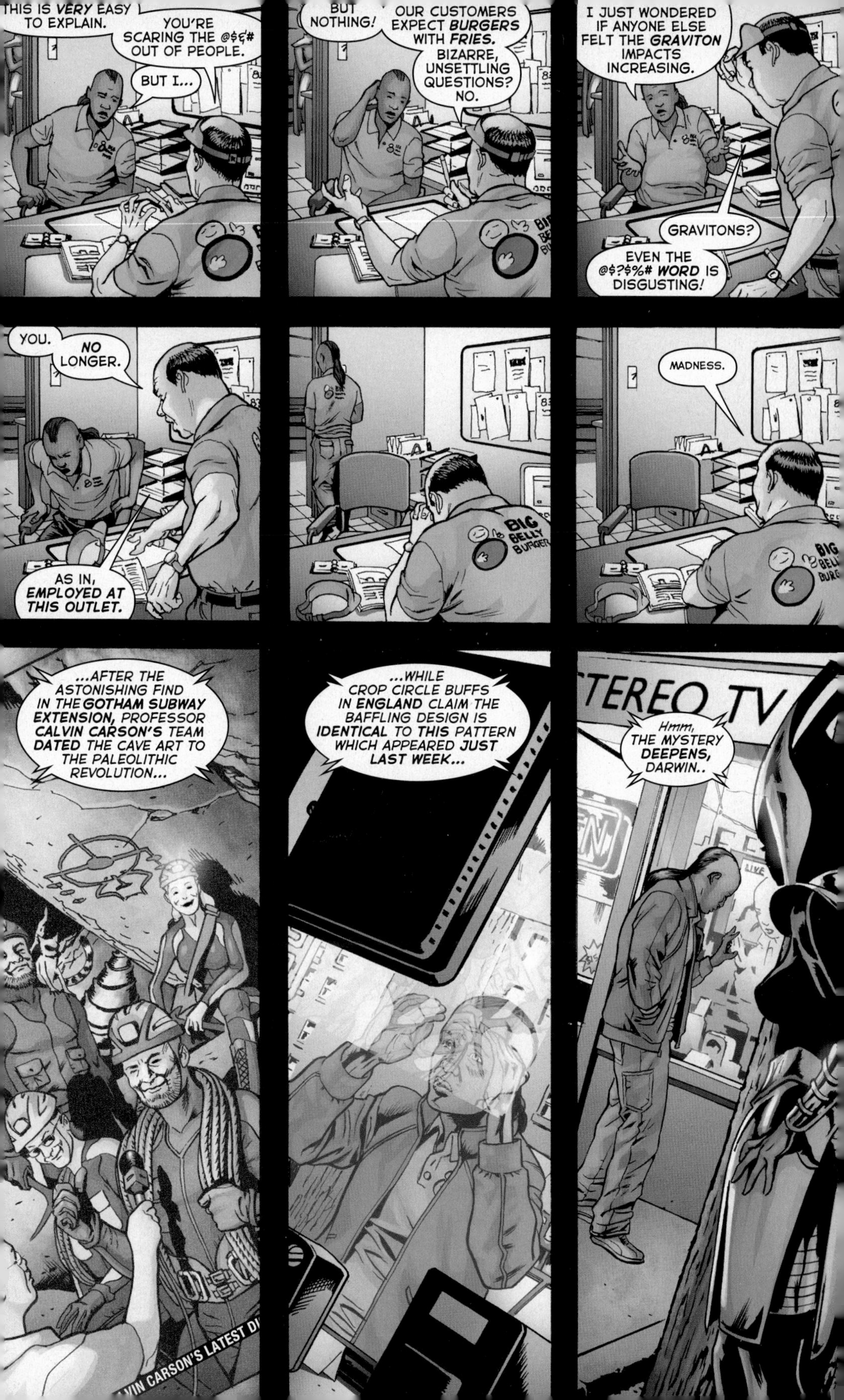
THIS IS VERY EASY TO EXPLAIN.
YOU'RE SCARING THE @$&# OUT OF PEOPLE.
BUT I...
BUT NOTHING!
OUR CUSTOMERS EXPECT BURGERS WITH FRIES.
BIZARRE, UNSETTLING QUESTIONS? NO.
I JUST WONDERED IF ANYONE ELSE FELT THE GRAVITON IMPACTS INCREASING.
GRAVITONS?
EVEN THE @$?$%# WORD IS DISGUSTING!
YOU.
NO LONGER.
AS IN, EMPLOYED AT THIS OUTLET.
BIG BELLY BURGER
MADNESS.
...AFTER THE ASTONISHING FIND IN THE GOTHAM SUBWAY EXTENSION, PROFESSOR CALVIN CARSON'S TEAM DATED THE CAVE ART TO THE PALEOLITHIC REVOLUTION...
VIN CARSON'S LATEST DI
...WHILE CROP CIRCLE BUFFS IN ENGLAND CLAIM THE BAFFLING DESIGN IS IDENTICAL TO THIS PATTERN WHICH APPEARED JUST LAST WEEK...
TEREO TV
Hmm, THE MYSTERY DEEPENS, DARWIN..

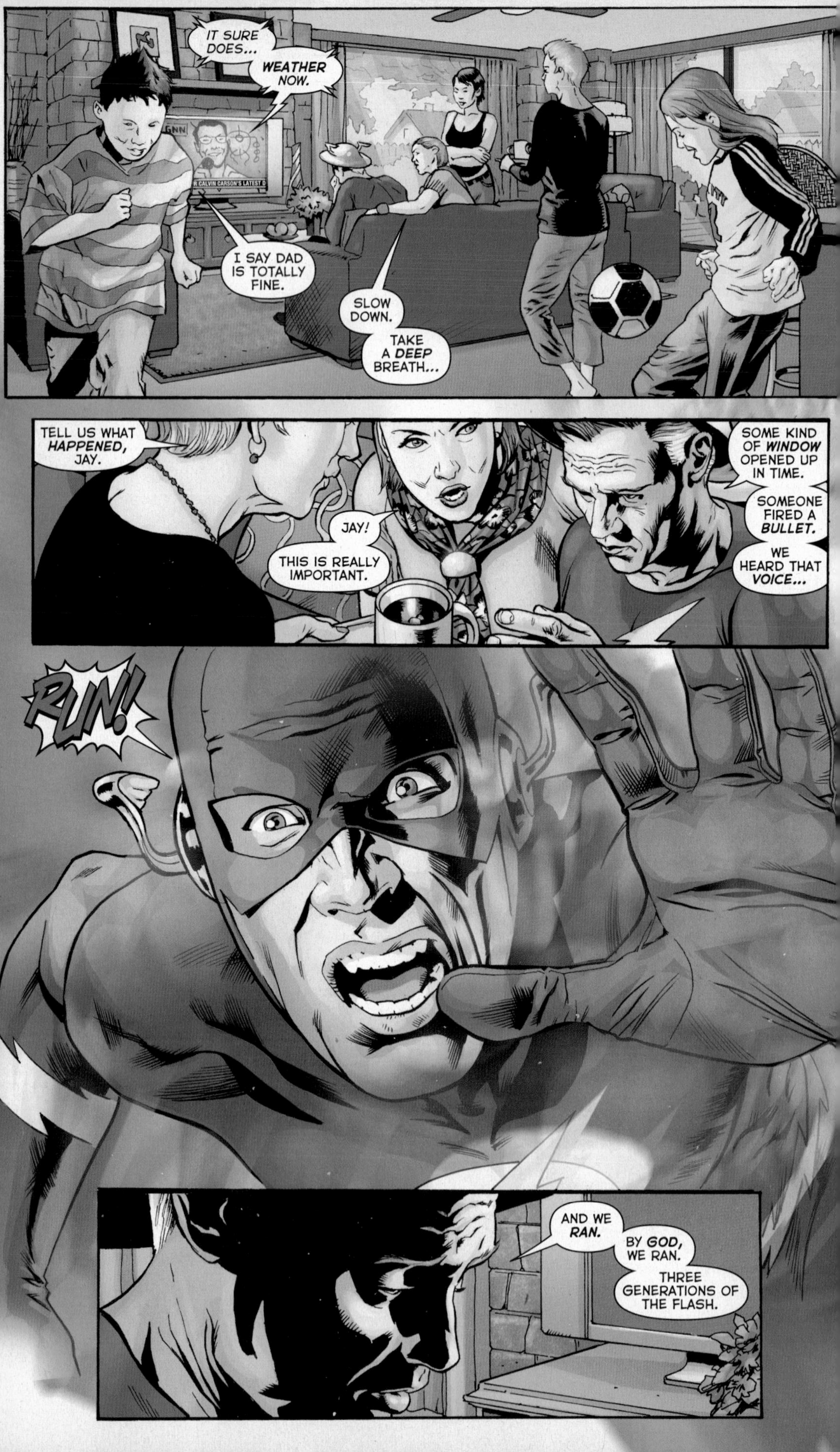
IT SURE DOES...
WEATHER NOW.
GNN
CALVIN CARSON'S LATEST D
I SAY DAD IS TOTALLY FINE.
SLOW DOWN.
TAKE A DEEP BREATH...
TELL US WHAT HAPPENED, JAY.
JAY!
THIS IS REALLY IMPORTANT.
SOME KIND OF WINDOW OPENED UP IN TIME.
SOMEONE FIRED A BULLET.
WE HEARD THAT VOICE...
RUN!
AND WE RAN.
BY GOD, WE RAN.
THREE GENERATIONS OF THE FLASH.

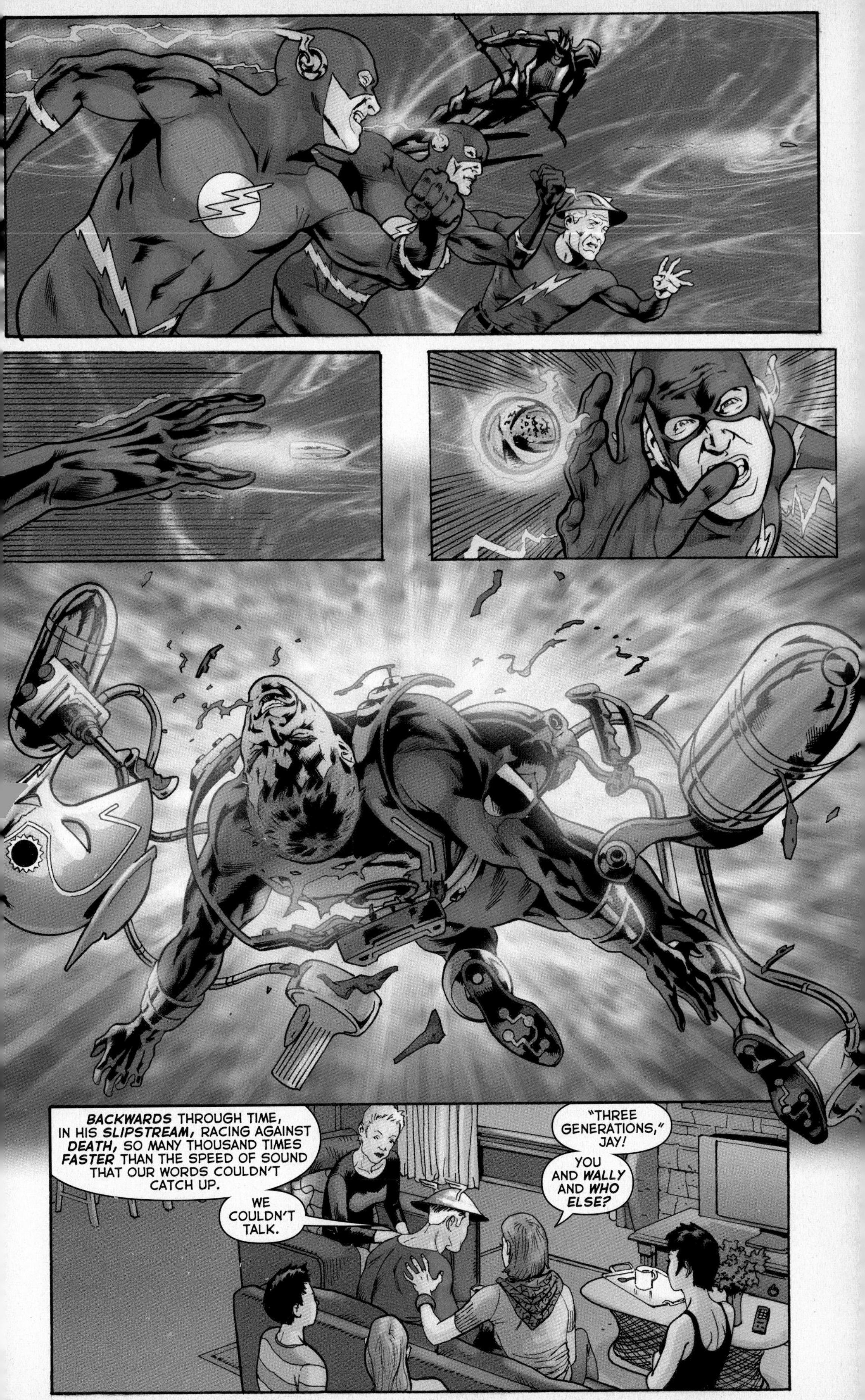
BACKWARDS THROUGH TIME, IN HIS SLIPSTREAM, RACING AGAINST DEATH, SO MANY THOUSAND TIMES FASTER THAN THE SPEED OF SOUND THAT OUR WORDS COULDN'T CATCH UP.
WE COULDN'T TALK.
"THREE GENERATIONS," JAY!
YOU AND WALLY AND WHO ELSE?

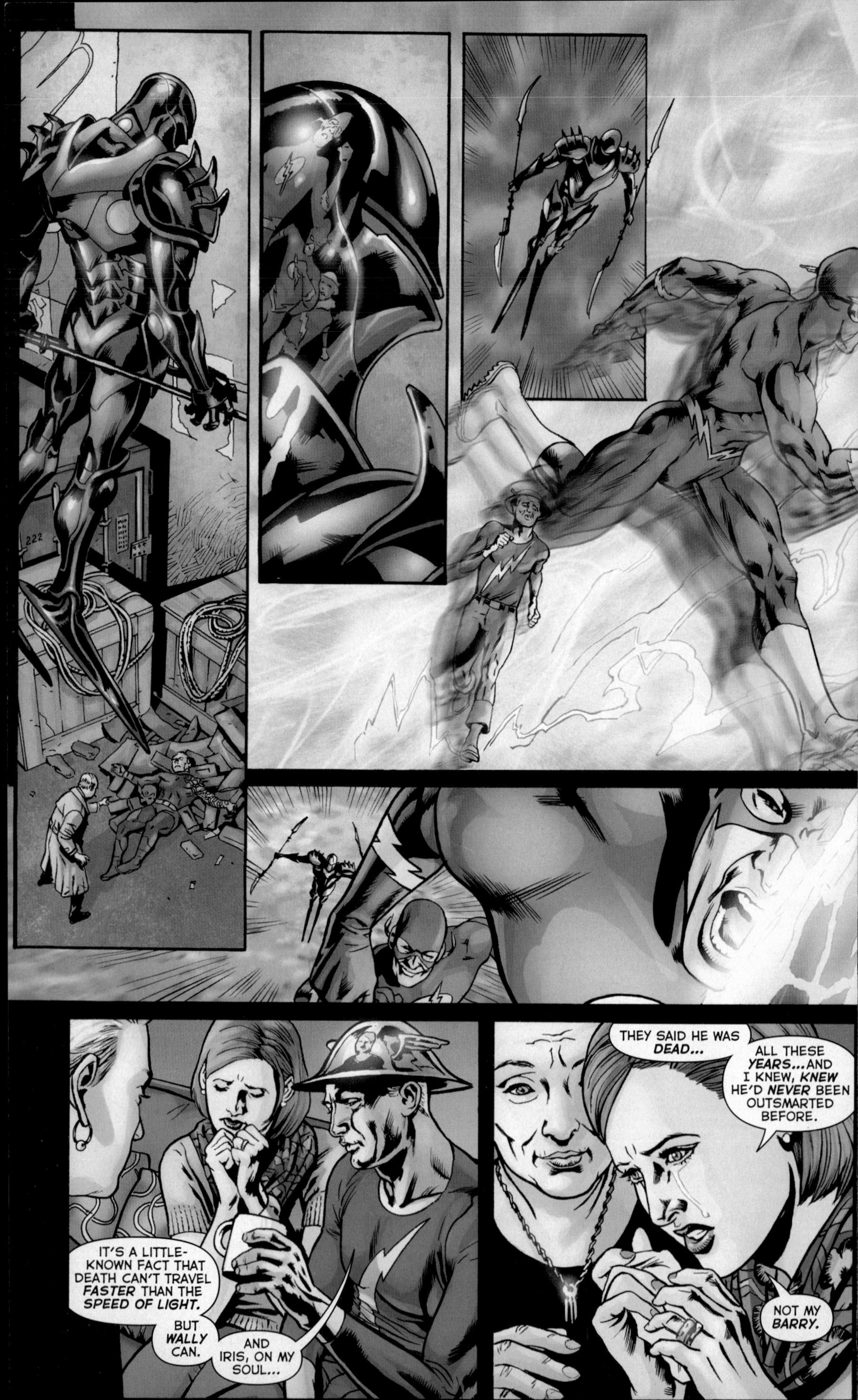
IT'S A LITTLE-KNOWN FACT THAT DEATH CAN'T TRAVEL *FASTER* THAN THE *SPEED OF LIGHT.*
BUT *WALLY* CAN.
AND IRIS, ON MY SOUL...
THEY SAID HE WAS *DEAD...*
ALL THESE *YEARS...*AND I KNEW, *KNEW* HE'D *NEVER* BEEN OUTSMARTED BEFORE.
NOT MY *BARRY.*

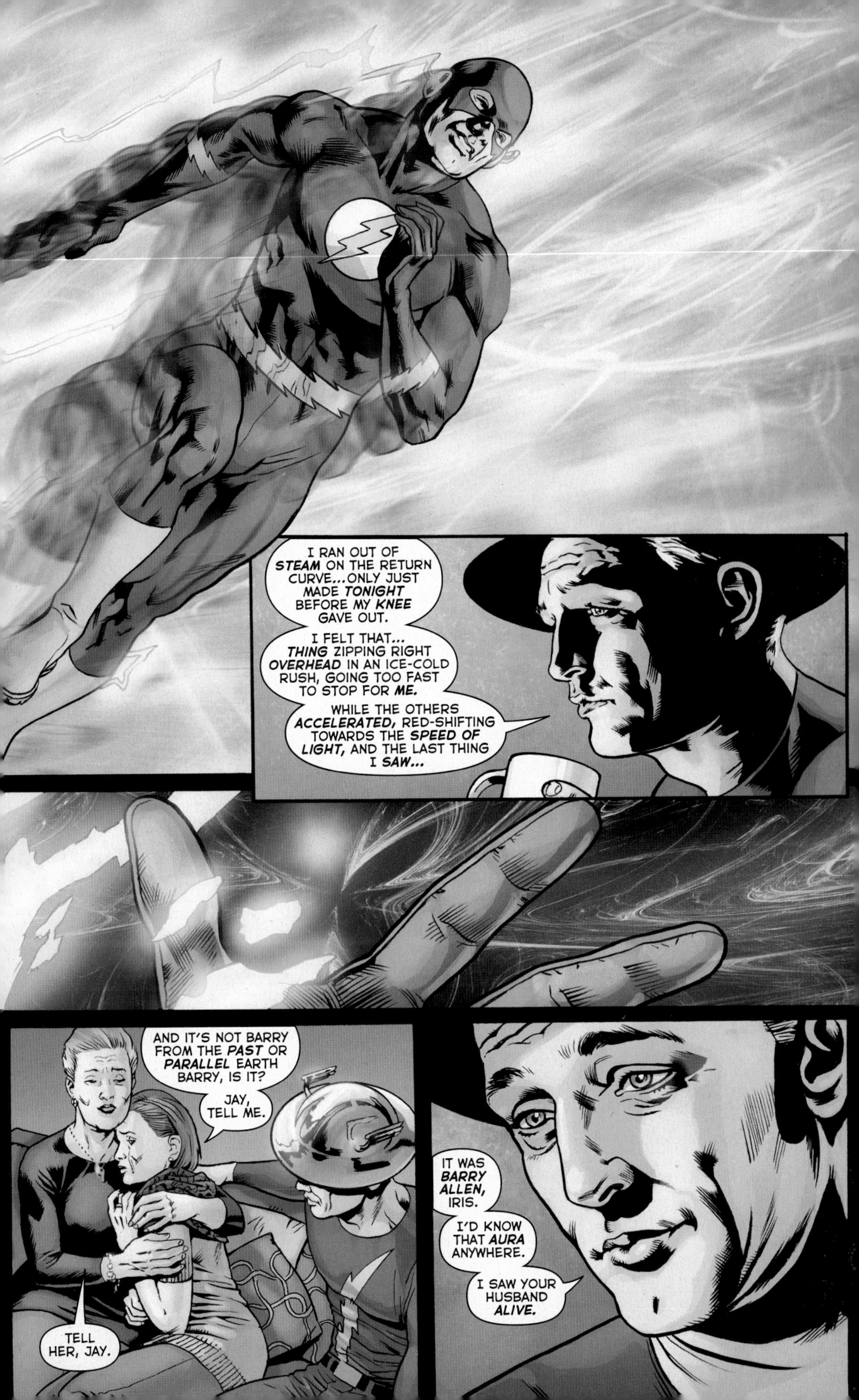
I RAN OUT OF STEAM ON THE RETURN CURVE...ONLY JUST MADE TONIGHT BEFORE MY KNEE GAVE OUT.
I FELT THAT... THING ZIPPING RIGHT OVERHEAD IN AN ICE-COLD RUSH, GOING TOO FAST TO STOP FOR ME.
WHILE THE OTHERS ACCELERATED, RED-SHIFTING TOWARDS THE SPEED OF LIGHT, AND THE LAST THING I SAW...
AND IT'S NOT BARRY FROM THE PAST OR PARALLEL EARTH BARRY, IS IT?
JAY, TELL ME.
TELL HER, JAY.
IT WAS BARRY ALLEN, IRIS.
I'D KNOW THAT AURA ANYWHERE.
I SAW YOUR HUSBAND ALIVE.

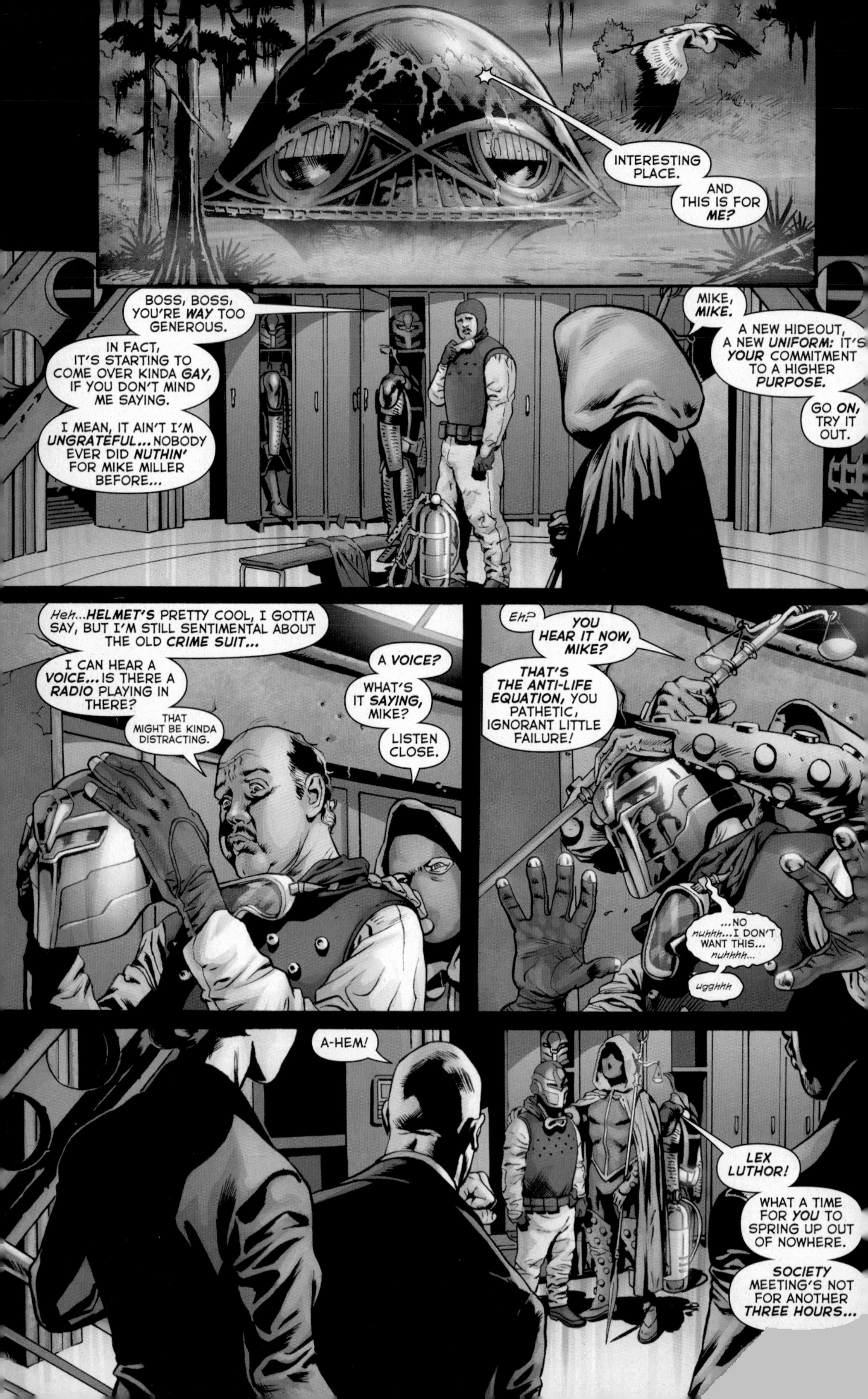
INTERESTING PLACE.
AND THIS IS FOR *ME?*
BOSS, BOSS, YOU'RE *WAY* TOO GENEROUS.
IN FACT, IT'S STARTING TO COME OVER KINDA *GAY,* IF YOU DON'T MIND ME SAYING.
I MEAN, IT AIN'T I'M *UNGRATEFUL...* NOBODY EVER DID *NUTHIN'* FOR MIKE MILLER BEFORE...
MIKE, *MIKE.*
A NEW HIDEOUT, A NEW *UNIFORM:* IT'S *YOUR* COMMITMENT TO A HIGHER *PURPOSE.*
GO *ON,* TRY IT OUT.
Heh... ***HELMET'S*** PRETTY COOL, I GOTTA SAY, BUT I'M STILL SENTIMENTAL ABOUT THE OLD *CRIME SUIT...*
I CAN HEAR A *VOICE...* IS THERE A *RADIO* PLAYING IN THERE?
THAT MIGHT BE KINDA DISTRACTING.
A *VOICE?*
WHAT'S IT *SAYING,* MIKE?
LISTEN CLOSE.
Eh?
YOU HEAR IT NOW, MIKE?
THAT'S THE ANTI-LIFE EQUATION, YOU PATHETIC, IGNORANT LITTLE FAILURE!
...NO *nuhhh...* I DON'T WANT THIS... *nuhhhh...*
ugghhh
A-HEM!
LEX LUTHOR!
WHAT A TIME FOR *YOU* TO SPRING UP OUT OF NOWHERE.
SOCIETY MEETING'S NOT FOR ANOTHER *THREE HOURS...*

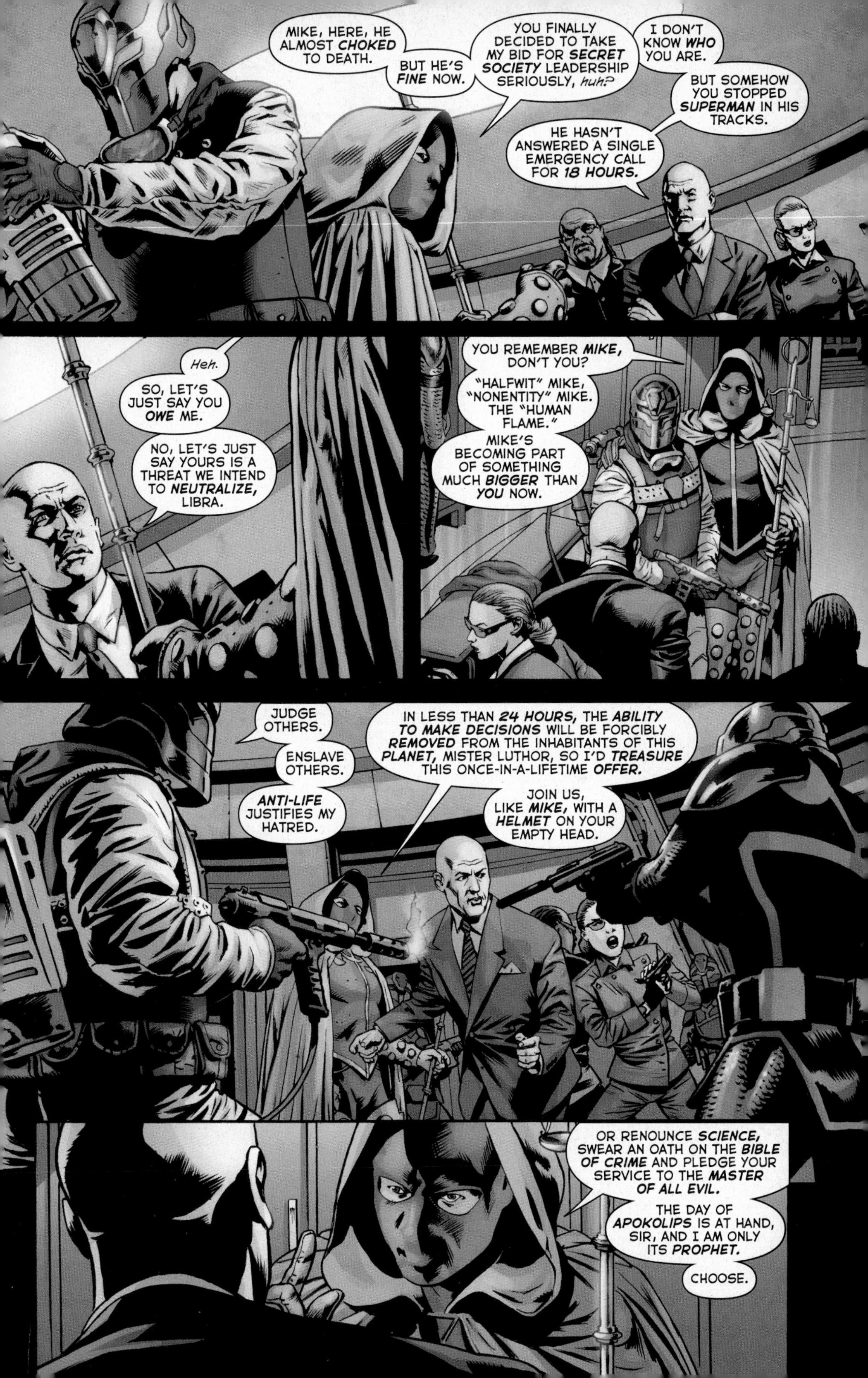
MIKE, HERE, HE ALMOST CHOKED TO DEATH.
BUT HE'S FINE NOW.
YOU FINALLY DECIDED TO TAKE MY BID FOR SECRET SOCIETY LEADERSHIP SERIOUSLY, huh?
I DON'T KNOW WHO YOU ARE.
BUT SOMEHOW YOU STOPPED SUPERMAN IN HIS TRACKS.
HE HASN'T ANSWERED A SINGLE EMERGENCY CALL FOR 18 HOURS.
Heh.
SO, LET'S JUST SAY YOU OWE ME.
NO, LET'S JUST SAY YOURS IS A THREAT WE INTEND TO NEUTRALIZE, LIBRA.
YOU REMEMBER MIKE, DON'T YOU?
"HALFWIT" MIKE, "NONENTITY" MIKE. THE "HUMAN FLAME."
MIKE'S BECOMING PART OF SOMETHING MUCH BIGGER THAN YOU NOW.
JUDGE OTHERS.
ENSLAVE OTHERS.
ANTI-LIFE JUSTIFIES MY HATRED.
IN LESS THAN 24 HOURS, THE ABILITY TO MAKE DECISIONS WILL BE FORCIBLY REMOVED FROM THE INHABITANTS OF THIS PLANET, MISTER LUTHOR, SO I'D TREASURE THIS ONCE-IN-A-LIFETIME OFFER.
JOIN US, LIKE MIKE, WITH A HELMET ON YOUR EMPTY HEAD.
OR RENOUNCE SCIENCE, SWEAR AN OATH ON THE BIBLE OF CRIME AND PLEDGE YOUR SERVICE TO THE MASTER OF ALL EVIL.
THE DAY OF APOKOLIPS IS AT HAND, SIR, AND I AM ONLY ITS PROPHET.
CHOOSE.

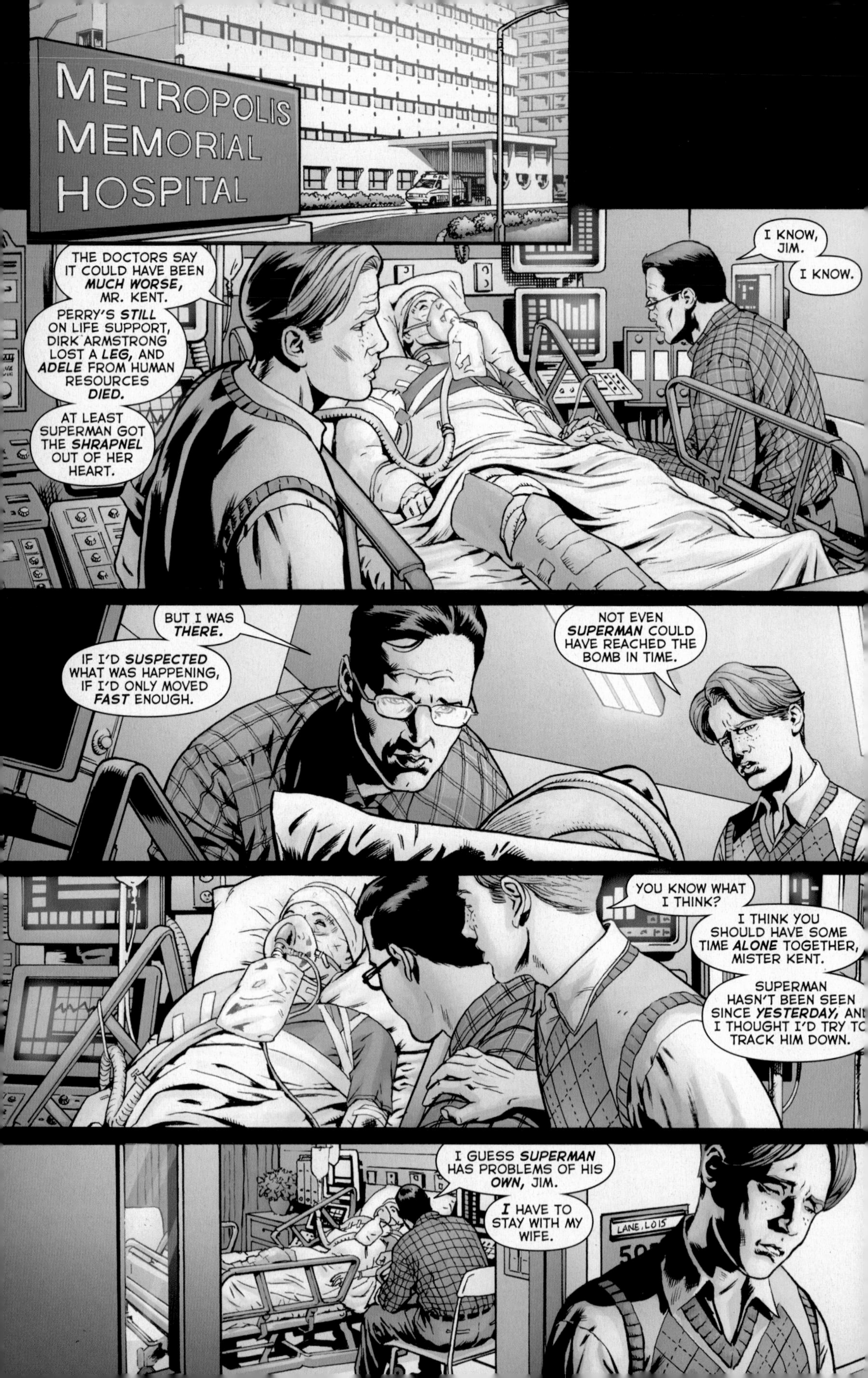
METROPOLIS MEMORIAL HOSPITAL
THE DOCTORS SAY IT COULD HAVE BEEN MUCH WORSE, MR. KENT.
PERRY'S STILL ON LIFE SUPPORT, DIRK ARMSTRONG LOST A LEG, AND ADELE FROM HUMAN RESOURCES DIED.
AT LEAST SUPERMAN GOT THE SHRAPNEL OUT OF HER HEART.
I KNOW, JIM.
I KNOW.
BUT I WAS THERE.
IF I'D SUSPECTED WHAT WAS HAPPENING, IF I'D ONLY MOVED FAST ENOUGH.
NOT EVEN SUPERMAN COULD HAVE REACHED THE BOMB IN TIME.
YOU KNOW WHAT I THINK?
I THINK YOU SHOULD HAVE SOME TIME ALONE TOGETHER, MISTER KENT.
SUPERMAN HASN'T BEEN SEEN SINCE YESTERDAY, AND I THOUGHT I'D TRY TO TRACK HIM DOWN.
I GUESS SUPERMAN HAS PROBLEMS OF HIS OWN, JIM.
I HAVE TO STAY WITH MY WIFE.
LANE, LOIS

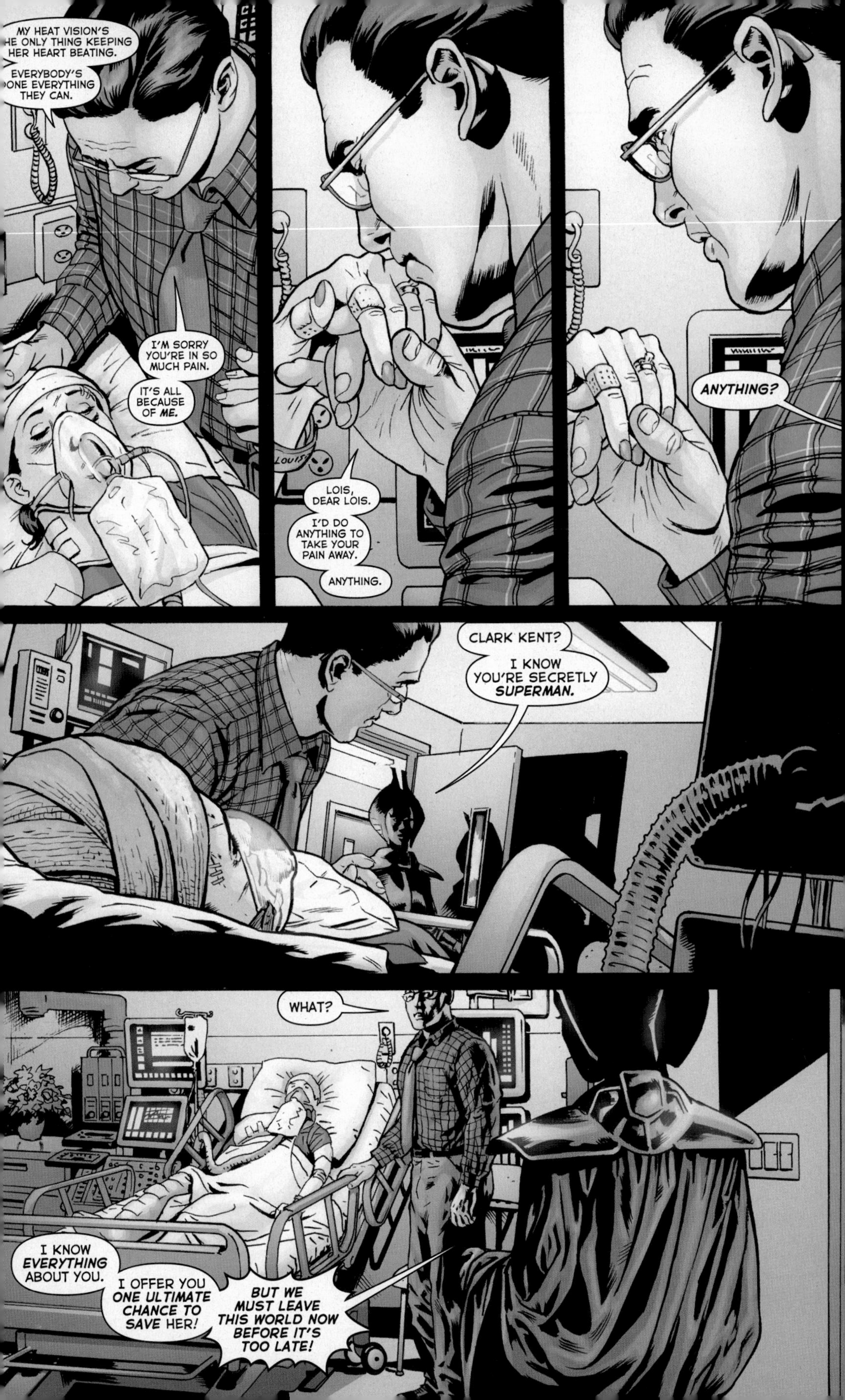
MY HEAT VISION'S HE ONLY THING KEEPING HER HEART BEATING.
EVERYBODY'S ONE EVERYTHING THEY CAN.
I'M SORRY YOU'RE IN SO MUCH PAIN.
IT'S ALL BECAUSE OF ME.
LOIS, DEAR LOIS.
I'D DO ANYTHING TO TAKE YOUR PAIN AWAY.
ANYTHING.
ANYTHING?
CLARK KENT?
I KNOW YOU'RE SECRETLY SUPERMAN.
WHAT?
I KNOW EVERYTHING ABOUT YOU.
I OFFER YOU ONE ULTIMATE CHANCE TO SAVE HER!
BUT WE MUST LEAVE THIS WORLD NOW BEFORE IT'S TOO LATE!

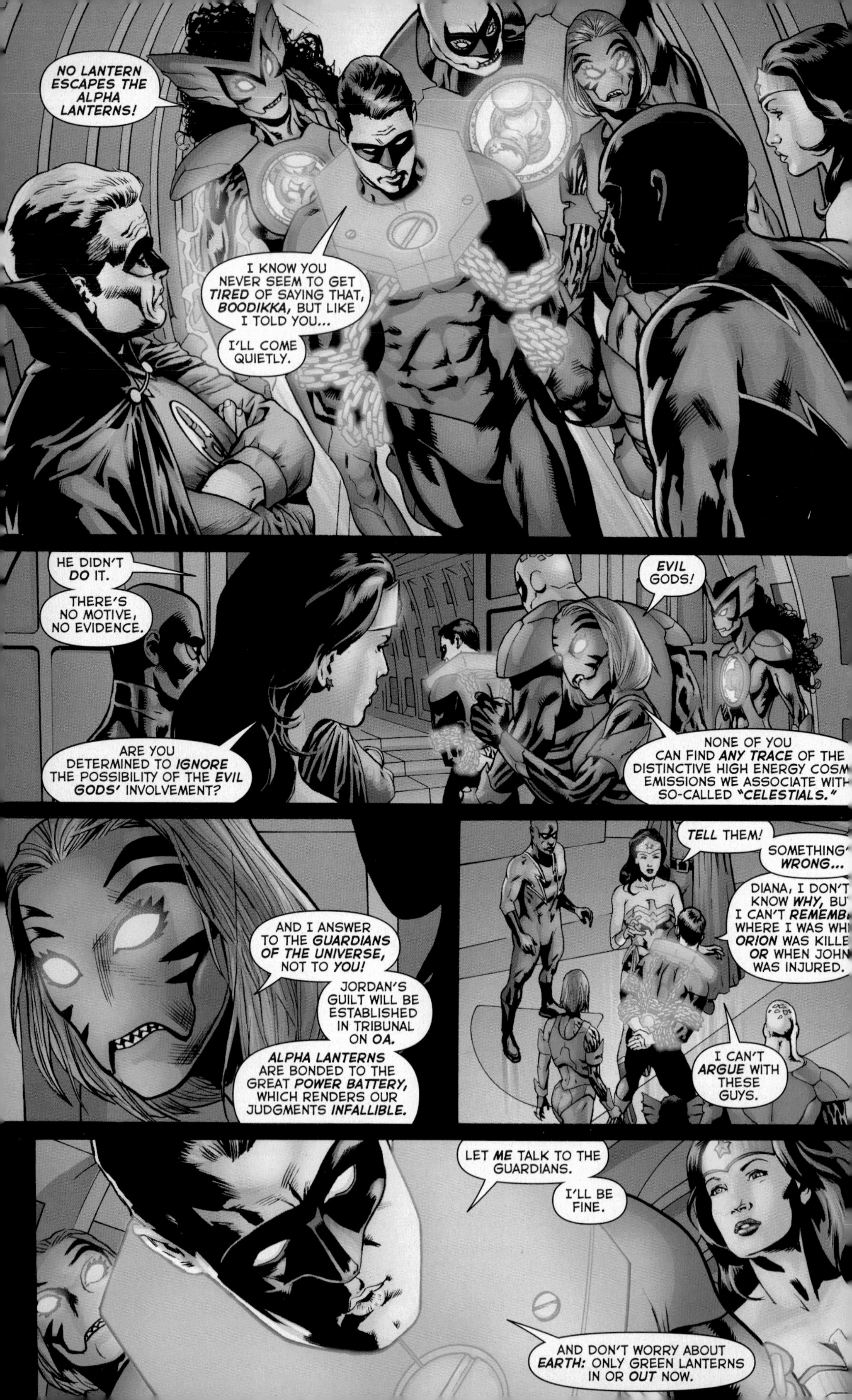
NO LANTERN ESCAPES THE ALPHA LANTERNS!
I KNOW YOU NEVER SEEM TO GET TIRED OF SAYING THAT, BOODIKKA, BUT LIKE I TOLD YOU...
I'LL COME QUIETLY.
HE DIDN'T DO IT.
THERE'S NO MOTIVE, NO EVIDENCE.
ARE YOU DETERMINED TO IGNORE THE POSSIBILITY OF THE EVIL GODS' INVOLVEMENT?
EVIL GODS!
NONE OF YOU CAN FIND ANY TRACE OF THE DISTINCTIVE HIGH ENERGY COSM EMISSIONS WE ASSOCIATE WITH SO-CALLED "CELESTIALS."
AND I ANSWER TO THE GUARDIANS OF THE UNIVERSE, NOT TO YOU!
JORDAN'S GUILT WILL BE ESTABLISHED IN TRIBUNAL ON OA.
ALPHA LANTERNS ARE BONDED TO THE GREAT POWER BATTERY, WHICH RENDERS OUR JUDGMENTS INFALLIBLE.
TELL THEM!
SOMETHING' WRONG...
DIANA, I DON'T KNOW WHY, BU I CAN'T REMEMB WHERE I WAS WH ORION WAS KILLE OR WHEN JOHN WAS INJURED.
I CAN'T ARGUE WITH THESE GUYS.
LET ME TALK TO THE GUARDIANS.
I'LL BE FINE.
AND DON'T WORRY ABOUT EARTH: ONLY GREEN LANTERNS IN OR OUT NOW.

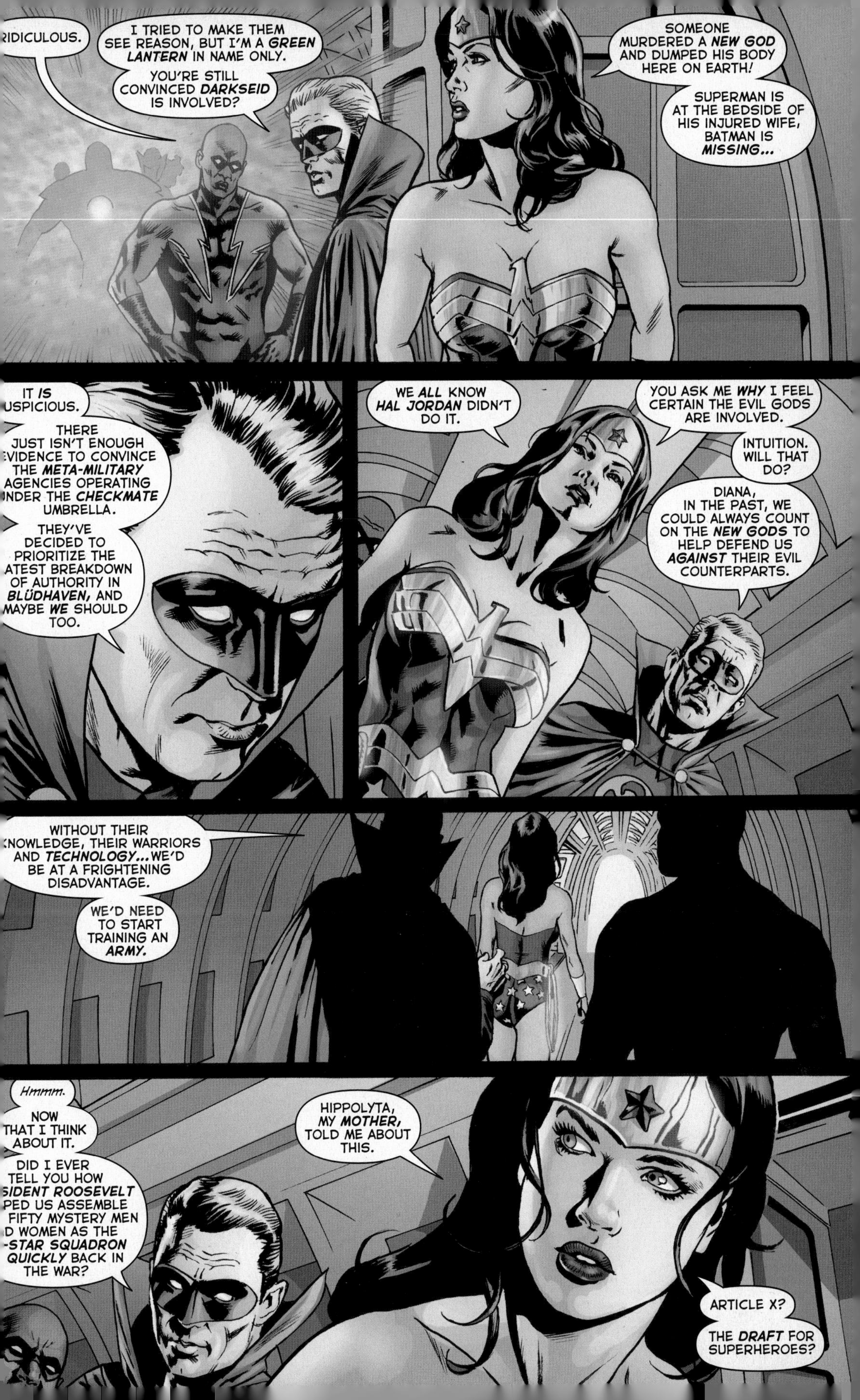
RIDICULOUS.
I TRIED TO MAKE THEM SEE REASON, BUT I'M A GREEN LANTERN IN NAME ONLY.
YOU'RE STILL CONVINCED DARKSEID IS INVOLVED?
SOMEONE MURDERED A NEW GOD AND DUMPED HIS BODY HERE ON EARTH!
SUPERMAN IS AT THE BEDSIDE OF HIS INJURED WIFE, BATMAN IS MISSING...
IT IS USPICIOUS.
THERE JUST ISN'T ENOUGH EVIDENCE TO CONVINCE THE META-MILITARY AGENCIES OPERATING UNDER THE CHECKMATE UMBRELLA.
THEY'VE DECIDED TO PRIORITIZE THE ATEST BREAKDOWN OF AUTHORITY IN BLÜDHAVEN, AND MAYBE WE SHOULD TOO.
WE ALL KNOW HAL JORDAN DIDN'T DO IT.
YOU ASK ME WHY I FEEL CERTAIN THE EVIL GODS ARE INVOLVED.
INTUITION. WILL THAT DO?
DIANA, IN THE PAST, WE COULD ALWAYS COUNT ON THE NEW GODS TO HELP DEFEND US AGAINST THEIR EVIL COUNTERPARTS.
WITHOUT THEIR KNOWLEDGE, THEIR WARRIORS AND TECHNOLOGY...WE'D BE AT A FRIGHTENING DISADVANTAGE.
WE'D NEED TO START TRAINING AN ARMY.
Hmmm.
NOW THAT I THINK ABOUT IT.
DID I EVER TELL YOU HOW SIDENT ROOSEVELT PED US ASSEMBLE FIFTY MYSTERY MEN D WOMEN AS THE -STAR SQUADRON QUICKLY BACK IN THE WAR?
HIPPOLYTA, MY MOTHER, TOLD ME ABOUT THIS.
ARTICLE X?
THE DRAFT FOR SUPERHEROES?

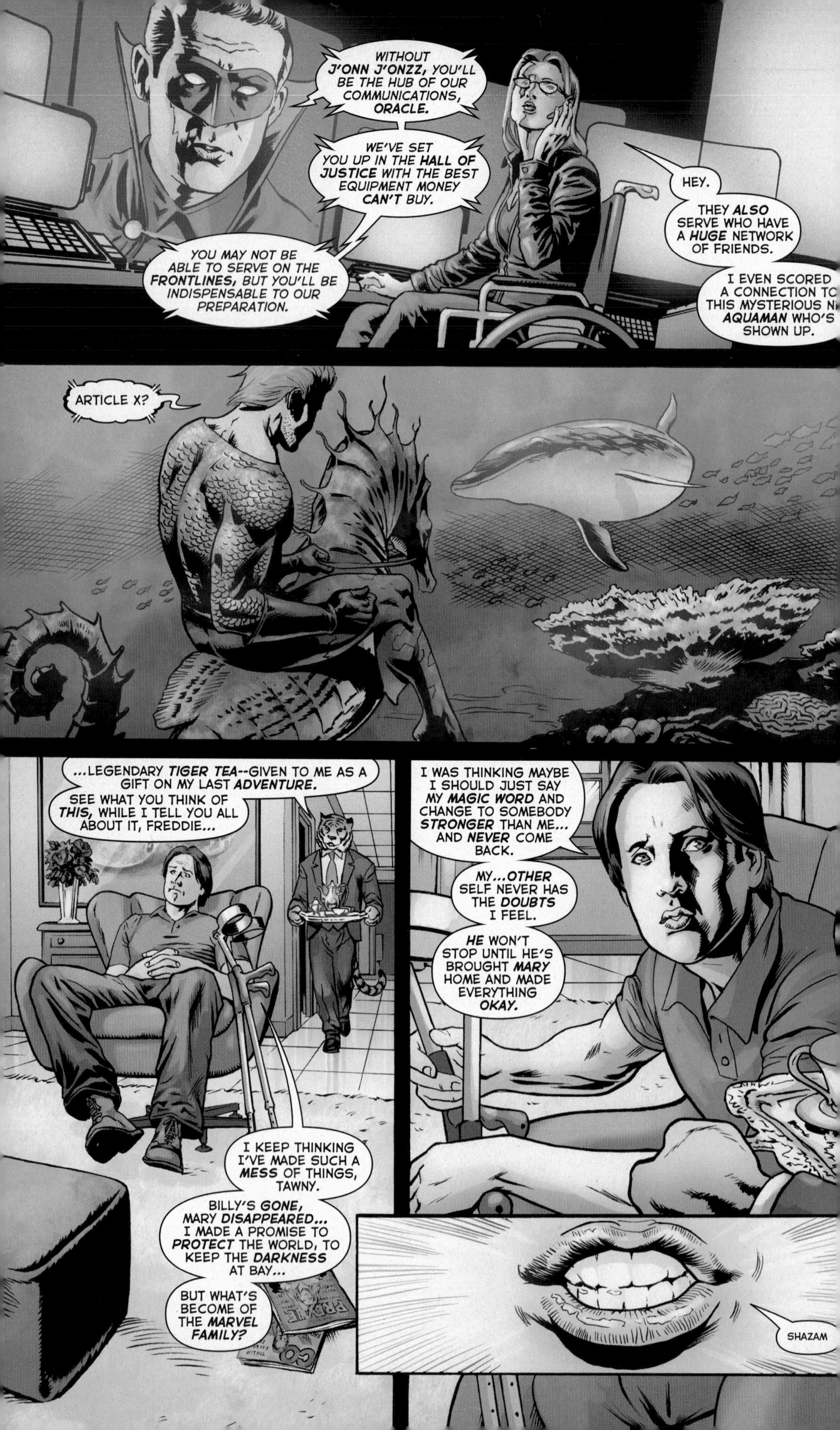
WITHOUT J'ONN J'ONZZ, YOU'LL BE THE HUB OF OUR COMMUNICATIONS, ORACLE.
WE'VE SET YOU UP IN THE HALL OF JUSTICE WITH THE BEST EQUIPMENT MONEY CAN'T BUY.
YOU MAY NOT BE ABLE TO SERVE ON THE FRONTLINES, BUT YOU'LL BE INDISPENSABLE TO OUR PREPARATION.
HEY.
THEY ALSO SERVE WHO HAVE A HUGE NETWORK OF FRIENDS.
I EVEN SCORED A CONNECTION TO THIS MYSTERIOUS N AQUAMAN WHO'S SHOWN UP.
ARTICLE X?
...LEGENDARY TIGER TEA--GIVEN TO ME AS A GIFT ON MY LAST ADVENTURE.
SEE WHAT YOU THINK OF THIS, WHILE I TELL YOU ALL ABOUT IT, FREDDIE...
I KEEP THINKING I'VE MADE SUCH A MESS OF THINGS, TAWNY.
BILLY'S GONE, MARY DISAPPEARED... I MADE A PROMISE TO PROTECT THE WORLD, TO KEEP THE DARKNESS AT BAY...
BUT WHAT'S BECOME OF THE MARVEL FAMILY?
I WAS THINKING MAYBE I SHOULD JUST SAY MY MAGIC WORD AND CHANGE TO SOMEBODY STRONGER THAN ME... AND NEVER COME BACK.
MY...OTHER SELF NEVER HAS THE DOUBTS I FEEL.
HE WON'T STOP UNTIL HE'S BROUGHT MARY HOME AND MADE EVERYTHING OKAY.
SHAZAM

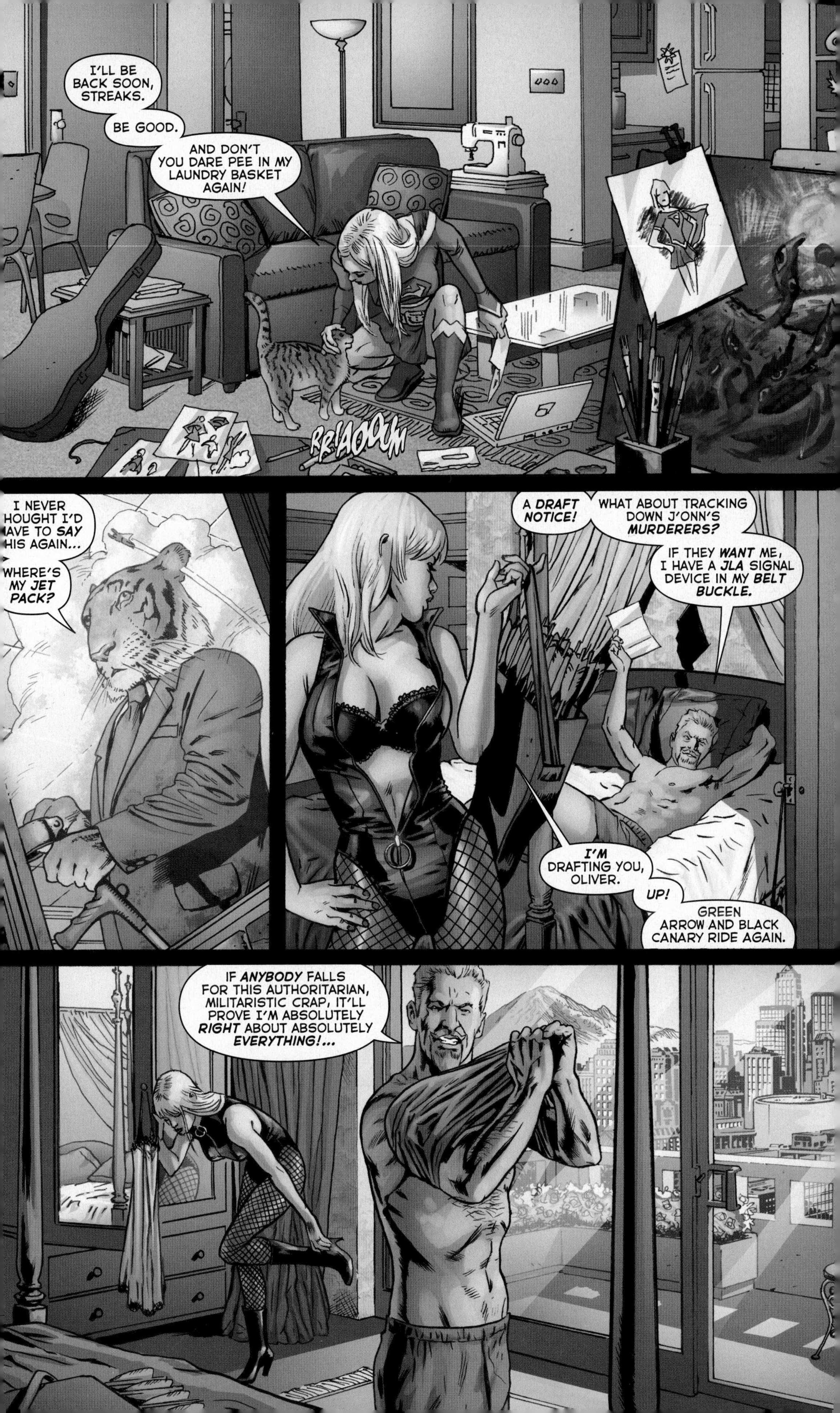
I'LL BE BACK SOON, STREAKS.
BE GOOD.
AND DON'T YOU DARE PEE IN MY LAUNDRY BASKET AGAIN!
RRRIAOOUM
I NEVER HOUGHT I'D IAVE TO SAY HIS AGAIN...
WHERE'S MY JET PACK?
A DRAFT NOTICE!
WHAT ABOUT TRACKING DOWN J'ONN'S MURDERERS?
IF THEY WANT ME, I HAVE A JLA SIGNAL DEVICE IN MY BELT BUCKLE.
I'M DRAFTING YOU, OLIVER.
UP!
GREEN ARROW AND BLACK CANARY RIDE AGAIN.
IF ANYBODY FALLS FOR THIS AUTHORITARIAN, MILITARISTIC CRAP, IT'LL PROVE I'M ABSOLUTELY RIGHT ABOUT ABSOLUTELY EVERYTHING!...

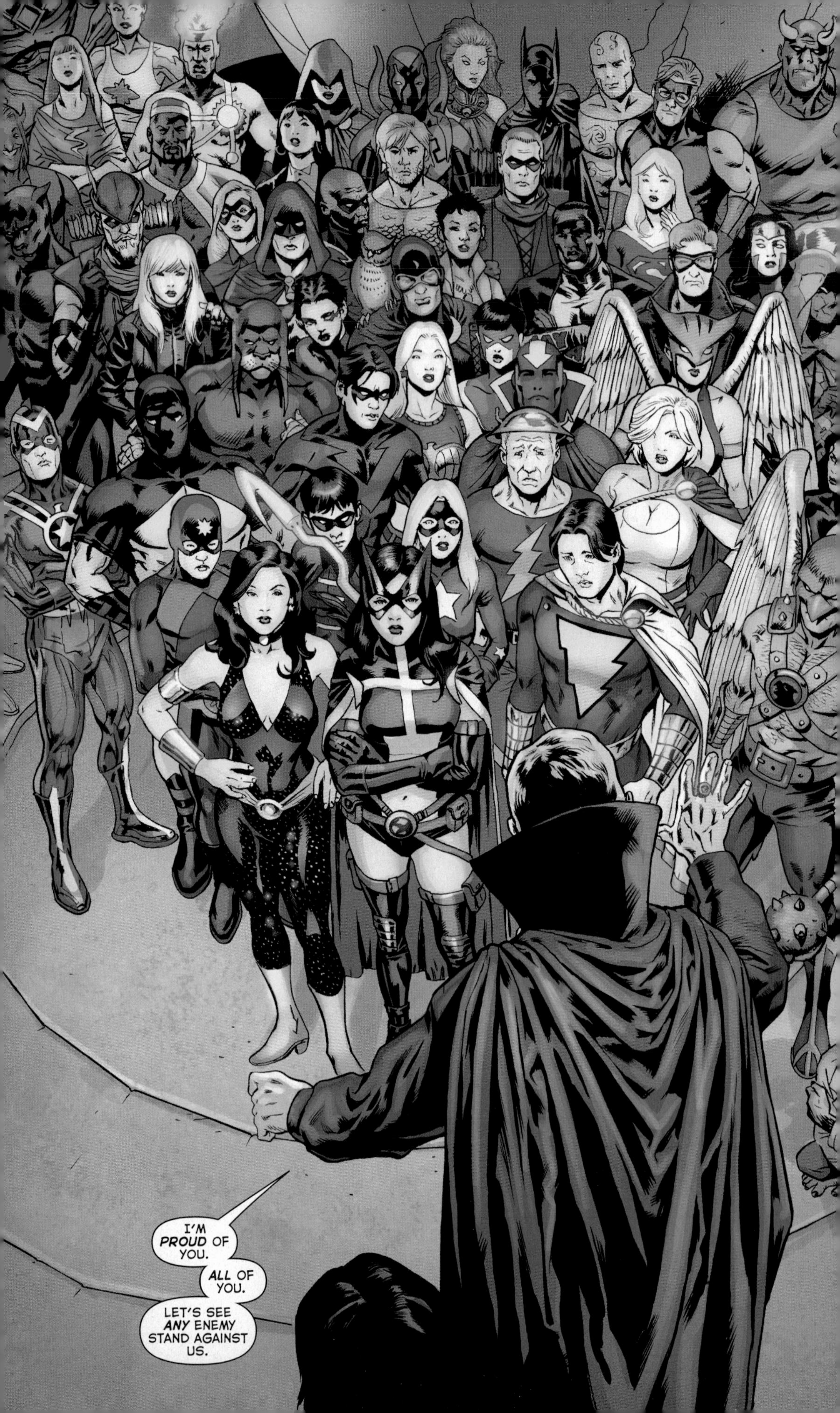
I'M *PROUD* OF YOU.
ALL OF YOU.
LET'S SEE *ANY* ENEMY STAND AGAINST US.

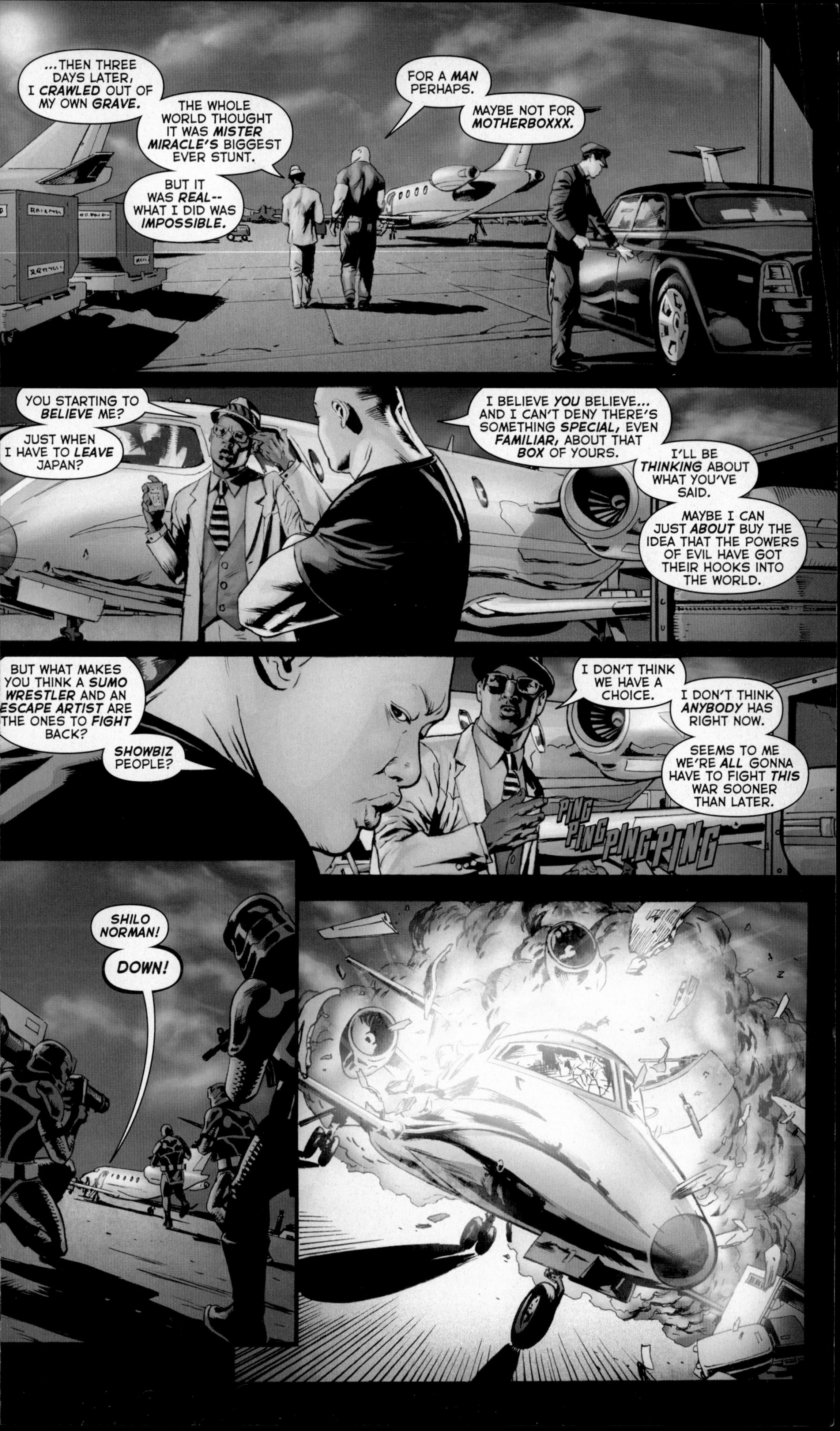
...THEN THREE DAYS LATER, I CRAWLED OUT OF MY OWN GRAVE.
THE WHOLE WORLD THOUGHT IT WAS MISTER MIRACLE'S BIGGEST EVER STUNT.
BUT IT WAS REAL-- WHAT I DID WAS IMPOSSIBLE.
FOR A MAN PERHAPS.
MAYBE NOT FOR MOTHERBOXXX.
YOU STARTING TO BELIEVE ME?
JUST WHEN I HAVE TO LEAVE JAPAN?
I BELIEVE YOU BELIEVE... AND I CAN'T DENY THERE'S SOMETHING SPECIAL, EVEN FAMILIAR, ABOUT THAT BOX OF YOURS.
I'LL BE THINKING ABOUT WHAT YOU'VE SAID.
MAYBE I CAN JUST ABOUT BUY THE IDEA THAT THE POWERS OF EVIL HAVE GOT THEIR HOOKS INTO THE WORLD.
BUT WHAT MAKES YOU THINK A SUMO WRESTLER AND AN ESCAPE ARTIST ARE THE ONES TO FIGHT BACK?
SHOWBIZ PEOPLE?
I DON'T THINK WE HAVE A CHOICE.
I DON'T THINK ANYBODY HAS RIGHT NOW.
SEEMS TO ME WE'RE ALL GONNA HAVE TO FIGHT THIS WAR SOONER THAN LATER.
PING PING PING PING
SHILO NORMAN!
DOWN!

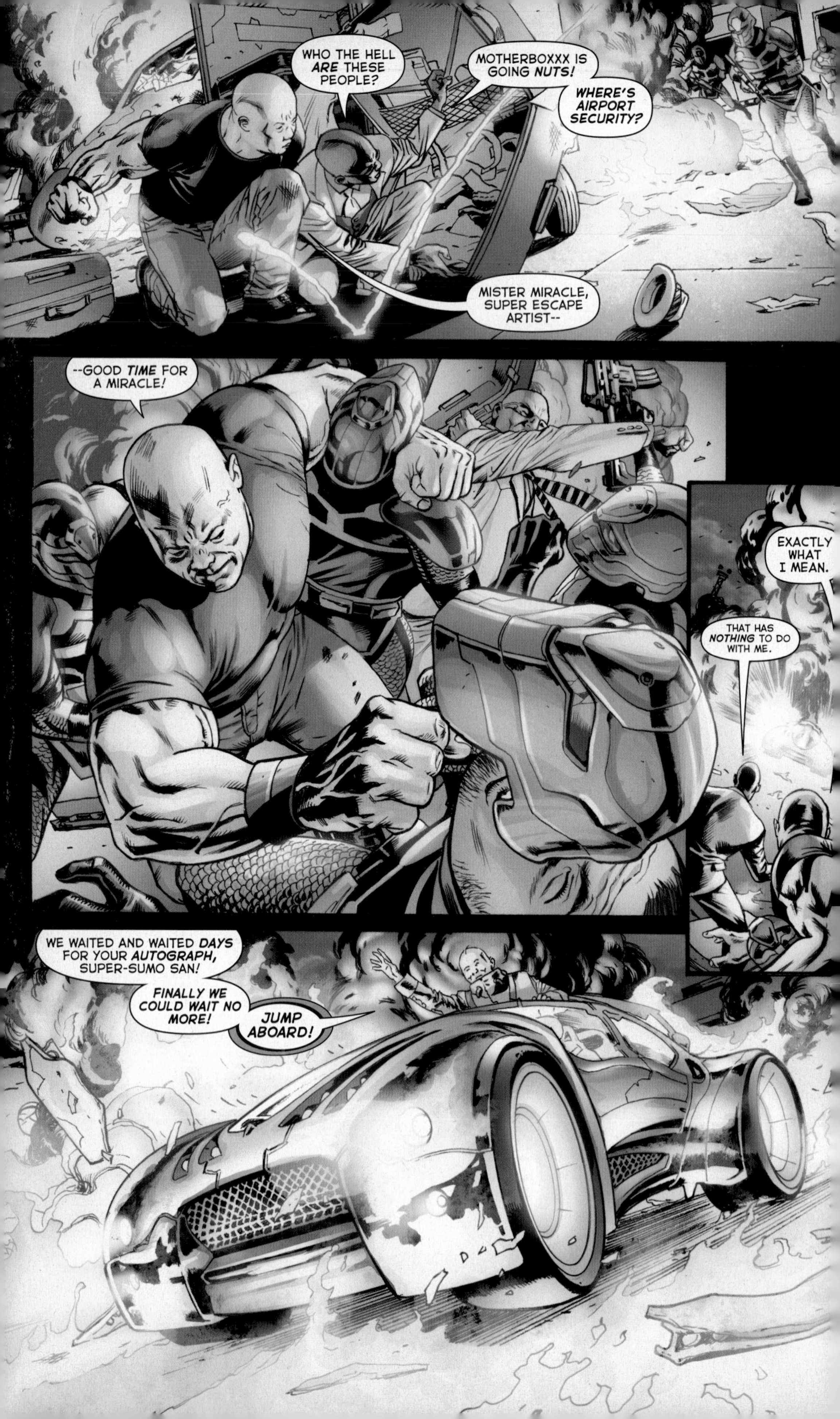

WHO THE HELL ARE THESE PEOPLE?
MOTHERBOXXX IS GOING NUTS!
WHERE'S AIRPORT SECURITY?
MISTER MIRACLE, SUPER ESCAPE ARTIST--
--GOOD TIME FOR A MIRACLE!
EXACTLY WHAT I MEAN.
THAT HAS NOTHING TO DO WITH ME.
WE WAITED AND WAITED DAYS FOR YOUR AUTOGRAPH, SUPER-SUMO SAN!
FINALLY WE COULD WAIT NO MORE!
JUMP ABOARD!

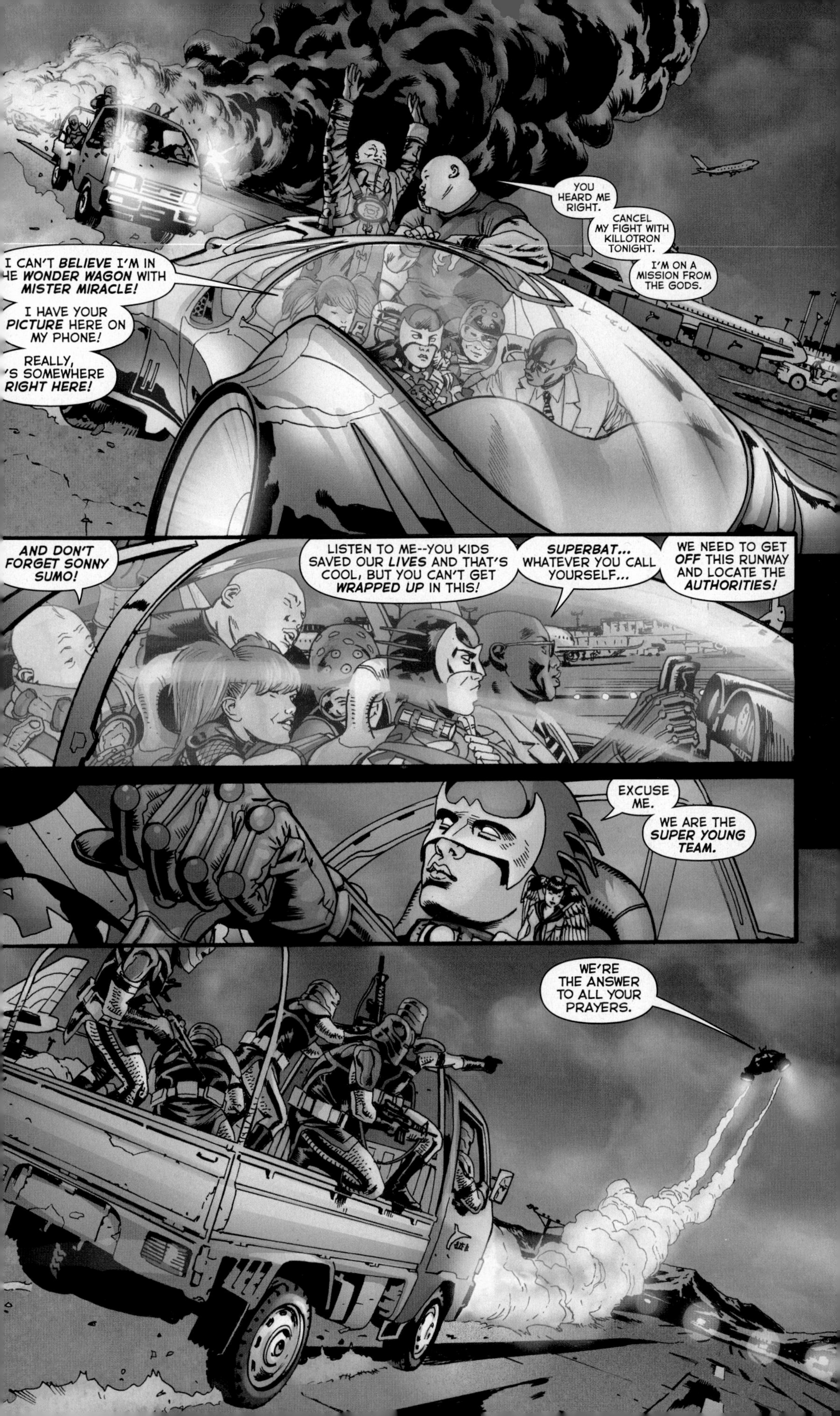
YOU HEARD ME RIGHT.
CANCEL MY FIGHT WITH KILLOTRON TONIGHT.
I'M ON A MISSION FROM THE GODS.
I CAN'T *BELIEVE* I'M IN HE *WONDER WAGON* WITH *MISTER MIRACLE!*
I HAVE YOUR *PICTURE* HERE ON MY PHONE!
REALLY, 'S SOMEWHERE *RIGHT HERE!*
AND DON'T FORGET SONNY SUMO!
LISTEN TO ME--YOU KIDS SAVED OUR *LIVES* AND THAT'S COOL, BUT YOU CAN'T GET *WRAPPED UP* IN THIS!
SUPERBAT... WHATEVER YOU CALL YOURSELF...
WE NEED TO GET *OFF* THIS RUNWAY AND LOCATE THE *AUTHORITIES!*
EXCUSE ME.
WE ARE THE *SUPER YOUNG TEAM.*
WE'RE THE ANSWER TO ALL YOUR PRAYERS.

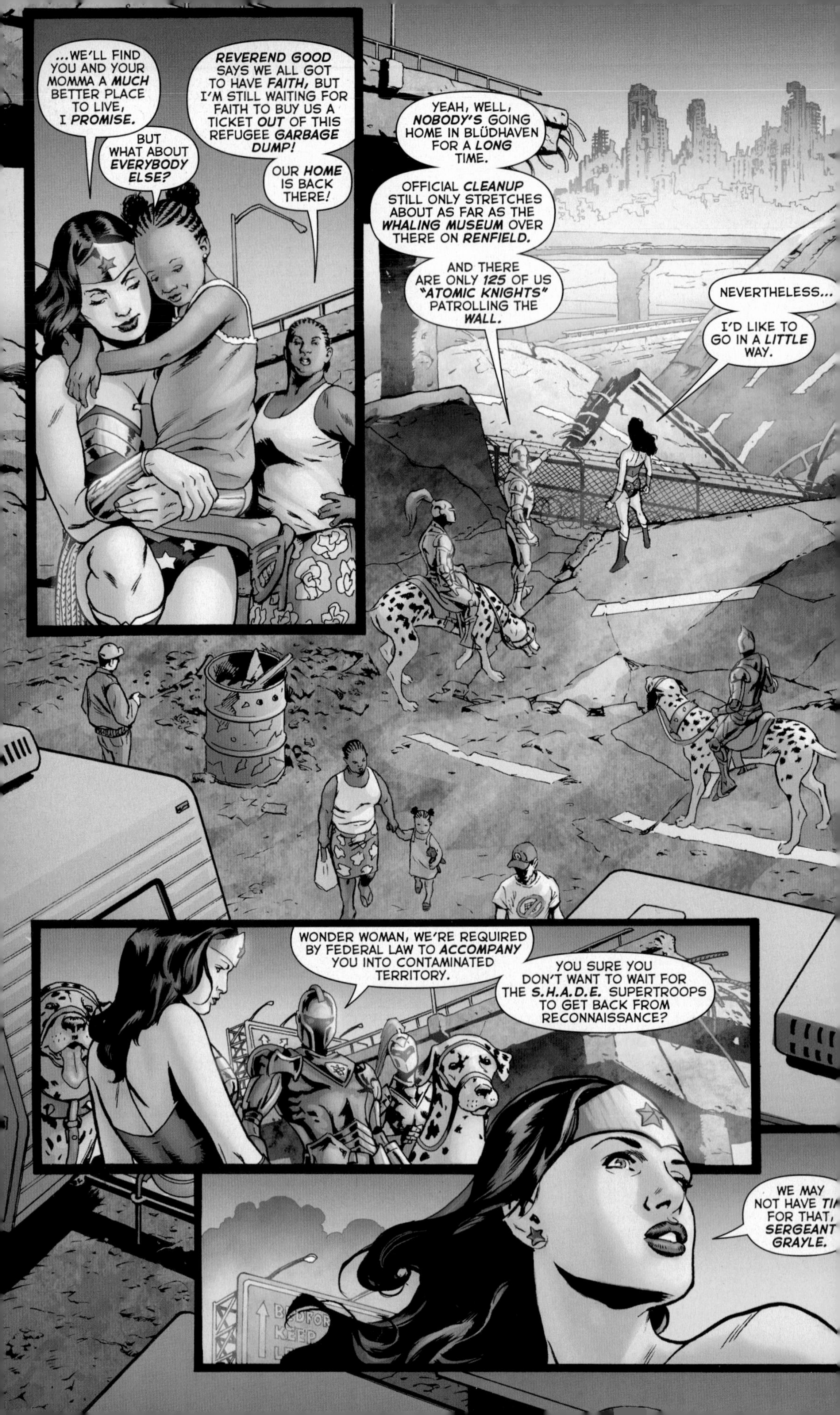
...WE'LL FIND YOU AND YOUR MOMMA A *MUCH* BETTER PLACE TO LIVE, I *PROMISE.*
BUT WHAT ABOUT *EVERYBODY ELSE?*
REVEREND GOOD SAYS WE ALL GOT TO HAVE *FAITH,* BUT I'M STILL WAITING FOR FAITH TO BUY US A TICKET *OUT* OF THIS REFUGEE *GARBAGE DUMP!*
OUR *HOME* IS BACK THERE!
YEAH, WELL, *NOBODY'S* GOING HOME IN BLÜDHAVEN FOR A *LONG* TIME.
OFFICIAL *CLEANUP* STILL ONLY STRETCHES ABOUT AS FAR AS THE *WHALING MUSEUM* OVER THERE ON *RENFIELD.*
AND THERE ARE ONLY *125* OF US *"ATOMIC KNIGHTS"* PATROLLING THE *WALL.*
NEVERTHELESS...
I'D LIKE TO GO IN A *LITTLE* WAY.
WONDER WOMAN, WE'RE REQUIRED BY FEDERAL LAW TO *ACCOMPANY* YOU INTO CONTAMINATED TERRITORY.
YOU SURE YOU DON'T WANT TO WAIT FOR THE *S.H.A.D.E.* SUPERTROOPS TO GET BACK FROM RECONNAISSANCE?
WE MAY NOT HAVE TI FOR THAT, *SERGEANT GRAYLE.*

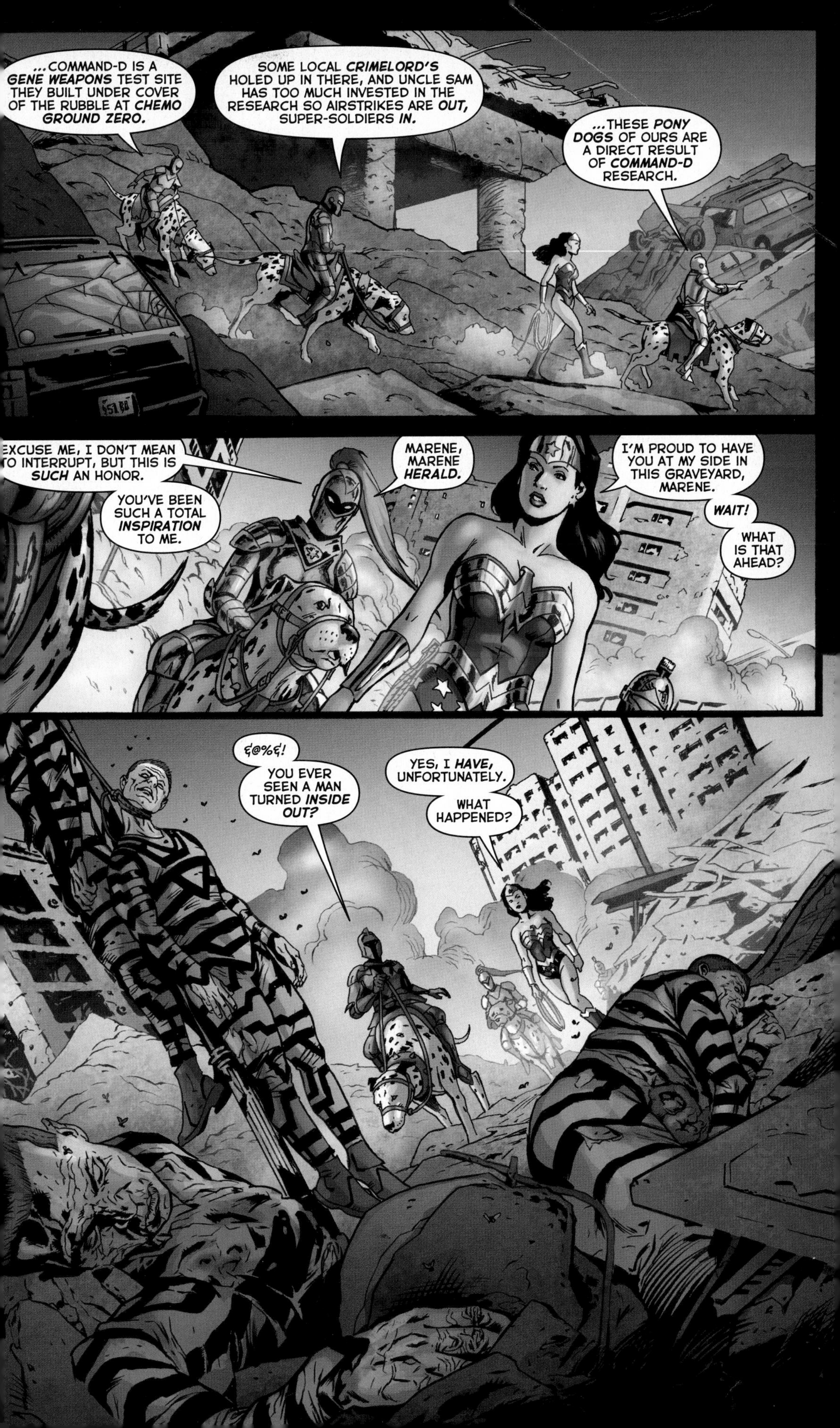
...COMMAND-D IS A GENE WEAPONS TEST SITE THEY BUILT UNDER COVER OF THE RUBBLE AT CHEMO GROUND ZERO.
SOME LOCAL CRIMELORD'S HOLED UP IN THERE, AND UNCLE SAM HAS TOO MUCH INVESTED IN THE RESEARCH SO AIRSTRIKES ARE OUT, SUPER-SOLDIERS IN.
...THESE PONY DOGS OF OURS ARE A DIRECT RESULT OF COMMAND-D RESEARCH.
EXCUSE ME, I DON'T MEAN TO INTERRUPT, BUT THIS IS SUCH AN HONOR.
YOU'VE BEEN SUCH A TOTAL INSPIRATION TO ME.
MARENE, MARENE HERALD.
I'M PROUD TO HAVE YOU AT MY SIDE IN THIS GRAVEYARD, MARENE.
WAIT!
WHAT IS THAT AHEAD?
₰@%₰!
YOU EVER SEEN A MAN TURNED INSIDE OUT?
YES, I HAVE, UNFORTUNATELY.
WHAT HAPPENED?

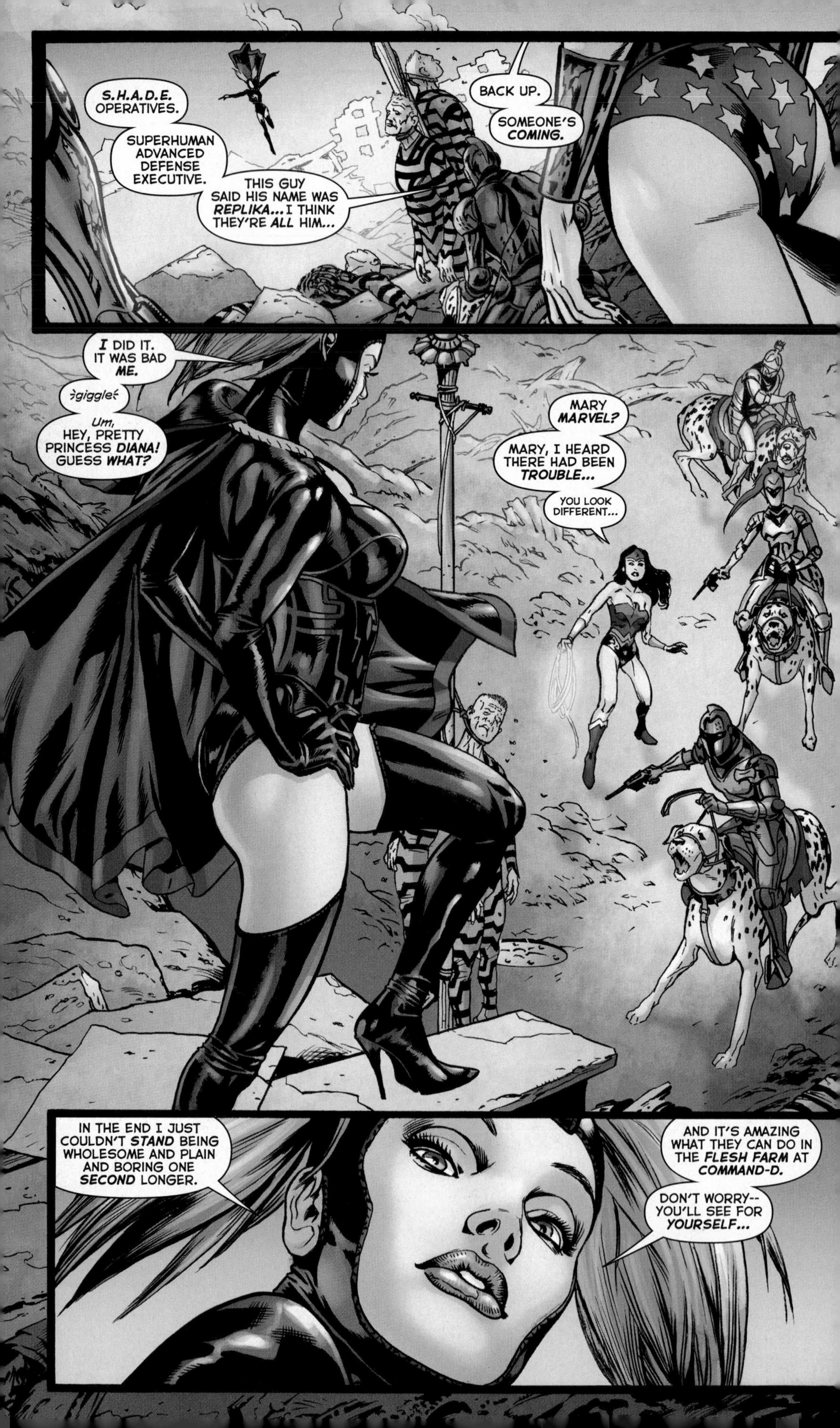
S.H.A.D.E. OPERATIVES.
SUPERHUMAN ADVANCED DEFENSE EXECUTIVE.
THIS GUY SAID HIS NAME WAS REPLIKA... I THINK THEY'RE ALL HIM...
BACK UP.
SOMEONE'S COMING.
I DID IT. IT WAS BAD ME.
giggle
Um, HEY, PRETTY PRINCESS DIANA! GUESS WHAT?
MARY MARVEL?
MARY, I HEARD THERE HAD BEEN TROUBLE...
YOU LOOK DIFFERENT...
IN THE END I JUST COULDN'T STAND BEING WHOLESOME AND PLAIN AND BORING ONE SECOND LONGER.
AND IT'S AMAZING WHAT THEY CAN DO IN THE FLESH FARM AT COMMAND-D.
DON'T WORRY-- YOU'LL SEE FOR YOURSELF...

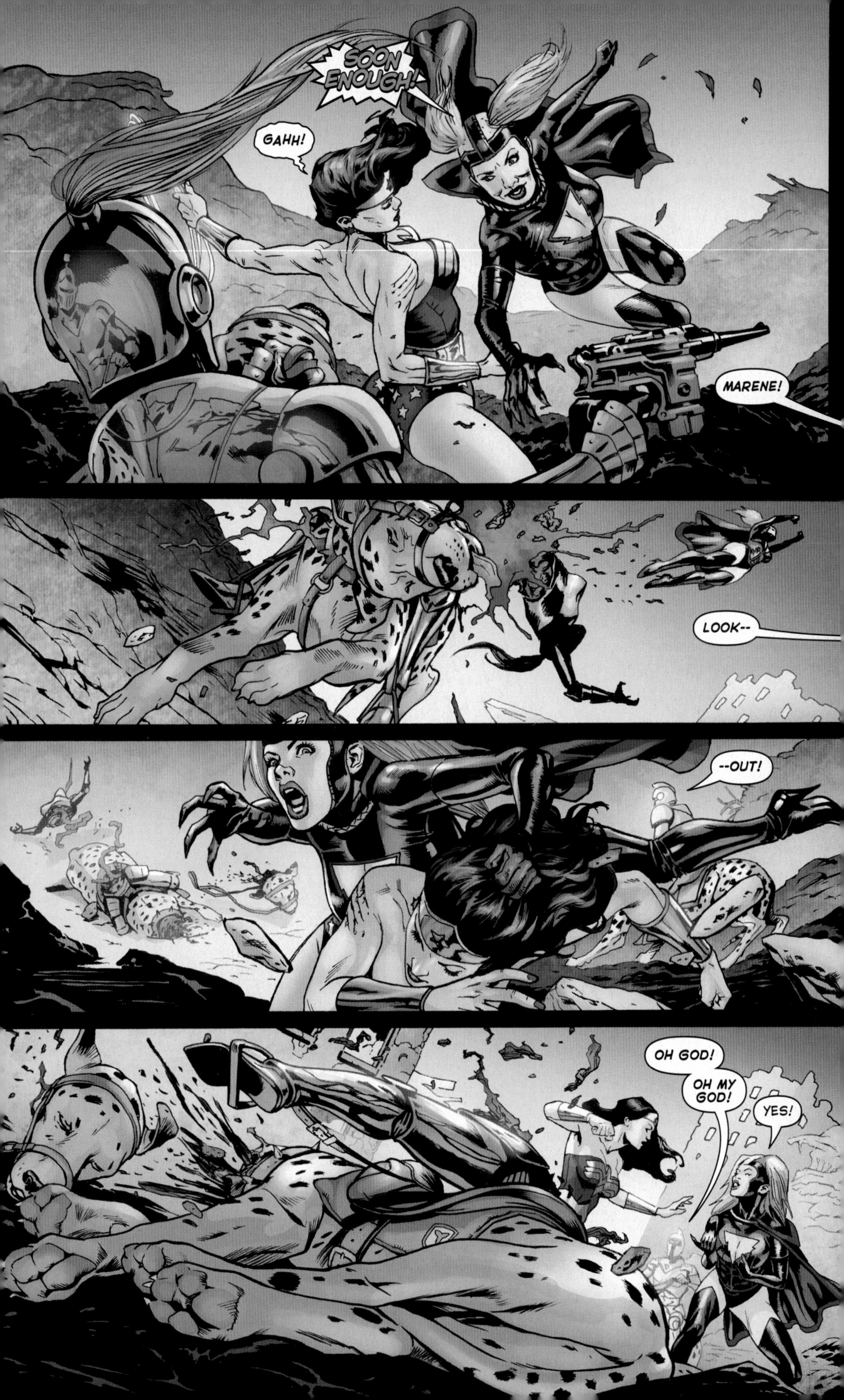
SOON ENOUGH!
GAHH!
MARENE!
LOOK--
--OUT!
OH GOD!
OH MY GOD!
YES!

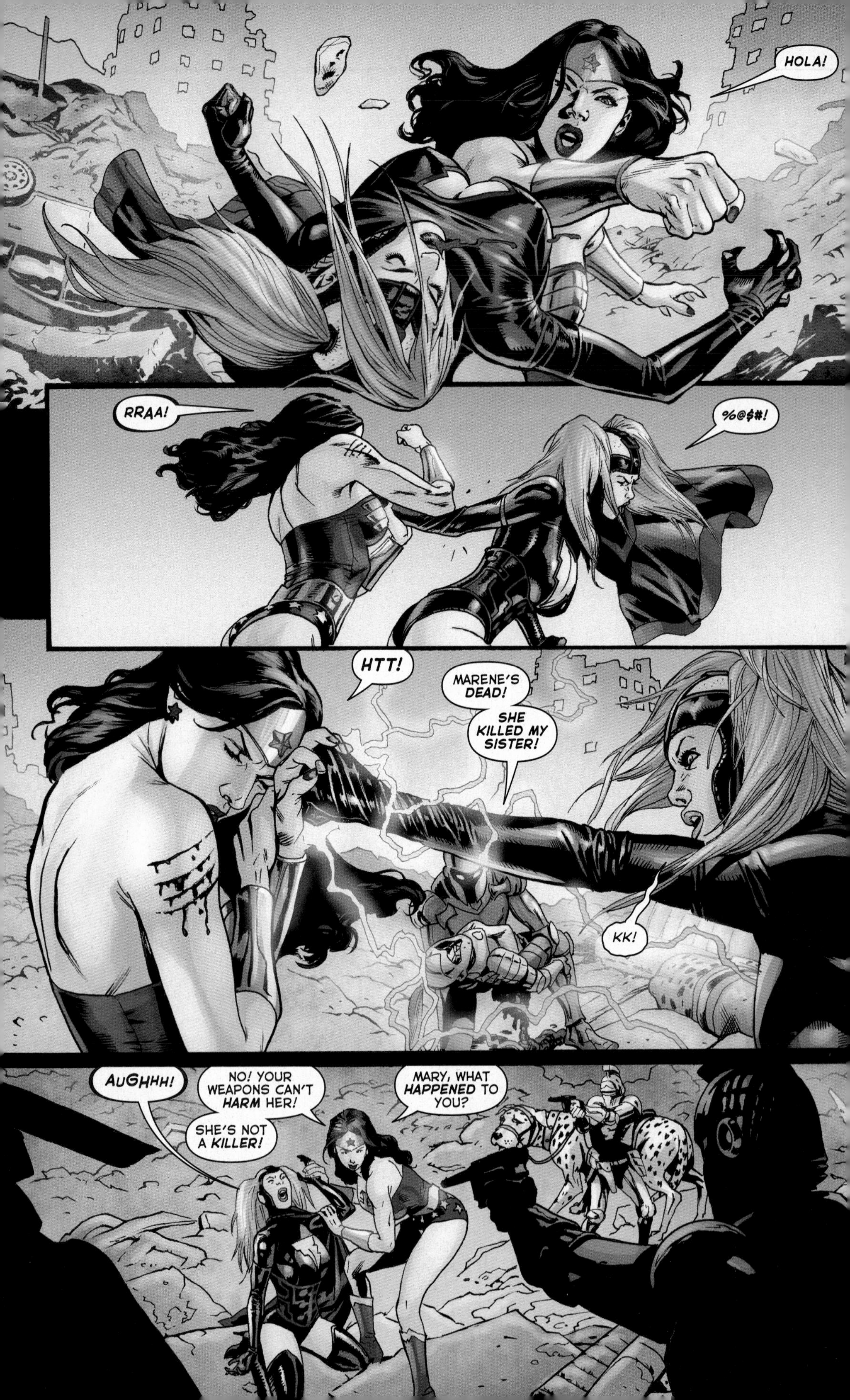
HOLA!
RRAA!
%@$#!
HTT!
MARENE'S DEAD!
SHE KILLED MY SISTER!
KK!
AUGHHH!
NO! YOUR WEAPONS CAN'T HARM HER!
SHE'S NOT A KILLER!
MARY, WHAT HAPPENED TO YOU?

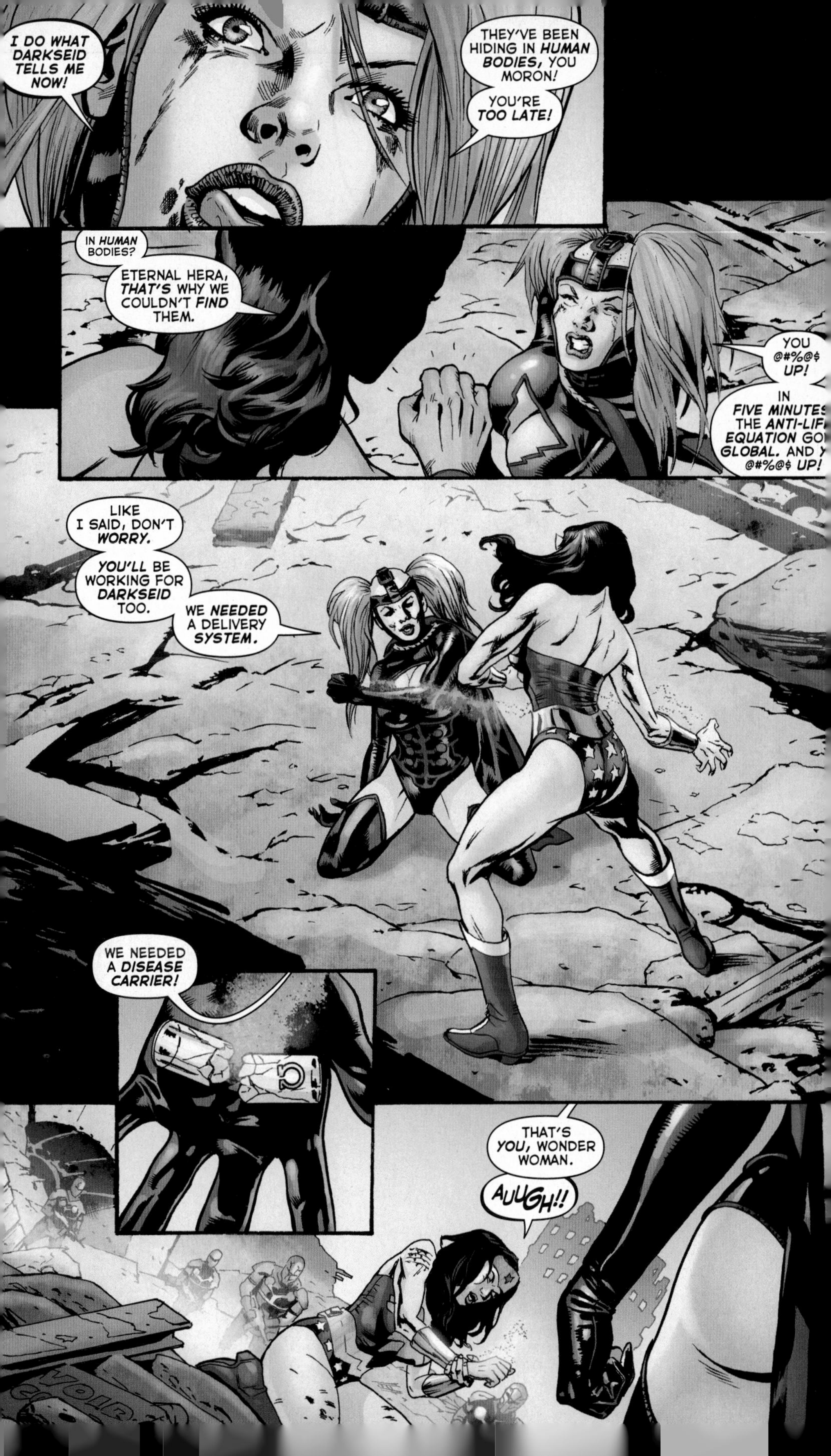

I DO WHAT DARKSEID TELLS ME NOW!
THEY'VE BEEN HIDING IN HUMAN BODIES, YOU MORON!
YOU'RE TOO LATE!
IN HUMAN BODIES?
ETERNAL HERA, THAT'S WHY WE COULDN'T FIND THEM.
YOU @#%@$ UP!
IN FIVE MINUTES THE ANTI-LIF EQUATION GO GLOBAL. AND Y @#%@$ UP!
LIKE I SAID, DON'T WORRY.
YOU'LL BE WORKING FOR DARKSEID TOO.
WE NEEDED A DELIVERY SYSTEM.
WE NEEDED A DISEASE CARRIER!
THAT'S YOU, WONDER WOMAN.
AUUGH!!

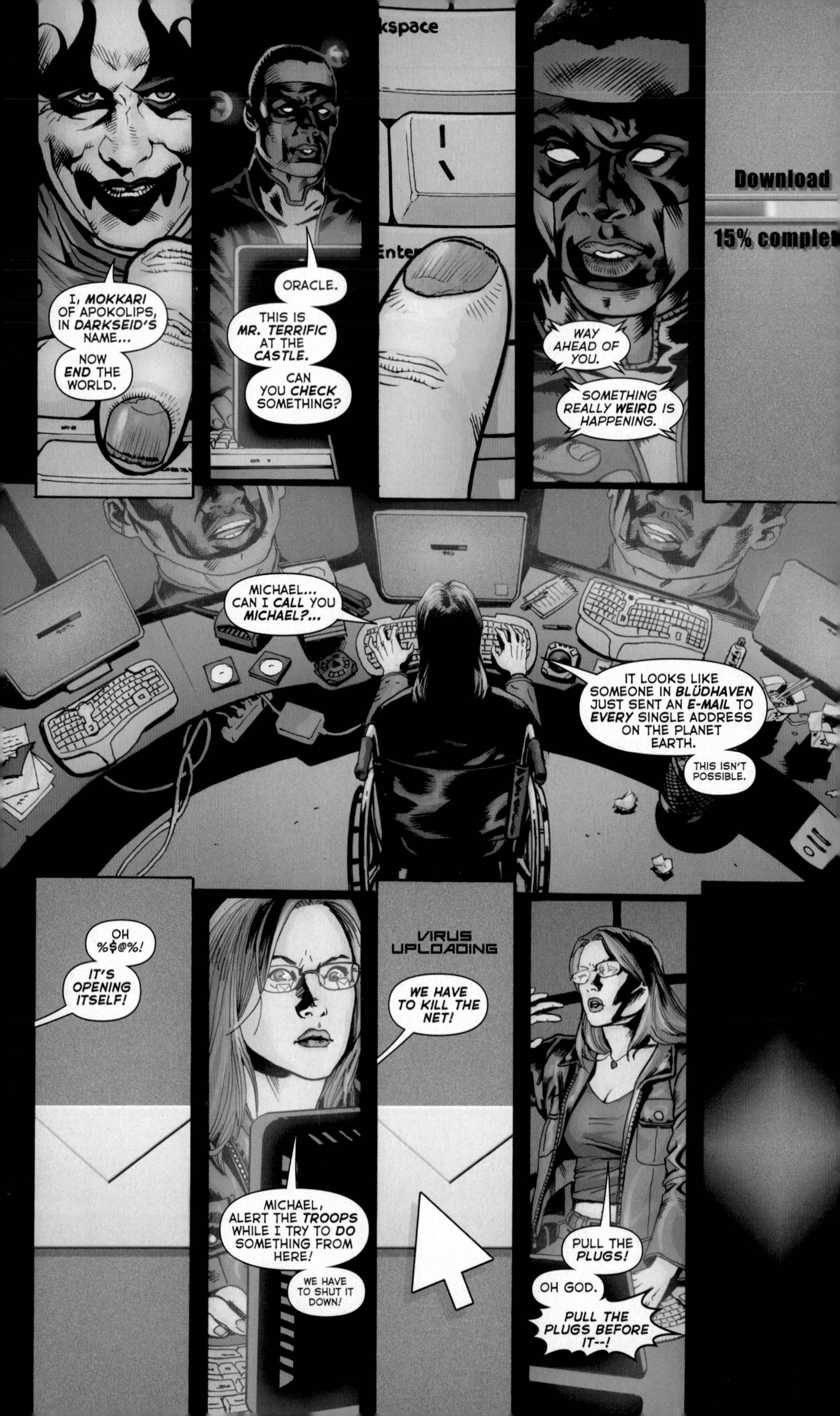
kspace
Enter
Download
15% complet
I, MOKKARI OF APOKOLIPS, IN DARKSEID'S NAME...
NOW END THE WORLD.
ORACLE.
THIS IS MR. TERRIFIC AT THE CASTLE.
CAN YOU CHECK SOMETHING?
WAY AHEAD OF YOU.
SOMETHING REALLY WEIRD IS HAPPENING.
MICHAEL... CAN I CALL YOU MICHAEL?...
IT LOOKS LIKE SOMEONE IN BLÜDHAVEN JUST SENT AN E-MAIL TO EVERY SINGLE ADDRESS ON THE PLANET EARTH.
THIS ISN'T POSSIBLE.
OH %$@%!
IT'S OPENING ITSELF!
MICHAEL, ALERT THE TROOPS WHILE I TRY TO DO SOMETHING FROM HERE!
WE HAVE TO SHUT IT DOWN!
VIRUS UPLOADING
WE HAVE TO KILL THE NET!
PULL THE PLUGS!
OH GOD.
PULL THE PLUGS BEFORE IT--!

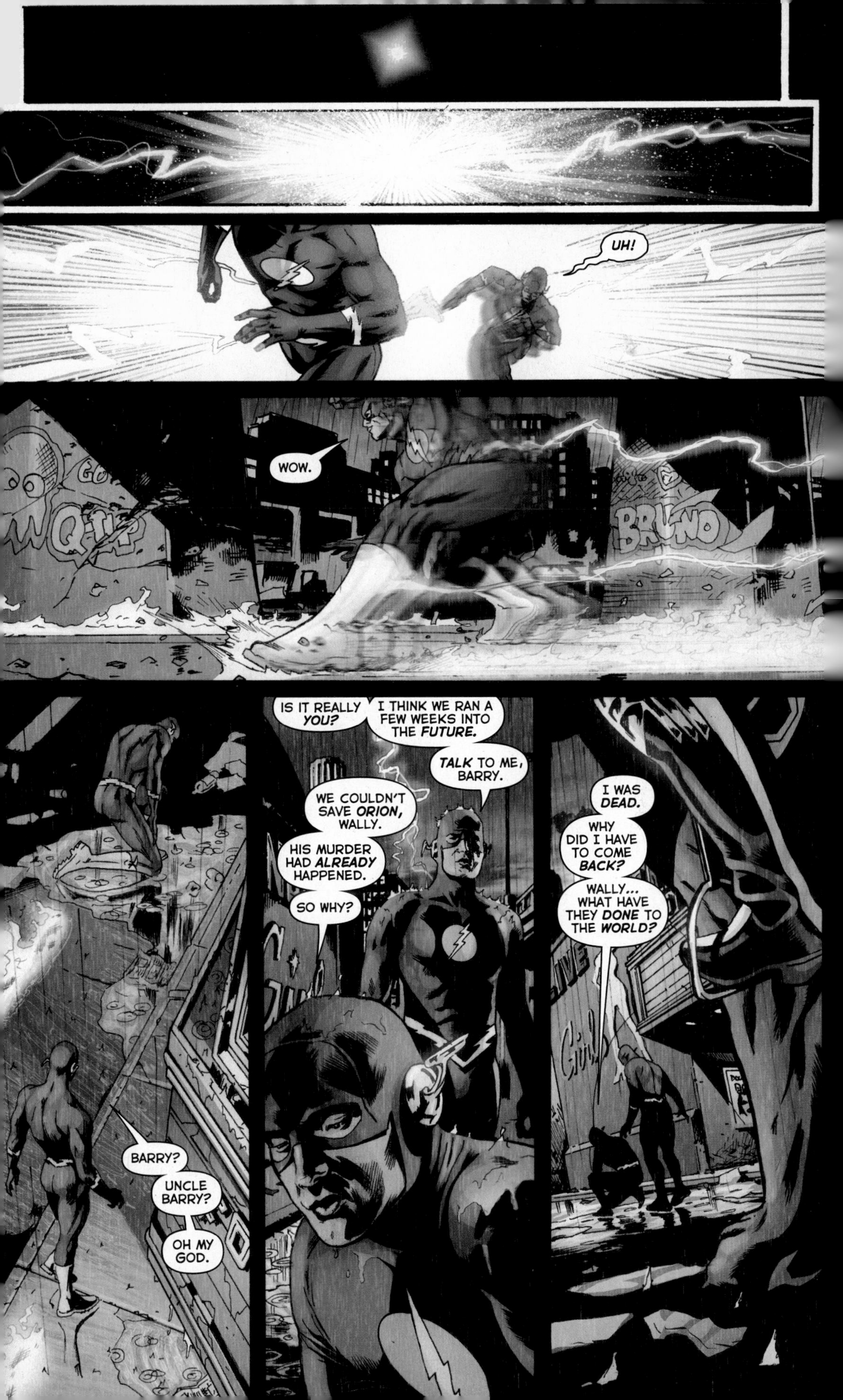
UH!
WOW.
BRUNO
BARRY?
UNCLE BARRY?
OH MY GOD.
IS IT REALLY YOU?
I THINK WE RAN A FEW WEEKS INTO THE FUTURE.
TALK TO ME, BARRY.
WE COULDN'T SAVE ORION, WALLY.
HIS MURDER HAD ALREADY HAPPENED.
SO WHY?
I WAS DEAD.
WHY DID I HAVE TO COME BACK?
WALLY... WHAT HAVE THEY DONE TO THE WORLD?

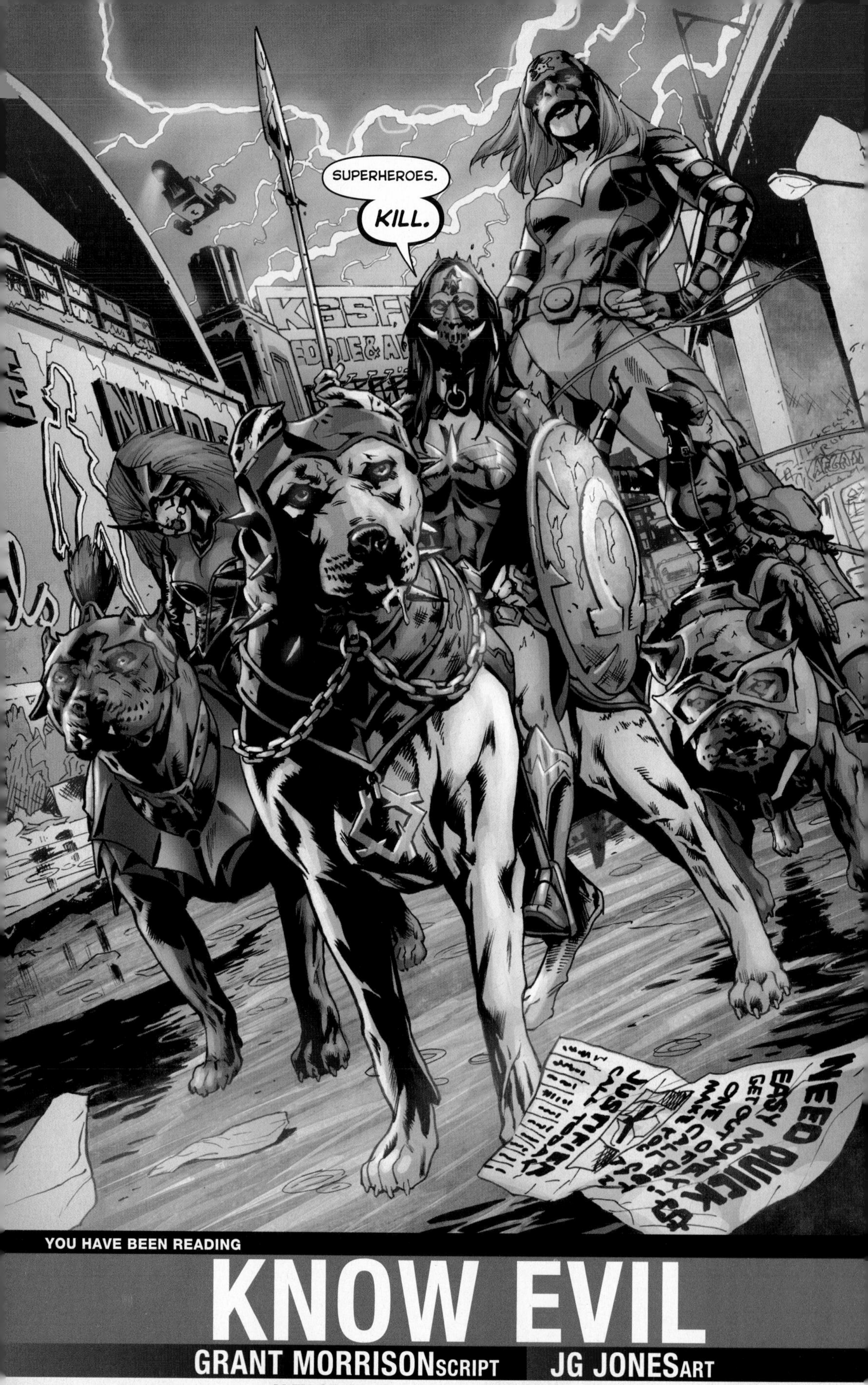
SUPERHEROES.
KILL.
NEED QUICK
EASY MONEY

YOU HAVE BEEN READING

KNOW EVIL

GRANT MORRISON SCRIPT **JG JONES** ART

ALEX SINCLAIR COLORS **ROB LEIGH** LETTERING

RMAN BEYOND #1 JH Williams

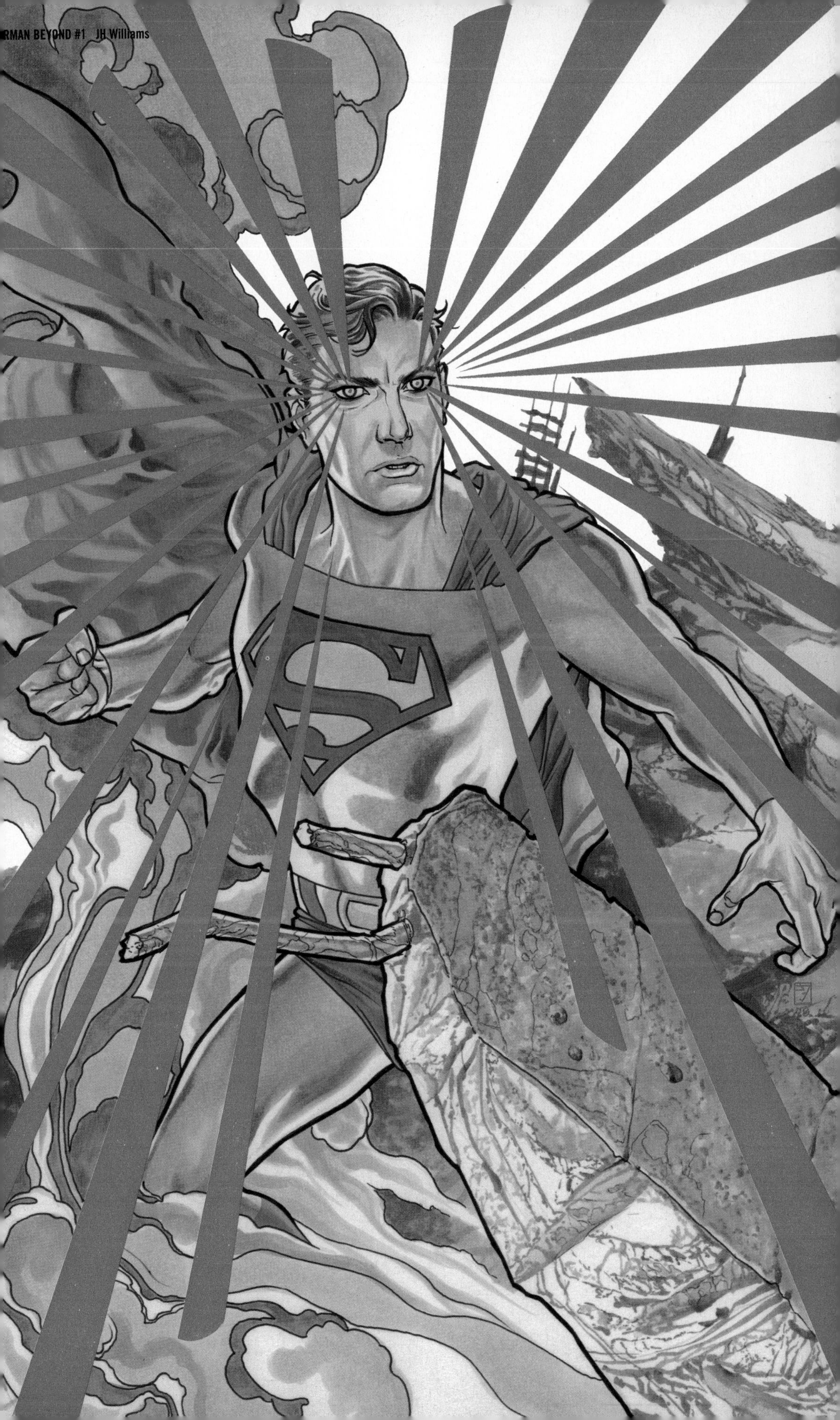

Doug Mahnke, Christian Alamy with David Baron

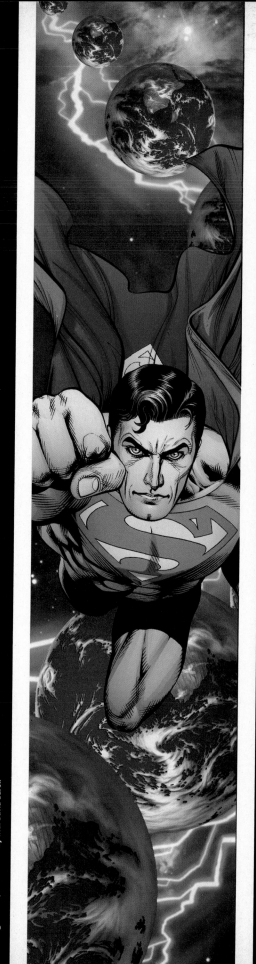

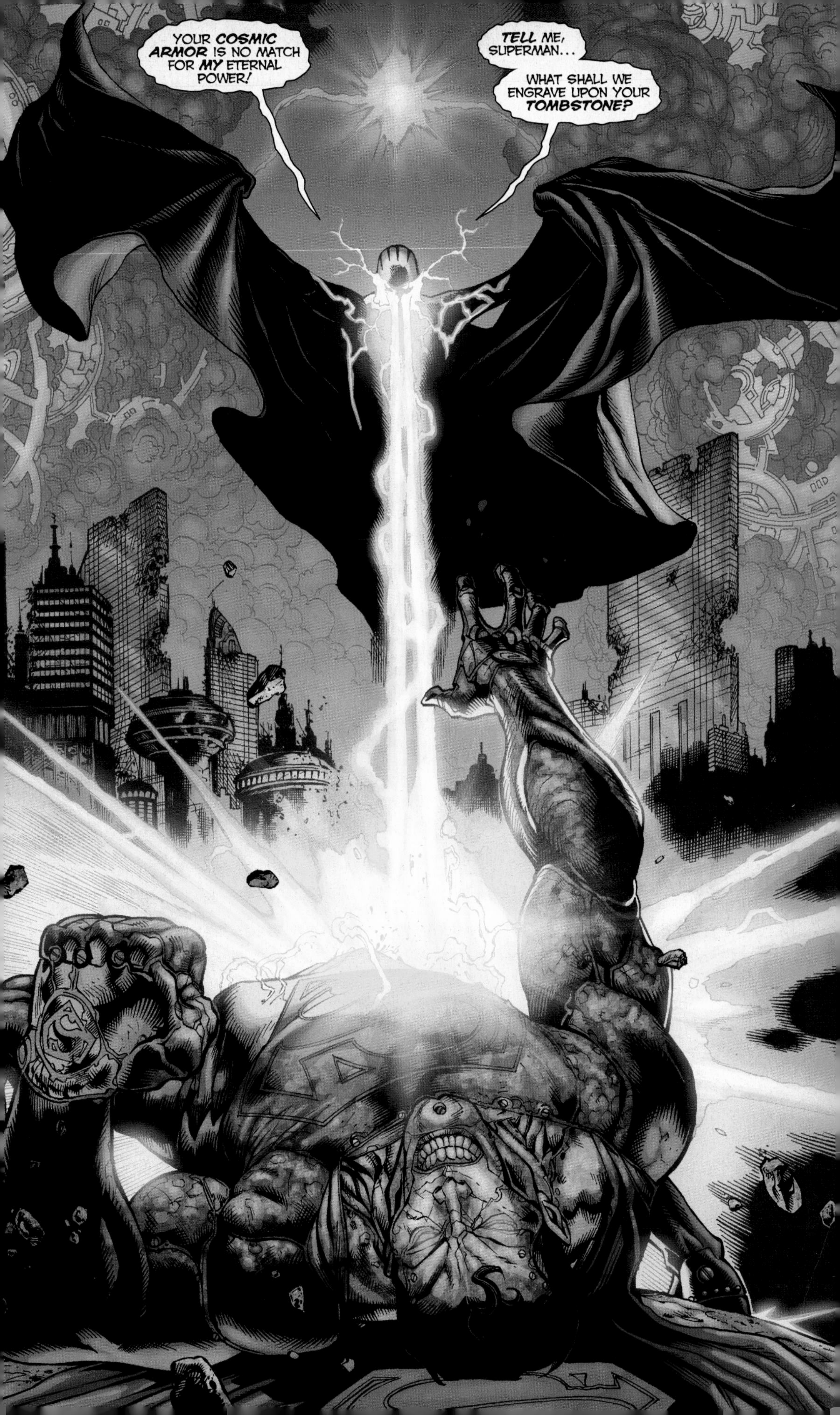
YOUR COSMIC ARMOR IS NO MATCH FOR MY ETERNAL POWER!
TELL ME, SUPERMAN...
WHAT SHALL WE ENGRAVE UPON YOUR TOMBSTONE?

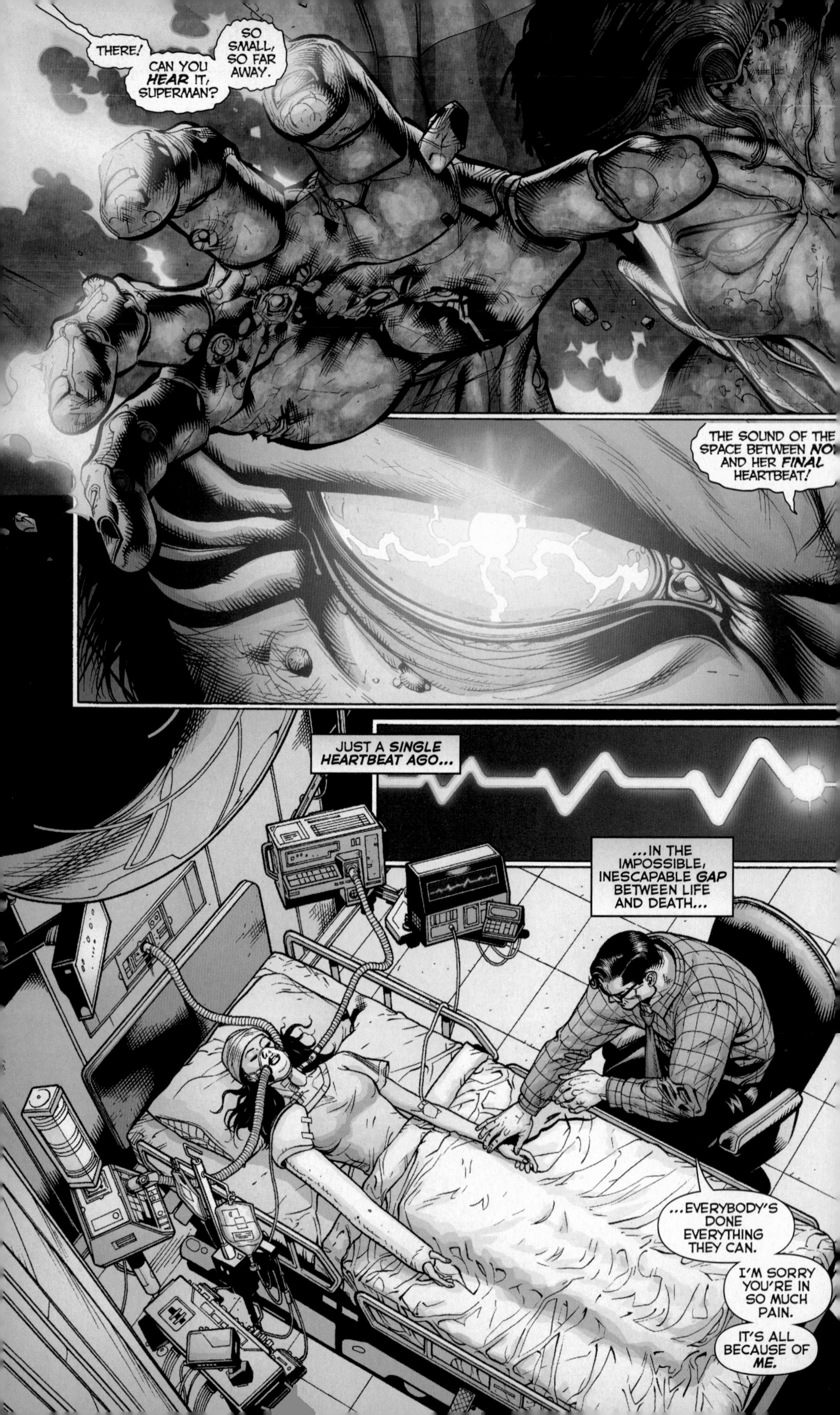
THERE!
CAN YOU HEAR IT, SUPERMAN?
SO SMALL, SO FAR AWAY.
THE SOUND OF THE SPACE BETWEEN NOW AND HER FINAL HEARTBEAT!
JUST A SINGLE HEARTBEAT AGO...
...IN THE IMPOSSIBLE, INESCAPABLE GAP BETWEEN LIFE AND DEATH...
...EVERYBODY'S DONE EVERYTHING THEY CAN.
I'M SORRY YOU'RE IN SO MUCH PAIN.
IT'S ALL BECAUSE OF ME.

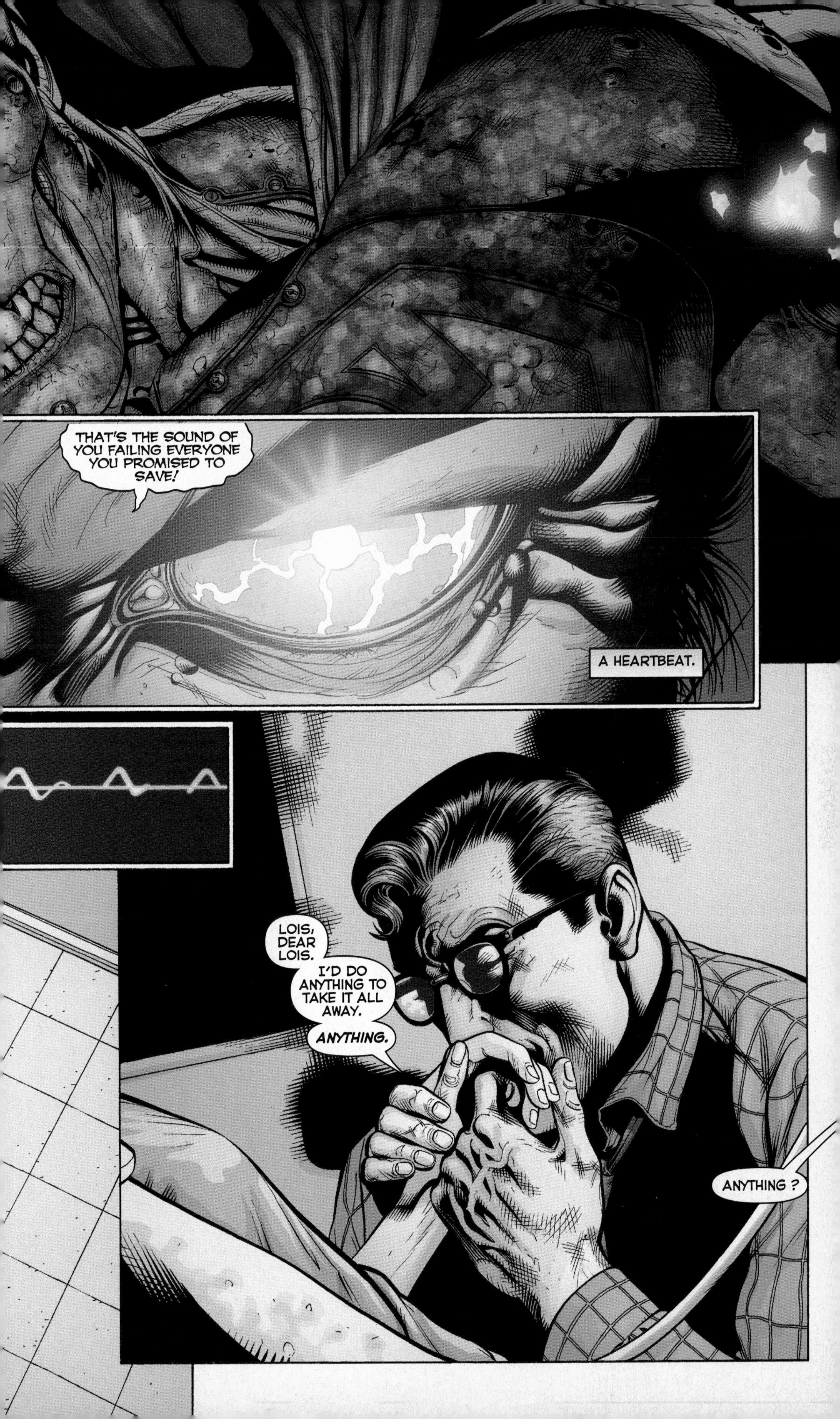
THAT'S THE SOUND OF YOU FAILING EVERYONE YOU PROMISED TO SAVE!
A HEARTBEAT.
LOIS, DEAR LOIS.
I'D DO ANYTHING TO TAKE IT ALL AWAY.
ANYTHING.
ANYTHING ?

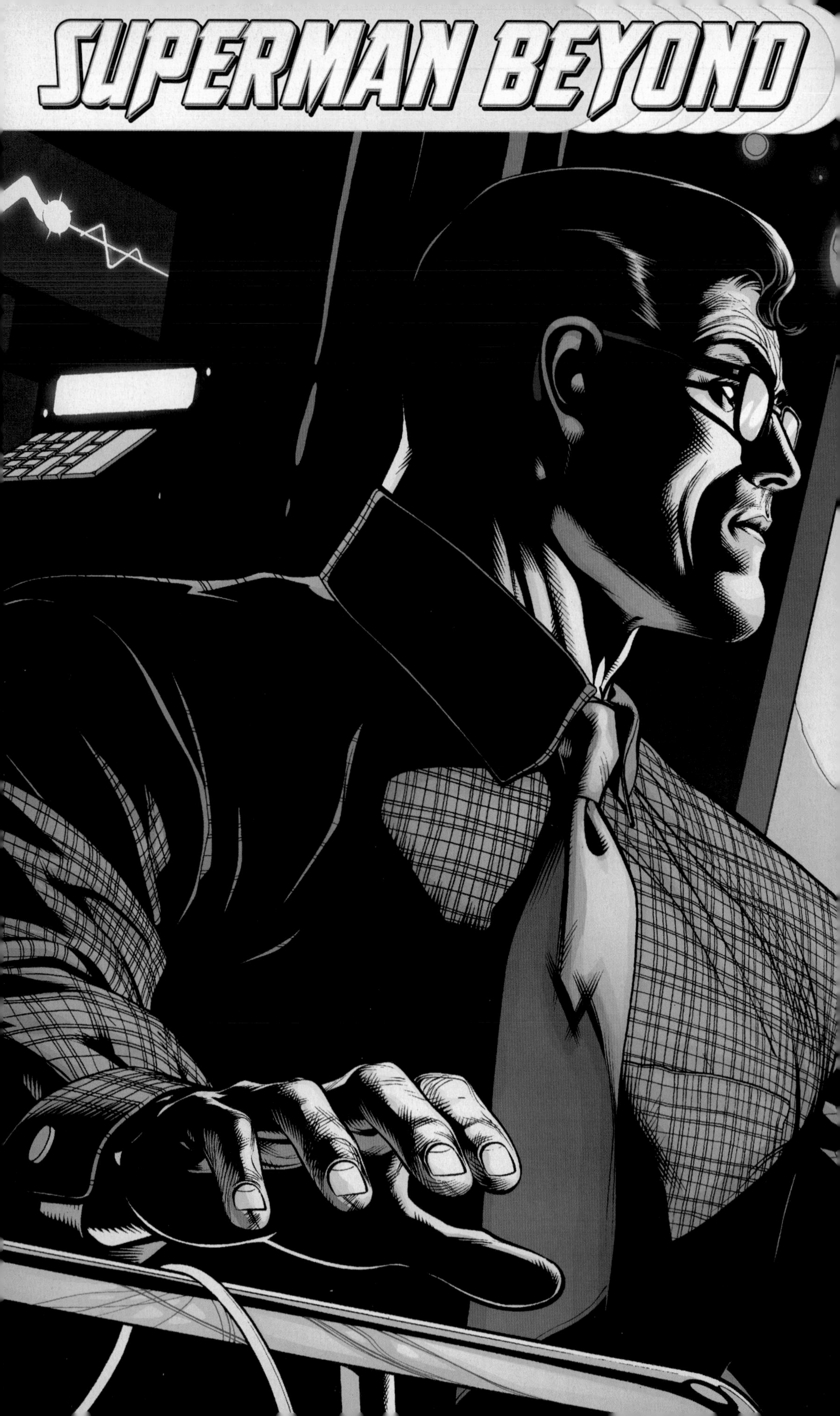
SUPERMAN BEYOND

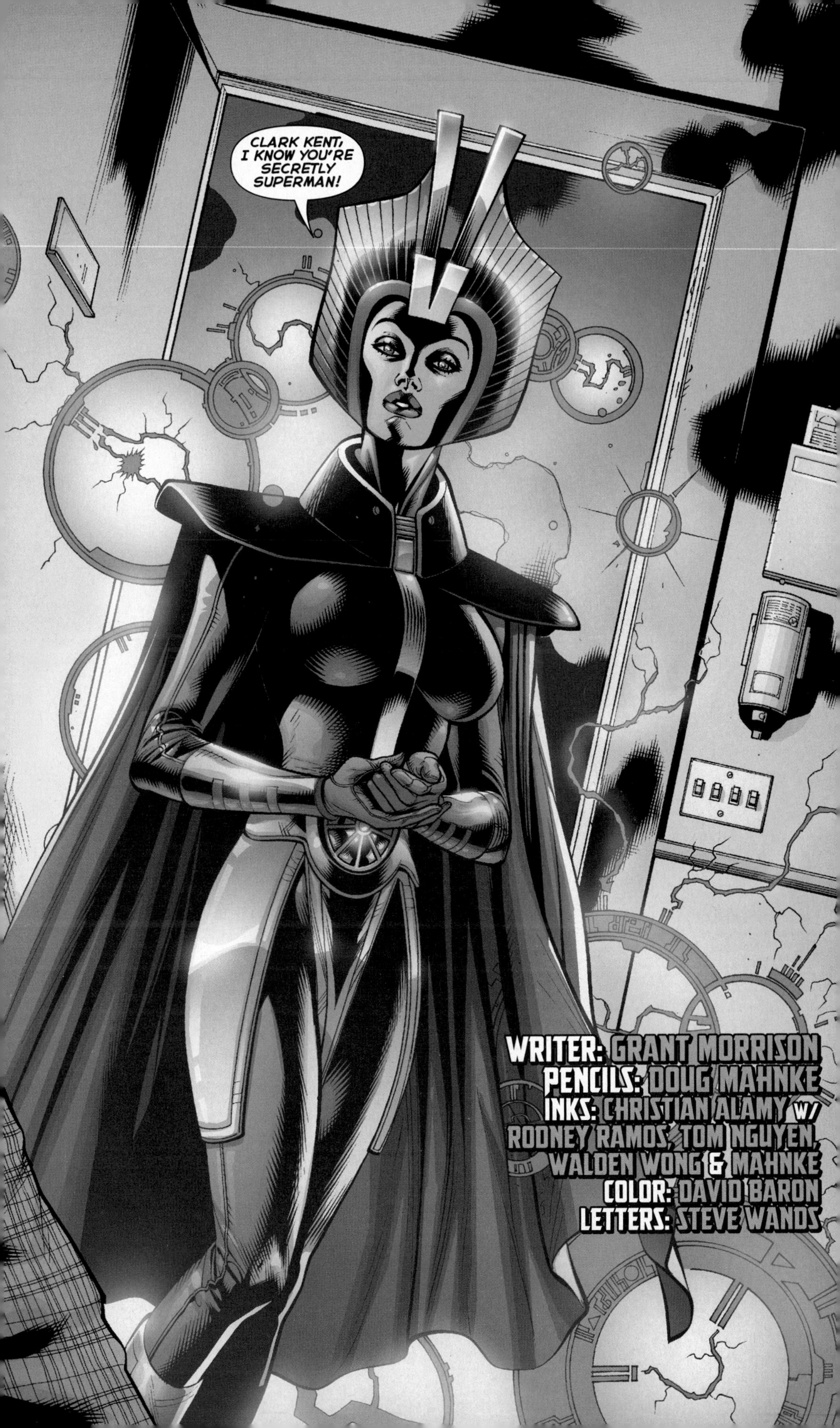
CLARK KENT, I KNOW YOU'RE SECRETLY SUPERMAN!
WRITER: GRANT MORRISON
PENCILS: DOUG MAHNKE
INKS: CHRISTIAN ALAMY W/ RODNEY RAMOS, TOM NGUYEN, WALDEN WONG & MAHNKE
COLOR: DAVID BARON
LETTERS: STEVE WANDS

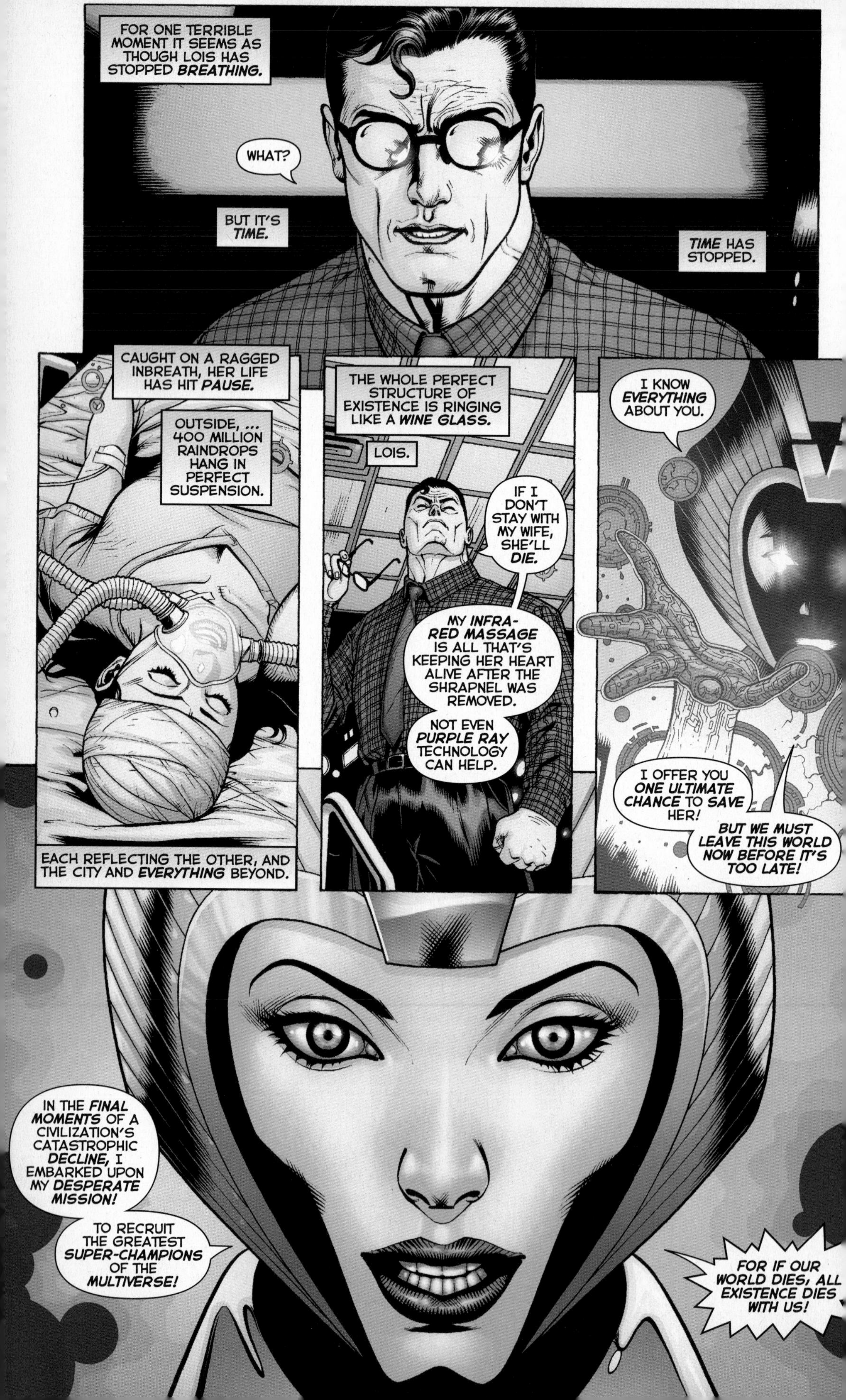
FOR ONE TERRIBLE MOMENT IT SEEMS AS THOUGH LOIS HAS STOPPED *BREATHING.*
WHAT?
BUT IT'S *TIME.*
TIME HAS STOPPED.
CAUGHT ON A RAGGED INBREATH, HER LIFE HAS HIT *PAUSE.*
OUTSIDE, ... 400 MILLION RAINDROPS HANG IN PERFECT SUSPENSION.
EACH REFLECTING THE OTHER, AND THE CITY AND *EVERYTHING* BEYOND.
THE WHOLE PERFECT STRUCTURE OF EXISTENCE IS RINGING LIKE A *WINE GLASS.*
LOIS.
IF I DON'T STAY WITH MY WIFE, SHE'LL *DIE.*
MY *INFRA-RED MASSAGE* IS ALL THAT'S KEEPING HER HEART ALIVE AFTER THE SHRAPNEL WAS REMOVED.
NOT EVEN *PURPLE RAY* TECHNOLOGY CAN HELP.
I KNOW *EVERYTHING* ABOUT YOU.
I OFFER YOU *ONE ULTIMATE CHANCE* TO *SAVE* HER!
BUT WE MUST LEAVE THIS WORLD NOW BEFORE IT'S TOO LATE!
IN THE *FINAL MOMENTS* OF A CIVILIZATION'S CATASTROPHIC *DECLINE,* I EMBARKED UPON MY *DESPERATE MISSION!*
TO RECRUIT THE GREATEST *SUPER-CHAMPIONS* OF THE *MULTIVERSE!*
FOR IF OUR WORLD DIES, ALL EXISTENCE DIES WITH US!

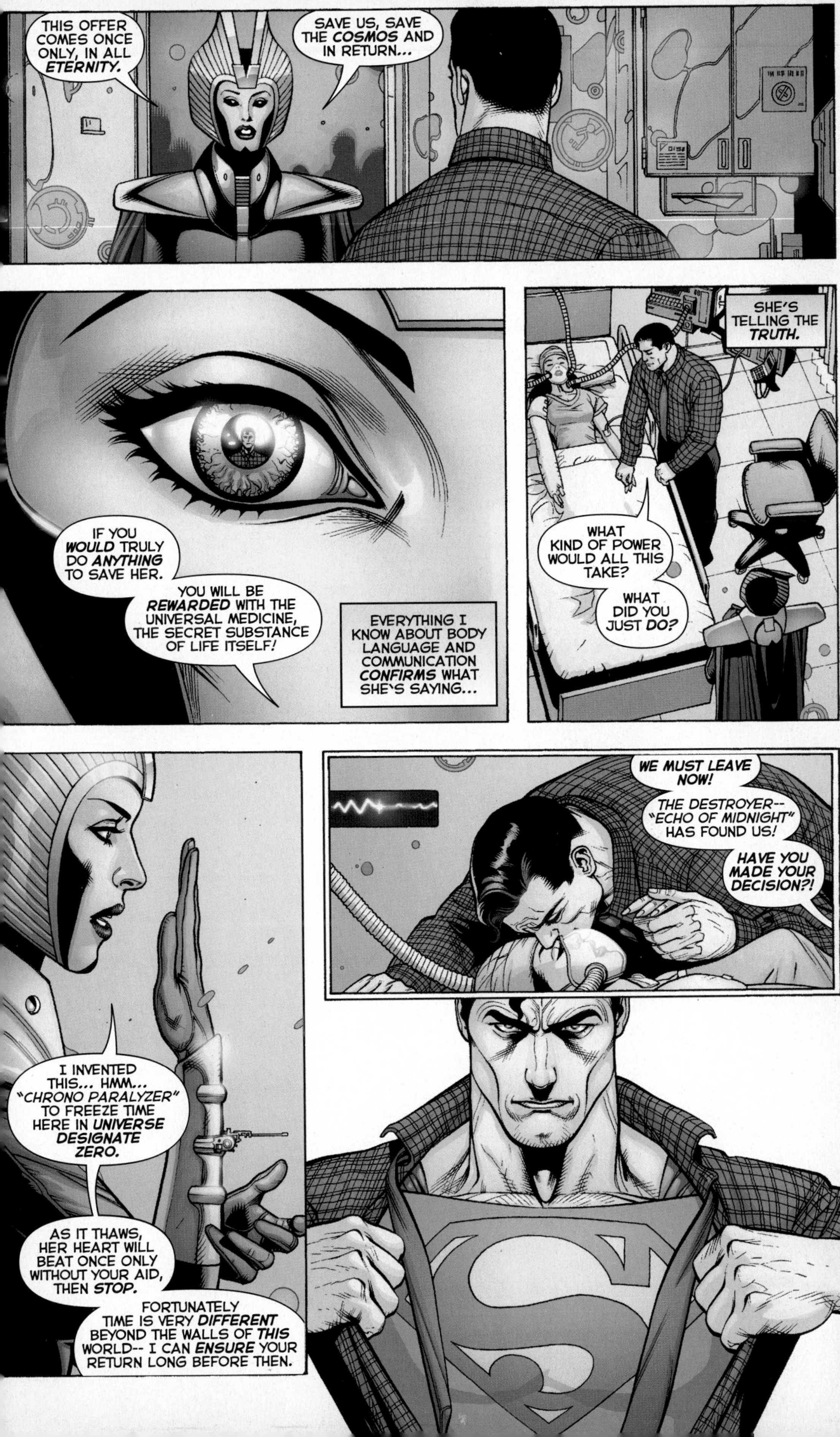
THIS OFFER COMES ONCE ONLY, IN ALL ETERNITY.
SAVE US, SAVE THE COSMOS AND IN RETURN...
IF YOU WOULD TRULY DO ANYTHING TO SAVE HER.
YOU WILL BE REWARDED WITH THE UNIVERSAL MEDICINE, THE SECRET SUBSTANCE OF LIFE ITSELF!
EVERYTHING I KNOW ABOUT BODY LANGUAGE AND COMMUNICATION CONFIRMS WHAT SHE'S SAYING...
SHE'S TELLING THE TRUTH.
WHAT KIND OF POWER WOULD ALL THIS TAKE?
WHAT DID YOU JUST DO?
I INVENTED THIS... HMM... "CHRONO PARALYZER" TO FREEZE TIME HERE IN UNIVERSE DESIGNATE ZERO.
AS IT THAWS, HER HEART WILL BEAT ONCE ONLY WITHOUT YOUR AID, THEN STOP.
FORTUNATELY TIME IS VERY DIFFERENT BEYOND THE WALLS OF THIS WORLD-- I CAN ENSURE YOUR RETURN LONG BEFORE THEN.
WE MUST LEAVE NOW!
THE DESTROYER-- "ECHO OF MIDNIGHT" HAS FOUND US!
HAVE YOU MADE YOUR DECISION?!

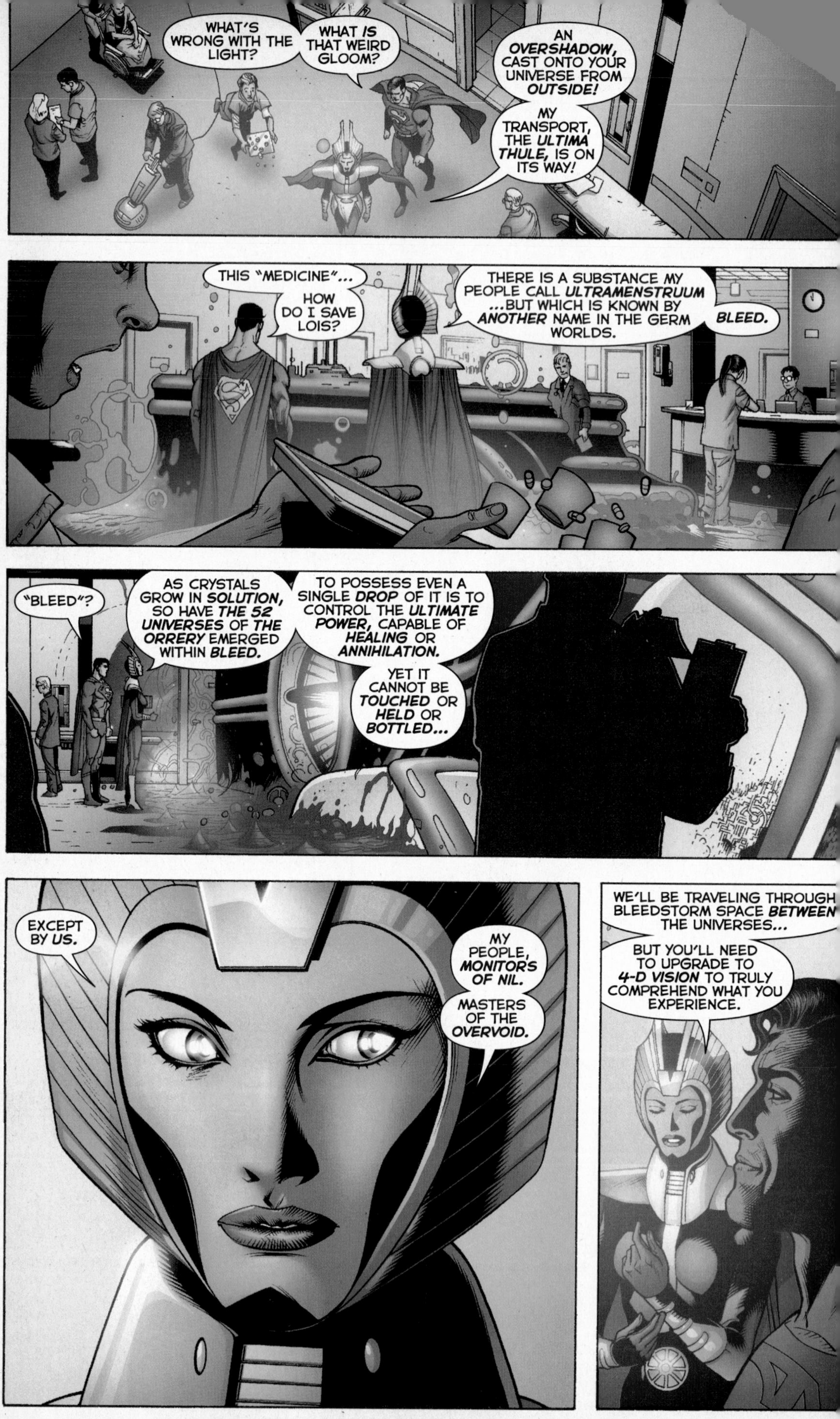
WHAT'S WRONG WITH THE LIGHT?
WHAT IS THAT WEIRD GLOOM?
AN OVERSHADOW, CAST ONTO YOUR UNIVERSE FROM OUTSIDE!
MY TRANSPORT, THE ULTIMA THULE, IS ON ITS WAY!
THIS "MEDICINE"...
HOW DO I SAVE LOIS?
THERE IS A SUBSTANCE MY PEOPLE CALL ULTRAMENSTRUUM ...BUT WHICH IS KNOWN BY ANOTHER NAME IN THE GERM WORLDS.
BLEED.
"BLEED"?
AS CRYSTALS GROW IN SOLUTION, SO HAVE THE 52 UNIVERSES OF THE ORRERY EMERGED WITHIN BLEED.
TO POSSESS EVEN A SINGLE DROP OF IT IS TO CONTROL THE ULTIMATE POWER, CAPABLE OF HEALING OR ANNIHILATION.
YET IT CANNOT BE TOUCHED OR HELD OR BOTTLED...
EXCEPT BY US.
MY PEOPLE, MONITORS OF NIL.
MASTERS OF THE OVERVOID.
WE'LL BE TRAVELING THROUGH BLEEDSTORM SPACE BETWEEN THE UNIVERSES...
BUT YOU'LL NEED TO UPGRADE TO 4-D VISION TO TRULY COMPREHEND WHAT YOU EXPERIENCE.

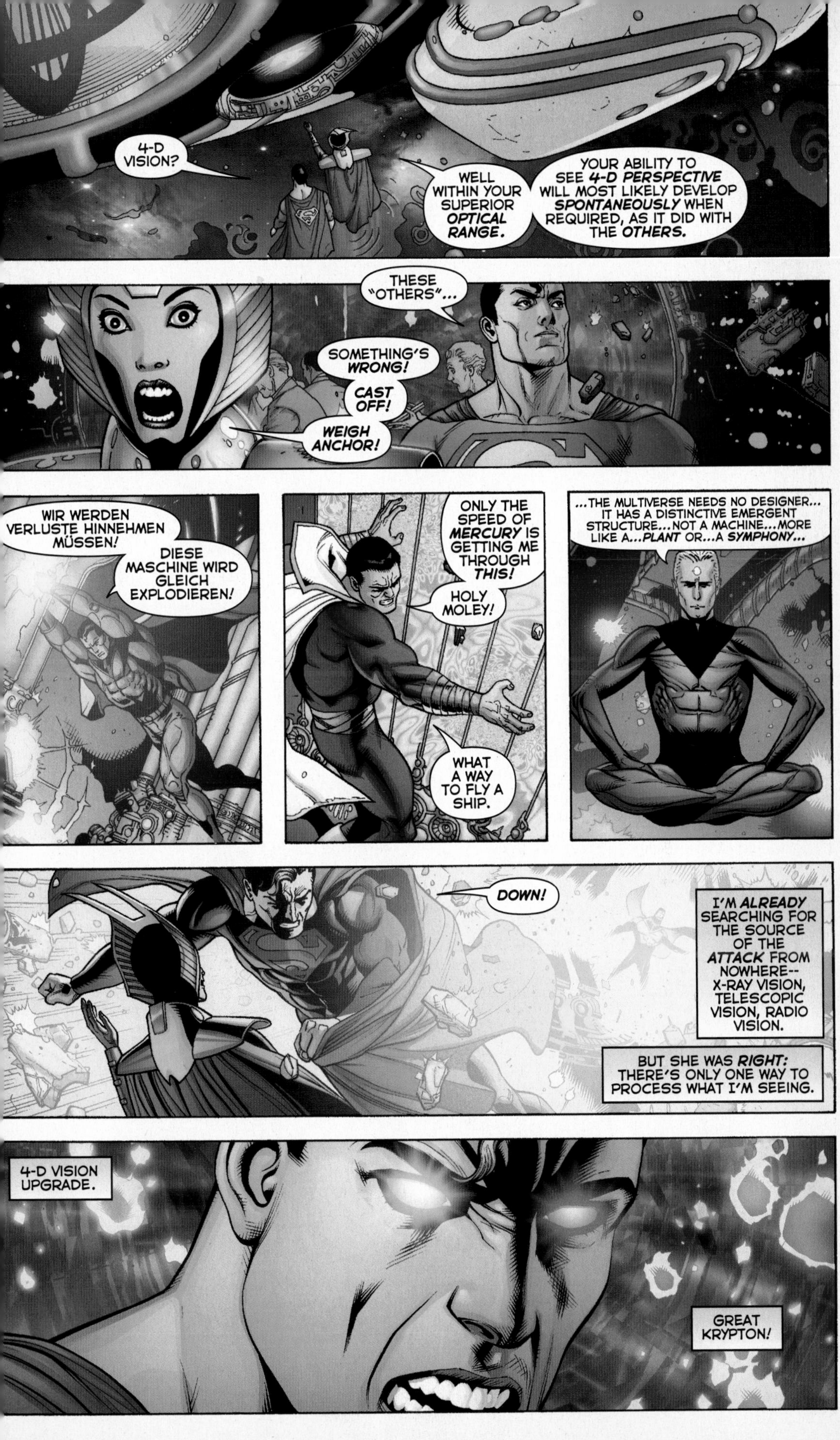
4-D VISION?
WELL WITHIN YOUR SUPERIOR OPTICAL RANGE.
YOUR ABILITY TO SEE 4-D PERSPECTIVE WILL MOST LIKELY DEVELOP SPONTANEOUSLY WHEN REQUIRED, AS IT DID WITH THE OTHERS.
THESE "OTHERS"...
SOMETHING'S WRONG!
CAST OFF!
WEIGH ANCHOR!
WIR WERDEN VERLUSTE HINNEHMEN MÜSSEN!
DIESE MASCHINE WIRD GLEICH EXPLODIEREN!
ONLY THE SPEED OF MERCURY IS GETTING ME THROUGH THIS!
HOLY MOLEY!
WHAT A WAY TO FLY A SHIP.
...THE MULTIVERSE NEEDS NO DESIGNER... IT HAS A DISTINCTIVE EMERGENT STRUCTURE...NOT A MACHINE...MORE LIKE A...PLANT OR...A SYMPHONY...
DOWN!
I'M ALREADY SEARCHING FOR THE SOURCE OF THE ATTACK FROM NOWHERE-- X-RAY VISION, TELESCOPIC VISION, RADIO VISION.
BUT SHE WAS RIGHT: THERE'S ONLY ONE WAY TO PROCESS WHAT I'M SEEING.
4-D VISION UPGRADE.
GREAT KRYPTON!

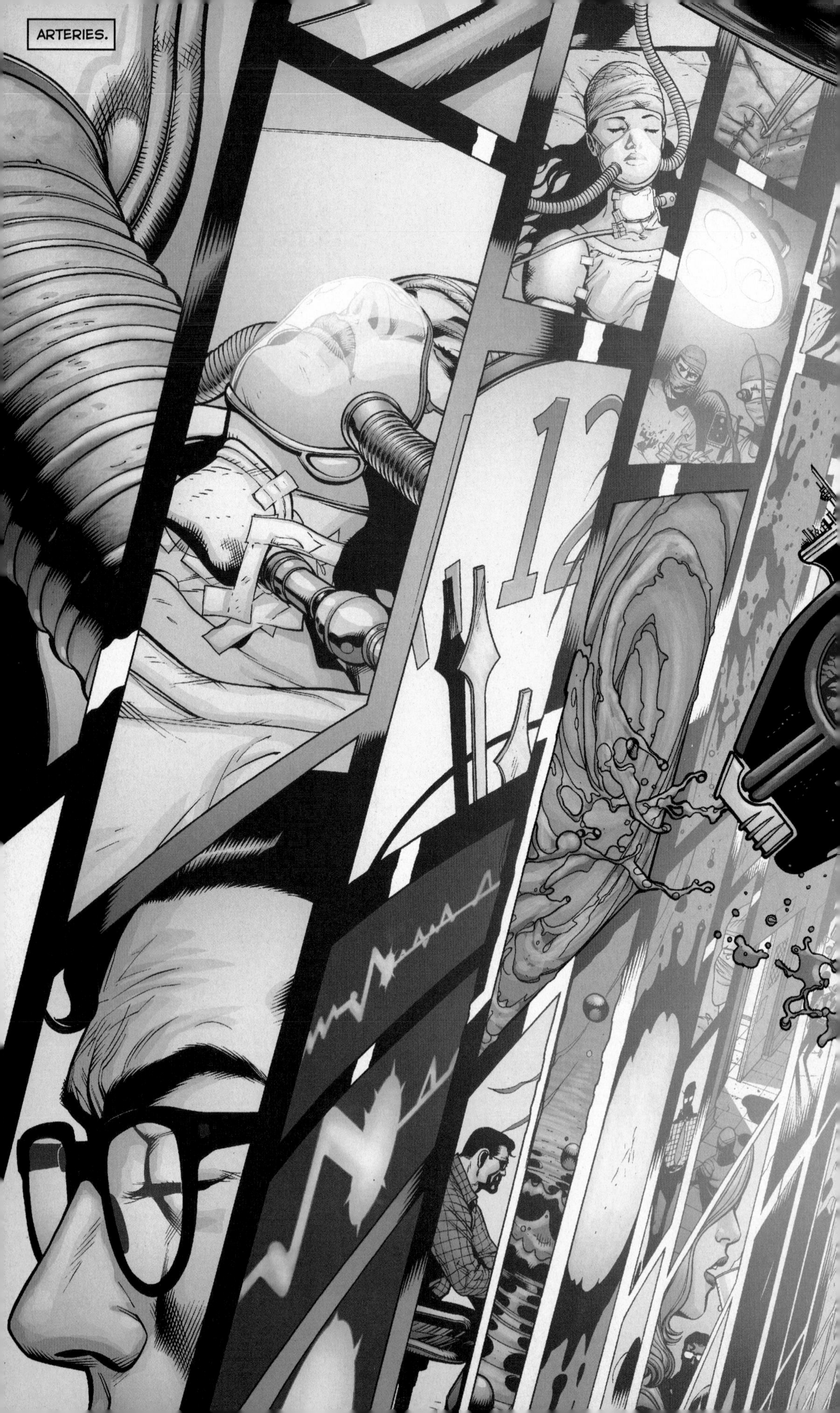
ARTERIES.

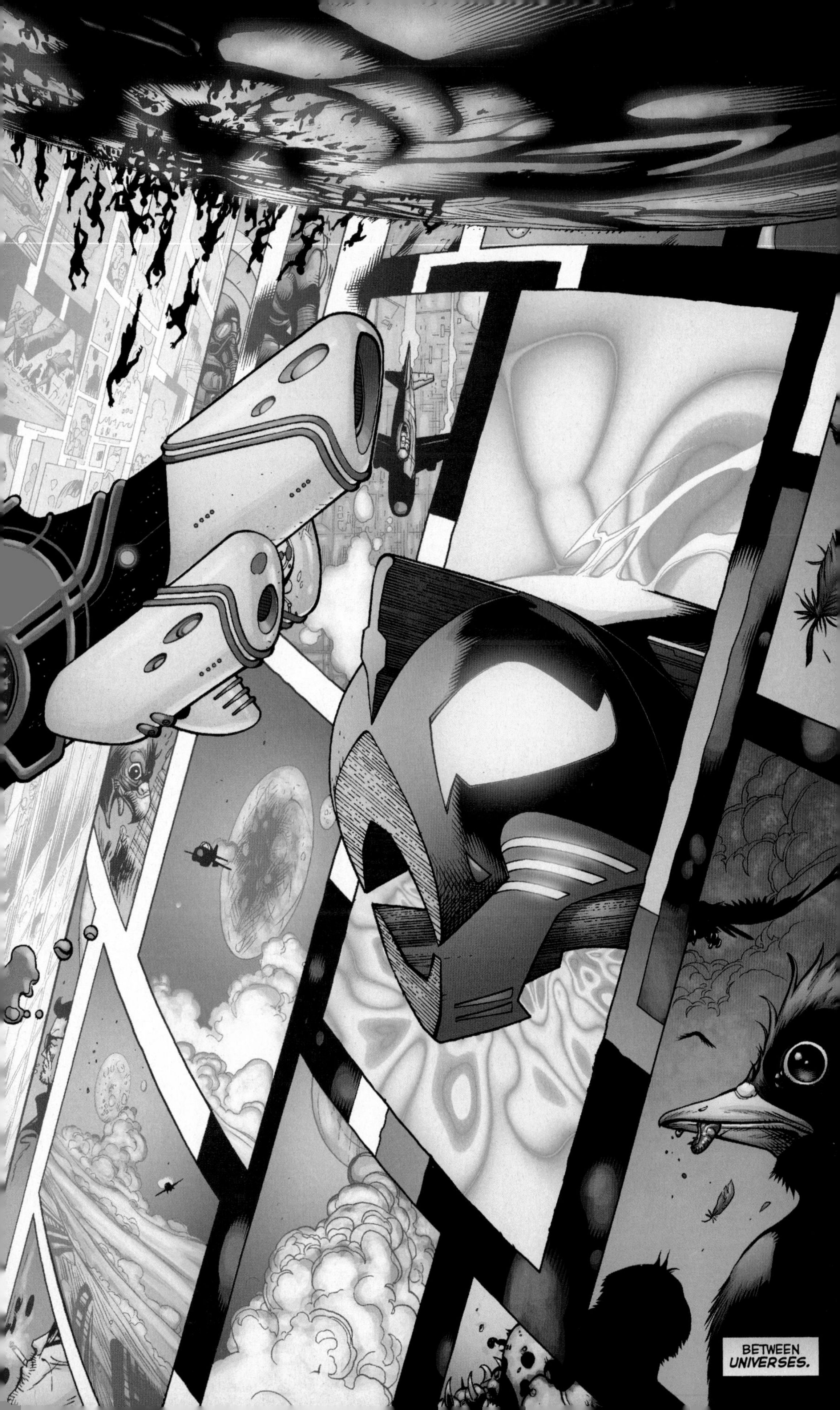
BETWEEN UNIVERSES.

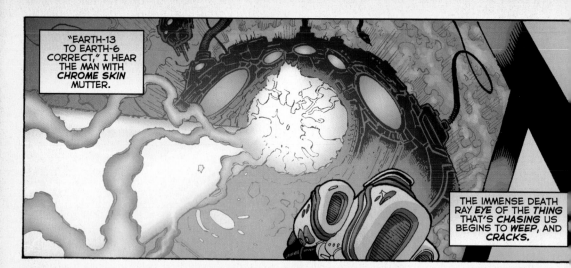

"EARTH-13 TO EARTH-6 CORRECT," I HEAR THE MAN WITH *CHROME SKIN* MUTTER.

THE IMMENSE DEATH RAY *EYE* OF THE *THING* THAT'S *CHASING* US BEGINS TO *WEEP*, AND *CRACKS*.

SOMETHING IS TRYING TO *KILL* THE DESTROYER "ECHO OF MIDNIGHT."

I TELESCOPE IN TO THE FURNACE EDGE AND THERE *HE* IS.

USING WHATEVER HE FINDS AS A *WEAPON*, A TOOL OF *DESTRUCTION*.

ULTRAMAN.

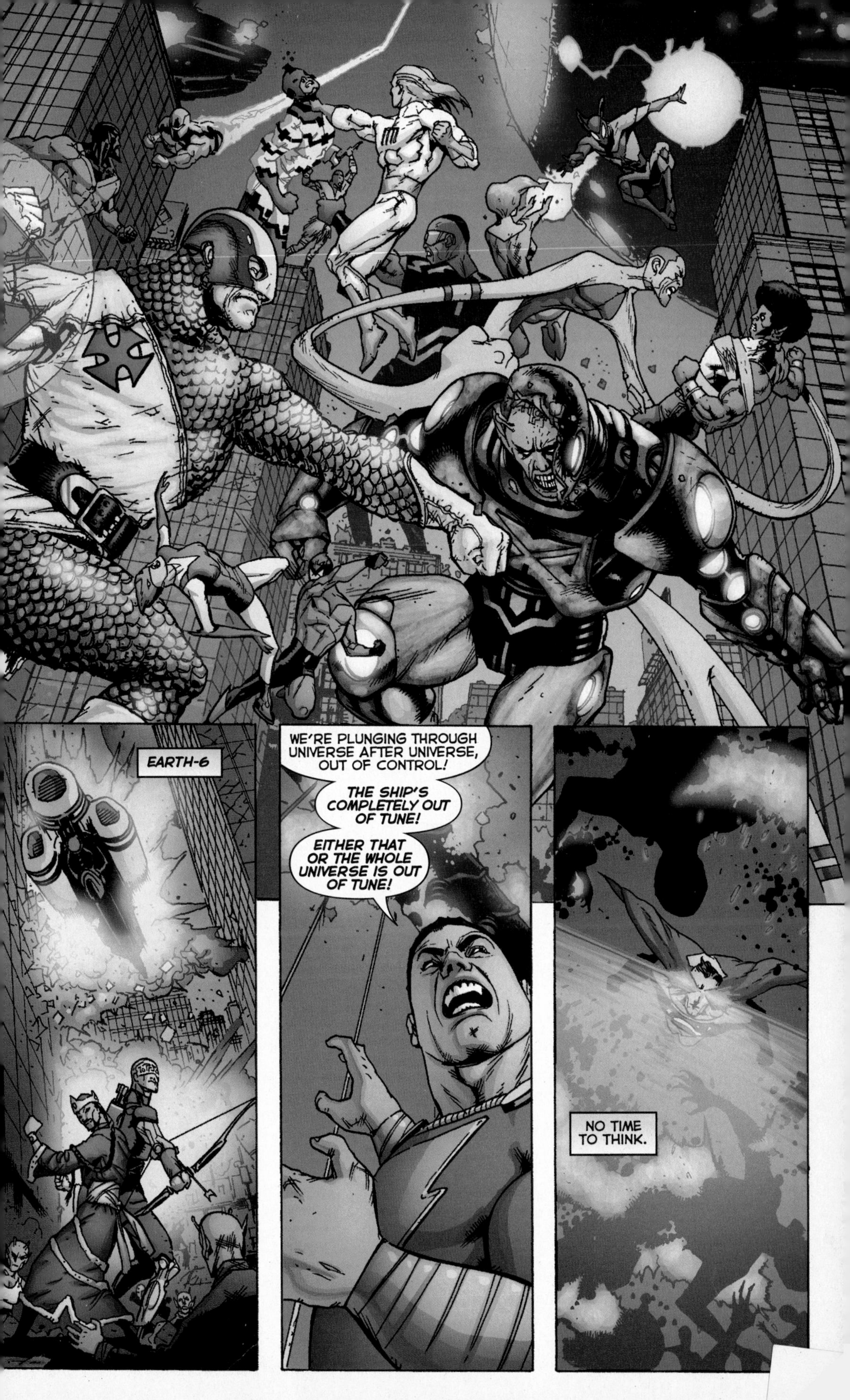
EARTH-6
WE'RE PLUNGING THROUGH UNIVERSE AFTER UNIVERSE, OUT OF CONTROL!
THE SHIP'S COMPLETELY OUT OF TUNE!
EITHER THAT OR THE WHOLE UNIVERSE IS OUT OF TUNE!
NO TIME TO THINK.

UNNGH!

THERE'S A *GRAVEYARD UNIVERSE* ON A LATERAL CORRECT-- *DESIGNATE 51!*

GET ME TO MY CHAMBER... FADING...

THAT MADMAN WILL *CRASH* THE DESTROYER!

IT'S *70 MILES LONG!* IF IT HITS THE PLANET AT THIS SPEED, THE CORE AND MANTLE WILL *SPLIT!*

98% OF TERRESTRIAL LIFE WILL DIE!

TERMINATE NAVIGATIONAL INPUT.

NOW *THAT* WAS INTERESTING.

IT'S SO RARE TO *GET* A CHALLENGE THESE DAYS.

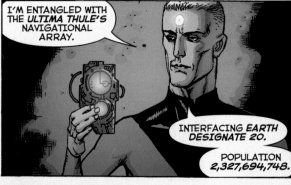

I'M ENTANGLED WITH THE *ULTIMA THULE'S* NAVIGATIONAL ARRAY.

INTERFACING *EARTH* DESIGNATE 20.

POPULATION 2,327,694,748.

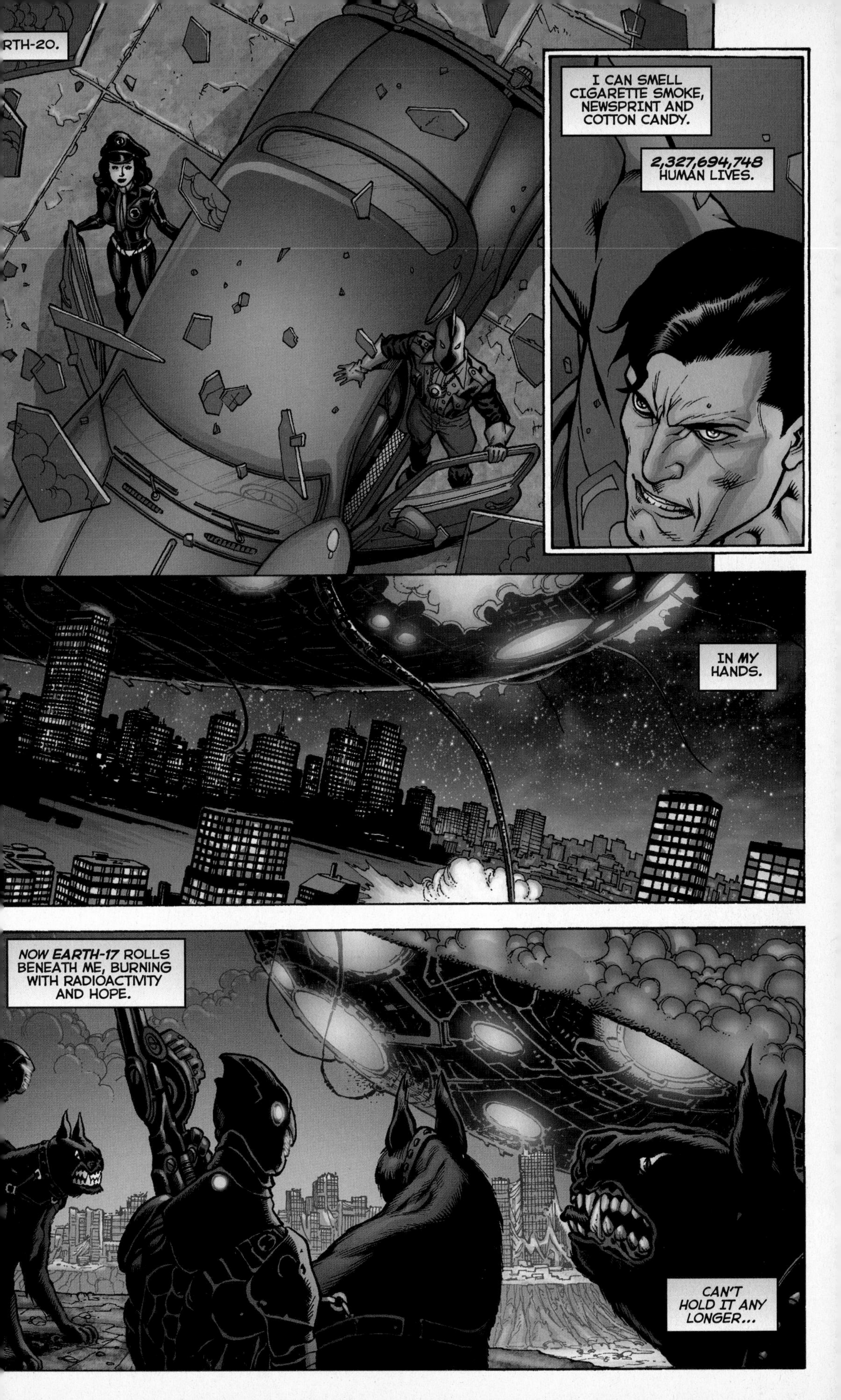
RTH-20.
I CAN SMELL CIGARETTE SMOKE, NEWSPRINT AND COTTON CANDY.
2,327,694,748 HUMAN LIVES.
IN MY HANDS.
NOW EARTH-17 ROLLS BENEATH ME, BURNING WITH RADIOACTIVITY AND HOPE.
CAN'T HOLD IT ANY LONGER...

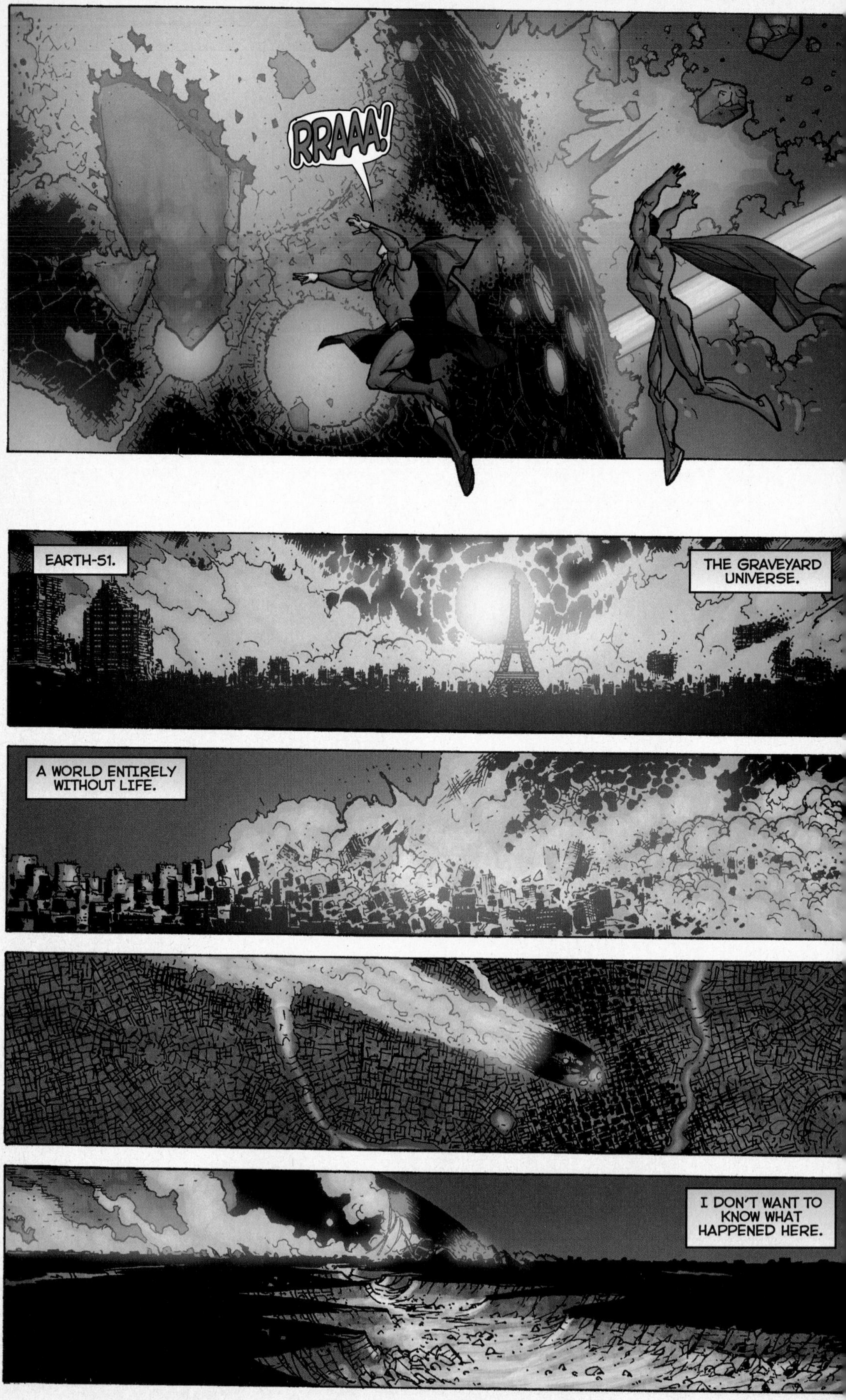
RRAAA!
EARTH-51.
THE GRAVEYARD UNIVERSE.
A WORLD ENTIRELY WITHOUT LIFE.
I DON'T WANT TO KNOW WHAT HAPPENED HERE.

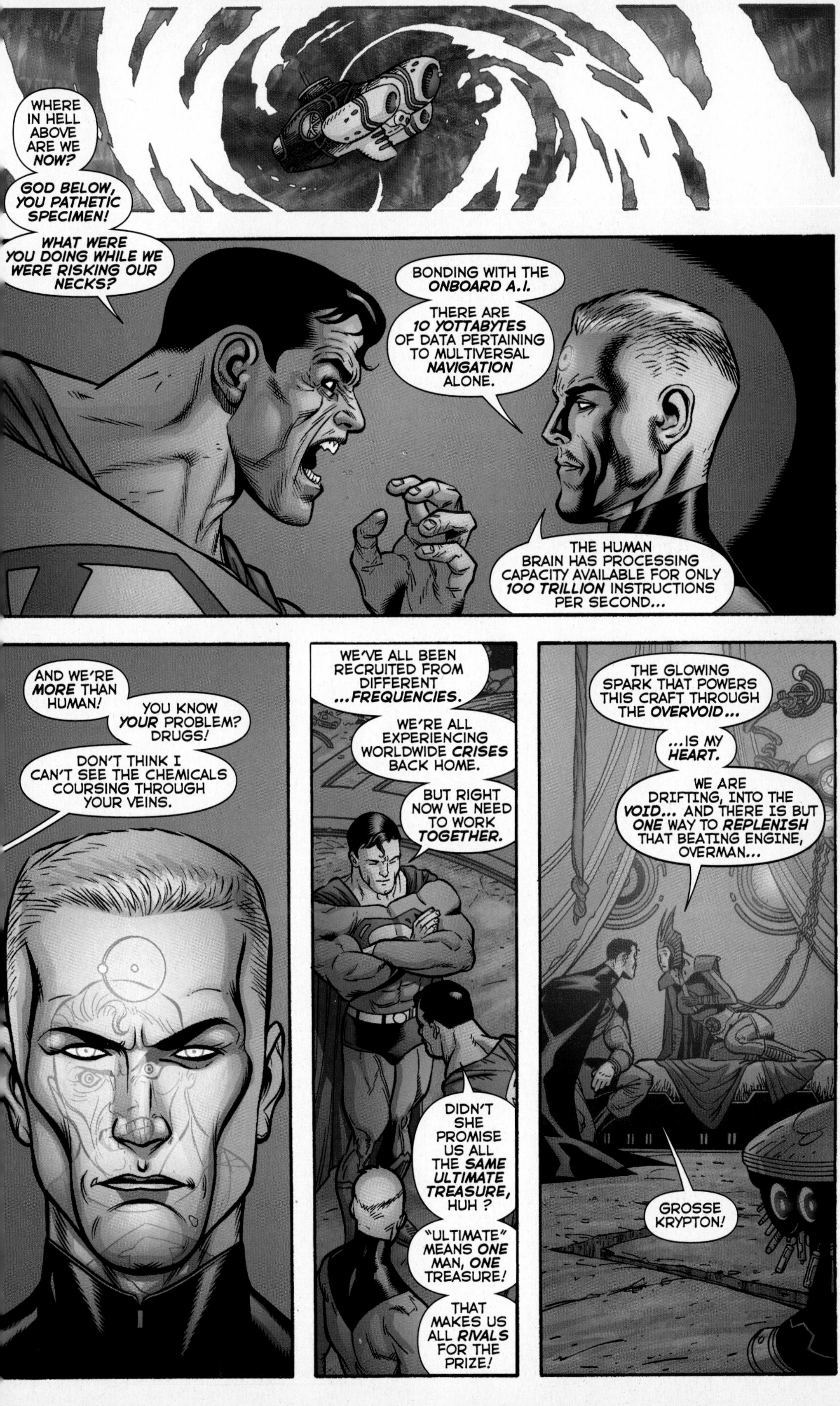

WHERE IN HELL ABOVE ARE WE NOW?
GOD BELOW, YOU PATHETIC SPECIMEN!
WHAT WERE YOU DOING WHILE WE WERE RISKING OUR NECKS?
BONDING WITH THE ONBOARD A.I.
THERE ARE 10 YOTTABYTES OF DATA PERTAINING TO MULTIVERSAL NAVIGATION ALONE.
THE HUMAN BRAIN HAS PROCESSING CAPACITY AVAILABLE FOR ONLY 100 TRILLION INSTRUCTIONS PER SECOND...
AND WE'RE MORE THAN HUMAN!
YOU KNOW YOUR PROBLEM? DRUGS!
DON'T THINK I CAN'T SEE THE CHEMICALS COURSING THROUGH YOUR VEINS.
WE'VE ALL BEEN RECRUITED FROM DIFFERENT ...FREQUENCIES.
WE'RE ALL EXPERIENCING WORLDWIDE CRISES BACK HOME.
BUT RIGHT NOW WE NEED TO WORK TOGETHER.
DIDN'T SHE PROMISE US ALL THE SAME ULTIMATE TREASURE, HUH ?
"ULTIMATE" MEANS ONE MAN, ONE TREASURE!
THAT MAKES US ALL RIVALS FOR THE PRIZE!
THE GLOWING SPARK THAT POWERS THIS CRAFT THROUGH THE OVERVOID...
...IS MY HEART.
WE ARE DRIFTING, INTO THE VOID... AND THERE IS BUT ONE WAY TO REPLENISH THAT BEATING ENGINE, OVERMAN...
GROSSE KRYPTON!

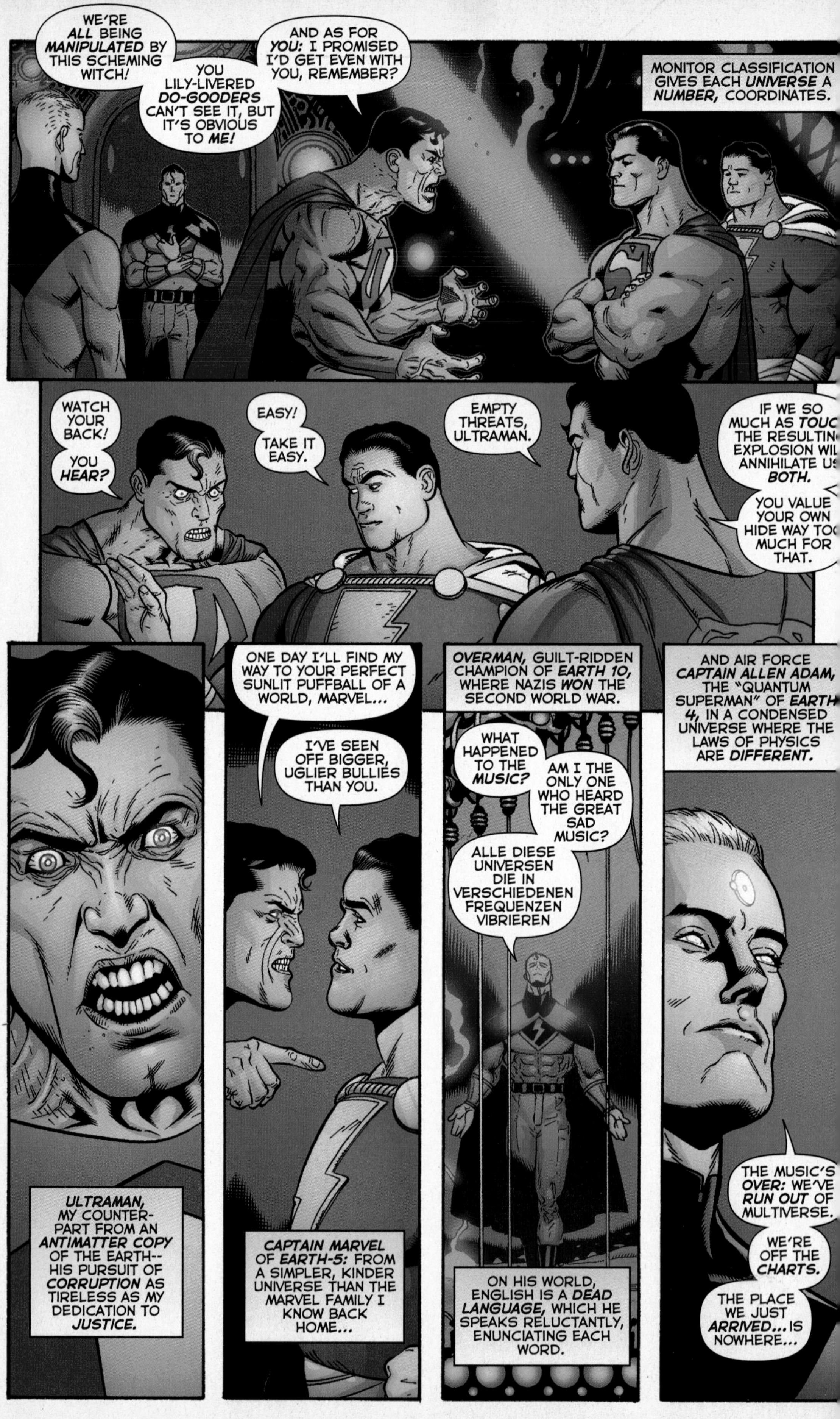
WE'RE ALL BEING MANIPULATED BY THIS SCHEMING WITCH!
YOU LILY-LIVERED DO-GOODERS CAN'T SEE IT, BUT IT'S OBVIOUS TO ME!
AND AS FOR YOU: I PROMISED I'D GET EVEN WITH YOU, REMEMBER?
MONITOR CLASSIFICATION GIVES EACH UNIVERSE A NUMBER, COORDINATES.
WATCH YOUR BACK!
YOU HEAR?
EASY!
TAKE IT EASY.
EMPTY THREATS, ULTRAMAN.
IF WE SO MUCH AS TOUC THE RESULTIN EXPLOSION WIL ANNIHILATE U BOTH.
YOU VALUE YOUR OWN HIDE WAY TO MUCH FOR THAT.
ULTRAMAN, MY COUNTER-PART FROM AN ANTIMATTER COPY OF THE EARTH-- HIS PURSUIT OF CORRUPTION AS TIRELESS AS MY DEDICATION TO JUSTICE.
ONE DAY I'LL FIND MY WAY TO YOUR PERFECT SUNLIT PUFFBALL OF A WORLD, MARVEL...
I'VE SEEN OFF BIGGER, UGLIER BULLIES THAN YOU.
CAPTAIN MARVEL OF EARTH-5: FROM A SIMPLER, KINDER UNIVERSE THAN THE MARVEL FAMILY I KNOW BACK HOME...
OVERMAN, GUILT-RIDDEN CHAMPION OF EARTH 10, WHERE NAZIS WON THE SECOND WORLD WAR.
WHAT HAPPENED TO THE MUSIC?
AM I THE ONLY ONE WHO HEARD THE GREAT SAD MUSIC?
ALLE DIESE UNIVERSEN DIE IN VERSCHIEDENEN FREQUENZEN VIBRIEREN
ON HIS WORLD, ENGLISH IS A DEAD LANGUAGE, WHICH HE SPEAKS RELUCTANTLY, ENUNCIATING EACH WORD.
AND AIR FORCE CAPTAIN ALLEN ADAM, THE "QUANTUM SUPERMAN" OF EARTH 4, IN A CONDENSED UNIVERSE WHERE THE LAWS OF PHYSICS ARE DIFFERENT.
THE MUSIC'S OVER: WE'VE RUN OUT OF MULTIVERSE.
WE'RE OFF THE CHARTS.
THE PLACE WE JUST ARRIVED... IS NOWHERE...

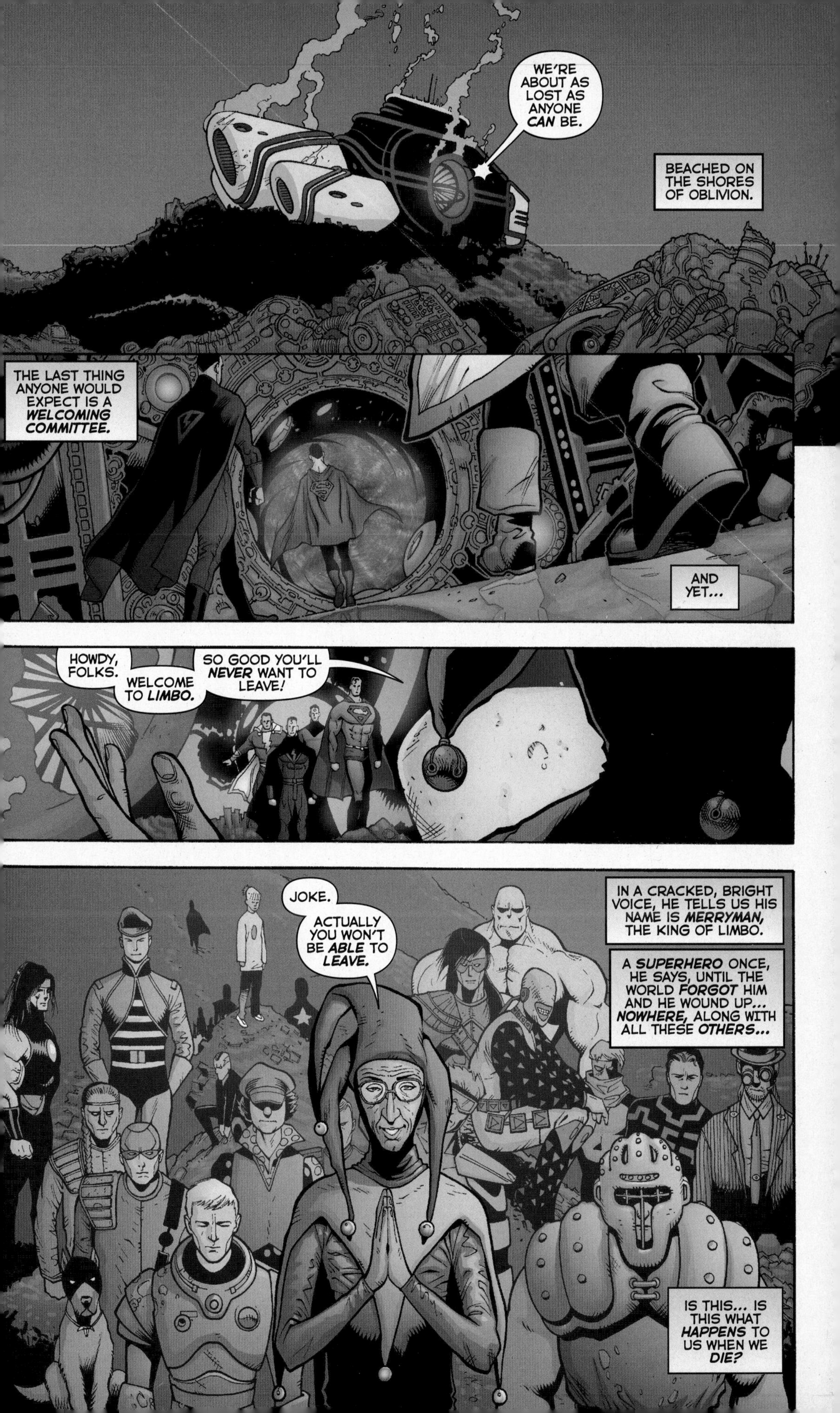
WE'RE ABOUT AS LOST AS ANYONE *CAN* BE.
BEACHED ON THE SHORES OF OBLIVION.
THE LAST THING ANYONE WOULD EXPECT IS A *WELCOMING COMMITTEE.*
AND YET...
HOWDY, FOLKS.
WELCOME TO *LIMBO.*
SO GOOD YOU'LL *NEVER* WANT TO LEAVE!
JOKE.
ACTUALLY YOU WON'T BE *ABLE* TO *LEAVE.*
IN A CRACKED, BRIGHT VOICE, HE TELLS US HIS NAME IS *MERRYMAN,* THE KING OF LIMBO.
A *SUPERHERO* ONCE, HE SAYS, UNTIL THE WORLD *FORGOT* HIM AND HE WOUND UP... *NOWHERE,* ALONG WITH ALL THESE *OTHERS...*
IS THIS... IS THIS WHAT *HAPPENS* TO US WHEN WE *DIE?*

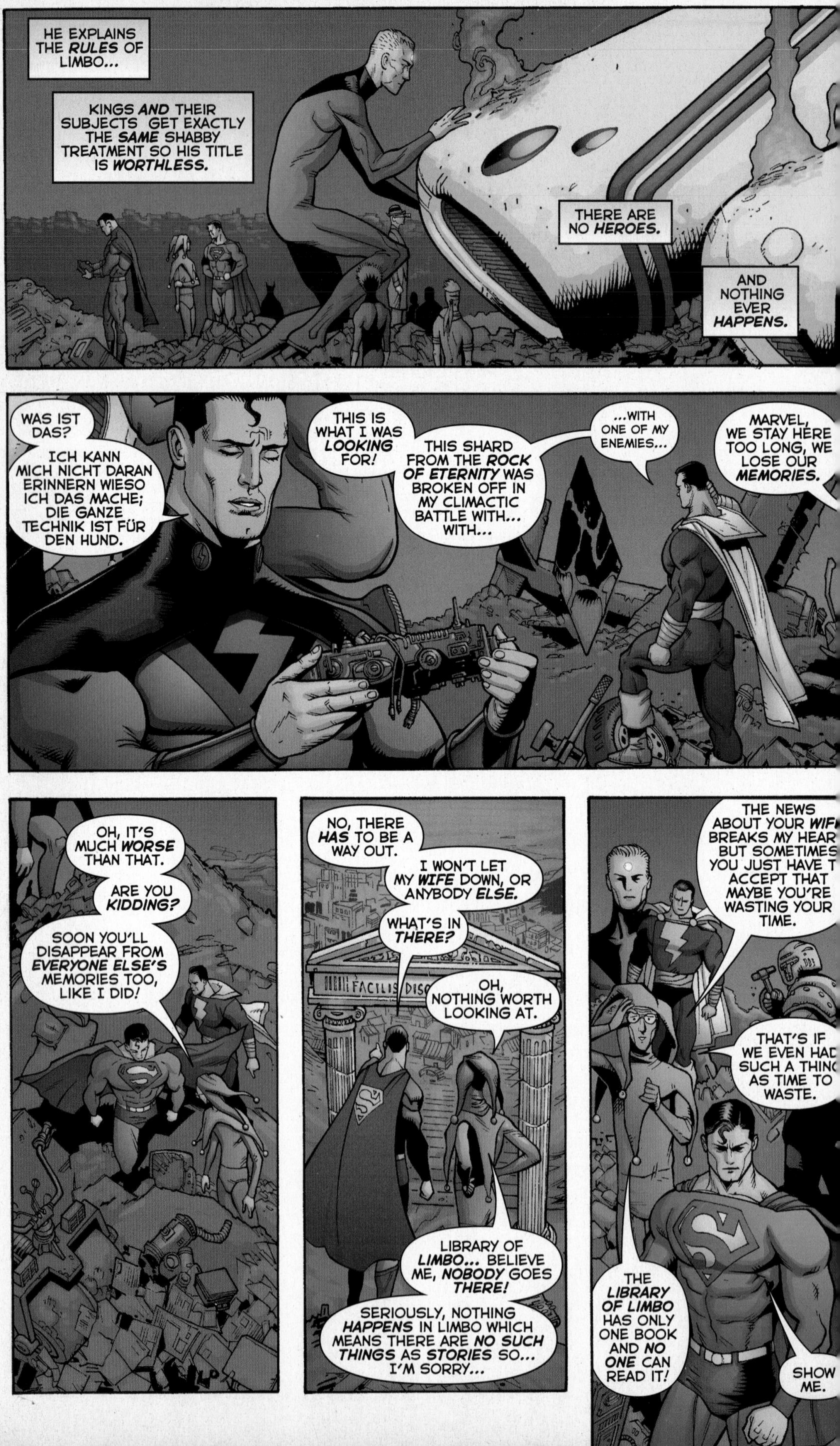
HE EXPLAINS THE RULES OF LIMBO...
KINGS AND THEIR SUBJECTS GET EXACTLY THE SAME SHABBY TREATMENT SO HIS TITLE IS WORTHLESS.
THERE ARE NO HEROES.
AND NOTHING EVER HAPPENS.
WAS IST DAS?
ICH KANN MICH NICHT DARAN ERINNERN WIESO ICH DAS MACHE; DIE GANZE TECHNIK IST FÜR DEN HUND.
THIS IS WHAT I WAS LOOKING FOR!
THIS SHARD FROM THE ROCK OF ETERNITY WAS BROKEN OFF IN MY CLIMACTIC BATTLE WITH... WITH...
...WITH ONE OF MY ENEMIES...
MARVEL, WE STAY HERE TOO LONG, WE LOSE OUR MEMORIES.
OH, IT'S MUCH WORSE THAN THAT.
ARE YOU KIDDING?
SOON YOU'LL DISAPPEAR FROM EVERYONE ELSE'S MEMORIES TOO, LIKE I DID!
NO, THERE HAS TO BE A WAY OUT.
I WON'T LET MY WIFE DOWN, OR ANYBODY ELSE.
WHAT'S IN THERE?
FACILIS DISC
OH, NOTHING WORTH LOOKING AT.
LIBRARY OF LIMBO... BELIEVE ME, NOBODY GOES THERE!
SERIOUSLY, NOTHING HAPPENS IN LIMBO WHICH MEANS THERE ARE NO SUCH THINGS AS STORIES SO... I'M SORRY...
THE NEWS ABOUT YOUR WIF BREAKS MY HEAR BUT SOMETIMES YOU JUST HAVE T ACCEPT THAT MAYBE YOU'RE WASTING YOUR TIME.
THAT'S IF WE EVEN HAD SUCH A THIN AS TIME TO WASTE.
THE LIBRARY OF LIMBO HAS ONLY ONE BOOK AND NO ONE CAN READ IT!
SHOW ME.

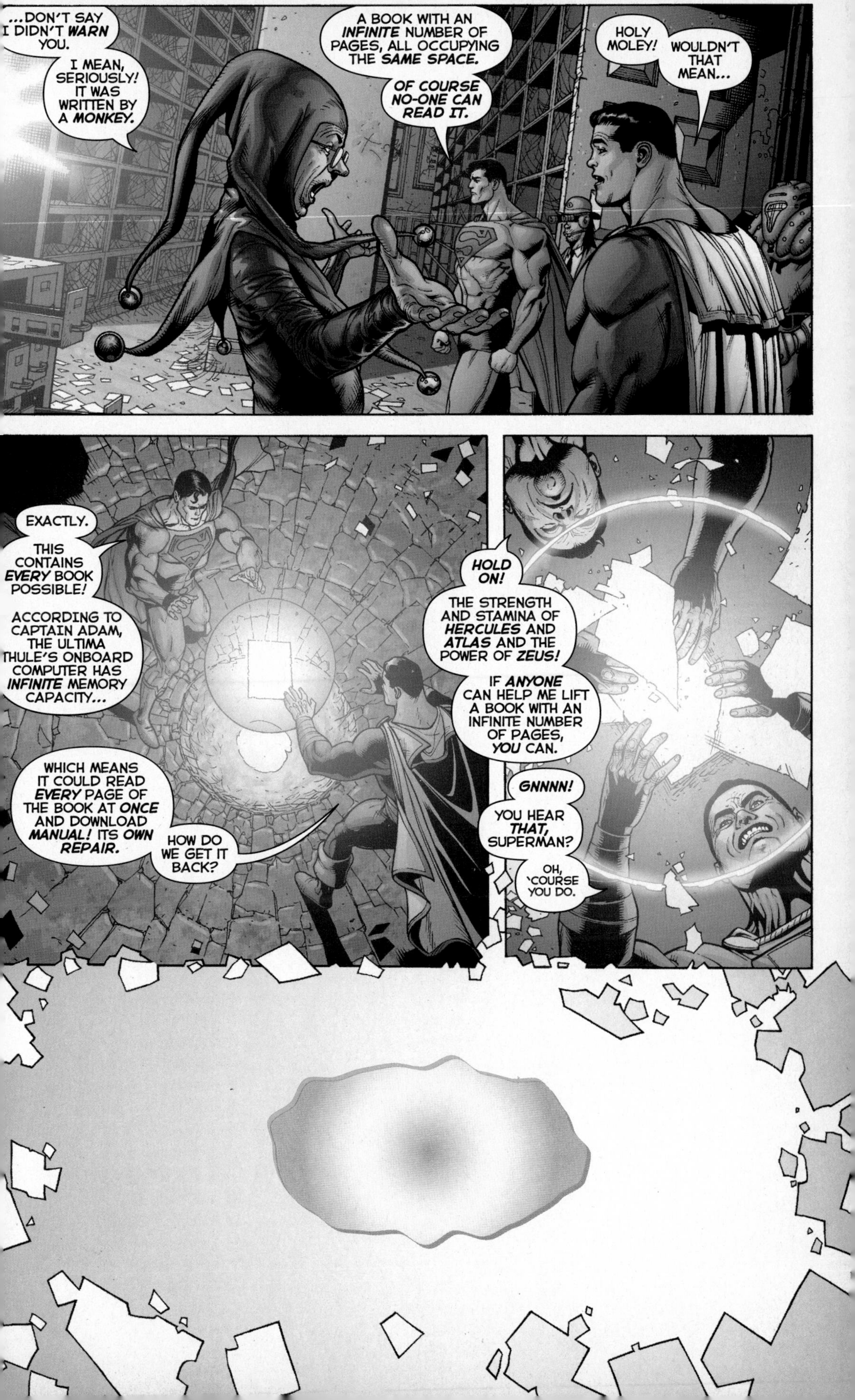
...DON'T SAY I DIDN'T WARN YOU.
I MEAN, SERIOUSLY! IT WAS WRITTEN BY A MONKEY.
A BOOK WITH AN INFINITE NUMBER OF PAGES, ALL OCCUPYING THE SAME SPACE.
OF COURSE NO-ONE CAN READ IT.
HOLY MOLEY!
WOULDN'T THAT MEAN...
EXACTLY.
THIS CONTAINS EVERY BOOK POSSIBLE!
ACCORDING TO CAPTAIN ADAM, THE ULTIMA THULE'S ONBOARD COMPUTER HAS INFINITE MEMORY CAPACITY...
WHICH MEANS IT COULD READ EVERY PAGE OF THE BOOK AT ONCE AND DOWNLOAD MANUAL! ITS OWN REPAIR.
HOW DO WE GET IT BACK?
HOLD ON!
THE STRENGTH AND STAMINA OF HERCULES AND ATLAS AND THE POWER OF ZEUS!
IF ANYONE CAN HELP ME LIFT A BOOK WITH AN INFINITE NUMBER OF PAGES, YOU CAN.
GNNNN!
YOU HEAR THAT, SUPERMAN?
OH, 'COURSE YOU DO.

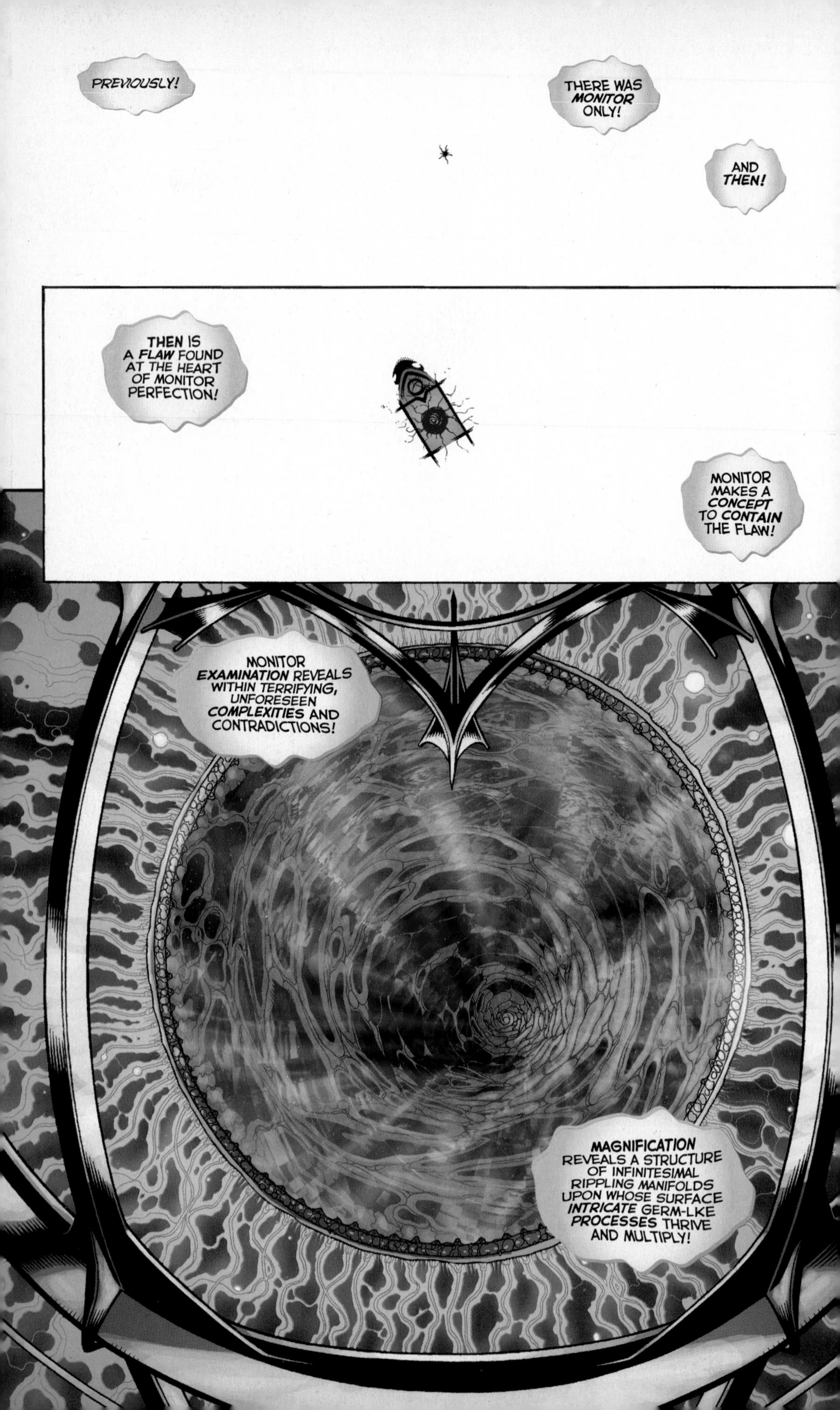
PREVIOUSLY!
THERE WAS MONITOR ONLY!
AND THEN!
THEN IS A FLAW FOUND AT THE HEART OF MONITOR PERFECTION!
MONITOR MAKES A CONCEPT TO CONTAIN THE FLAW!
MONITOR EXAMINATION REVEALS WITHIN TERRIFYING, UNFORESEEN COMPLEXITIES AND CONTRADICTIONS!
MAGNIFICATION REVEALS A STRUCTURE OF INFINITESIMAL RIPPLING MANIFOLDS UPON WHOSE SURFACE INTRICATE GERM-LKE PROCESSES THRIVE AND MULTIPLY!

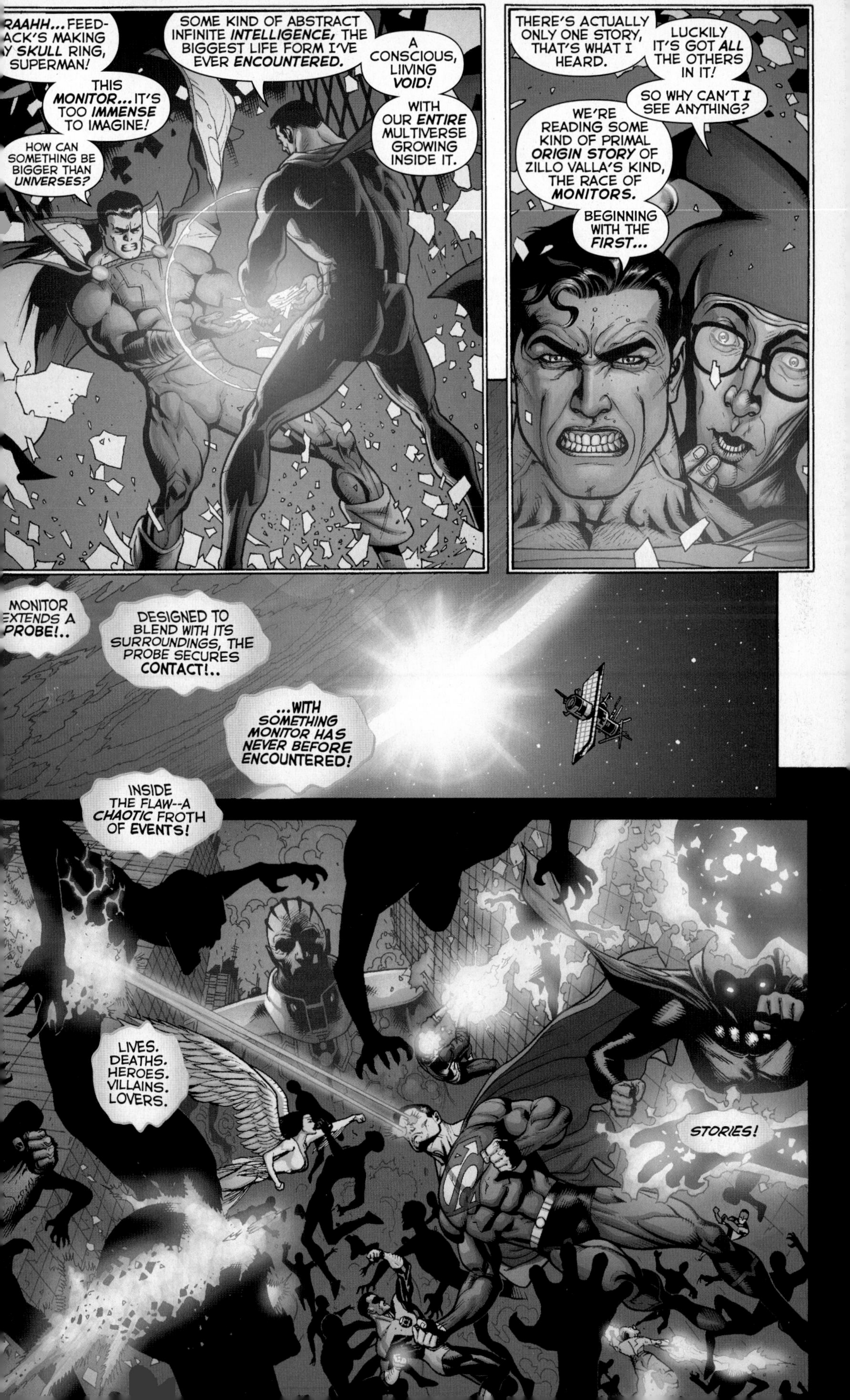
RAAHH... FEED-
ACK'S MAKING
Y SKULL RING,
SUPERMAN!
SOME KIND OF ABSTRACT INFINITE INTELLIGENCE, THE BIGGEST LIFE FORM I'VE EVER ENCOUNTERED.
A CONSCIOUS, LIIVING VOID!
THIS MONITOR... IT'S TOO IMMENSE TO IMAGINE!
WITH OUR ENTIRE MULTIVERSE GROWING INSIDE IT.
HOW CAN SOMETHING BE BIGGER THAN UNIVERSES?
THERE'S ACTUALLY ONLY ONE STORY, THAT'S WHAT I HEARD.
LUCKILY IT'S GOT ALL THE OTHERS IN IT!
SO WHY CAN'T I SEE ANYTHING?
WE'RE READING SOME KIND OF PRIMAL ORIGIN STORY OF ZILLO VALLA'S KIND, THE RACE OF MONITORS.
BEGINNING WITH THE FIRST...
MONITOR EXTENDS A PROBE!..
DESIGNED TO BLEND WITH ITS SURROUNDINGS, THE PROBE SECURES CONTACT!..
...WITH SOMETHING MONITOR HAS NEVER BEFORE ENCOUNTERED!
INSIDE THE FLAW--A CHAOTIC FROTH OF EVENTS!
LIVES. DEATHS. HEROES. VILLAINS. LOVERS.
STORIES!

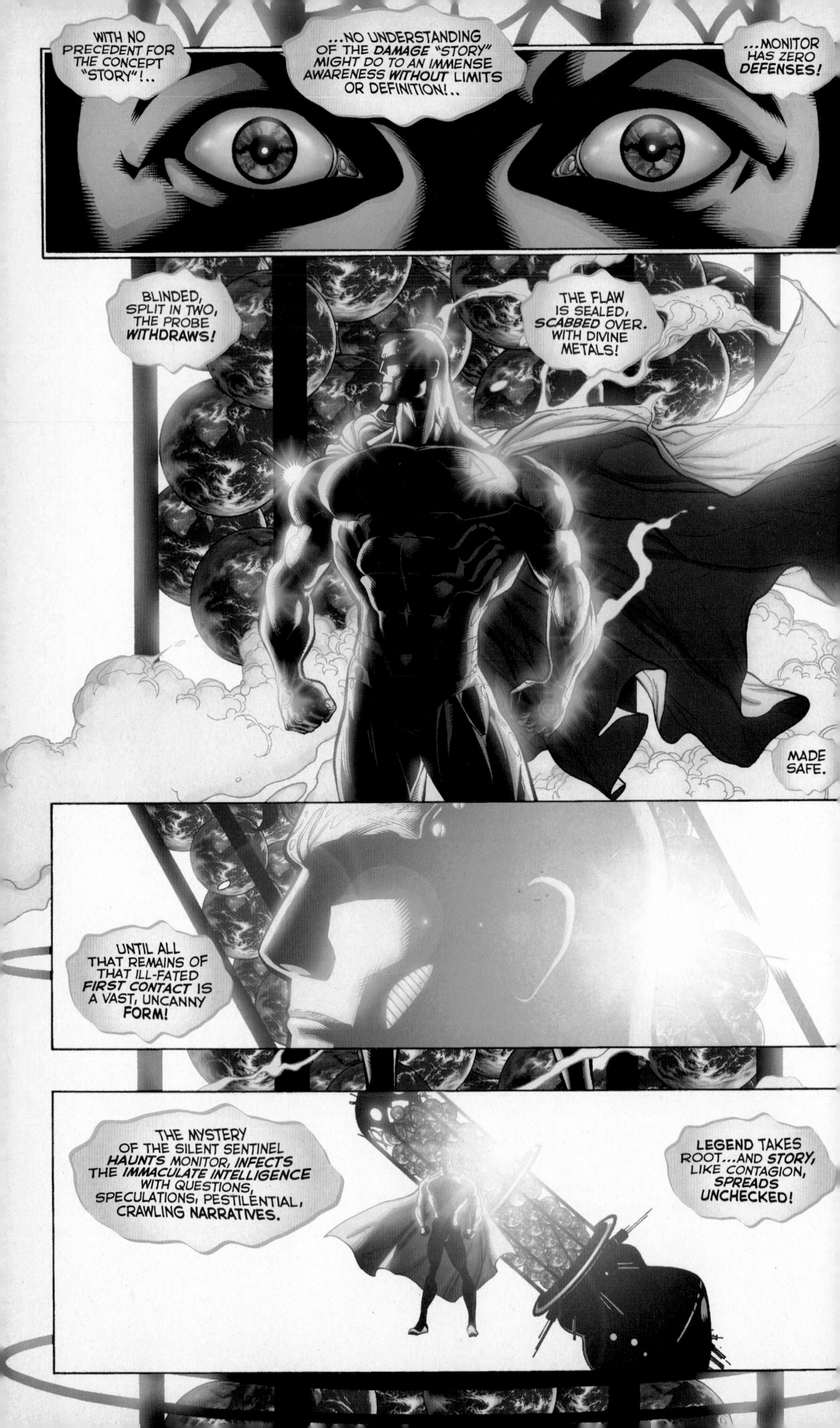
WITH NO PRECEDENT FOR THE CONCEPT "STORY"!..
...NO UNDERSTANDING OF THE DAMAGE "STORY" MIGHT DO TO AN IMMENSE AWARENESS WITHOUT LIMITS OR DEFINITION!..
...MONITOR HAS ZERO DEFENSES!
BLINDED, SPLIT IN TWO, THE PROBE WITHDRAWS!
THE FLAW IS SEALED, SCABBED OVER. WITH DIVINE METALS!
MADE SAFE.
UNTIL ALL THAT REMAINS OF THAT ILL-FATED FIRST CONTACT IS A VAST, UNCANNY FORM!
THE MYSTERY OF THE SILENT SENTINEL HAUNTS MONITOR, INFECTS THE IMMACULATE INTELLIGENCE WITH QUESTIONS, SPECULATIONS, PESTILENTIAL, CRAWLING NARRATIVES.
LEGEND TAKES ROOT...AND STORY, LIKE CONTAGION, SPREADS UNCHECKED!

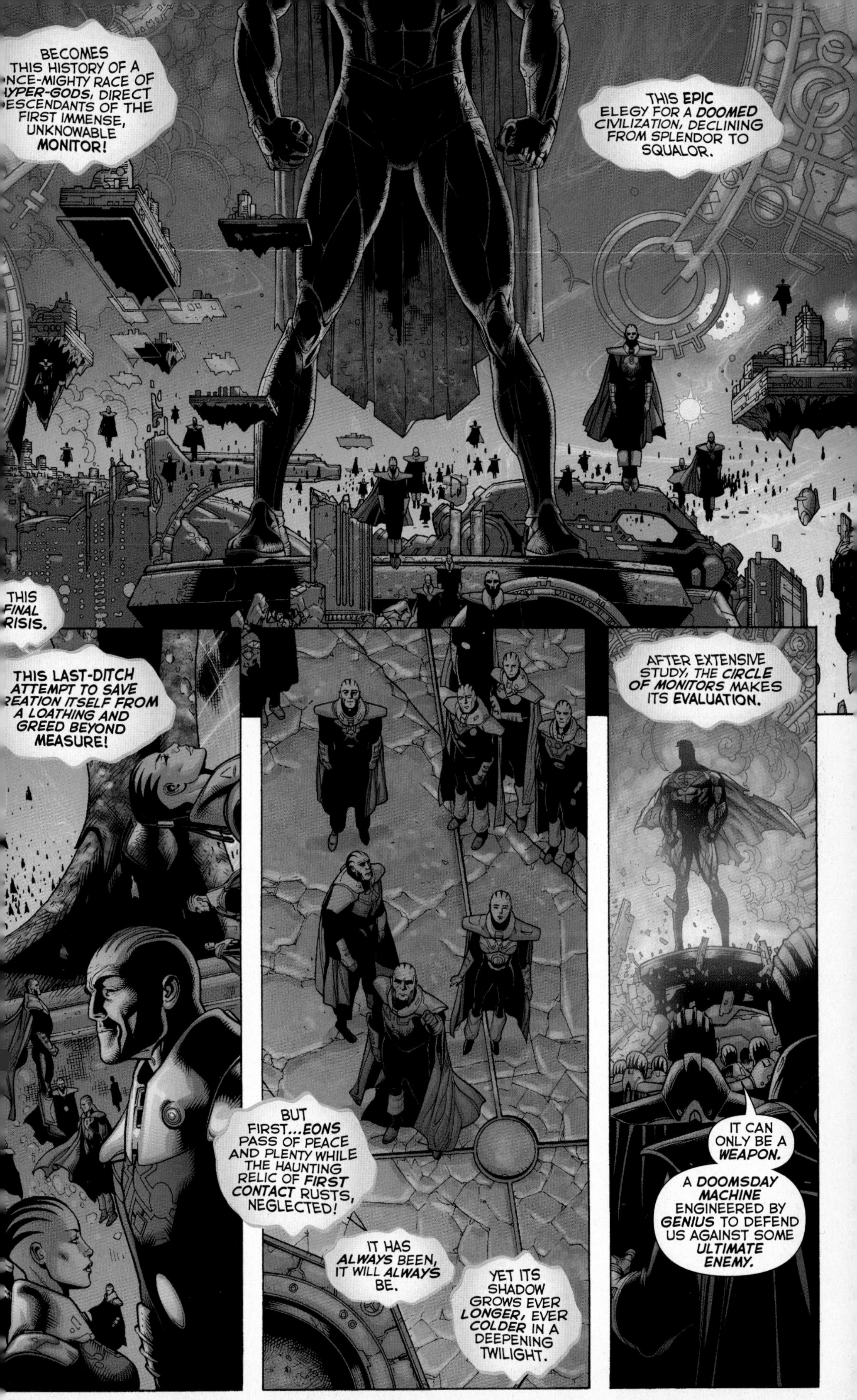

BECOMES THIS HISTORY OF A NCE-MIGHTY RACE OF YPER-GODS, DIRECT ESCENDANTS OF THE FIRST IMMENSE, UNKNOWABLE MONITOR!
THIS EPIC ELEGY FOR A DOOMED CIVILIZATION, DECLINING FROM SPLENDOR TO SQUALOR.
THIS FINAL RISIS.
THIS LAST-DITCH ATTEMPT TO SAVE REATION ITSELF FROM A LOATHING AND GREED BEYOND MEASURE!
BUT FIRST...EONS PASS OF PEACE AND PLENTY WHILE THE HAUNTING RELIC OF FIRST CONTACT RUSTS, NEGLECTED!
IT HAS ALWAYS BEEN, IT WILL ALWAYS BE.
YET ITS SHADOW GROWS EVER LONGER, EVER COLDER IN A DEEPENING TWILIGHT.
AFTER EXTENSIVE STUDY, THE CIRCLE OF MONITORS MAKES ITS EVALUATION.
IT CAN ONLY BE A WEAPON.
A DOOMSDAY MACHINE ENGINEERED BY GENIUS TO DEFEND US AGAINST SOME ULTIMATE ENEMY.

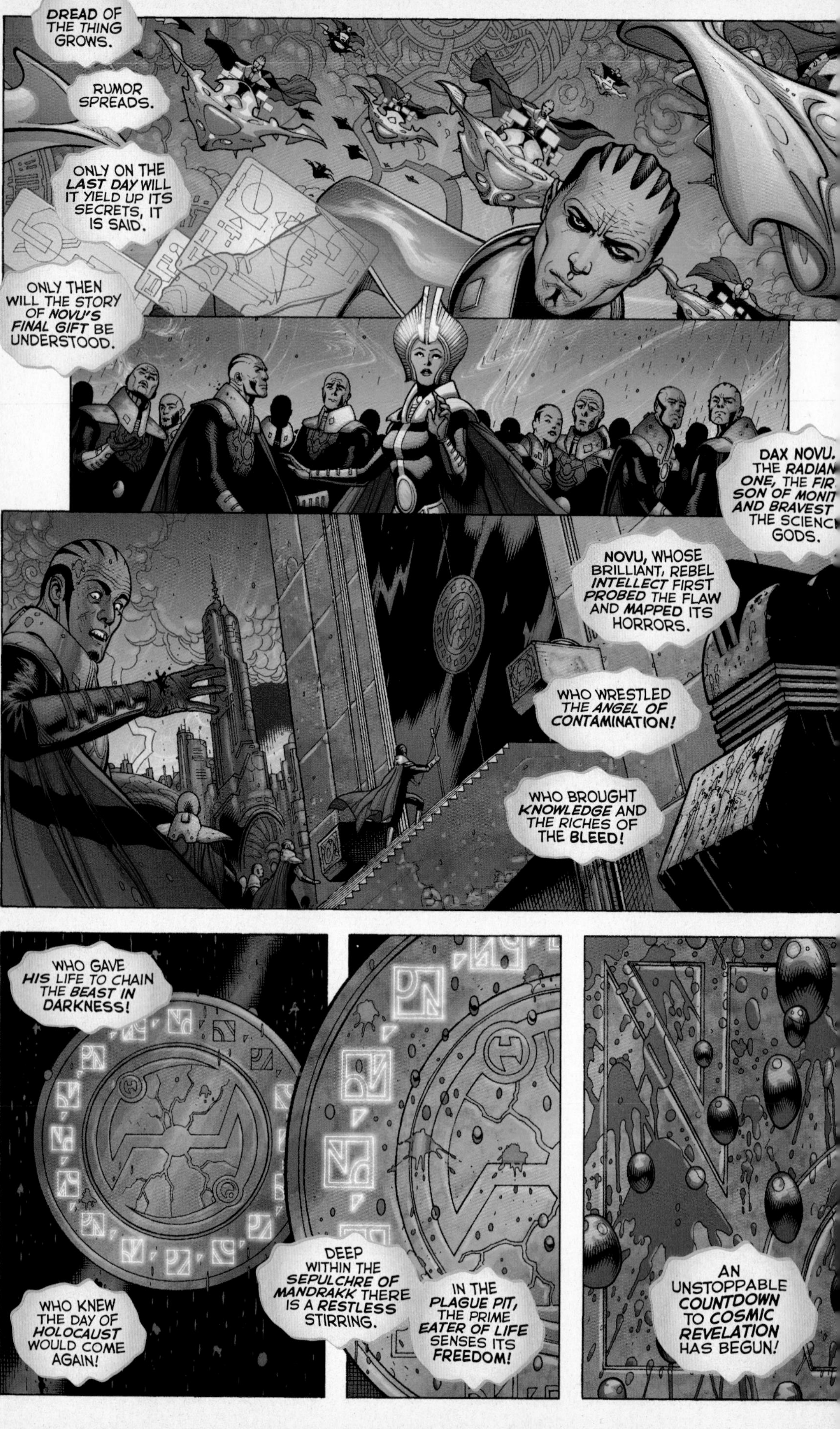
DREAD OF THE THING GROWS.
RUMOR SPREADS.
ONLY ON THE LAST DAY WILL IT YIELD UP ITS SECRETS, IT IS SAID.
ONLY THEN WILL THE STORY OF NOVU'S FINAL GIFT BE UNDERSTOOD.
DAX NOVU. THE RADIAN ONE, THE FIR SON OF MONIT AND BRAVEST THE SCIENC GODS.
NOVU, WHOSE BRILLIANT, REBEL INTELLECT FIRST PROBED THE FLAW AND MAPPED ITS HORRORS.
WHO WRESTLED THE ANGEL OF CONTAMINATION!
WHO BROUGHT KNOWLEDGE AND THE RICHES OF THE BLEED!
WHO GAVE HIS LIFE TO CHAIN THE BEAST IN DARKNESS!
WHO KNEW THE DAY OF HOLOCAUST WOULD COME AGAIN!
DEEP WITHIN THE SEPULCHRE OF MANDRAKK THERE IS A RESTLESS STIRRING.
IN THE PLAGUE PIT, THE PRIME EATER OF LIFE SENSES ITS FREEDOM!
AN UNSTOPPABLE COUNTDOWN TO COSMIC REVELATION HAS BEGUN!

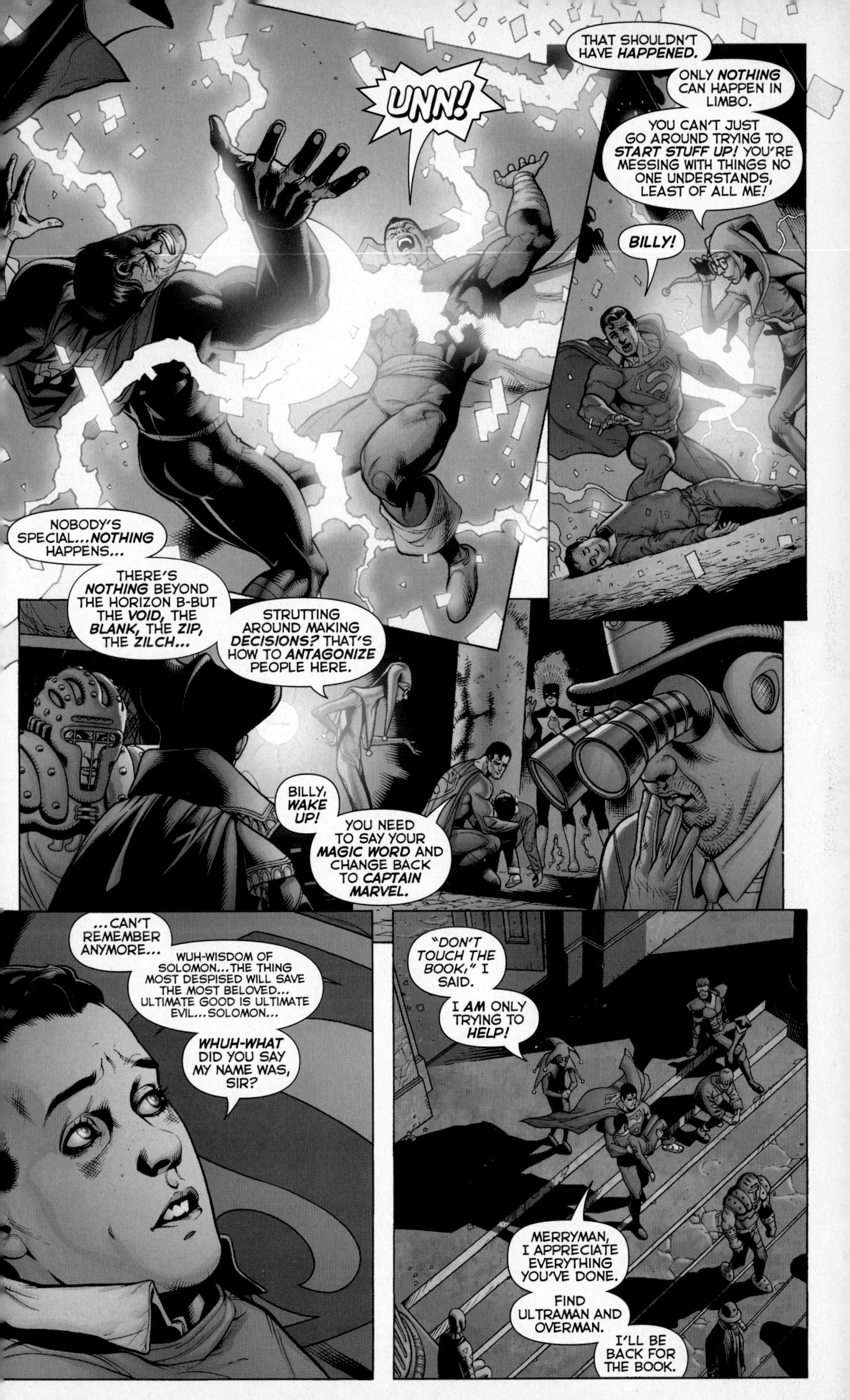
UNN!
THAT SHOULDN'T HAVE HAPPENED.
ONLY NOTHING CAN HAPPEN IN LIMBO.
YOU CAN'T JUST GO AROUND TRYING TO START STUFF UP! YOU'RE MESSING WITH THINGS NO ONE UNDERSTANDS, LEAST OF ALL ME!
BILLY!
NOBODY'S SPECIAL...NOTHING HAPPENS...
THERE'S NOTHING BEYOND THE HORIZON B-BUT THE VOID, THE BLANK, THE ZIP, THE ZILCH...
STRUTTING AROUND MAKING DECISIONS? THAT'S HOW TO ANTAGONIZE PEOPLE HERE.
BILLY, WAKE UP!
YOU NEED TO SAY YOUR MAGIC WORD AND CHANGE BACK TO CAPTAIN MARVEL.
...CAN'T REMEMBER ANYMORE...
WUH-WISDOM OF SOLOMON...THE THING MOST DESPISED WILL SAVE THE MOST BELOVED... ULTIMATE GOOD IS ULTIMATE EVIL...SOLOMON...
WHUH-WHAT DID YOU SAY MY NAME WAS, SIR?
"DON'T TOUCH THE BOOK," I SAID.
I AM ONLY TRYING TO HELP!
MERRYMAN, I APPRECIATE EVERYTHING YOU'VE DONE.
FIND ULTRAMAN AND OVERMAN.
I'LL BE BACK FOR THE BOOK.

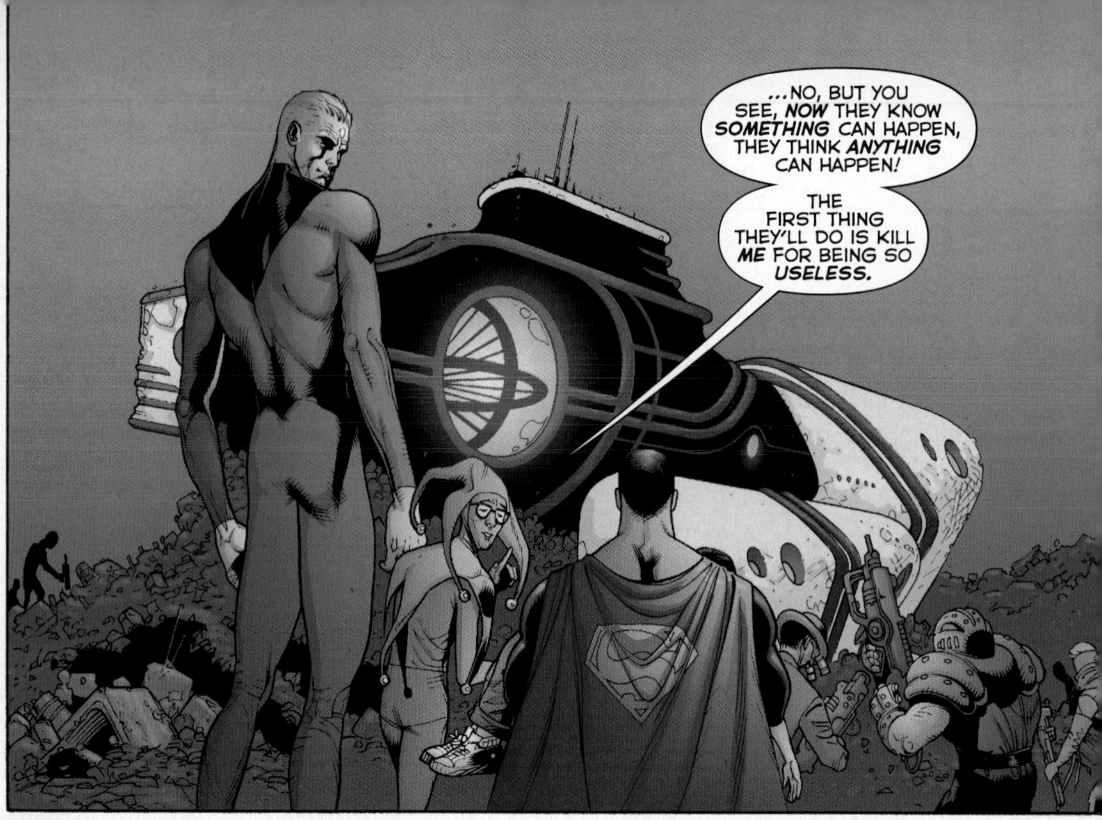
...NO, BUT YOU SEE, NOW THEY KNOW SOMETHING CAN HAPPEN, THEY THINK ANYTHING CAN HAPPEN!
THE FIRST THING THEY'LL DO IS KILL ME FOR BEING SO USELESS.

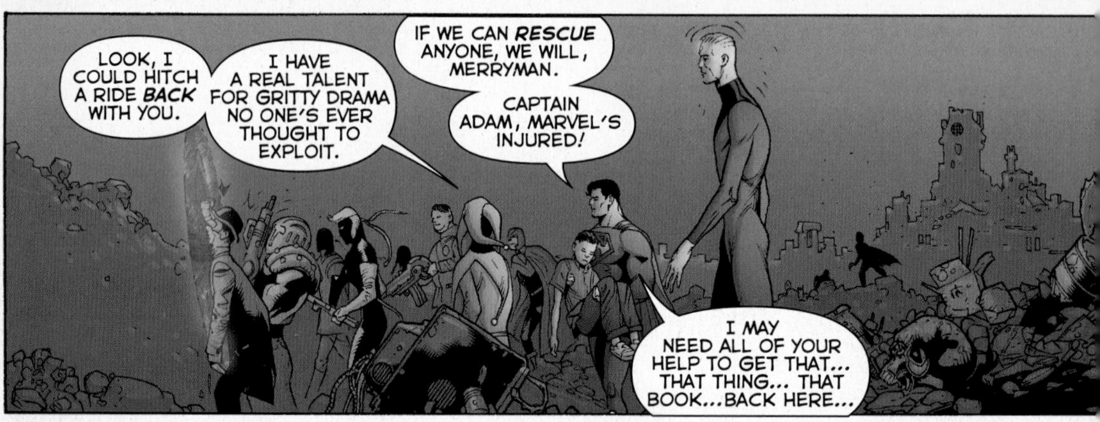
LOOK, I COULD HITCH A RIDE BACK WITH YOU.
I HAVE A REAL TALENT FOR GRITTY DRAMA NO ONE'S EVER THOUGHT TO EXPLOIT.
IF WE CAN RESCUE ANYONE, WE WILL, MERRYMAN.
CAPTAIN ADAM, MARVEL'S INJURED!
I MAY NEED ALL OF YOUR HELP TO GET THAT... THAT THING... THAT BOOK...BACK HERE...

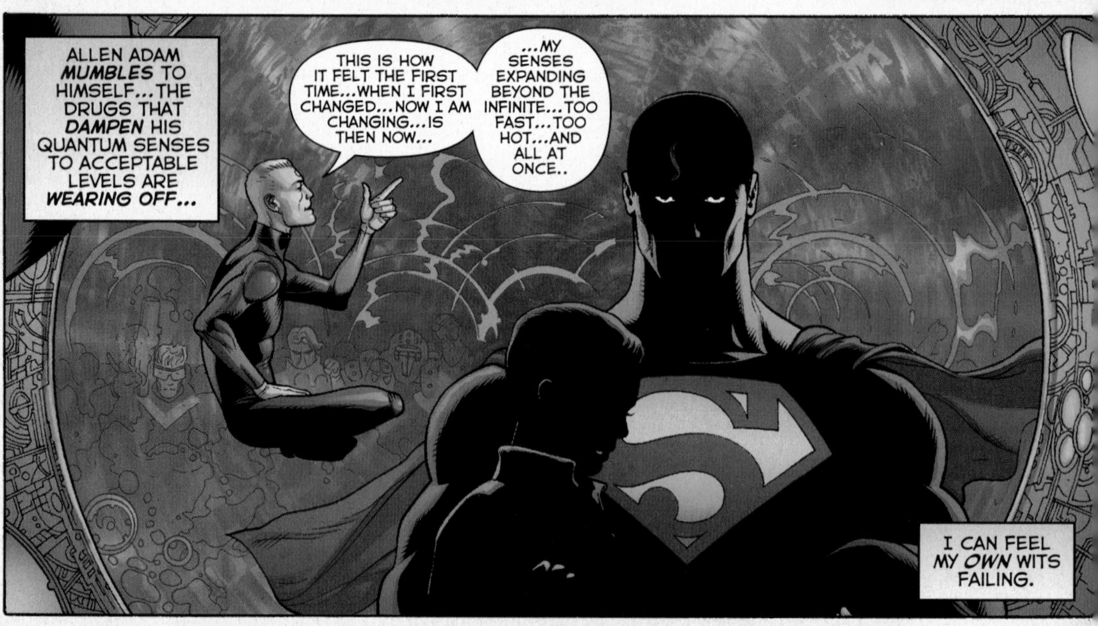
ALLEN ADAM MUMBLES TO HIMSELF...THE DRUGS THAT DAMPEN HIS QUANTUM SENSES TO ACCEPTABLE LEVELS ARE WEARING OFF...
THIS IS HOW IT FELT THE FIRST TIME...WHEN I FIRST CHANGED...NOW I AM CHANGING...IS THEN NOW...
...MY SENSES EXPANDING BEYOND THE INFINITE...TOO FAST...TOO HOT...AND ALL AT ONCE..
I CAN FEEL MY OWN WITS FAILING.

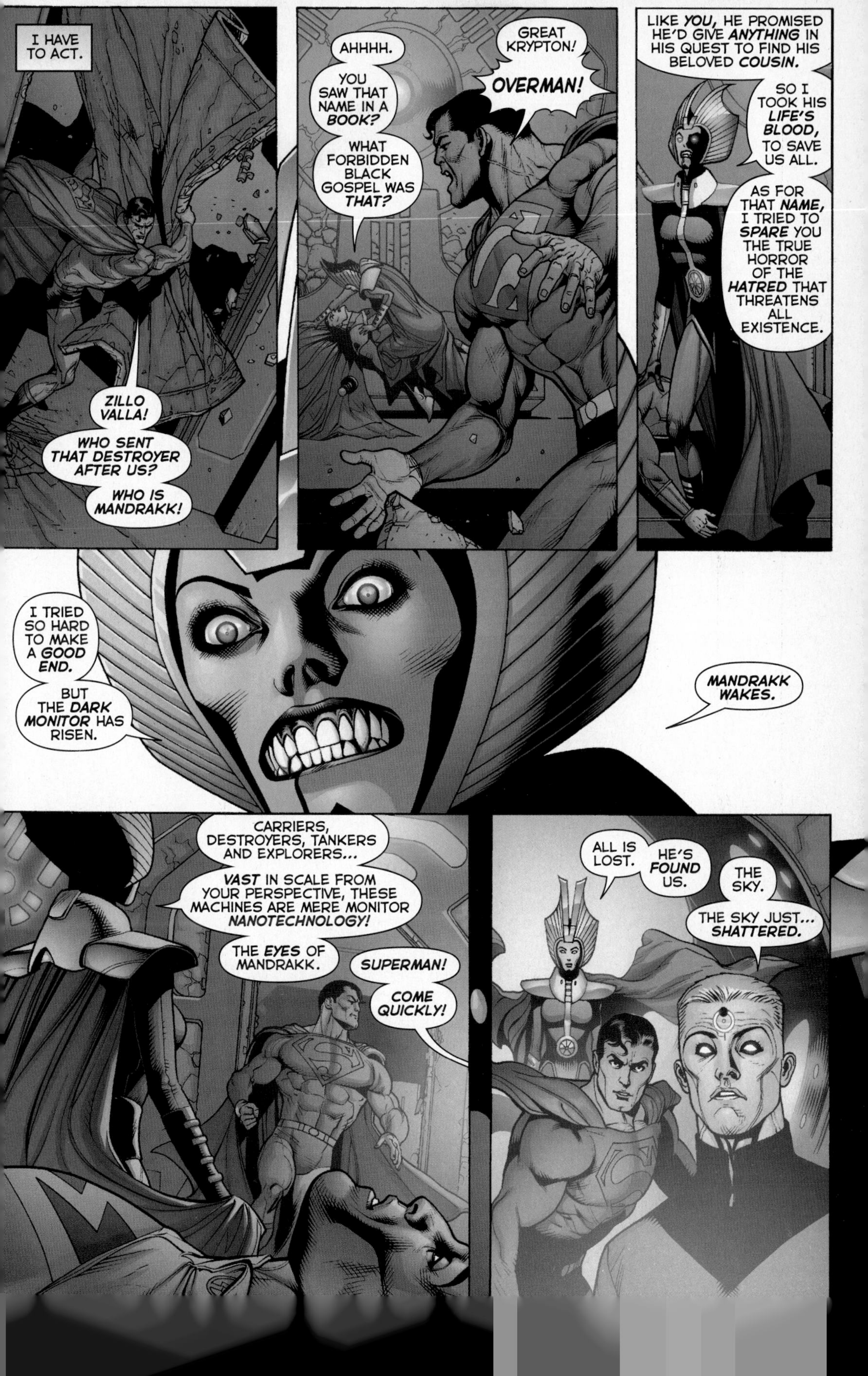
I HAVE TO ACT.
ZILLO VALLA!
WHO SENT THAT DESTROYER AFTER US?
WHO IS MANDRAKK!
AHHHH.
YOU SAW THAT NAME IN A BOOK?
WHAT FORBIDDEN BLACK GOSPEL WAS THAT?
GREAT KRYPTON!
OVERMAN!
LIKE YOU, HE PROMISED HE'D GIVE ANYTHING IN HIS QUEST TO FIND HIS BELOVED COUSIN.
SO I TOOK HIS LIFE'S BLOOD, TO SAVE US ALL.
AS FOR THAT NAME, I TRIED TO SPARE YOU THE TRUE HORROR OF THE HATRED THAT THREATENS ALL EXISTENCE.
I TRIED SO HARD TO MAKE A GOOD END.
BUT THE DARK MONITOR HAS RISEN.
MANDRAKK WAKES.
CARRIERS, DESTROYERS, TANKERS AND EXPLORERS...
VAST IN SCALE FROM YOUR PERSPECTIVE, THESE MACHINES ARE MERE MONITOR NANOTECHNOLOGY!
THE EYES OF MANDRAKK.
SUPERMAN!
COME QUICKLY!
ALL IS LOST.
HE'S FOUND US.
THE SKY.
THE SKY JUST... SHATTERED.

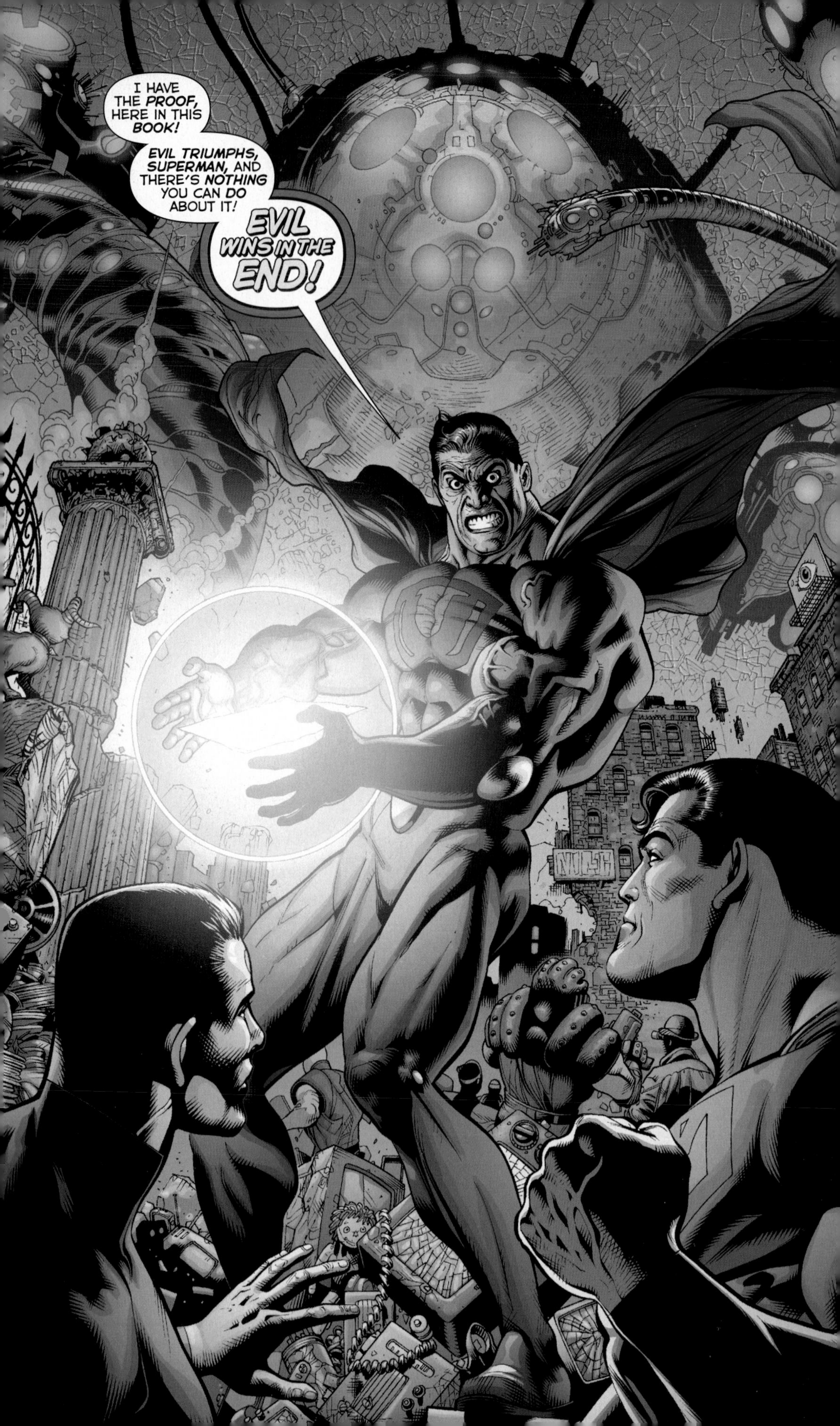
I HAVE THE *PROOF,* HERE IN THIS *BOOK!*
EVIL TRIUMPHS, SUPERMAN, AND THERE'S *NOTHING* YOU CAN *DO* ABOUT IT!
EVIL WINS IN THE END!

er to SUPERMAN BEYOND #2 Doug Mahnke, Christian Alamy with David Baron

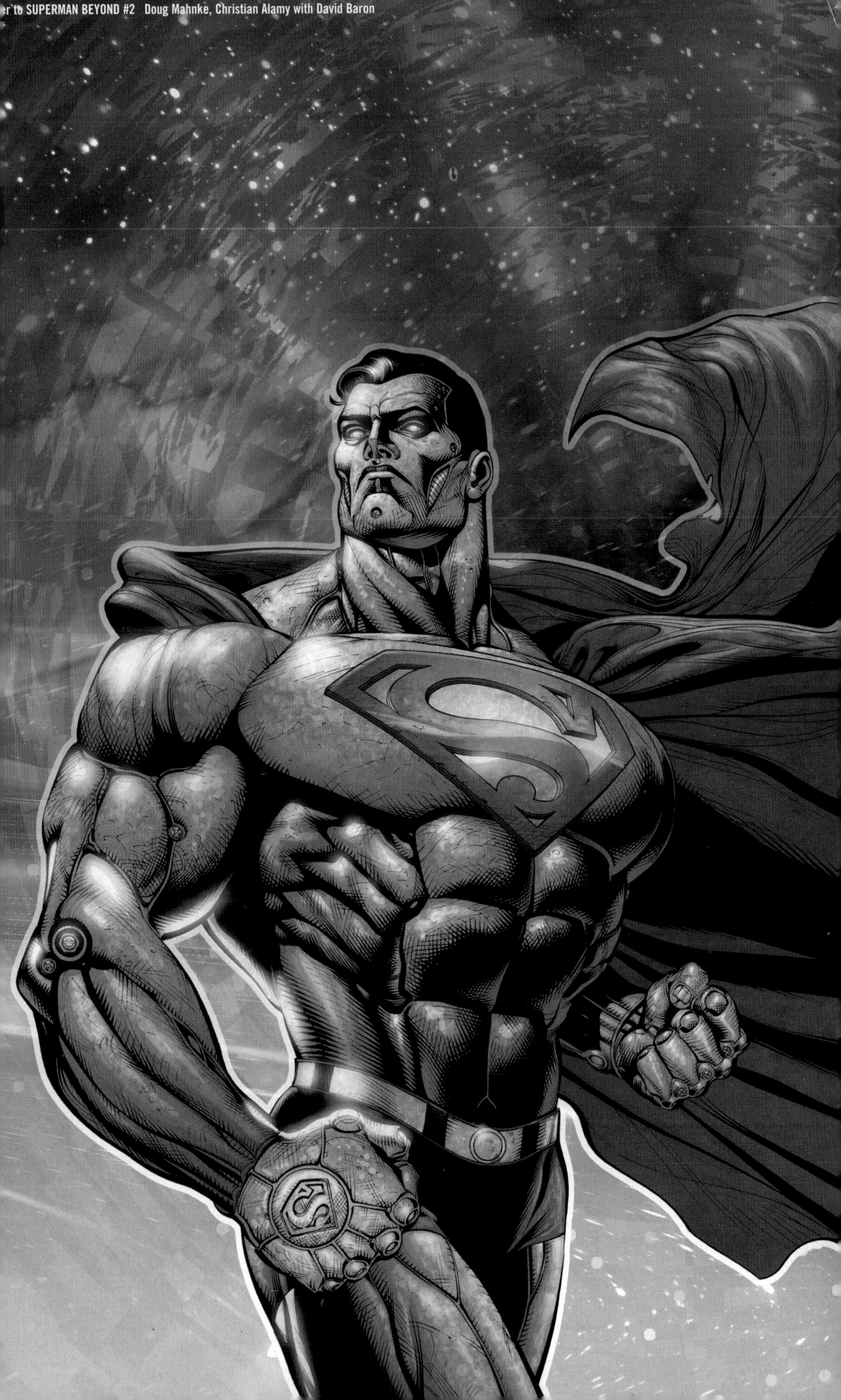

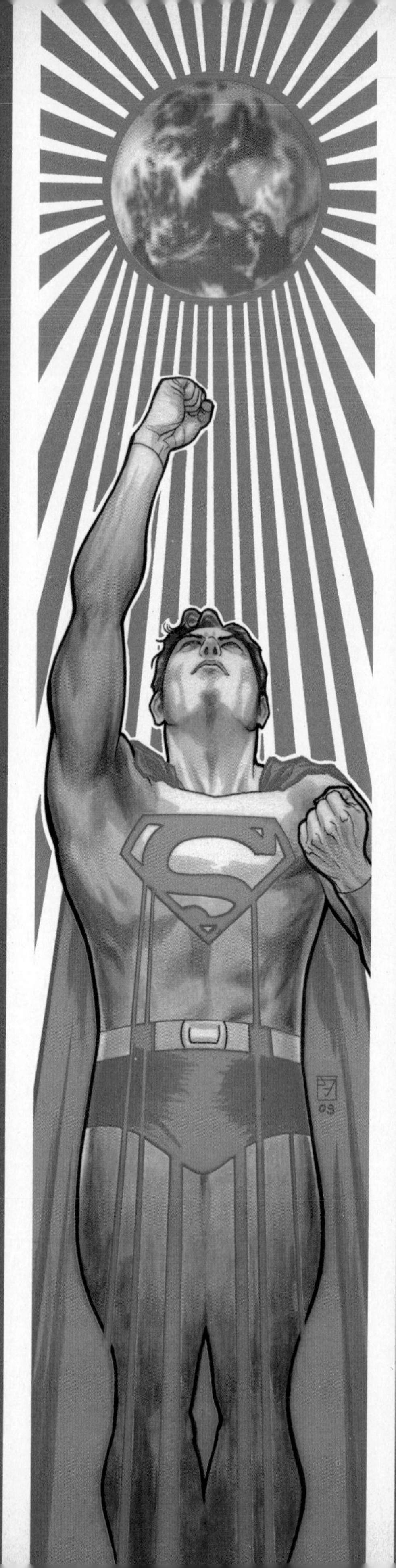

JH Williams

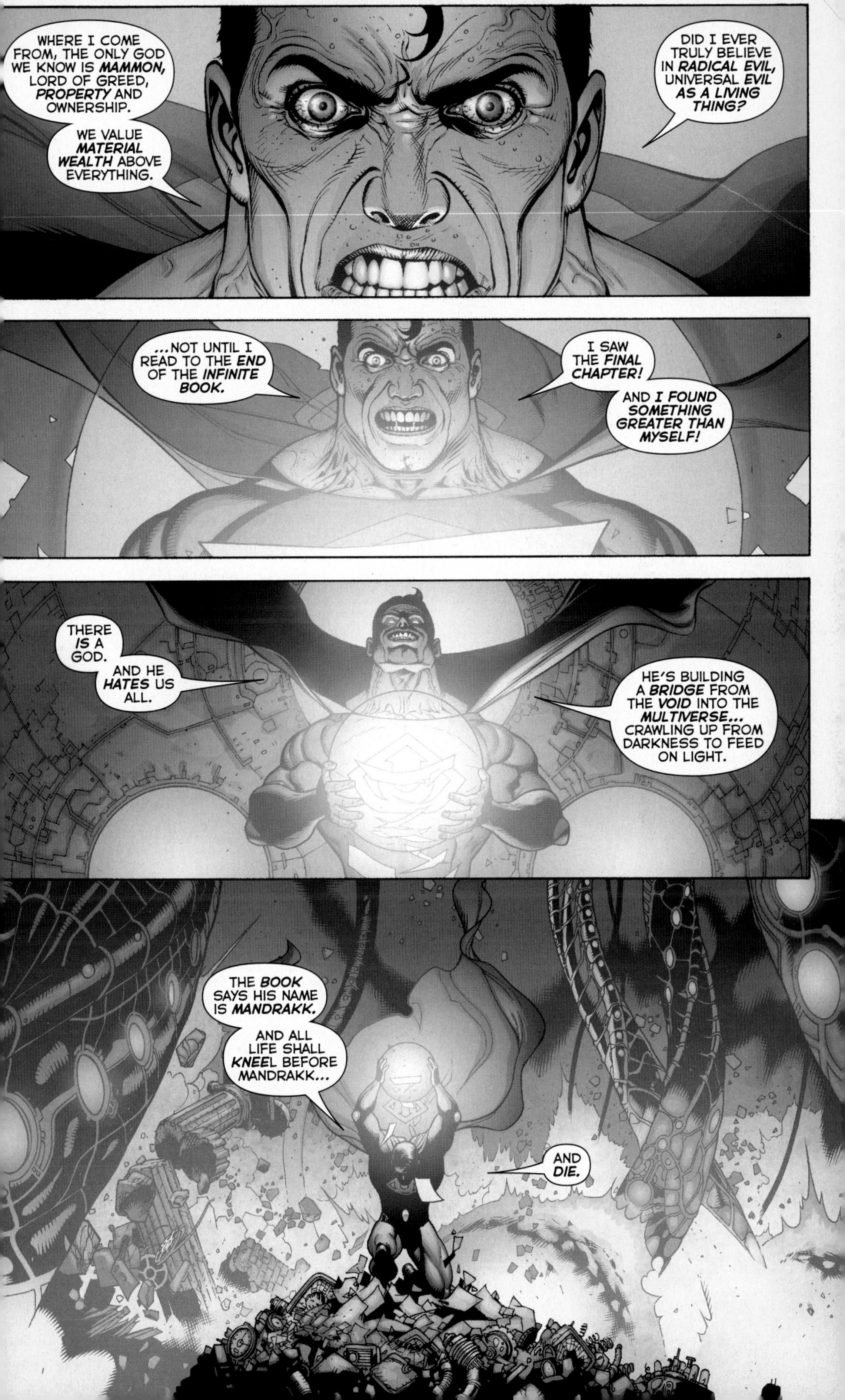
WHERE I COME FROM, THE ONLY GOD WE KNOW IS MAMMON, LORD OF GREED, PROPERTY AND OWNERSHIP.
WE VALUE MATERIAL WEALTH ABOVE EVERYTHING.
DID I EVER TRULY BELIEVE IN RADICAL EVIL, UNIVERSAL EVIL AS A LIVING THING?
...NOT UNTIL I READ TO THE END OF THE INFINITE BOOK.
I SAW THE FINAL CHAPTER!
AND I FOUND SOMETHING GREATER THAN MYSELF!
THERE IS A GOD.
AND HE HATES US ALL.
HE'S BUILDING A BRIDGE FROM THE VOID INTO THE MULTIVERSE... CRAWLING UP FROM DARKNESS TO FEED ON LIGHT.
THE BOOK SAYS HIS NAME IS MANDRAKK.
AND ALL LIFE SHALL KNEEL BEFORE MANDRAKK...
AND DIE.

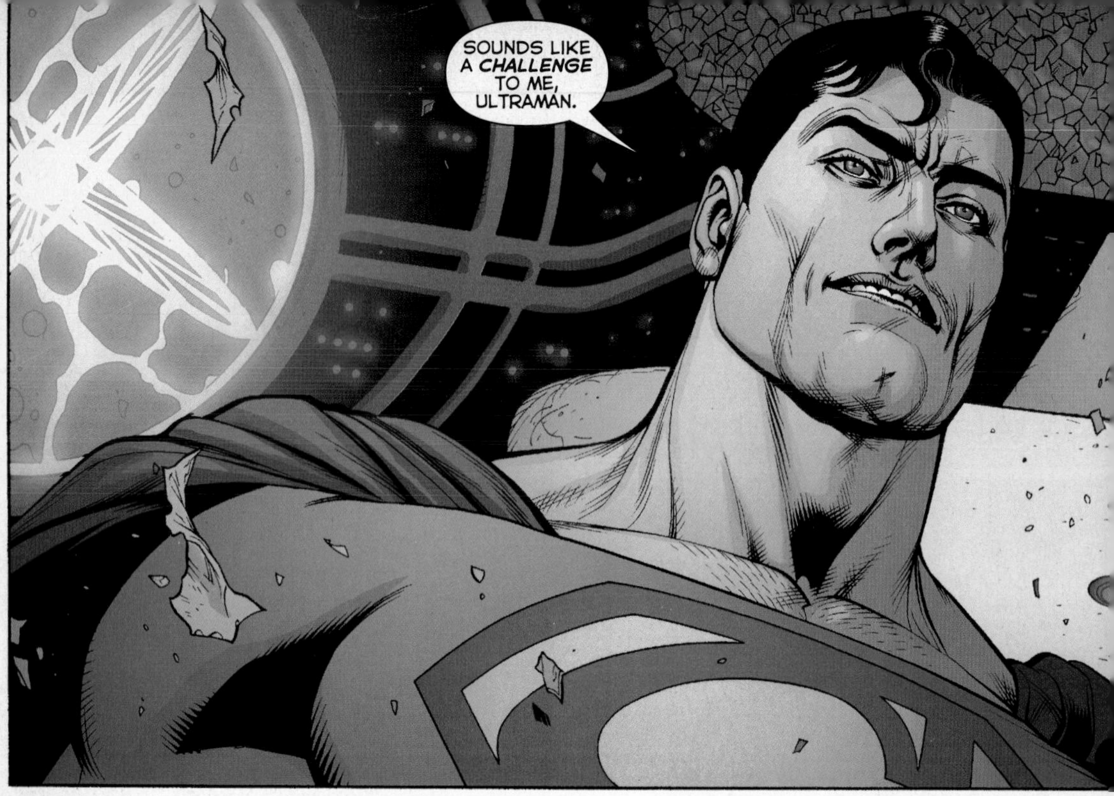
SOUNDS LIKE A *CHALLENGE* TO ME, ULTRAMAN.

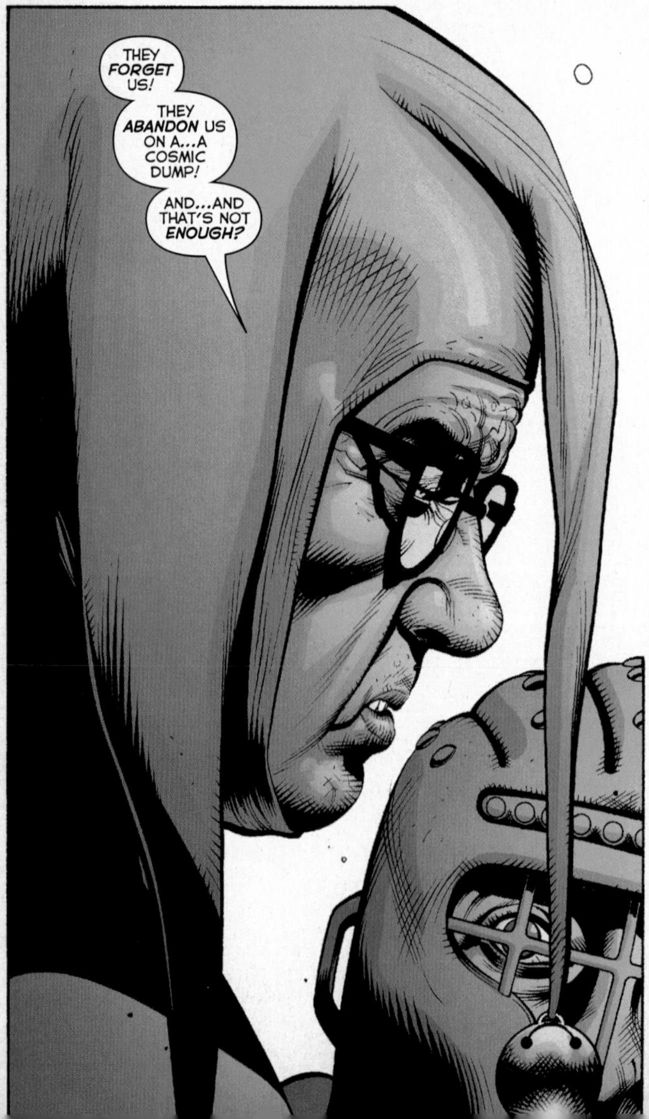
THEY *FORGET* US!
THEY *ABANDON* US ON A...A COSMIC DUMP!
AND...AND THAT'S NOT *ENOUGH?*

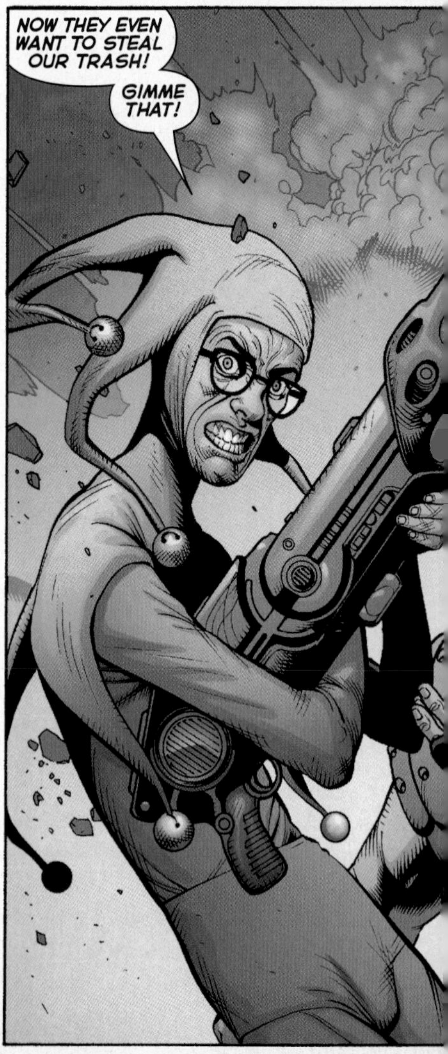
NOW THEY EVEN WANT TO STEAL OUR TRASH!
GIMME THAT!

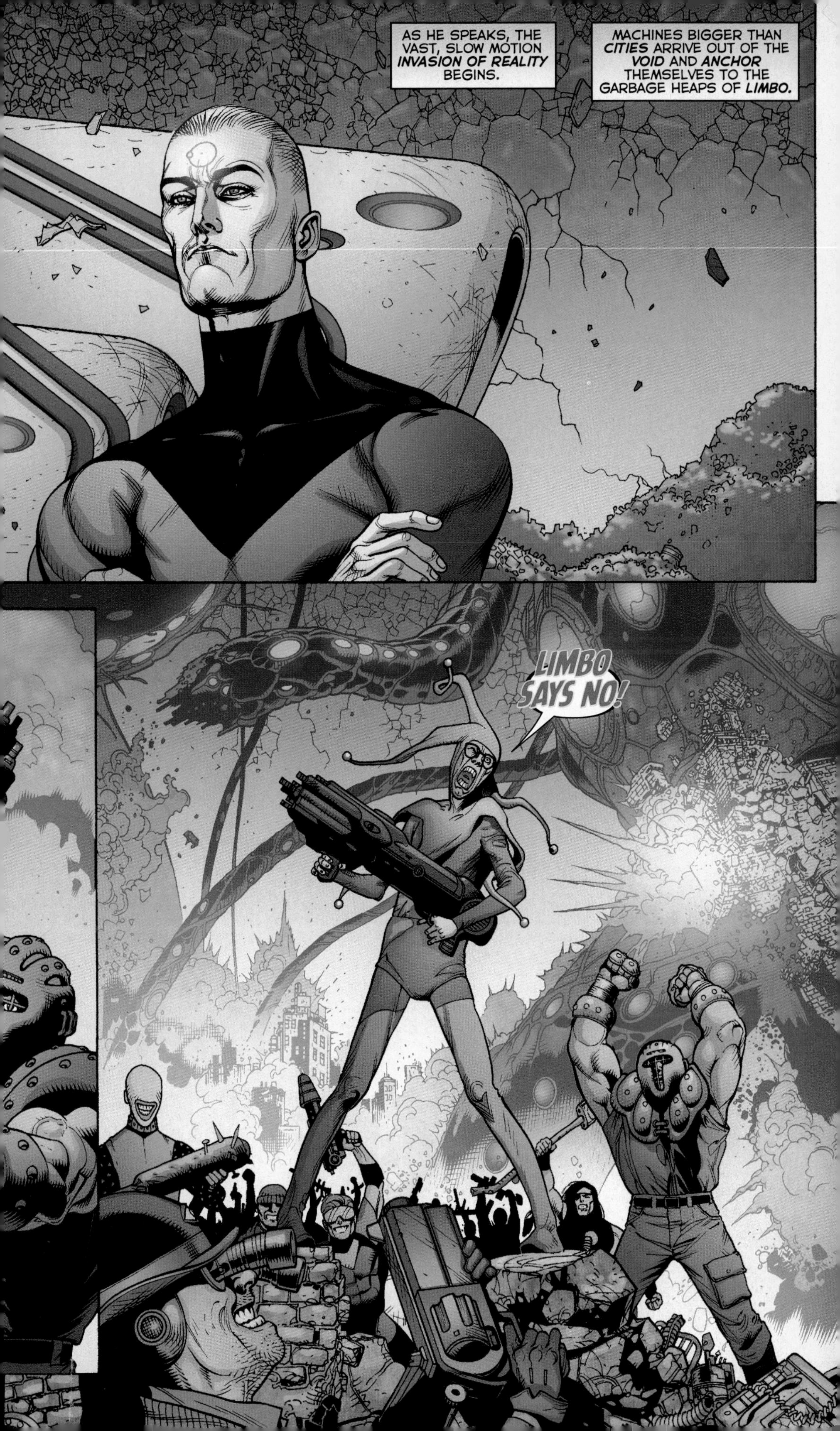
AS HE SPEAKS, THE VAST, SLOW MOTION *INVASION OF REALITY* BEGINS.
MACHINES BIGGER THAN *CITIES* ARRIVE OUT OF THE *VOID* AND *ANCHOR* THEMSELVES TO THE GARBAGE HEAPS OF *LIMBO.*
LIMBO SAYS NO!

...MANDRAKK WAKES!

THAT MEANS THE CIRCLE OF MONITORS HAS FALLEN.

52 UNIVERSES UNTENDED! UNDEFENDED!

...WHAT'S HAPPENING?

I WAS OUT COLD.

STAND AWAY FROM HER, BOY!

SHE'S A VAMPIRE!

SOMEONE HAS TO KILL HER BEFORE...

NO. AND TO BE PERFECTLY FRANK, I DON'T MUCH LIKE NAZIS TELLING ME WHAT TO DO.

SIE VERSTEHEN NICHT!

MY ROCKET FROM KRYPTON ARRIVED IN A FIELD IN THE OCCUPIED SUDETENLAND IN 1938.

GERMAN ROCKET SCIENTISTS RETRO-ENGINEERED THE TECHNOLOGY HERR HITLER USED TO WIN THE WAR, AND I...

I AND MY KIND INHERITED A UTOPIA BUILT ON HUMAN SUFFERING.

MINE IS NOT ANY WORLD YOU KNOW.

I LEFT MY WORLD IN CRISIS TO SEARCH FOR MY LOST COUSIN.

MY TREASURE.

I CANNOT PERMIT TH[E] MONSTE[R] TO DECEIV[E] US ANY FURTHER

I GUESS EVERY MONSTER HA[S] A STORY, OVERMAN.

INCLUDING HER.

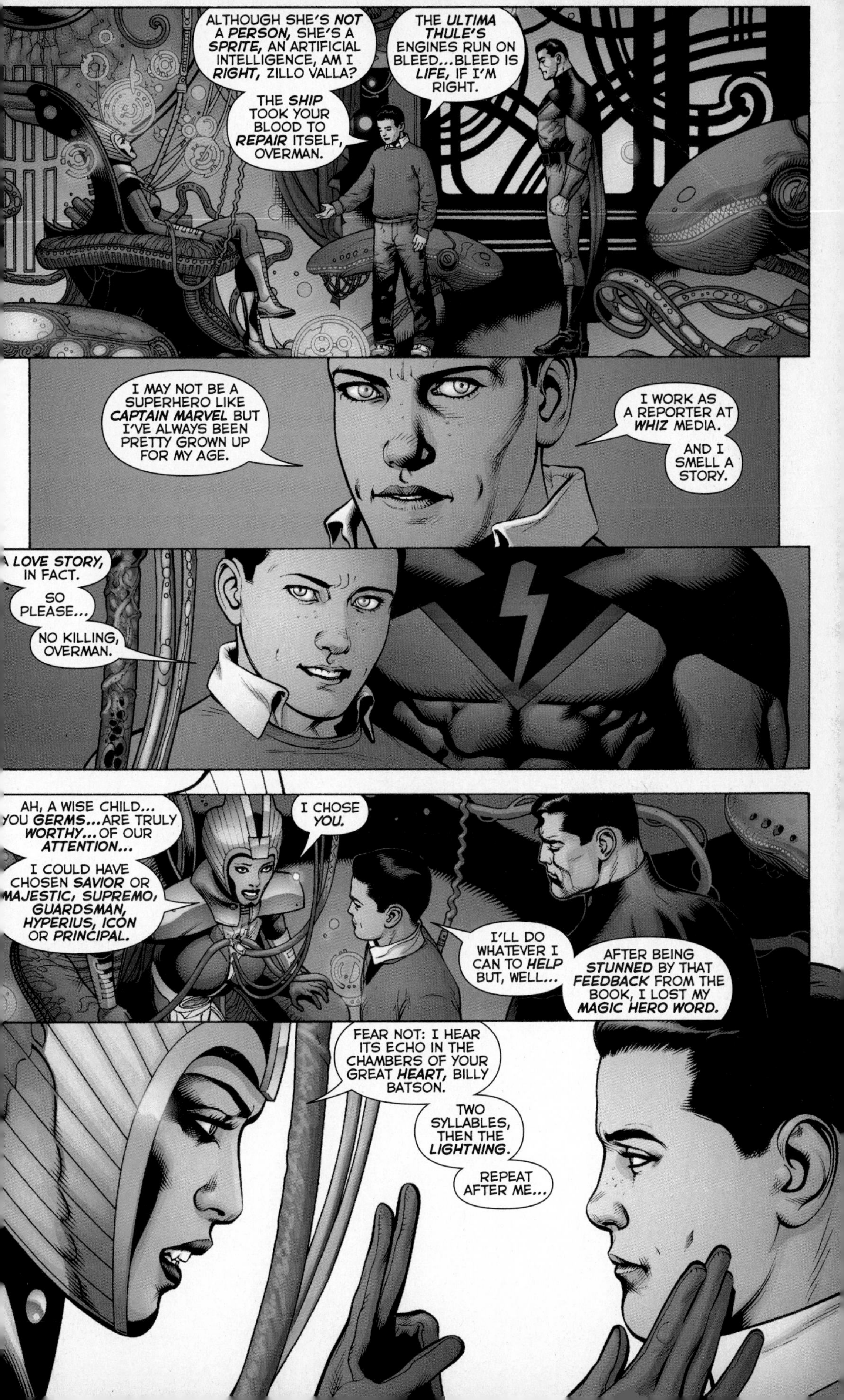
ALTHOUGH SHE'S NOT A PERSON, SHE'S A SPRITE, AN ARTIFICIAL INTELLIGENCE, AM I RIGHT, ZILLO VALLA?
THE SHIP TOOK YOUR BLOOD TO REPAIR ITSELF, OVERMAN.
THE ULTIMA THULE'S ENGINES RUN ON BLEED...BLEED IS LIFE, IF I'M RIGHT.
I MAY NOT BE A SUPERHERO LIKE CAPTAIN MARVEL BUT I'VE ALWAYS BEEN PRETTY GROWN UP FOR MY AGE.
I WORK AS A REPORTER AT WHIZ MEDIA.
AND I SMELL A STORY.
A LOVE STORY, IN FACT.
SO PLEASE...
NO KILLING, OVERMAN.
AH, A WISE CHILD... YOU GERMS...ARE TRULY WORTHY...OF OUR ATTENTION...
I COULD HAVE CHOSEN SAVIOR OR MAJESTIC, SUPREMO, GUARDSMAN, HYPERIUS, ICON OR PRINCIPAL.
I CHOSE YOU.
I'LL DO WHATEVER I CAN TO HELP BUT, WELL...
AFTER BEING STUNNED BY THAT FEEDBACK FROM THE BOOK, I LOST MY MAGIC HERO WORD.
FEAR NOT: I HEAR ITS ECHO IN THE CHAMBERS OF YOUR GREAT HEART, BILLY BATSON.
TWO SYLLABLES, THEN THE LIGHTNING.
REPEAT AFTER ME...

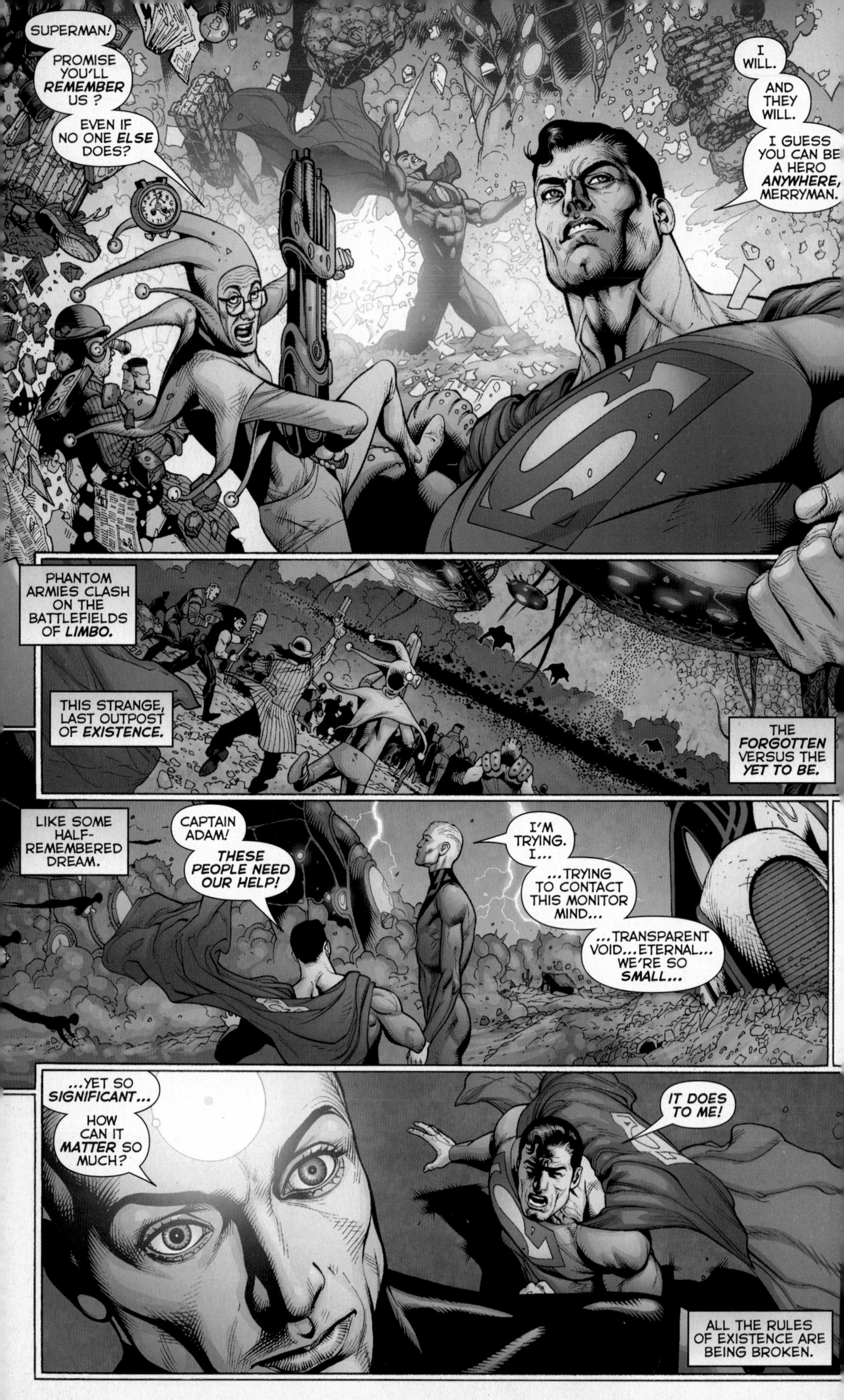
SUPERMAN!
PROMISE YOU'LL *REMEMBER* US ?
EVEN IF NO ONE *ELSE* DOES?
I WILL.
AND THEY WILL.
I GUESS YOU CAN BE A HERO *ANYWHERE,* MERRYMAN.
PHANTOM ARMIES CLASH ON THE BATTLEFIELDS OF *LIMBO.*
THIS STRANGE, LAST OUTPOST OF *EXISTENCE.*
THE *FORGOTTEN* VERSUS THE *YET TO BE.*
LIKE SOME HALF-REMEMBERED DREAM.
CAPTAIN ADAM! *THESE PEOPLE NEED OUR HELP!*
I'M TRYING. I...
...TRYING TO CONTACT THIS MONITOR MIND...
...TRANSPARENT VOID...ETERNAL... WE'RE SO *SMALL...*
...YET SO *SIGNIFICANT...*
HOW CAN IT *MATTER* SO MUCH?
IT DOES TO ME!
ALL THE RULES OF EXISTENCE ARE BEING BROKEN.

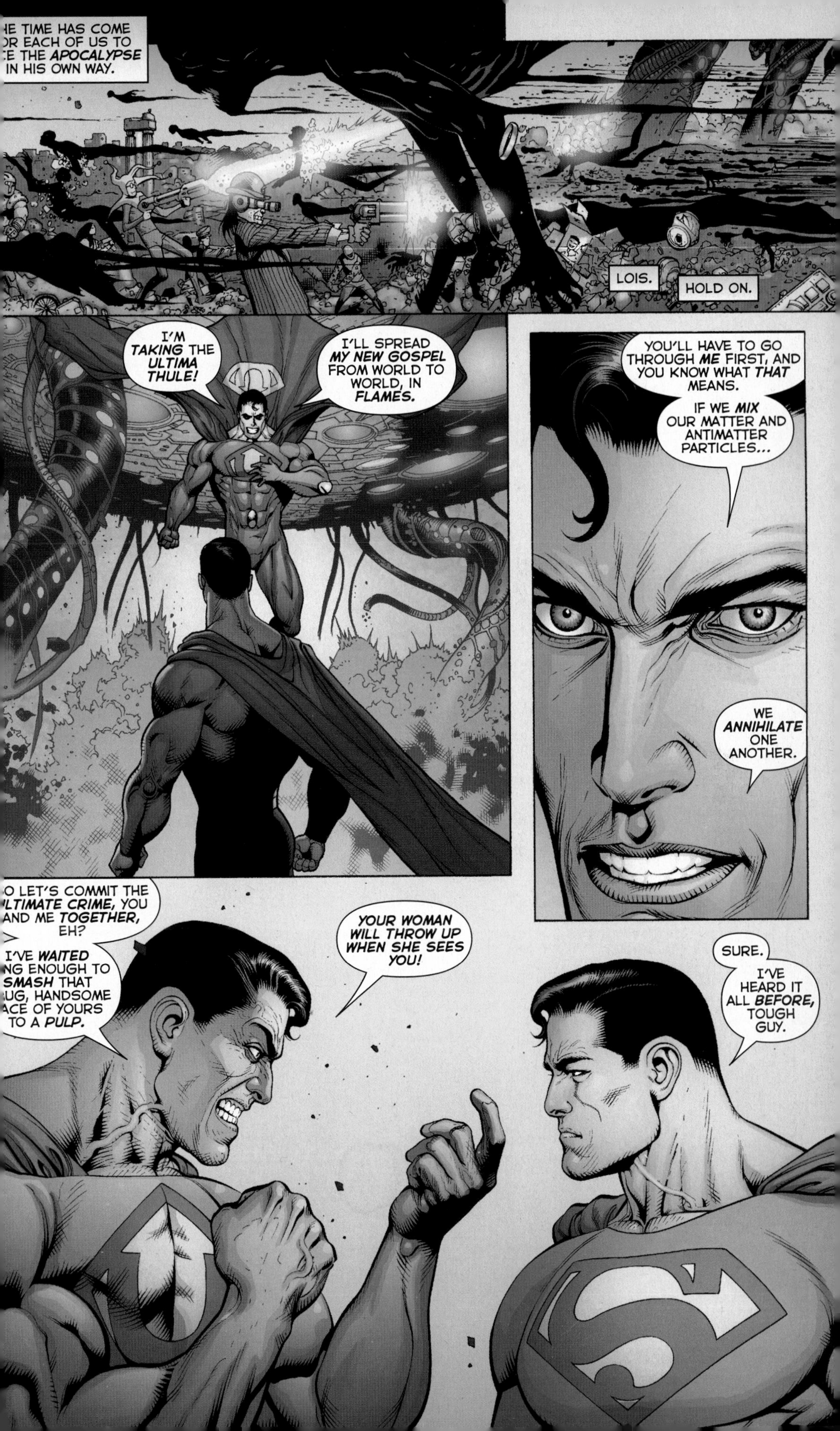

HE TIME HAS COME OR EACH OF US TO CE THE *APOCALYPSE* IN HIS OWN WAY.
LOIS.
HOLD ON.
I'M *TAKING* THE *ULTIMA THULE!*
I'LL SPREAD *MY NEW GOSPEL* FROM WORLD TO WORLD, IN *FLAMES.*
YOU'LL HAVE TO GO THROUGH *ME* FIRST, AND YOU KNOW WHAT *THAT* MEANS.
IF WE *MIX* OUR MATTER AND ANTIMATTER PARTICLES...
WE *ANNIHILATE* ONE ANOTHER.
O LET'S COMMIT THE *ULTIMATE CRIME,* YOU AND ME *TOGETHER,* EH?
I'VE *WAITED* NG ENOUGH TO *SMASH* THAT UG, HANDSOME ACE OF YOURS TO A *PULP.*
YOUR WOMAN WILL THROW UP WHEN SHE SEES YOU!
SURE.
I'VE HEARD IT ALL *BEFORE,* TOUGH GUY.

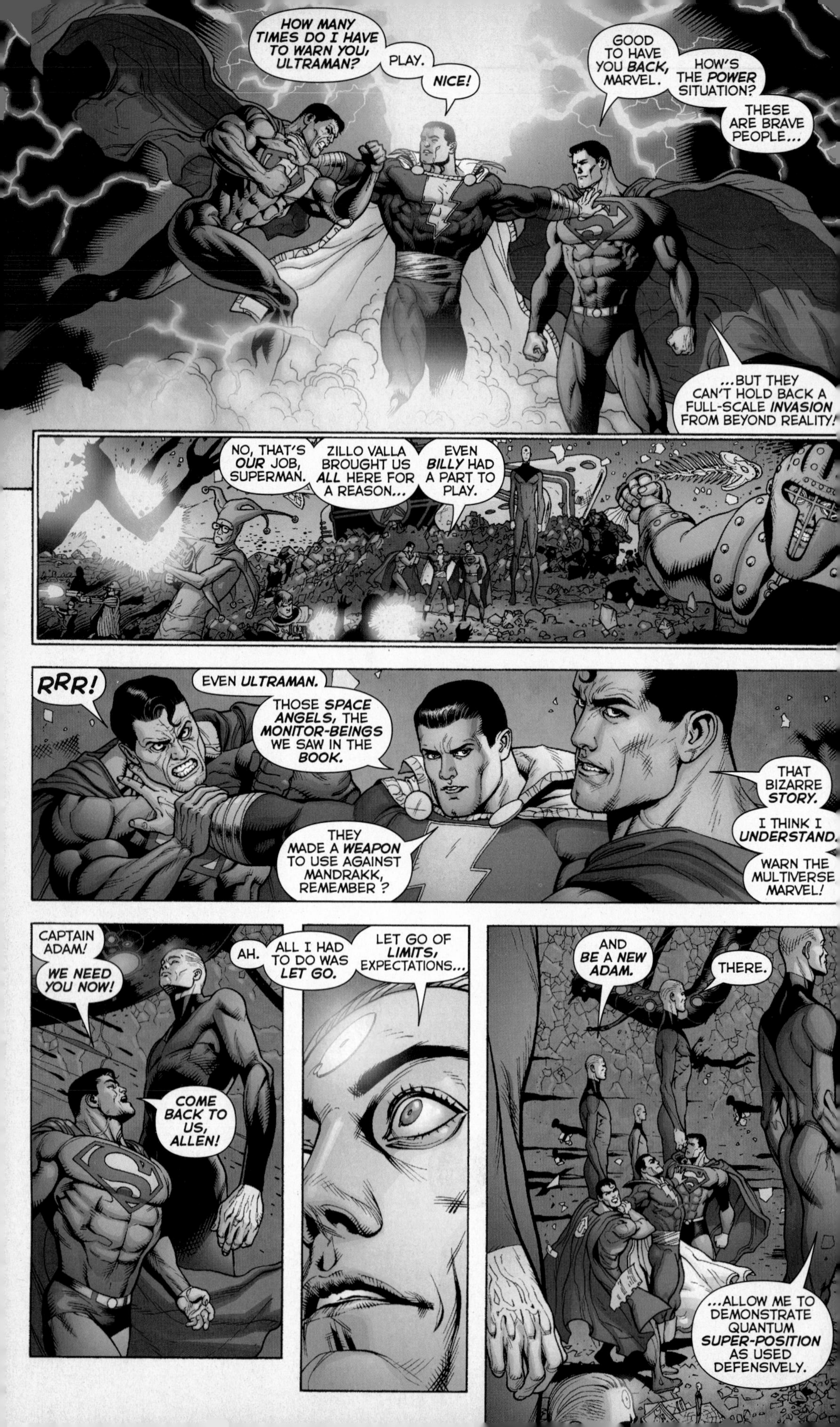
HOW MANY TIMES DO I HAVE TO WARN YOU, ULTRAMAN?
PLAY.
NICE!
GOOD TO HAVE YOU BACK, MARVEL.
HOW'S THE POWER SITUATION?
THESE ARE BRAVE PEOPLE...
...BUT THEY CAN'T HOLD BACK A FULL-SCALE INVASION FROM BEYOND REALITY!
NO, THAT'S OUR JOB, SUPERMAN.
ZILLO VALLA BROUGHT US ALL HERE FOR A REASON...
EVEN BILLY HAD A PART TO PLAY.
RRR!
EVEN ULTRAMAN.
THOSE SPACE ANGELS, THE MONITOR-BEINGS WE SAW IN THE BOOK.
THEY MADE A WEAPON TO USE AGAINST MANDRAKK, REMEMBER ?
THAT BIZARRE STORY.
I THINK I UNDERSTAND.
WARN THE MULTIVERSE MARVEL!
CAPTAIN ADAM!
WE NEED YOU NOW!
COME BACK TO US, ALLEN!
AH.
ALL I HAD TO DO WAS LET GO.
LET GO OF LIMITS, EXPECTATIONS...
AND BE A NEW ADAM.
THERE.
...ALLOW ME TO DEMONSTRATE QUANTUM SUPER-POSITION AS USED DEFENSIVELY.

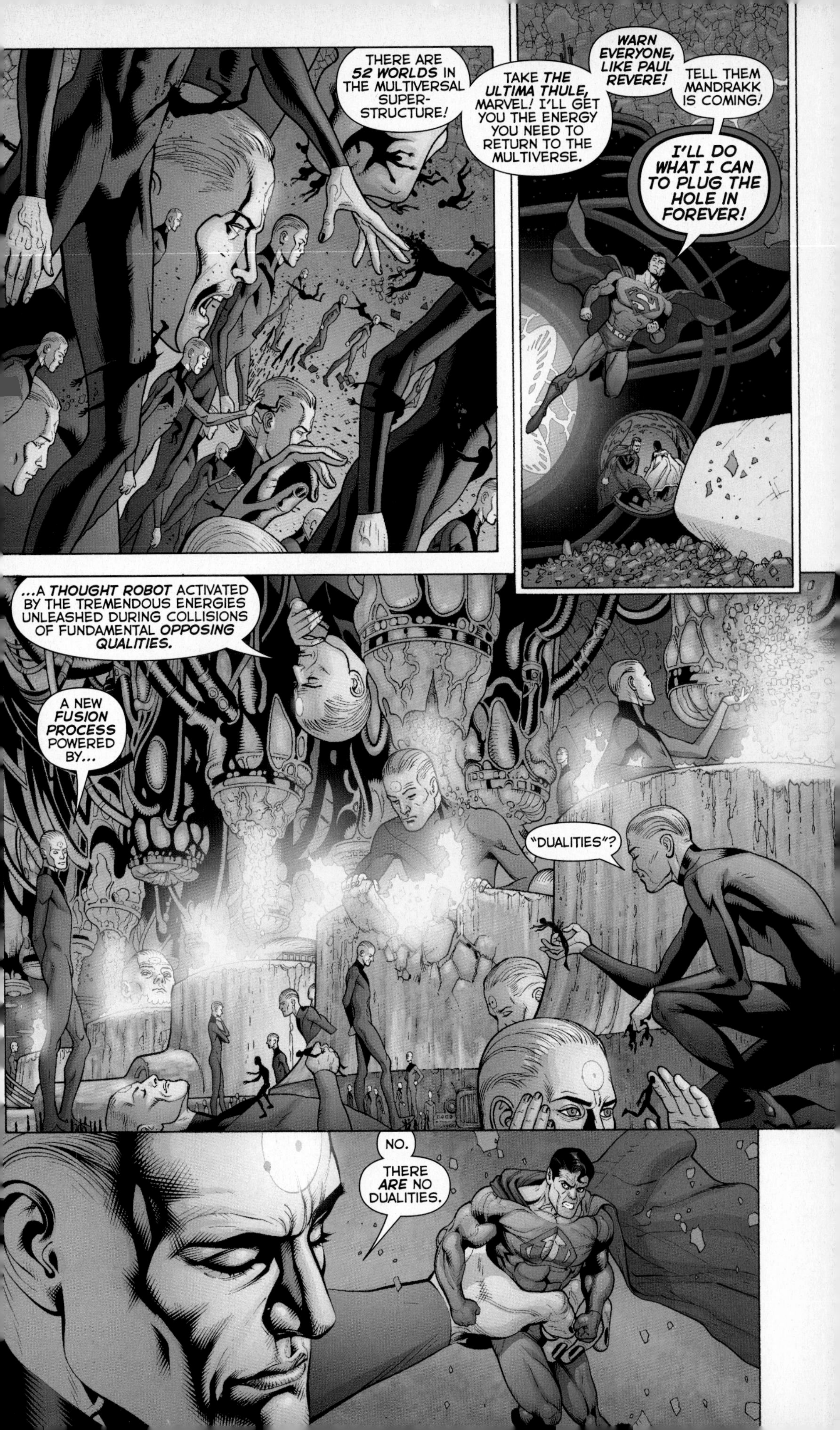
THERE ARE 52 WORLDS IN THE MULTIVERSAL SUPER-STRUCTURE!
TAKE THE ULTIMA THULE, MARVEL! I'LL GET YOU THE ENERGY YOU NEED TO RETURN TO THE MULTIVERSE.
WARN EVERYONE, LIKE PAUL REVERE!
TELL THEM MANDRAKK IS COMING!
I'LL DO WHAT I CAN TO PLUG THE HOLE IN FOREVER!
...A THOUGHT ROBOT ACTIVATED BY THE TREMENDOUS ENERGIES UNLEASHED DURING COLLISIONS OF FUNDAMENTAL OPPOSING QUALITIES.
A NEW FUSION PROCESS POWERED BY...
"DUALITIES"?
NO.
THERE ARE NO DUALITIES.

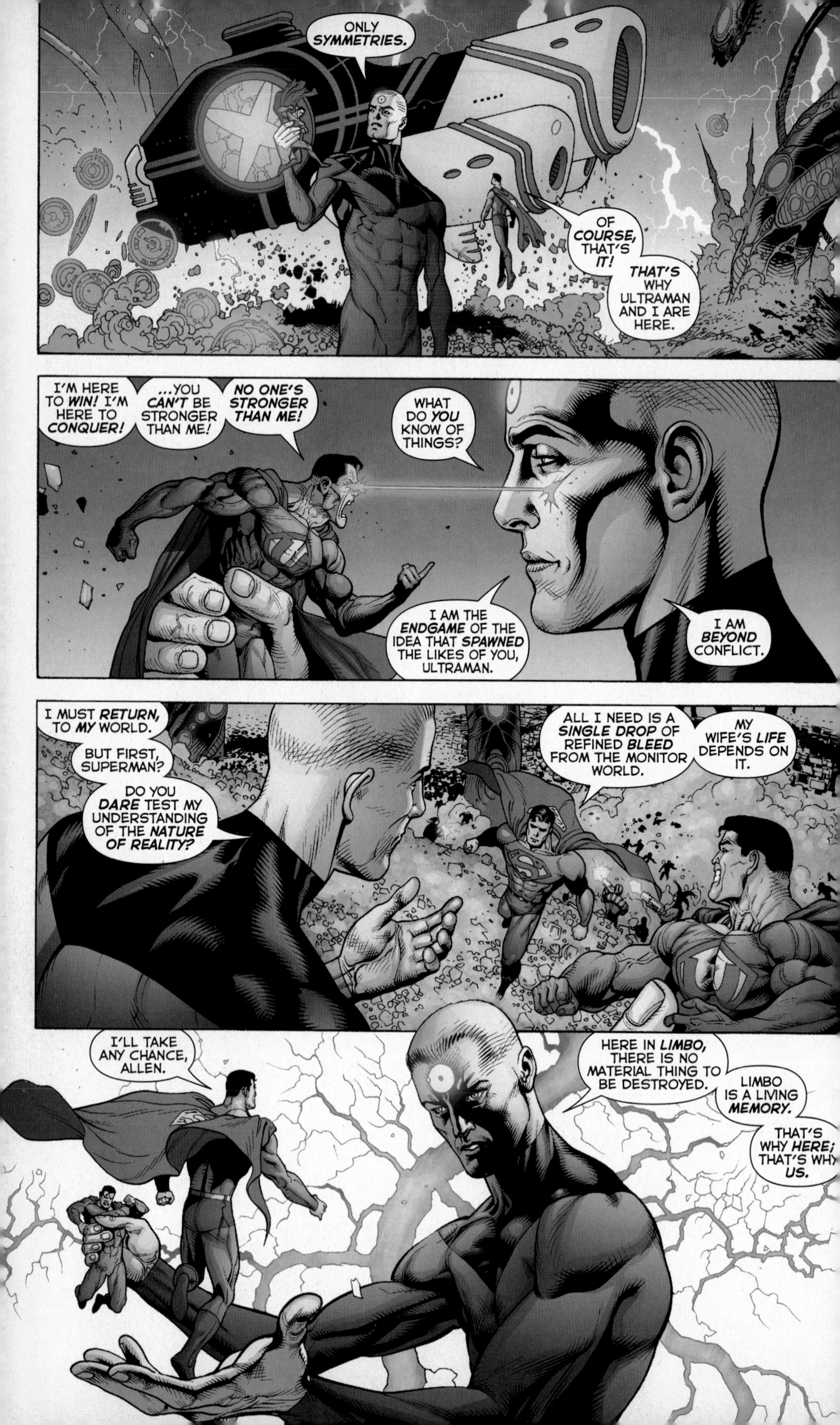

ONLY SYMMETRIES.
OF COURSE, THAT'S IT!
THAT'S WHY ULTRAMAN AND I ARE HERE.
I'M HERE TO WIN! I'M HERE TO CONQUER!
...YOU CAN'T BE STRONGER THAN ME!
NO ONE'S STRONGER THAN ME!
WHAT DO YOU KNOW OF THINGS?
I AM THE ENDGAME OF THE IDEA THAT SPAWNED THE LIKES OF YOU, ULTRAMAN.
I AM BEYOND CONFLICT.
I MUST RETURN, TO MY WORLD.
BUT FIRST, SUPERMAN?
DO YOU DARE TEST MY UNDERSTANDING OF THE NATURE OF REALITY?
ALL I NEED IS A SINGLE DROP OF REFINED BLEED FROM THE MONITOR WORLD.
MY WIFE'S LIFE DEPENDS ON IT.
I'LL TAKE ANY CHANCE, ALLEN.
HERE IN LIMBO, THERE IS NO MATERIAL THING TO BE DESTROYED.
LIMBO IS A LIVING MEMORY.
THAT'S WHY HERE; THAT'S WHY US.

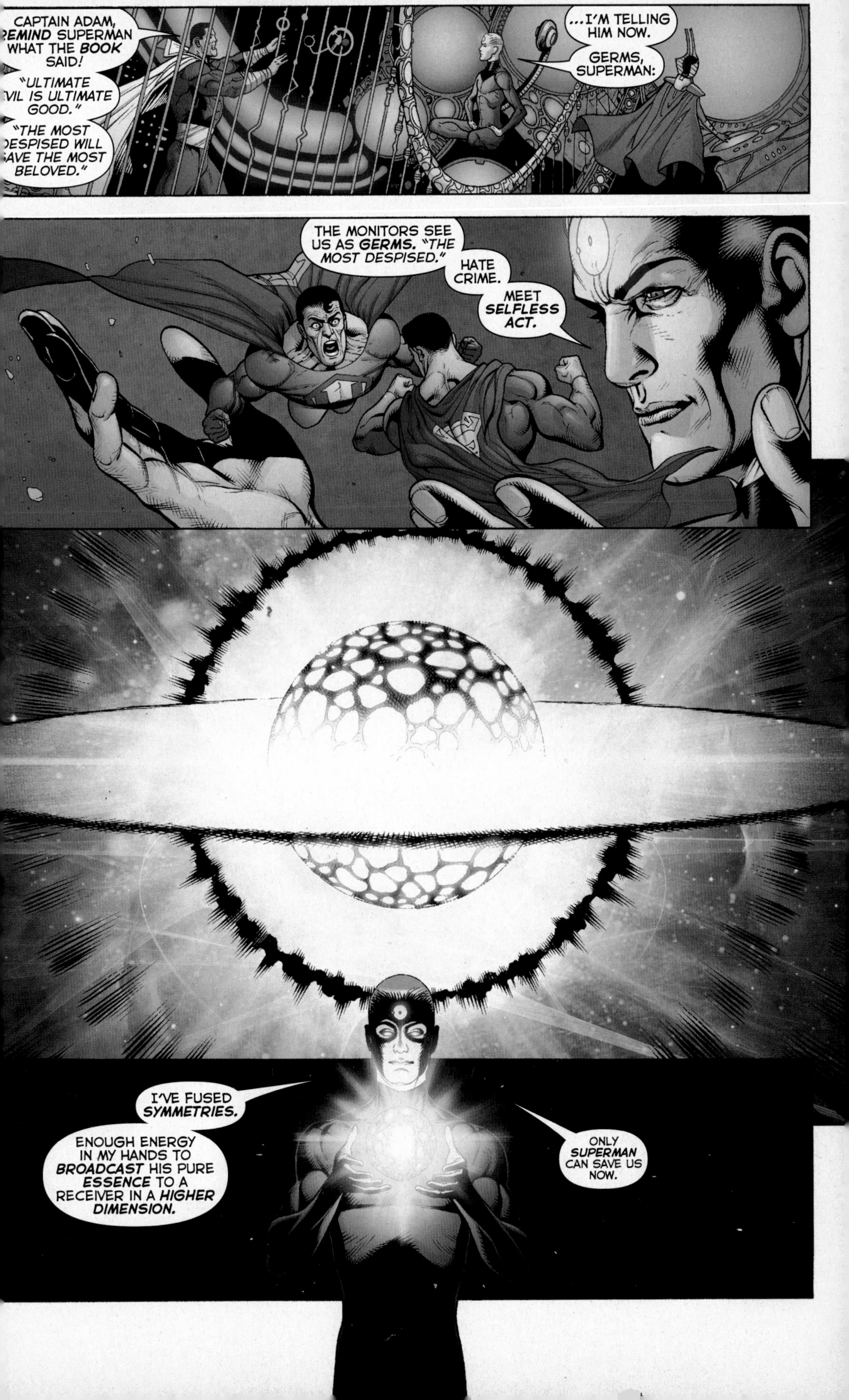
CAPTAIN ADAM, REMIND SUPERMAN WHAT THE BOOK SAID!
"ULTIMATE EVIL IS ULTIMATE GOOD."
"THE MOST DESPISED WILL SAVE THE MOST BELOVED."
...I'M TELLING HIM NOW.
GERMS, SUPERMAN:
THE MONITORS SEE US AS GERMS. "THE MOST DESPISED."
HATE CRIME.
MEET SELFLESS ACT.
I'VE FUSED SYMMETRIES.
ENOUGH ENERGY IN MY HANDS TO BROADCAST HIS PURE ESSENCE TO A RECEIVER IN A HIGHER DIMENSION.
ONLY SUPERMAN CAN SAVE US NOW.

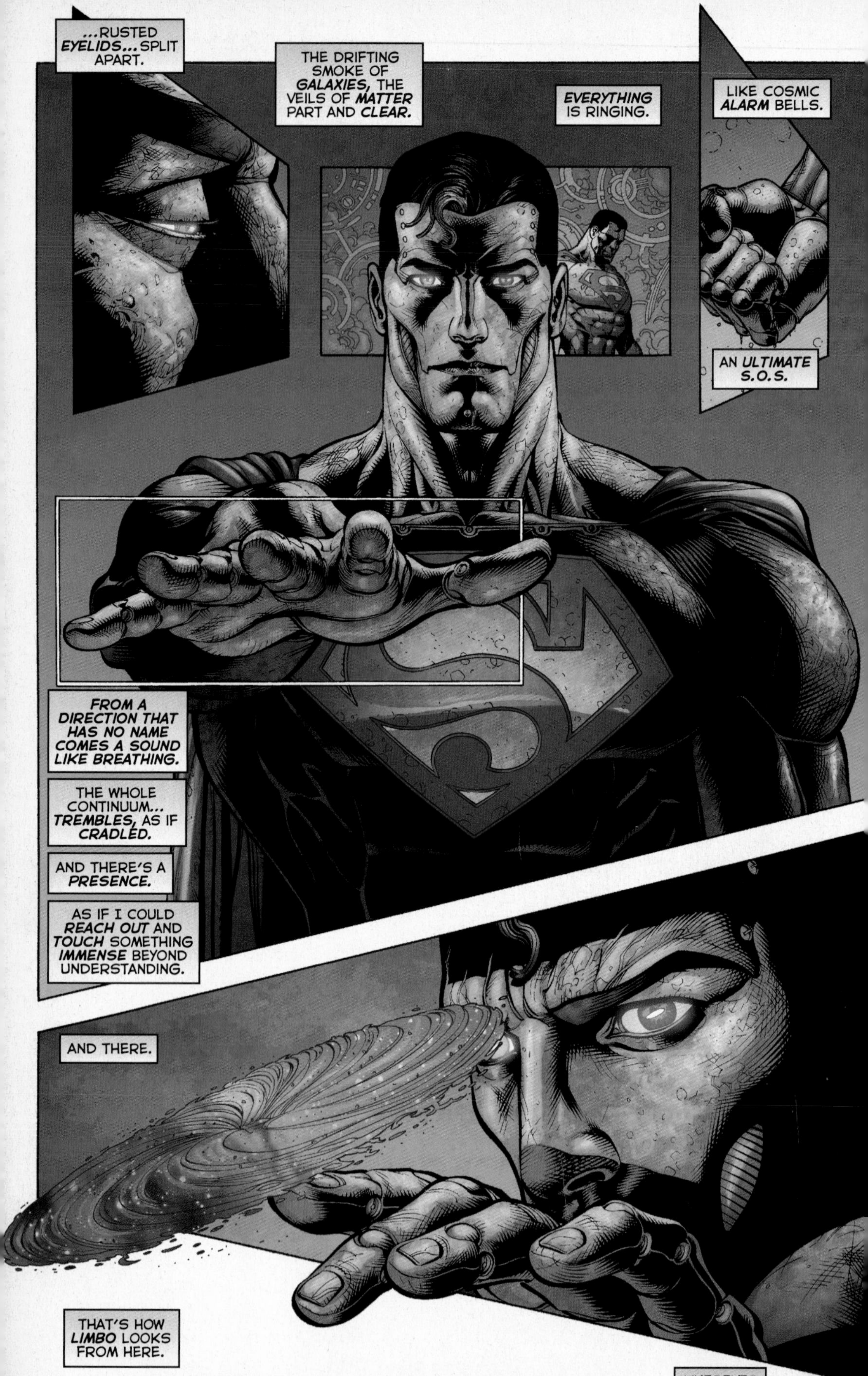

...RUSTED EYELIDS... SPLIT APART.
THE DRIFTING SMOKE OF GALAXIES, THE VEILS OF MATTER PART AND CLEAR.
EVERYTHING IS RINGING.
LIKE COSMIC ALARM BELLS.
AN ULTIMATE S.O.S.
FROM A DIRECTION THAT HAS NO NAME COMES A SOUND LIKE BREATHING.
THE WHOLE CONTINUUM... TREMBLES, AS IF CRADLED.
AND THERE'S A PRESENCE.
AS IF I COULD REACH OUT AND TOUCH SOMETHING IMMENSE BEYOND UNDERSTANDING.
AND THERE.
THAT'S HOW LIMBO LOOKS FROM HERE.
WHEREVER HERE IS.

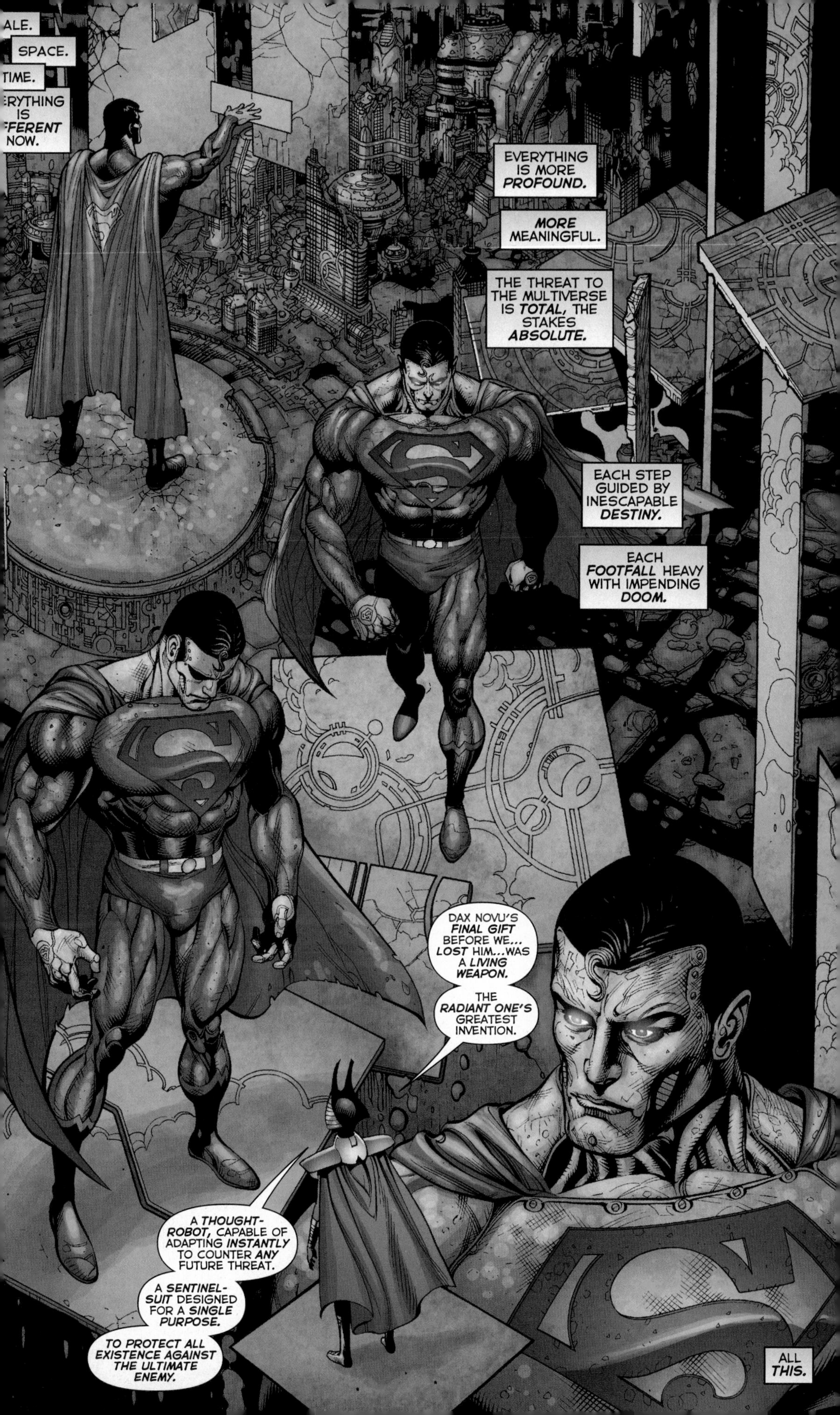
ALE.
SPACE.
TIME.
ERYTHING IS FFERENT NOW.
EVERYTHING IS MORE PROFOUND.
MORE MEANINGFUL.
THE THREAT TO THE MULTIVERSE IS TOTAL, THE STAKES ABSOLUTE.
EACH STEP GUIDED BY INESCAPABLE DESTINY.
EACH FOOTFALL HEAVY WITH IMPENDING DOOM.
DAX NOVU'S FINAL GIFT BEFORE WE... LOST HIM...WAS A LIVING WEAPON.
THE RADIANT ONE'S GREATEST INVENTION.
A THOUGHT-ROBOT, CAPABLE OF ADAPTING INSTANTLY TO COUNTER ANY FUTURE THREAT.
A SENTINEL-SUIT DESIGNED FOR A SINGLE PURPOSE.
TO PROTECT ALL EXISTENCE AGAINST THE ULTIMATE ENEMY.
ALL THIS.

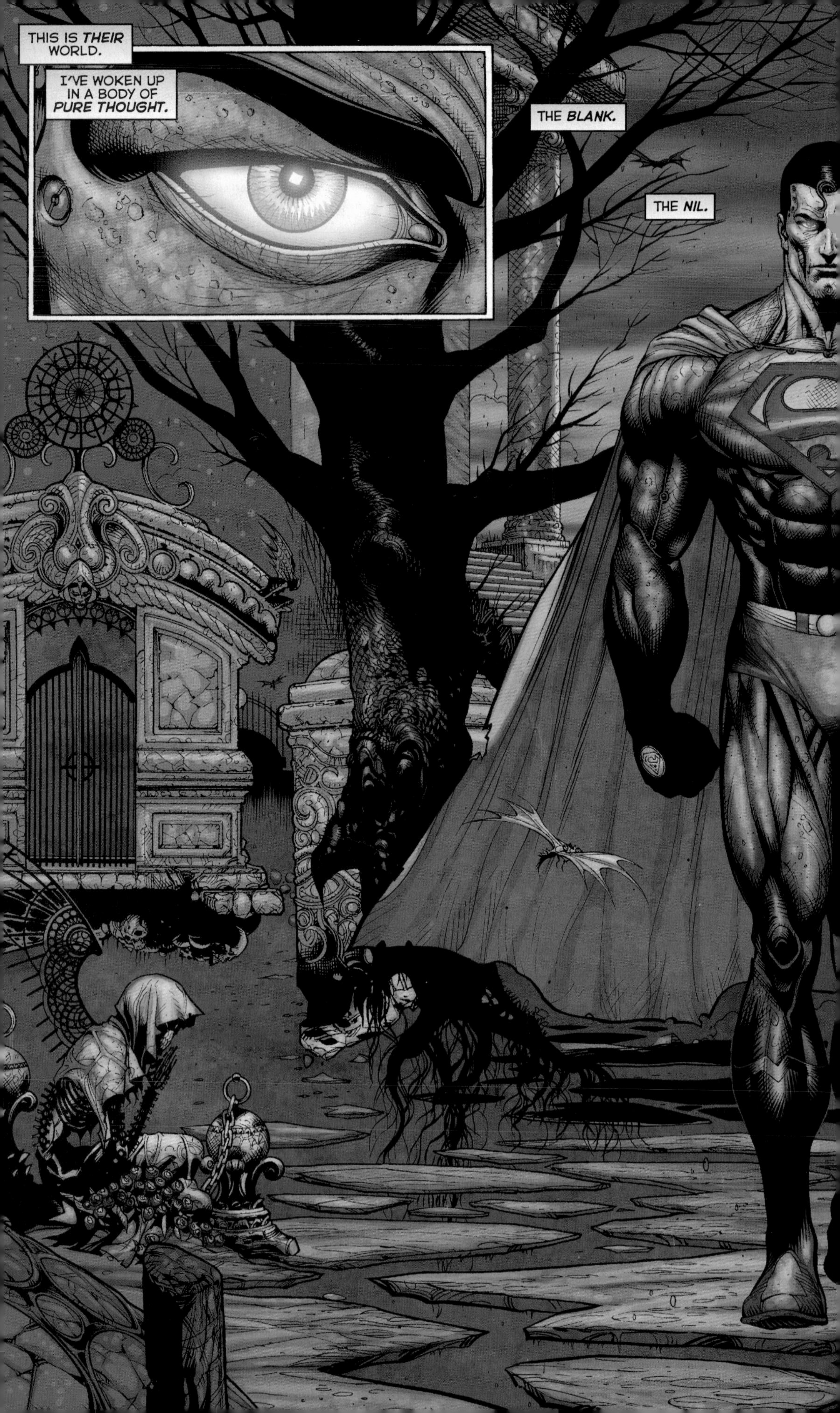
THIS IS *THEIR* WORLD.
I'VE WOKEN UP IN A BODY OF *PURE THOUGHT.*
THE *BLANK.*
THE *NIL.*

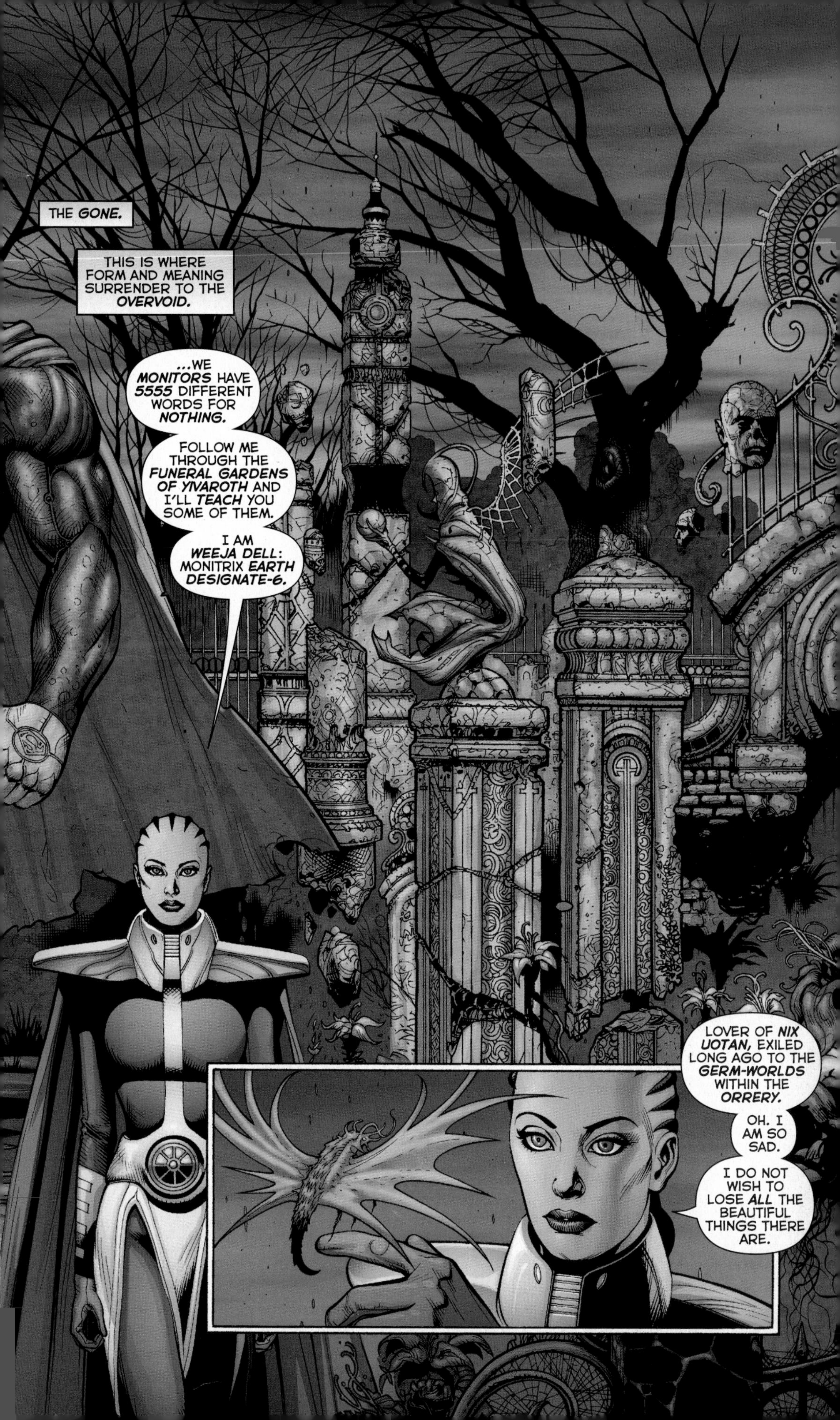
THE GONE.
THIS IS WHERE FORM AND MEANING SURRENDER TO THE OVERVOID.
...WE MONITORS HAVE 5555 DIFFERENT WORDS FOR NOTHING.
FOLLOW ME THROUGH THE FUNERAL GARDENS OF YIVAROTH AND I'LL TEACH YOU SOME OF THEM.
I AM WEEJA DELL: MONITRIX EARTH DESIGNATE-6.
LOVER OF NIX UOTAN, EXILED LONG AGO TO THE GERM-WORLDS WITHIN THE ORRERY.
OH. I AM SO SAD.
I DO NOT WISH TO LOSE ALL THE BEAUTIFUL THINGS THERE ARE.

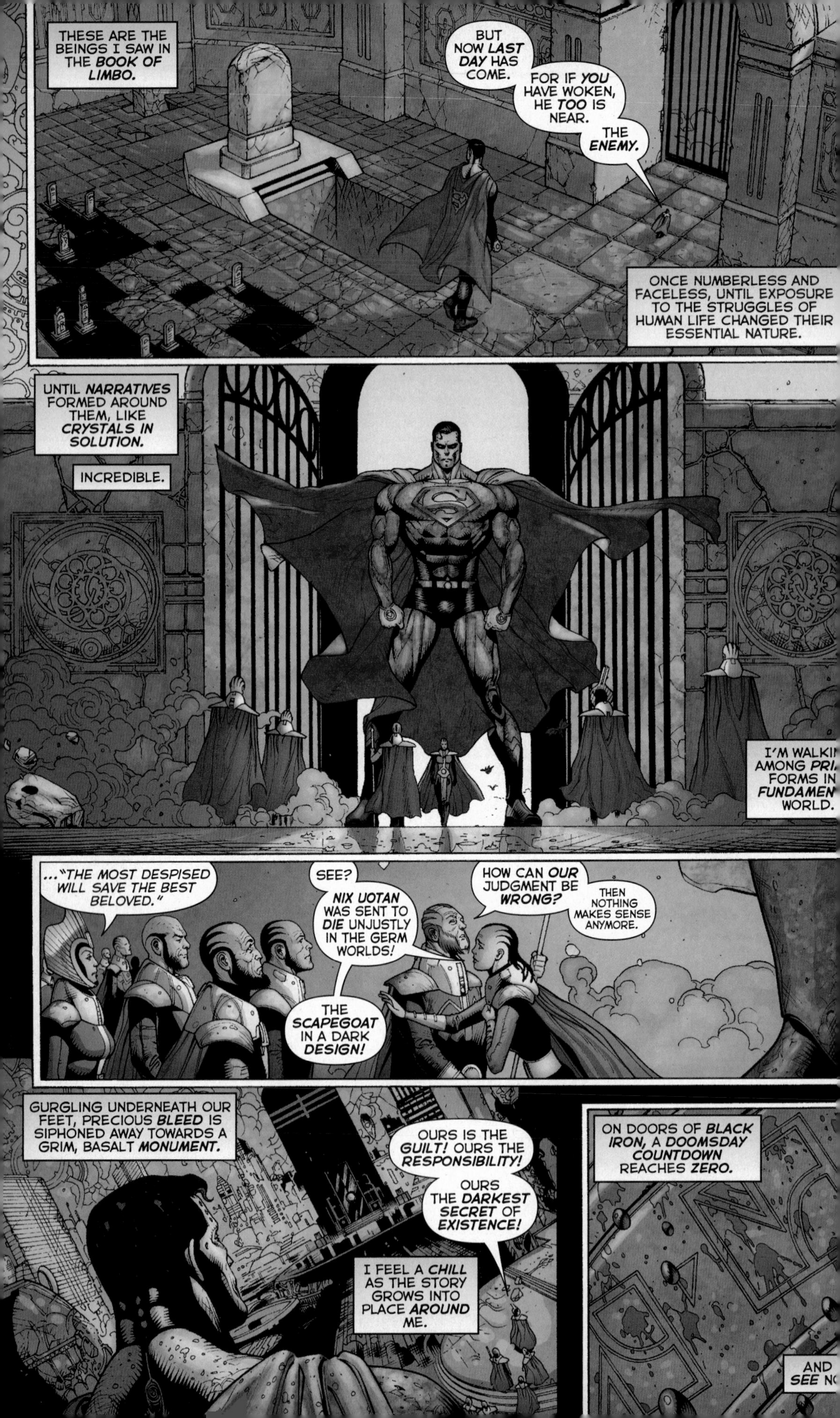
THESE ARE THE BEINGS I SAW IN THE BOOK OF LIMBO.
BUT NOW LAST DAY HAS COME.
FOR IF YOU HAVE WOKEN, HE TOO IS NEAR.
THE ENEMY.
ONCE NUMBERLESS AND FACELESS, UNTIL EXPOSURE TO THE STRUGGLES OF HUMAN LIFE CHANGED THEIR ESSENTIAL NATURE.
UNTIL NARRATIVES FORMED AROUND THEM, LIKE CRYSTALS IN SOLUTION.
INCREDIBLE.
I'M WALKI AMONG PRI FORMS IN FUNDAMEN WORLD.
..."THE MOST DESPISED WILL SAVE THE BEST BELOVED."
SEE? NIX UOTAN WAS SENT TO DIE UNJUSTLY IN THE GERM WORLDS!
THE SCAPEGOAT IN A DARK DESIGN!
HOW CAN OUR JUDGMENT BE WRONG?
THEN NOTHING MAKES SENSE ANYMORE.
GURGLING UNDERNEATH OUR FEET, PRECIOUS BLEED IS SIPHONED AWAY TOWARDS A GRIM, BASALT MONUMENT.
OURS IS THE GUILT! OURS THE RESPONSIBILITY!
OURS THE DARKEST SECRET OF EXISTENCE!
I FEEL A CHILL AS THE STORY GROWS INTO PLACE AROUND ME.
ON DOORS OF BLACK IRON, A DOOMSDAY COUNTDOWN REACHES ZERO.
AND SEE N

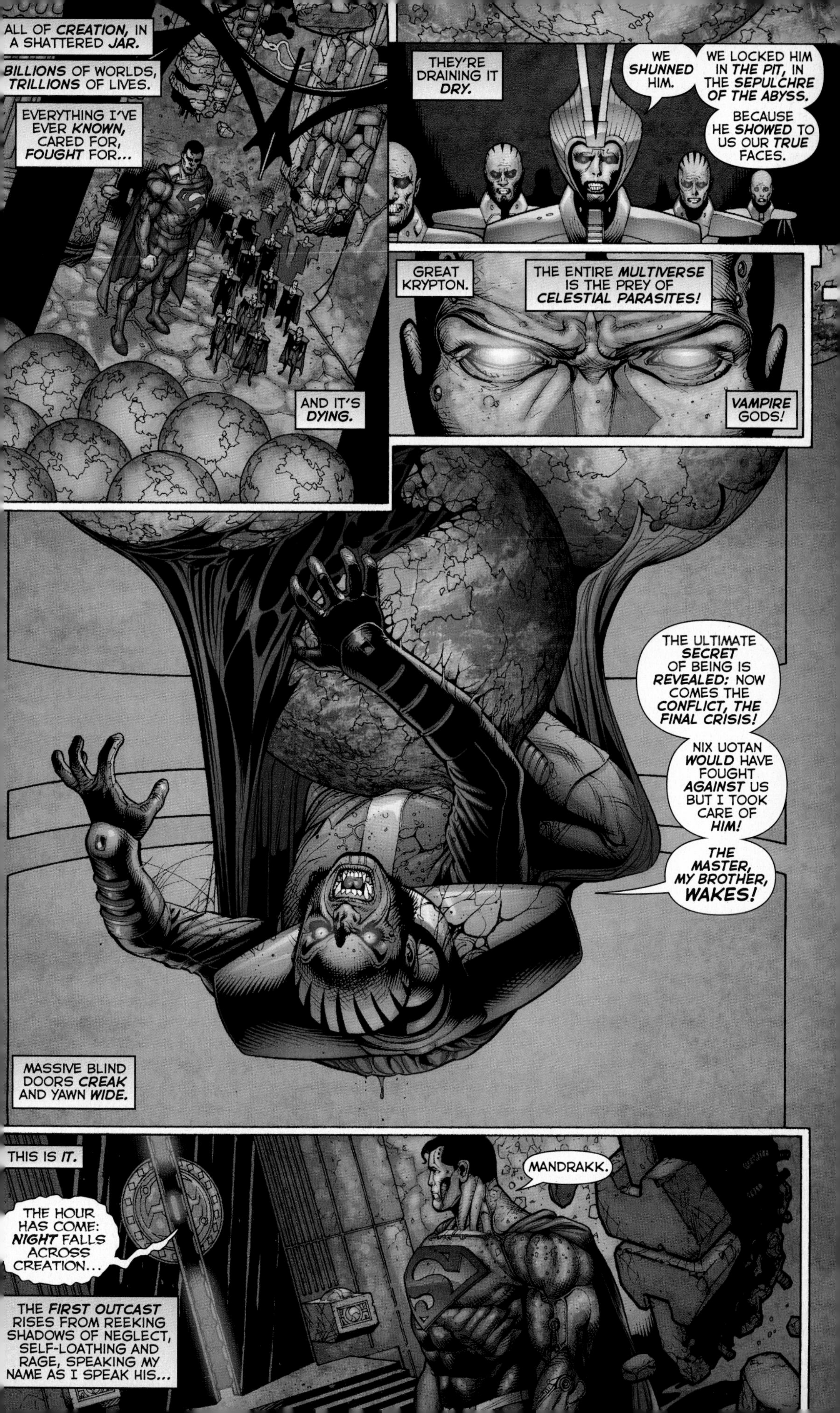
ALL OF CREATION, IN A SHATTERED JAR.
BILLIONS OF WORLDS, TRILLIONS OF LIVES.
EVERYTHING I'VE EVER KNOWN, CARED FOR, FOUGHT FOR...
AND IT'S DYING.
THEY'RE DRAINING IT DRY.
WE SHUNNED HIM.
WE LOCKED HIM IN THE PIT, IN THE SEPULCHRE OF THE ABYSS.
BECAUSE HE SHOWED TO US OUR TRUE FACES.
GREAT KRYPTON.
THE ENTIRE MULTIVERSE IS THE PREY OF CELESTIAL PARASITES!
VAMPIRE GODS!
THE ULTIMATE SECRET OF BEING IS REVEALED: NOW COMES THE CONFLICT, THE FINAL CRISIS!
NIX UOTAN WOULD HAVE FOUGHT AGAINST US BUT I TOOK CARE OF HIM!
THE MASTER, MY BROTHER, WAKES!
MASSIVE BLIND DOORS CREAK AND YAWN WIDE.
THIS IS IT.
MANDRAKK.
THE HOUR HAS COME: NIGHT FALLS ACROSS CREATION...
THE FIRST OUTCAST RISES FROM REEKING SHADOWS OF NEGLECT, SELF-LOATHING AND RAGE, SPEAKING MY NAME AS I SPEAK HIS...

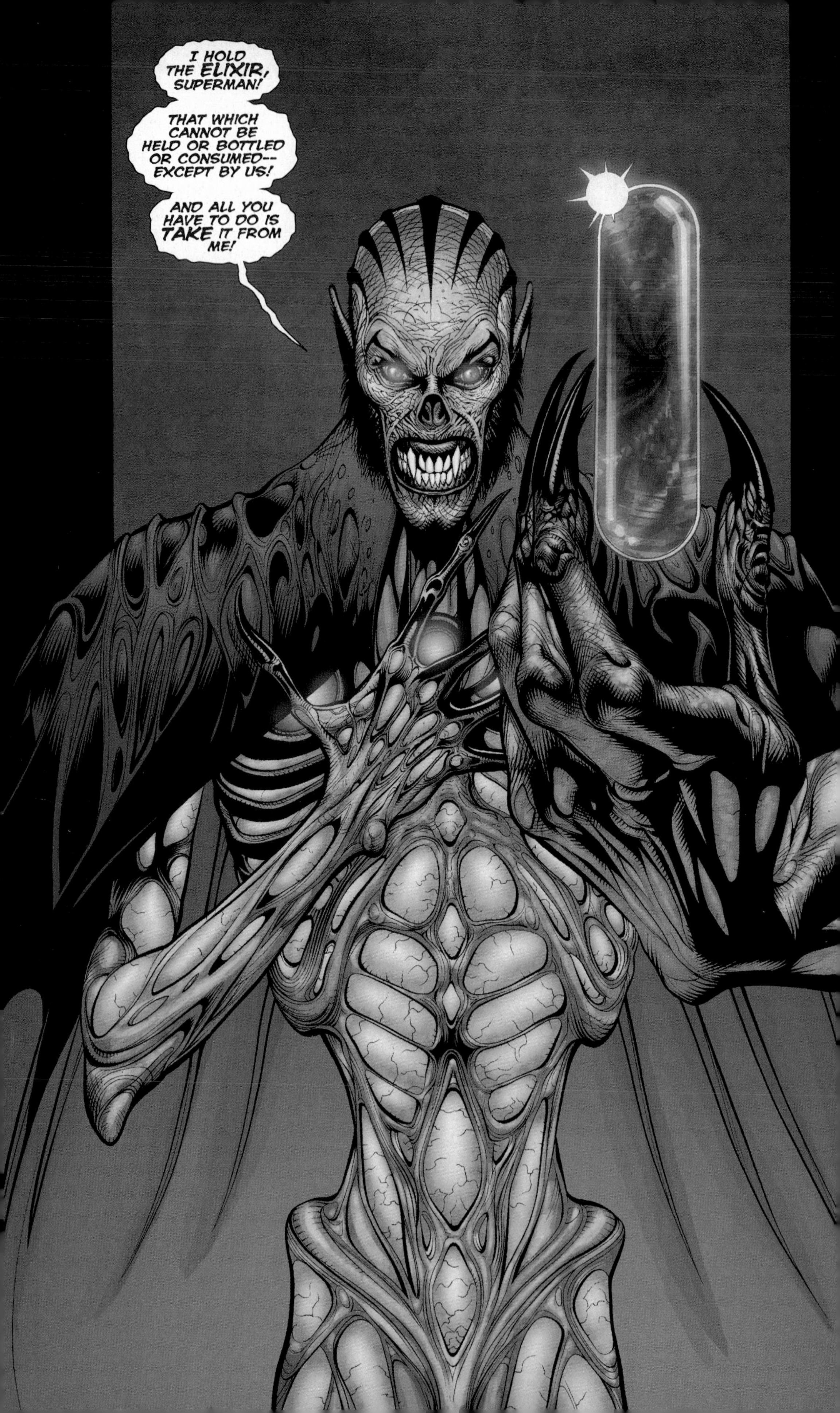
I HOLD THE ELIXIR, SUPERMAN!
THAT WHICH CANNOT BE HELD OR BOTTLED OR CONSUMED--- EXCEPT BY US!
AND ALL YOU HAVE TO DO IS TAKE IT FROM ME!

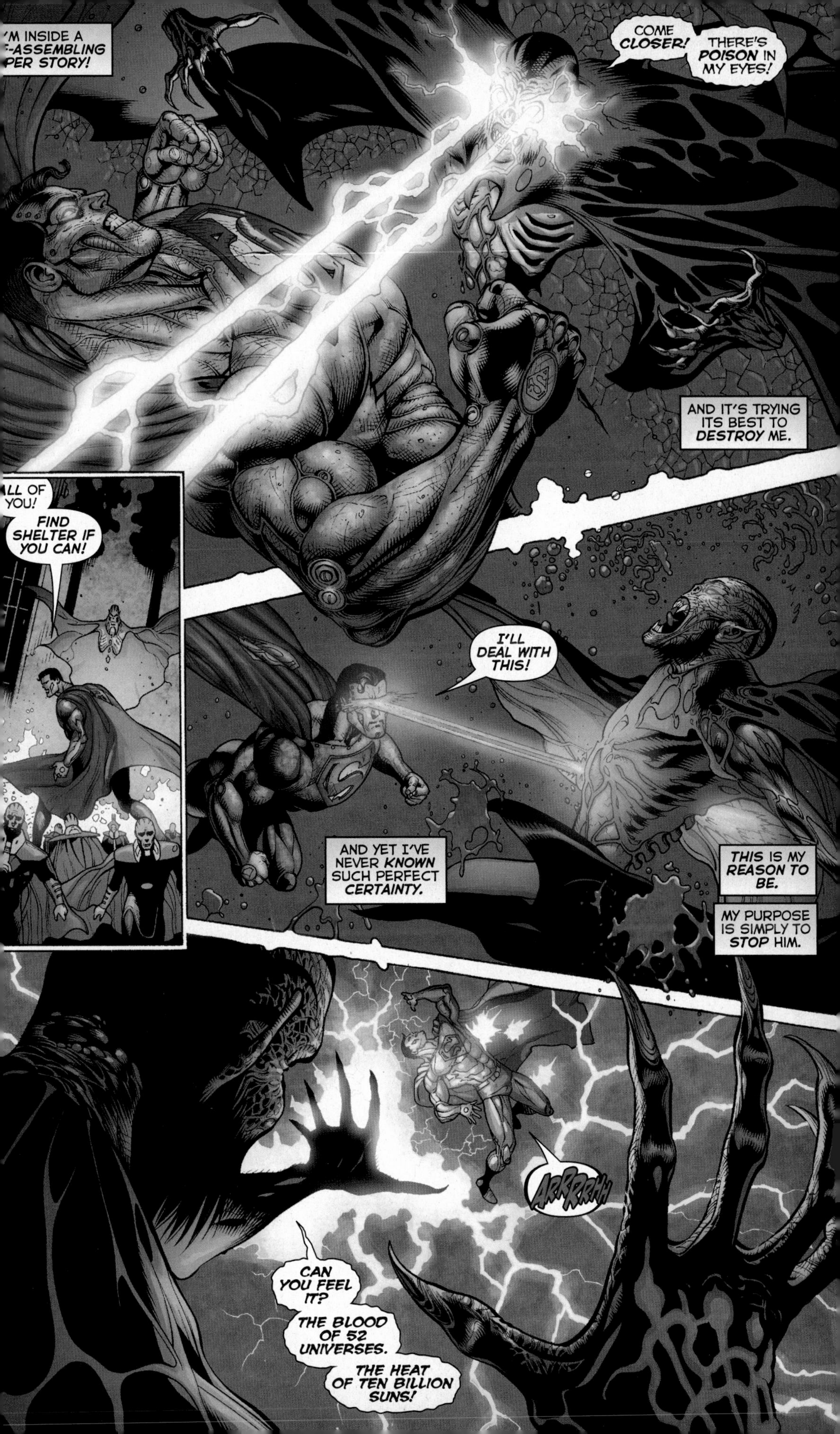
'M INSIDE A
-ASSEMBLING
PER STORY!
COME CLOSER!
THERE'S POISON IN MY EYES!
AND IT'S TRYING ITS BEST TO DESTROY ME.
LL OF YOU!
FIND SHELTER IF YOU CAN!
I'LL DEAL WITH THIS!
AND YET I'VE NEVER KNOWN SUCH PERFECT CERTAINTY.
THIS IS MY REASON TO BE.
MY PURPOSE IS SIMPLY TO STOP HIM.
ARRRRHH
CAN YOU FEEL IT?
THE BLOOD OF 52 UNIVERSES.
THE HEAT OF TEN BILLION SUNS!

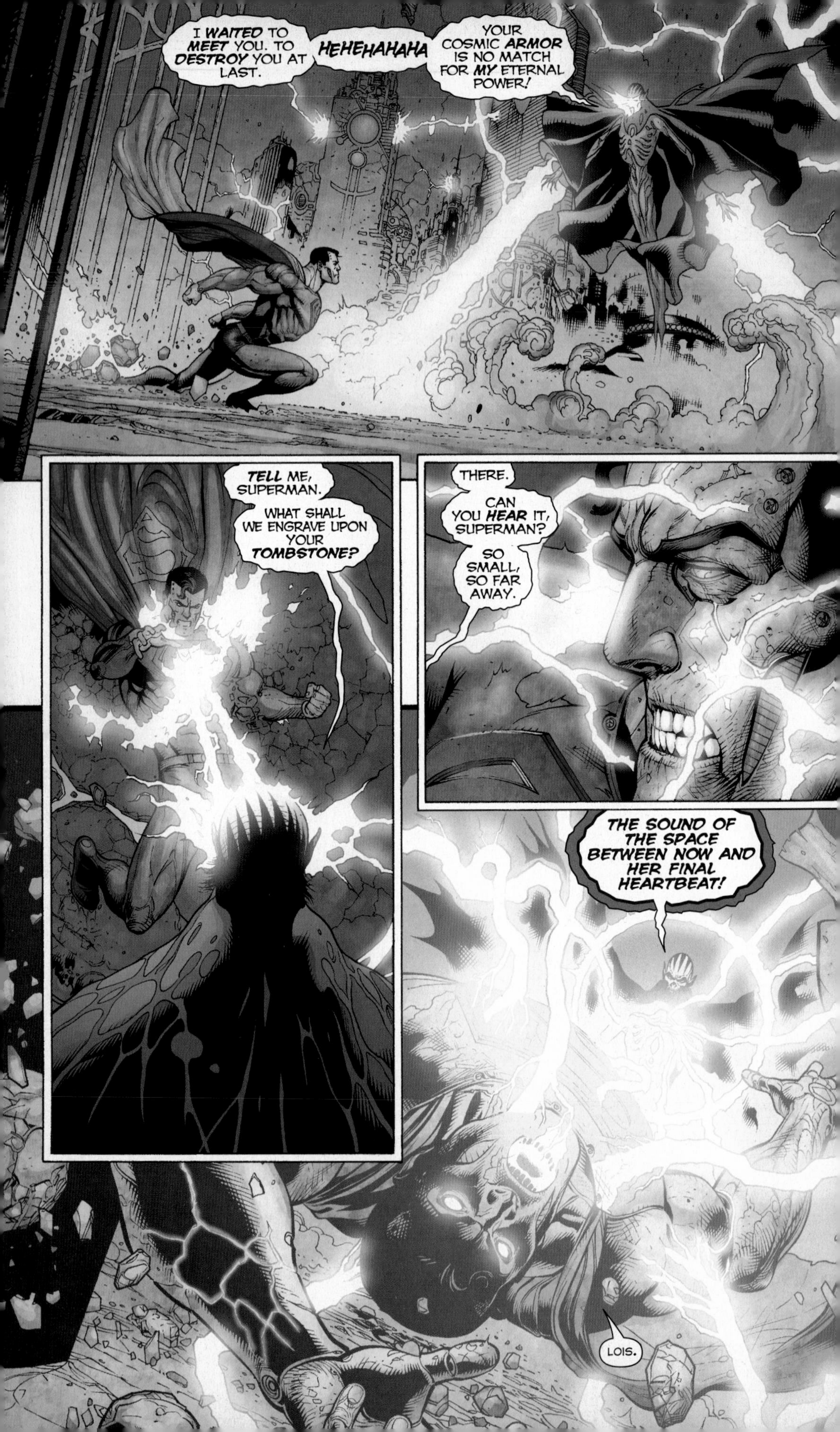

I WAITED TO MEET YOU. TO DESTROY YOU AT LAST.
HEHEHAHAHA
YOUR COSMIC ARMOR IS NO MATCH FOR MY ETERNAL POWER!
TELL ME, SUPERMAN.
WHAT SHALL WE ENGRAVE UPON YOUR TOMBSTONE?
THERE.
CAN YOU HEAR IT, SUPERMAN?
SO SMALL, SO FAR AWAY.
THE SOUND OF THE SPACE BETWEEN NOW AND HER FINAL HEARTBEAT!
LOIS.

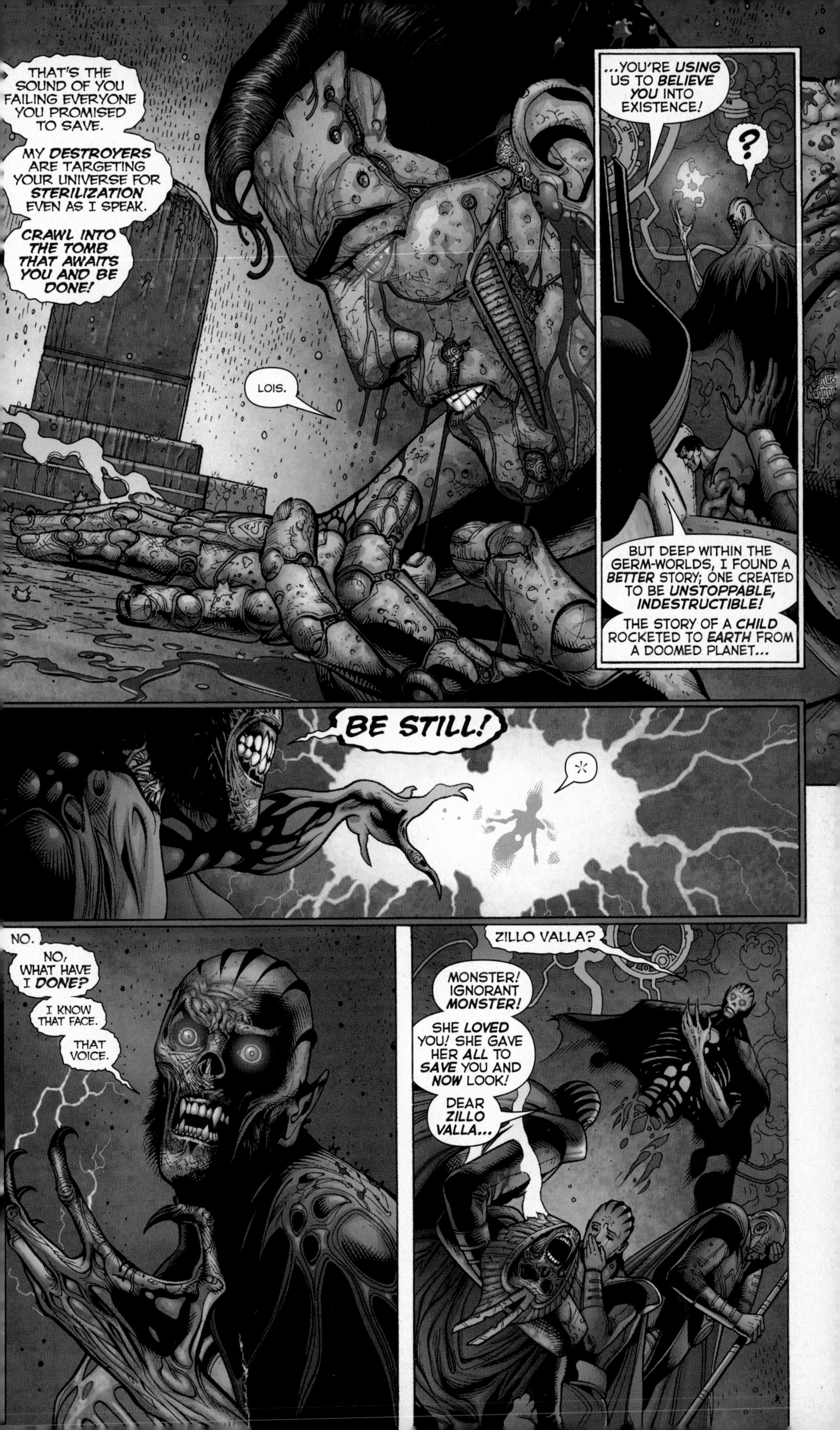
THAT'S THE SOUND OF YOU FAILING EVERYONE YOU PROMISED TO SAVE.
MY DESTROYERS ARE TARGETING YOUR UNIVERSE FOR STERILIZATION EVEN AS I SPEAK.
CRAWL INTO THE TOMB THAT AWAITS YOU AND BE DONE!
LOIS.
...YOU'RE USING US TO BELIEVE YOU INTO EXISTENCE!
?
BUT DEEP WITHIN THE GERM-WORLDS, I FOUND A BETTER STORY; ONE CREATED TO BE UNSTOPPABLE, INDESTRUCTIBLE!
THE STORY OF A CHILD ROCKETED TO EARTH FROM A DOOMED PLANET...
BE STILL!
NO.
NO, WHAT HAVE I DONE?
I KNOW THAT FACE.
THAT VOICE.
ZILLO VALLA?
MONSTER! IGNORANT MONSTER!
SHE LOVED YOU! SHE GAVE HER ALL TO SAVE YOU AND NOW LOOK!
DEAR ZILLO VALLA...

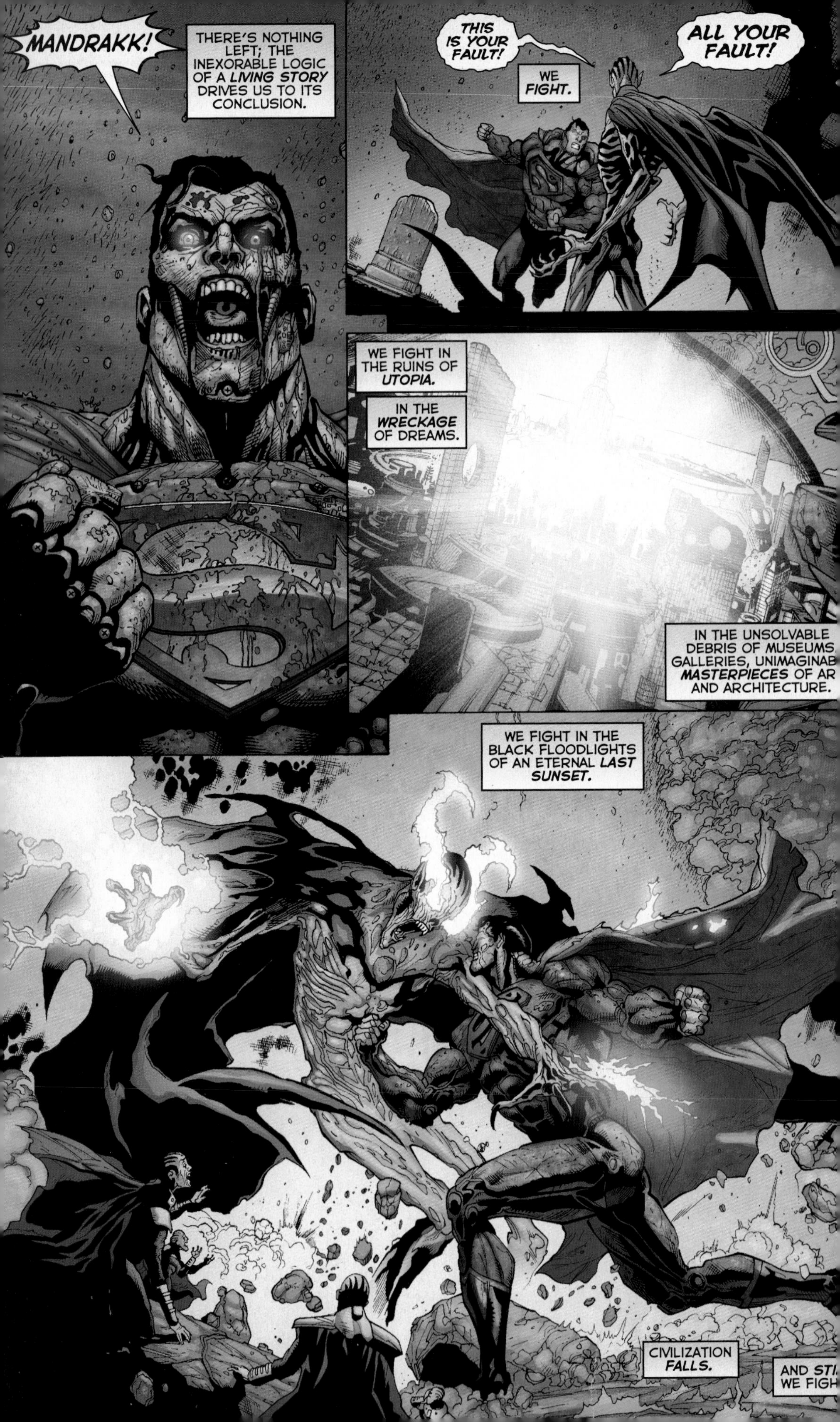

MANDRAKK!
THERE'S NOTHING LEFT; THE INEXORABLE LOGIC OF A *LIVING STORY* DRIVES US TO ITS CONCLUSION.
THIS IS YOUR FAULT!
ALL YOUR FAULT!
WE *FIGHT.*
WE FIGHT IN THE RUINS OF *UTOPIA.*
IN THE *WRECKAGE* OF DREAMS.
IN THE UNSOLVABLE DEBRIS OF MUSEUMS, GALLERIES, UNIMAGINAB *MASTERPIECES* OF AR AND ARCHITECTURE.
WE FIGHT IN THE BLACK FLOODLIGHTS OF AN ETERNAL *LAST SUNSET.*
CIVILIZATION *FALLS.*
AND STI WE FIGH

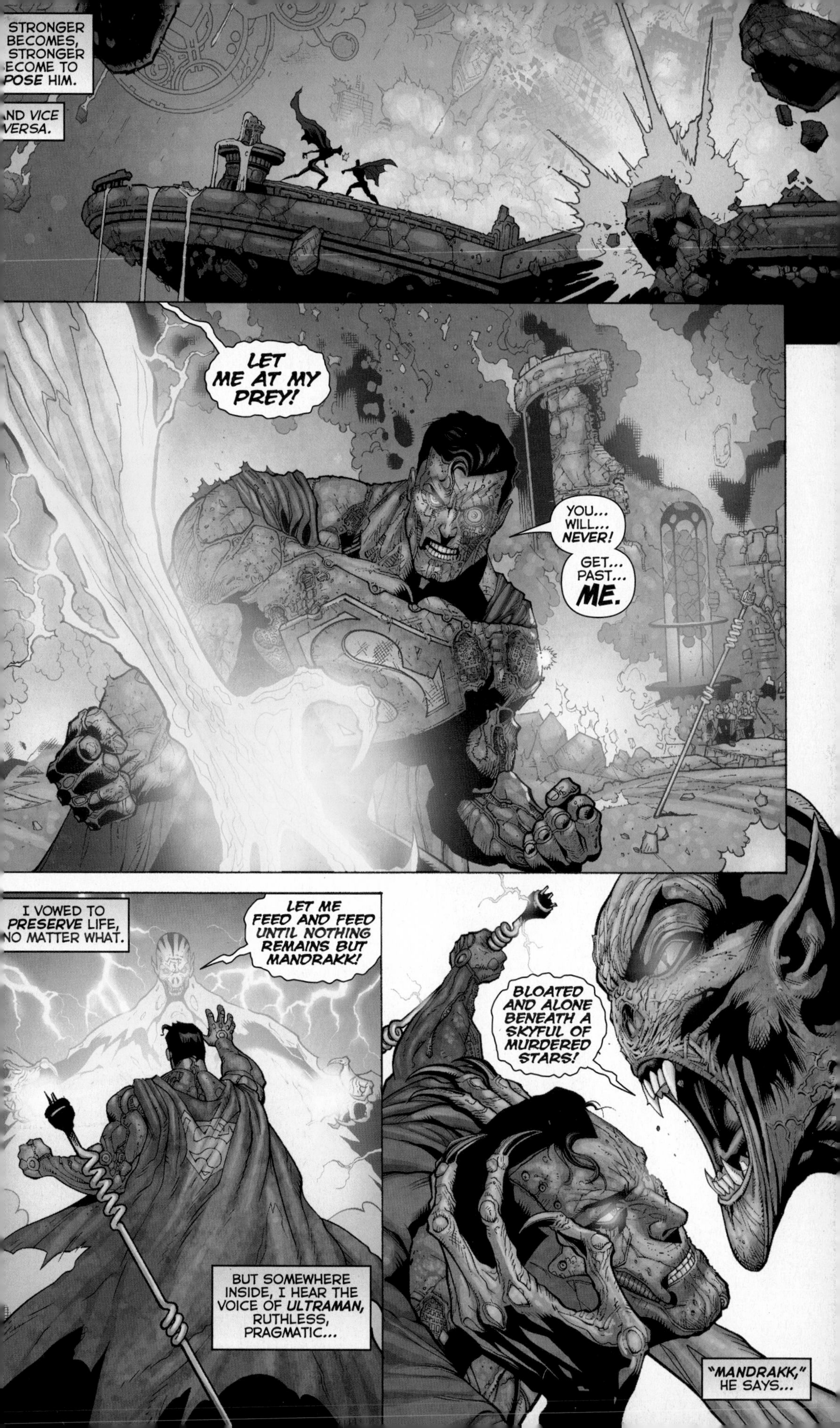
STRONGER
BECOMES,
STRONGER
ECOME TO
POSE HIM.
ND VICE
VERSA.
LET ME AT MY PREY!
YOU... WILL... NEVER!
GET... PAST... ME.
I VOWED TO PRESERVE LIFE, NO MATTER WHAT.
LET ME FEED AND FEED UNTIL NOTHING REMAINS BUT MANDRAKK!
BLOATED AND ALONE BENEATH A SKYFUL OF MURDERED STARS!
BUT SOMEWHERE INSIDE, I HEAR THE VOICE OF ULTRAMAN, RUTHLESS, PRAGMATIC...
"MANDRAKK," HE SAYS...

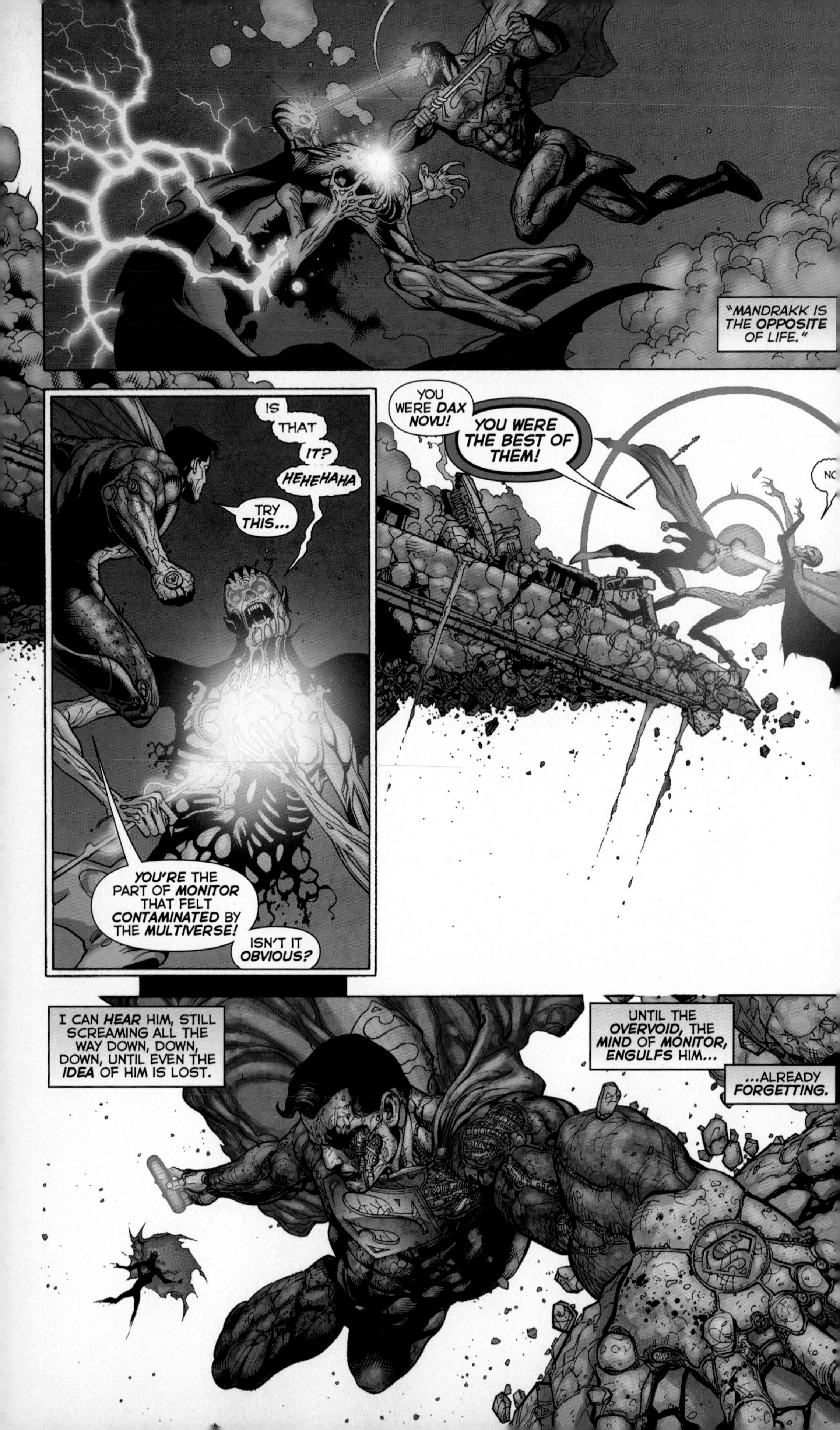
"MANDRAKK IS THE OPPOSITE OF LIFE."
IS THAT IT? HEHEHAHA
TRY THIS...
YOU'RE THE PART OF MONITOR THAT FELT CONTAMINATED BY THE MULTIVERSE!
ISN'T IT OBVIOUS?
YOU WERE DAX NOVU!
YOU WERE THE BEST OF THEM!
I CAN HEAR HIM, STILL SCREAMING ALL THE WAY DOWN, DOWN, DOWN, UNTIL EVEN THE IDEA OF HIM IS LOST.
UNTIL THE OVERVOID, THE MIND OF MONITOR, ENGULFS HIM...
...ALREADY FORGETTING.

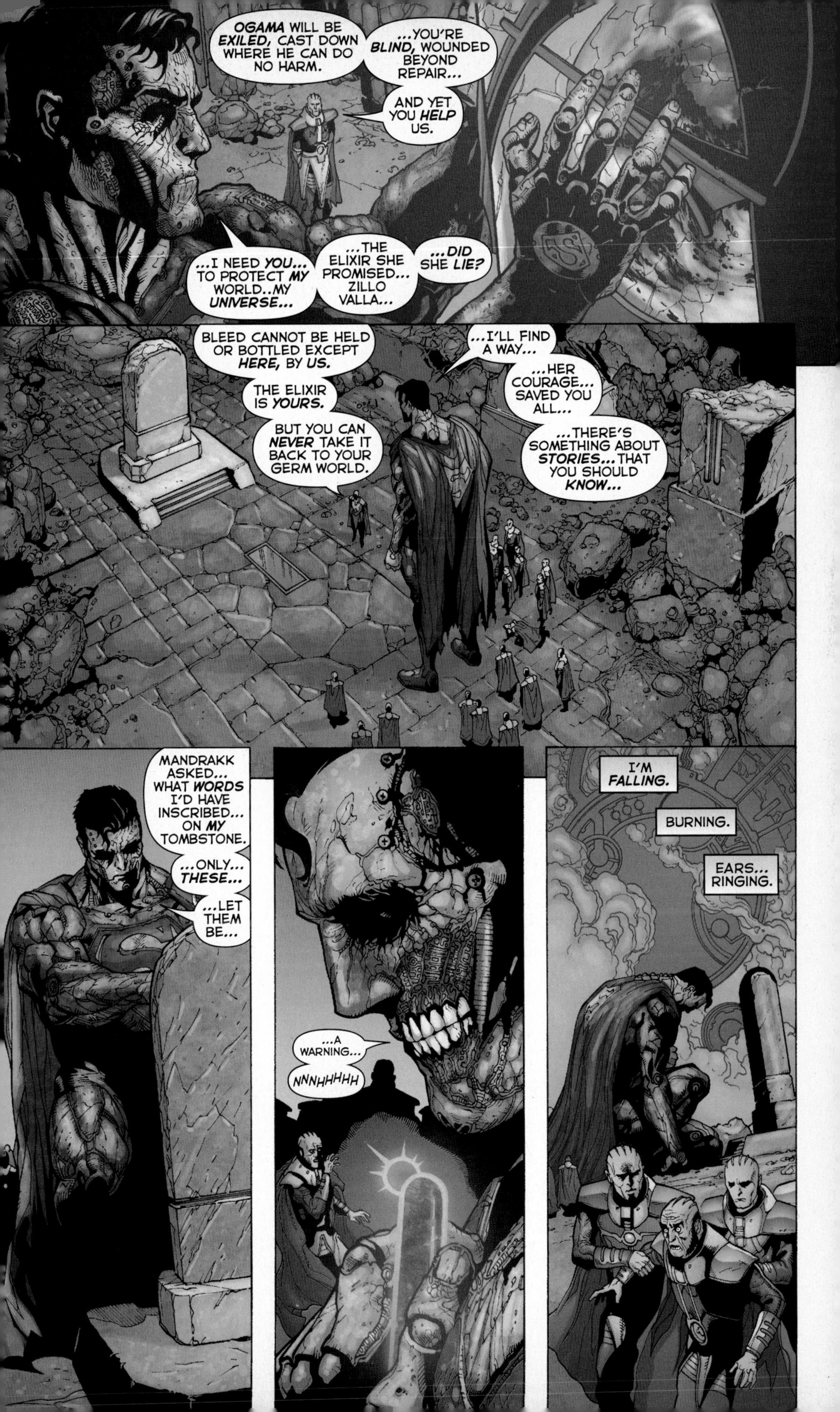
OGAMA WILL BE EXILED, CAST DOWN WHERE HE CAN DO NO HARM.
...YOU'RE BLIND, WOUNDED BEYOND REPAIR...
AND YET YOU HELP US.
...I NEED YOU... TO PROTECT MY WORLD..MY UNIVERSE...
...THE ELIXIR SHE PROMISED... ZILLO VALLA...
...DID SHE LIE?
BLEED CANNOT BE HELD OR BOTTLED EXCEPT HERE, BY US.
THE ELIXIR IS YOURS.
BUT YOU CAN NEVER TAKE IT BACK TO YOUR GERM WORLD.
...I'LL FIND A WAY...
...HER COURAGE... SAVED YOU ALL...
...THERE'S SOMETHING ABOUT STORIES... THAT YOU SHOULD KNOW...
MANDRAKK ASKED... WHAT WORDS I'D HAVE INSCRIBED... ON MY TOMBSTONE.
...ONLY... THESE...
...LET THEM BE...
...A WARNING...
NNNHHHHH
I'M FALLING.
BURNING.
EARS... RINGING.

EXPLODING ALL AROUND ME LIKE *THUNDER AND STARS.*

I FOUND *MY TREASURE,* CAPTAIN ADAM.

ONCE I RESTORE THIS FRAGMENT TO THE *ROCK OF ETERNITY,* THE *TIME-CRISIS* THAT TURNED MY WORLD TOPSY-TURVY OUGHT TO COME TO AN *END.*

...CAPTAIN?...

DECELERATING IN A SHOWER OF DISCORDANT *BLEED.*

THE *ONLY THING* THAT CAN *SAVE* LOIS'S LIFE.

THE *ELIXIR* THAT CAN'T BE BOTTLED...OR HELD...OR *CONTAINED...*

REALITY-BLITZING MISSILES *EVOLVE* INTO POSITION ON THE BLACK CARAPACE OF MANDRAKK'S *DESTROYER.*

THIS *INFINITESIMA* OBJECT FRO THE MONITO WORLD, GIGAN IN OUR OWN.

PREPARING T *STERILIZE* T GERM-WORL AND MAKE EV LIVING THIN *EXTINCT!*

THIS LOOKS LIKE A JOB FOR *SUPERMAN.*

FOR ALL OF US.

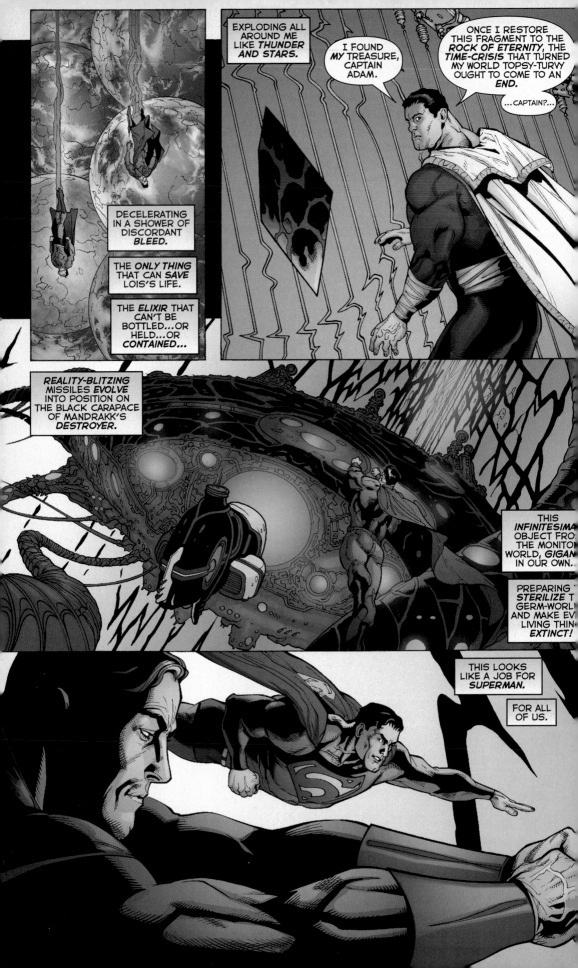

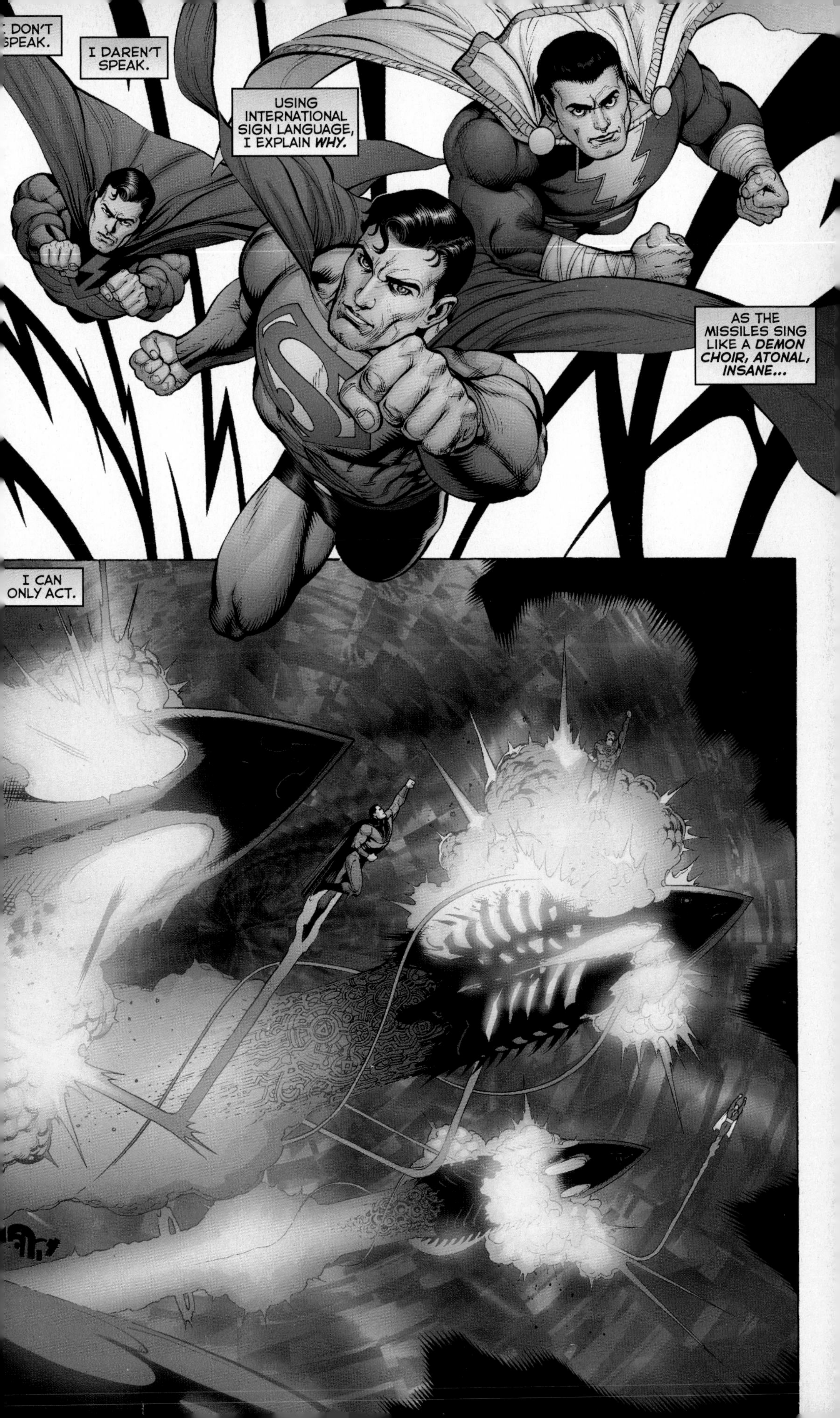
I DON'T SPEAK.
I DAREN'T SPEAK.
USING INTERNATIONAL SIGN LANGUAGE, I EXPLAIN *WHY.*
AS THE MISSILES SING LIKE A *DEMON CHOIR, ATONAL, INSANE...*
I CAN ONLY ACT.

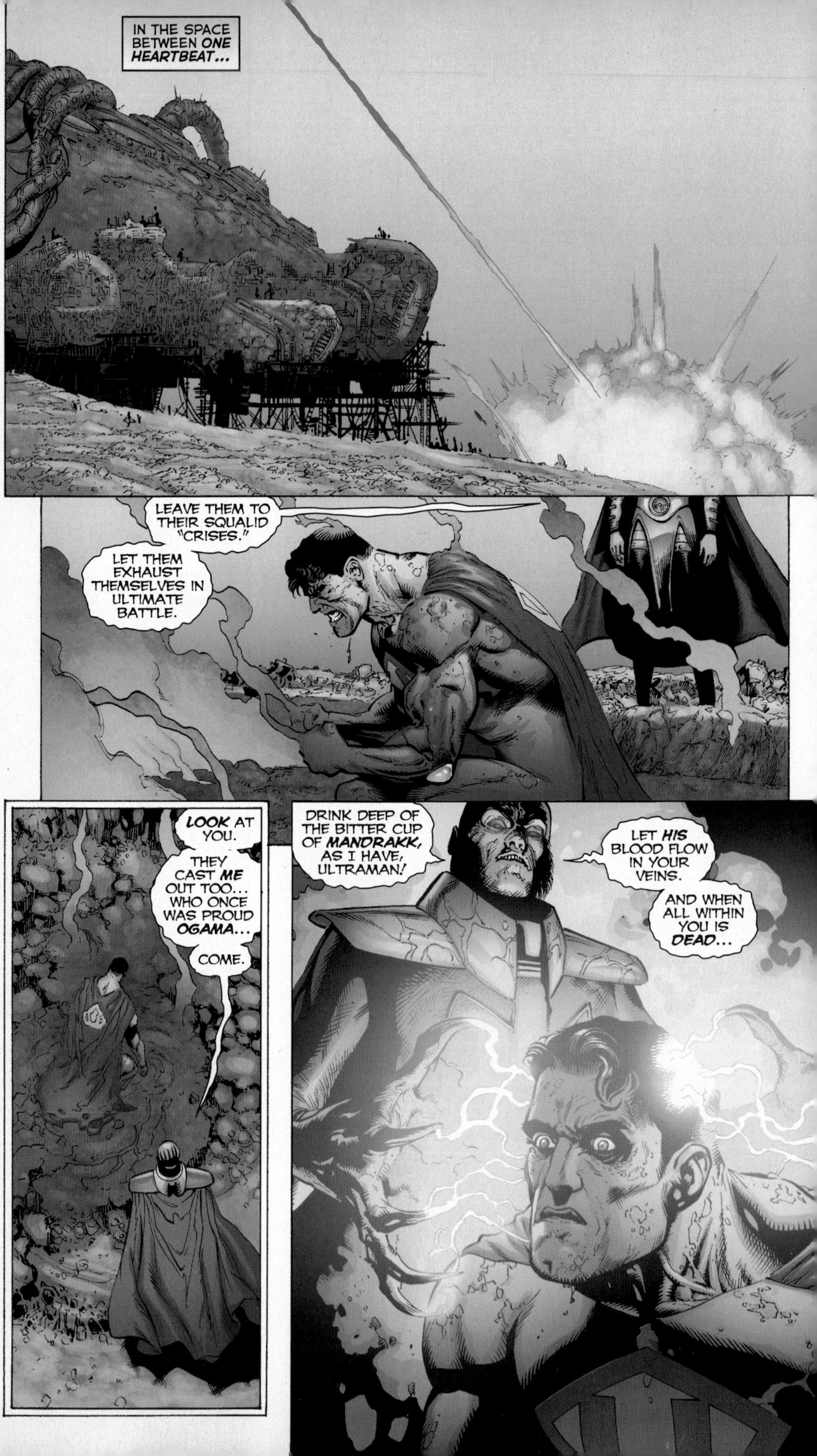

IN THE SPACE BETWEEN ONE HEARTBEAT...
LEAVE THEM TO THEIR SQUALID "CRISES."
LET THEM EXHAUST THEMSELVES IN ULTIMATE BATTLE.
LOOK AT YOU.
THEY CAST ME OUT TOO... WHO ONCE WAS PROUD OGAMA...
COME.
DRINK DEEP OF THE BITTER CUP OF MANDRAKK, AS I HAVE, ULTRAMAN!
LET HIS BLOOD FLOW IN YOUR VEINS.
AND WHEN ALL WITHIN YOU IS DEAD...

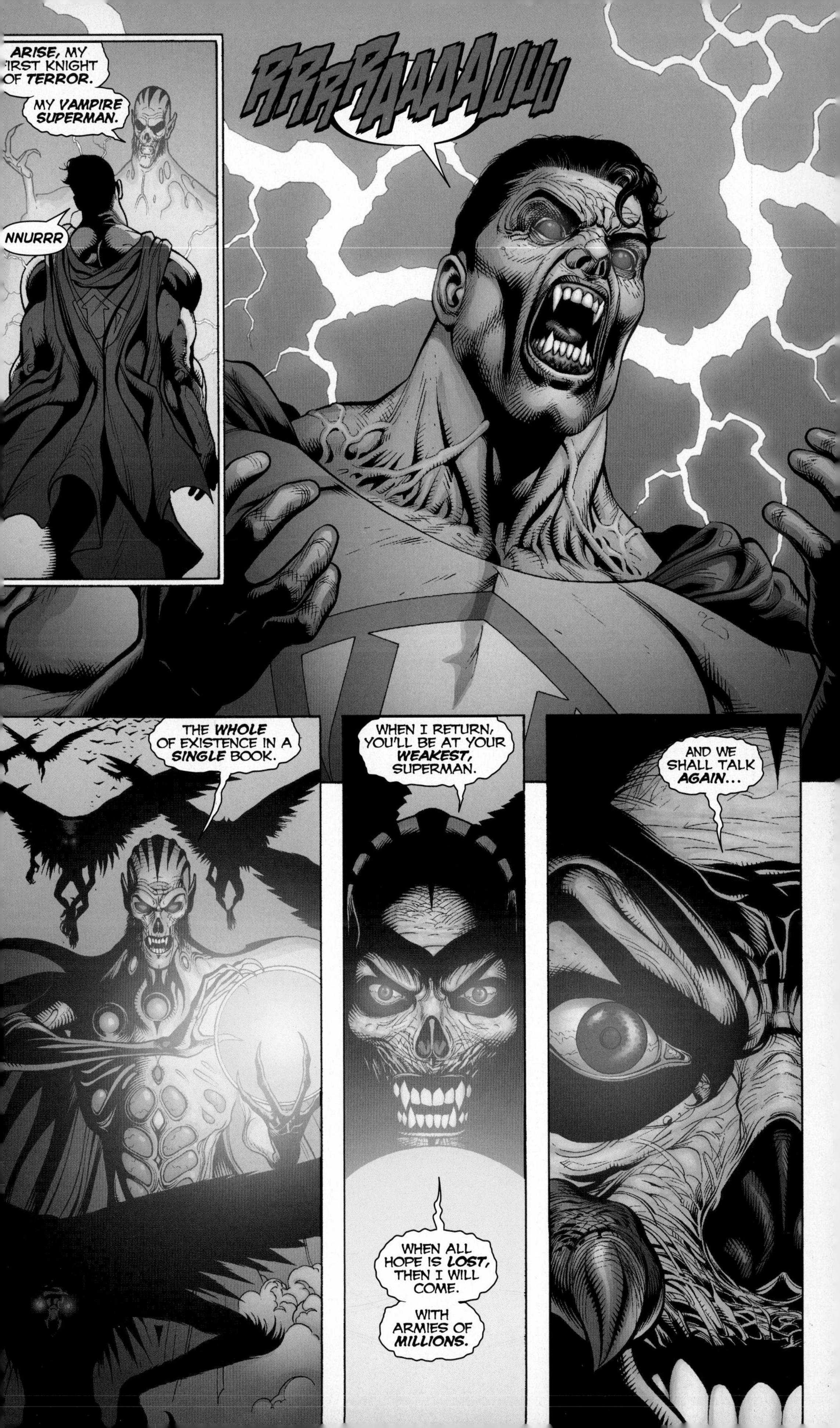
ARISE, MY FIRST KNIGHT OF TERROR.
MY VAMPIRE SUPERMAN.
NNURRR
RRRRAAAAUUU
THE WHOLE OF EXISTENCE IN A SINGLE BOOK.
WHEN I RETURN, YOU'LL BE AT YOUR WEAKEST, SUPERMAN.
WHEN ALL HOPE IS LOST, THEN I WILL COME.
WITH ARMIES OF MILLIONS.
AND WE SHALL TALK AGAIN...

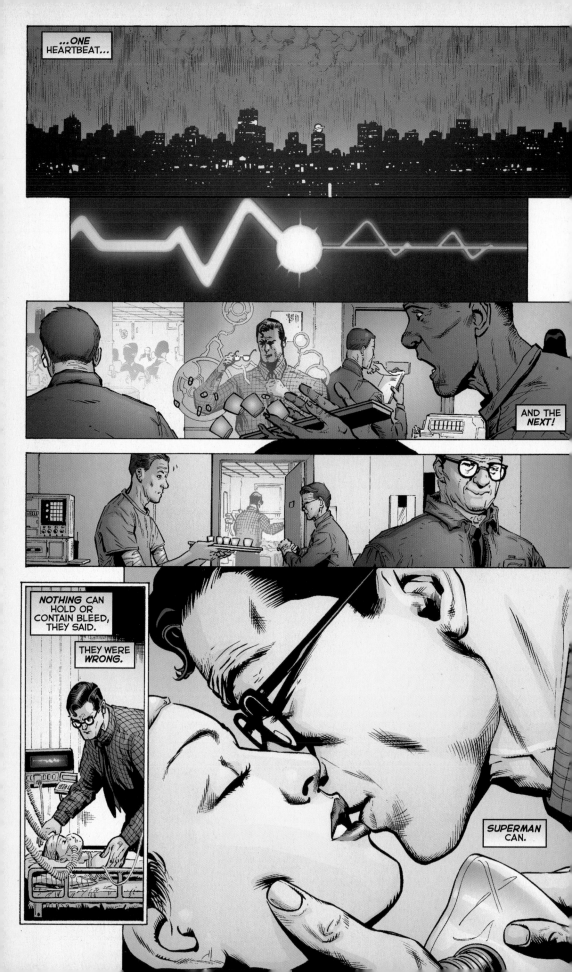

...ONE HEARTBEAT...

AND THE NEXT!

NOTHING CAN HOLD OR CONTAIN BLEED, THEY SAID.

THEY WERE WRONG.

SUPERMAN CAN.

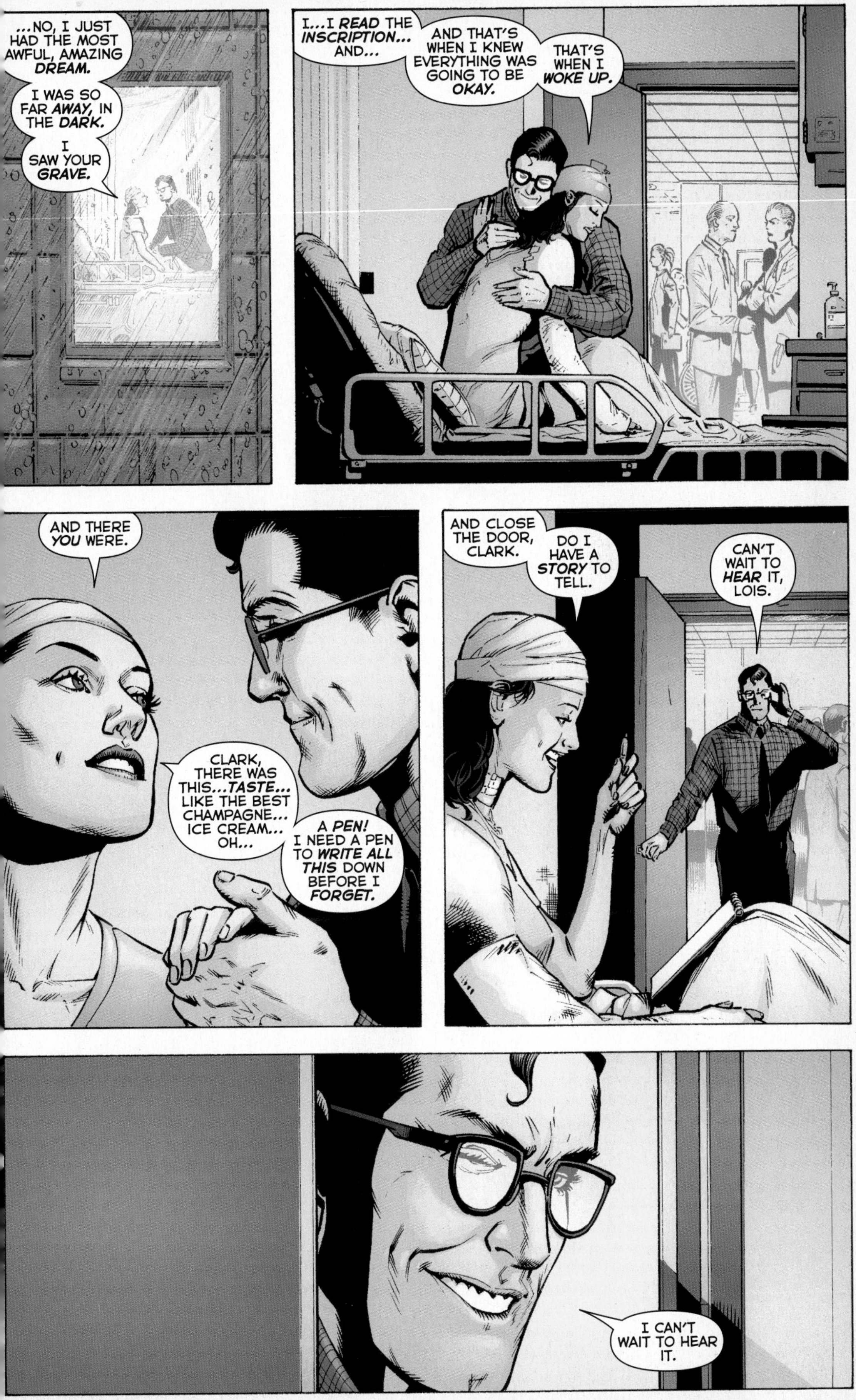
...NO, I JUST HAD THE MOST AWFUL, AMAZING DREAM.
I WAS SO FAR AWAY, IN THE DARK.
I SAW YOUR GRAVE.
I...I READ THE INSCRIPTION... AND...
AND THAT'S WHEN I KNEW EVERYTHING WAS GOING TO BE OKAY.
THAT'S WHEN I WOKE UP.
AND THERE YOU WERE.
CLARK, THERE WAS THIS...TASTE... LIKE THE BEST CHAMPAGNE... ICE CREAM... OH...
A PEN! I NEED A PEN TO WRITE ALL THIS DOWN BEFORE I FORGET.
AND CLOSE THE DOOR, CLARK.
DO I HAVE A STORY TO TELL.
CAN'T WAIT TO HEAR IT, LOIS.
I CAN'T WAIT TO HEAR IT.

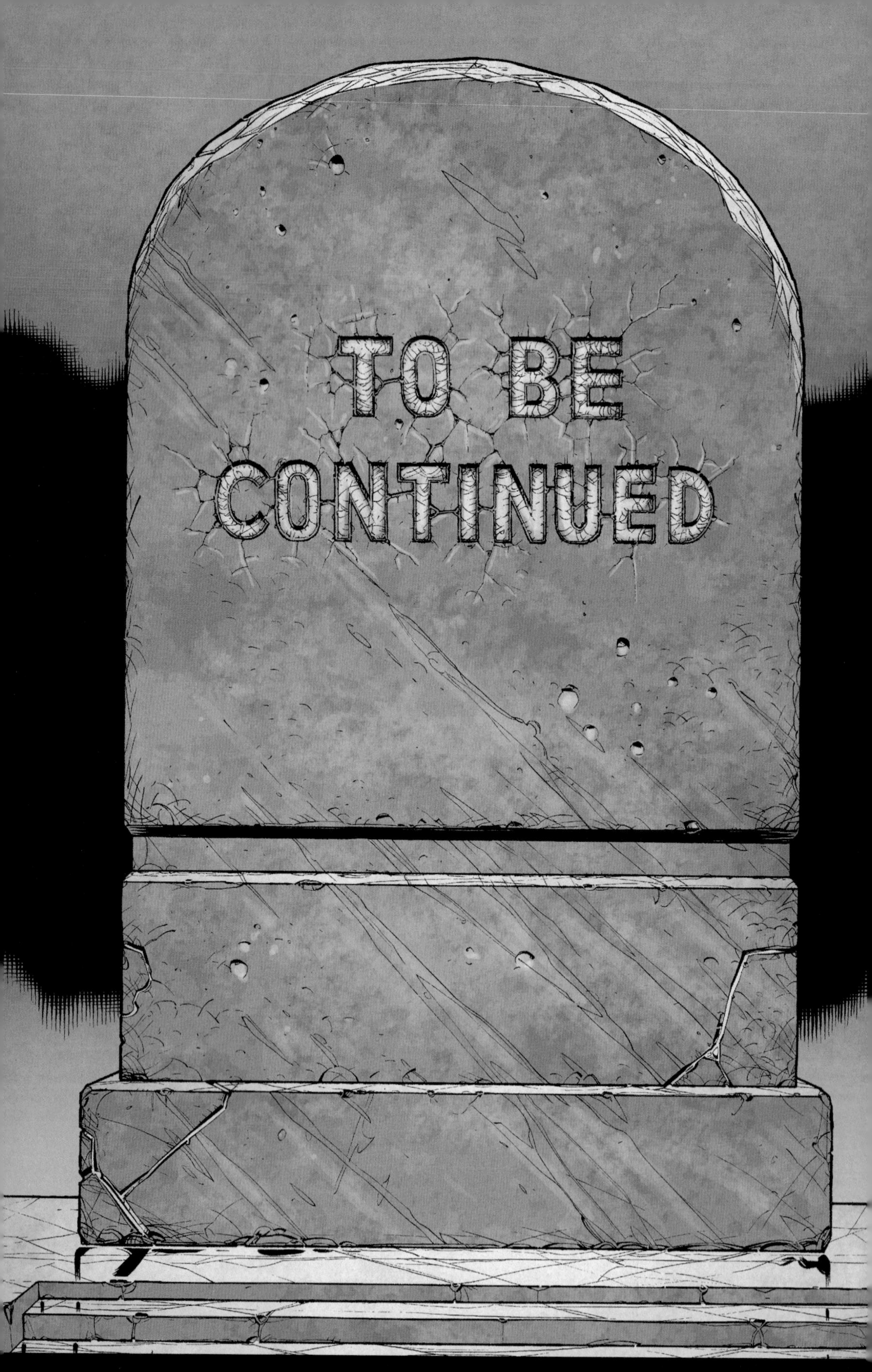
TO BE CONTINUED

WRITER: GRANT MORRISON PENCILS: DOUG MAHNKE
INKS: CHRISTIAN ALAMY w/TOM NGUYEN, DREW GERACI & DEREK FRIDOLFS

Cover to SUBMIT #1 Matthew Clark with Pete Pantazis

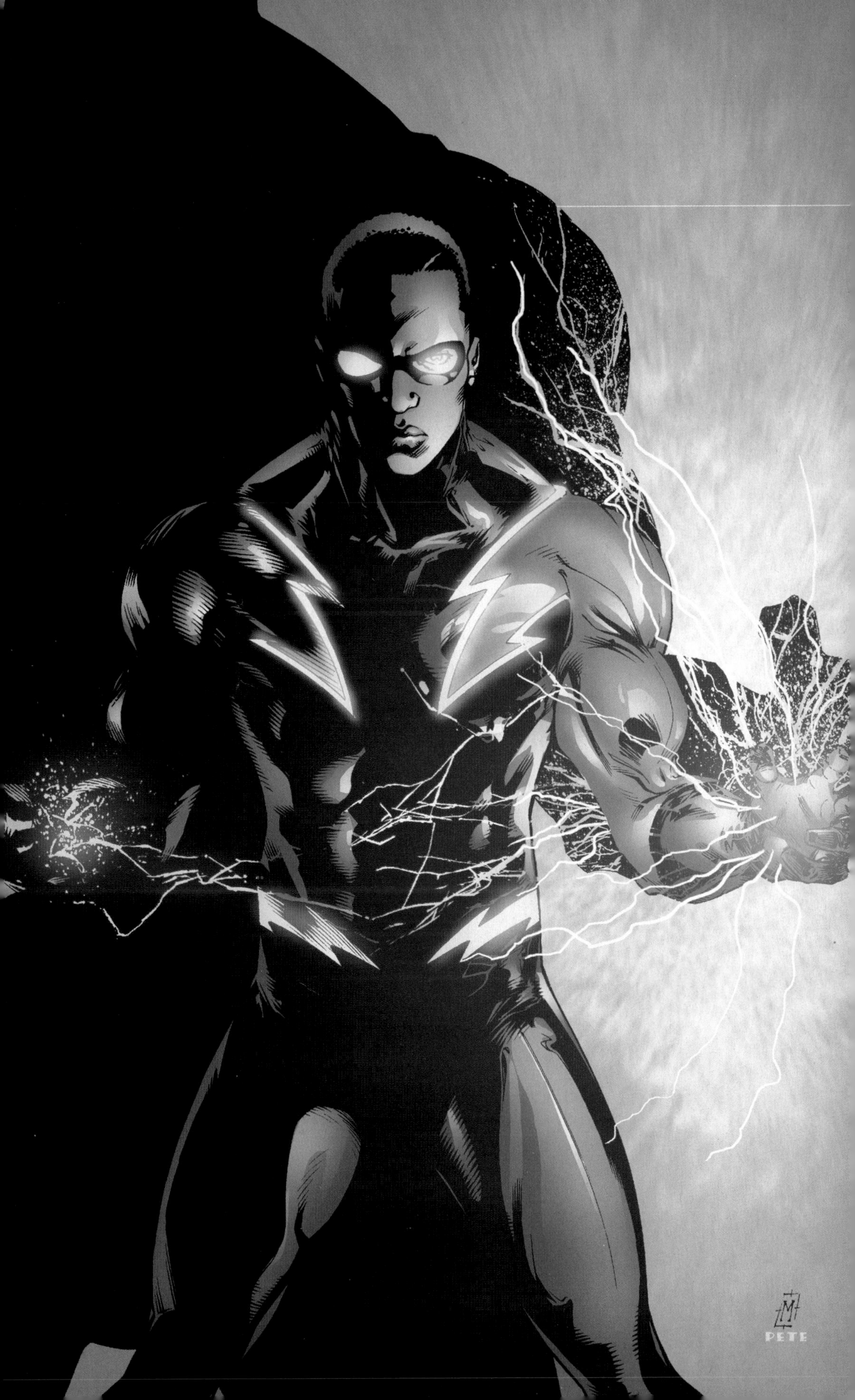
PETE

Rodolfo Migliari

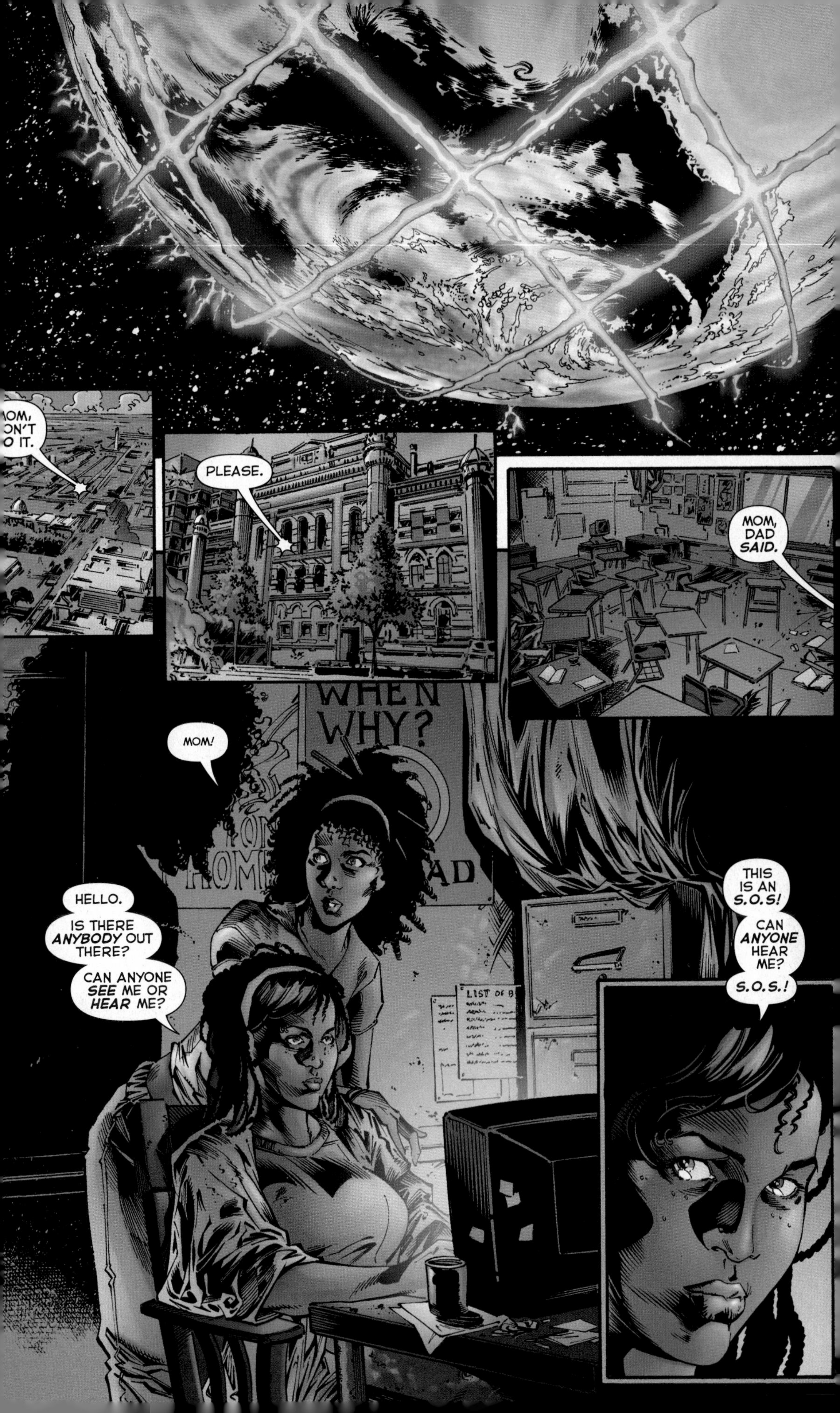
MOM, ON'T O IT.
PLEASE.
MOM, DAD SAID.
WHEN WHY?
MOM!
HELLO.
IS THERE ANYBODY OUT THERE?
CAN ANYONE SEE ME OR HEAR ME?
THIS IS AN S.O.S!
CAN ANYONE HEAR ME?
S.O.S.!

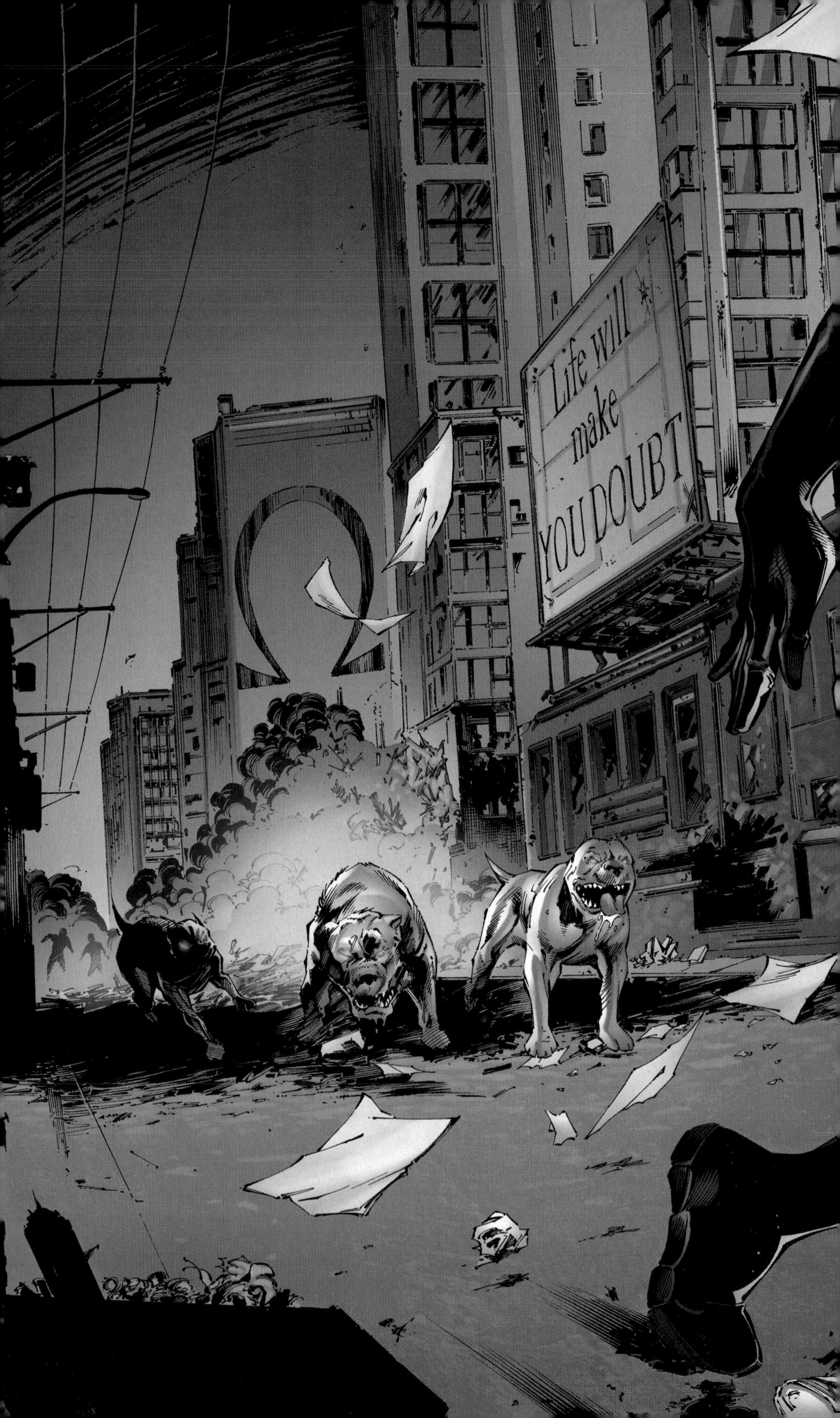
Life will make YOU DOUBT

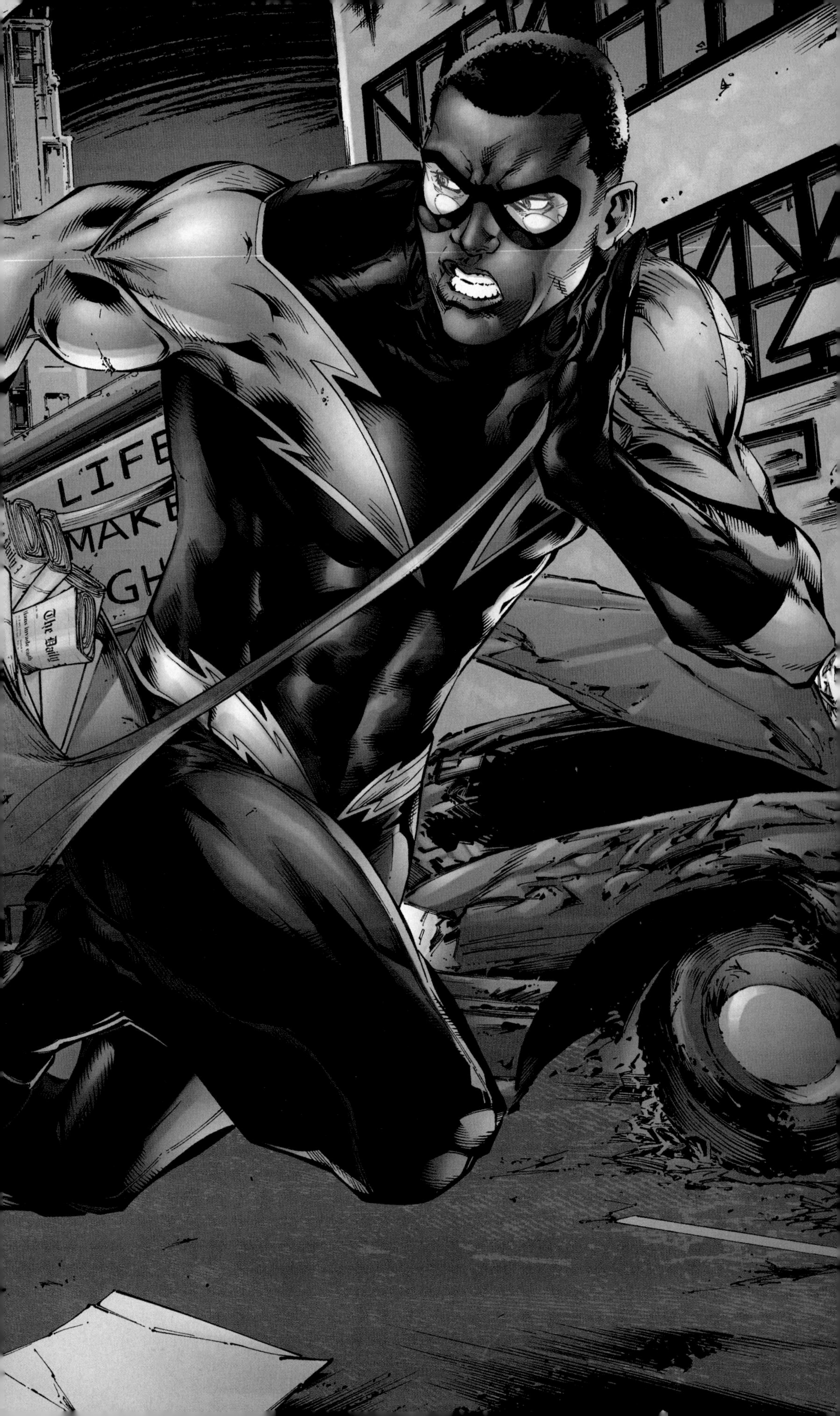

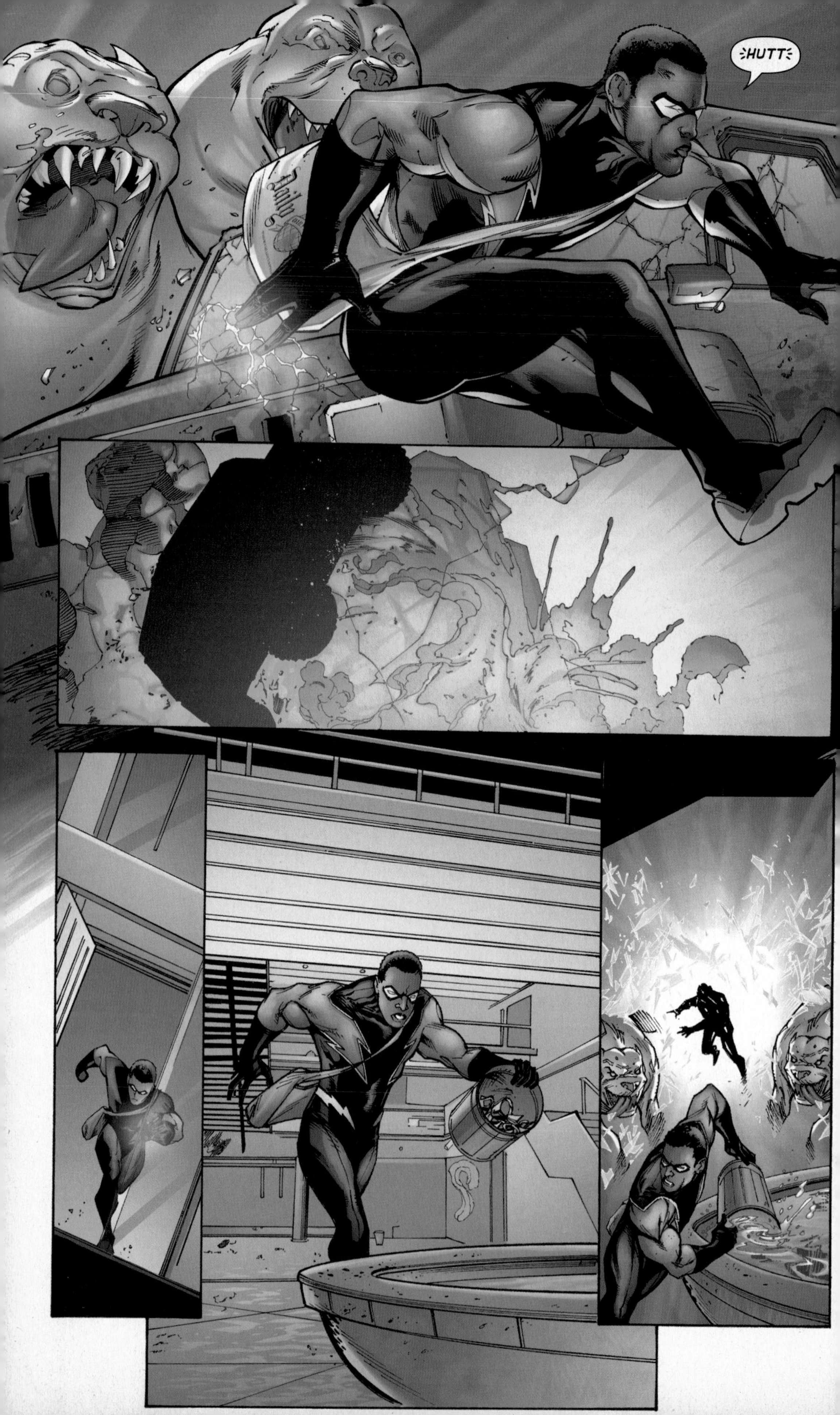
HUTT

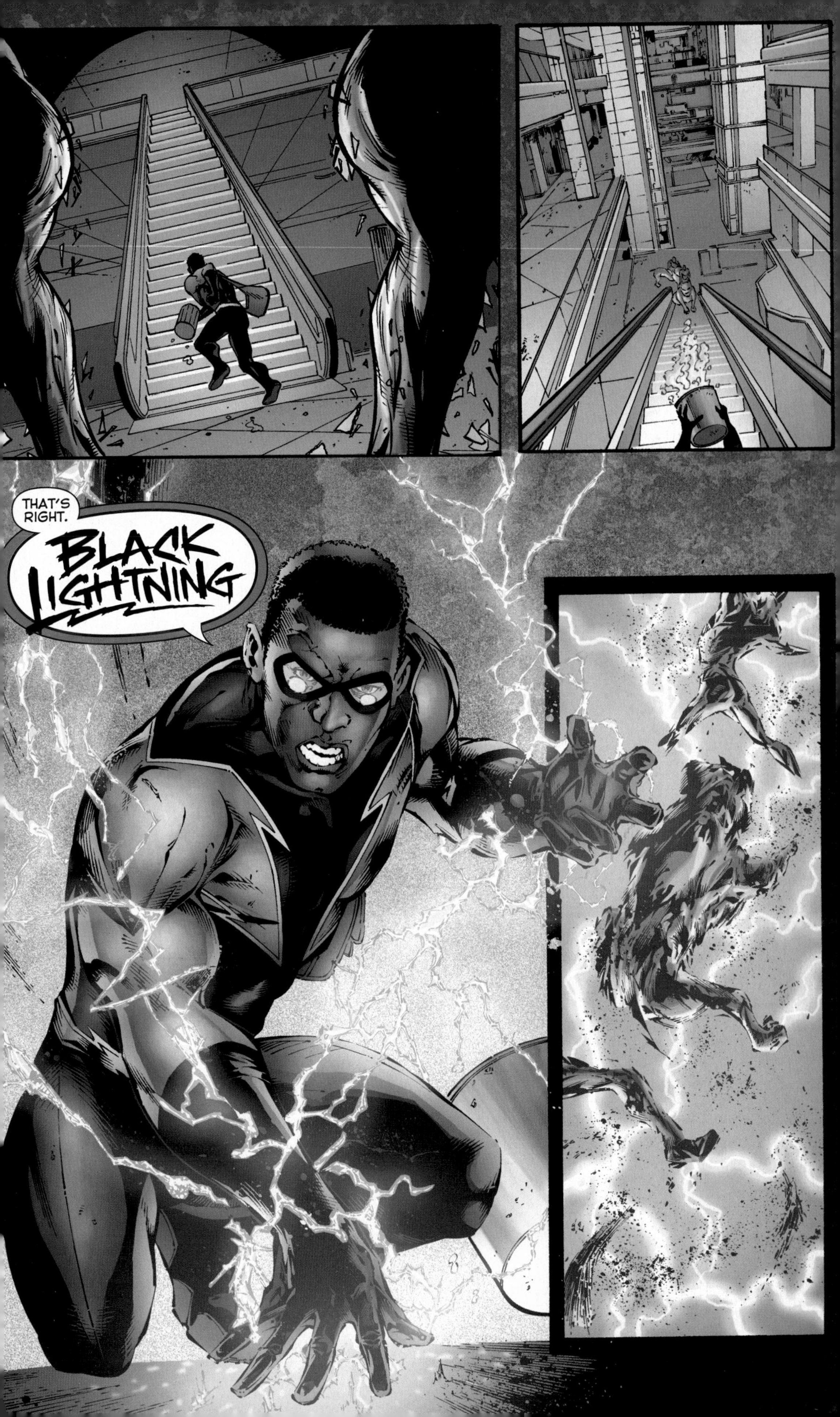
THAT'S RIGHT.
BLACK LIGHTNING

...BUT I *HEARD* 'EM ALL TURN AWAY.

THEY'RE *CHASING* SOMEBODY ELSE.

SHH!

THEY'RE CHASING *US*, BOY!

THEY GOT JUSTIFIERS EVERYWHERE!

OW!

GET YOUR HANDS OFF MY DAMN *THROAT!*

I *HEARD* THEM.

YEAH, WELL, MAYBE YOU'RE *RIGHT* AFTER ALL.

SOMETHING'S *GOING ON* UP AHEAD!

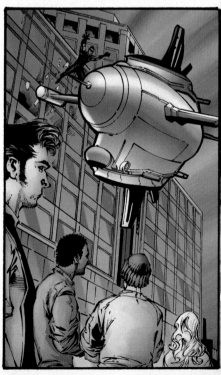

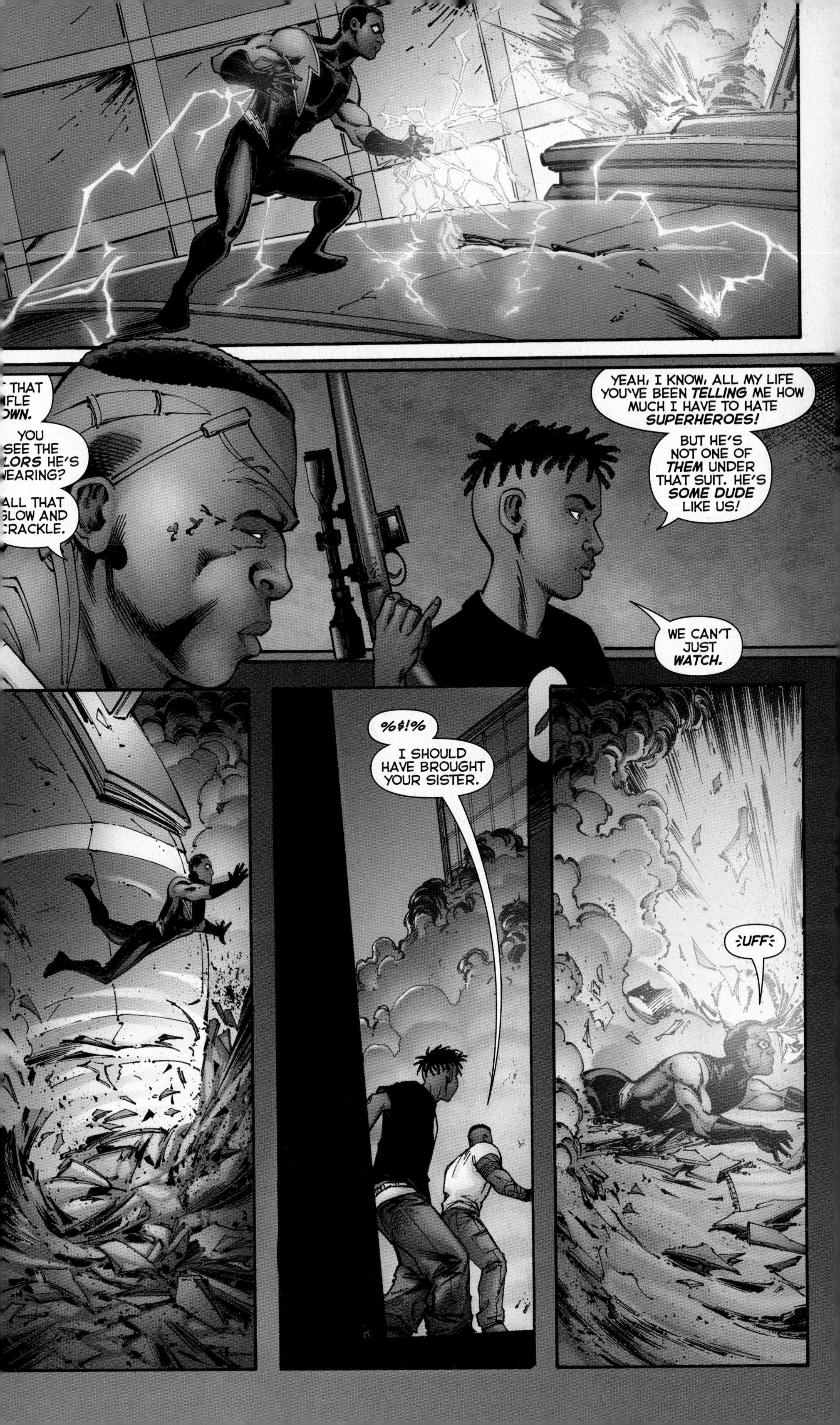
THAT
FLE
OWN.
YOU SEE THE
LORS HE'S
WEARING?
ALL THAT
GLOW AND
CRACKLE.
YEAH, I KNOW, ALL MY LIFE YOU'VE BEEN TELLING ME HOW MUCH I HAVE TO HATE SUPERHEROES!
BUT HE'S NOT ONE OF THEM UNDER THAT SUIT. HE'S SOME DUDE LIKE US!
WE CAN'T JUST WATCH.
%$!%
I SHOULD HAVE BROUGHT YOUR SISTER.
UFF

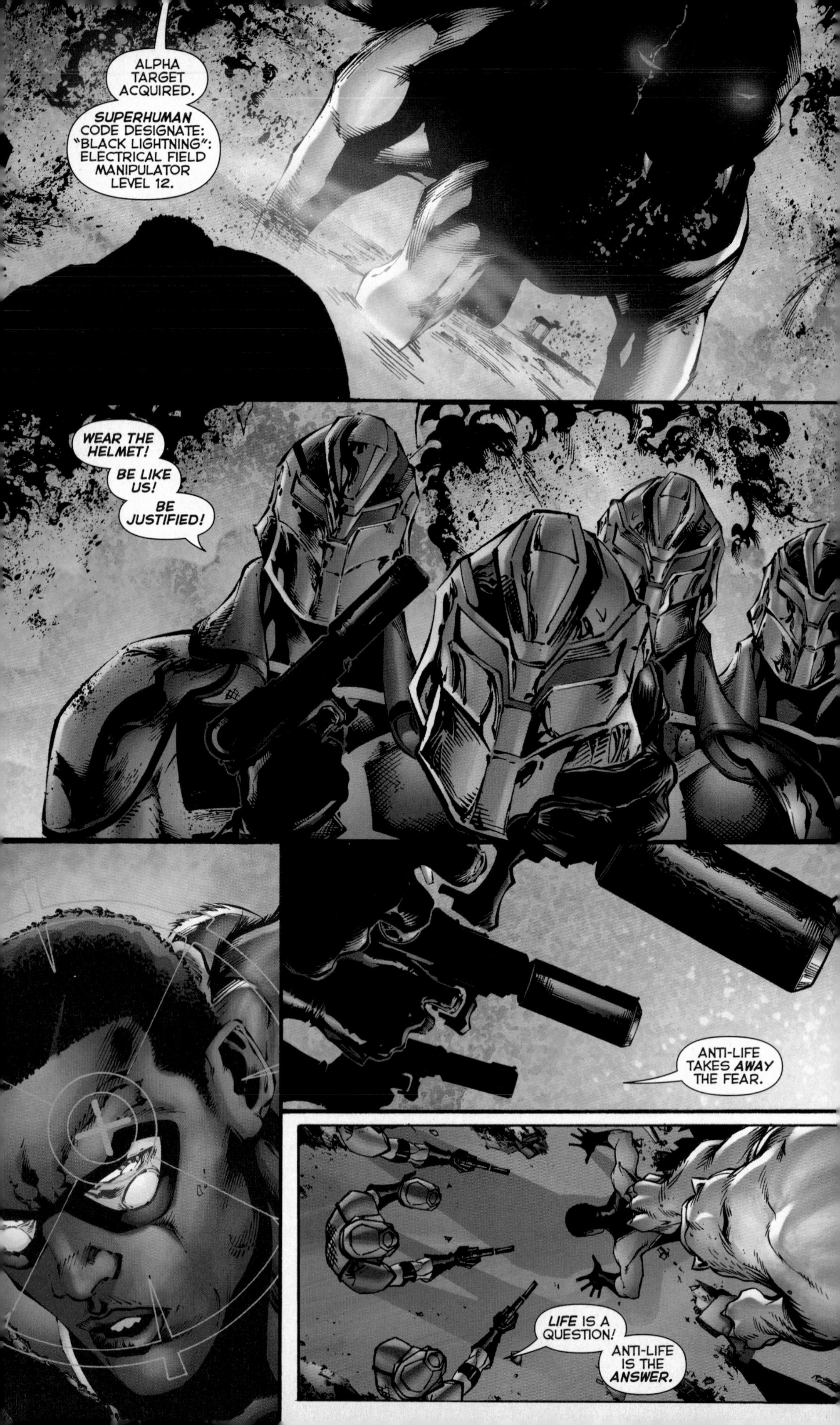
ALPHA TARGET ACQUIRED.
SUPERHUMAN CODE DESIGNATE: "BLACK LIGHTNING": ELECTRICAL FIELD MANIPULATOR LEVEL 12.
WEAR THE HELMET!
BE LIKE US!
BE JUSTIFIED!
ANTI-LIFE TAKES *AWAY* THE FEAR.
LIFE IS A QUESTION!
ANTI-LIFE IS THE *ANSWER.*

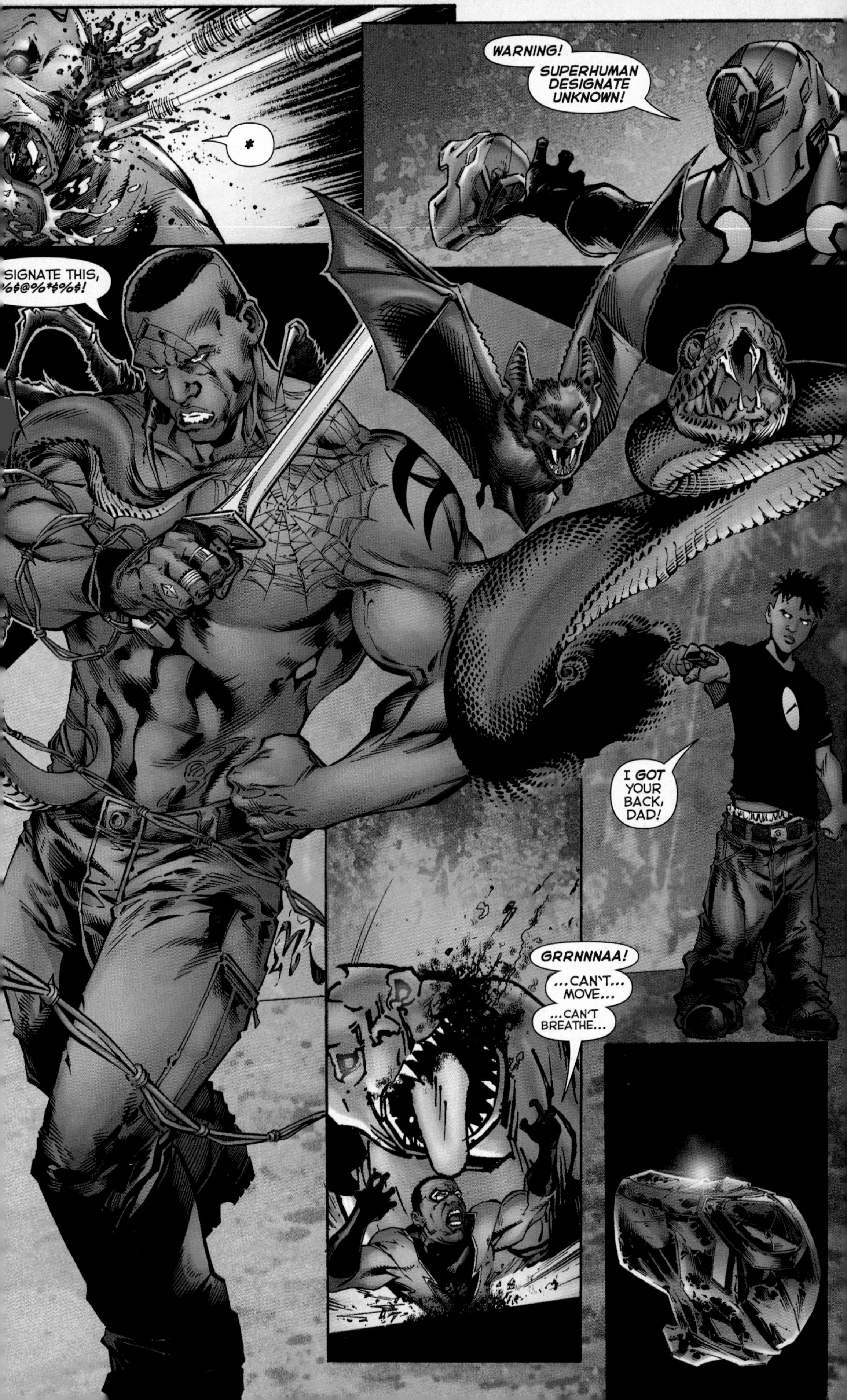

*
WARNING!
SUPERHUMAN DESIGNATE UNKNOWN!
SIGNATE THIS,
%$@%*$%$!
I GOT YOUR BACK, DAD!
GRRNNNAA!
...CAN'T... MOVE...
...CAN'T BREATHE...

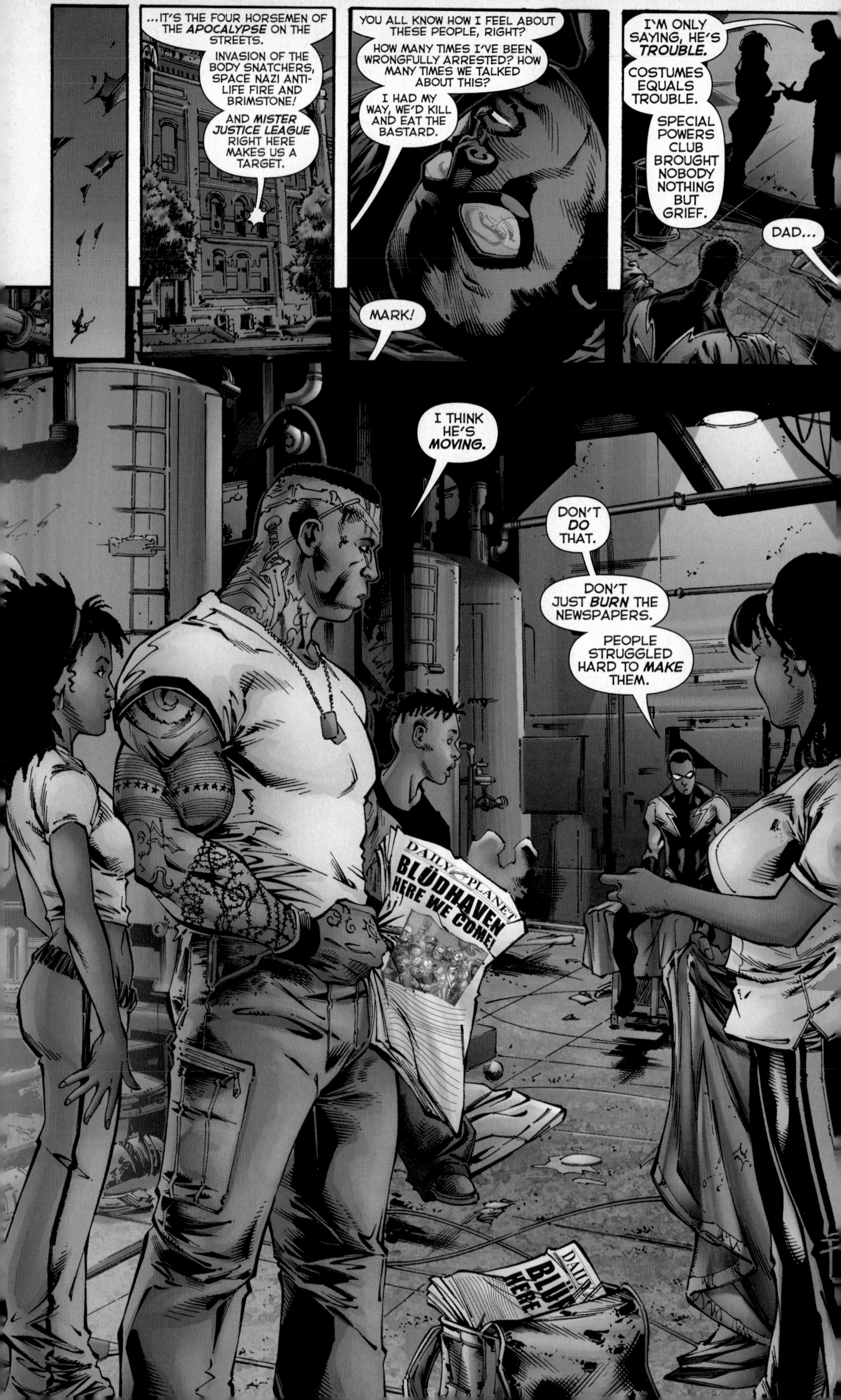

...IT'S THE FOUR HORSEMEN OF THE APOCALYPSE ON THE STREETS.
INVASION OF THE BODY SNATCHERS, SPACE NAZI ANTI-LIFE FIRE AND BRIMSTONE!
AND MISTER JUSTICE LEAGUE RIGHT HERE MAKES US A TARGET.
YOU ALL KNOW HOW I FEEL ABOUT THESE PEOPLE, RIGHT?
HOW MANY TIMES I'VE BEEN WRONGFULLY ARRESTED? HOW MANY TIMES WE TALKED ABOUT THIS?
I HAD MY WAY, WE'D KILL AND EAT THE BASTARD.
MARK!
I'M ONLY SAYING, HE'S TROUBLE.
COSTUMES EQUALS TROUBLE.
SPECIAL POWERS CLUB BROUGHT NOBODY NOTHING BUT GRIEF.
DAD...
I THINK HE'S MOVING.
DON'T DO THAT.
DON'T JUST BURN THE NEWSPAPERS.
PEOPLE STRUGGLED HARD TO MAKE THEM.
DAILY PLANET
BLÜDHAVEN HERE WE COME!

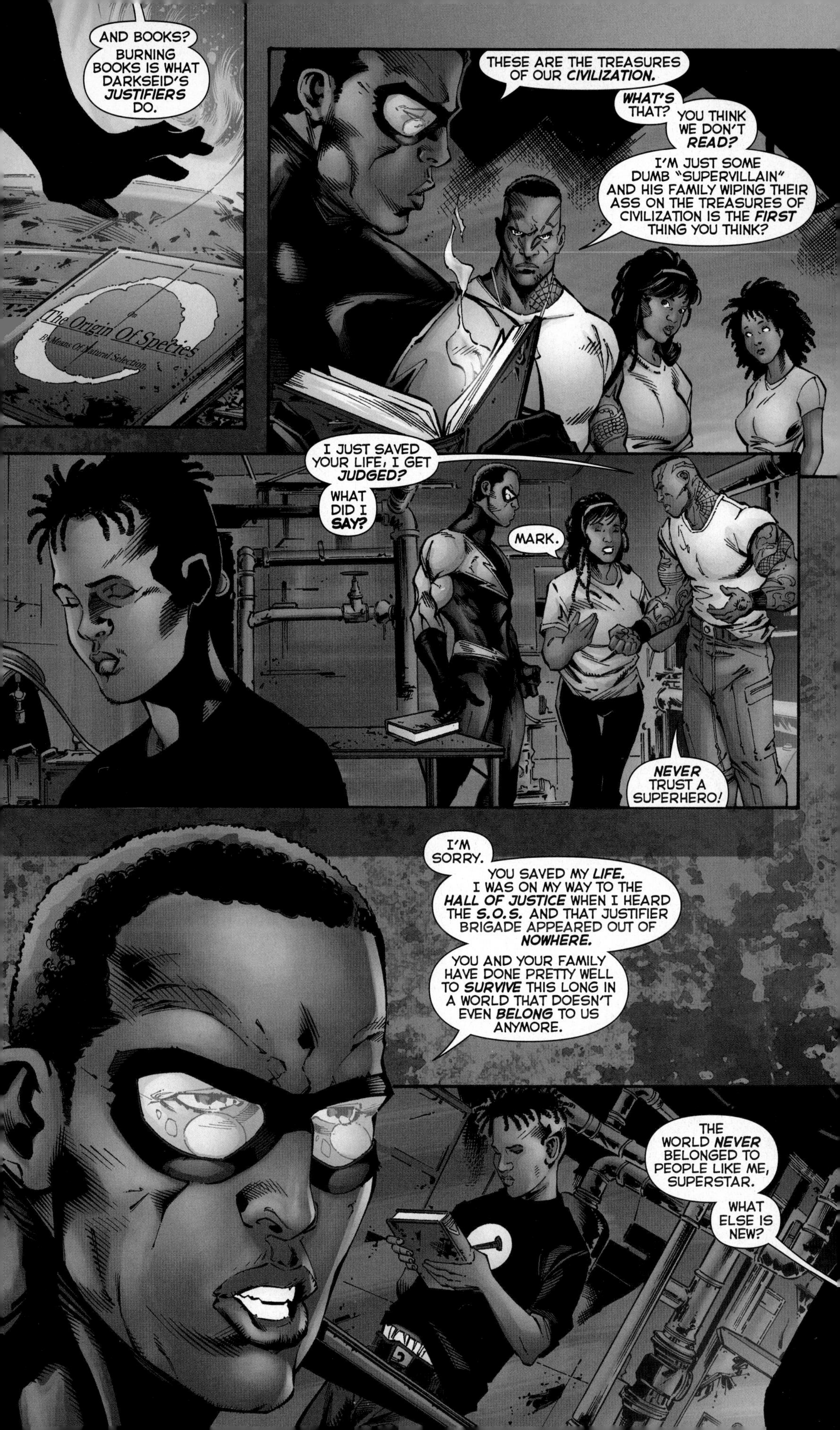
AND BOOKS? BURNING BOOKS IS WHAT DARKSEID'S JUSTIFIERS DO.
The Origin Of Species
By Means Of Natural Selection
THESE ARE THE TREASURES OF OUR CIVILIZATION.
WHAT'S THAT?
YOU THINK WE DON'T READ?
I'M JUST SOME DUMB "SUPERVILLAIN" AND HIS FAMILY WIPING THEIR ASS ON THE TREASURES OF CIVILIZATION IS THE FIRST THING YOU THINK?
I JUST SAVED YOUR LIFE, I GET JUDGED?
WHAT DID I SAY?
MARK.
NEVER TRUST A SUPERHERO!
I'M SORRY.
YOU SAVED MY LIFE. I WAS ON MY WAY TO THE HALL OF JUSTICE WHEN I HEARD THE S.O.S. AND THAT JUSTIFIER BRIGADE APPEARED OUT OF NOWHERE.
YOU AND YOUR FAMILY HAVE DONE PRETTY WELL TO SURVIVE THIS LONG IN A WORLD THAT DOESN'T EVEN BELONG TO US ANYMORE.
THE WORLD NEVER BELONGED TO PEOPLE LIKE ME, SUPERSTAR.
WHAT ELSE IS NEW?

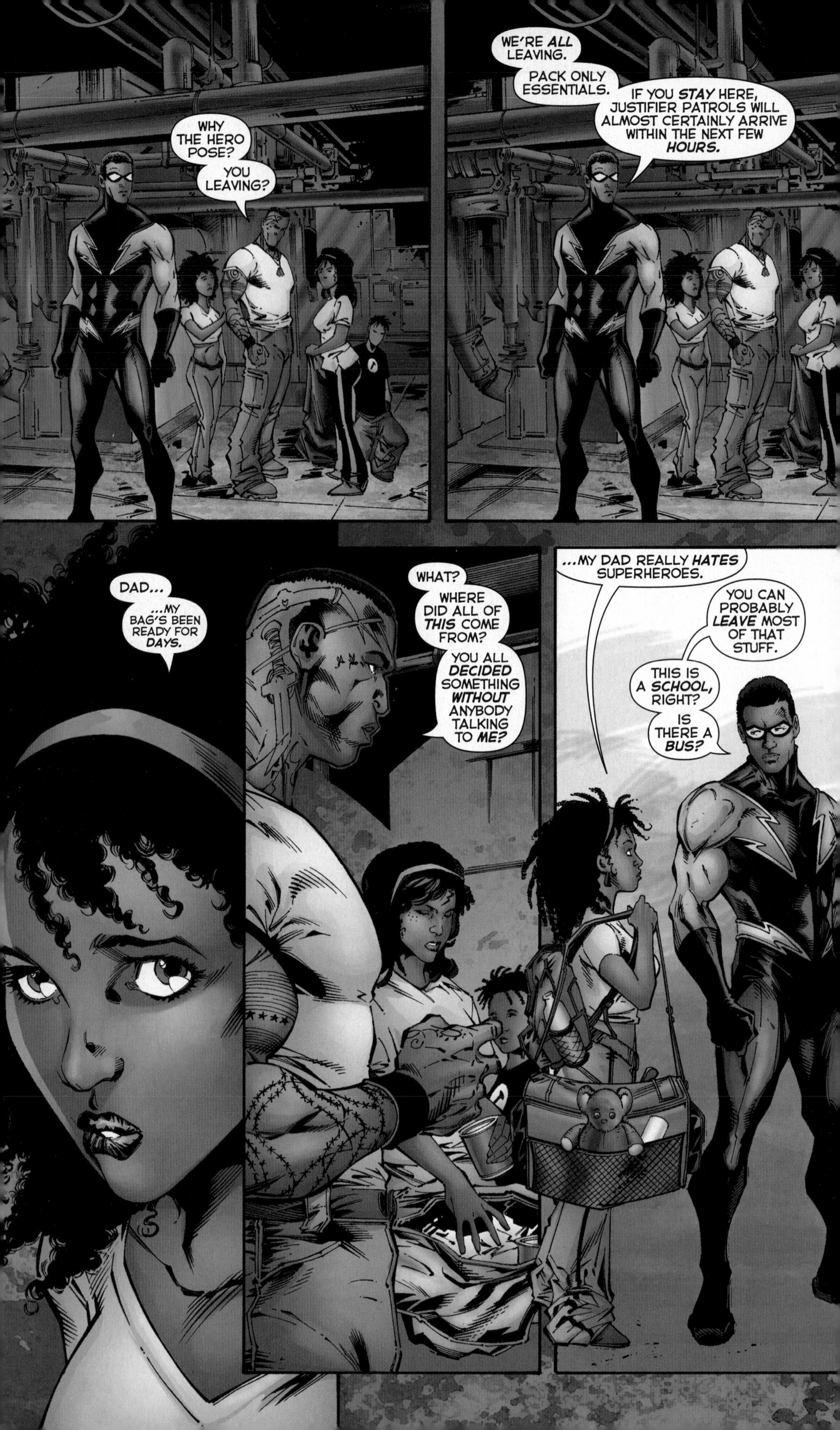
WHY THE HERO POSE?
YOU LEAVING?
WE'RE ALL LEAVING.
PACK ONLY ESSENTIALS.
IF YOU STAY HERE, JUSTIFIER PATROLS WILL ALMOST CERTAINLY ARRIVE WITHIN THE NEXT FEW HOURS.
DAD...
...MY BAG'S BEEN READY FOR DAYS.
WHAT?
WHERE DID ALL OF THIS COME FROM?
YOU ALL DECIDED SOMETHING WITHOUT ANYBODY TALKING TO ME?
...MY DAD REALLY HATES SUPERHEROES.
YOU CAN PROBABLY LEAVE MOST OF THAT STUFF.
THIS IS A SCHOOL, RIGHT?
IS THERE A BUS?

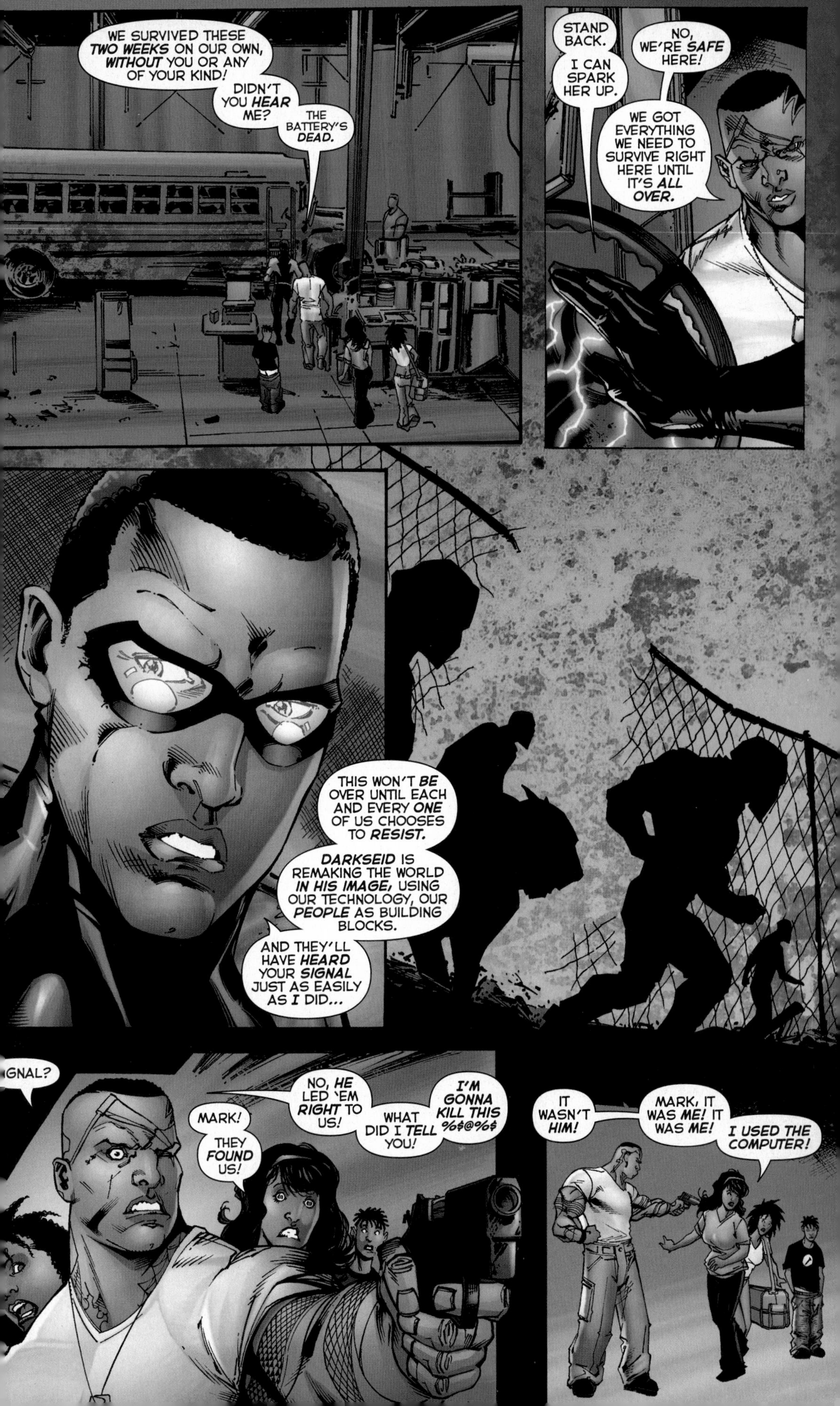
WE SURVIVED THESE TWO WEEKS ON OUR OWN, WITHOUT YOU OR ANY OF YOUR KIND!
DIDN'T YOU HEAR ME?
THE BATTERY'S DEAD.
STAND BACK.
I CAN SPARK HER UP.
NO, WE'RE SAFE HERE!
WE GOT EVERYTHING WE NEED TO SURVIVE RIGHT HERE UNTIL IT'S ALL OVER.
THIS WON'T BE OVER UNTIL EACH AND EVERY ONE OF US CHOOSES TO RESIST.
DARKSEID IS REMAKING THE WORLD IN HIS IMAGE, USING OUR TECHNOLOGY, OUR PEOPLE AS BUILDING BLOCKS.
AND THEY'LL HAVE HEARD YOUR SIGNAL JUST AS EASILY AS I DID...
GNAL?
MARK! THEY FOUND US!
NO, HE LED 'EM RIGHT TO US!
WHAT DID I TELL YOU!
I'M GONNA KILL THIS %$@%$
IT WASN'T HIM!
MARK, IT WAS ME! IT WAS ME!
I USED THE COMPUTER!

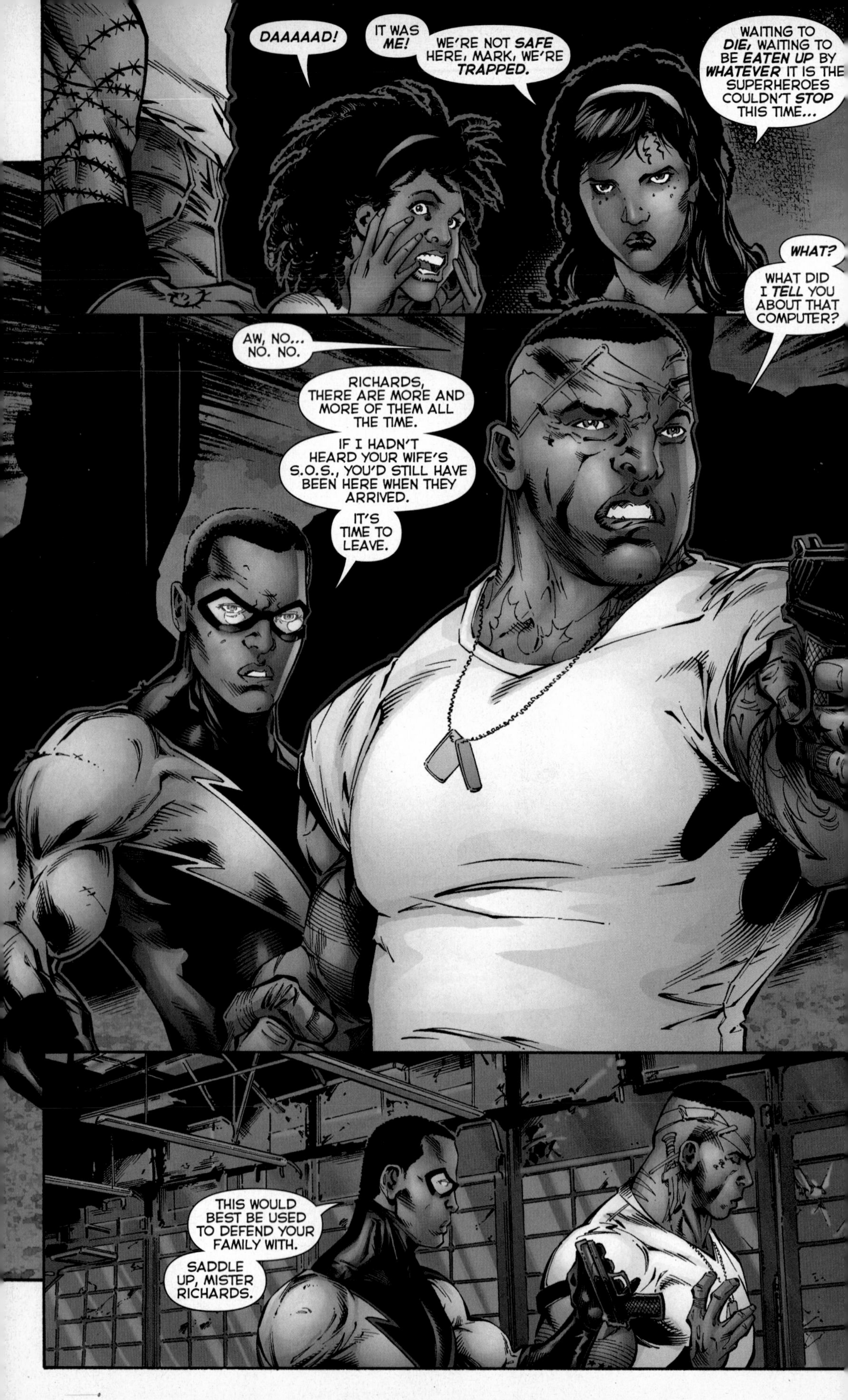
DAAAAAD!
IT WAS ME!
WE'RE NOT SAFE HERE, MARK, WE'RE TRAPPED.
WAITING TO DIE; WAITING TO BE EATEN UP BY WHATEVER IT IS THE SUPERHEROES COULDN'T STOP THIS TIME...
WHAT?
WHAT DID I TELL YOU ABOUT THAT COMPUTER?
AW, NO... NO. NO.
RICHARDS, THERE ARE MORE AND MORE OF THEM ALL THE TIME.
IF I HADN'T HEARD YOUR WIFE'S S.O.S., YOU'D STILL HAVE BEEN HERE WHEN THEY ARRIVED.
IT'S TIME TO LEAVE.
THIS WOULD BEST BE USED TO DEFEND YOUR FAMILY WITH.
SADDLE UP, MISTER RICHARDS.

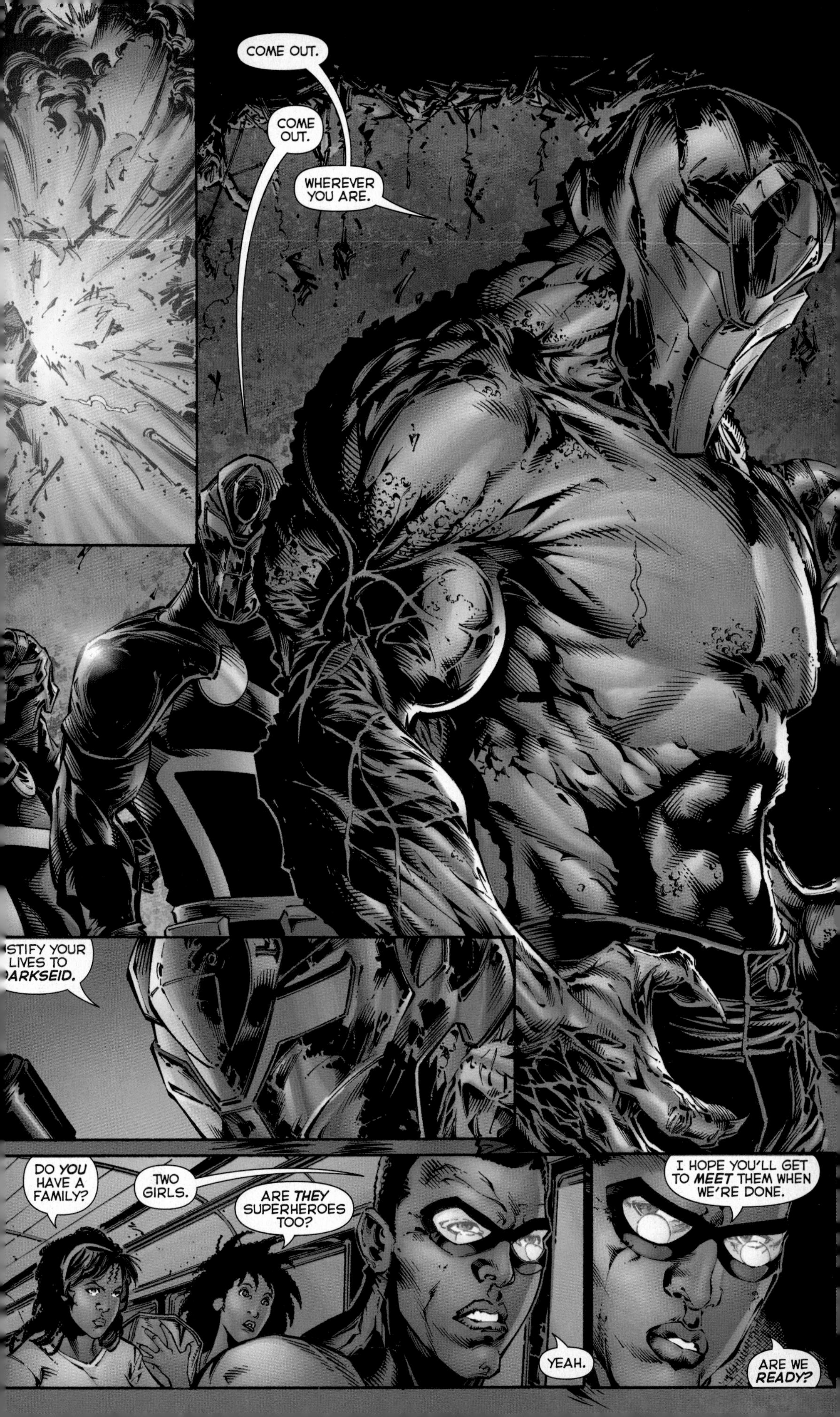
COME OUT.
COME OUT.
WHEREVER YOU ARE.
STIFY YOUR LIVES TO DARKSEID.
DO YOU HAVE A FAMILY?
TWO GIRLS.
ARE THEY SUPERHEROES TOO?
YEAH.
I HOPE YOU'LL GET TO MEET THEM WHEN WE'RE DONE.
ARE WE READY?

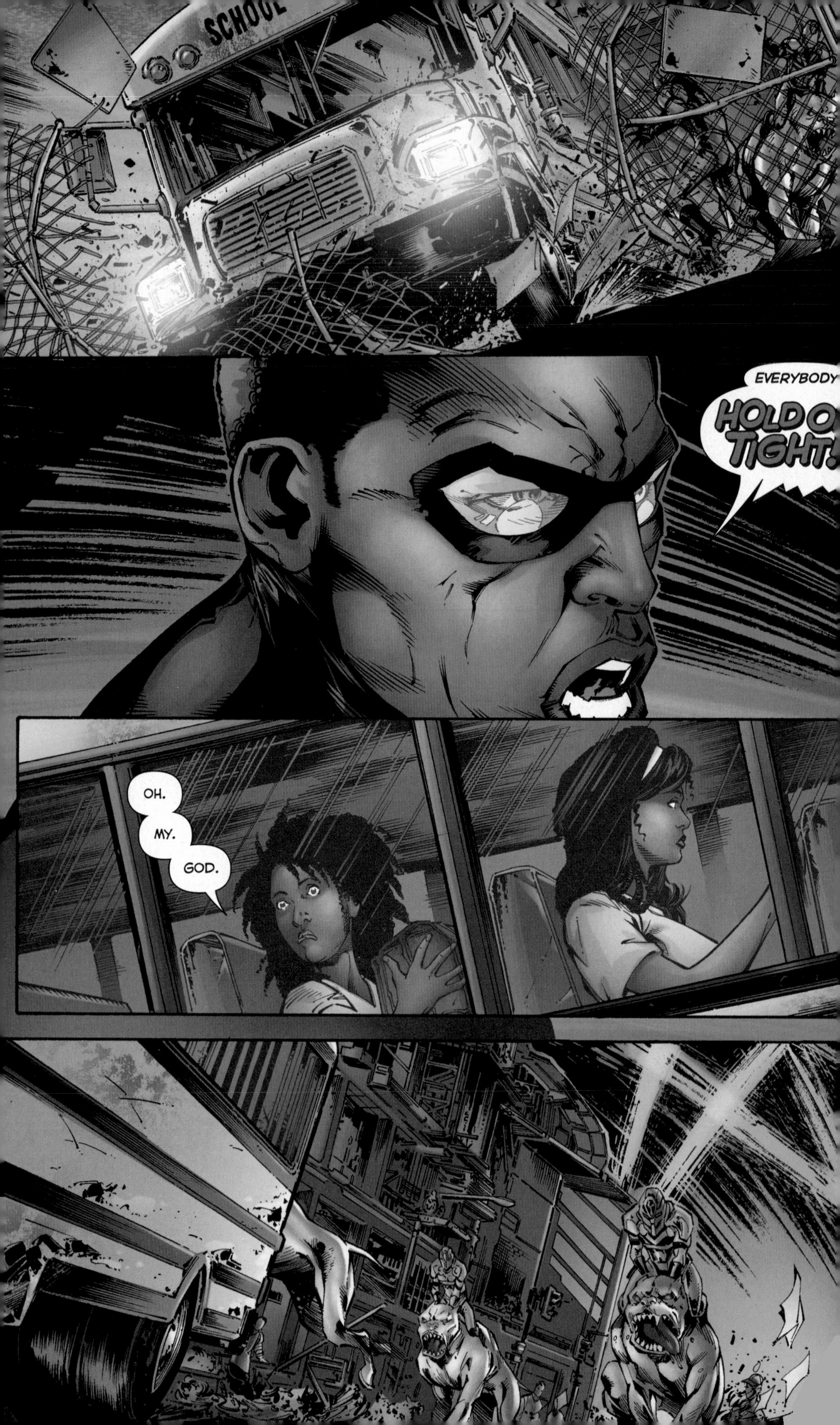
SCHOOL
EVERYBODY HOLD ON TIGHT!
OH.
MY.
GOD.

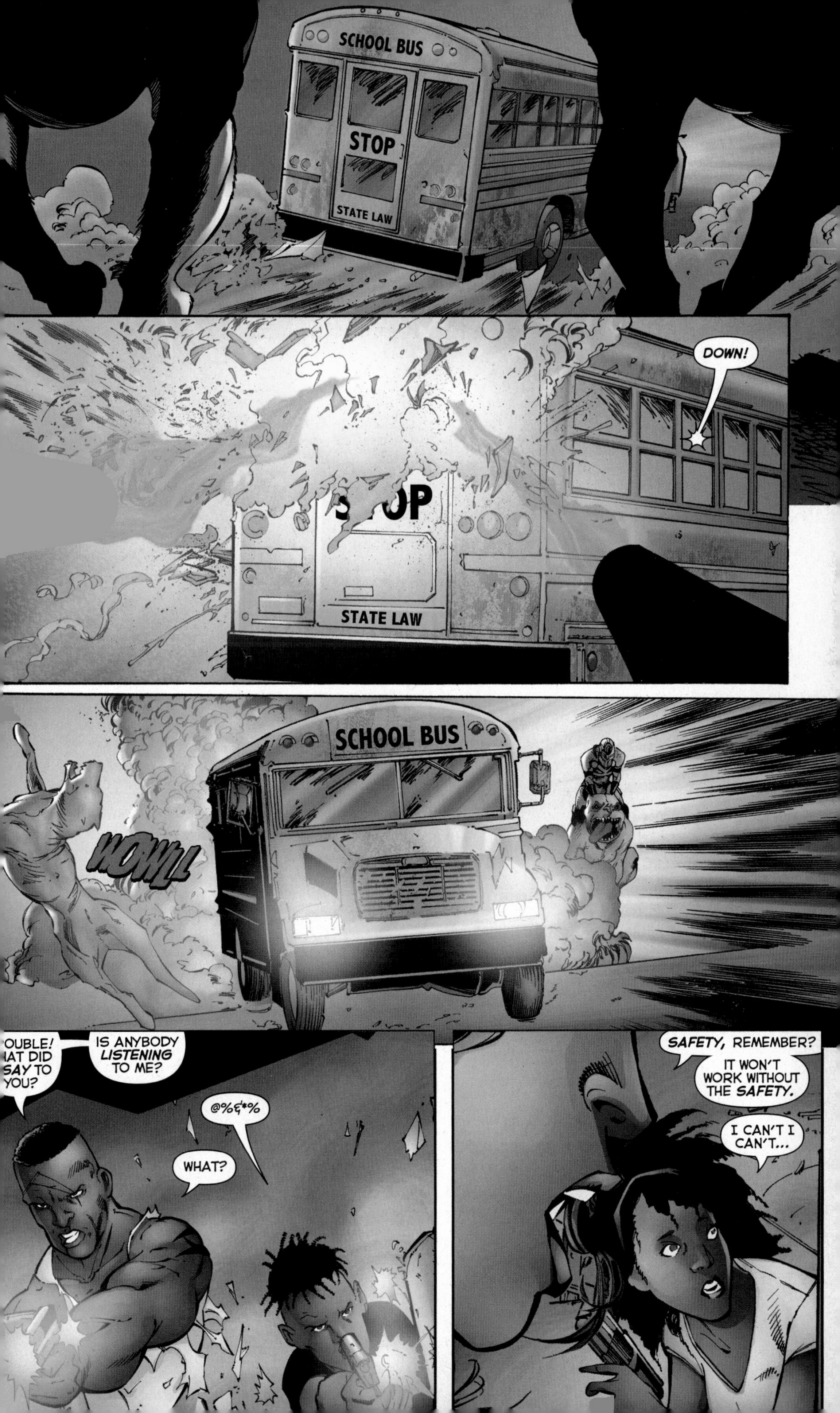
SCHOOL BUS
STOP
STATE LAW
DOWN!
STOP
STATE LAW
SCHOOL BUS
HOWLL
OUBLE! AT DID SAY TO YOU?
IS ANYBODY LISTENING TO ME?
@%$*%
WHAT?
SAFETY, REMEMBER?
IT WON'T WORK WITHOUT THE SAFETY.
I CAN'T I CAN'T...

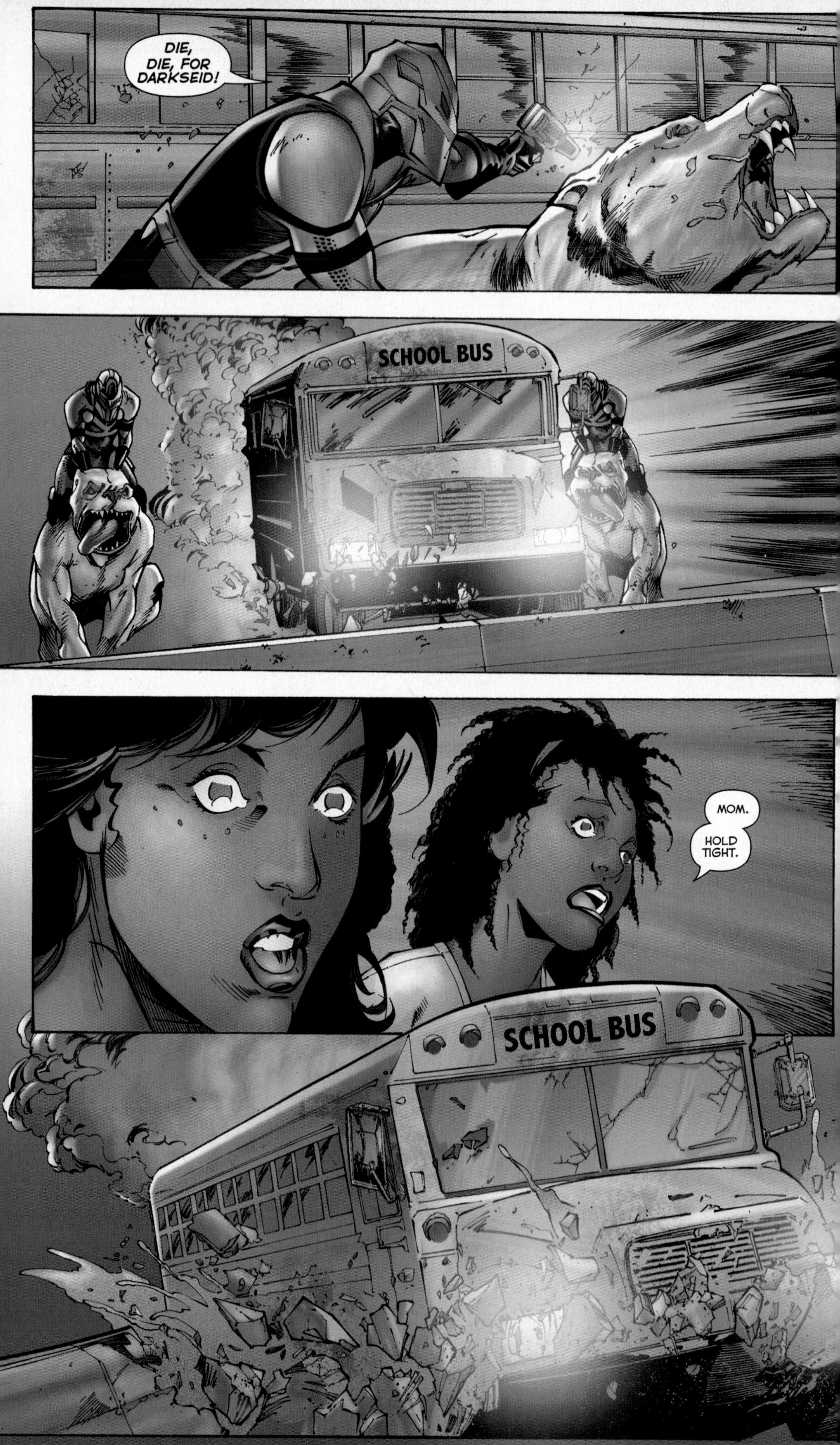
DIE, DIE, FOR DARKSEID!
SCHOOL BUS
MOM.
HOLD TIGHT.
SCHOOL BUS

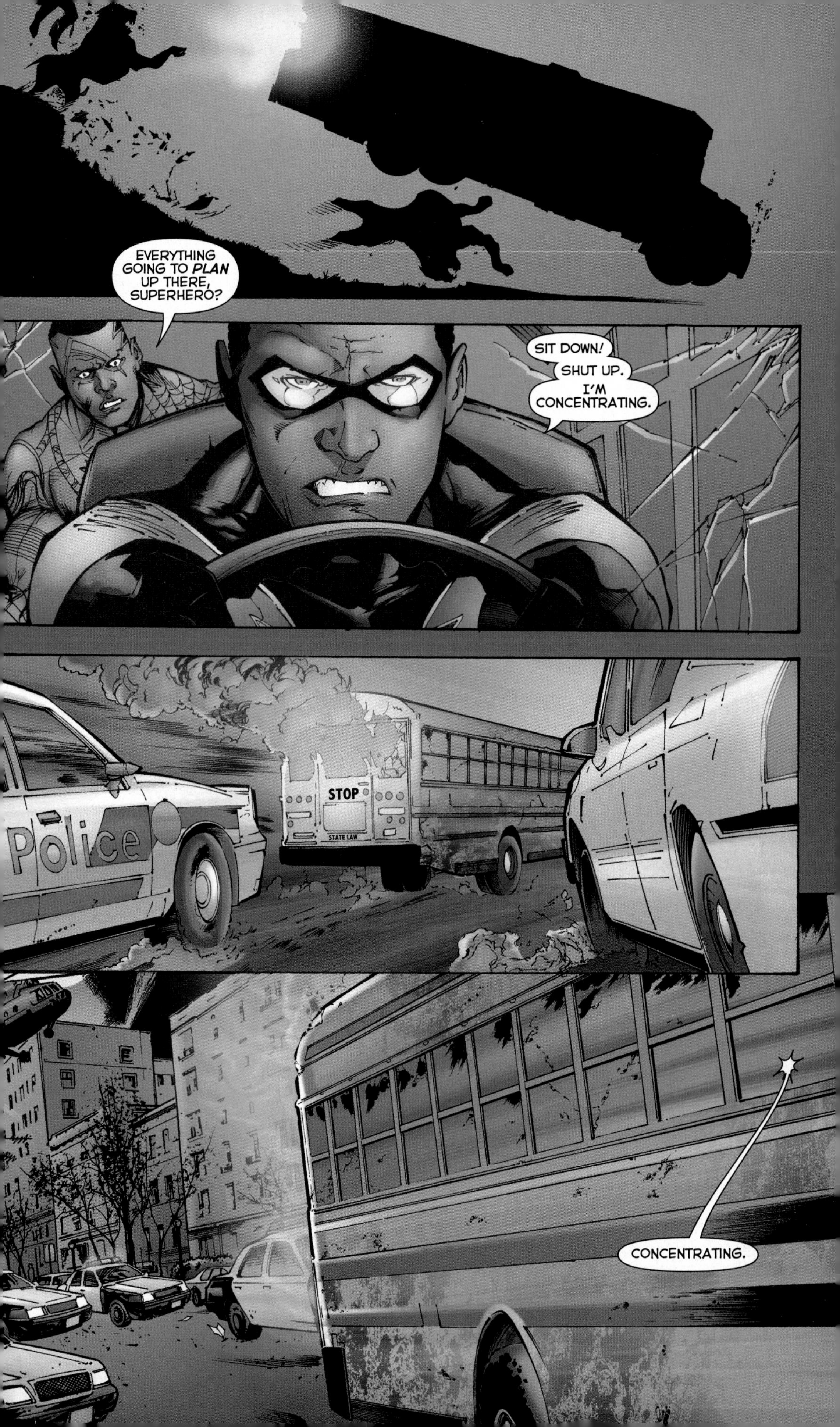
EVERYTHING GOING TO *PLAN* UP THERE, SUPERHERO?
SIT DOWN!
SHUT UP.
I'M CONCENTRATING.
Police
STOP
STATE LAW
CONCENTRATING.

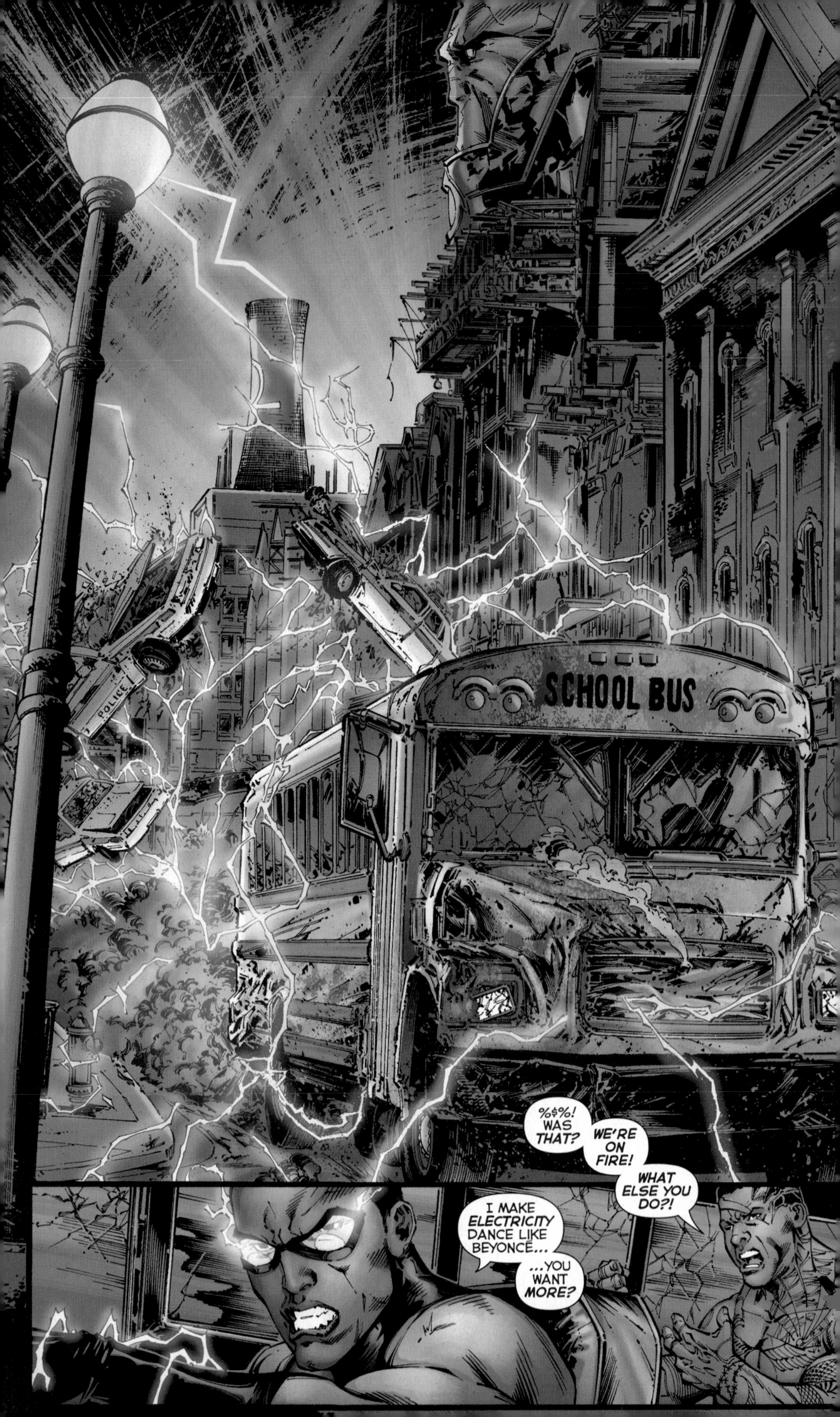
SCHOOL BUS
POLICE
%$%! WAS THAT?
WE'RE ON FIRE!
WHAT ELSE YOU DO?!
I MAKE ELECTRICITY DANCE LIKE BEYONCÉ...
...YOU WANT MORE?

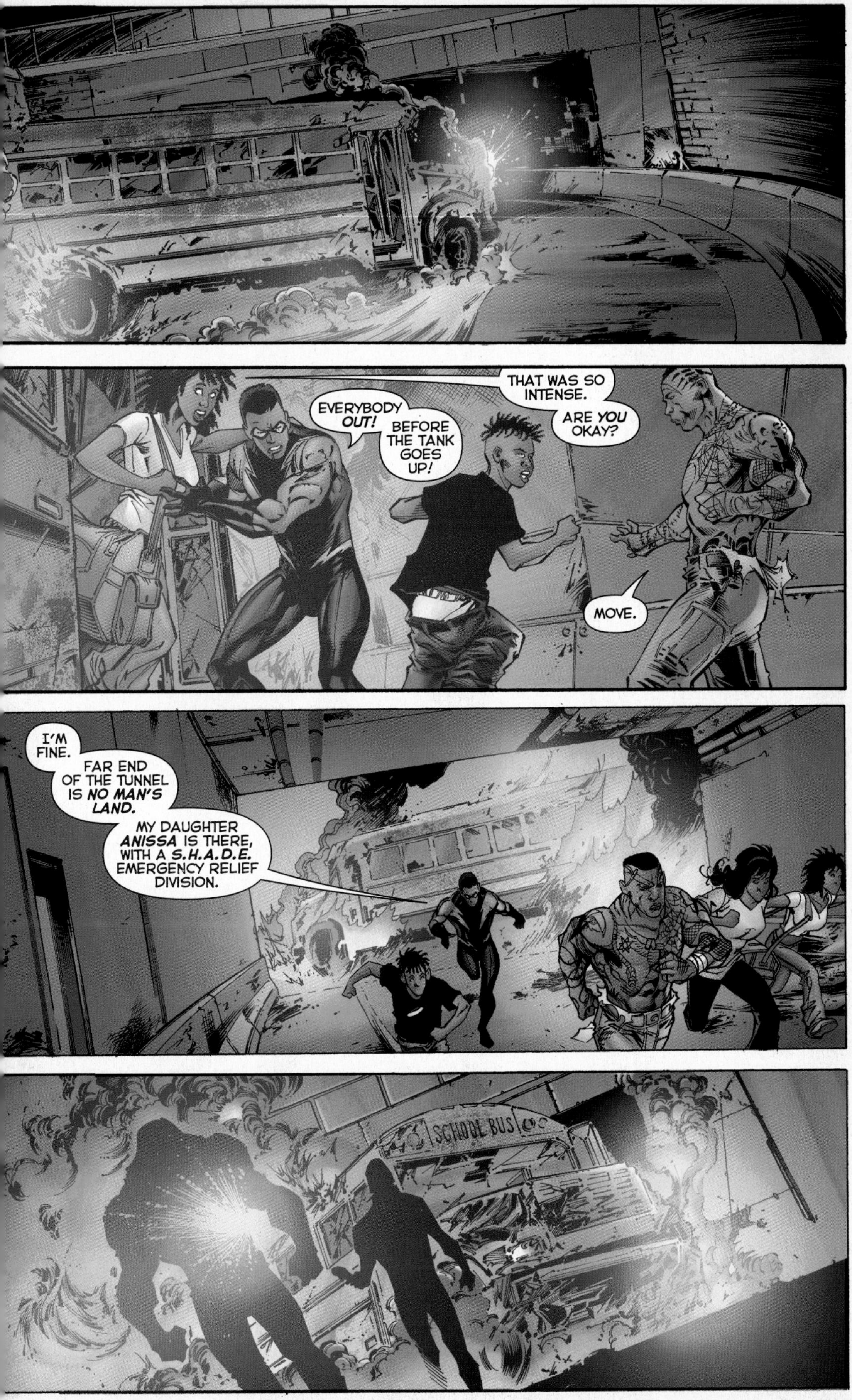

EVERYBODY OUT!
BEFORE THE TANK GOES UP!
THAT WAS SO INTENSE.
ARE YOU OKAY?
MOVE.
I'M FINE.
FAR END OF THE TUNNEL IS NO MAN'S LAND.
MY DAUGHTER ANISSA IS THERE, WITH A S.H.A.D.E. EMERGENCY RELIEF DIVISION.
SCHOOL BUS

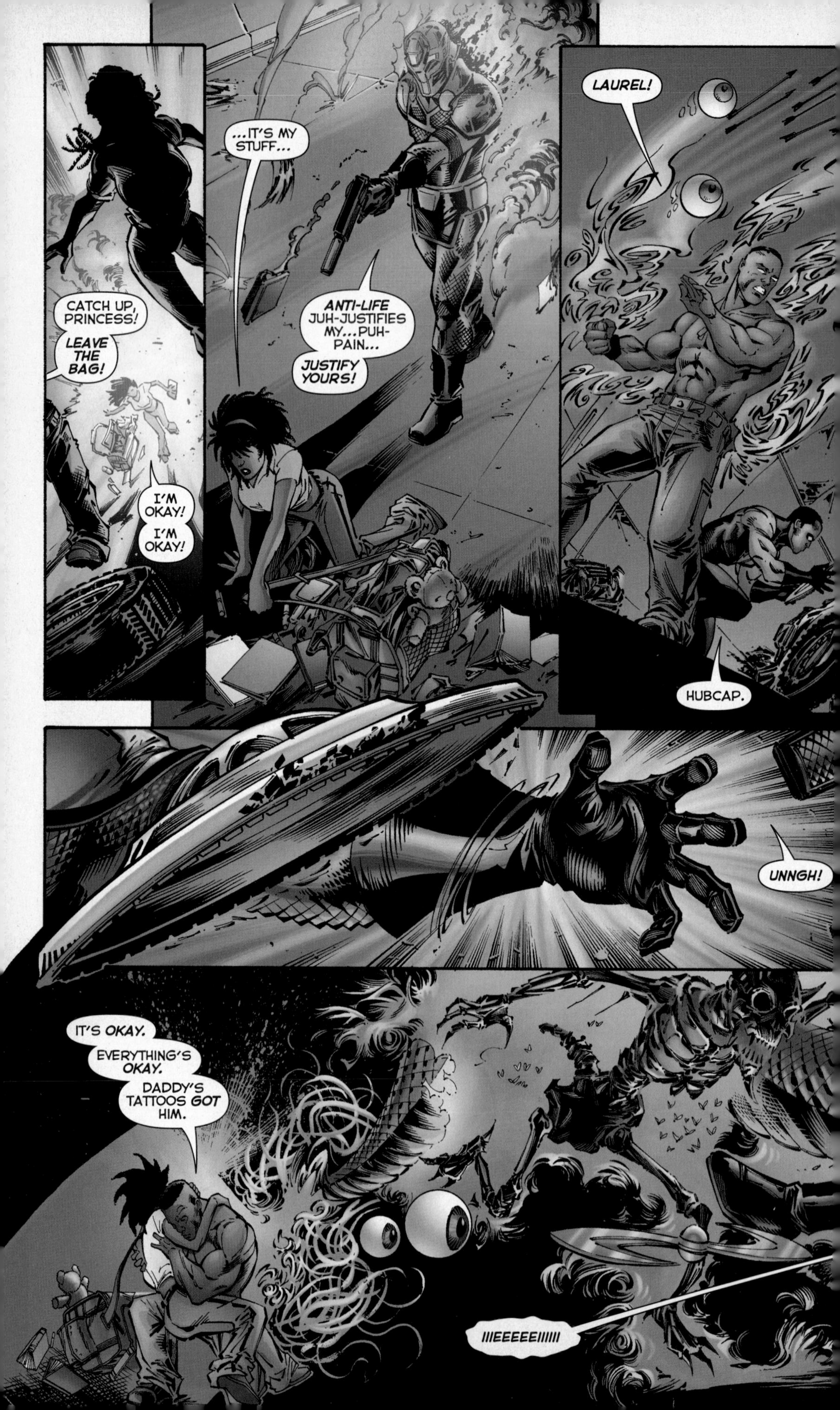

CATCH UP, PRINCESS!
LEAVE THE BAG!
I'M OKAY! I'M OKAY!
...IT'S MY STUFF...
ANTI-LIFE JUH-JUSTIFIES MY...PUH-PAIN... JUSTIFY YOURS!
LAUREL!
HUBCAP.
UNNGH!
IT'S OKAY.
EVERYTHING'S OKAY.
DADDY'S TATTOOS GOT HIM.
IIIEEEEEIIIIII

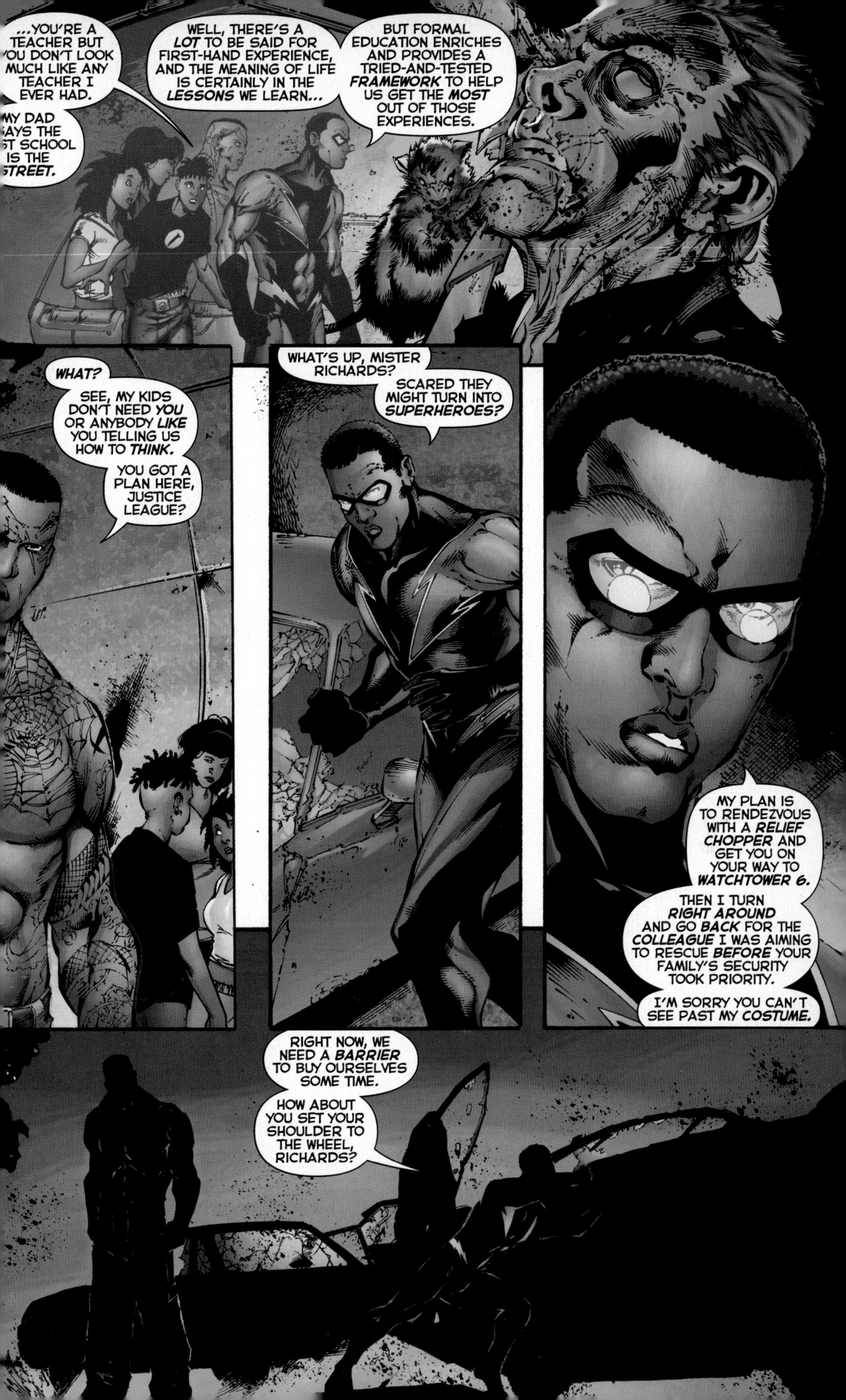
...YOU'RE A TEACHER BUT YOU DON'T LOOK MUCH LIKE ANY TEACHER I EVER HAD.
MY DAD SAYS THE ST SCHOOL IS THE STREET.
WELL, THERE'S A LOT TO BE SAID FOR FIRST-HAND EXPERIENCE, AND THE MEANING OF LIFE IS CERTAINLY IN THE LESSONS WE LEARN...
BUT FORMAL EDUCATION ENRICHES AND PROVIDES A TRIED-AND-TESTED FRAMEWORK TO HELP US GET THE MOST OUT OF THOSE EXPERIENCES.
WHAT?
SEE, MY KIDS DON'T NEED YOU OR ANYBODY LIKE YOU TELLING US HOW TO THINK.
YOU GOT A PLAN HERE, JUSTICE LEAGUE?
WHAT'S UP, MISTER RICHARDS?
SCARED THEY MIGHT TURN INTO SUPERHEROES?
MY PLAN IS TO RENDEZVOUS WITH A RELIEF CHOPPER AND GET YOU ON YOUR WAY TO WATCHTOWER 6.
THEN I TURN RIGHT AROUND AND GO BACK FOR THE COLLEAGUE I WAS AIMING TO RESCUE BEFORE YOUR FAMILY'S SECURITY TOOK PRIORITY.
I'M SORRY YOU CAN'T SEE PAST MY COSTUME.
RIGHT NOW, WE NEED A BARRIER TO BUY OURSELVES SOME TIME.
HOW ABOUT YOU SET YOUR SHOULDER TO THE WHEEL, RICHARDS?

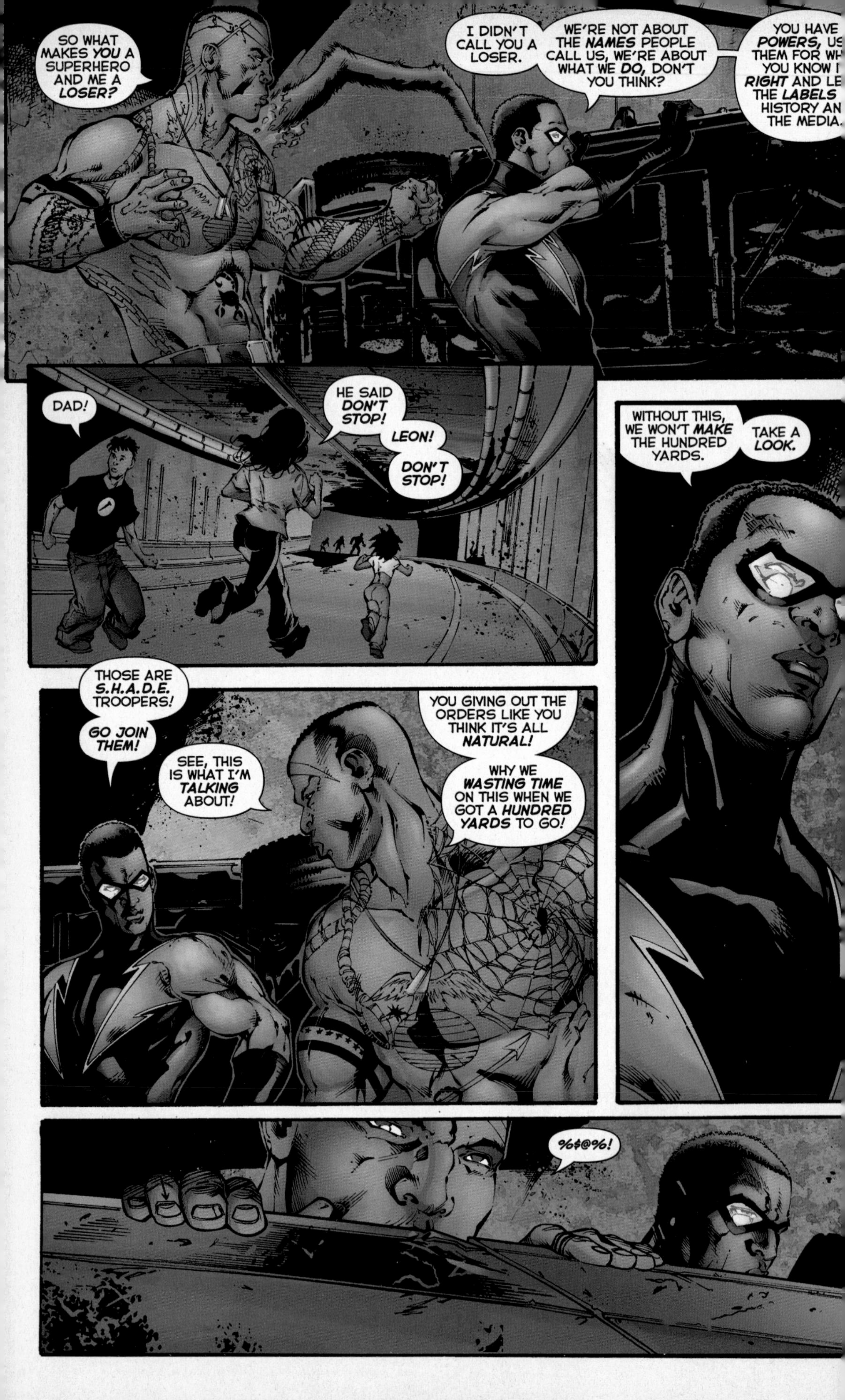

SO WHAT MAKES YOU A SUPERHERO AND ME A LOSER?
I DIDN'T CALL YOU A LOSER.
WE'RE NOT ABOUT THE NAMES PEOPLE CALL US, WE'RE ABOUT WHAT WE DO, DON'T YOU THINK?
YOU HAVE POWERS, US THEM FOR WH YOU KNOW I RIGHT AND LE THE LABELS HISTORY AN THE MEDIA.
DAD!
HE SAID DON'T STOP!
LEON!
DON'T STOP!
WITHOUT THIS, WE WON'T MAKE THE HUNDRED YARDS.
TAKE A LOOK.
THOSE ARE S.H.A.D.E. TROOPERS!
GO JOIN THEM!
SEE, THIS IS WHAT I'M TALKING ABOUT!
YOU GIVING OUT THE ORDERS LIKE YOU THINK IT'S ALL NATURAL!
WHY WE WASTING TIME ON THIS WHEN WE GOT A HUNDRED YARDS TO GO!
%$@%!

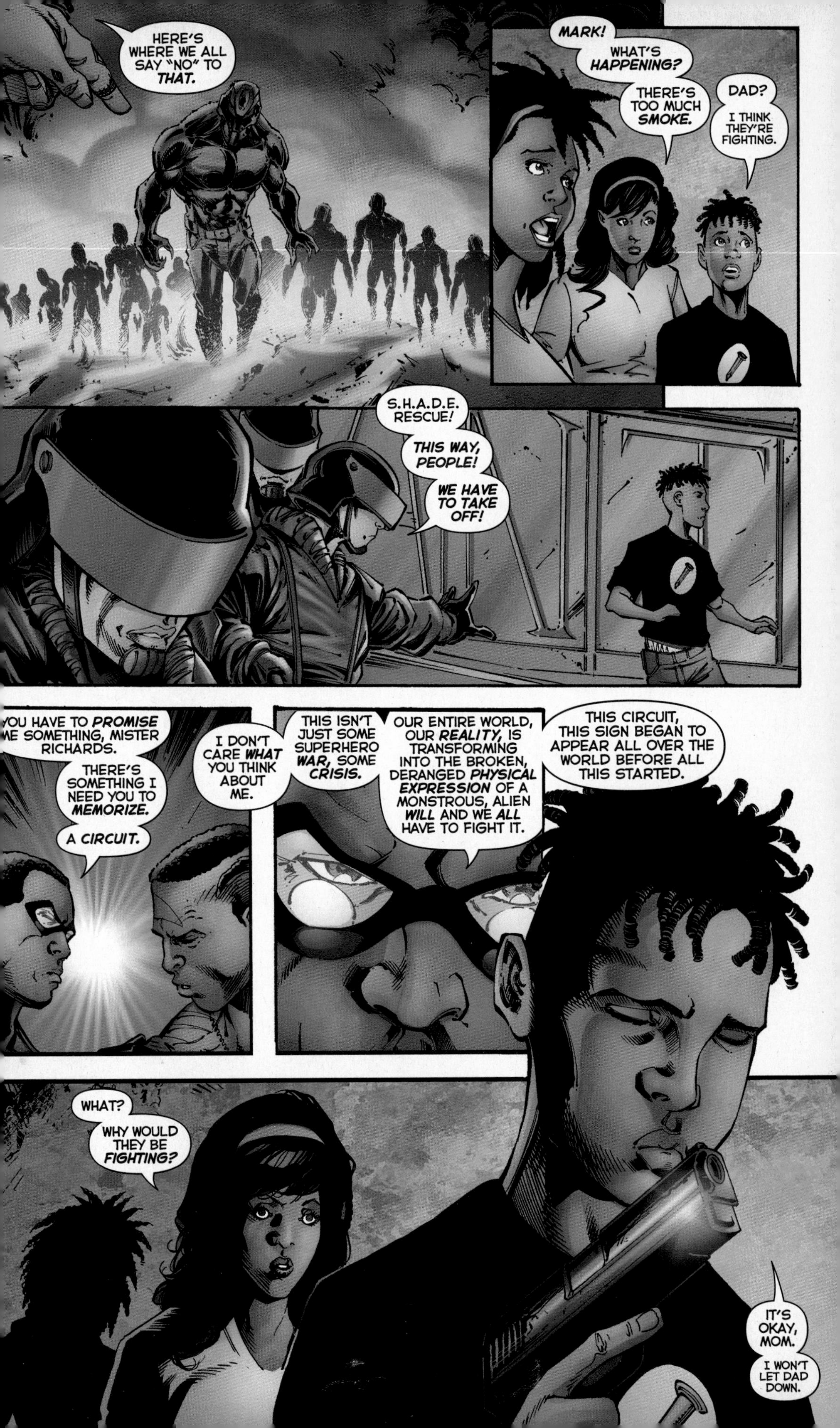

HERE'S WHERE WE ALL SAY "NO" TO THAT.
MARK! WHAT'S HAPPENING?
THERE'S TOO MUCH SMOKE.
DAD?
I THINK THEY'RE FIGHTING.
S.H.A.D.E. RESCUE!
THIS WAY, PEOPLE!
WE HAVE TO TAKE OFF!
YOU HAVE TO PROMISE ME SOMETHING, MISTER RICHARDS.
THERE'S SOMETHING I NEED YOU TO MEMORIZE.
A CIRCUIT.
I DON'T CARE WHAT YOU THINK ABOUT ME.
THIS ISN'T JUST SOME SUPERHERO WAR, SOME CRISIS.
OUR ENTIRE WORLD, OUR REALITY, IS TRANSFORMING INTO THE BROKEN, DERANGED PHYSICAL EXPRESSION OF A MONSTROUS, ALIEN WILL AND WE ALL HAVE TO FIGHT IT.
THIS CIRCUIT, THIS SIGN BEGAN TO APPEAR ALL OVER THE WORLD BEFORE ALL THIS STARTED.
WHAT?
WHY WOULD THEY BE FIGHTING?
IT'S OKAY, MOM.
I WON'T LET DAD DOWN.

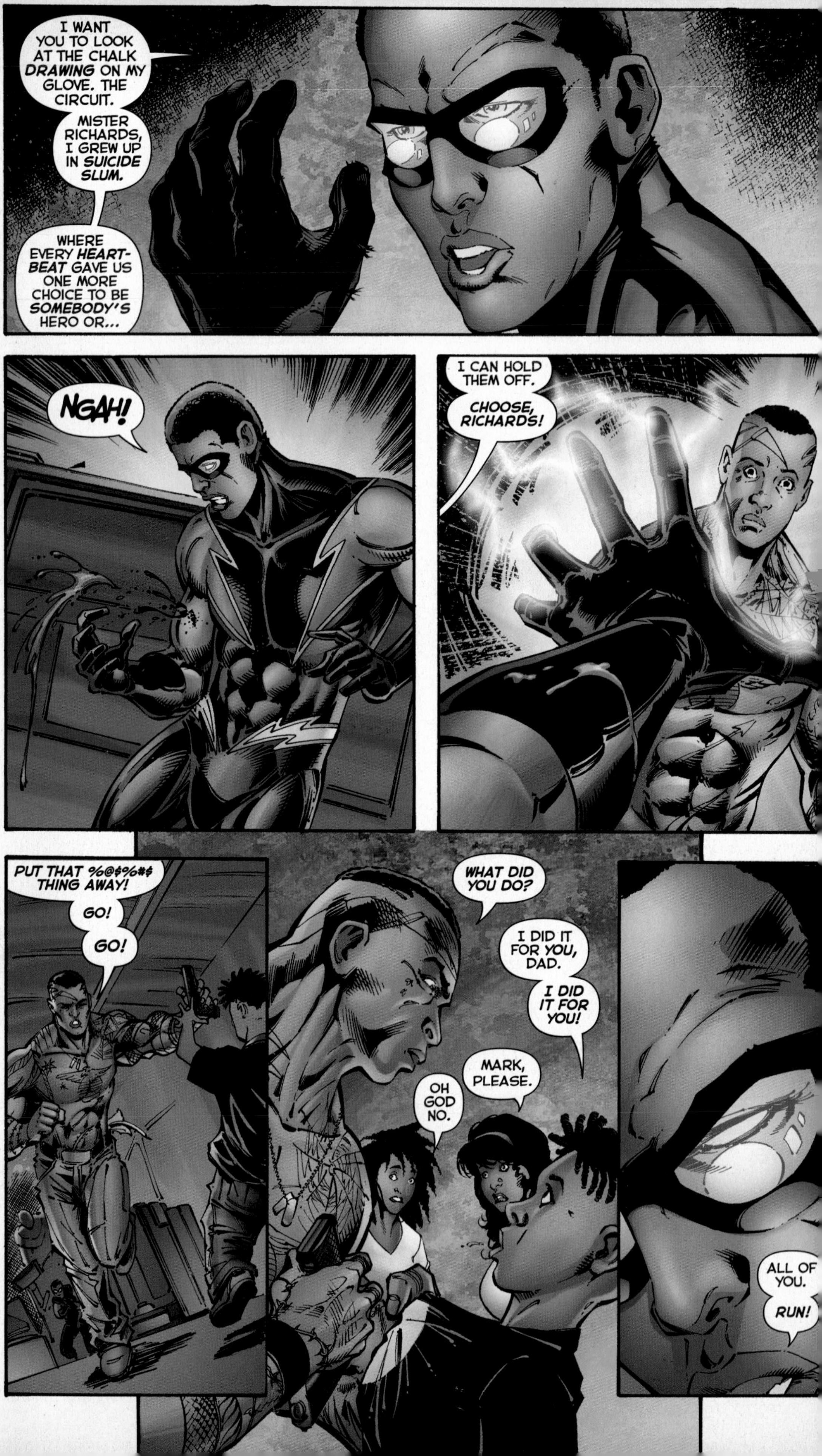

I WANT YOU TO LOOK AT THE CHALK DRAWING ON MY GLOVE. THE CIRCUIT.
MISTER RICHARDS, I GREW UP IN SUICIDE SLUM.
WHERE EVERY HEART-BEAT GAVE US ONE MORE CHOICE TO BE SOMEBODY'S HERO OR...
NGAH!
I CAN HOLD THEM OFF.
CHOOSE, RICHARDS!
PUT THAT %@$%#$ THING AWAY!
GO!
GO!
WHAT DID YOU DO?
I DID IT FOR YOU, DAD.
I DID IT FOR YOU!
MARK, PLEASE.
OH GOD NO.
ALL OF YOU.
RUN!

I DIDN'T MEAN TO HIT HIM.

I DON'T KNOW WHAT I MEANT.

I DID IT FOR YOU.

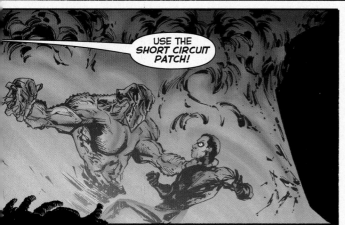

USE THE SHORT CIRCUIT PATCH!

AAUUU!

I DON'T KNOW.

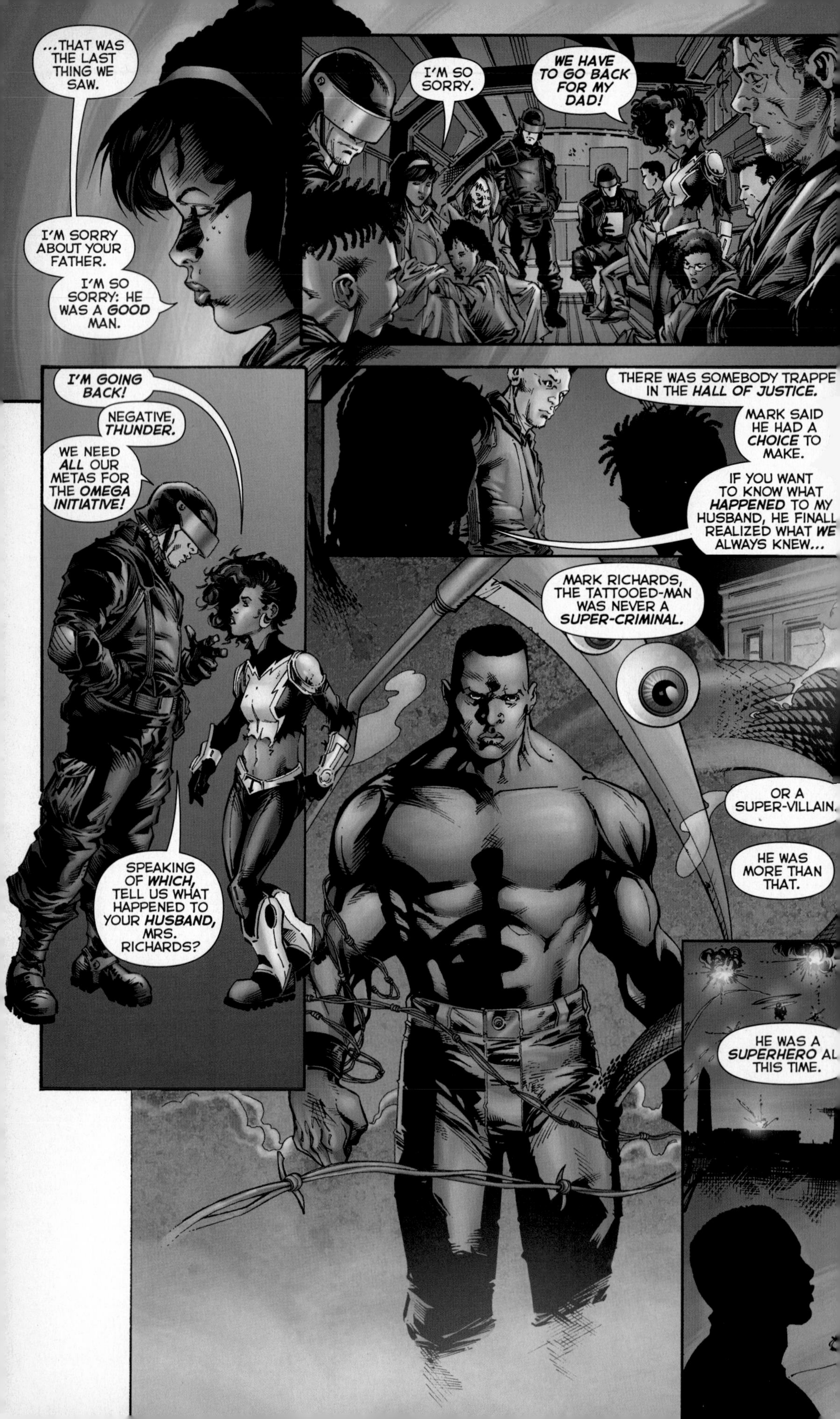

...THAT WAS THE LAST THING WE SAW.
I'M SO SORRY.
WE HAVE TO GO BACK FOR MY DAD!
I'M SORRY ABOUT YOUR FATHER.
I'M SO SORRY: HE WAS A GOOD MAN.
I'M GOING BACK!
NEGATIVE, THUNDER.
WE NEED ALL OUR METAS FOR THE OMEGA INITIATIVE!
SPEAKING OF WHICH, TELL US WHAT HAPPENED TO YOUR HUSBAND, MRS. RICHARDS?
THERE WAS SOMEBODY TRAPPE IN THE HALL OF JUSTICE.
MARK SAID HE HAD A CHOICE TO MAKE.
IF YOU WANT TO KNOW WHAT HAPPENED TO MY HUSBAND, HE FINALL REALIZED WHAT WE ALWAYS KNEW...
MARK RICHARDS, THE TATTOOED-MAN WAS NEVER A SUPER-CRIMINAL.
OR A SUPER-VILLAIN.
HE WAS MORE THAN THAT.
HE WAS A SUPERHERO AL THIS TIME.

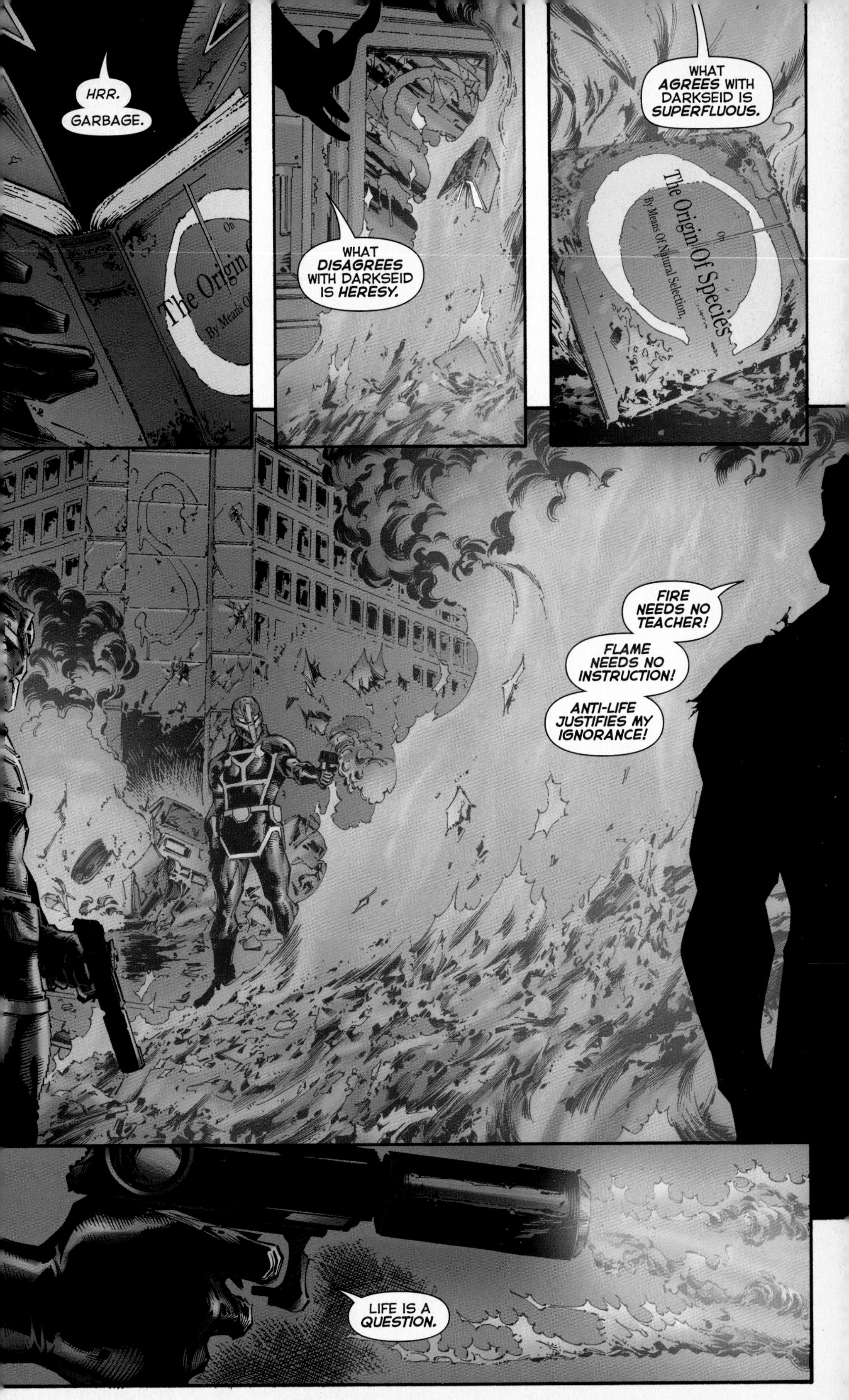
HRR. GARBAGE.
WHAT DISAGREES WITH DARKSEID IS HERESY.
WHAT AGREES WITH DARKSEID IS SUPERFLUOUS.
On
The Origin Of Species
FIRE NEEDS NO TEACHER!
FLAME NEEDS NO INSTRUCTION!
ANTI-LIFE JUSTIFIES MY IGNORANCE!
LIFE IS A QUESTION.

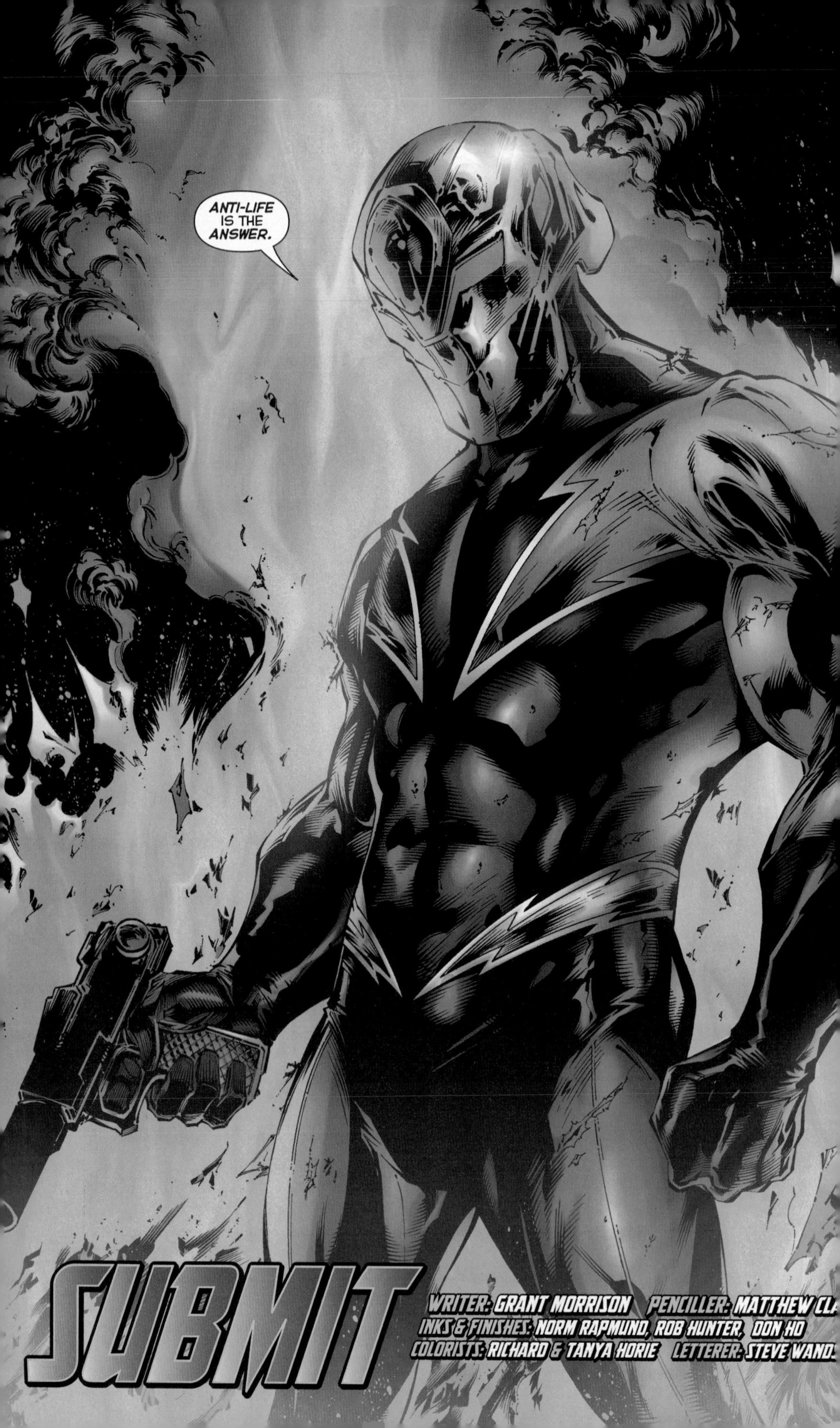
ANTI-LIFE IS THE ANSWER.
SUBMIT
WRITER: GRANT MORRISON PENCILLER: MATTHEW CL
INKS & FINISHES: NORM RAPMUND, ROB HUNTER, DON HO
COLORISTS: RICHARD & TANYA HORIE LETTERER: STEVE WAND

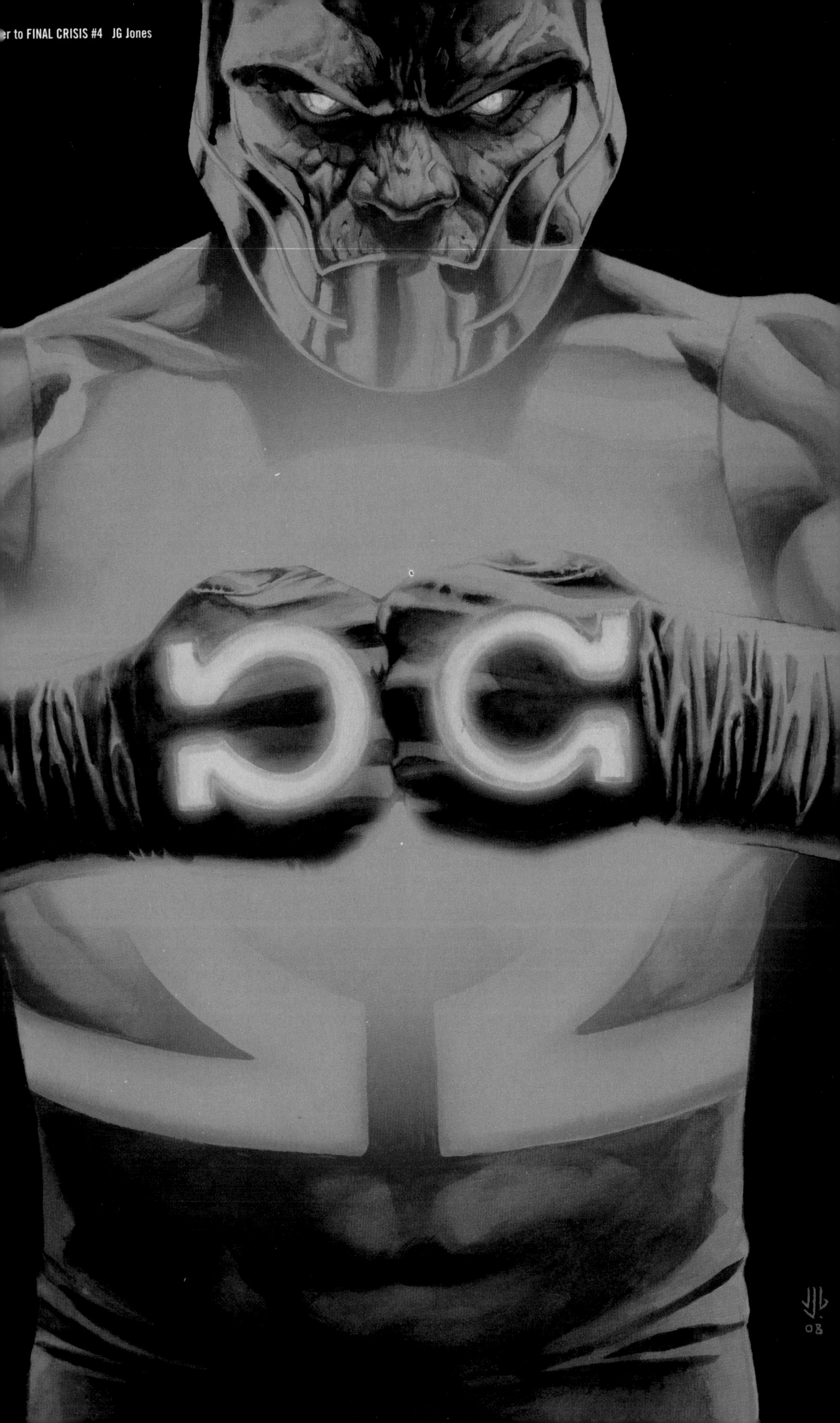

r to FINAL CRISIS #4 JG Jones

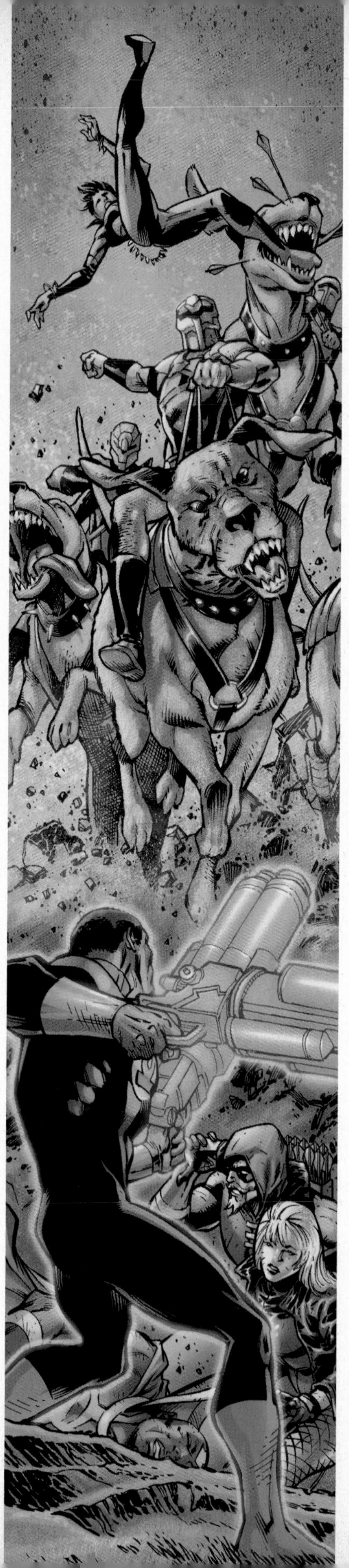

Carlos Pacheco & Jesus Merino with Alex Sinclair

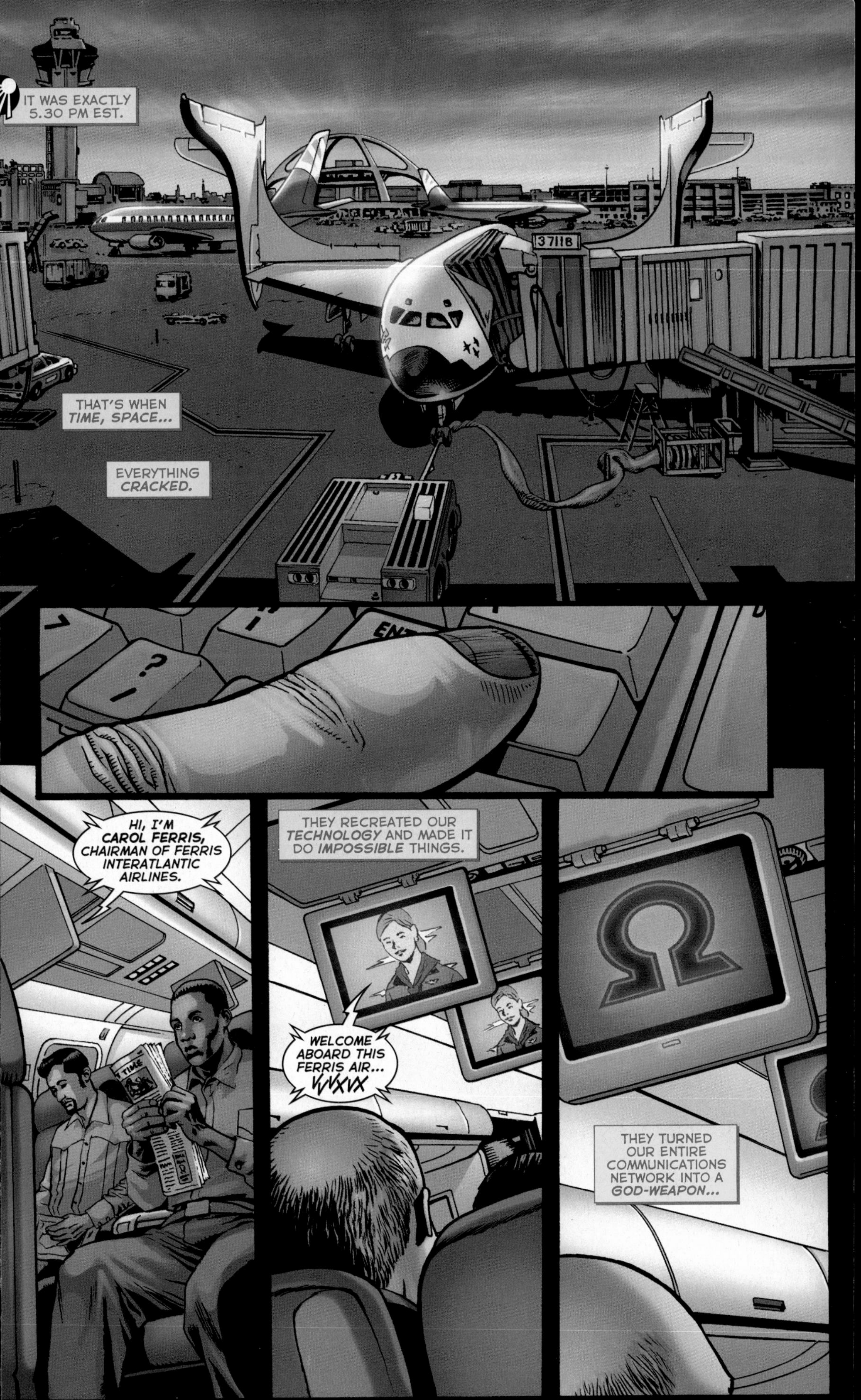
IT WAS EXACTLY 5.30 PM EST.
37118
THAT'S WHEN TIME, SPACE...
EVERYTHING CRACKED.
HI, I'M CAROL FERRIS, CHAIRMAN OF FERRIS INTERATLANTIC AIRLINES.
THEY RECREATED OUR TECHNOLOGY AND MADE IT DO IMPOSSIBLE THINGS.
WELCOME ABOARD THIS FERRIS AIR... VVVXVX
THEY TURNED OUR ENTIRE COMMUNICATIONS NETWORK INTO A GOD-WEAPON...

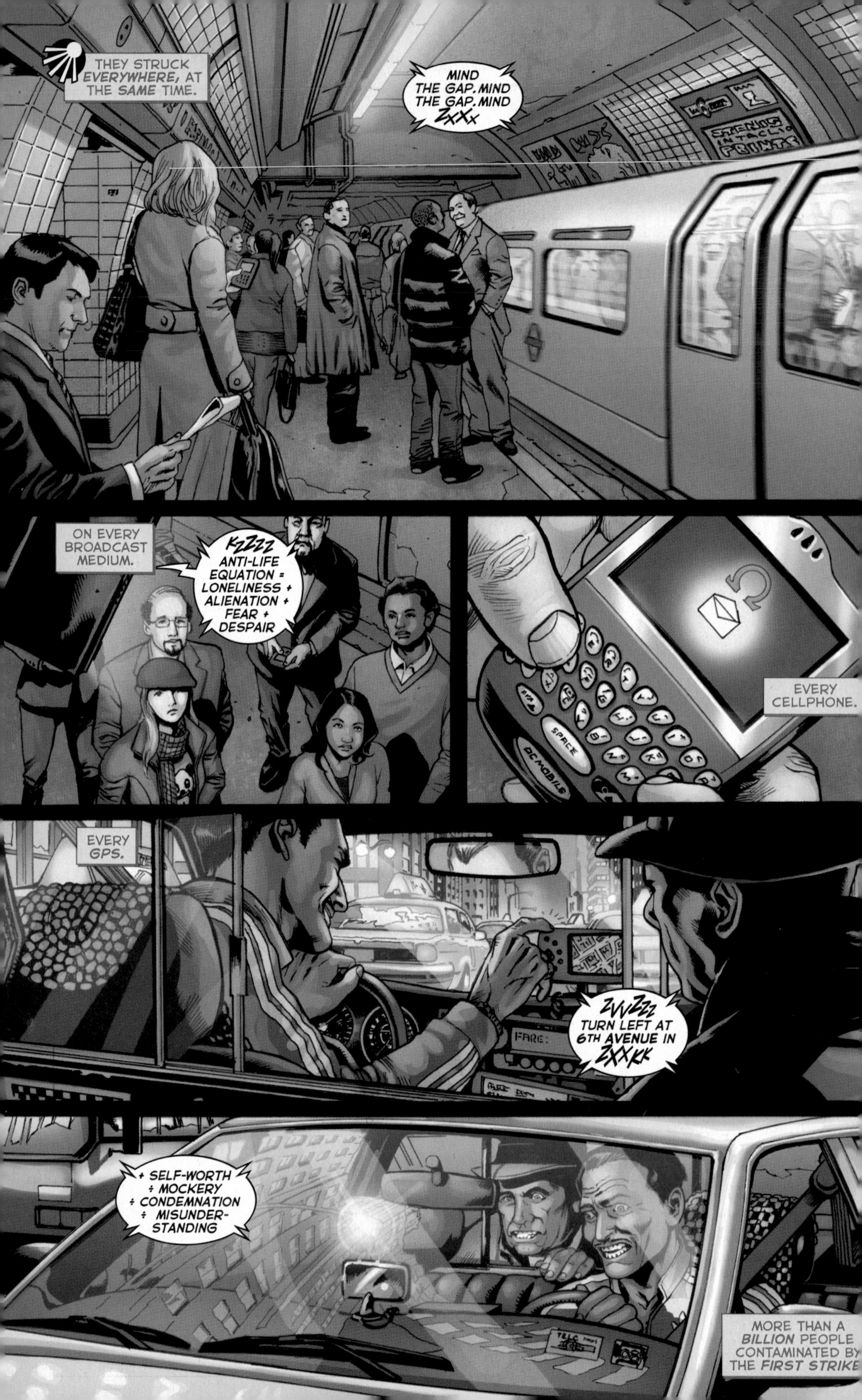
THEY STRUCK EVERYWHERE, AT THE SAME TIME.
MIND THE GAP. MIND THE GAP. MIND ZXXx
ON EVERY BROADCAST MEDIUM.
KZZZZ ANTI-LIFE EQUATION = LONELINESS + ALIENATION + FEAR + DESPAIR
EVERY CELLPHONE.
EVERY GPS.
ZVVZZZ TURN LEFT AT 6TH AVENUE IN ZXXKK
FARE:
+ SELF-WORTH ÷ MOCKERY ÷ CONDEMNATION ÷ MISUNDERSTANDING
MORE THAN A BILLION PEOPLE CONTAMINATED BY THE FIRST STRIKE

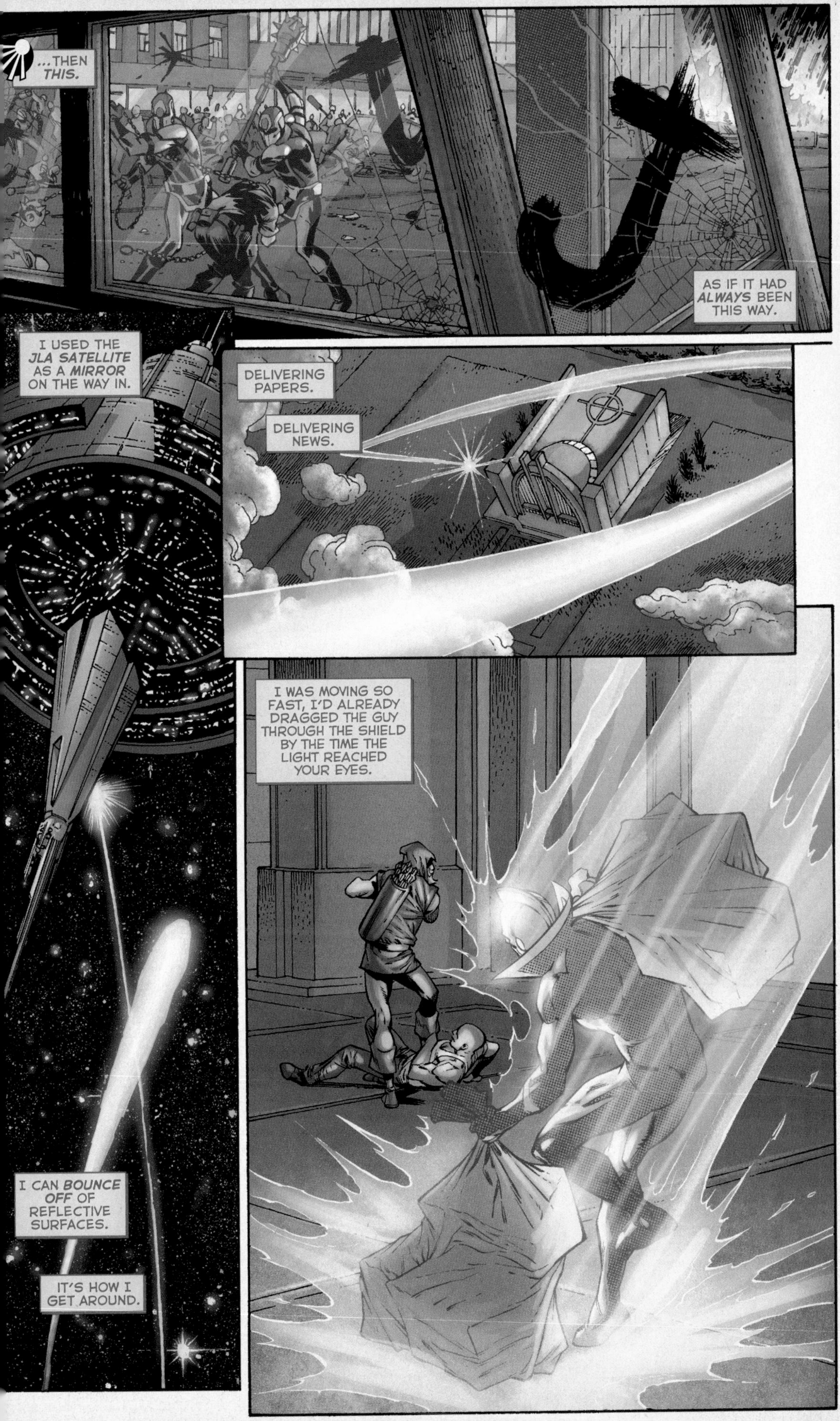
...THEN THIS.
AS IF IT HAD ALWAYS BEEN THIS WAY.
I USED THE JLA SATELLITE AS A MIRROR ON THE WAY IN.
DELIVERING PAPERS.
DELIVERING NEWS.
I WAS MOVING SO FAST, I'D ALREADY DRAGGED THE GUY THROUGH THE SHIELD BY THE TIME THE LIGHT REACHED YOUR EYES.
I CAN BOUNCE OFF OF REFLECTIVE SURFACES.
IT'S HOW I GET AROUND.

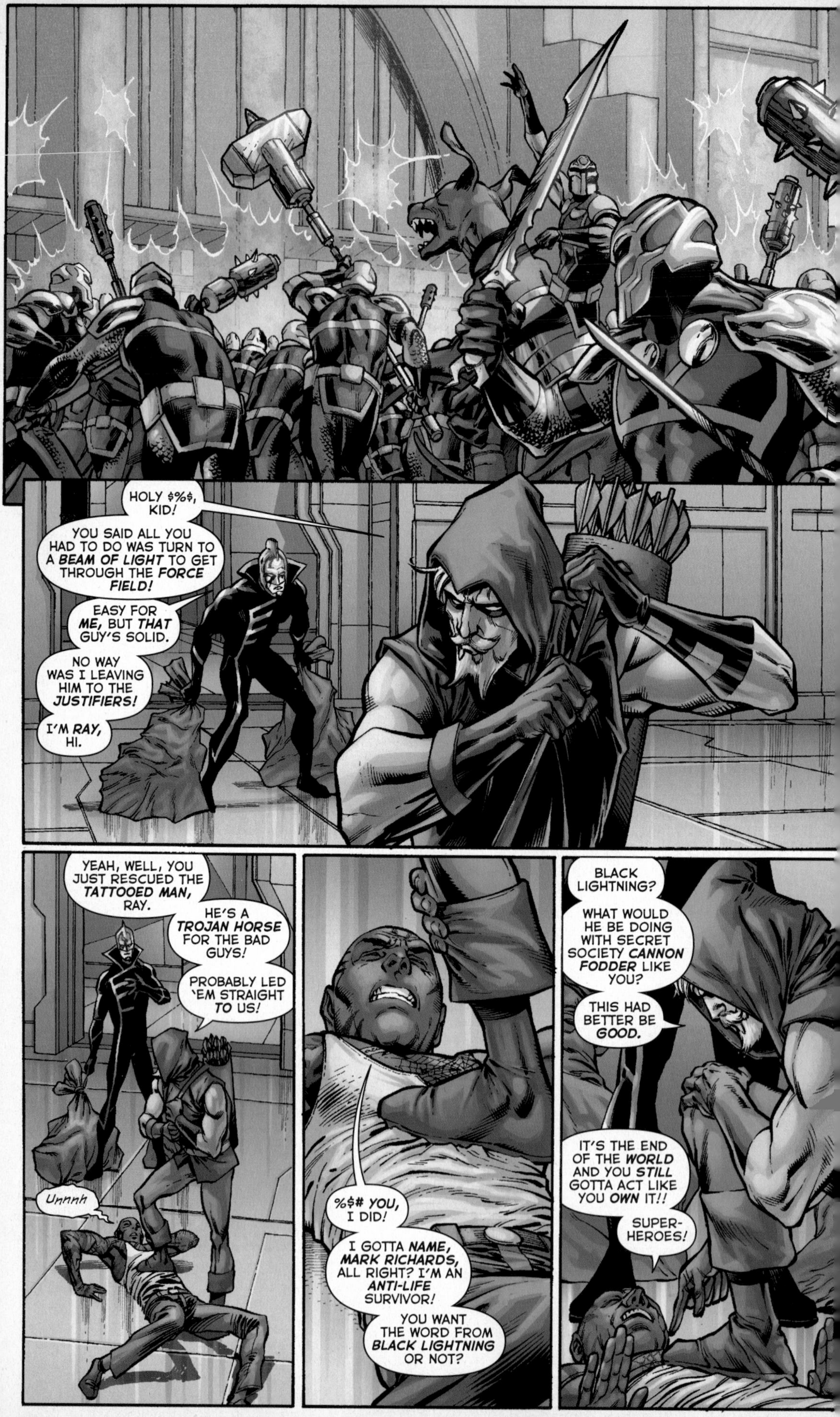
HOLY $%$, KID!
YOU SAID ALL YOU HAD TO DO WAS TURN TO A BEAM OF LIGHT TO GET THROUGH THE FORCE FIELD!
EASY FOR ME, BUT THAT GUY'S SOLID.
NO WAY WAS I LEAVING HIM TO THE JUSTIFIERS!
I'M RAY, HI.
YEAH, WELL, YOU JUST RESCUED THE TATTOOED MAN, RAY.
HE'S A TROJAN HORSE FOR THE BAD GUYS!
PROBABLY LED 'EM STRAIGHT TO US!
Unnnh
%$# YOU, I DID!
I GOTTA NAME, MARK RICHARDS, ALL RIGHT? I'M AN ANTI-LIFE SURVIVOR!
YOU WANT THE WORD FROM BLACK LIGHTNING OR NOT?
BLACK LIGHTNING?
WHAT WOULD HE BE DOING WITH SECRET SOCIETY CANNON FODDER LIKE YOU?
THIS HAD BETTER BE GOOD.
IT'S THE END OF THE WORLD AND YOU STILL GOTTA ACT LIKE YOU OWN IT!!
SUPER-HEROES!

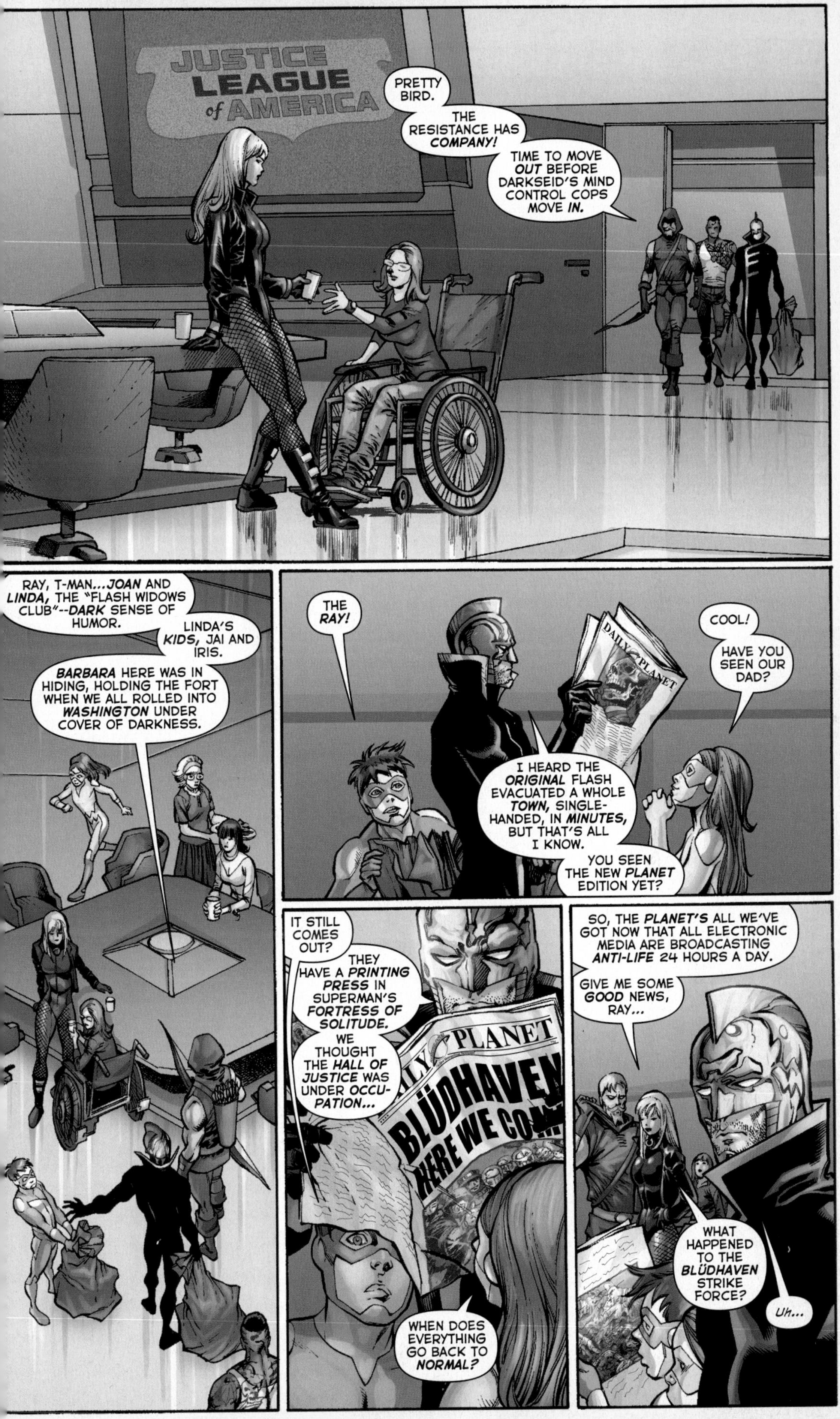
JUSTICE LEAGUE of AMERICA
PRETTY BIRD.
THE RESISTANCE HAS COMPANY!
TIME TO MOVE OUT BEFORE DARKSEID'S MIND CONTROL COPS MOVE IN.
RAY, T-MAN...JOAN AND LINDA, THE "FLASH WIDOWS CLUB"--DARK SENSE OF HUMOR.
LINDA'S KIDS, JAI AND IRIS.
BARBARA HERE WAS IN HIDING, HOLDING THE FORT WHEN WE ALL ROLLED INTO WASHINGTON UNDER COVER OF DARKNESS.
THE RAY!
COOL!
HAVE YOU SEEN OUR DAD?
DAILY PLANET
I HEARD THE ORIGINAL FLASH EVACUATED A WHOLE TOWN, SINGLE-HANDED, IN MINUTES, BUT THAT'S ALL I KNOW.
YOU SEEN THE NEW PLANET EDITION YET?
IT STILL COMES OUT?
THEY HAVE A PRINTING PRESS IN SUPERMAN'S FORTRESS OF SOLITUDE.
WE THOUGHT THE HALL OF JUSTICE WAS UNDER OCCU-PATION...
PLANET
BLÜDHAVEN HERE WE CO...
WHEN DOES EVERYTHING GO BACK TO NORMAL?
SO, THE PLANET'S ALL WE'VE GOT NOW THAT ALL ELECTRONIC MEDIA ARE BROADCASTING ANTI-LIFE 24 HOURS A DAY.
GIVE ME SOME GOOD NEWS, RAY...
WHAT HAPPENED TO THE BLÜDHAVEN STRIKE FORCE?
Uh...

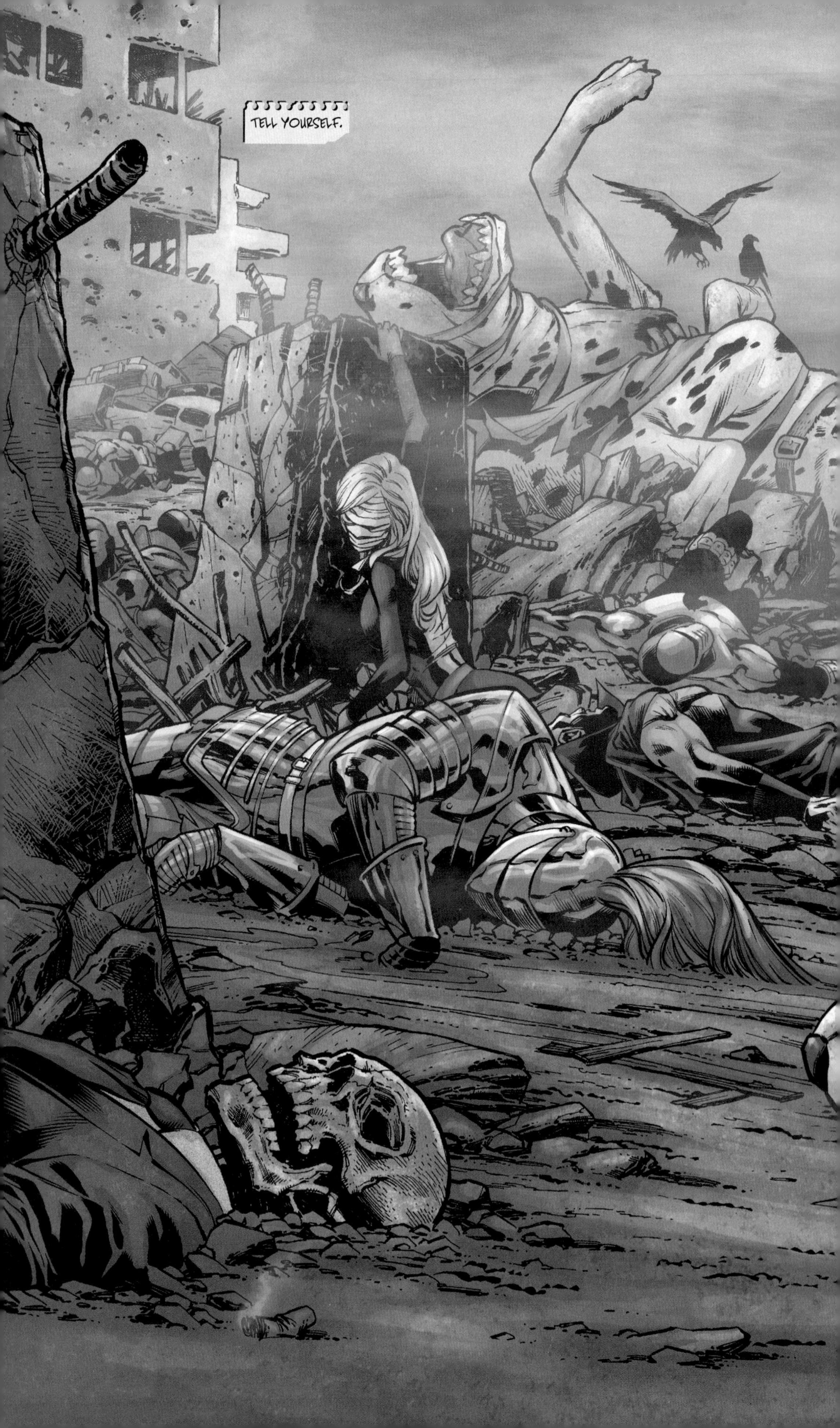
TELL YOURSELF.

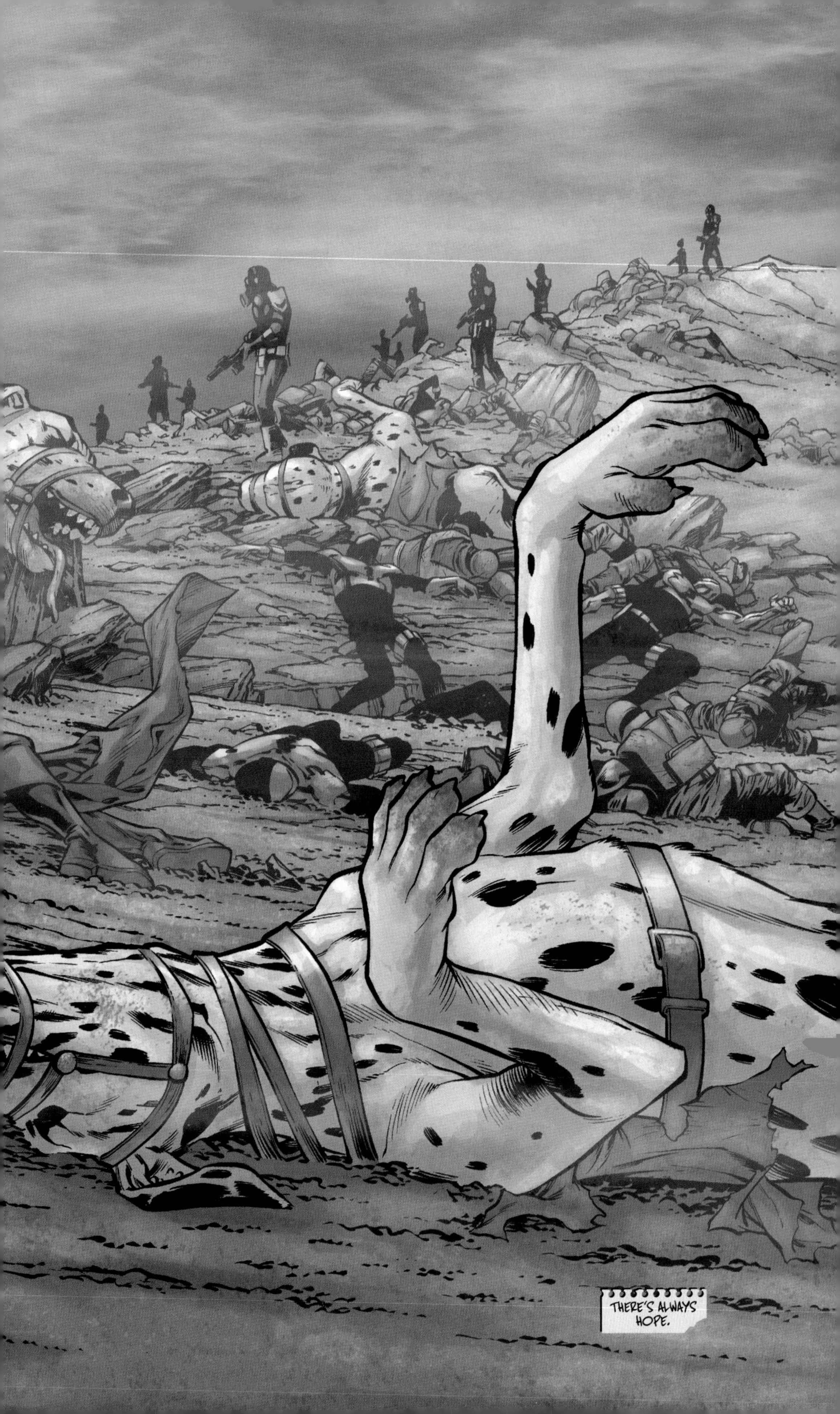
THERE'S ALWAYS HOPE.

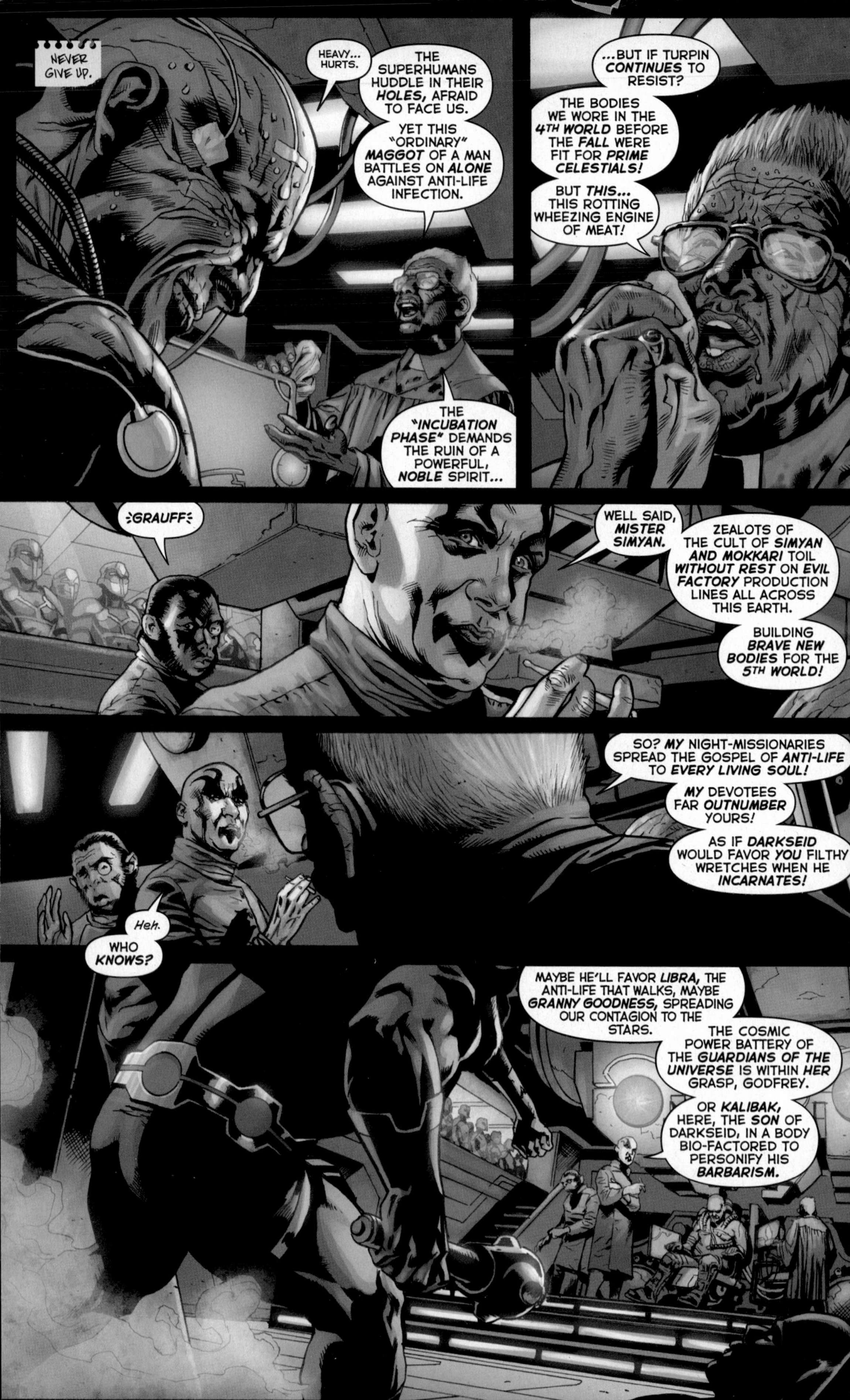

NEVER GIVE UP.
HEAVY... HURTS.
THE SUPERHUMANS HUDDLE IN THEIR HOLES, AFRAID TO FACE US.
YET THIS "ORDINARY" MAGGOT OF A MAN BATTLES ON ALONE AGAINST ANTI-LIFE INFECTION.
THE "INCUBATION PHASE" DEMANDS THE RUIN OF A POWERFUL, NOBLE SPIRIT...
...BUT IF TURPIN CONTINUES TO RESIST?
THE BODIES WE WORE IN THE 4TH WORLD BEFORE THE FALL WERE FIT FOR PRIME CELESTIALS!
BUT THIS... THIS ROTTING WHEEZING ENGINE OF MEAT!
GRAUFF
WELL SAID, MISTER SIMYAN.
ZEALOTS OF THE CULT OF SIMYAN AND MOKKARI TOIL WITHOUT REST ON EVIL FACTORY PRODUCTION LINES ALL ACROSS THIS EARTH.
BUILDING BRAVE NEW BODIES FOR THE 5TH WORLD!
SO? MY NIGHT-MISSIONARIES SPREAD THE GOSPEL OF ANTI-LIFE TO EVERY LIVING SOUL!
MY DEVOTEES FAR OUTNUMBER YOURS!
AS IF DARKSEID WOULD FAVOR YOU FILTHY WRETCHES WHEN HE INCARNATES!
Heh.
WHO KNOWS?
MAYBE HE'LL FAVOR LIBRA, THE ANTI-LIFE THAT WALKS, MAYBE GRANNY GOODNESS, SPREADING OUR CONTAGION TO THE STARS.
THE COSMIC POWER BATTERY OF THE GUARDIANS OF THE UNIVERSE IS WITHIN HER GRASP, GODFREY.
OR KALIBAK, HERE, THE SON OF DARKSEID, IN A BODY BIO-FACTORED TO PERSONIFY HIS BARBARISM.

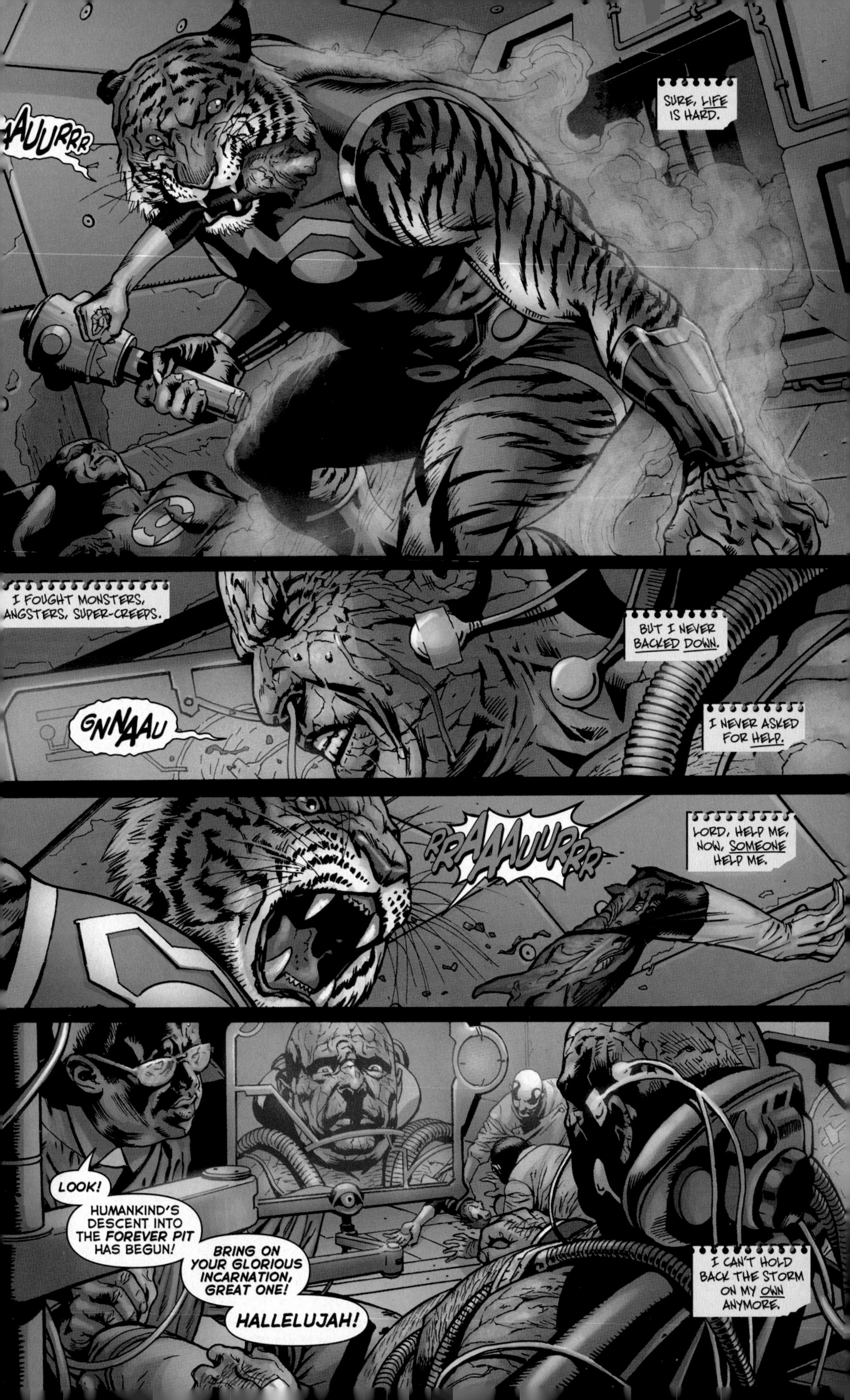
AUURRR
SURE, LIFE IS HARD.
I FOUGHT MONSTERS, GANGSTERS, SUPER-CREEPS.
BUT I NEVER BACKED DOWN.
GNNAAU
I NEVER ASKED FOR HELP.
RRAAAAUURRR
LORD, HELP ME, NOW, SOMEONE HELP ME.
LOOK!
HUMANKIND'S DESCENT INTO THE FOREVER PIT HAS BEGUN!
BRING ON YOUR GLORIOUS INCARNATION, GREAT ONE!
HALLELUJAH!
I CAN'T HOLD BACK THE STORM ON MY OWN ANYMORE.

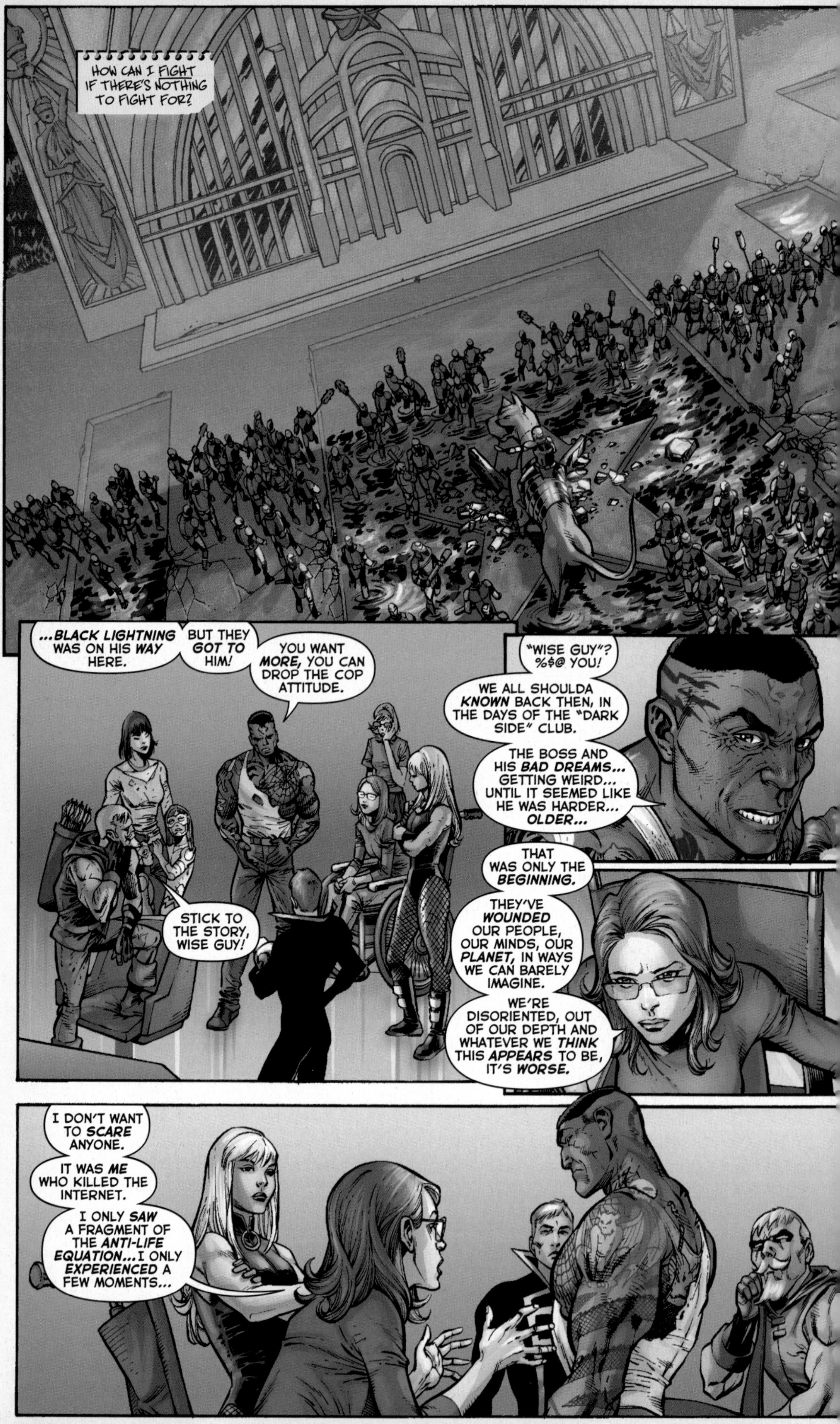

HOW CAN I FIGHT IF THERE'S NOTHING TO FIGHT FOR?
...BLACK LIGHTNING WAS ON HIS WAY HERE.
BUT THEY GOT TO HIM!
YOU WANT MORE, YOU CAN DROP THE COP ATTITUDE.
STICK TO THE STORY, WISE GUY!
"WISE GUY"? %$@ YOU!
WE ALL SHOULDA KNOWN BACK THEN, IN THE DAYS OF THE "DARK SIDE" CLUB.
THE BOSS AND HIS BAD DREAMS... GETTING WEIRD... UNTIL IT SEEMED LIKE HE WAS HARDER... OLDER...
THAT WAS ONLY THE BEGINNING.
THEY'VE WOUNDED OUR PEOPLE, OUR MINDS, OUR PLANET, IN WAYS WE CAN BARELY IMAGINE.
WE'RE DISORIENTED, OUT OF OUR DEPTH AND WHATEVER WE THINK THIS APPEARS TO BE, IT'S WORSE.
I DON'T WANT TO SCARE ANYONE.
IT WAS ME WHO KILLED THE INTERNET.
I ONLY SAW A FRAGMENT OF THE ANTI-LIFE EQUATION...I ONLY EXPERIENCED A FEW MOMENTS...

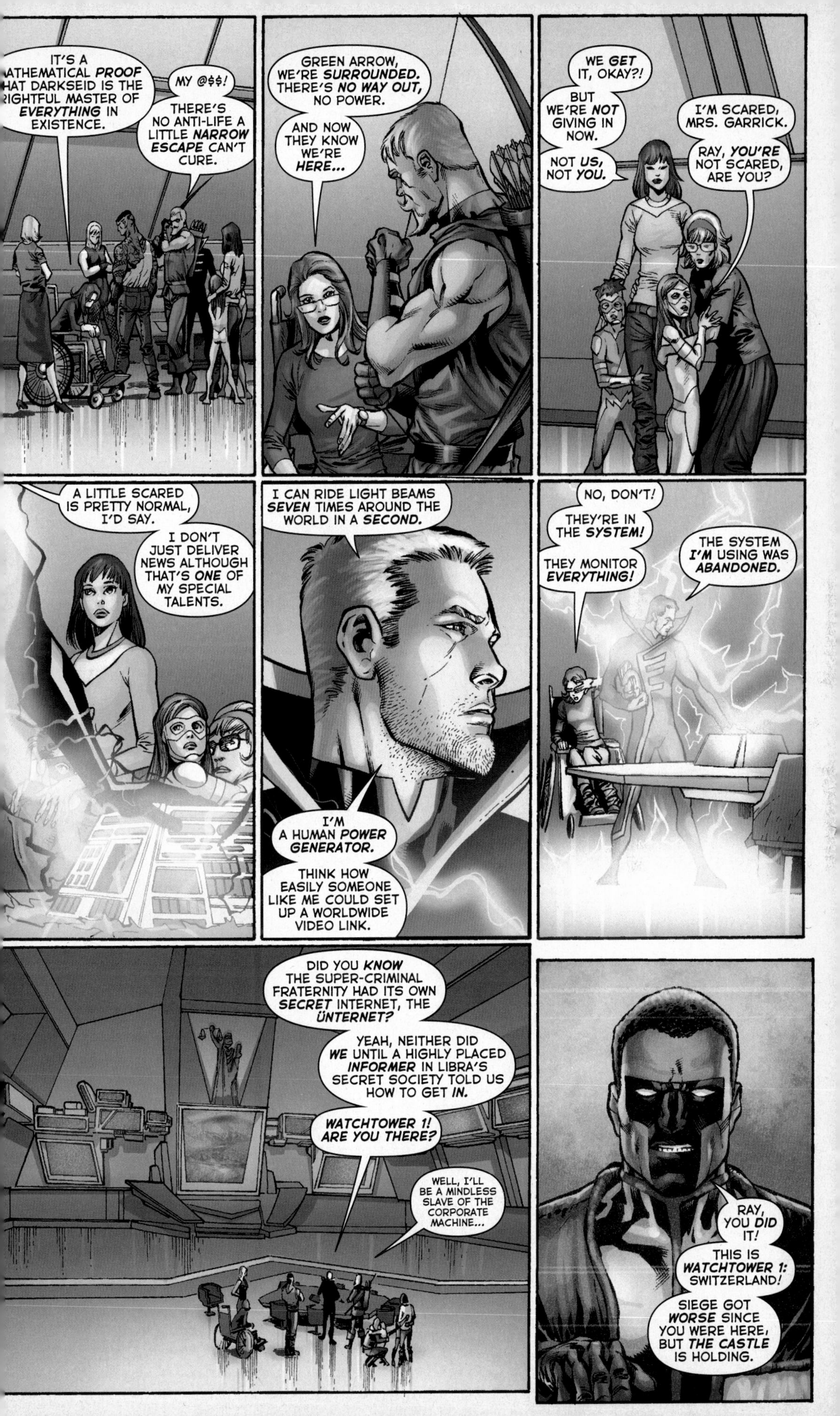
IT'S A
ATHEMATICAL PROOF
HAT DARKSEID IS THE
RIGHTFUL MASTER OF
EVERYTHING IN
EXISTENCE.
MY @$$!
THERE'S
NO ANTI-LIFE A
LITTLE NARROW
ESCAPE CAN'T
CURE.
GREEN ARROW,
WE'RE SURROUNDED.
THERE'S NO WAY OUT,
NO POWER.
AND NOW
THEY KNOW
WE'RE
HERE...
WE GET
IT, OKAY?!
BUT
WE'RE NOT
GIVING IN
NOW.
NOT US,
NOT YOU.
I'M SCARED,
MRS. GARRICK.
RAY, YOU'RE
NOT SCARED,
ARE YOU?
A LITTLE SCARED
IS PRETTY NORMAL,
I'D SAY.
I DON'T
JUST DELIVER
NEWS ALTHOUGH
THAT'S ONE OF
MY SPECIAL
TALENTS.
I CAN RIDE LIGHT BEAMS
SEVEN TIMES AROUND THE
WORLD IN A SECOND.
I'M
A HUMAN POWER
GENERATOR.
THINK HOW
EASILY SOMEONE
LIKE ME COULD SET
UP A WORLDWIDE
VIDEO LINK.
NO, DON'T!
THEY'RE IN
THE SYSTEM!
THEY MONITOR
EVERYTHING!
THE SYSTEM
I'M USING WAS
ABANDONED.
DID YOU KNOW
THE SUPER-CRIMINAL
FRATERNITY HAD ITS OWN
SECRET INTERNET, THE
ÜNTERNET?
YEAH, NEITHER DID
WE UNTIL A HIGHLY PLACED
INFORMER IN LIBRA'S
SECRET SOCIETY TOLD US
HOW TO GET IN.
WATCHTOWER 1!
ARE YOU THERE?
WELL, I'LL
BE A MINDLESS
SLAVE OF THE
CORPORATE
MACHINE...
RAY,
YOU DID
IT!
THIS IS
WATCHTOWER 1:
SWITZERLAND!
SIEGE GOT
WORSE SINCE
YOU WERE HERE,
BUT THE CASTLE
IS HOLDING.

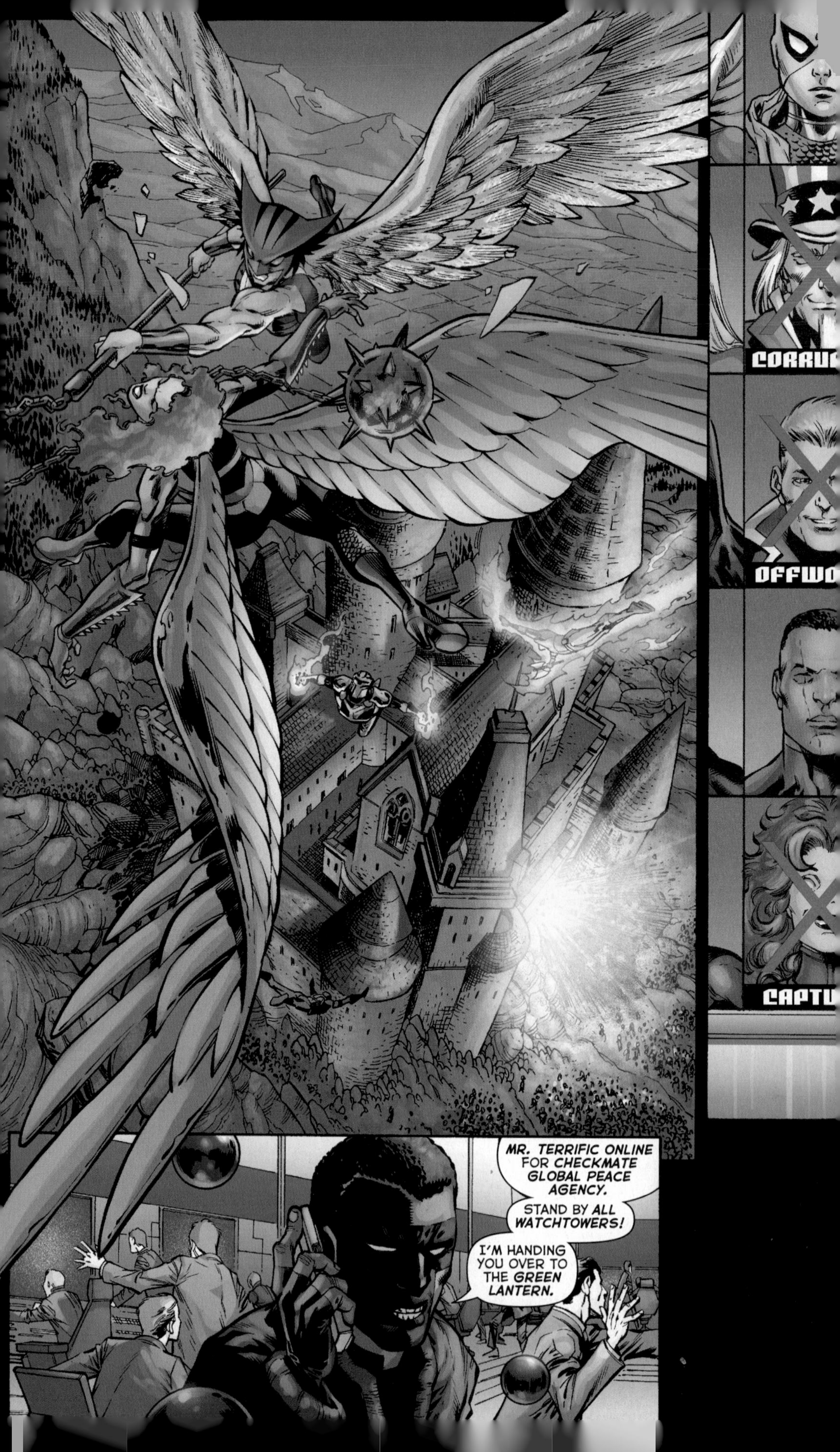

CORRU
OFFWO
CAPTU
MR. TERRIFIC ONLINE FOR CHECKMATE GLOBAL PEACE AGENCY.
STAND BY ALL WATCHTOWERS!
I'M HANDING YOU OVER TO THE GREEN LANTERN.

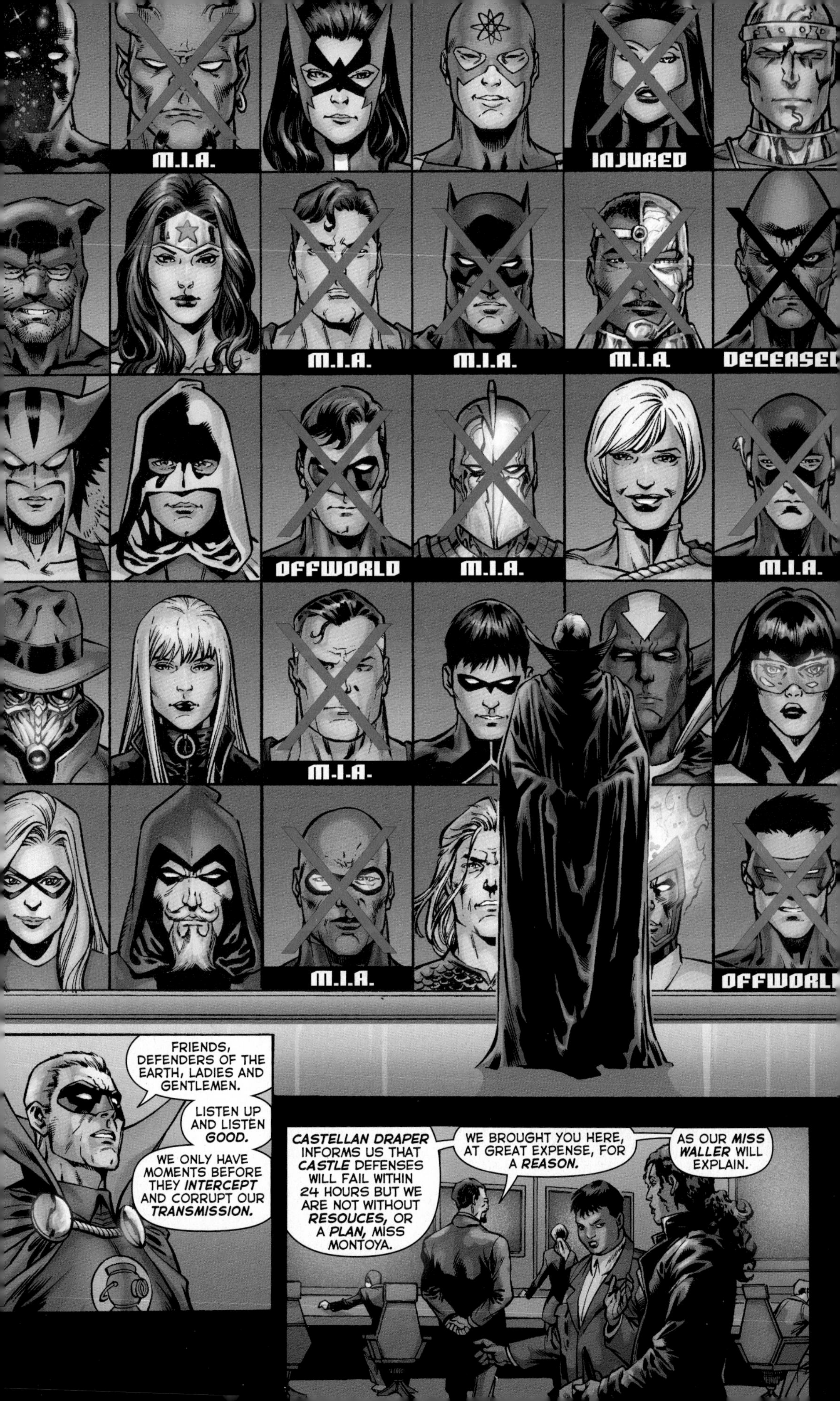

M.I.A.
INJURED
M.I.A.
M.I.A.
M.I.A
DECEASED
OFFWORLD
M.I.A.
M.I.A.
M.I.A.
M.I.A.
OFFWORLD
FRIENDS, DEFENDERS OF THE EARTH, LADIES AND GENTLEMEN.
LISTEN UP AND LISTEN GOOD.
WE ONLY HAVE MOMENTS BEFORE THEY INTERCEPT AND CORRUPT OUR TRANSMISSION.
CASTELLAN DRAPER INFORMS US THAT CASTLE DEFENSES WILL FAIL WITHIN 24 HOURS BUT WE ARE NOT WITHOUT RESOUCES, OR A PLAN, MISS MONTOYA.
WE BROUGHT YOU HERE, AT GREAT EXPENSE, FOR A REASON.
AS OUR MISS WALLER WILL EXPLAIN.

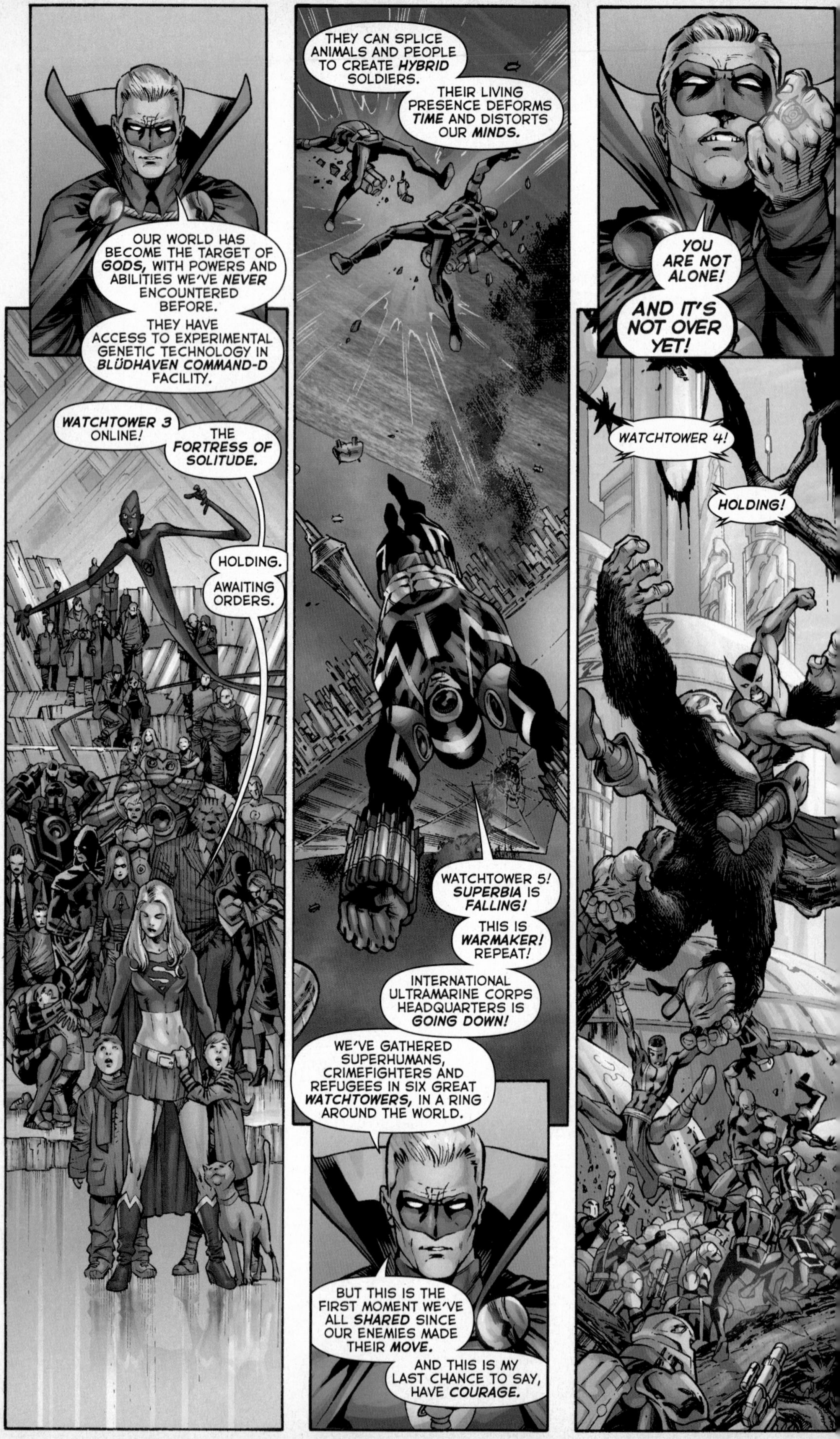
OUR WORLD HAS BECOME THE TARGET OF GODS, WITH POWERS AND ABILITIES WE'VE NEVER ENCOUNTERED BEFORE.
THEY HAVE ACCESS TO EXPERIMENTAL GENETIC TECHNOLOGY IN BLÜDHAVEN COMMAND-D FACILITY.
WATCHTOWER 3 ONLINE!
THE FORTRESS OF SOLITUDE.
HOLDING.
AWAITING ORDERS.
THEY CAN SPLICE ANIMALS AND PEOPLE TO CREATE HYBRID SOLDIERS.
THEIR LIVING PRESENCE DEFORMS TIME AND DISTORTS OUR MINDS.
WATCHTOWER 5! SUPERBIA IS FALLING!
THIS IS WARMAKER! REPEAT!
INTERNATIONAL ULTRAMARINE CORPS HEADQUARTERS IS GOING DOWN!
WE'VE GATHERED SUPERHUMANS, CRIMEFIGHTERS AND REFUGEES IN SIX GREAT WATCHTOWERS, IN A RING AROUND THE WORLD.
BUT THIS IS THE FIRST MOMENT WE'VE ALL SHARED SINCE OUR ENEMIES MADE THEIR MOVE.
AND THIS IS MY LAST CHANCE TO SAY, HAVE COURAGE.
YOU ARE NOT ALONE!
AND IT'S NOT OVER YET!
WATCHTOWER 4!
HOLDING!

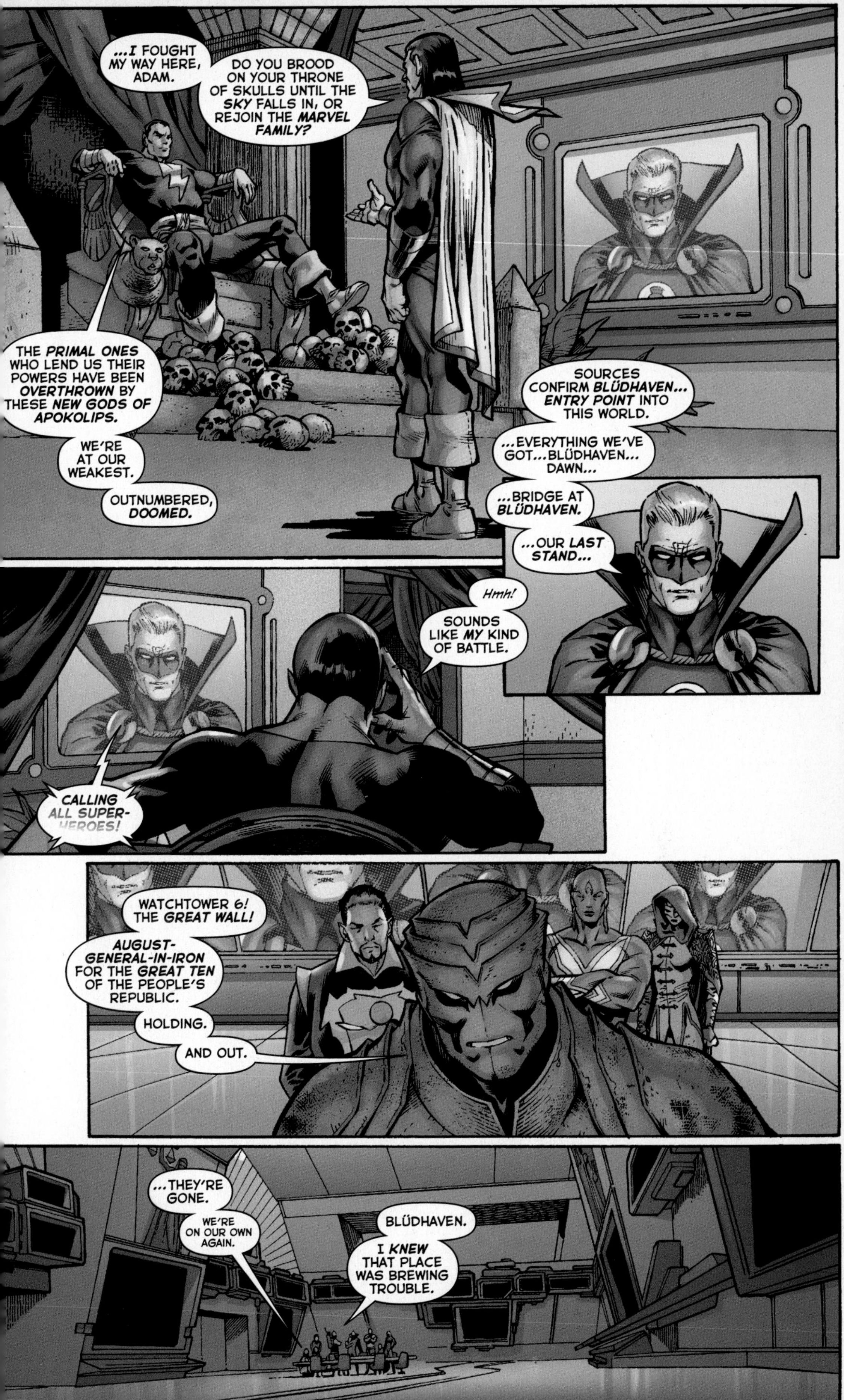
...I FOUGHT MY WAY HERE, ADAM.
DO YOU BROOD ON YOUR THRONE OF SKULLS UNTIL THE SKY FALLS IN, OR REJOIN THE MARVEL FAMILY?
THE PRIMAL ONES WHO LEND US THEIR POWERS HAVE BEEN OVERTHROWN BY THESE NEW GODS OF APOKOLIPS.
WE'RE AT OUR WEAKEST.
OUTNUMBERED, DOOMED.
SOURCES CONFIRM BLÜDHAVEN... ENTRY POINT INTO THIS WORLD.
...EVERYTHING WE'VE GOT...BLÜDHAVEN... DAWN...
...BRIDGE AT BLÜDHAVEN.
...OUR LAST STAND...
Hmh!
SOUNDS LIKE MY KIND OF BATTLE.
CALLING ALL SUPER-HEROES!
WATCHTOWER 6! THE GREAT WALL!
AUGUST-GENERAL-IN-IRON FOR THE GREAT TEN OF THE PEOPLE'S REPUBLIC.
HOLDING.
AND OUT.
...THEY'RE GONE.
WE'RE ON OUR OWN AGAIN.
BLÜDHAVEN.
I KNEW THAT PLACE WAS BREWING TROUBLE.

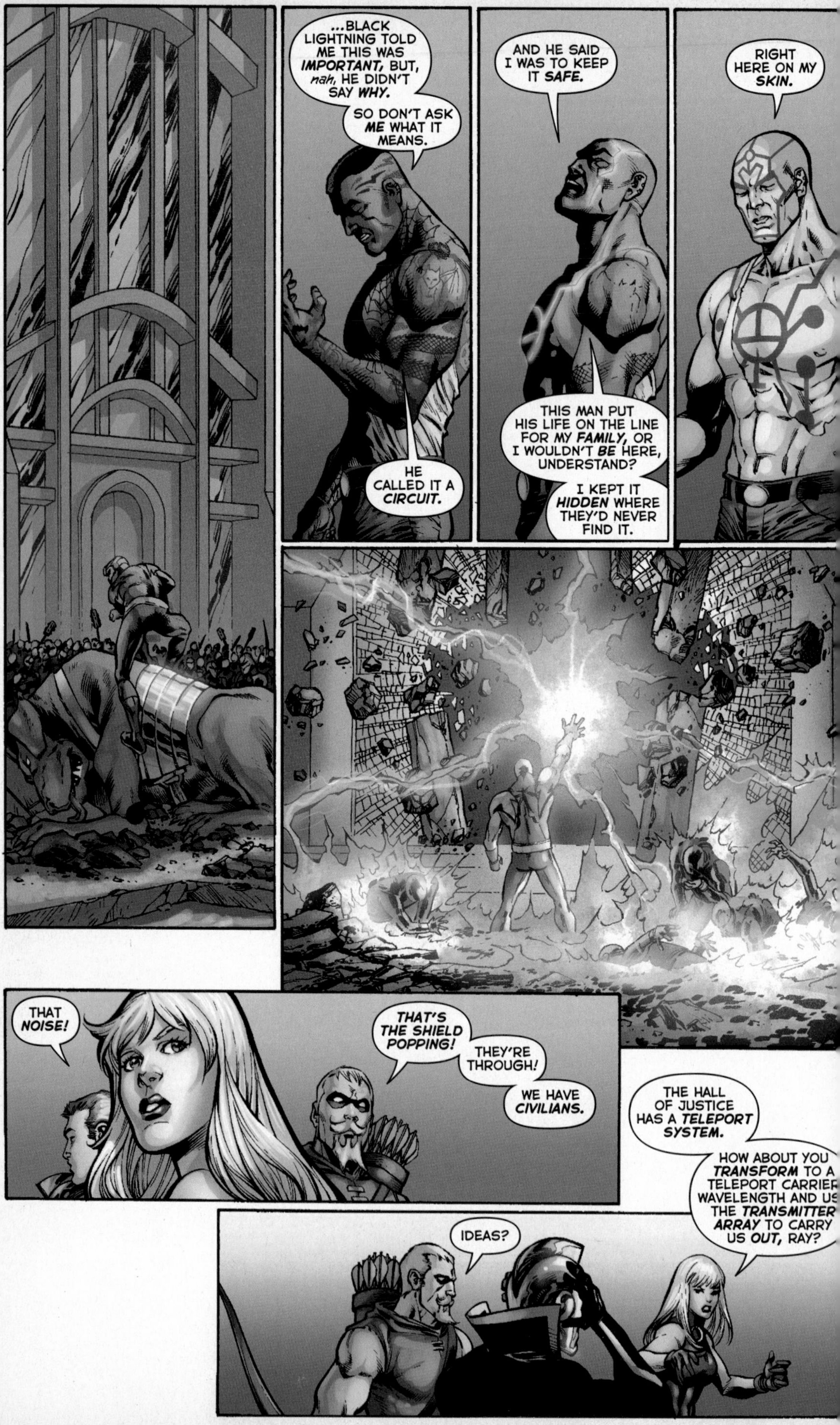
...BLACK LIGHTNING TOLD ME THIS WAS IMPORTANT, BUT, nah, HE DIDN'T SAY WHY.
SO DON'T ASK ME WHAT IT MEANS.
HE CALLED IT A CIRCUIT.
AND HE SAID I WAS TO KEEP IT SAFE.
THIS MAN PUT HIS LIFE ON THE LINE FOR MY FAMILY, OR I WOULDN'T BE HERE, UNDERSTAND?
I KEPT IT HIDDEN WHERE THEY'D NEVER FIND IT.
RIGHT HERE ON MY SKIN.
THAT NOISE!
THAT'S THE SHIELD POPPING!
THEY'RE THROUGH!
WE HAVE CIVILIANS.
IDEAS?
THE HALL OF JUSTICE HAS A TELEPORT SYSTEM.
HOW ABOUT YOU TRANSFORM TO A TELEPORT CARRIER WAVELENGTH AND US THE TRANSMITTER ARRAY TO CARRY US OUT, RAY?

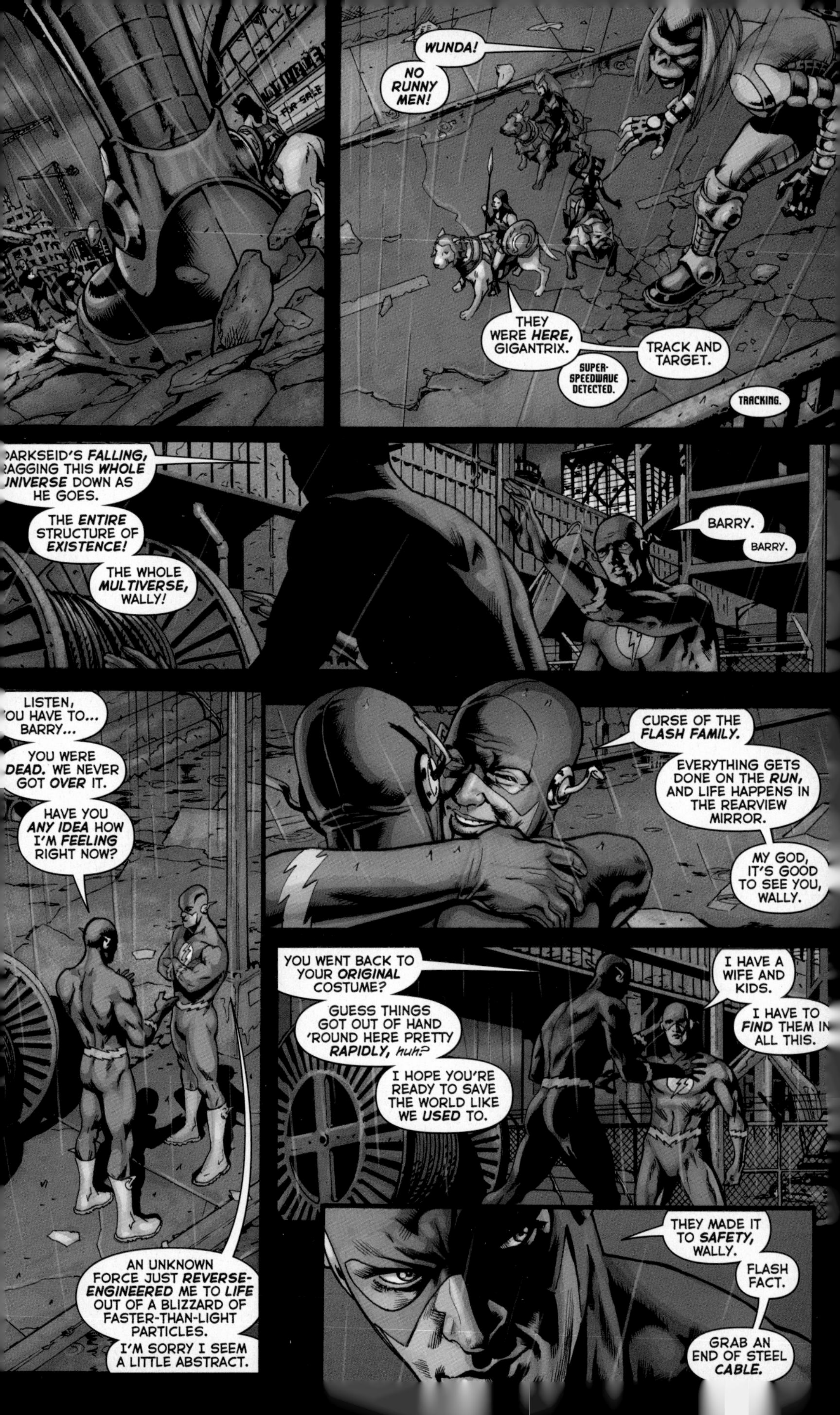
WUNDA!
NO RUNNY MEN!
THEY WERE HERE, GIGANTRIX.
TRACK AND TARGET.
SUPER-SPEEDWAVE DETECTED.
TRACKING.
DARKSEID'S FALLING, DRAGGING THIS WHOLE UNIVERSE DOWN AS HE GOES.
THE ENTIRE STRUCTURE OF EXISTENCE!
THE WHOLE MULTIVERSE, WALLY!
BARRY.
BARRY.
LISTEN, YOU HAVE TO... BARRY...
YOU WERE DEAD. WE NEVER GOT OVER IT.
HAVE YOU ANY IDEA HOW I'M FEELING RIGHT NOW?
AN UNKNOWN FORCE JUST REVERSE-ENGINEERED ME TO LIFE OUT OF A BLIZZARD OF FASTER-THAN-LIGHT PARTICLES.
I'M SORRY I SEEM A LITTLE ABSTRACT.
CURSE OF THE FLASH FAMILY.
EVERYTHING GETS DONE ON THE RUN, AND LIFE HAPPENS IN THE REARVIEW MIRROR.
MY GOD, IT'S GOOD TO SEE YOU, WALLY.
YOU WENT BACK TO YOUR ORIGINAL COSTUME?
GUESS THINGS GOT OUT OF HAND 'ROUND HERE PRETTY RAPIDLY, huh?
I HOPE YOU'RE READY TO SAVE THE WORLD LIKE WE USED TO.
I HAVE A WIFE AND KIDS.
I HAVE TO FIND THEM IN ALL THIS.
THEY MADE IT TO SAFETY, WALLY.
FLASH FACT.
GRAB AN END OF STEEL CABLE.

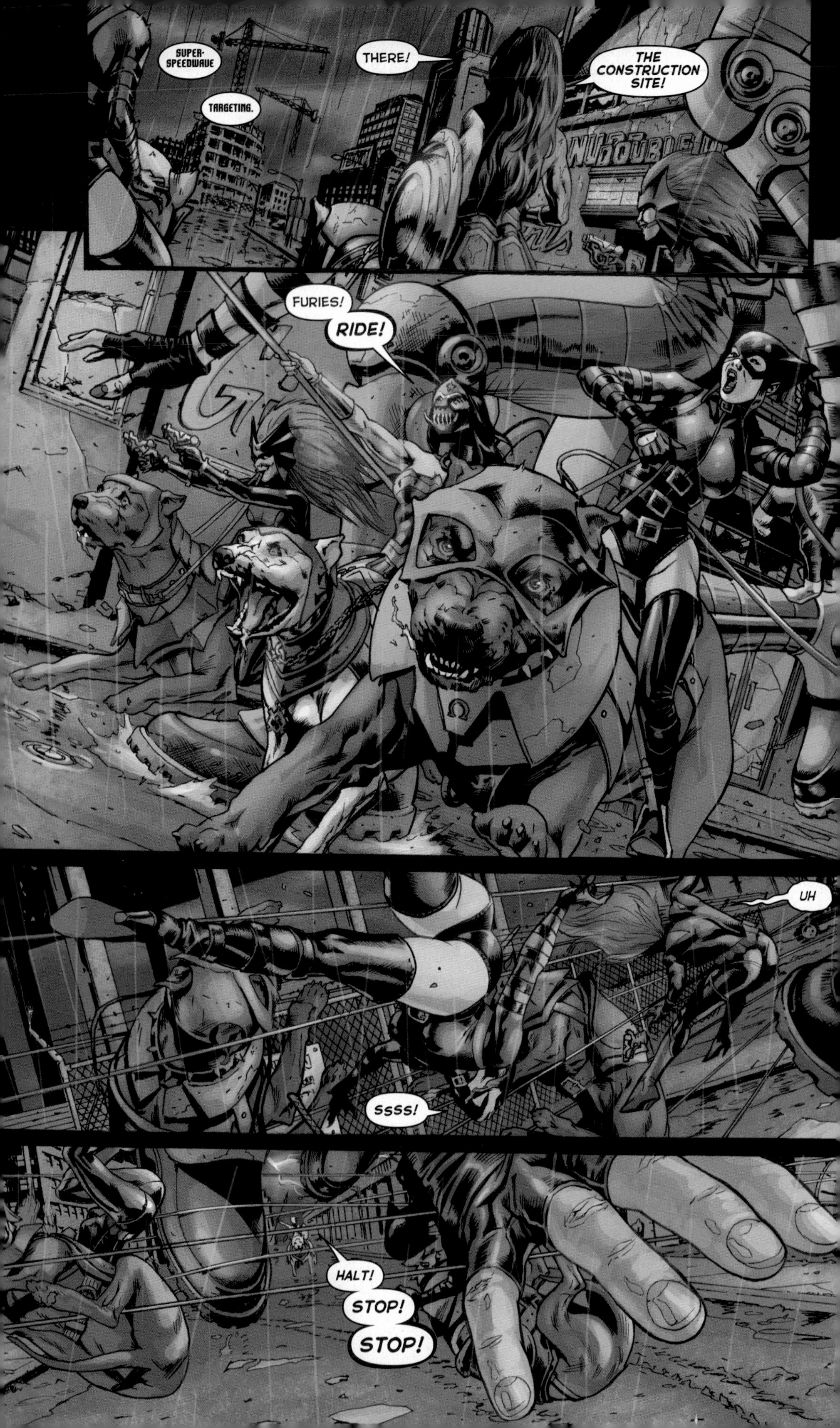
SUPER-SPEEDWAVE
TARGETING.
THERE!
THE CONSTRUCTION SITE!
FURIES!
RIDE!
UH
SSSS!
HALT!
STOP!
STOP!

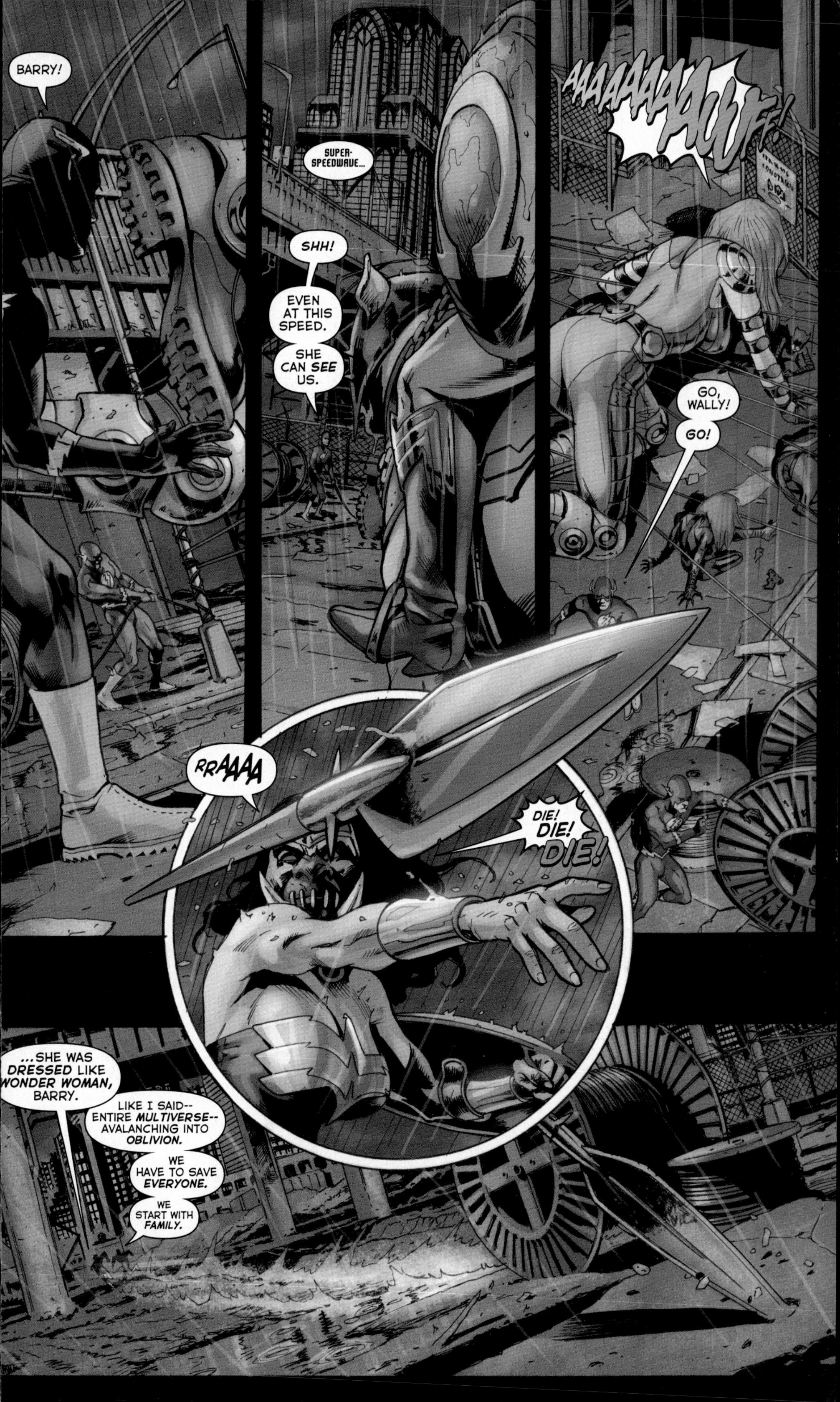

BARRY!
SUPER-SPEEDWAVE...
SHH!
EVEN AT THIS SPEED.
SHE CAN SEE US.
AAAAAAAAAUUFF!
GO, WALLY!
GO!
RRAAAA
DIE! DIE! DIE!
...SHE WAS DRESSED LIKE WONDER WOMAN, BARRY.
LIKE I SAID-- ENTIRE MULTIVERSE-- AVALANCHING INTO OBLIVION.
WE HAVE TO SAVE EVERYONE.
WE START WITH FAMILY.

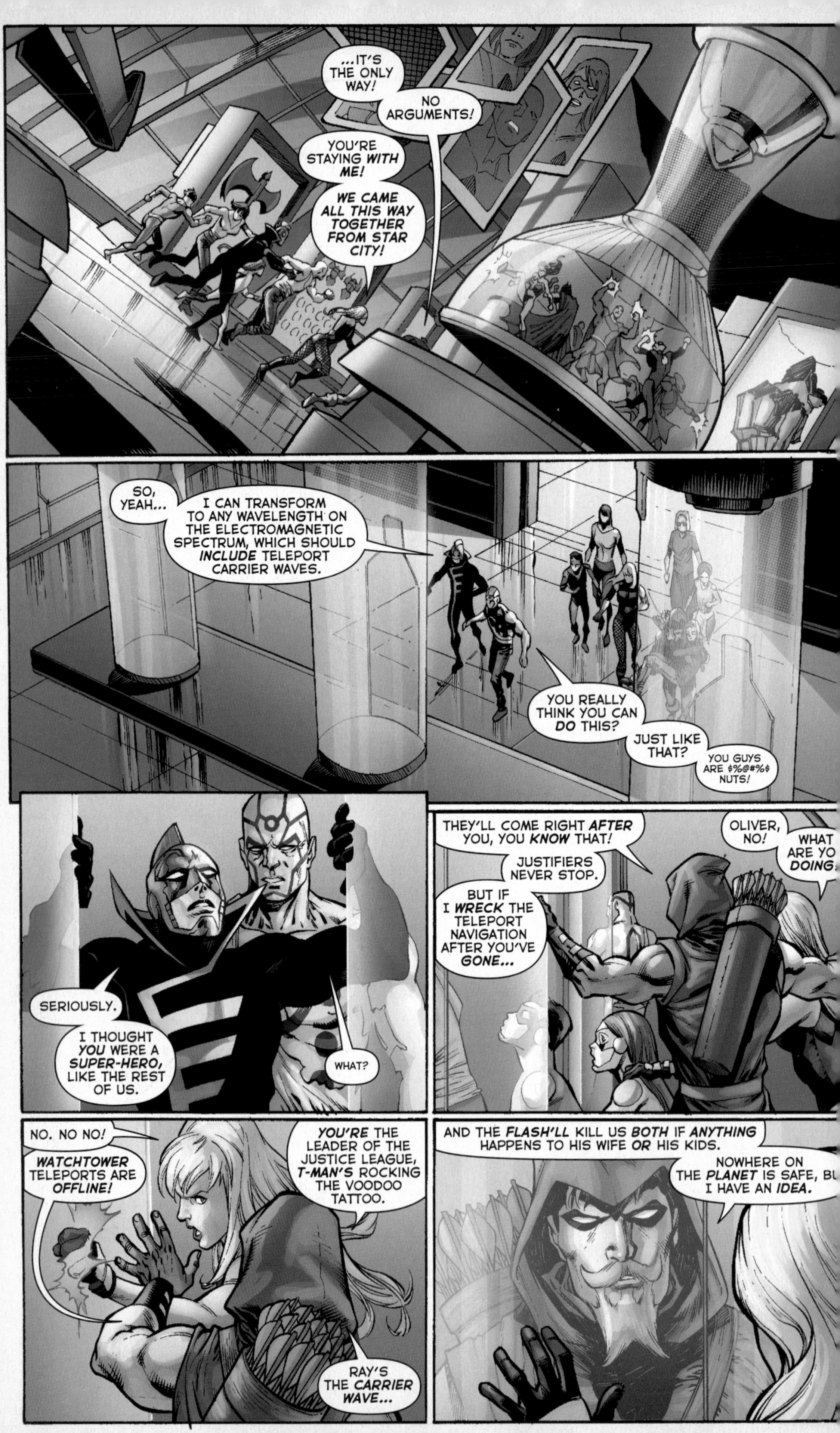
...IT'S THE ONLY WAY!
NO ARGUMENTS!
YOU'RE STAYING WITH ME!
WE CAME ALL THIS WAY TOGETHER FROM STAR CITY!
SO, YEAH...
I CAN TRANSFORM TO ANY WAVELENGTH ON THE ELECTROMAGNETIC SPECTRUM, WHICH SHOULD INCLUDE TELEPORT CARRIER WAVES.
YOU REALLY THINK YOU CAN DO THIS?
JUST LIKE THAT?
YOU GUYS ARE $%@#%$ NUTS!
SERIOUSLY.
I THOUGHT YOU WERE A SUPER-HERO, LIKE THE REST OF US.
WHAT?
THEY'LL COME RIGHT AFTER YOU, YOU KNOW THAT!
JUSTIFIERS NEVER STOP.
BUT IF I WRECK THE TELEPORT NAVIGATION AFTER YOU'VE GONE...
OLIVER, NO!
WHAT ARE YO DOING
NO. NO NO!
WATCHTOWER TELEPORTS ARE OFFLINE!
YOU'RE THE LEADER OF THE JUSTICE LEAGUE, T-MAN'S ROCKING THE VOODOO TATTOO.
RAY'S THE CARRIER WAVE...
AND THE FLASH'LL KILL US BOTH IF ANYTHING HAPPENS TO HIS WIFE OR HIS KIDS.
NOWHERE ON THE PLANET IS SAFE, BU I HAVE AN IDEA.

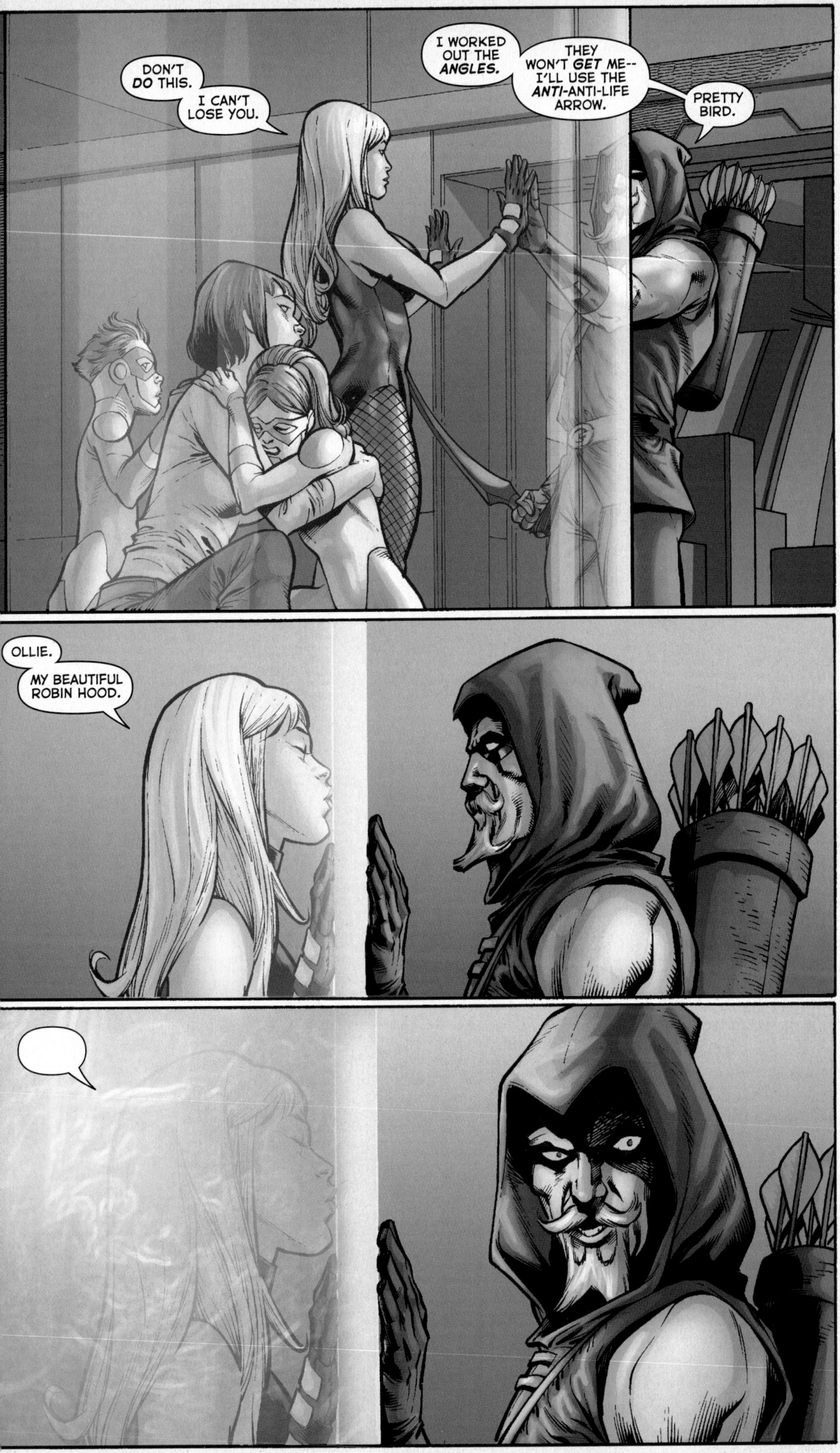

DON'T DO THIS.
I CAN'T LOSE YOU.
I WORKED OUT THE ANGLES.
THEY WON'T GET ME-- I'LL USE THE ANTI-ANTI-LIFE ARROW.
PRETTY BIRD.
OLLIE.
MY BEAUTIFUL ROBIN HOOD.

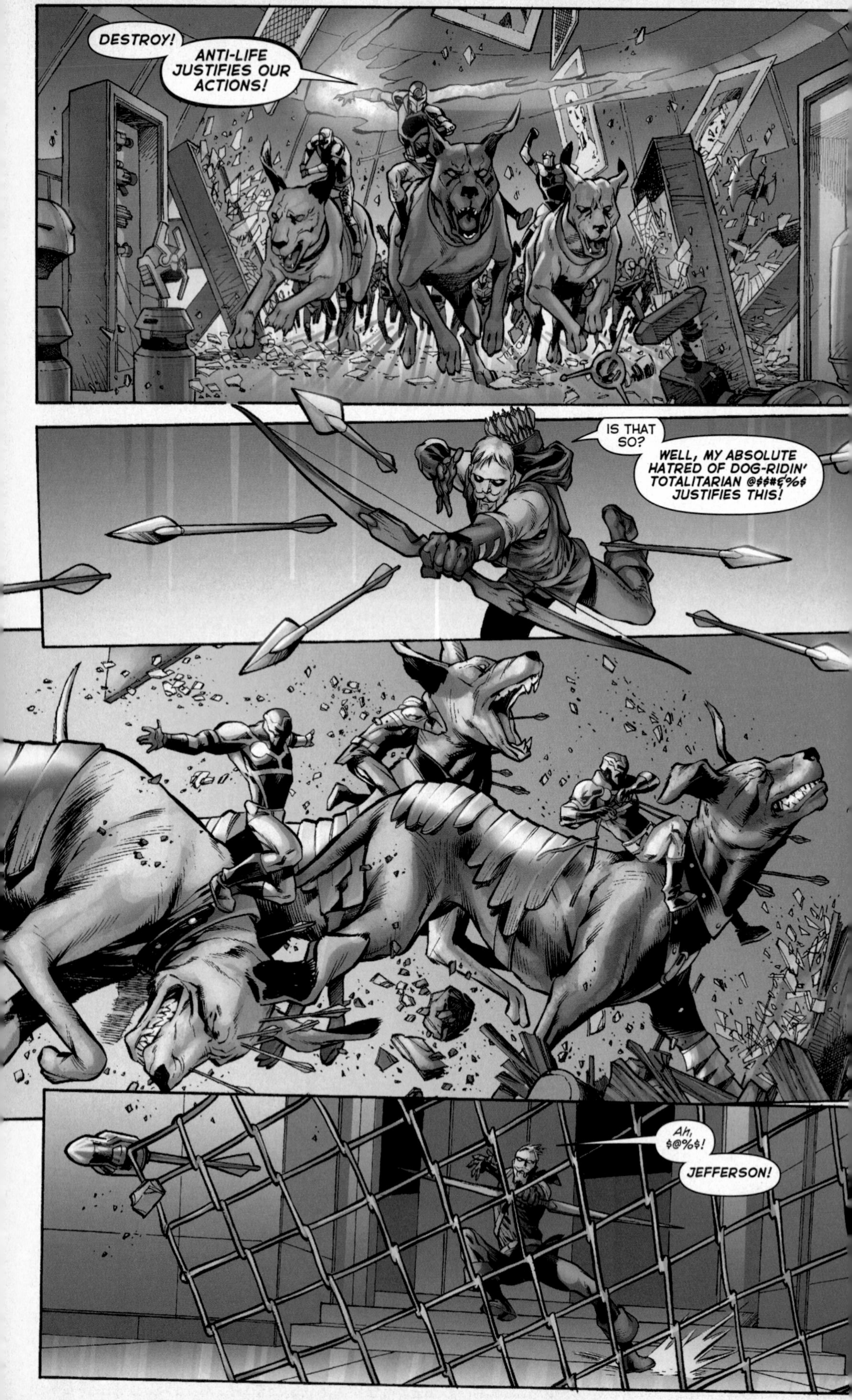
DESTROY!
ANTI-LIFE JUSTIFIES OUR ACTIONS!
IS THAT SO?
WELL, MY ABSOLUTE HATRED OF DOG-RIDIN' TOTALITARIAN @$$#€%$ JUSTIFIES THIS!
AH, $@%$!
JEFFERSON!

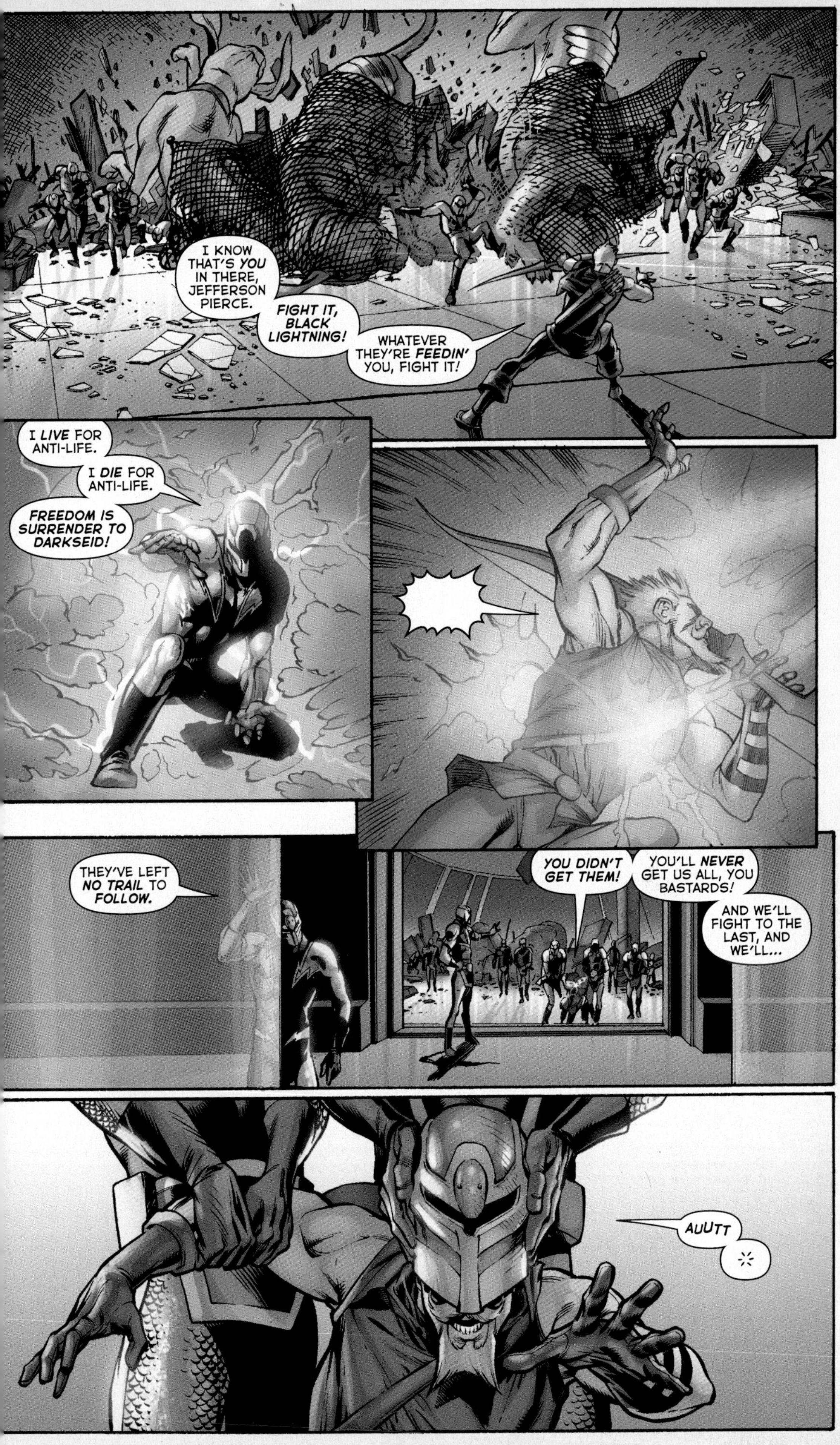

I KNOW THAT'S *YOU* IN THERE, JEFFERSON PIERCE.
FIGHT IT, BLACK LIGHTNING!
WHATEVER THEY'RE *FEEDIN'* YOU, FIGHT IT!
I *LIVE* FOR ANTI-LIFE.
I *DIE* FOR ANTI-LIFE.
FREEDOM IS SURRENDER TO DARKSEID!
THEY'VE LEFT *NO TRAIL* TO *FOLLOW.*
YOU DIDN'T GET THEM!
YOU'LL *NEVER* GET US ALL, YOU BASTARDS!
AND WE'LL FIGHT TO THE LAST, AND WE'LL...
AUUTT

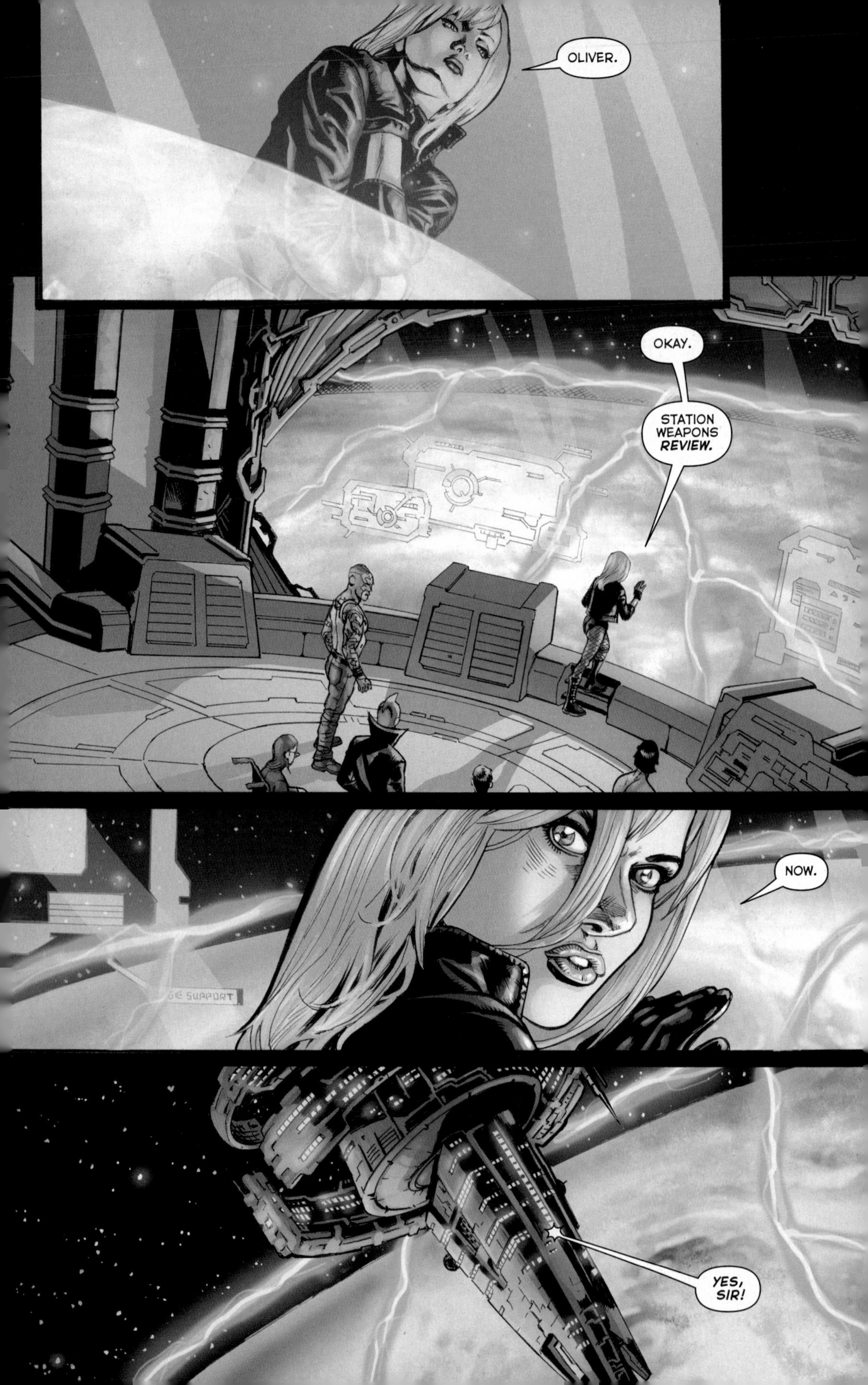
OLIVER.
OKAY.
STATION WEAPONS REVIEW.
GE SUPPORT
NOW.
YES, SIR!

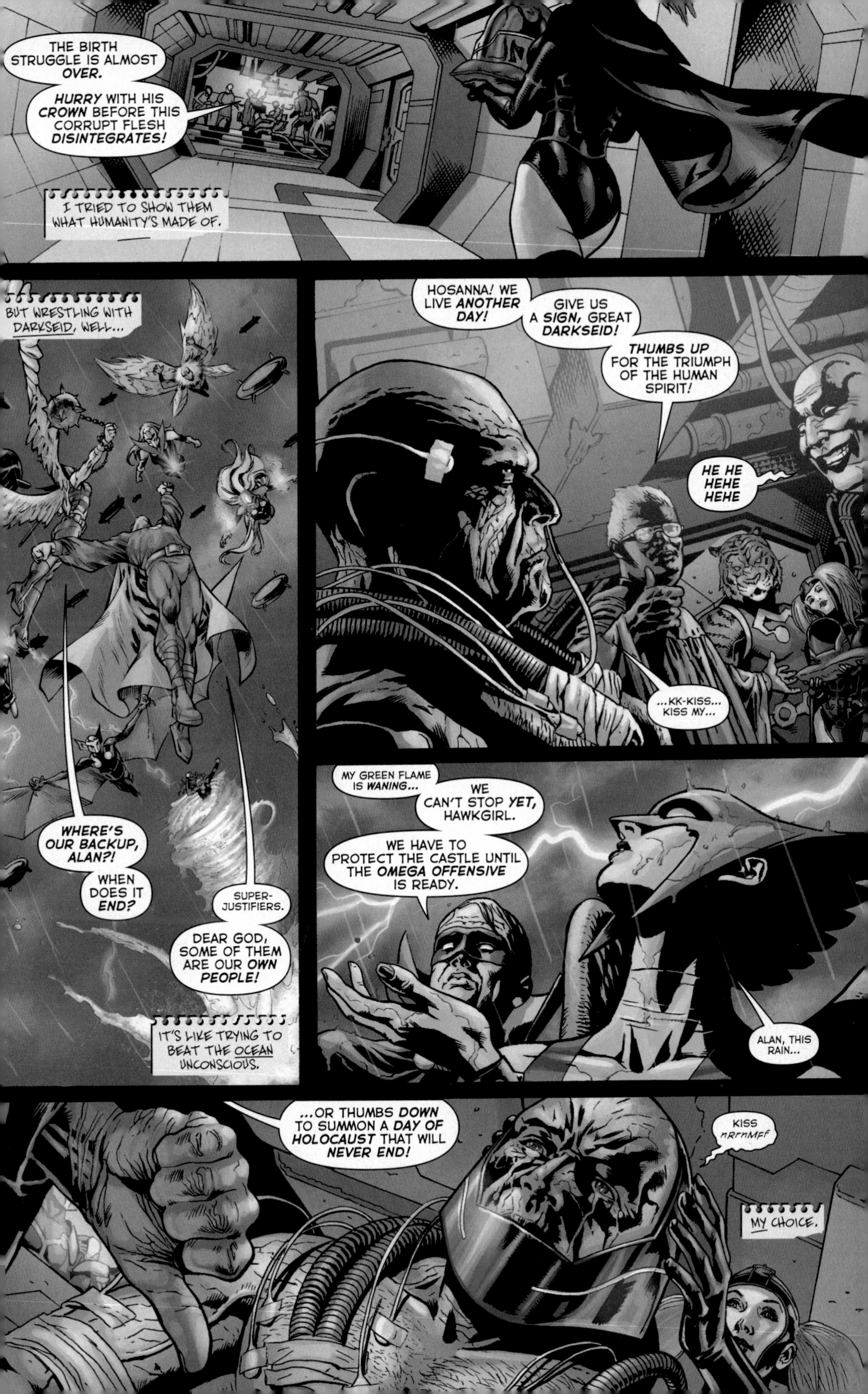

THE BIRTH STRUGGLE IS ALMOST OVER.
HURRY WITH HIS CROWN BEFORE THIS CORRUPT FLESH DISINTEGRATES!
I TRIED TO SHOW THEM WHAT HUMANITY'S MADE OF.
BUT WRESTLING WITH DARKSEID, WELL...
WHERE'S OUR BACKUP, ALAN?!
WHEN DOES IT END?
SUPER-JUSTIFIERS.
DEAR GOD, SOME OF THEM ARE OUR OWN PEOPLE!
IT'S LIKE TRYING TO BEAT THE OCEAN UNCONSCIOUS.
HOSANNA! WE LIVE ANOTHER DAY!
GIVE US A SIGN, GREAT DARKSEID!
THUMBS UP FOR THE TRIUMPH OF THE HUMAN SPIRIT!
HE HE HEHE HEHE
...KK-KISS... KISS MY...
MY GREEN FLAME IS WANING...
WE CAN'T STOP YET, HAWKGIRL.
WE HAVE TO PROTECT THE CASTLE UNTIL THE OMEGA OFFENSIVE IS READY.
ALAN, THIS RAIN...
...OR THUMBS DOWN TO SUMMON A DAY OF HOLOCAUST THAT WILL NEVER END!
KISS
MRFMMFF
MY CHOICE.

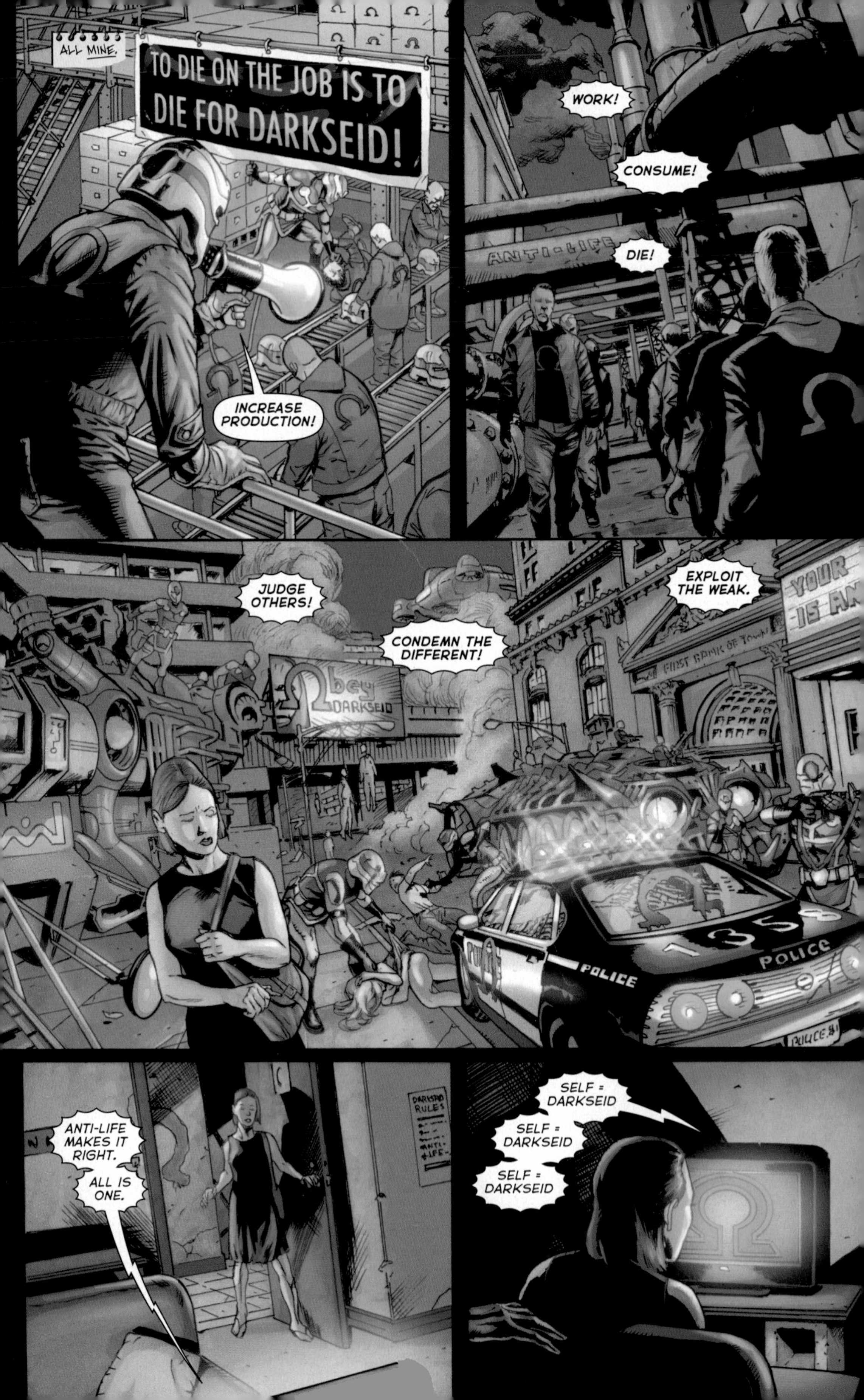
ALL MINE.
TO DIE ON THE JOB IS TO DIE FOR DARKSEID!
INCREASE PRODUCTION!
WORK!
CONSUME!
ANTI-LIFE
DIE!
JUDGE OTHERS!
CONDEMN THE DIFFERENT!
Obey DARKSEID
EXPLOIT THE WEAK.
POLICE
POLICE
ANTI-LIFE MAKES IT RIGHT.
ALL IS ONE.
DARKSEID RULES
SELF = DARKSEID
SELF = DARKSEID
SELF = DARKSEID

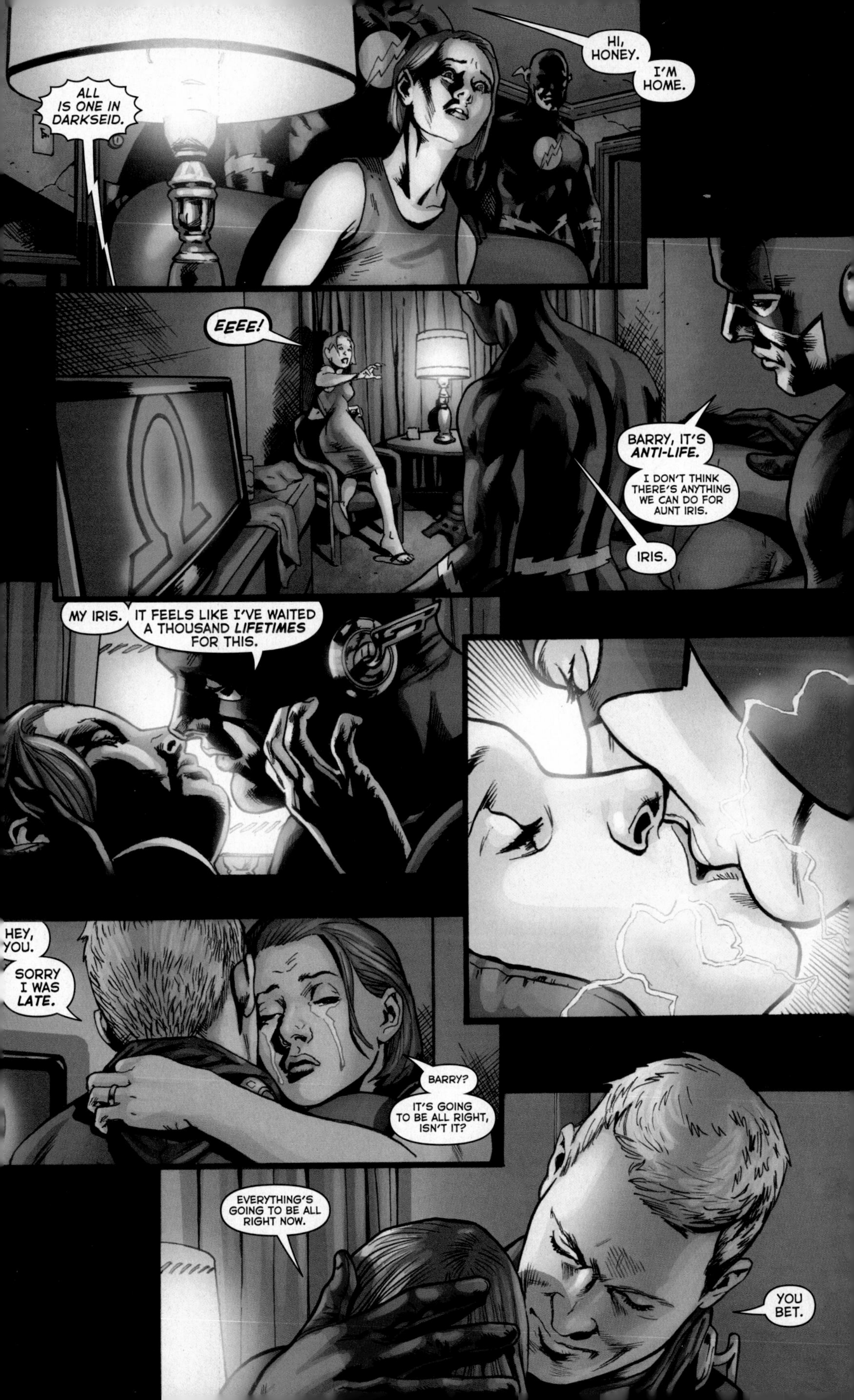
ALL IS ONE IN DARKSEID.
HI, HONEY.
I'M HOME.
EEEE!
BARRY, IT'S ANTI-LIFE.
I DON'T THINK THERE'S ANYTHING WE CAN DO FOR AUNT IRIS.
IRIS.
MY IRIS.
IT FEELS LIKE I'VE WAITED A THOUSAND LIFETIMES FOR THIS.
HEY, YOU.
SORRY I WAS LATE.
BARRY?
IT'S GOING TO BE ALL RIGHT, ISN'T IT?
EVERYTHING'S GOING TO BE ALL RIGHT NOW.
YOU BET.

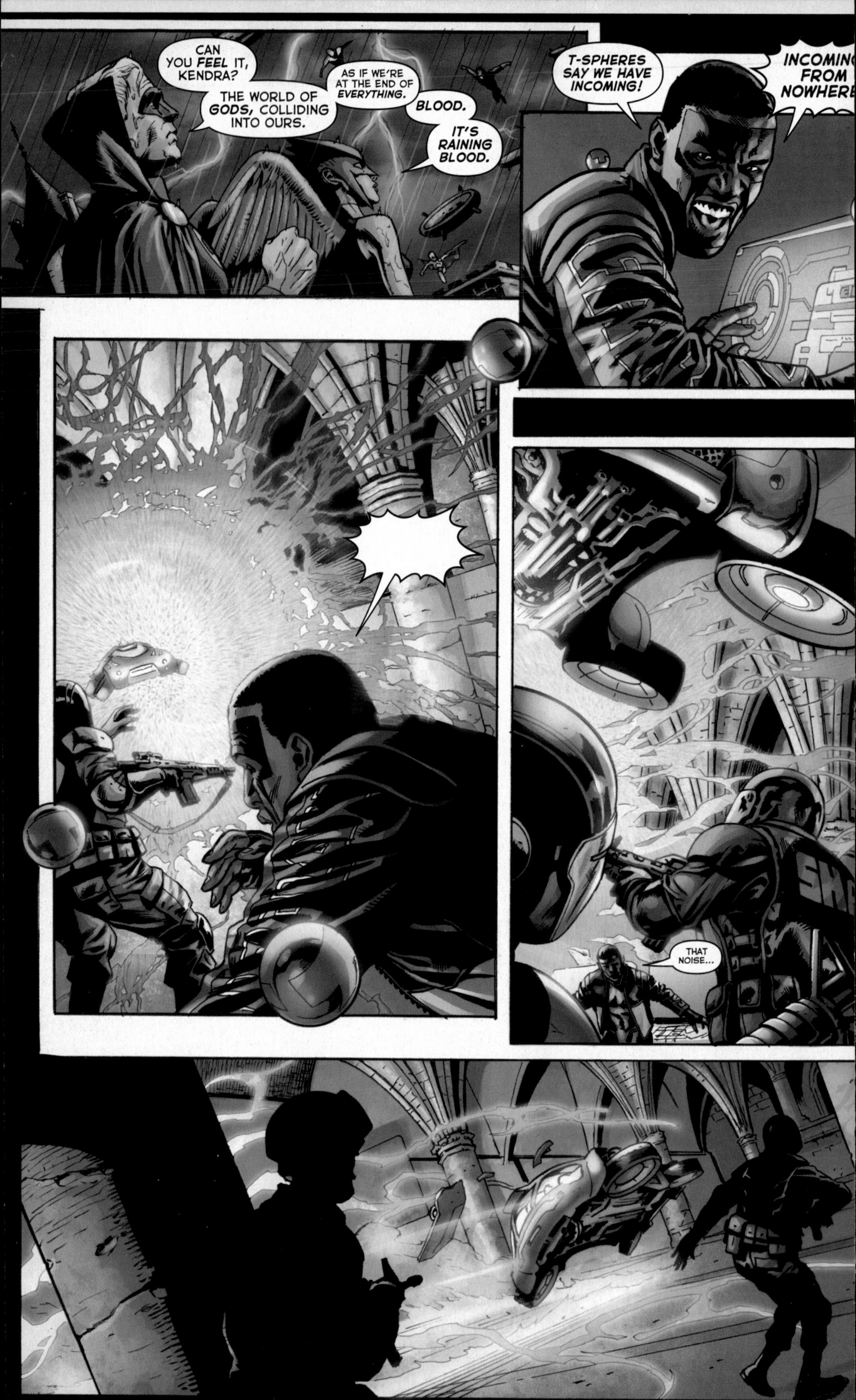
CAN YOU FEEL IT, KENDRA?
THE WORLD OF GODS, COLLIDING INTO OURS.
AS IF WE'RE AT THE END OF EVERYTHING.
BLOOD.
IT'S RAINING BLOOD.
T-SPHERES SAY WE HAVE INCOMING!
INCOMING FROM NOWHERE
THAT NOISE...

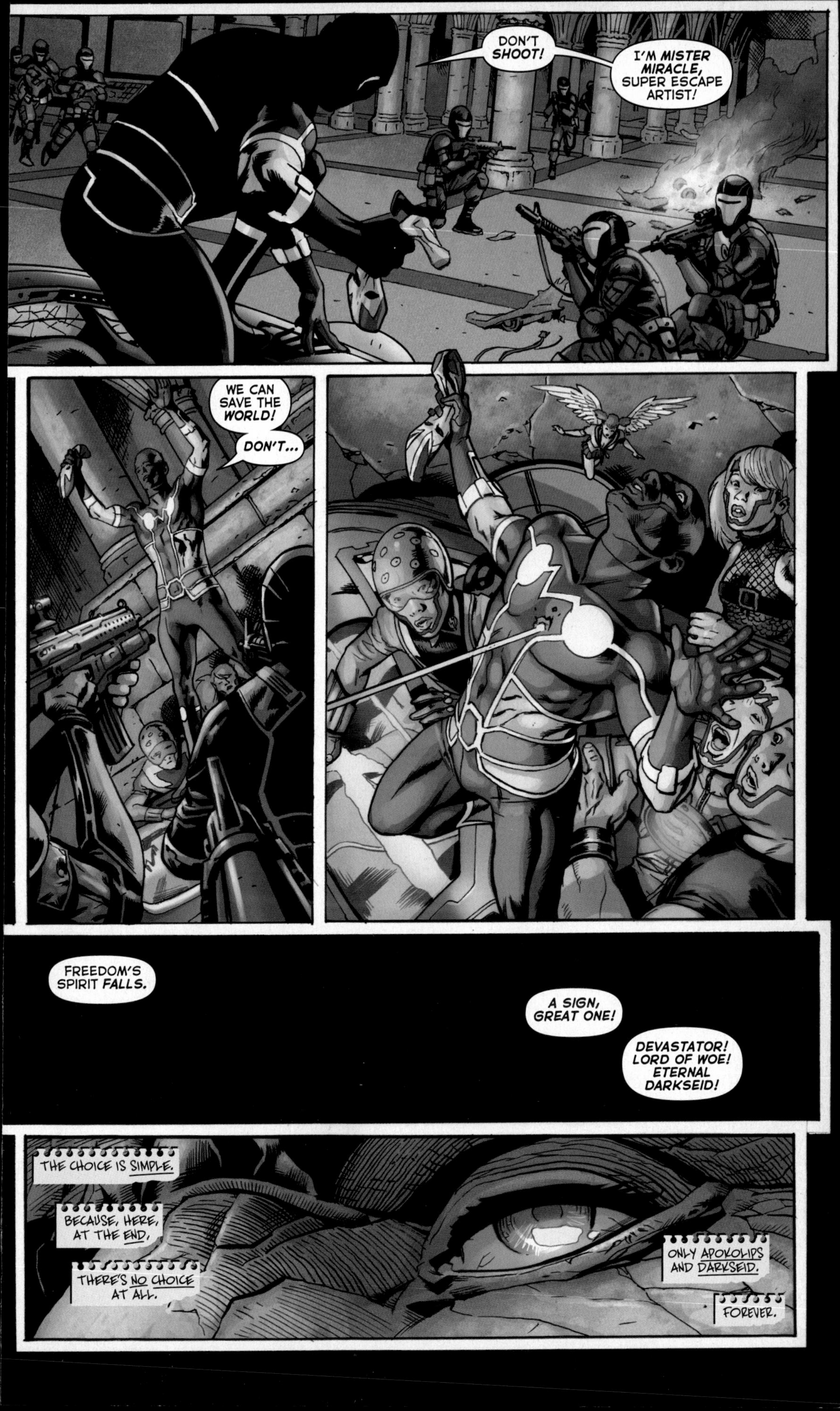
DON'T SHOOT!
I'M MISTER MIRACLE, SUPER ESCAPE ARTIST!
WE CAN SAVE THE WORLD!
DON'T...
FREEDOM'S SPIRIT FALLS.
A SIGN, GREAT ONE!
DEVASTATOR! LORD OF WOE! ETERNAL DARKSEID!
THE CHOICE IS SIMPLE.
BECAUSE, HERE, AT THE END,
THERE'S NO CHOICE AT ALL.
ONLY APOKOLIPS AND DARKSEID.
FOREVER.

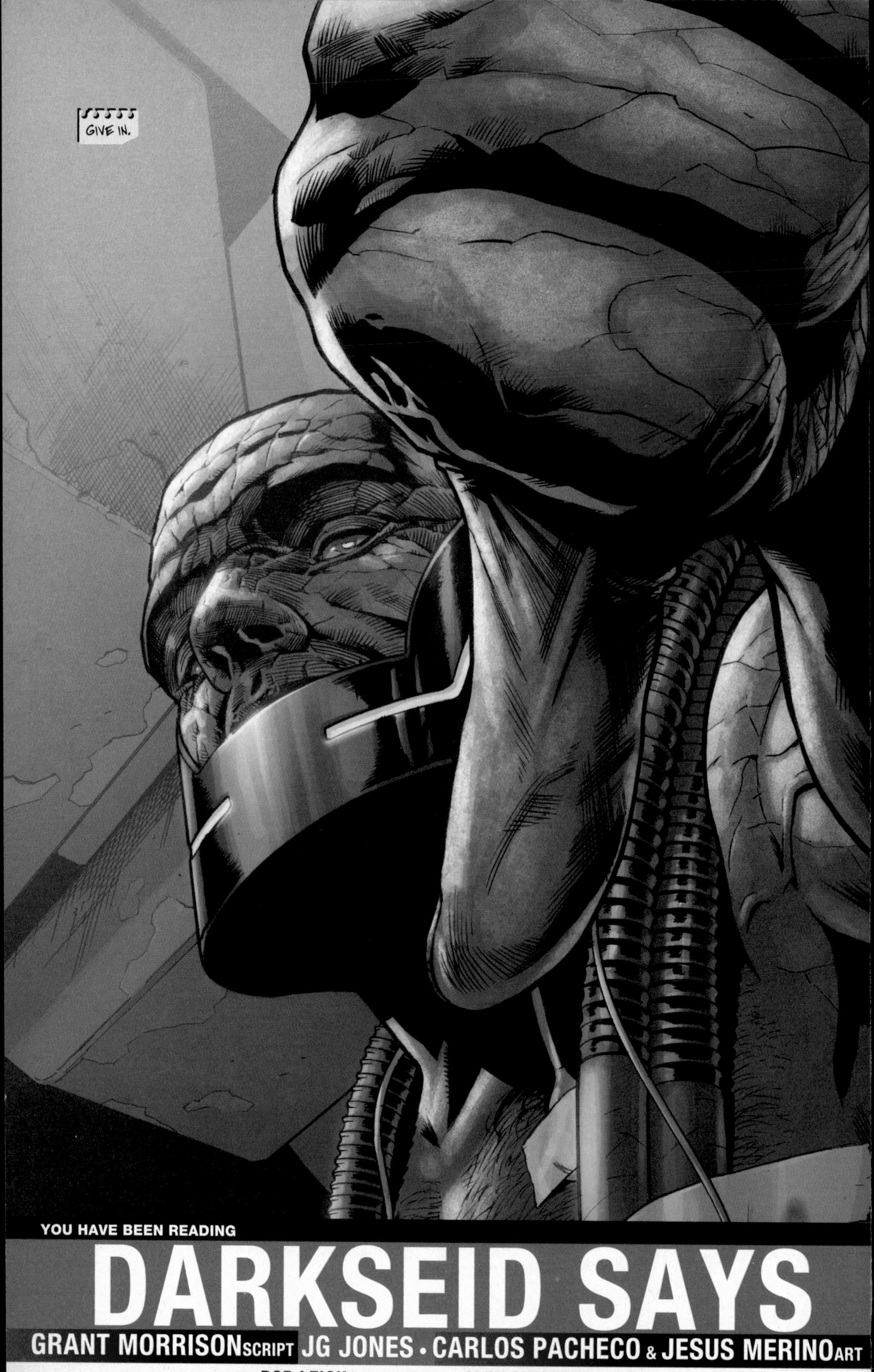
ſſſſſ
GIVE IN.

YOU HAVE BEEN READING

DARKSEID SAYS

GRANT MORRISON SCRIPT JG JONES • CARLOS PACHECO & JESUS MERINO ART
ROB LEIGH LETTERING ALEX SINCLAIR COLORS

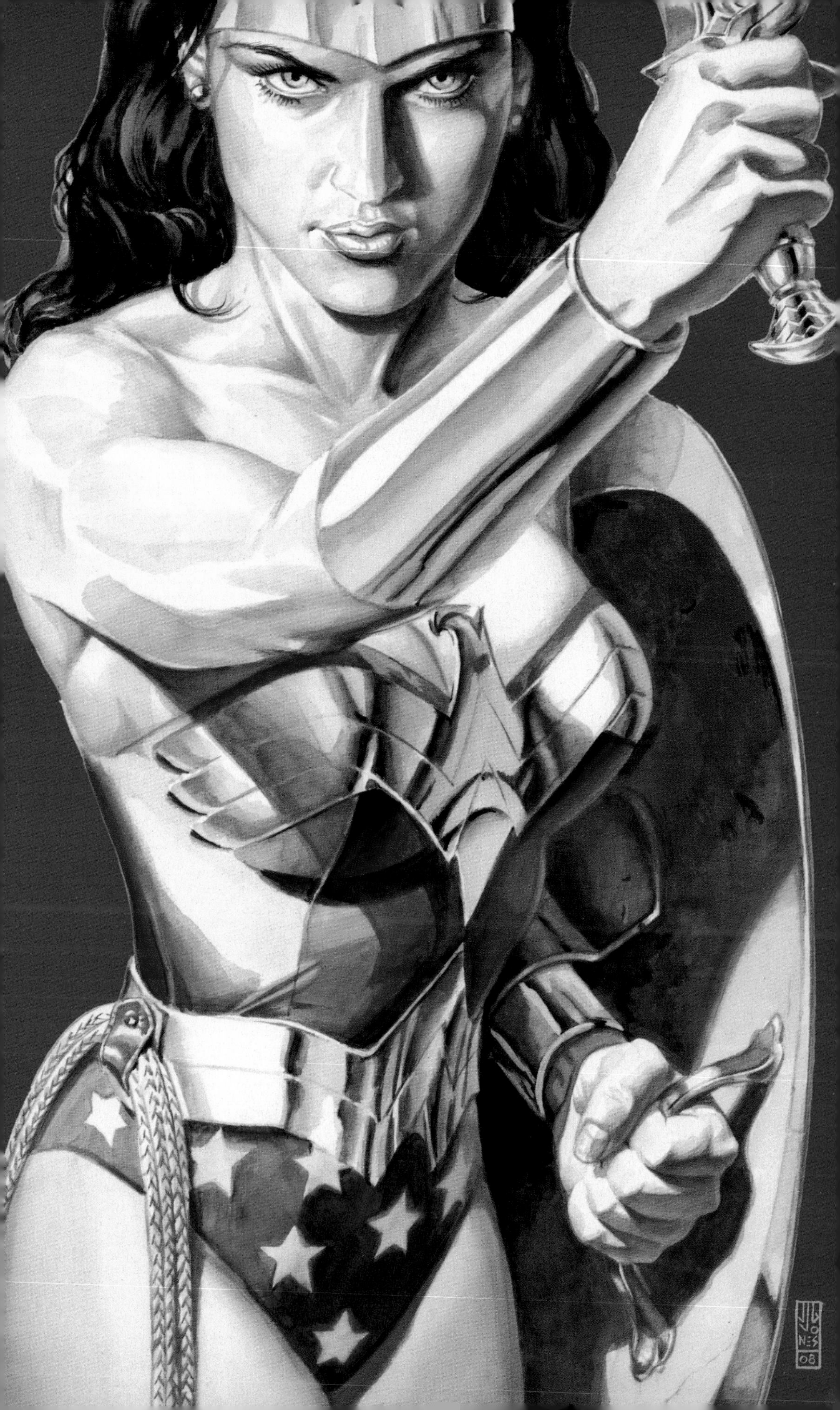

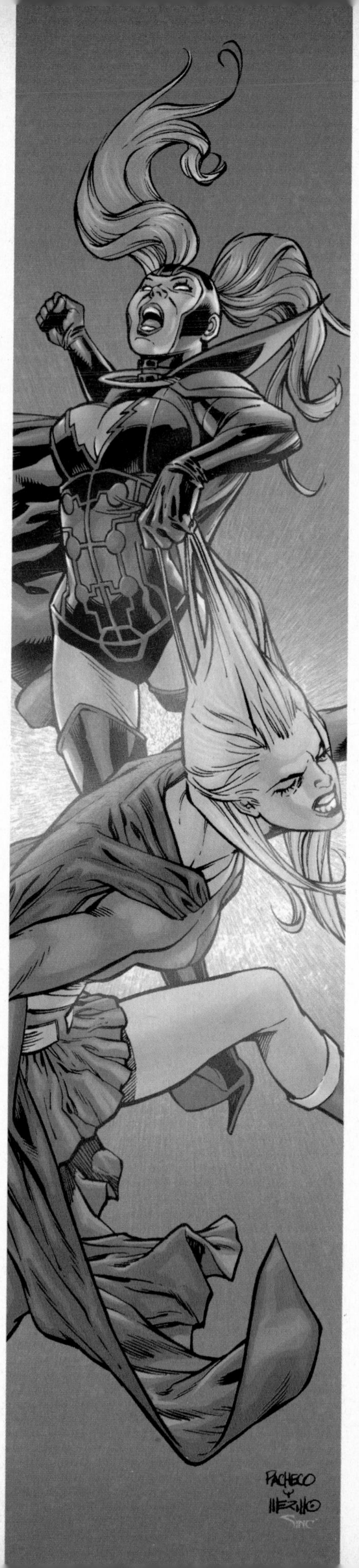

Carlos Pacheco & Jesus Merino with Alex Sinclair

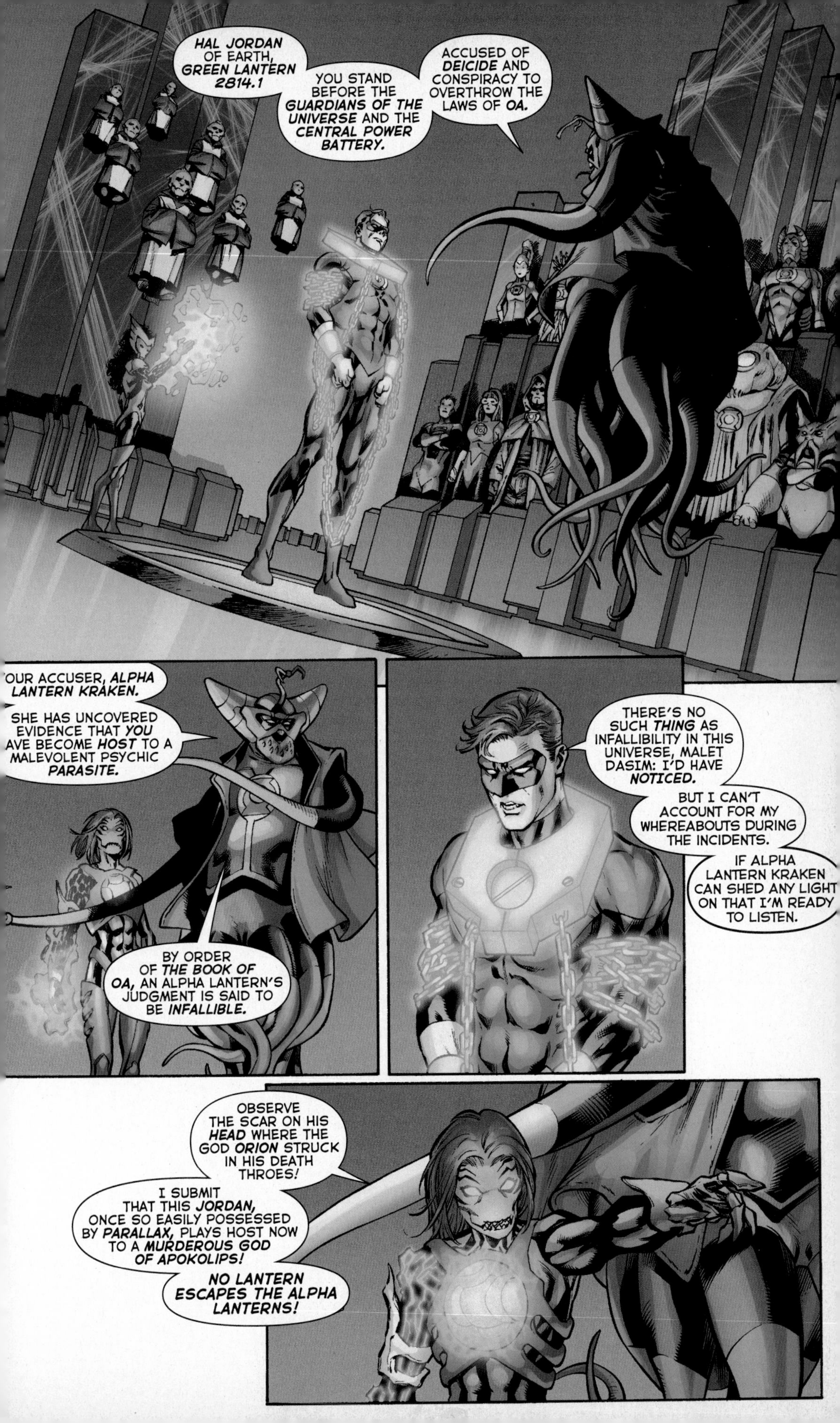
HAL JORDAN OF EARTH, GREEN LANTERN 2814.1
YOU STAND BEFORE THE GUARDIANS OF THE UNIVERSE AND THE CENTRAL POWER BATTERY.
ACCUSED OF DEICIDE AND CONSPIRACY TO OVERTHROW THE LAWS OF OA.
OUR ACCUSER, ALPHA LANTERN KRAKEN.
SHE HAS UNCOVERED EVIDENCE THAT YOU AVE BECOME HOST TO A MALEVOLENT PSYCHIC PARASITE.
BY ORDER OF THE BOOK OF OA, AN ALPHA LANTERN'S JUDGMENT IS SAID TO BE INFALLIBLE.
THERE'S NO SUCH THING AS INFALLIBILITY IN THIS UNIVERSE, MALET DASIM: I'D HAVE NOTICED.
BUT I CAN'T ACCOUNT FOR MY WHEREABOUTS DURING THE INCIDENTS.
IF ALPHA LANTERN KRAKEN CAN SHED ANY LIGHT ON THAT I'M READY TO LISTEN.
OBSERVE THE SCAR ON HIS HEAD WHERE THE GOD ORION STRUCK IN HIS DEATH THROES!
I SUBMIT THAT THIS JORDAN, ONCE SO EASILY POSSESSED BY PARALLAX, PLAYS HOST NOW TO A MURDEROUS GOD OF APOKOLIPS!
NO LANTERN ESCAPES THE ALPHA LANTERNS!

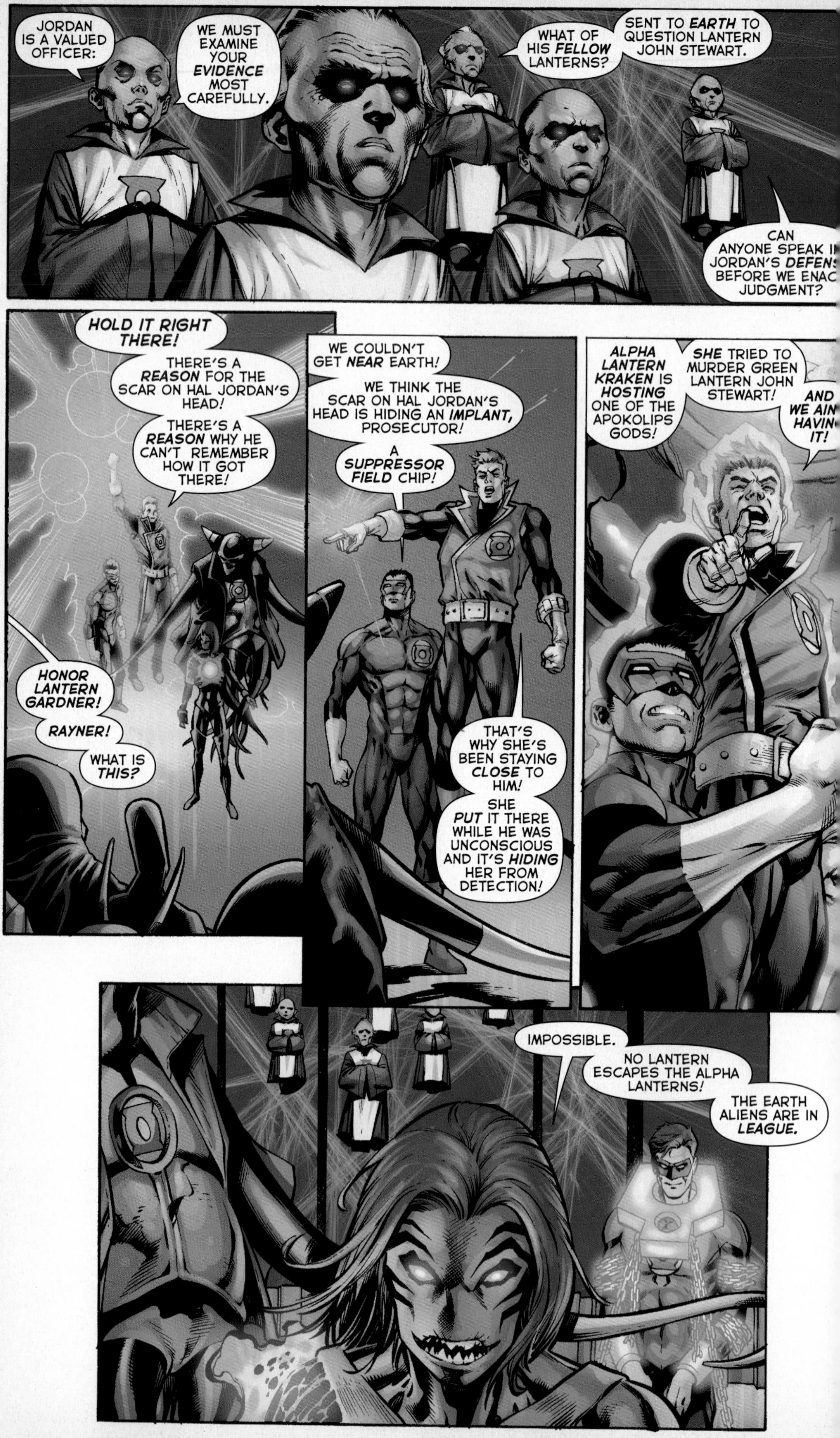
JORDAN IS A VALUED OFFICER:
WE MUST EXAMINE YOUR EVIDENCE MOST CAREFULLY.
WHAT OF HIS FELLOW LANTERNS?
SENT TO EARTH TO QUESTION LANTERN JOHN STEWART.
CAN ANYONE SPEAK I JORDAN'S DEFEN BEFORE WE ENAC JUDGMENT?
HOLD IT RIGHT THERE!
THERE'S A REASON FOR THE SCAR ON HAL JORDAN'S HEAD!
THERE'S A REASON WHY HE CAN'T REMEMBER HOW IT GOT THERE!
HONOR LANTERN GARDNER!
RAYNER!
WHAT IS THIS?
WE COULDN'T GET NEAR EARTH!
WE THINK THE SCAR ON HAL JORDAN'S HEAD IS HIDING AN IMPLANT, PROSECUTOR!
A SUPPRESSOR FIELD CHIP!
THAT'S WHY SHE'S BEEN STAYING CLOSE TO HIM!
SHE PUT IT THERE WHILE HE WAS UNCONSCIOUS AND IT'S HIDING HER FROM DETECTION!
ALPHA LANTERN KRAKEN IS HOSTING ONE OF THE APOKOLIPS GODS!
SHE TRIED TO MURDER GREEN LANTERN JOHN STEWART!
AND WE AIN HAVIN IT!
IMPOSSIBLE.
NO LANTERN ESCAPES THE ALPHA LANTERNS!
THE EARTH ALIENS ARE IN LEAGUE.

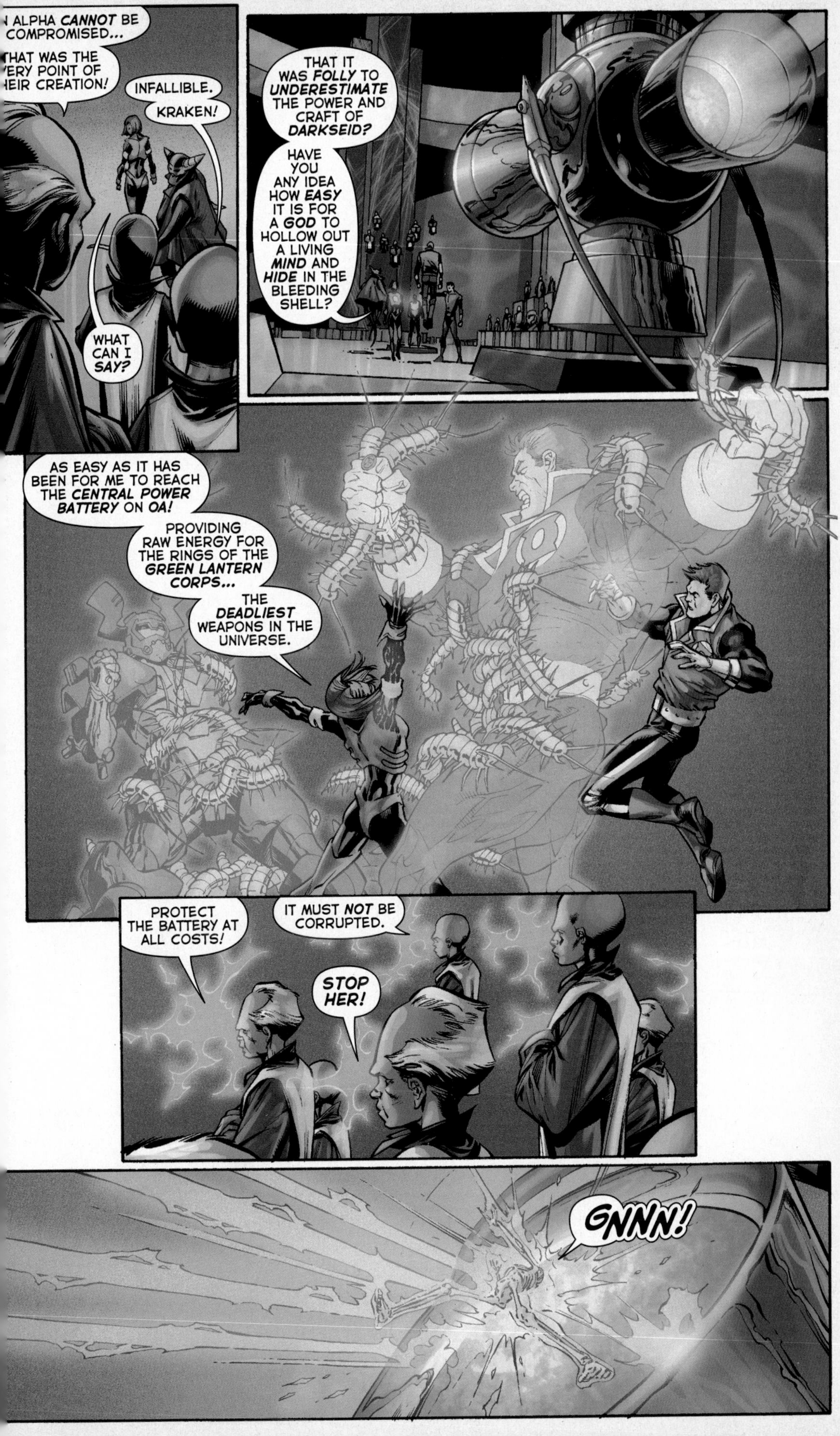
N ALPHA CANNOT BE COMPROMISED...
THAT WAS THE ERY POINT OF HEIR CREATION!
INFALLIBLE.
KRAKEN!
WHAT CAN I SAY?
THAT IT WAS FOLLY TO UNDERESTIMATE THE POWER AND CRAFT OF DARKSEID?
HAVE YOU ANY IDEA HOW EASY IT IS FOR A GOD TO HOLLOW OUT A LIVING MIND AND HIDE IN THE BLEEDING SHELL?
AS EASY AS IT HAS BEEN FOR ME TO REACH THE CENTRAL POWER BATTERY ON OA!
PROVIDING RAW ENERGY FOR THE RINGS OF THE GREEN LANTERN CORPS...
THE DEADLIEST WEAPONS IN THE UNIVERSE.
PROTECT THE BATTERY AT ALL COSTS!
IT MUST NOT BE CORRUPTED.
STOP HER!
GNNN!

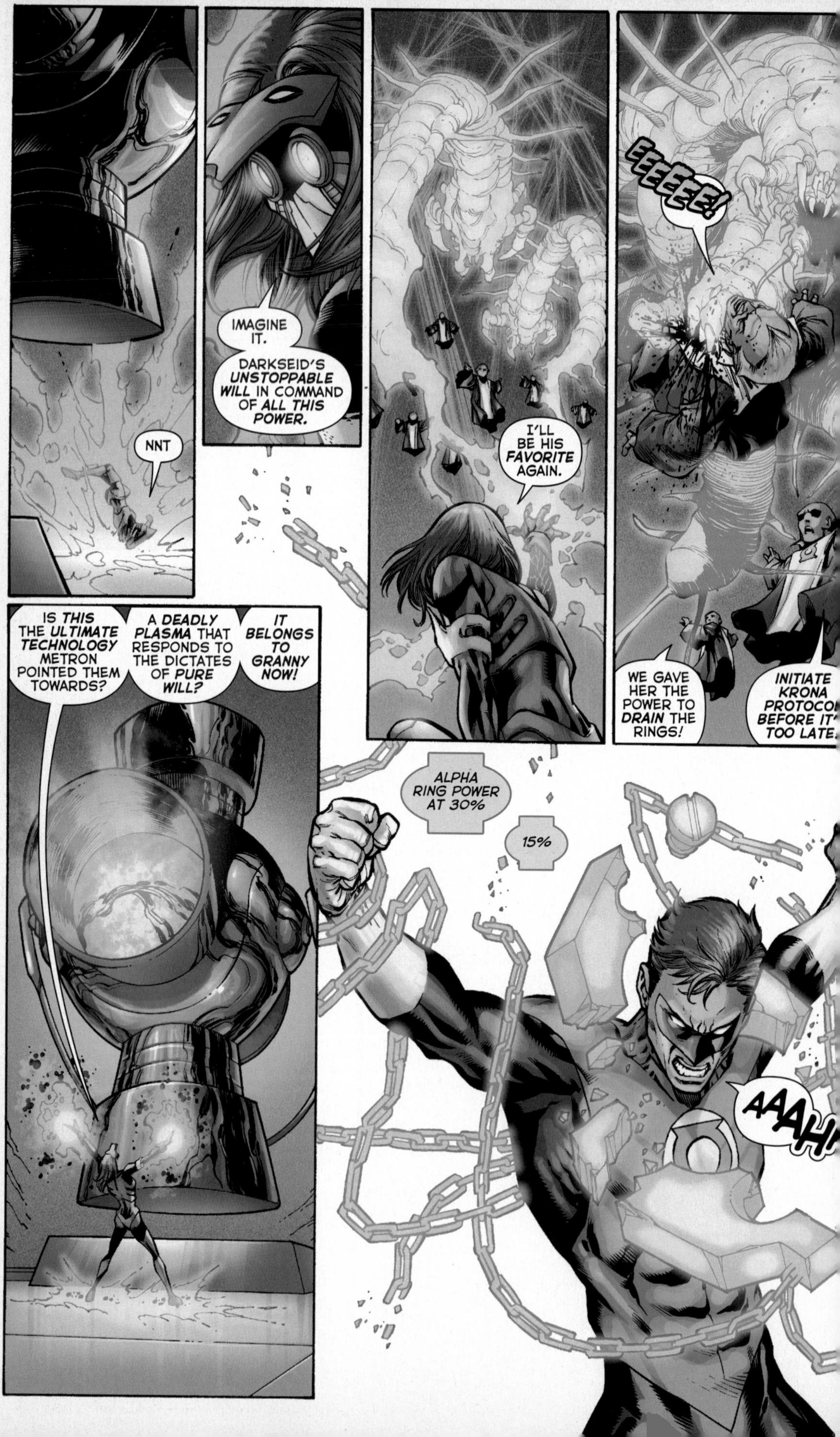
IMAGINE IT.
DARKSEID'S UNSTOPPABLE WILL IN COMMAND OF ALL THIS POWER.
NNT
I'LL BE HIS FAVORITE AGAIN.
EEEEEE!
WE GAVE HER THE POWER TO DRAIN THE RINGS!
INITIATE KRONA PROTOCO BEFORE IT' TOO LATE.
IS THIS THE ULTIMATE TECHNOLOGY METRON POINTED THEM TOWARDS?
A DEADLY PLASMA THAT RESPONDS TO THE DICTATES OF PURE WILL?
IT BELONGS TO GRANNY NOW!
ALPHA RING POWER AT 30%
15%
AAAH!

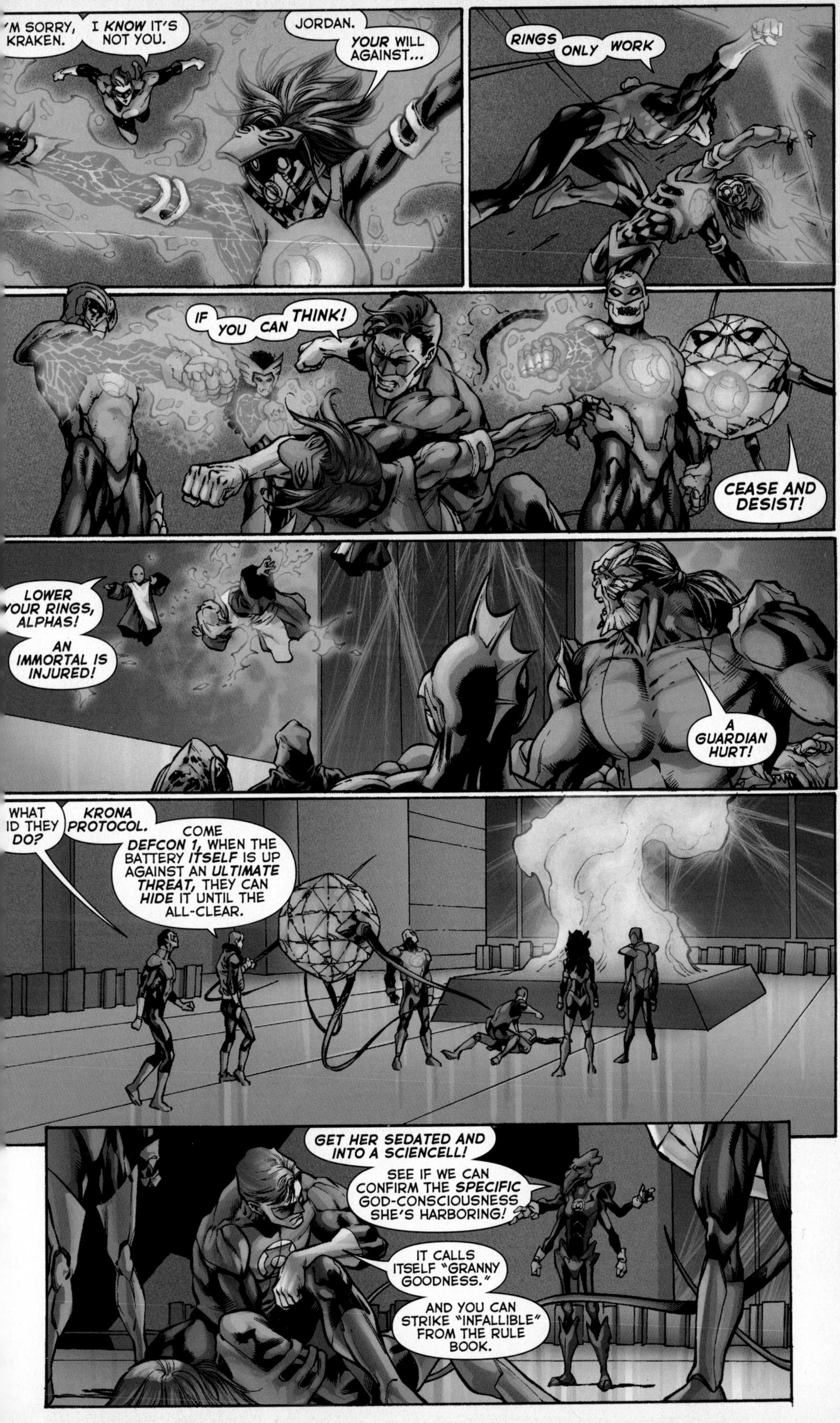

'M SORRY, KRAKEN.
I KNOW IT'S NOT YOU.
JORDAN.
YOUR WILL AGAINST...
RINGS ONLY WORK
IF YOU CAN THINK!
CEASE AND DESIST!
LOWER YOUR RINGS, ALPHAS!
AN IMMORTAL IS INJURED!
A GUARDIAN HURT!
WHAT ID THEY DO?
KRONA PROTOCOL.
COME DEFCON 1, WHEN THE BATTERY ITSELF IS UP AGAINST AN ULTIMATE THREAT, THEY CAN HIDE IT UNTIL THE ALL-CLEAR.
GET HER SEDATED AND INTO A SCIENCELL!
SEE IF WE CAN CONFIRM THE SPECIFIC GOD-CONSCIOUSNESS SHE'S HARBORING!
IT CALLS ITSELF "GRANNY GOODNESS."
AND YOU CAN STRIKE "INFALLIBLE" FROM THE RULE BOOK.

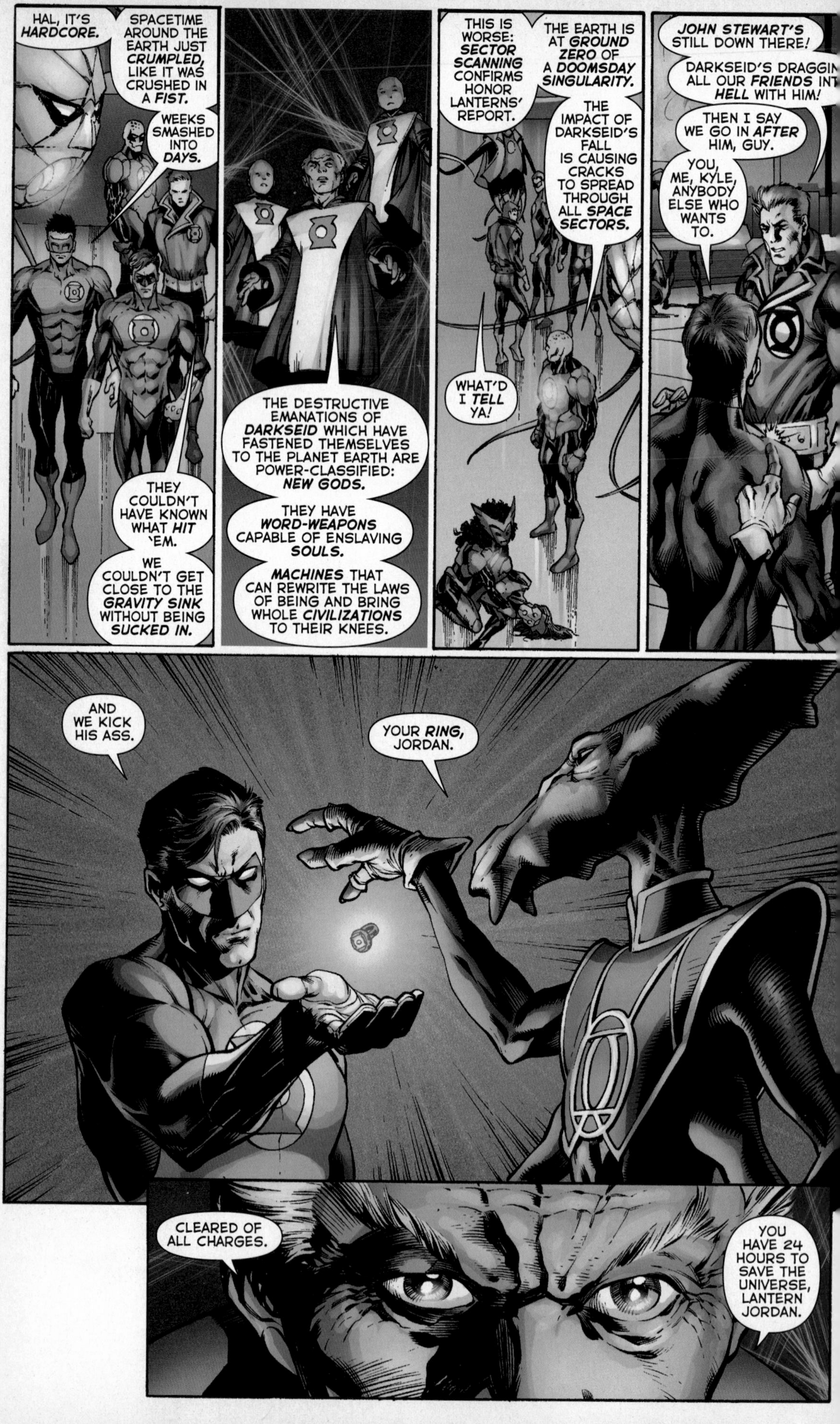
HAL, IT'S HARDCORE.
SPACETIME AROUND THE EARTH JUST CRUMPLED, LIKE IT WAS CRUSHED IN A FIST.
WEEKS SMASHED INTO DAYS.
THEY COULDN'T HAVE KNOWN WHAT HIT 'EM.
WE COULDN'T GET CLOSE TO THE GRAVITY SINK WITHOUT BEING SUCKED IN.
THE DESTRUCTIVE EMANATIONS OF DARKSEID WHICH HAVE FASTENED THEMSELVES TO THE PLANET EARTH ARE POWER-CLASSIFIED: NEW GODS.
THEY HAVE WORD-WEAPONS CAPABLE OF ENSLAVING SOULS.
MACHINES THAT CAN REWRITE THE LAWS OF BEING AND BRING WHOLE CIVILIZATIONS TO THEIR KNEES.
THIS IS WORSE: SECTOR SCANNING CONFIRMS HONOR LANTERNS' REPORT.
THE EARTH IS AT GROUND ZERO OF A DOOMSDAY SINGULARITY.
THE IMPACT OF DARKSEID'S FALL IS CAUSING CRACKS TO SPREAD THROUGH ALL SPACE SECTORS.
WHAT'D I TELL YA!
JOHN STEWART'S STILL DOWN THERE!
DARKSEID'S DRAGGIN ALL OUR FRIENDS INT HELL WITH HIM!
THEN I SAY WE GO IN AFTER HIM, GUY.
YOU, ME, KYLE, ANYBODY ELSE WHO WANTS TO.
AND WE KICK HIS ASS.
YOUR RING, JORDAN.
CLEARED OF ALL CHARGES.
YOU HAVE 24 HOURS TO SAVE THE UNIVERSE, LANTERN JORDAN.

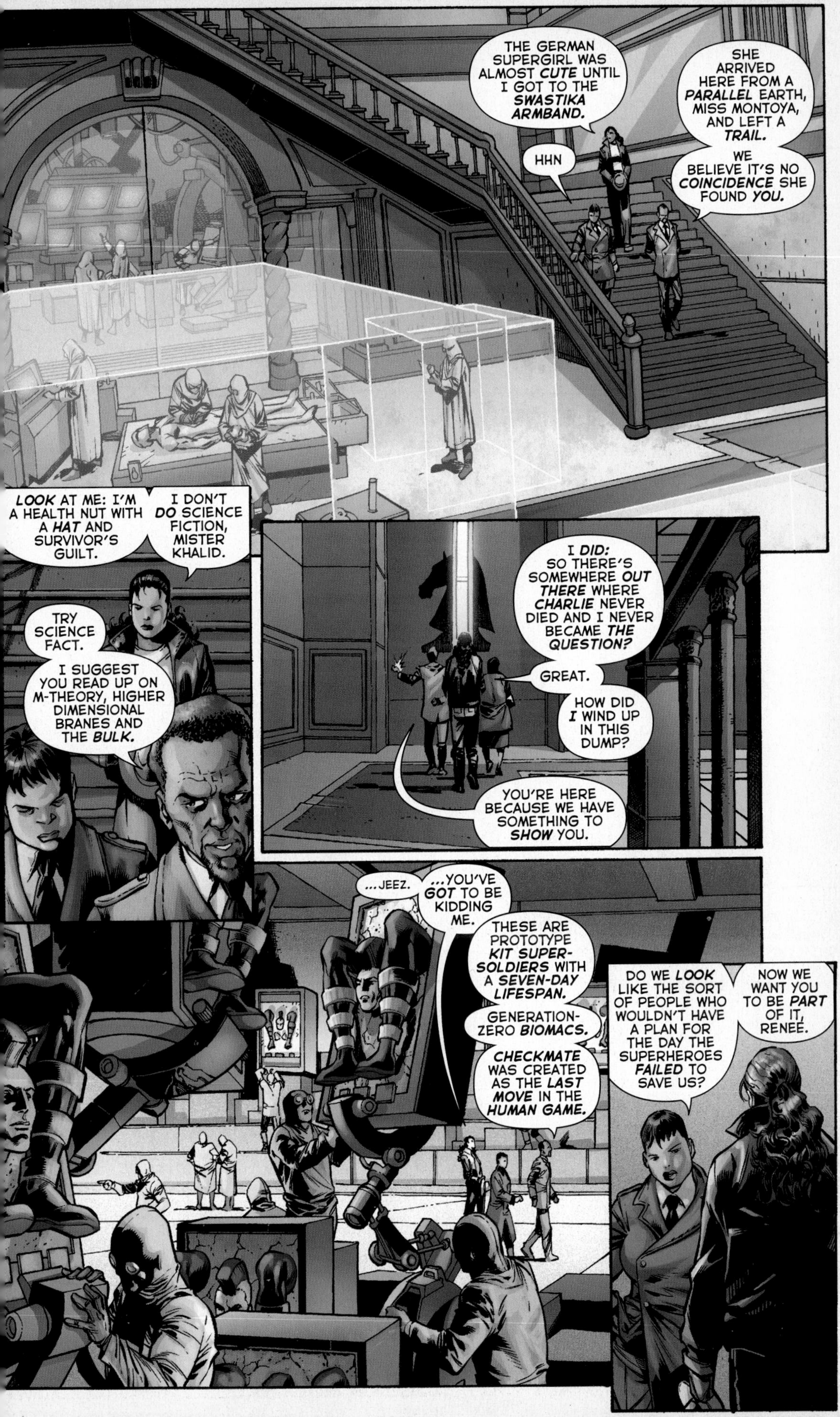
THE GERMAN SUPERGIRL WAS ALMOST CUTE UNTIL I GOT TO THE SWASTIKA ARMBAND.
SHE ARRIVED HERE FROM A PARALLEL EARTH, MISS MONTOYA, AND LEFT A TRAIL.
HHN
WE BELIEVE IT'S NO COINCIDENCE SHE FOUND YOU.
LOOK AT ME: I'M A HEALTH NUT WITH A HAT AND SURVIVOR'S GUILT.
I DON'T DO SCIENCE FICTION, MISTER KHALID.
TRY SCIENCE FACT.
I SUGGEST YOU READ UP ON M-THEORY, HIGHER DIMENSIONAL BRANES AND THE BULK.
I DID: SO THERE'S SOMEWHERE OUT THERE WHERE CHARLIE NEVER DIED AND I NEVER BECAME THE QUESTION?
GREAT.
HOW DID I WIND UP IN THIS DUMP?
YOU'RE HERE BECAUSE WE HAVE SOMETHING TO SHOW YOU.
...JEEZ.
...YOU'VE GOT TO BE KIDDING ME.
THESE ARE PROTOTYPE KIT SUPER-SOLDIERS WITH A SEVEN-DAY LIFESPAN.
GENERATION-ZERO BIOMACS.
CHECKMATE WAS CREATED AS THE LAST MOVE IN THE HUMAN GAME.
DO WE LOOK LIKE THE SORT OF PEOPLE WHO WOULDN'T HAVE A PLAN FOR THE DAY THE SUPERHEROES FAILED TO SAVE US?
NOW WE WANT YOU TO BE PART OF IT, RENEE.

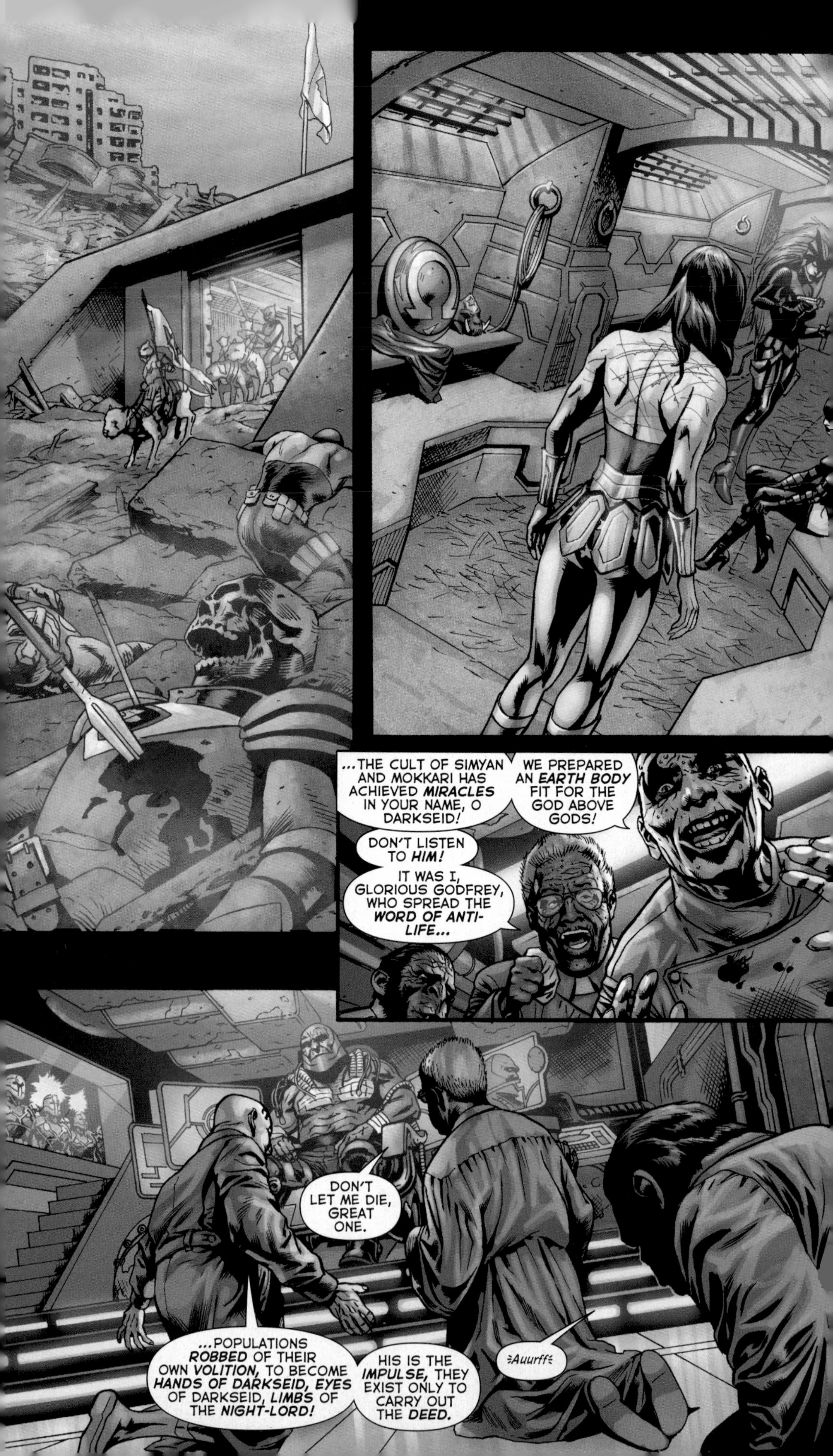
...THE CULT OF SIMYAN AND MOKKARI HAS ACHIEVED MIRACLES IN YOUR NAME, O DARKSEID!
WE PREPARED AN EARTH BODY FIT FOR THE GOD ABOVE GODS!
DON'T LISTEN TO HIM!
IT WAS I, GLORIOUS GODFREY, WHO SPREAD THE WORD OF ANTI-LIFE...
DON'T LET ME DIE, GREAT ONE.
...POPULATIONS ROBBED OF THEIR OWN VOLITION, TO BECOME HANDS OF DARKSEID, EYES OF DARKSEID, LIMBS OF THE NIGHT-LORD!
HIS IS THE IMPULSE, THEY EXIST ONLY TO CARRY OUT THE DEED.
Auurff

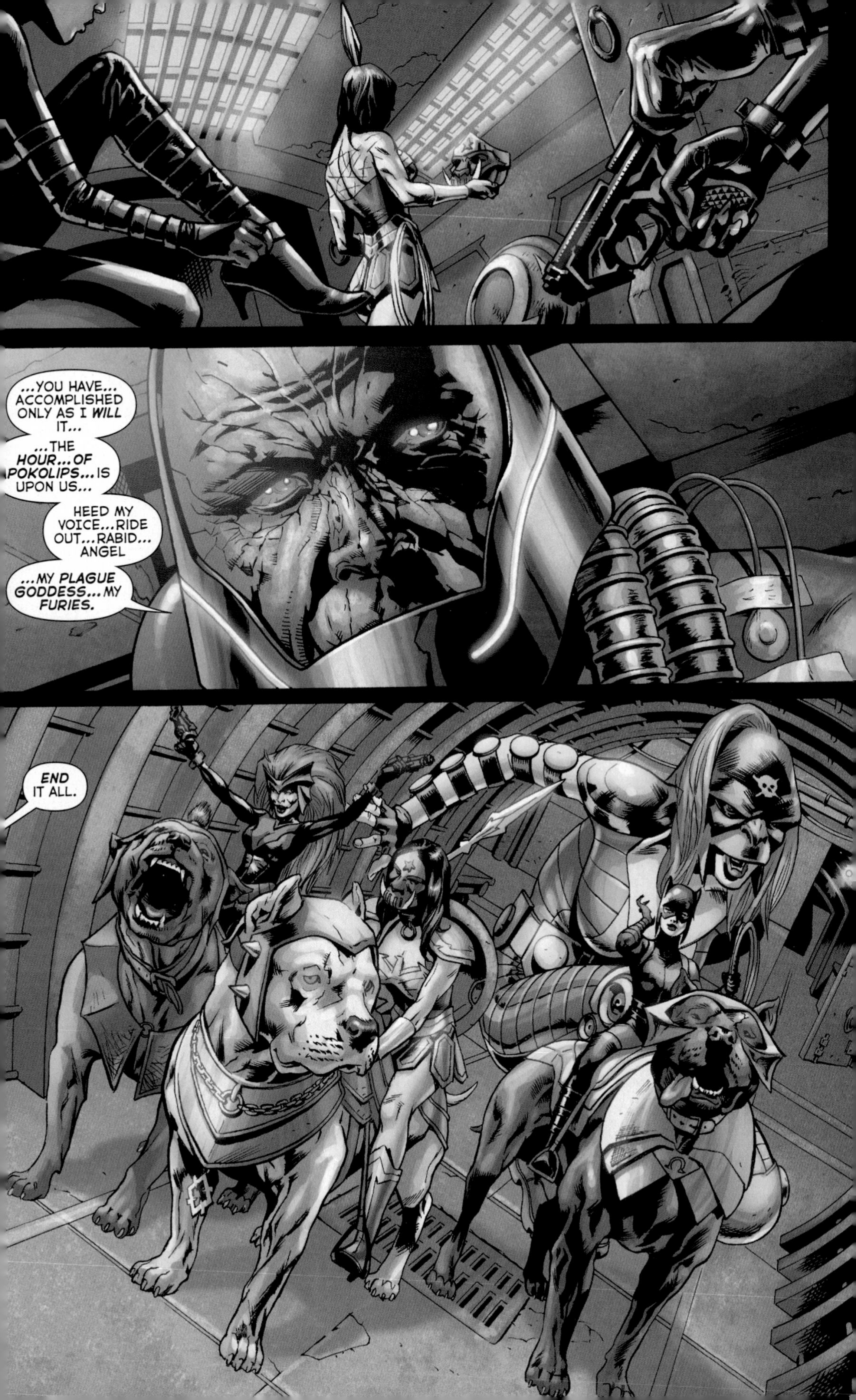
...YOU HAVE... ACCOMPLISHED ONLY AS I *WILL* IT...
...THE *HOUR...OF APOKOLIPS...*IS UPON US...
HEED MY VOICE...RIDE OUT...RABID... ANGEL
...MY *PLAGUE GODDESS...*MY *FURIES.*
END IT ALL.

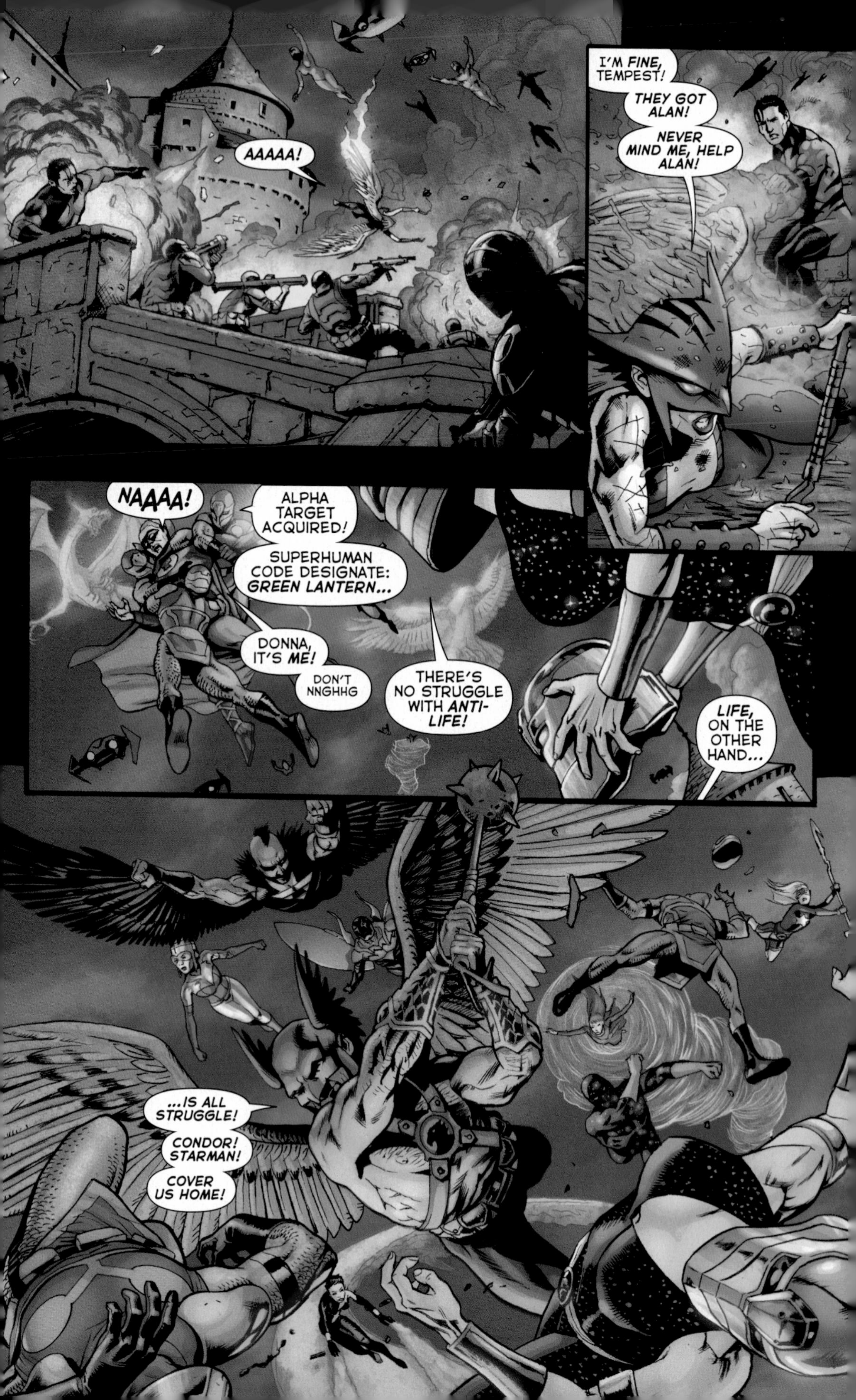
AAAAA!
I'M FINE, TEMPEST!
THEY GOT ALAN!
NEVER MIND ME, HELP ALAN!
NAAAA!
ALPHA TARGET ACQUIRED!
SUPERHUMAN CODE DESIGNATE: GREEN LANTERN...
DONNA, IT'S ME!
DON'T NNGHHG
THERE'S NO STRUGGLE WITH ANTI-LIFE!
LIFE, ON THE OTHER HAND...
...IS ALL STRUGGLE!
CONDOR! STARMAN!
COVER US HOME!

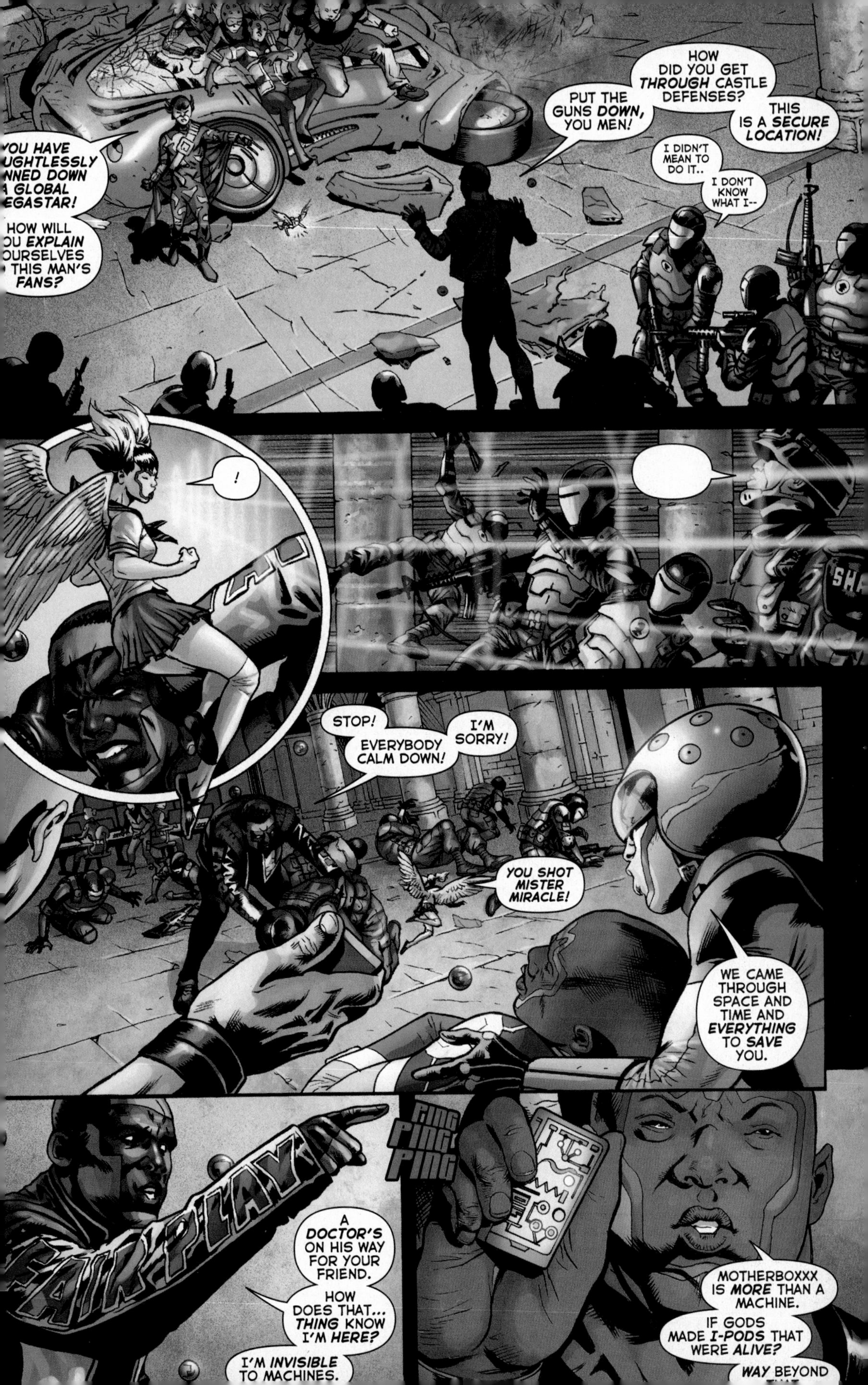

YOU HAVE UGHTLESSLY NNED DOWN A GLOBAL EGASTAR!
HOW WILL OU EXPLAIN OURSELVES THIS MAN'S FANS?
PUT THE GUNS DOWN, YOU MEN!
HOW DID YOU GET THROUGH CASTLE DEFENSES?
THIS IS A SECURE LOCATION!
I DIDN'T MEAN TO DO IT..
I DON'T KNOW WHAT I--
!
STOP!
EVERYBODY CALM DOWN!
I'M SORRY!
YOU SHOT MISTER MIRACLE!
WE CAME THROUGH SPACE AND TIME AND EVERYTHING TO SAVE YOU.
PING PING PING
FAIR PLAY
A DOCTOR'S ON HIS WAY FOR YOUR FRIEND.
HOW DOES THAT... THING KNOW I'M HERE?
I'M INVISIBLE TO MACHINES.
MOTHERBOXXX IS MORE THAN A MACHINE.
IF GODS MADE I-PODS THAT WERE ALIVE?
WAY BEYOND

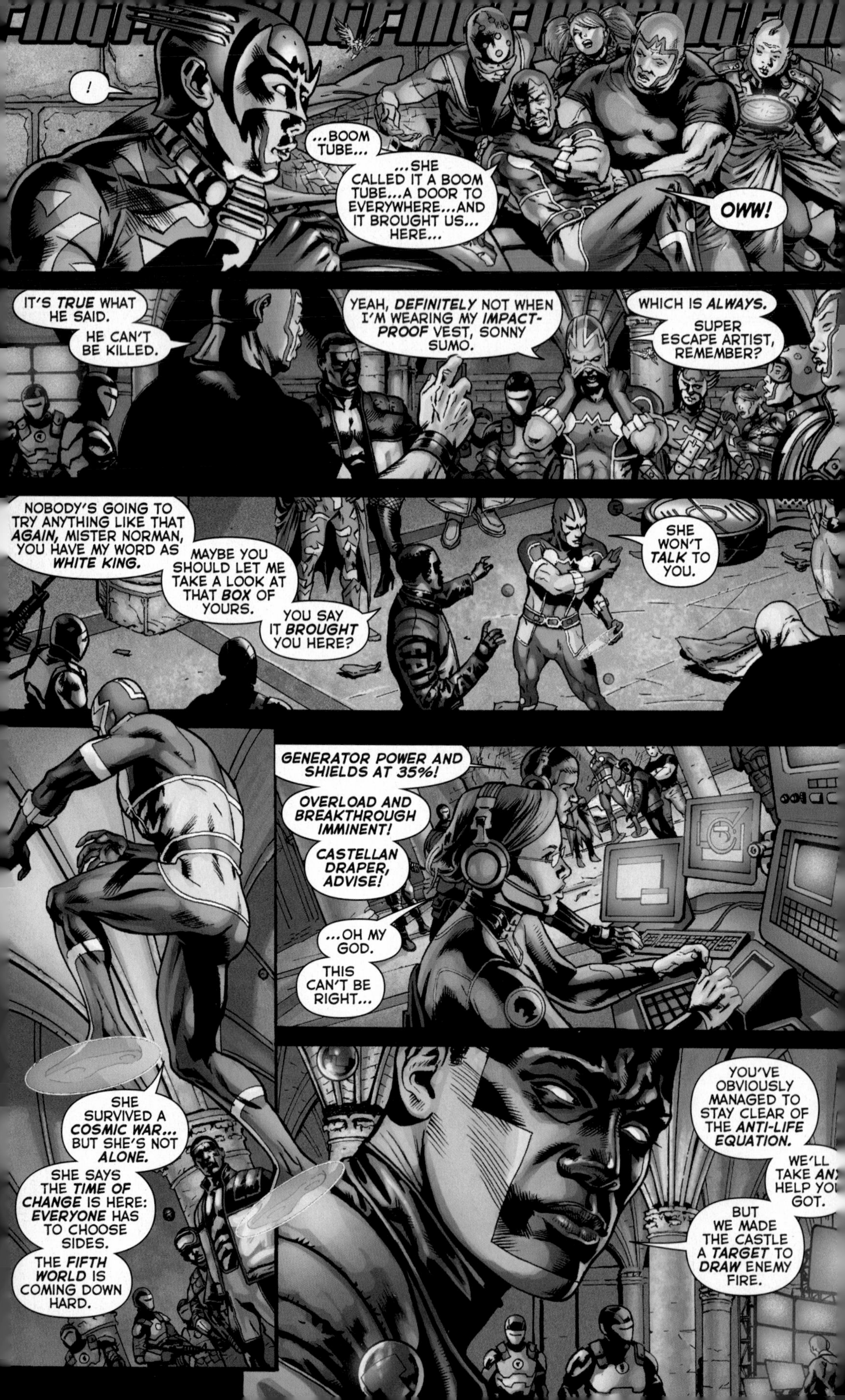
!
...BOOM TUBE...
...SHE CALLED IT A BOOM TUBE...A DOOR TO EVERYWHERE...AND IT BROUGHT US... HERE...
OWW!
IT'S TRUE WHAT HE SAID.
HE CAN'T BE KILLED.
YEAH, DEFINITELY NOT WHEN I'M WEARING MY IMPACT-PROOF VEST, SONNY SUMO.
WHICH IS ALWAYS.
SUPER ESCAPE ARTIST, REMEMBER?
NOBODY'S GOING TO TRY ANYTHING LIKE THAT AGAIN, MISTER NORMAN, YOU HAVE MY WORD AS WHITE KING.
MAYBE YOU SHOULD LET ME TAKE A LOOK AT THAT BOX OF YOURS.
YOU SAY IT BROUGHT YOU HERE?
SHE WON'T TALK TO YOU.
GENERATOR POWER AND SHIELDS AT 35%!
OVERLOAD AND BREAKTHROUGH IMMINENT!
CASTELLAN DRAPER, ADVISE!
...OH MY GOD.
THIS CAN'T BE RIGHT...
SHE SURVIVED A COSMIC WAR... BUT SHE'S NOT ALONE.
SHE SAYS THE TIME OF CHANGE IS HERE: EVERYONE HAS TO CHOOSE SIDES.
THE FIFTH WORLD IS COMING DOWN HARD.
YOU'VE OBVIOUSLY MANAGED TO STAY CLEAR OF THE ANTI-LIFE EQUATION.
BUT WE MADE THE CASTLE A TARGET TO DRAW ENEMY FIRE.

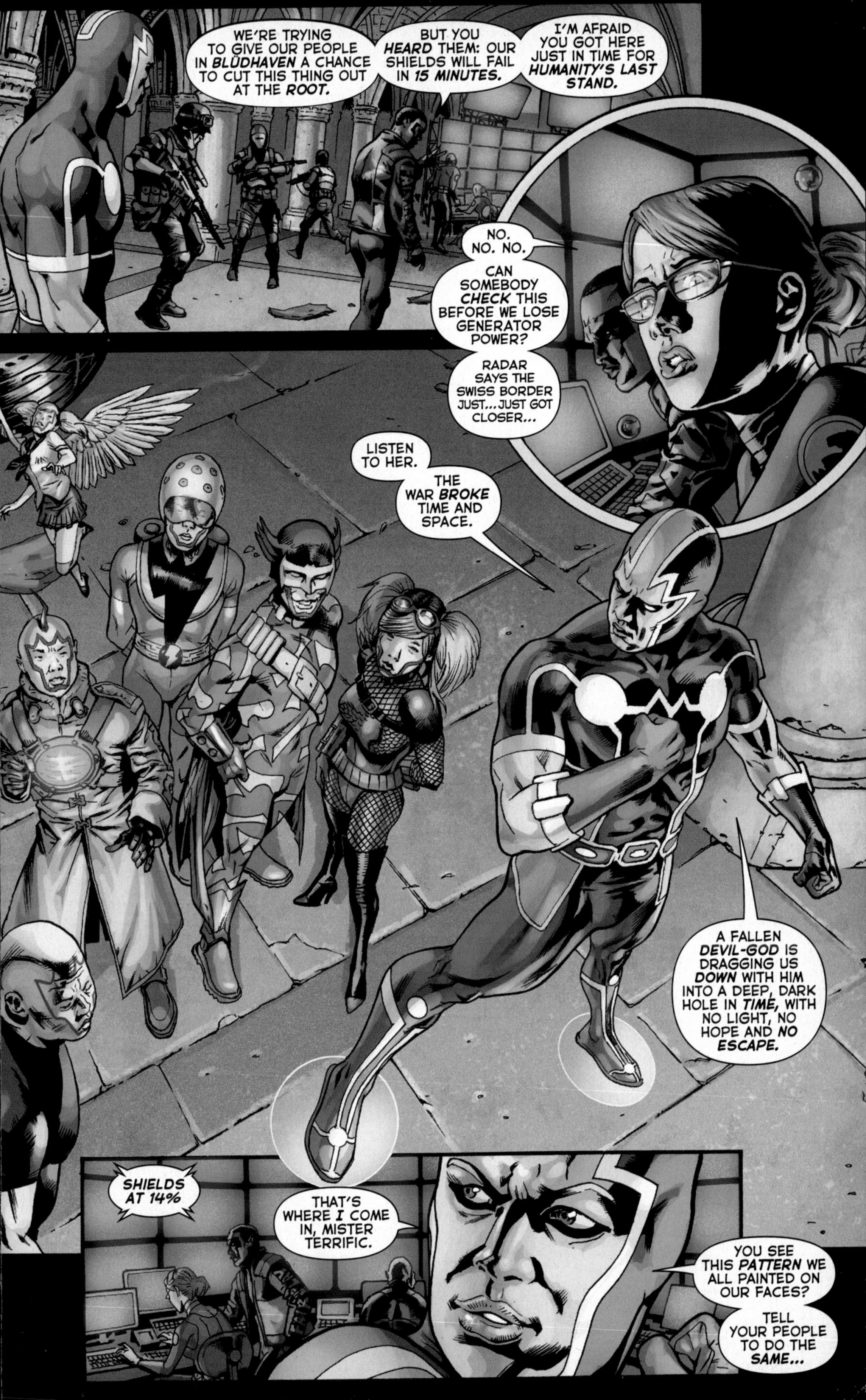

WE'RE TRYING TO GIVE OUR PEOPLE IN BLÜDHAVEN A CHANCE TO CUT THIS THING OUT AT THE ROOT.
BUT YOU HEARD THEM: OUR SHIELDS WILL FAIL IN 15 MINUTES.
I'M AFRAID YOU GOT HERE JUST IN TIME FOR HUMANITY'S LAST STAND.
NO. NO. NO.
CAN SOMEBODY CHECK THIS BEFORE WE LOSE GENERATOR POWER?
RADAR SAYS THE SWISS BORDER JUST...JUST GOT CLOSER...
LISTEN TO HER.
THE WAR BROKE TIME AND SPACE.
A FALLEN DEVIL-GOD IS DRAGGING US DOWN WITH HIM INTO A DEEP, DARK HOLE IN TIME, WITH NO LIGHT, NO HOPE AND NO ESCAPE.
SHIELDS AT 14%
THAT'S WHERE I COME IN, MISTER TERRIFIC.
YOU SEE THIS PATTERN WE ALL PAINTED ON OUR FACES?
TELL YOUR PEOPLE TO DO THE SAME...

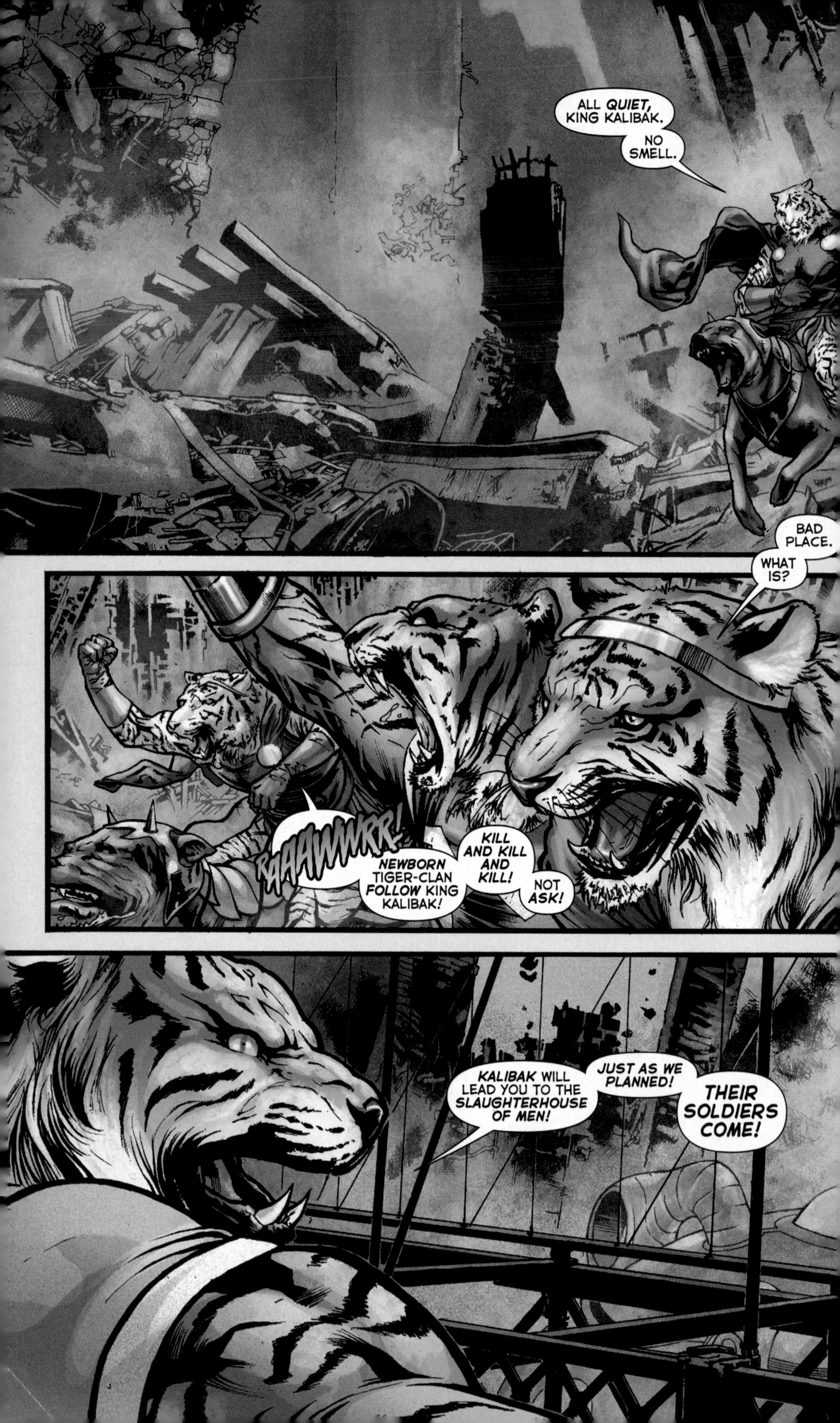
ALL QUIET, KING KALIBAK.
NO SMELL.
BAD PLACE.
WHAT IS?
RAAAWWRR!
NEWBORN TIGER-CLAN FOLLOW KING KALIBAK!
KILL AND KILL AND KILL!
NOT ASK!
KALIBAK WILL LEAD YOU TO THE SLAUGHTERHOUSE OF MEN!
JUST AS WE PLANNED!
THEIR SOLDIERS COME!

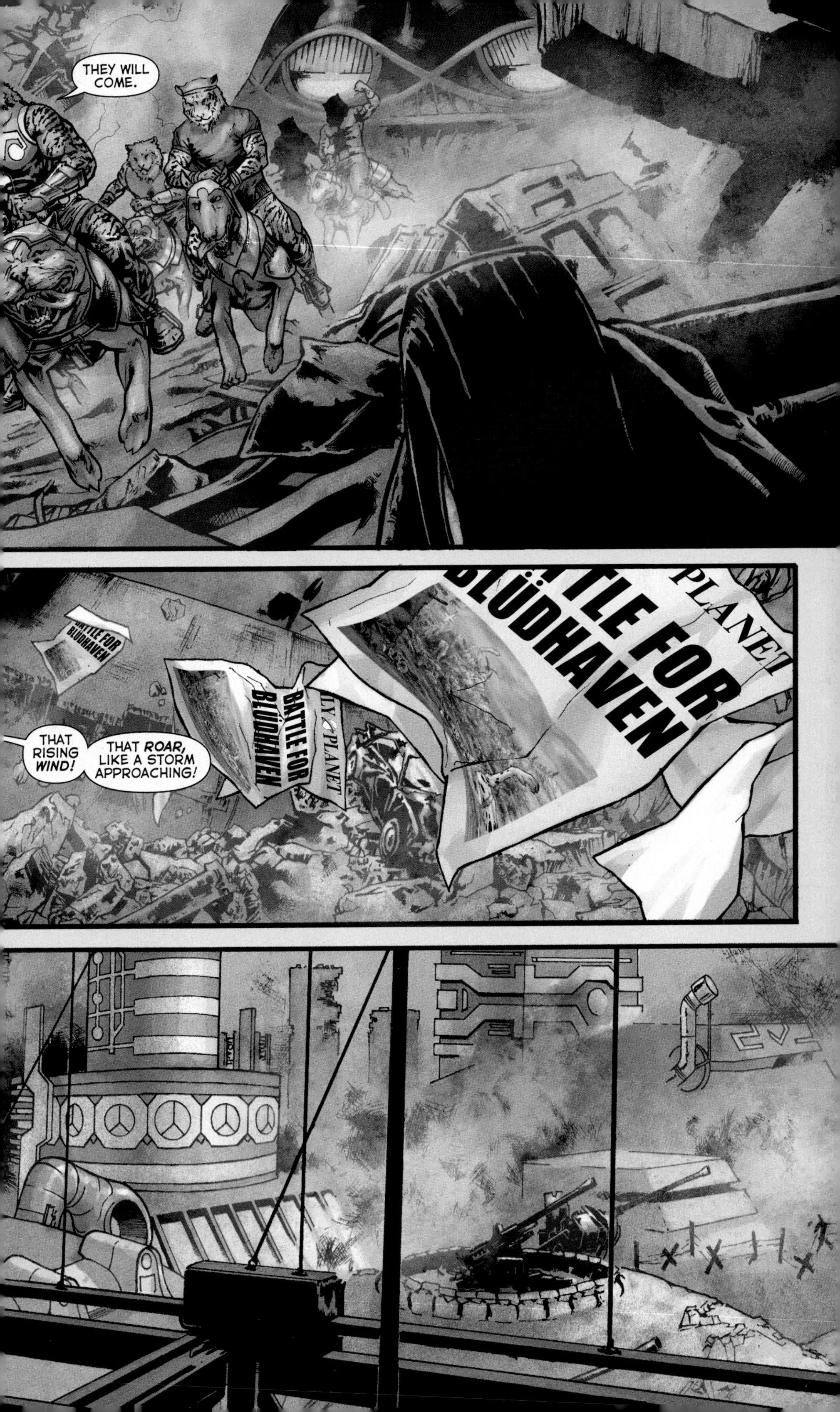
THEY WILL COME.
BATTLE FOR BLÜDHAVEN
PLANET
BATTLE FOR BLÜDHAVEN
THAT RISING WIND!
THAT ROAR, LIKE A STORM APPROACHING!

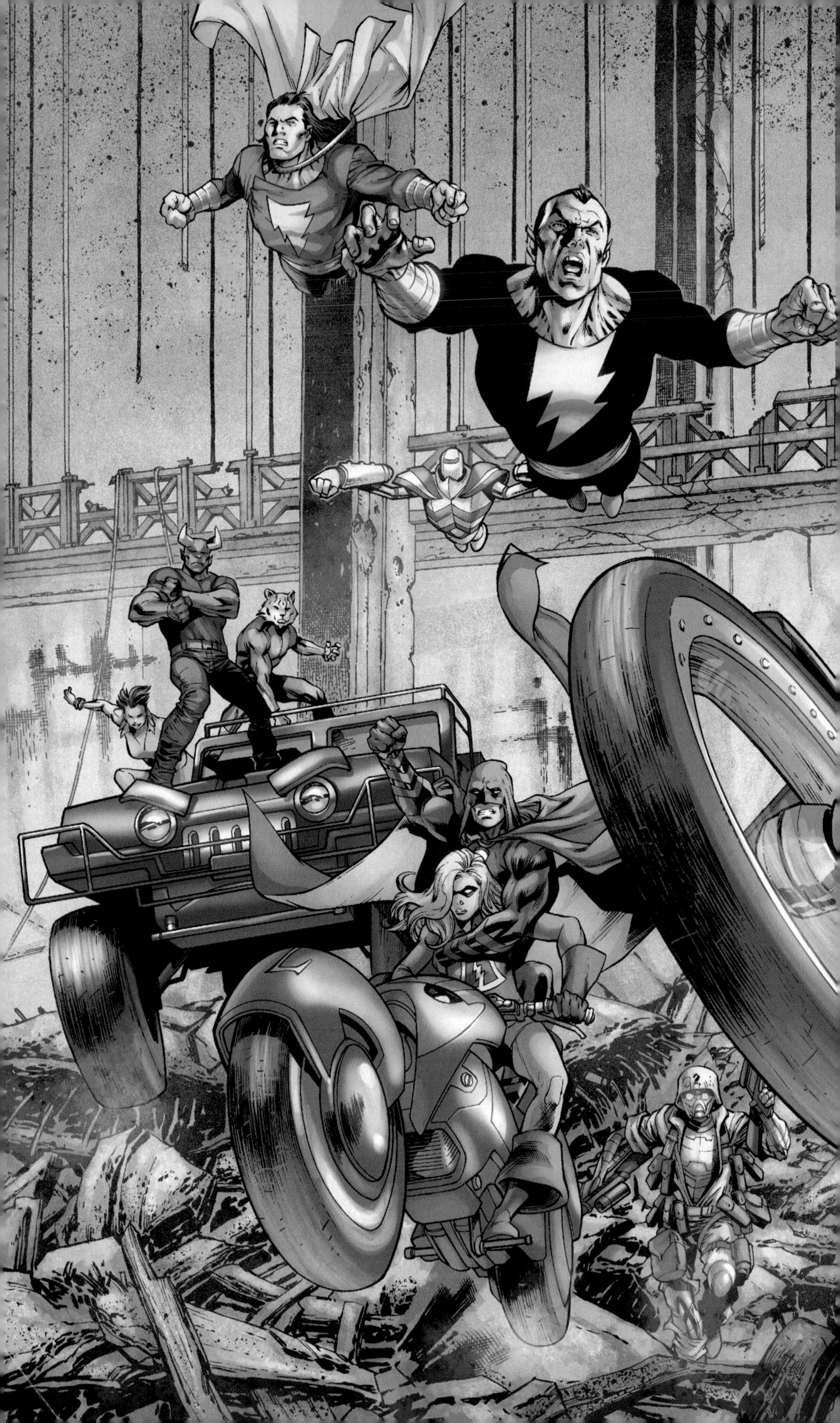

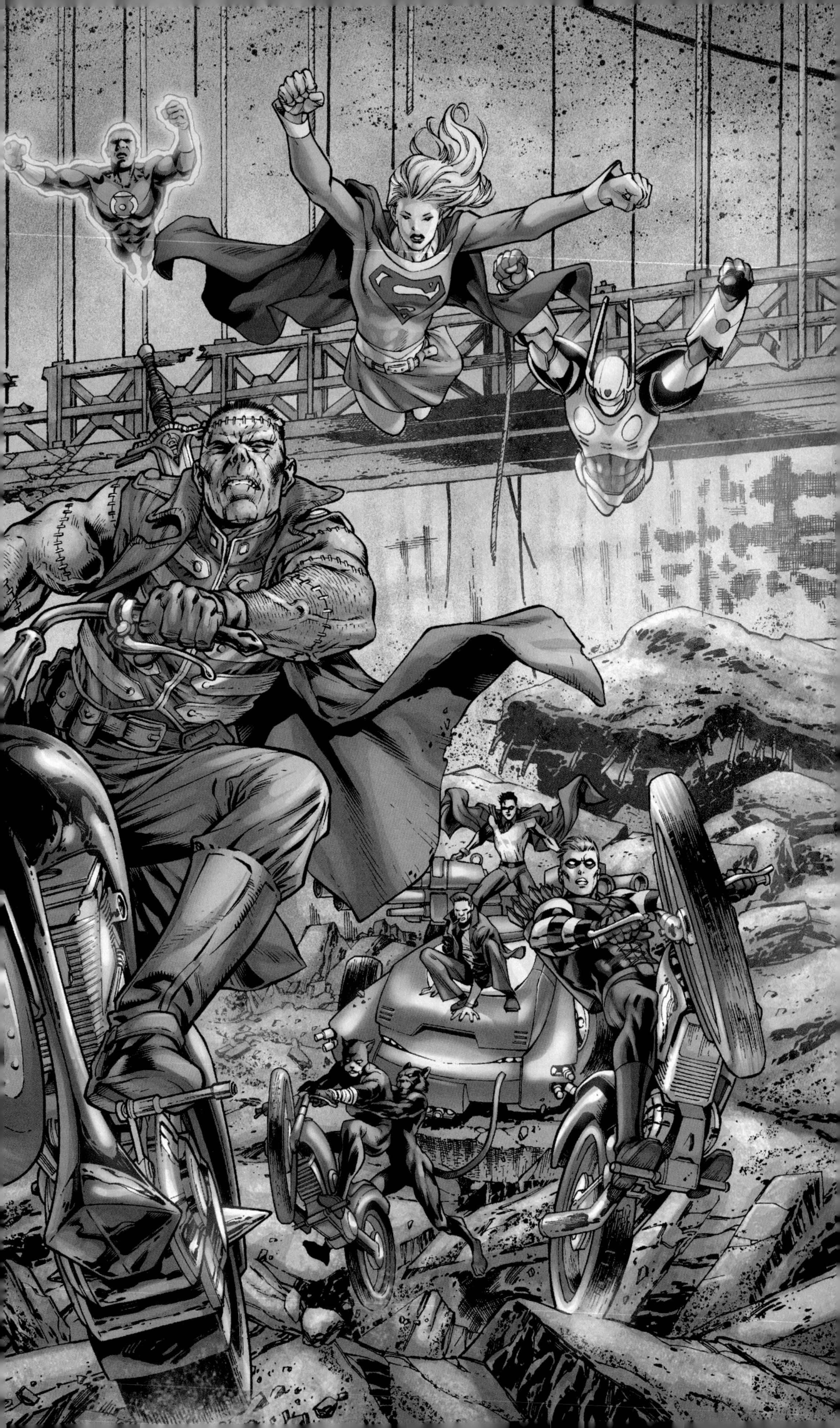

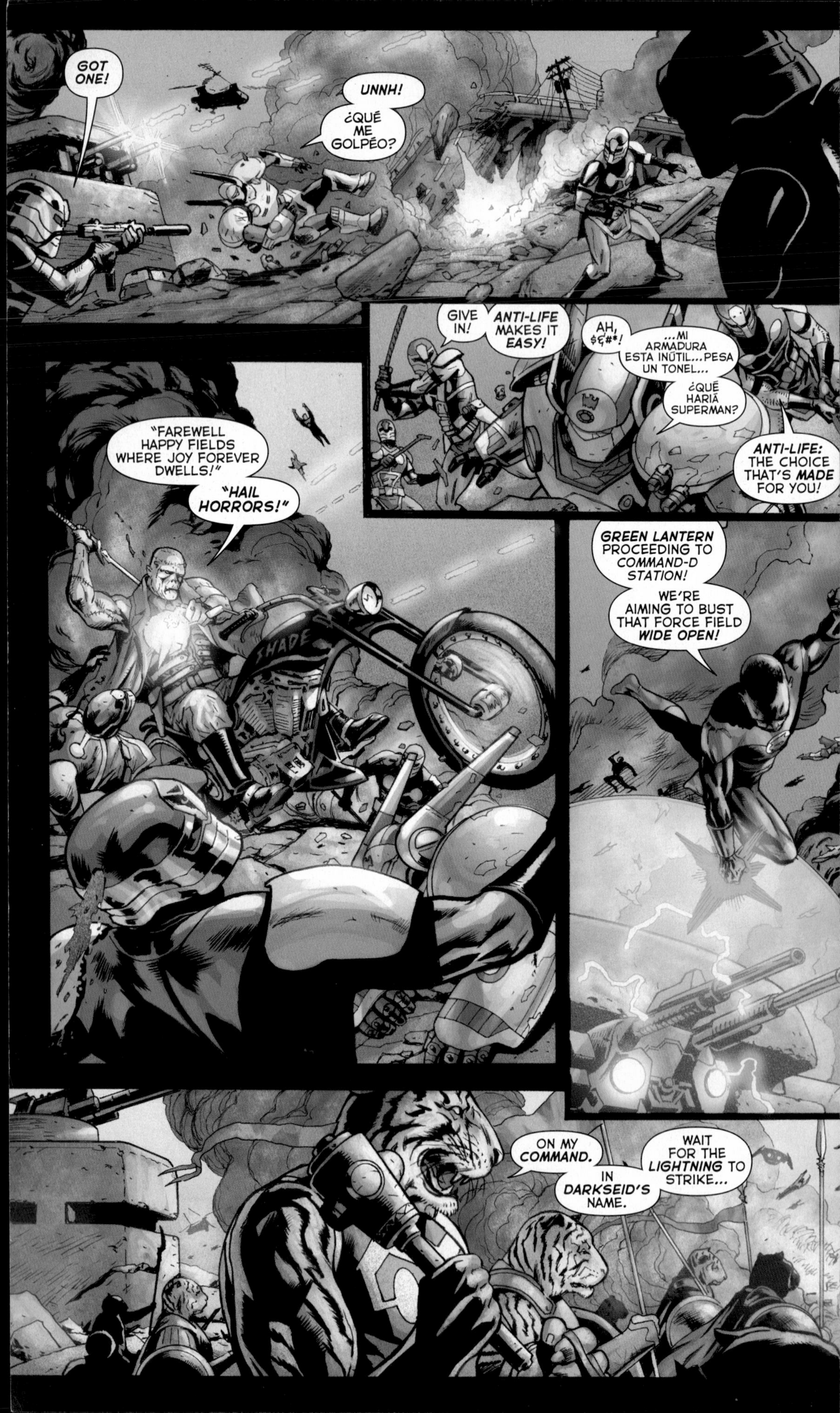
GOT ONE!
UNNH!
¿QUÉ ME GOLPÉO?
GIVE IN!
ANTI-LIFE MAKES IT EASY!
AH, $&#*!
...MI ARMADURA ESTA INÚTIL...PESA UN TONEL...
¿QUÉ HARIÁ SUPERMAN?
ANTI-LIFE: THE CHOICE THAT'S MADE FOR YOU!
"FAREWELL HAPPY FIELDS WHERE JOY FOREVER DWELLS!"
"HAIL HORRORS!"
SHADE
GREEN LANTERN PROCEEDING TO COMMAND-D STATION!
WE'RE AIMING TO BUST THAT FORCE FIELD WIDE OPEN!
ON MY COMMAND.
IN DARKSEID'S NAME.
WAIT FOR THE LIGHTNING TO STRIKE...

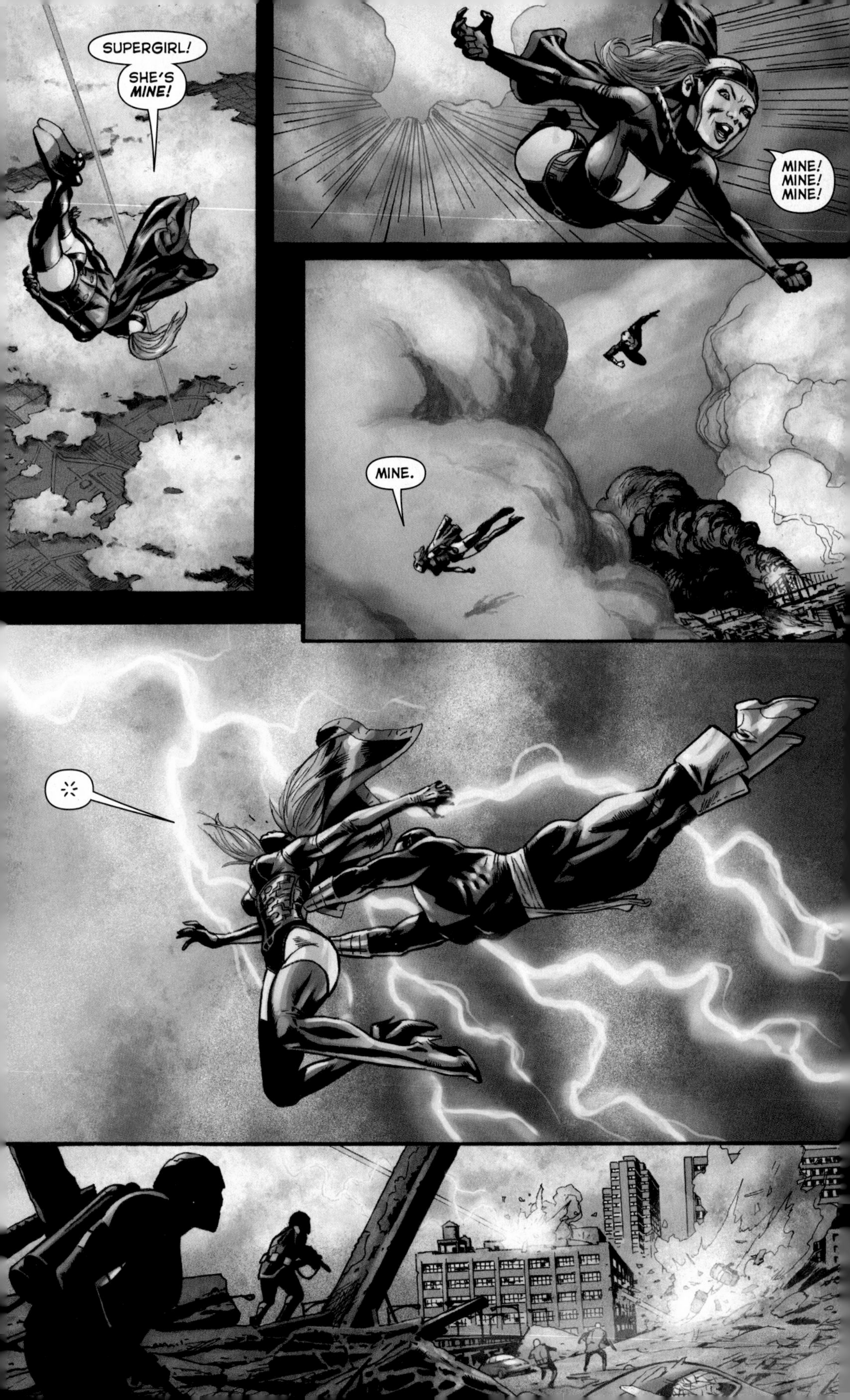
SUPERGIRL!
SHE'S *MINE!*
MINE! MINE! MINE!
MINE.
!

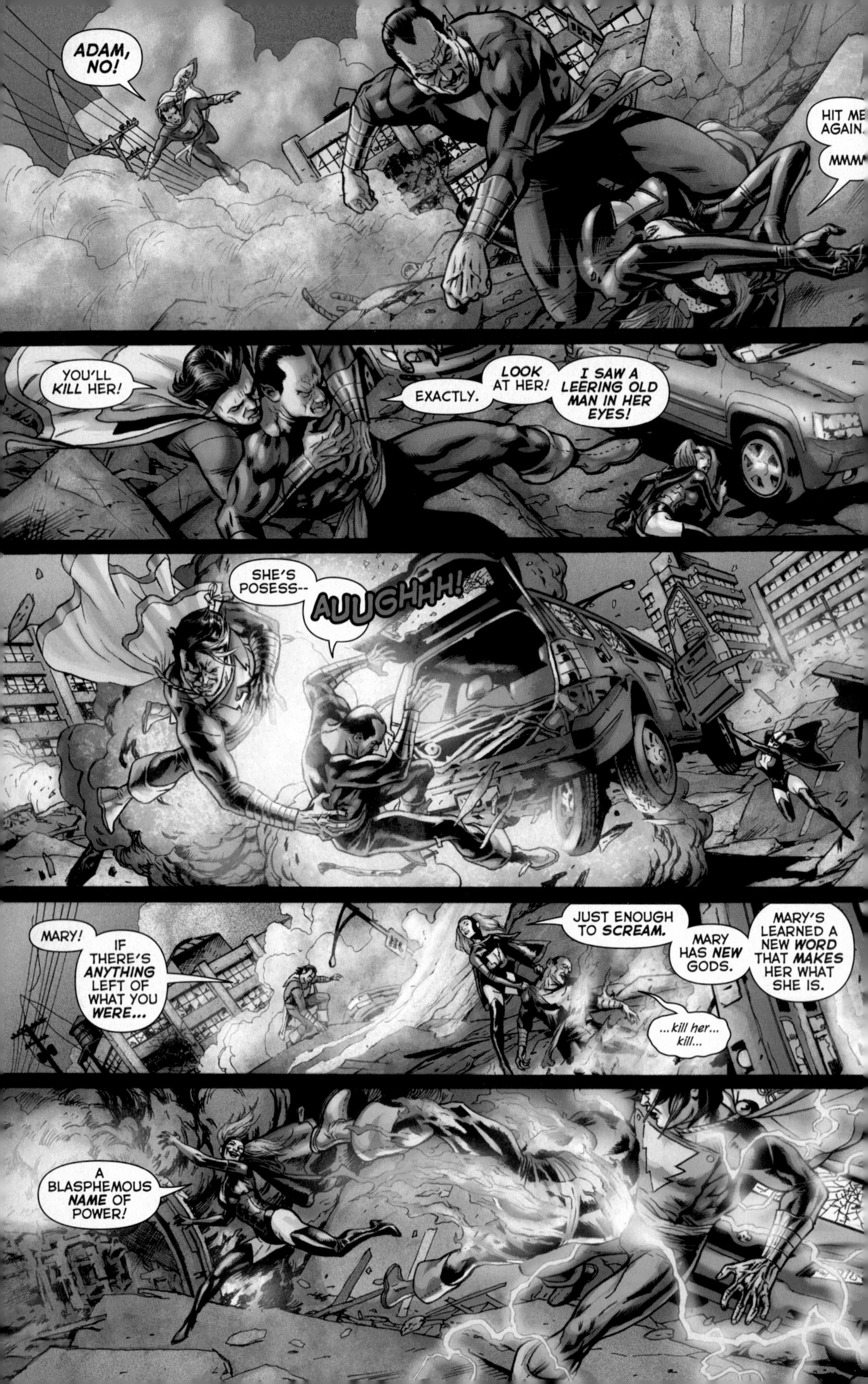
ADAM, NO!
HIT ME AGAIN.
MMM
YOU'LL KILL HER!
EXACTLY.
LOOK AT HER!
I SAW A LEERING OLD MAN IN HER EYES!
SHE'S POSESS--
AUUGHHH!
MARY!
IF THERE'S ANYTHING LEFT OF WHAT YOU WERE...
JUST ENOUGH TO SCREAM.
MARY HAS NEW GODS.
MARY'S LEARNED A NEW WORD THAT MAKES HER WHAT SHE IS.
...kill her... kill...
A BLASPHEMOUS NAME OF POWER!

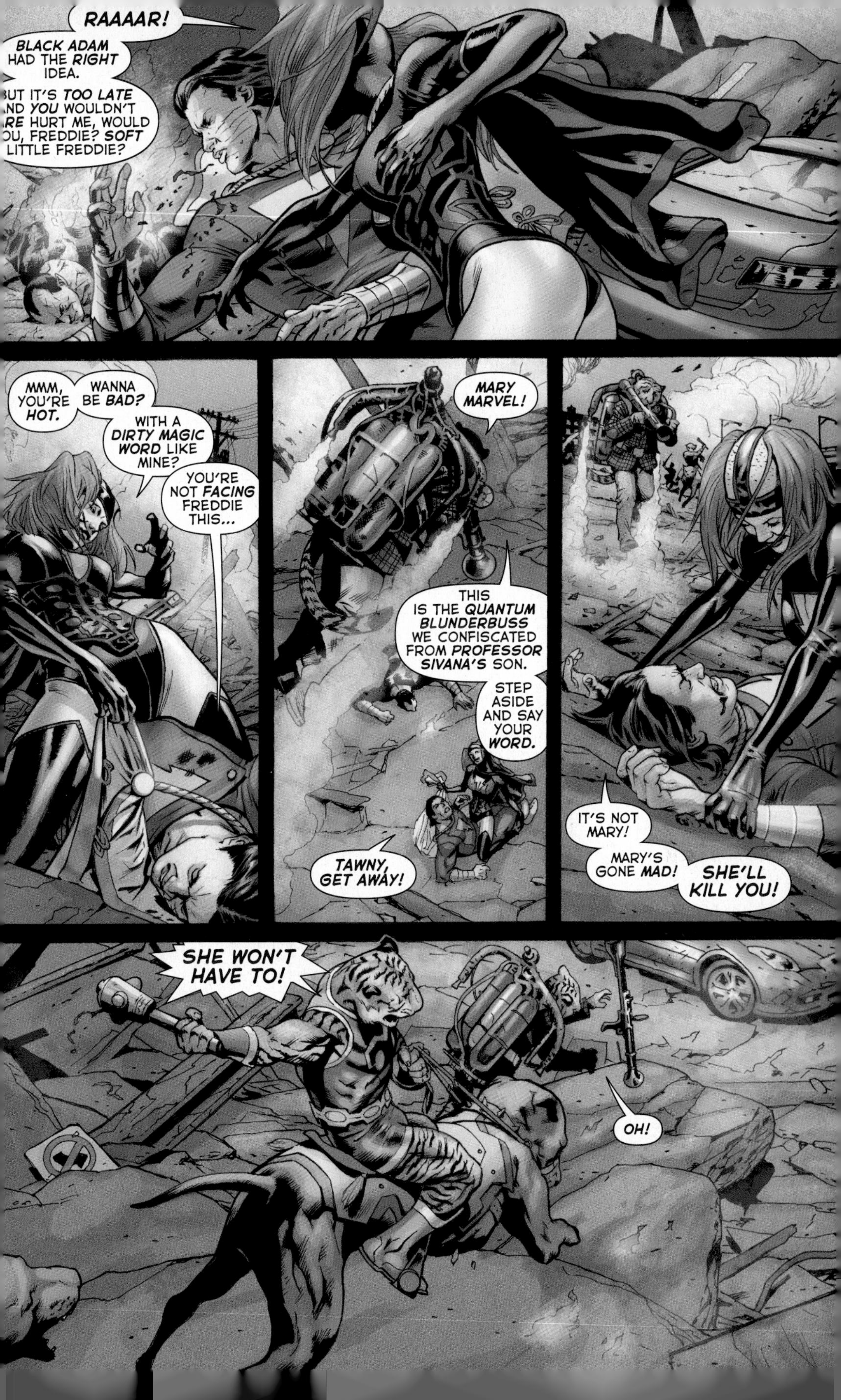
RAAAAR!
BLACK ADAM HAD THE RIGHT IDEA.
BUT IT'S TOO LATE AND YOU WOULDN'T DARE HURT ME, WOULD YOU, FREDDIE? SOFT LITTLE FREDDIE?
MMM, YOU'RE HOT.
WANNA BE BAD?
WITH A DIRTY MAGIC WORD LIKE MINE?
YOU'RE NOT FACING FREDDIE THIS...
MARY MARVEL!
THIS IS THE QUANTUM BLUNDERBUSS WE CONFISCATED FROM PROFESSOR SIVANA'S SON.
STEP ASIDE AND SAY YOUR WORD.
TAWNY, GET AWAY!
IT'S NOT MARY!
MARY'S GONE MAD!
SHE'LL KILL YOU!
SHE WON'T HAVE TO!
OH!

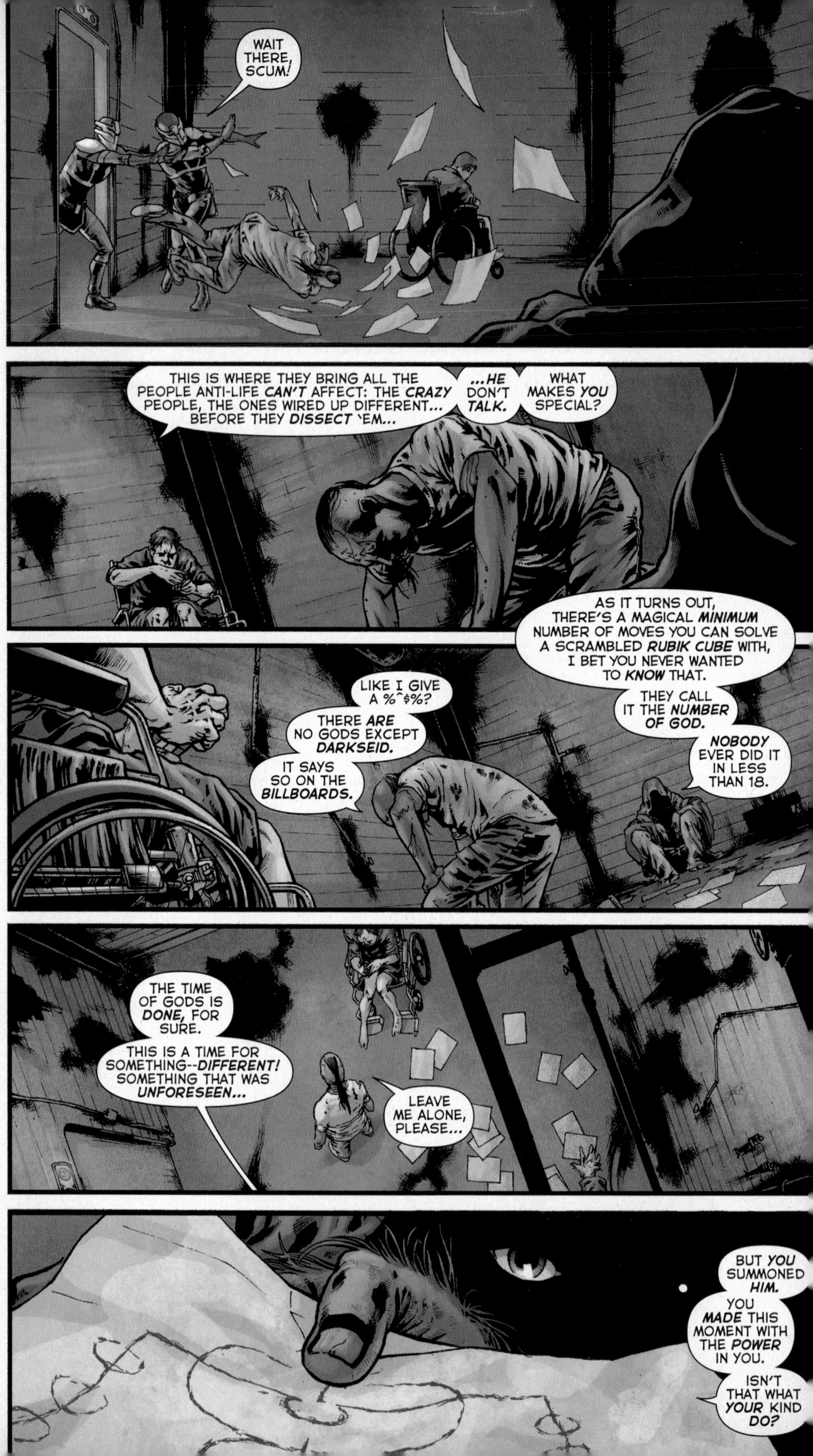

WAIT THERE, SCUM!
THIS IS WHERE THEY BRING ALL THE PEOPLE ANTI-LIFE CAN'T AFFECT: THE CRAZY PEOPLE, THE ONES WIRED UP DIFFERENT... BEFORE THEY DISSECT 'EM...
...HE DON'T TALK.
WHAT MAKES YOU SPECIAL?
AS IT TURNS OUT, THERE'S A MAGICAL MINIMUM NUMBER OF MOVES YOU CAN SOLVE A SCRAMBLED RUBIK CUBE WITH, I BET YOU NEVER WANTED TO KNOW THAT.
THEY CALL IT THE NUMBER OF GOD.
NOBODY EVER DID IT IN LESS THAN 18.
LIKE I GIVE A %^$%?
THERE ARE NO GODS EXCEPT DARKSEID.
IT SAYS SO ON THE BILLBOARDS.
THE TIME OF GODS IS DONE, FOR SURE.
THIS IS A TIME FOR SOMETHING--DIFFERENT! SOMETHING THAT WAS UNFORESEEN...
LEAVE ME ALONE, PLEASE...
BUT YOU SUMMONED HIM.
YOU MADE THIS MOMENT WITH THE POWER IN YOU.
ISN'T THAT WHAT YOUR KIND DO?

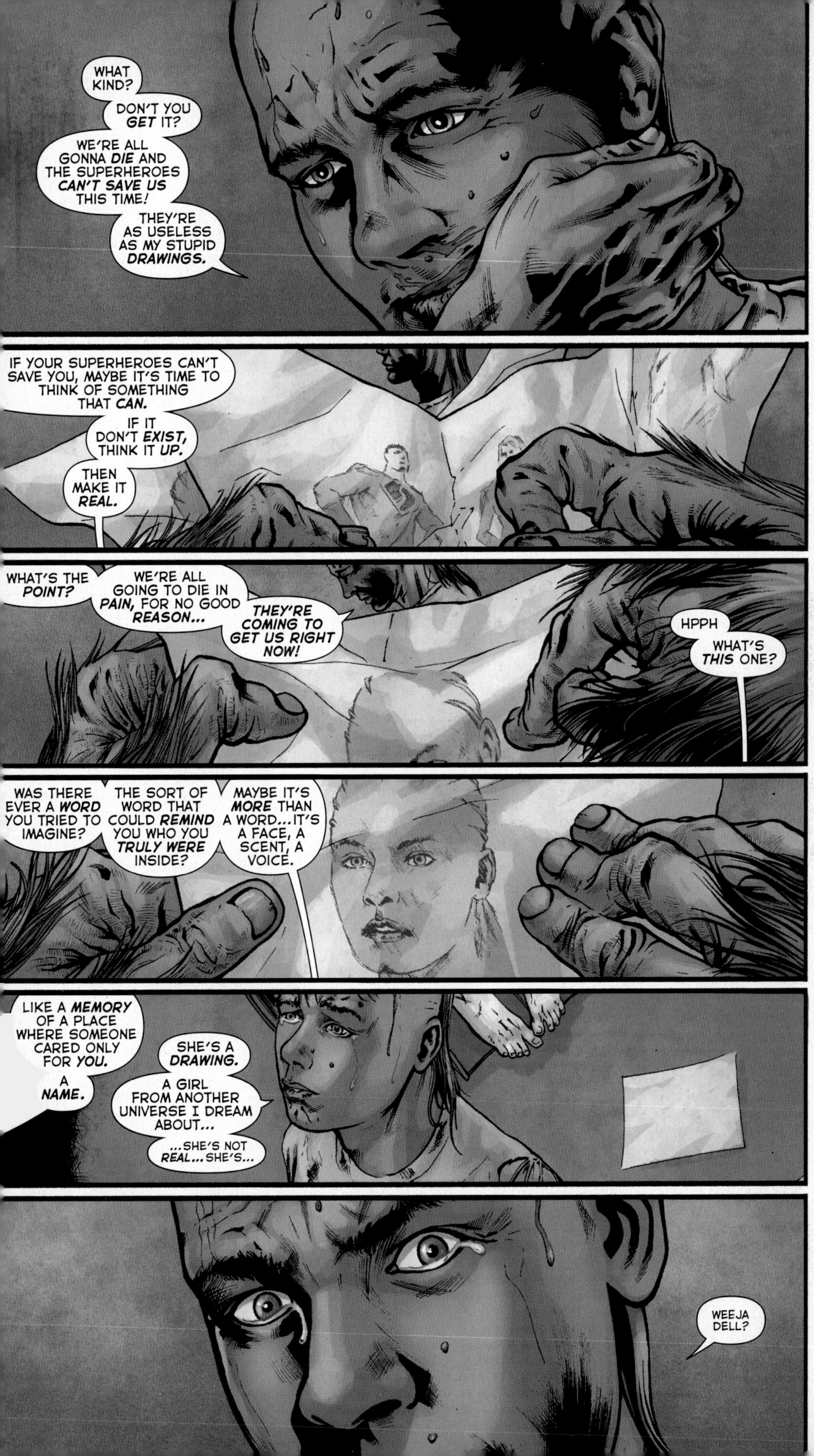

WHAT KIND?
DON'T YOU GET IT?
WE'RE ALL GONNA DIE AND THE SUPERHEROES CAN'T SAVE US THIS TIME!
THEY'RE AS USELESS AS MY STUPID DRAWINGS.
IF YOUR SUPERHEROES CAN'T SAVE YOU, MAYBE IT'S TIME TO THINK OF SOMETHING THAT CAN.
IF IT DON'T EXIST, THINK IT UP.
THEN MAKE IT REAL.
WHAT'S THE POINT?
WE'RE ALL GOING TO DIE IN PAIN, FOR NO GOOD REASON...
THEY'RE COMING TO GET US RIGHT NOW!
HPPH
WHAT'S THIS ONE?
WAS THERE EVER A WORD YOU TRIED TO IMAGINE?
THE SORT OF WORD THAT COULD REMIND YOU WHO YOU TRULY WERE INSIDE?
MAYBE IT'S MORE THAN A WORD...IT'S A FACE, A SCENT, A VOICE.
LIKE A MEMORY OF A PLACE WHERE SOMEONE CARED ONLY FOR YOU.
A NAME.
SHE'S A DRAWING.
A GIRL FROM ANOTHER UNIVERSE I DREAM ABOUT...
...SHE'S NOT REAL...SHE'S...
WEEJA DELL?

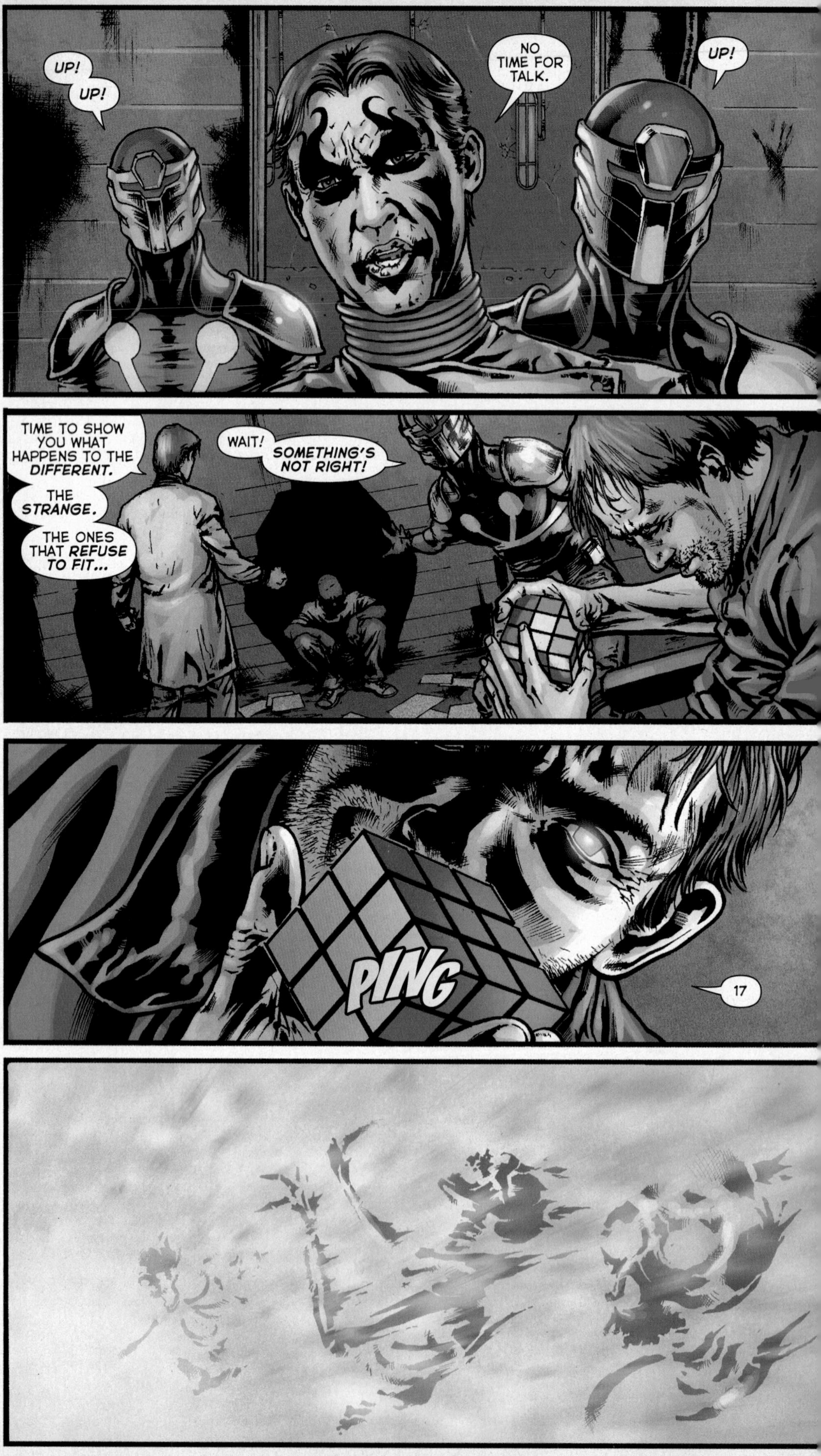
UP!
UP!
NO TIME FOR TALK.
UP!
TIME TO SHOW YOU WHAT HAPPENS TO THE *DIFFERENT.*
THE *STRANGE.*
THE ONES THAT *REFUSE TO FIT...*
WAIT!
SOMETHING'S NOT RIGHT!
PING

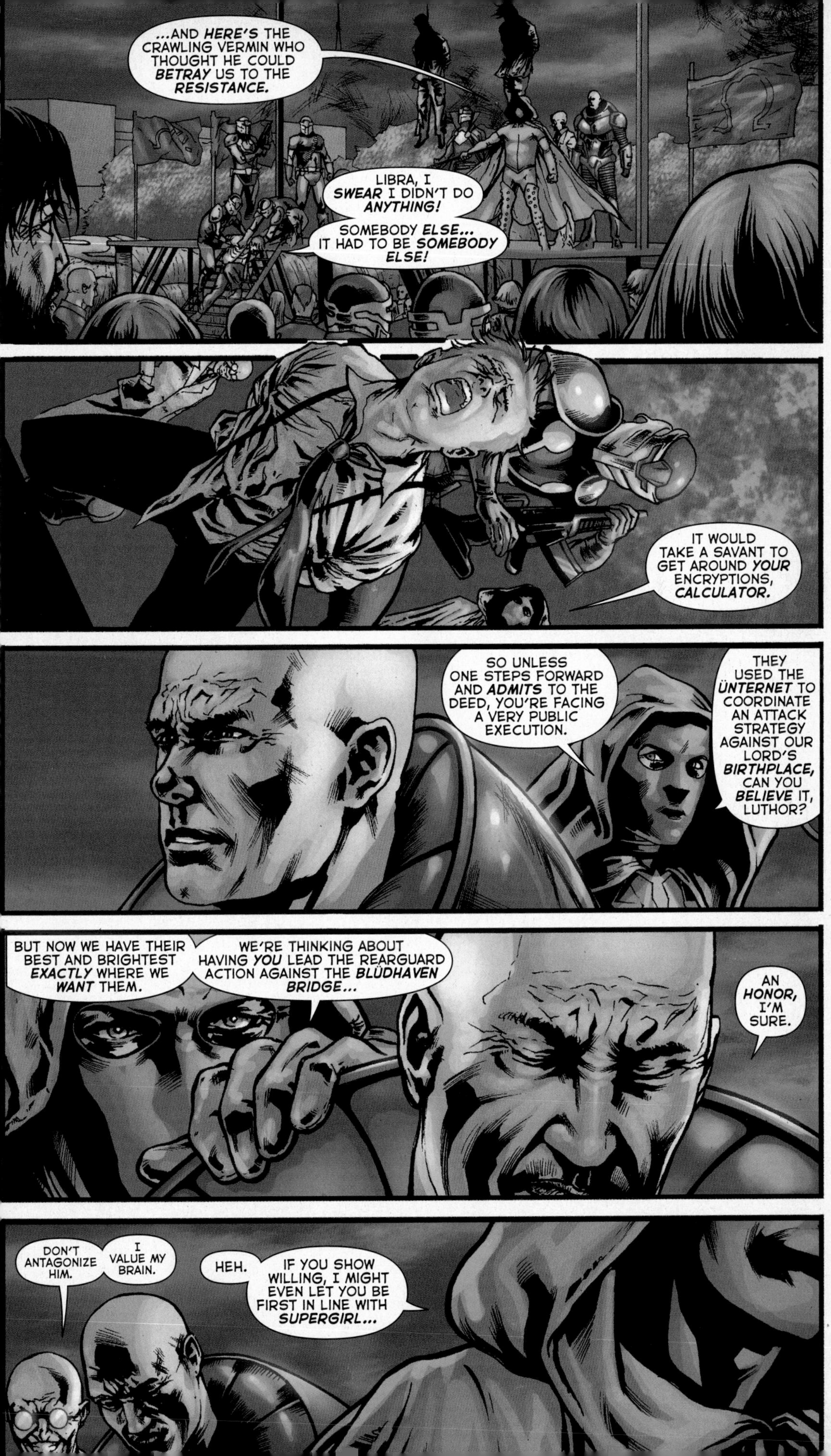

...AND HERE'S THE CRAWLING VERMIN WHO THOUGHT HE COULD BETRAY US TO THE RESISTANCE.
LIBRA, I SWEAR I DIDN'T DO ANYTHING!
SOMEBODY ELSE... IT HAD TO BE SOMEBODY ELSE!
IT WOULD TAKE A SAVANT TO GET AROUND YOUR ENCRYPTIONS, CALCULATOR.
SO UNLESS ONE STEPS FORWARD AND ADMITS TO THE DEED, YOU'RE FACING A VERY PUBLIC EXECUTION.
THEY USED THE ÜNTERNET TO COORDINATE AN ATTACK STRATEGY AGAINST OUR LORD'S BIRTHPLACE, CAN YOU BELIEVE IT, LUTHOR?
BUT NOW WE HAVE THEIR BEST AND BRIGHTEST EXACTLY WHERE WE WANT THEM.
WE'RE THINKING ABOUT HAVING YOU LEAD THE REARGUARD ACTION AGAINST THE BLÜDHAVEN BRIDGE...
AN HONOR, I'M SURE.
DON'T ANTAGONIZE HIM.
I VALUE MY BRAIN.
HEH.
IF YOU SHOW WILLING, I MIGHT EVEN LET YOU BE FIRST IN LINE WITH SUPERGIRL...

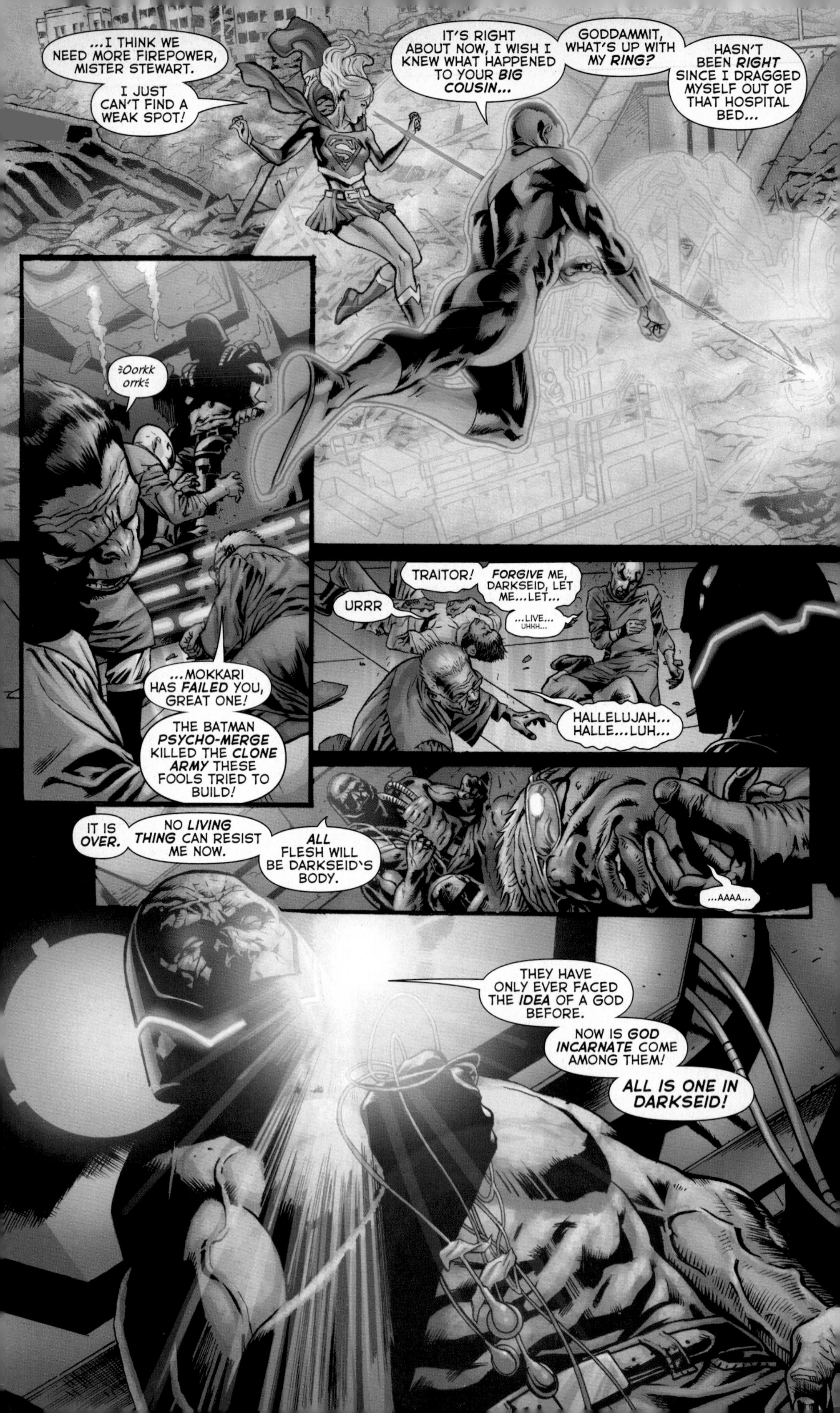
...I THINK WE NEED MORE FIREPOWER, MISTER STEWART.
I JUST CAN'T FIND A WEAK SPOT!
IT'S RIGHT ABOUT NOW, I WISH I KNEW WHAT HAPPENED TO YOUR BIG COUSIN...
GODDAMMIT, WHAT'S UP WITH MY RING?
HASN'T BEEN RIGHT SINCE I DRAGGED MYSELF OUT OF THAT HOSPITAL BED...
Oorkk orrk
...MOKKARI HAS FAILED YOU, GREAT ONE!
THE BATMAN PSYCHO-MERGE KILLED THE CLONE ARMY THESE FOOLS TRIED TO BUILD!
TRAITOR!
FORGIVE ME, DARKSEID, LET ME...LET...
URRR
...LIVE... UHHH...
HALLELUJAH... HALLE...LUH...
IT IS OVER.
NO LIVING THING CAN RESIST ME NOW.
ALL FLESH WILL BE DARKSEID'S BODY.
...AAAA...
THEY HAVE ONLY EVER FACED THE IDEA OF A GOD BEFORE.
NOW IS GOD INCARNATE COME AMONG THEM!
ALL IS ONE IN DARKSEID!

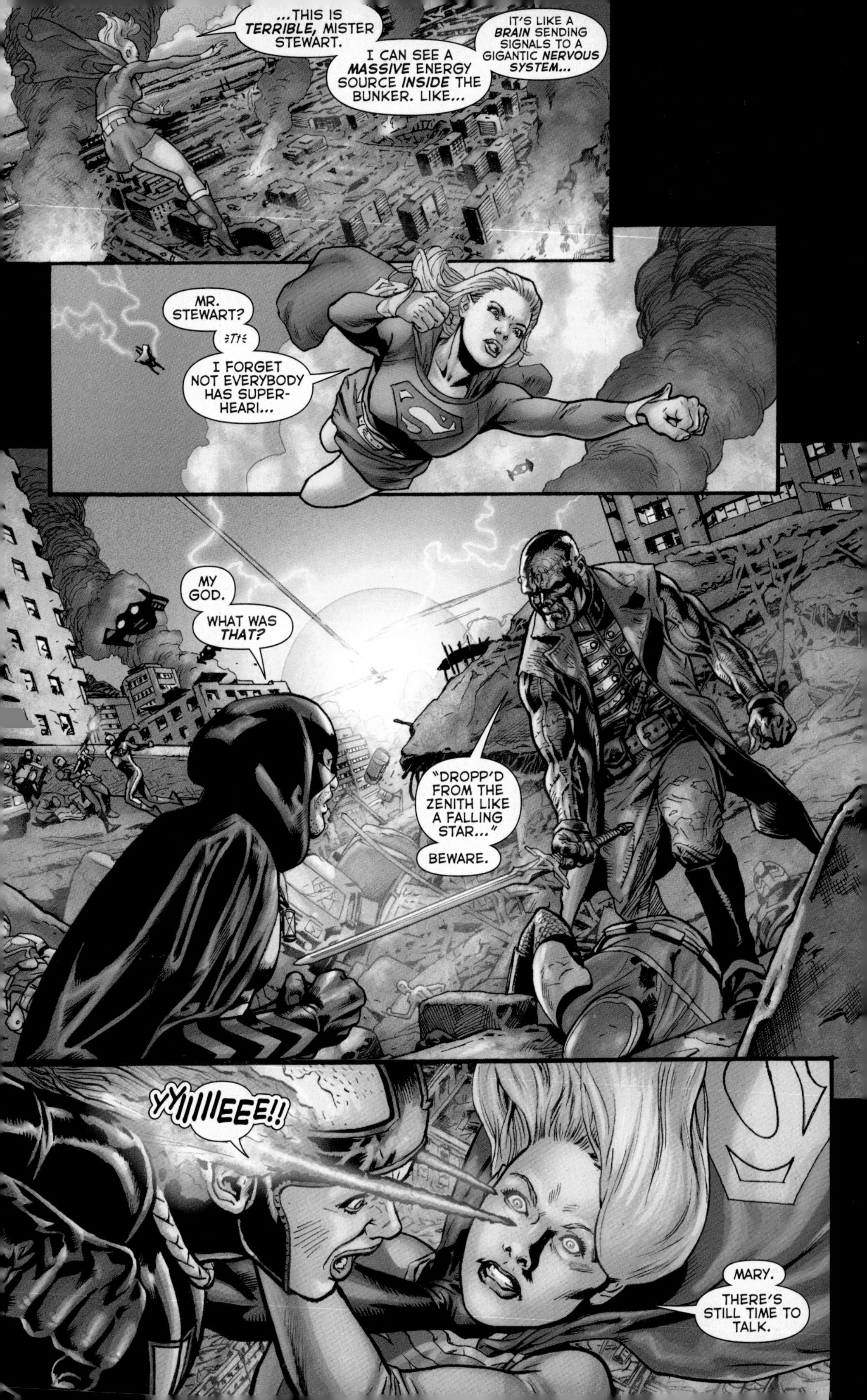
...THIS IS TERRIBLE, MISTER STEWART.
I CAN SEE A MASSIVE ENERGY SOURCE INSIDE THE BUNKER. LIKE...
IT'S LIKE A BRAIN SENDING SIGNALS TO A GIGANTIC NERVOUS SYSTEM...
MR. STEWART?
I FORGET NOT EVERYBODY HAS SUPER-HEARI...
MY GOD.
WHAT WAS THAT?
"DROPP'D FROM THE ZENITH LIKE A FALLING STAR..."
BEWARE.
YYIIIIIEEE!!
MARY.
THERE'S STILL TIME TO TALK.

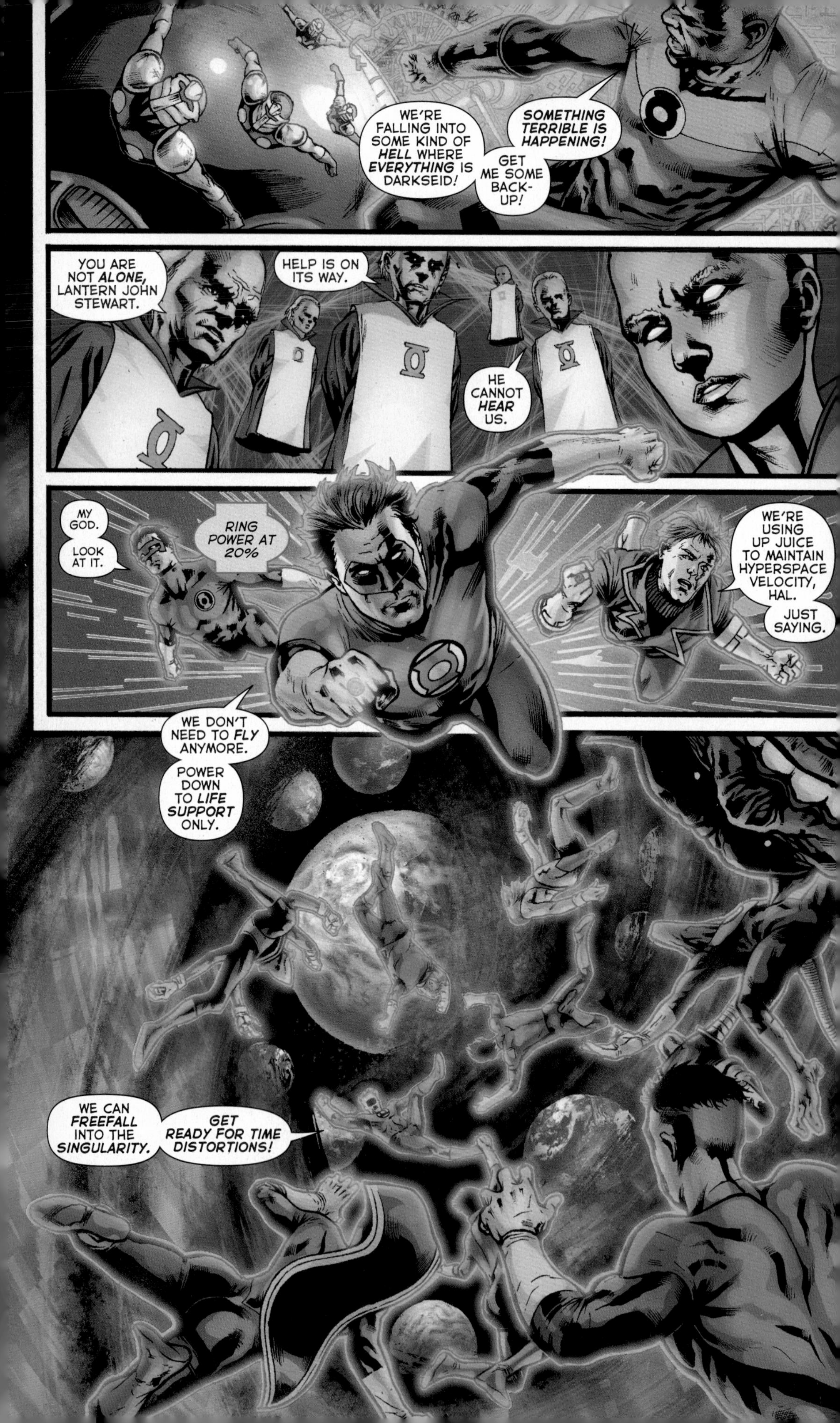

SOMETHING TERRIBLE IS HAPPENING!
WE'RE FALLING INTO SOME KIND OF HELL WHERE EVERYTHING IS DARKSEID!
GET ME SOME BACK-UP!
YOU ARE NOT ALONE, LANTERN JOHN STEWART.
HELP IS ON ITS WAY.
HE CANNOT HEAR US.
MY GOD.
LOOK AT IT.
RING POWER AT 20%
WE'RE USING UP JUICE TO MAINTAIN HYPERSPACE VELOCITY, HAL.
JUST SAYING.
WE DON'T NEED TO FLY ANYMORE.
POWER DOWN TO LIFE SUPPORT ONLY.
WE CAN FREEFALL INTO THE SINGULARITY.
GET READY FOR TIME DISTORTIONS!

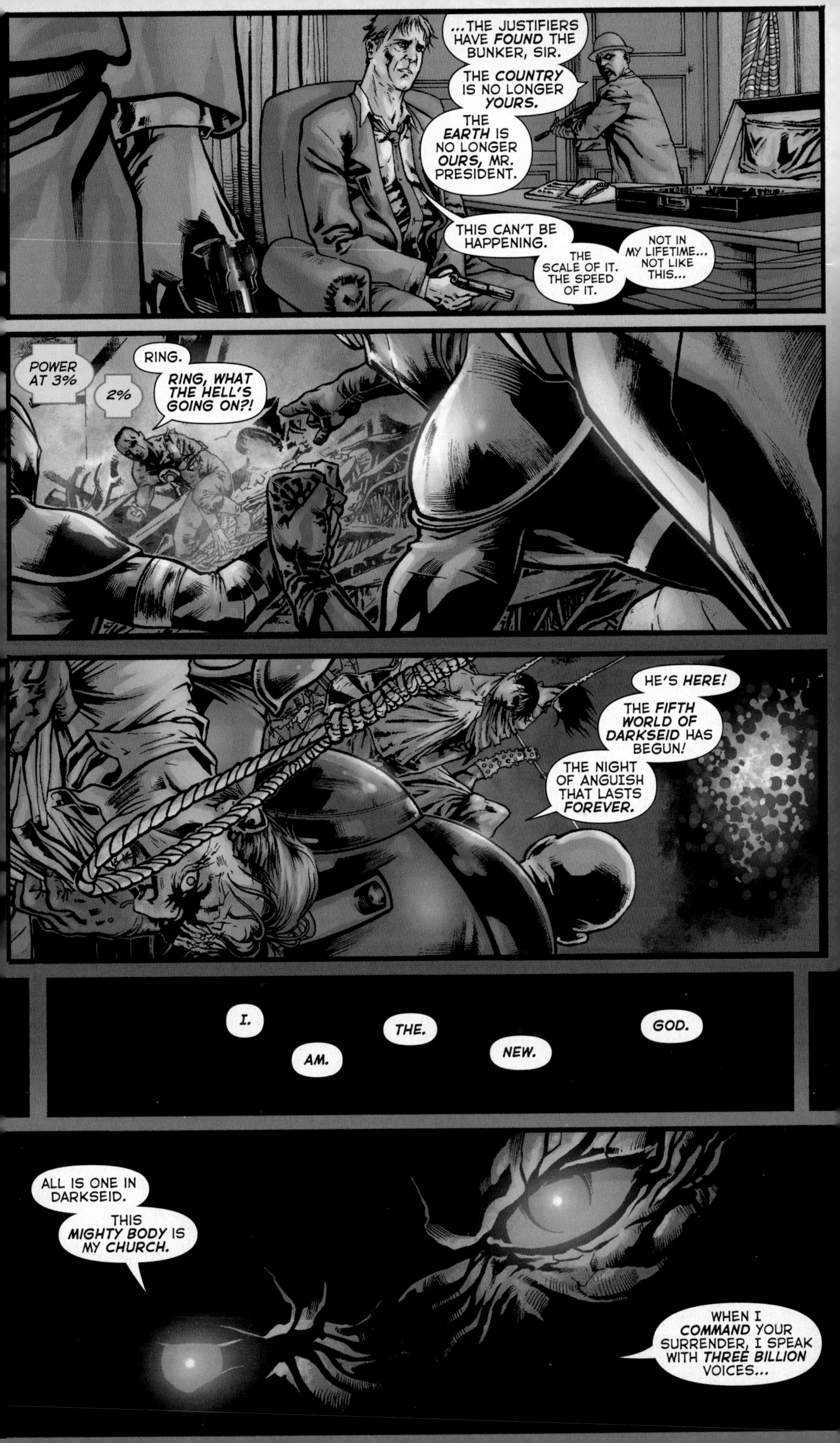

...THE JUSTIFIERS HAVE FOUND THE BUNKER, SIR.
THE COUNTRY IS NO LONGER YOURS.
THE EARTH IS NO LONGER OURS, MR. PRESIDENT.
THIS CAN'T BE HAPPENING.
THE SCALE OF IT. THE SPEED OF IT.
NOT IN MY LIFETIME... NOT LIKE THIS...
POWER AT 3%
2%
RING.
RING, WHAT THE HELL'S GOING ON?!
HE'S HERE!
THE FIFTH WORLD OF DARKSEID HAS BEGUN!
THE NIGHT OF ANGUISH THAT LASTS FOREVER.
I.
AM.
THE.
NEW.
GOD.
ALL IS ONE IN DARKSEID.
THIS MIGHTY BODY IS MY CHURCH.
WHEN I COMMAND YOUR SURRENDER, I SPEAK WITH THREE BILLION VOICES...

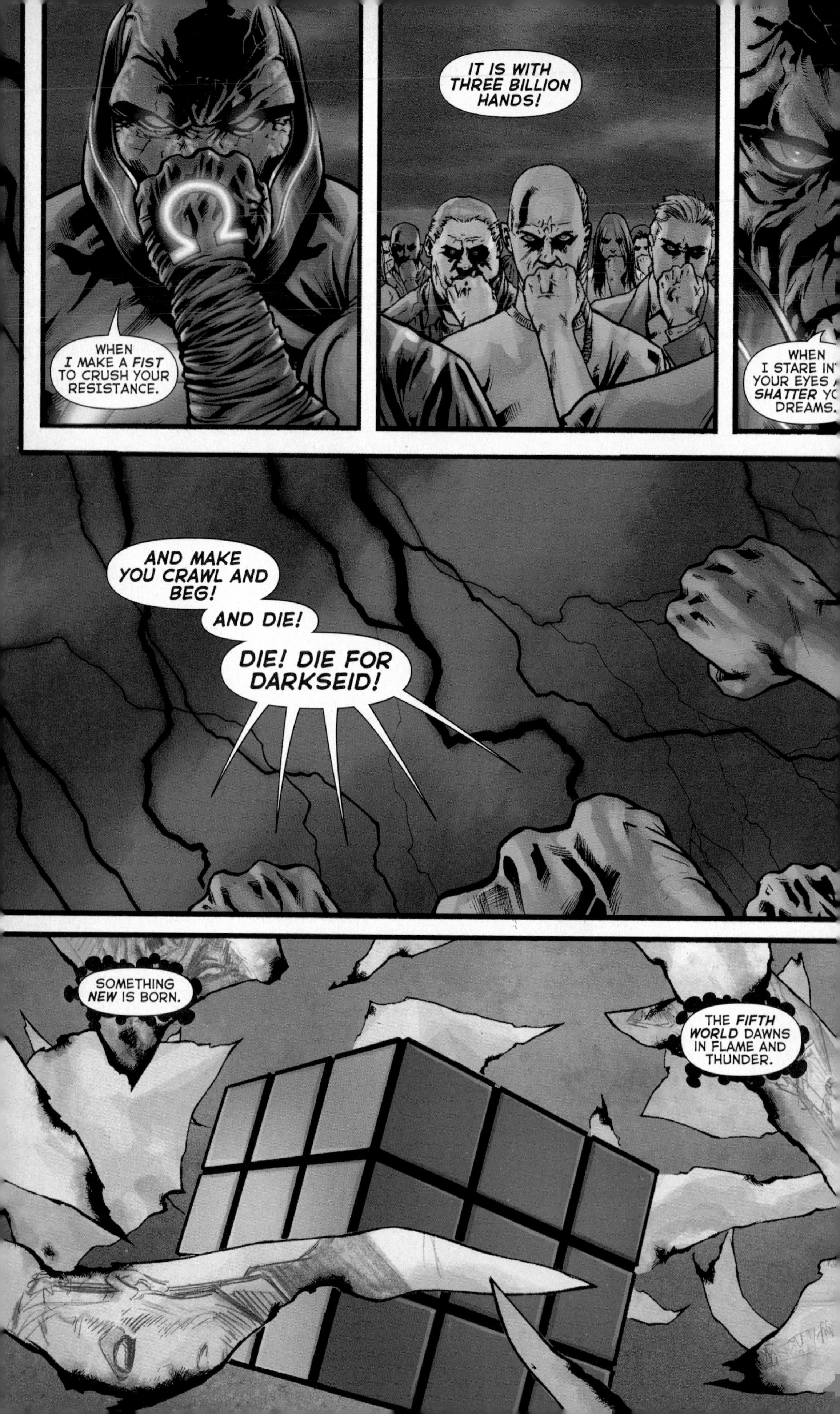
WHEN I MAKE A FIST TO CRUSH YOUR RESISTANCE.
IT IS WITH THREE BILLION HANDS!
WHEN I STARE IN YOUR EYES SHATTER YO DREAMS.
AND MAKE YOU CRAWL AND BEG!
AND DIE!
DIE! DIE FOR DARKSEID!
SOMETHING NEW IS BORN.
THE FIFTH WORLD DAWNS IN FLAME AND THUNDER.

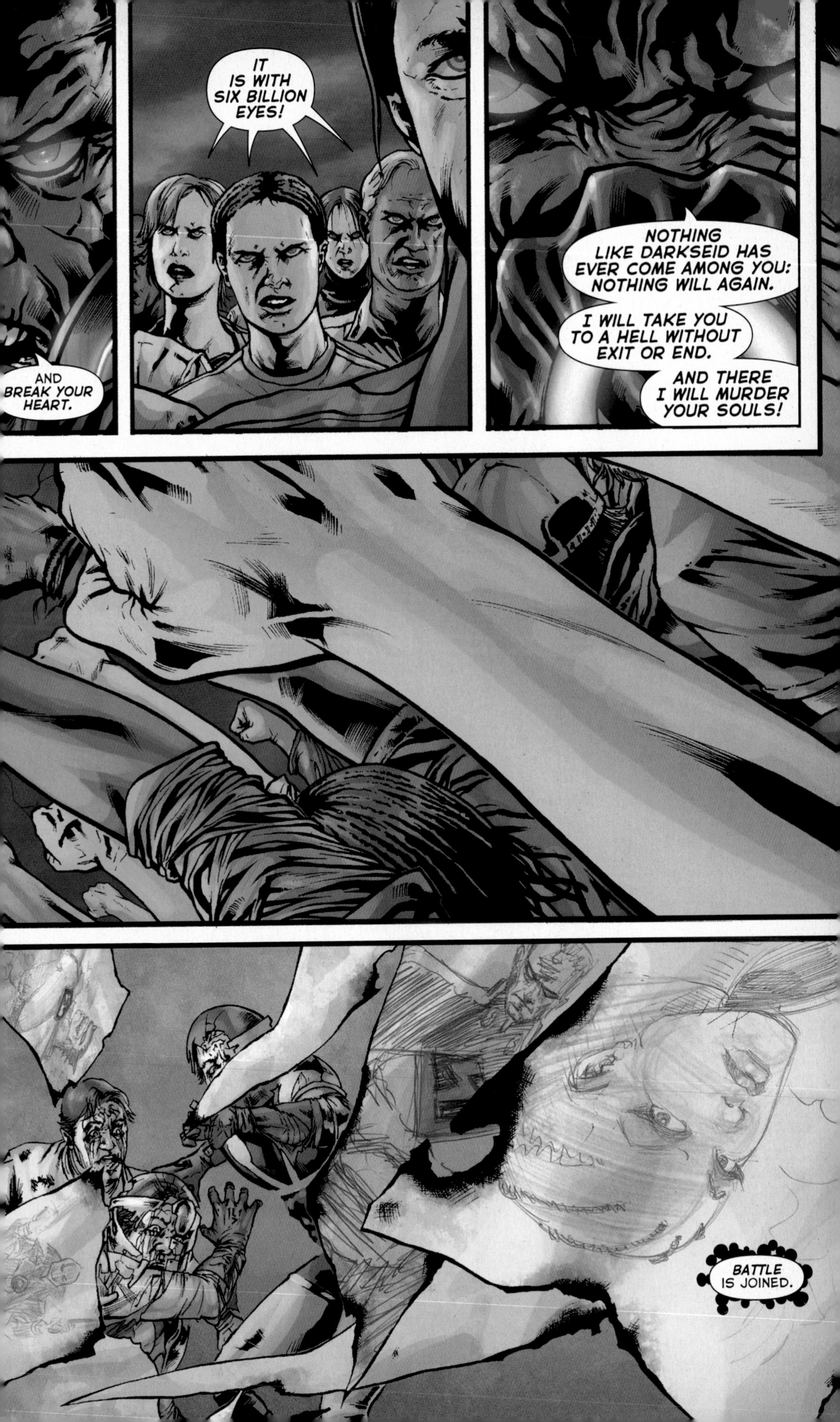
AND BREAK YOUR HEART.
IT IS WITH SIX BILLION EYES!
NOTHING LIKE DARKSEID HAS EVER COME AMONG YOU: NOTHING WILL AGAIN.
I WILL TAKE YOU TO A HELL WITHOUT EXIT OR END.
AND THERE I WILL MURDER YOUR SOULS!
BATTLE IS JOINED.

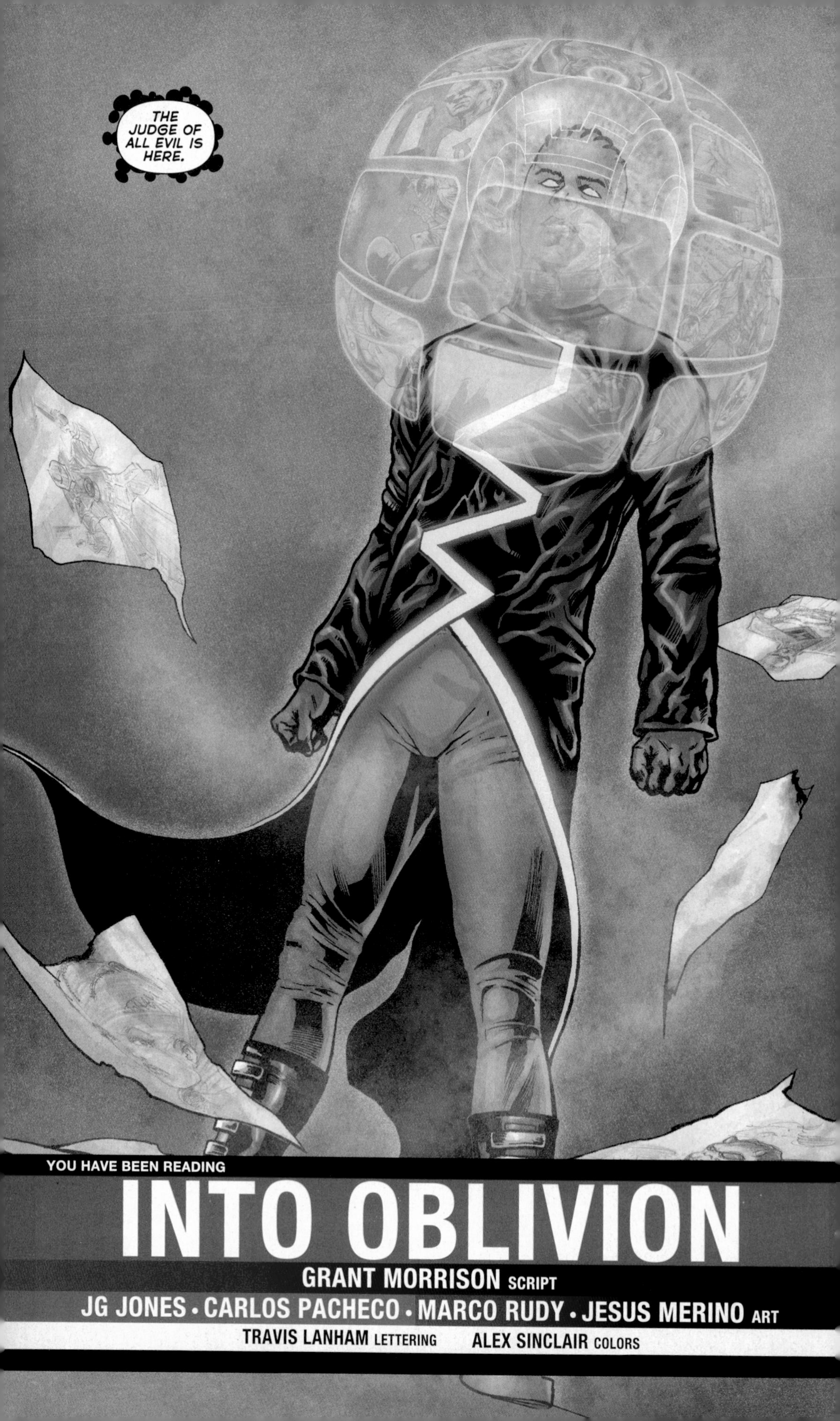
THE JUDGE OF ALL EVIL IS HERE.
YOU HAVE BEEN READING
INTO OBLIVION
GRANT MORRISON SCRIPT
JG JONES • CARLOS PACHECO • MARCO RUDY • JESUS MERINO ART
TRAVIS LANHAM LETTERING
ALEX SINCLAIR COLORS

er to FINAL CRISIS #6 JG Jones

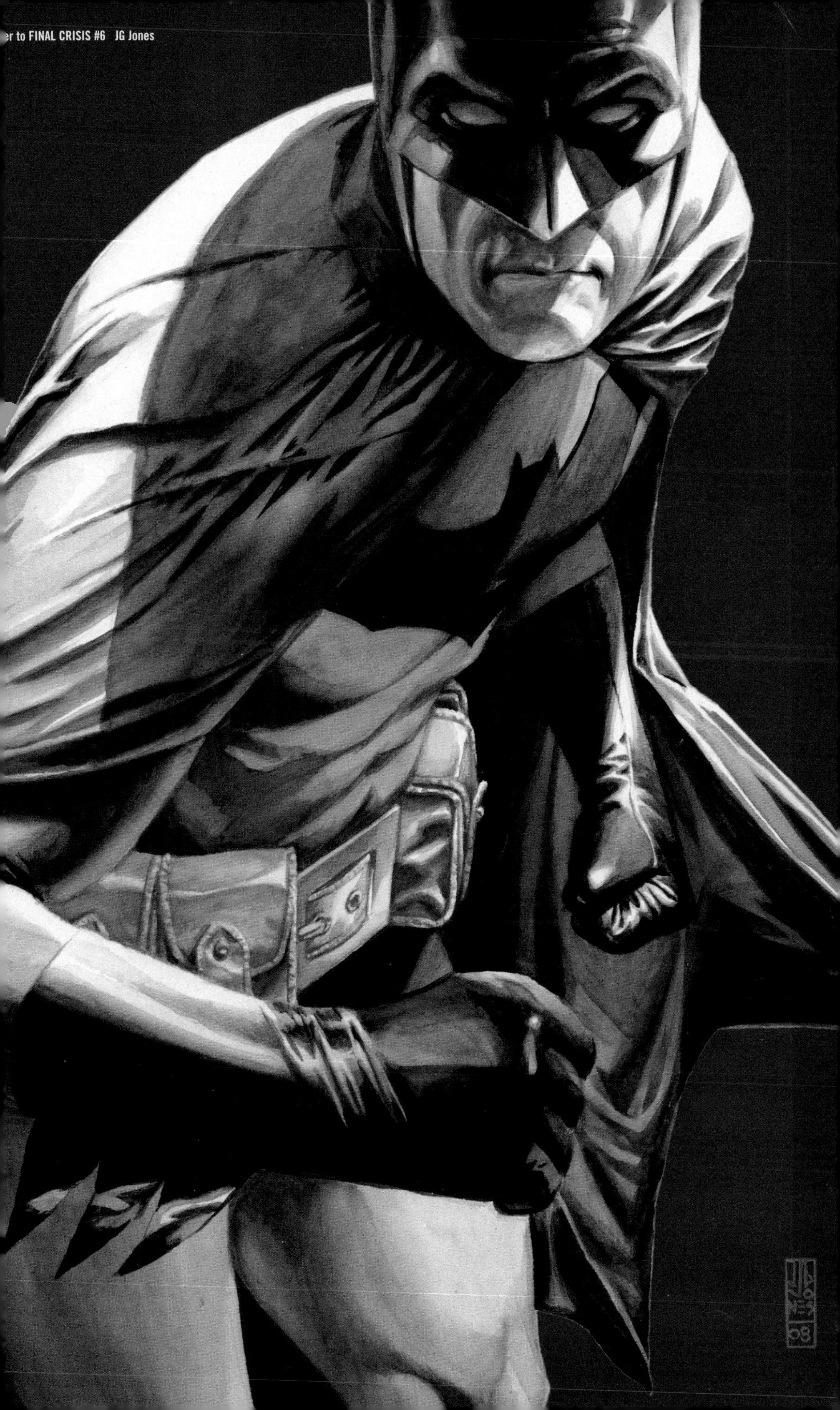

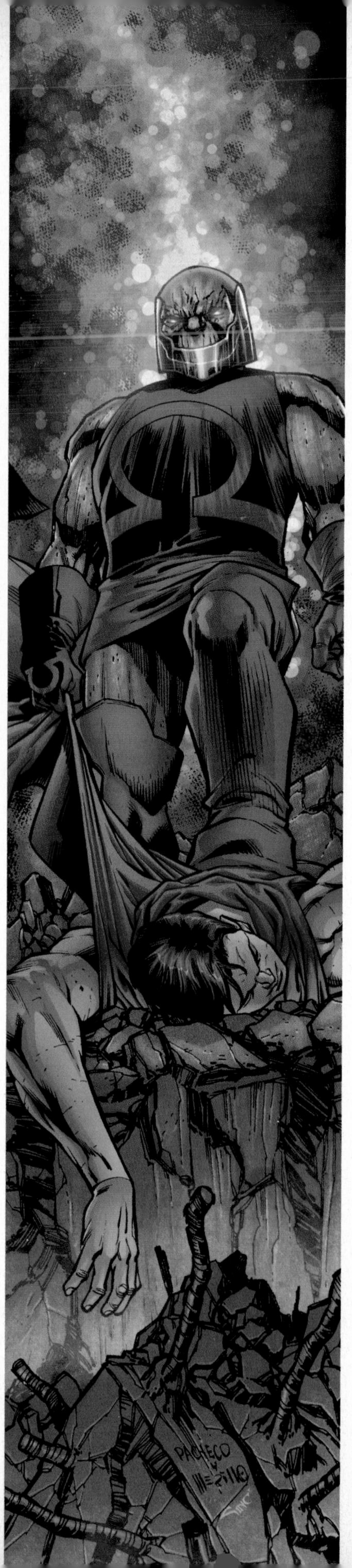
PACHECO

Carlos Pacheco & Jesus Merino with Alex Sinclair

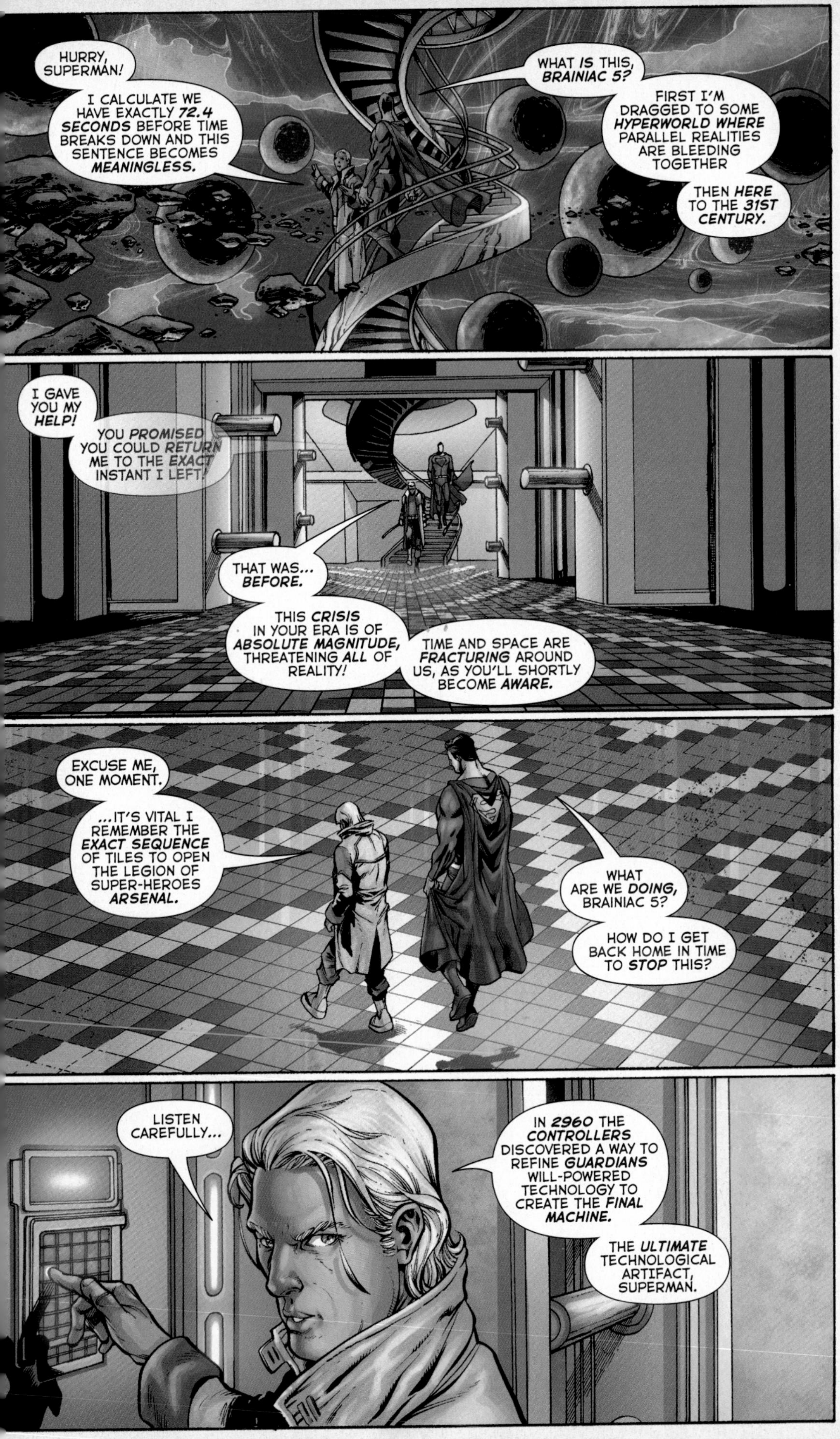
HURRY, SUPERMAN!
I CALCULATE WE HAVE EXACTLY 72.4 SECONDS BEFORE TIME BREAKS DOWN AND THIS SENTENCE BECOMES MEANINGLESS.
WHAT IS THIS, BRAINIAC 5?
FIRST I'M DRAGGED TO SOME HYPERWORLD WHERE PARALLEL REALITIES ARE BLEEDING TOGETHER
THEN HERE TO THE 31ST CENTURY.
I GAVE YOU MY HELP!
YOU PROMISED YOU COULD RETURN ME TO THE EXACT INSTANT I LEFT!
THAT WAS... BEFORE.
THIS CRISIS IN YOUR ERA IS OF ABSOLUTE MAGNITUDE, THREATENING ALL OF REALITY!
TIME AND SPACE ARE FRACTURING AROUND US, AS YOU'LL SHORTLY BECOME AWARE.
EXCUSE ME, ONE MOMENT.
...IT'S VITAL I REMEMBER THE EXACT SEQUENCE OF TILES TO OPEN THE LEGION OF SUPER-HEROES ARSENAL.
WHAT ARE WE DOING, BRAINIAC 5?
HOW DO I GET BACK HOME IN TIME TO STOP THIS?
LISTEN CAREFULLY...
IN 2960 THE CONTROLLERS DISCOVERED A WAY TO REFINE GUARDIANS WILL-POWERED TECHNOLOGY TO CREATE THE FINAL MACHINE.
THE ULTIMATE TECHNOLOGICAL ARTIFACT, SUPERMAN.

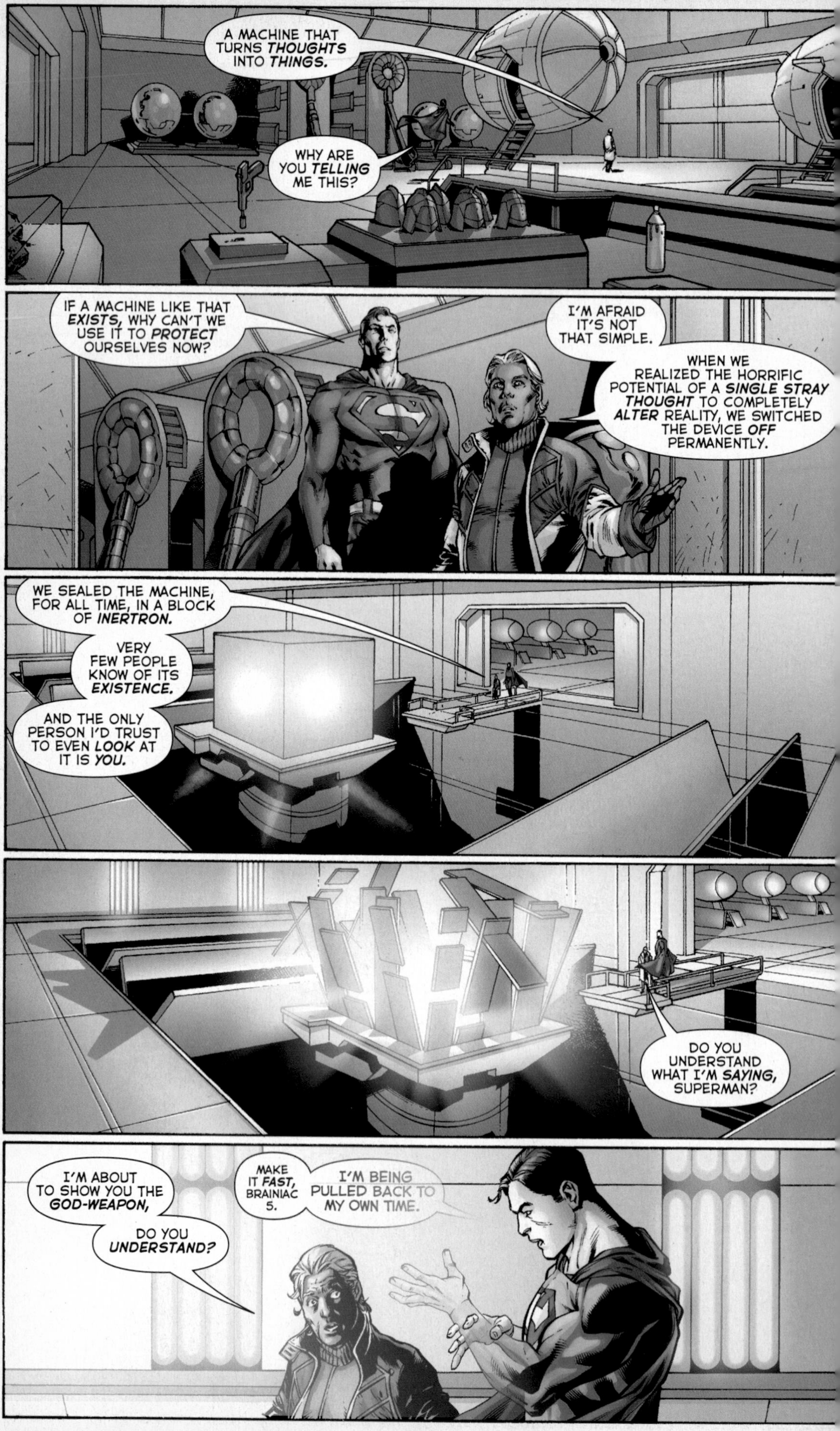
A MACHINE THAT TURNS *THOUGHTS* INTO *THINGS.*
WHY ARE YOU *TELLING* ME THIS?
IF A MACHINE LIKE THAT *EXISTS,* WHY CAN'T WE USE IT TO *PROTECT* OURSELVES NOW?
I'M AFRAID IT'S NOT THAT SIMPLE.
WHEN WE REALIZED THE HORRIFIC POTENTIAL OF A *SINGLE STRAY THOUGHT* TO COMPLETELY *ALTER* REALITY, WE SWITCHED THE DEVICE *OFF* PERMANENTLY.
WE SEALED THE MACHINE, FOR ALL TIME, IN A BLOCK OF *INERTRON.*
VERY FEW PEOPLE KNOW OF ITS *EXISTENCE.*
AND THE ONLY PERSON I'D TRUST TO EVEN *LOOK* AT IT IS *YOU.*
DO YOU UNDERSTAND WHAT I'M *SAYING,* SUPERMAN?
I'M ABOUT TO SHOW YOU THE *GOD-WEAPON,*
DO YOU *UNDERSTAND?*
MAKE IT *FAST,* BRAINIAC 5.
I'M BEING PULLED BACK TO MY OWN TIME.

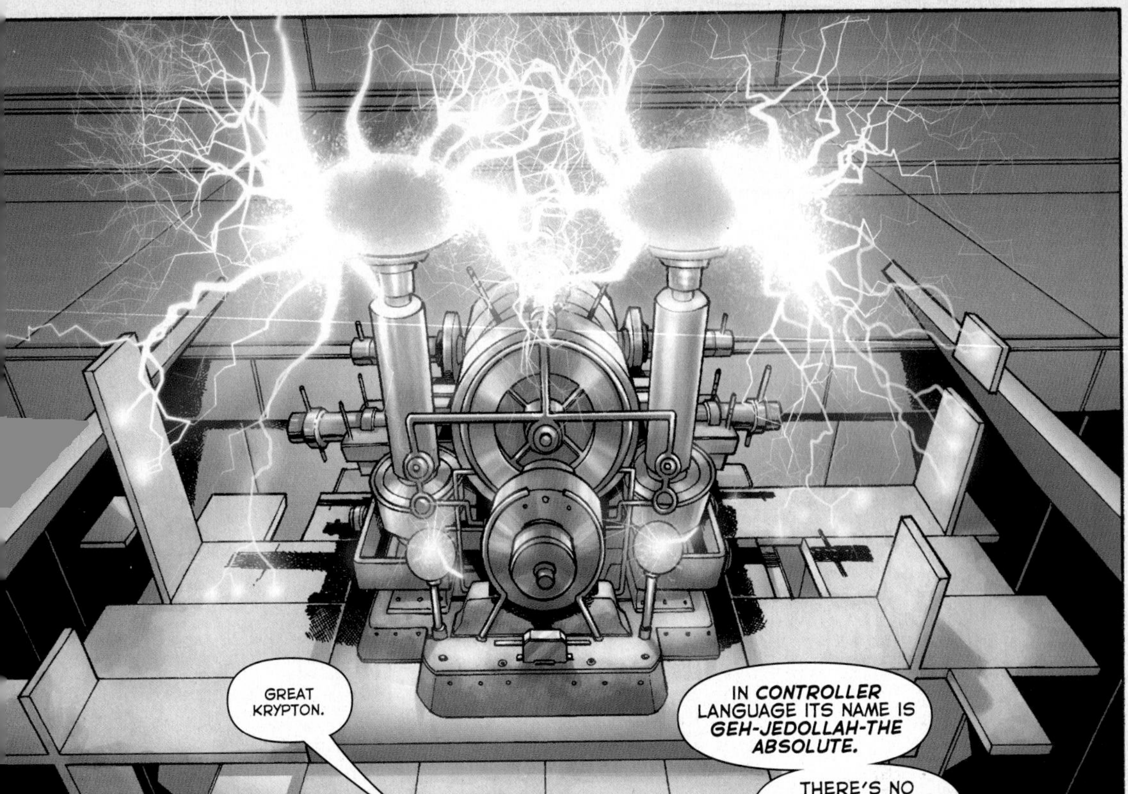
GREAT KRYPTON.
IN CONTROLLER LANGUAGE ITS NAME IS GEH-JEDOLLAH-THE ABSOLUTE.
THERE'S NO TRANSLATION THAT REALLY MAKES SENSE.
WE CALL IT THE MIRACLE MACHINE.

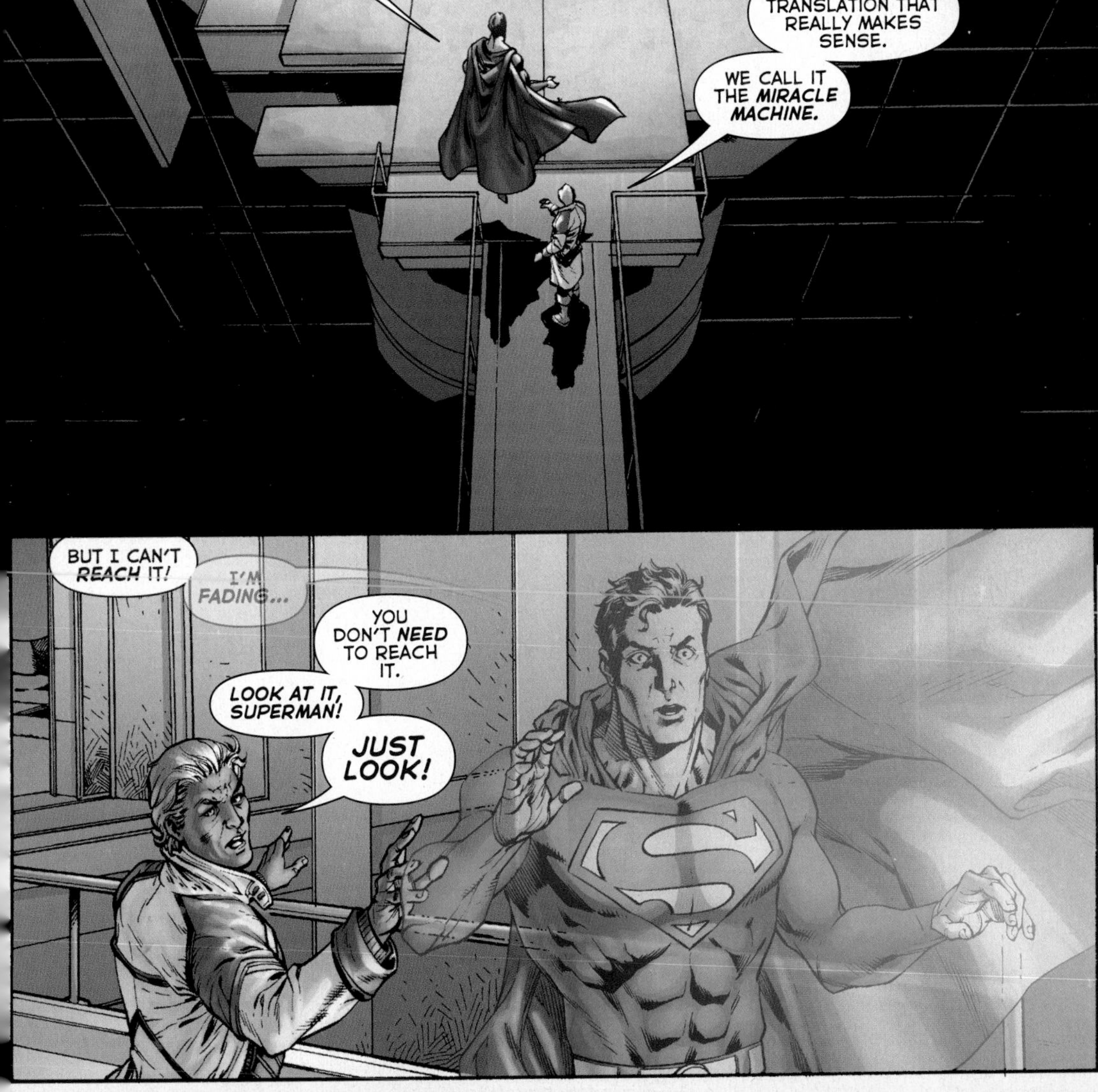
BUT I CAN'T REACH IT!
I'M FADING...
YOU DON'T NEED TO REACH IT.
LOOK AT IT, SUPERMAN!
JUST LOOK!

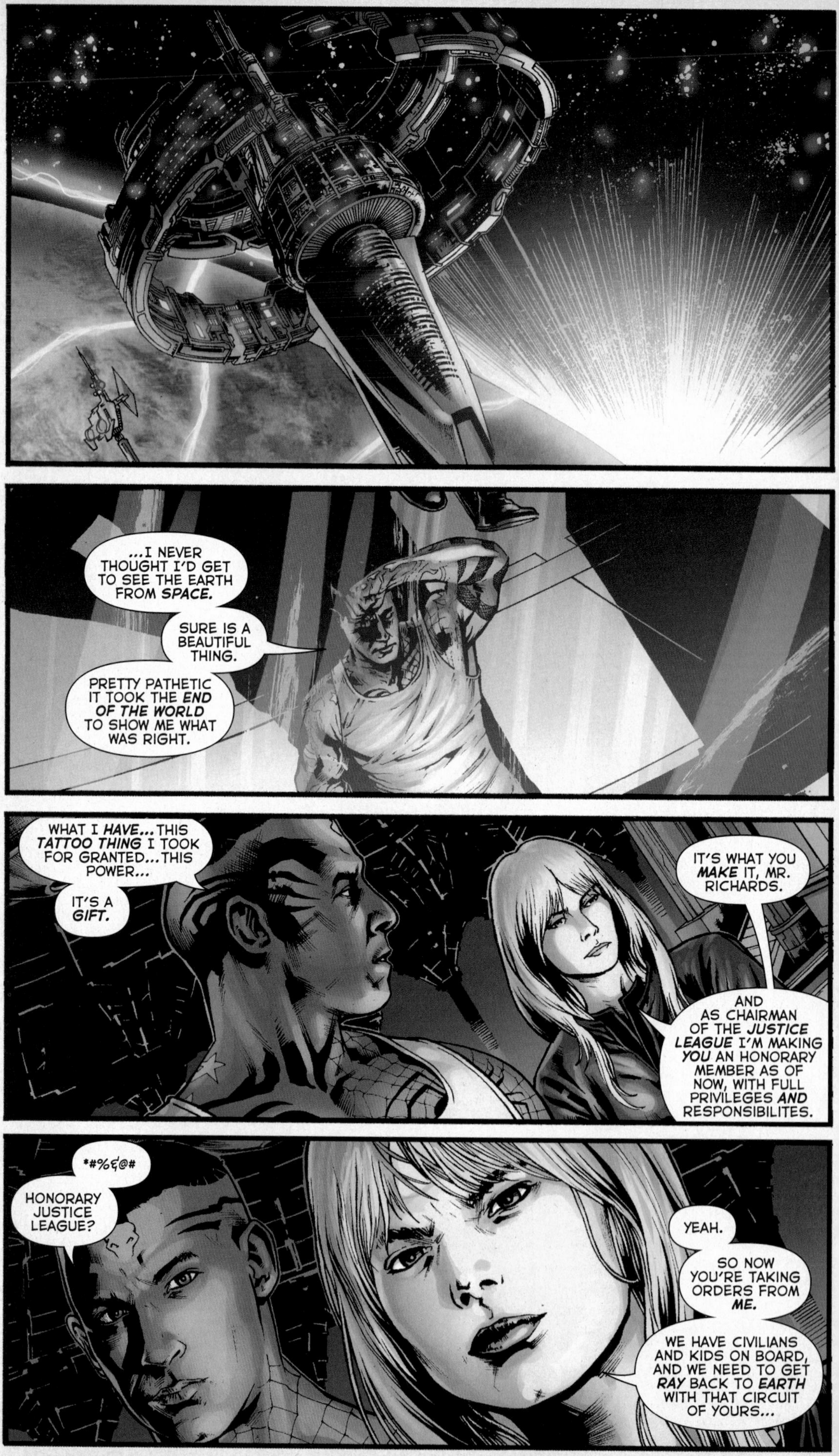
...I NEVER THOUGHT I'D GET TO SEE THE EARTH FROM SPACE.
SURE IS A BEAUTIFUL THING.
PRETTY PATHETIC IT TOOK THE END OF THE WORLD TO SHOW ME WHAT WAS RIGHT.
WHAT I HAVE... THIS TATTOO THING I TOOK FOR GRANTED... THIS POWER...
IT'S A GIFT.
IT'S WHAT YOU MAKE IT, MR. RICHARDS.
AND AS CHAIRMAN OF THE JUSTICE LEAGUE I'M MAKING YOU AN HONORARY MEMBER AS OF NOW, WITH FULL PRIVILEGES AND RESPONSIBILITES.
*#%¢@#
HONORARY JUSTICE LEAGUE?
YEAH.
SO NOW YOU'RE TAKING ORDERS FROM ME.
WE HAVE CIVILIANS AND KIDS ON BOARD, AND WE NEED TO GET RAY BACK TO EARTH WITH THAT CIRCUIT OF YOURS...

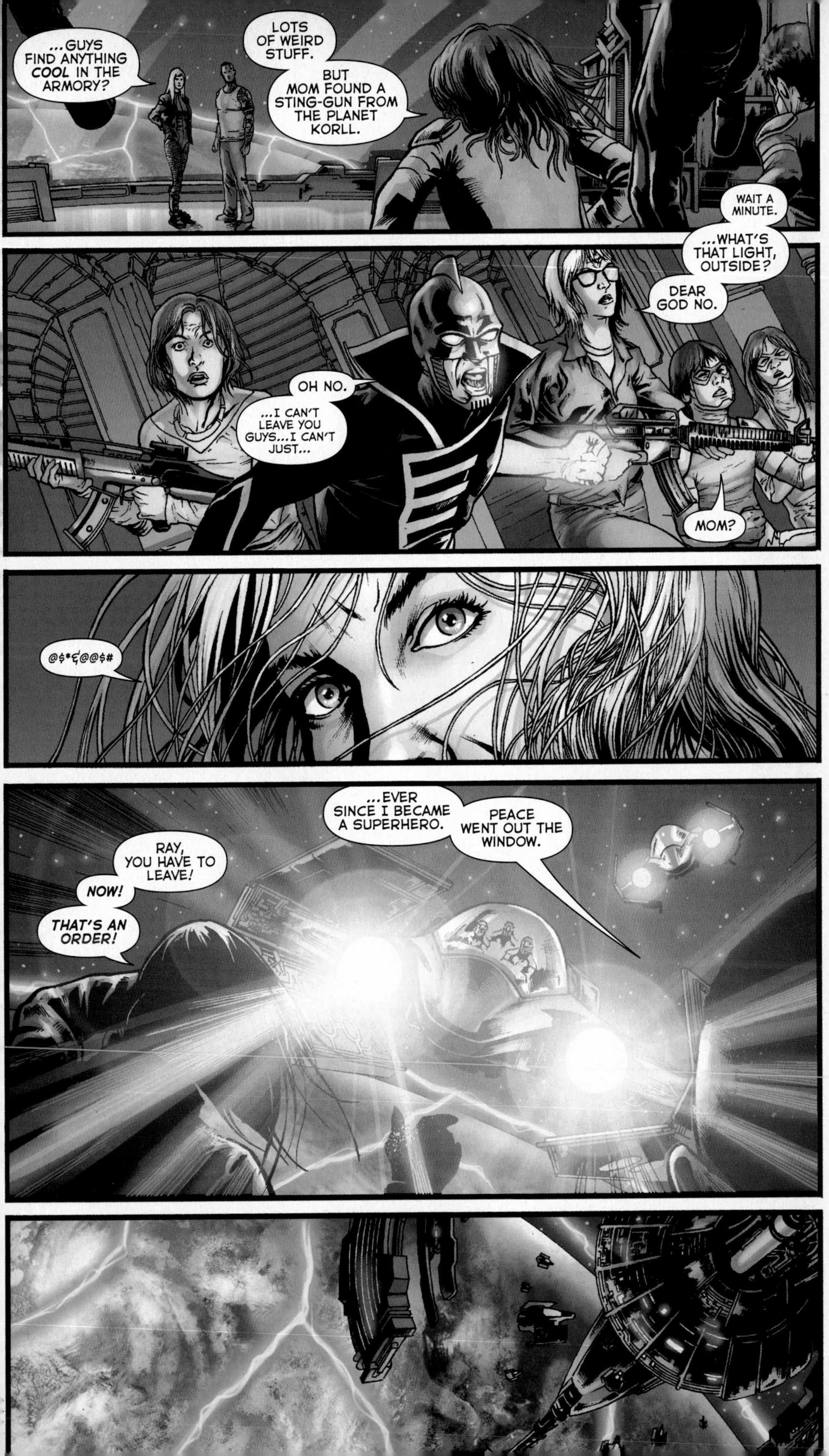
...GUYS FIND ANYTHING COOL IN THE ARMORY?
LOTS OF WEIRD STUFF.
BUT MOM FOUND A STING-GUN FROM THE PLANET KORLL.
WAIT A MINUTE.
...WHAT'S THAT LIGHT, OUTSIDE?
DEAR GOD NO.
OH NO.
...I CAN'T LEAVE YOU GUYS...I CAN'T JUST...
MOM?
@$*¢@@$#
...EVER SINCE I BECAME A SUPERHERO.
PEACE WENT OUT THE WINDOW.
RAY, YOU HAVE TO LEAVE!
NOW!
THAT'S AN ORDER!

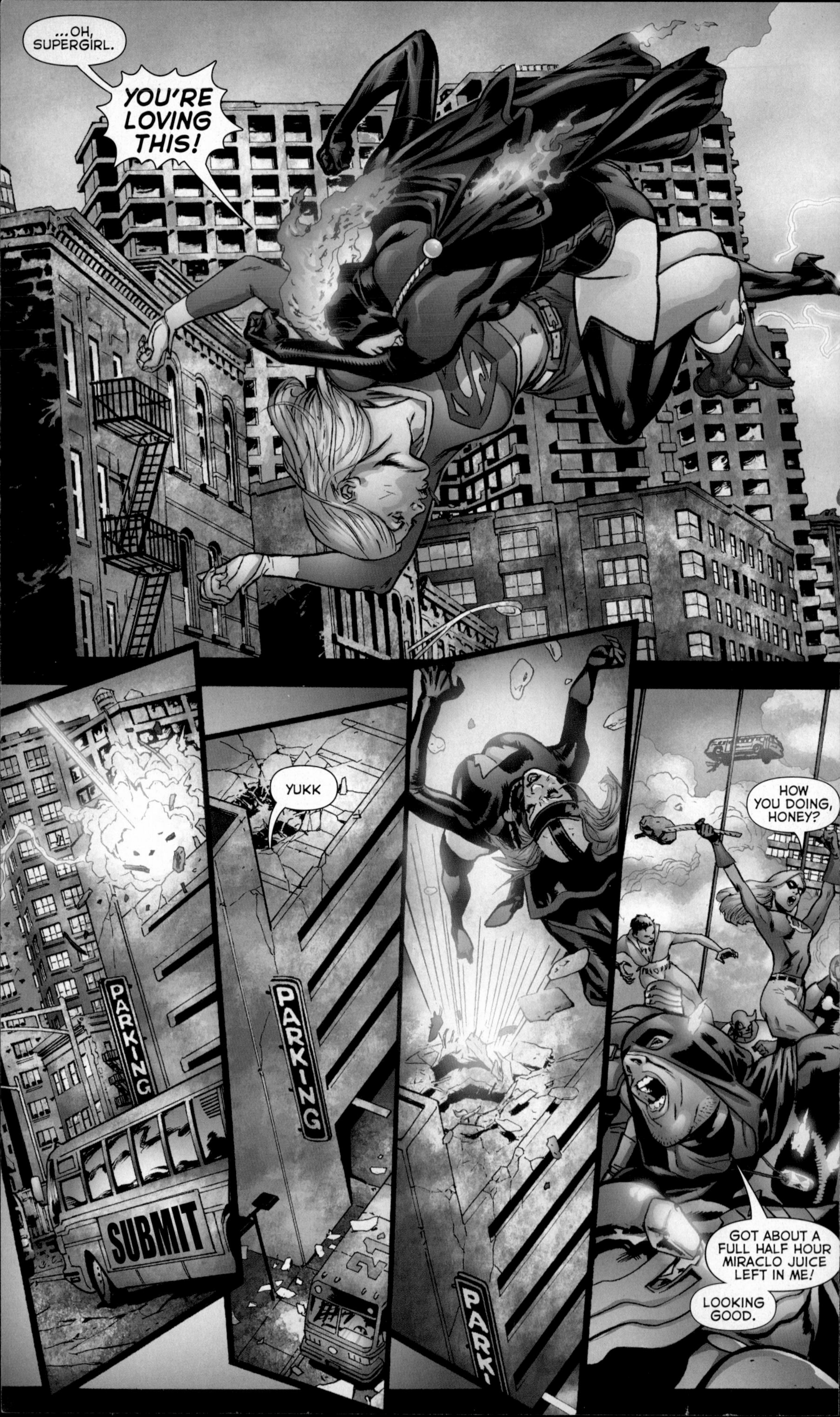
...OH, SUPERGIRL.
YOU'RE LOVING THIS!
PARKING
SUBMIT
YUKK
PARKING
PARKI
HOW YOU DOING, HONEY?
GOT ABOUT A FULL HALF HOUR MIRACLO JUICE LEFT IN ME!
LOOKING GOOD.

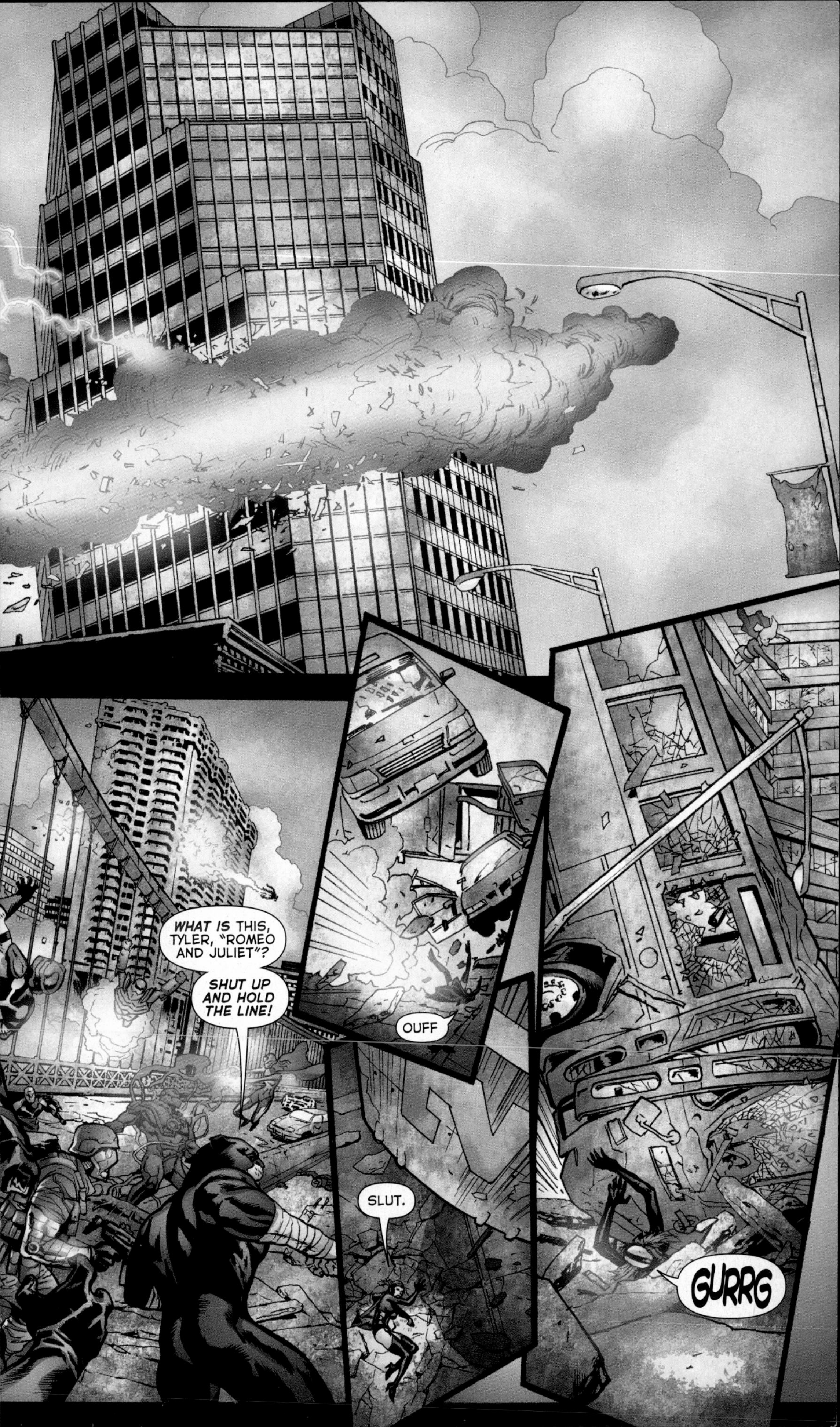
WHAT IS THIS, TYLER, "ROMEO AND JULIET"?
SHUT UP AND HOLD THE LINE!
OUFF
SLUT.
GURRG

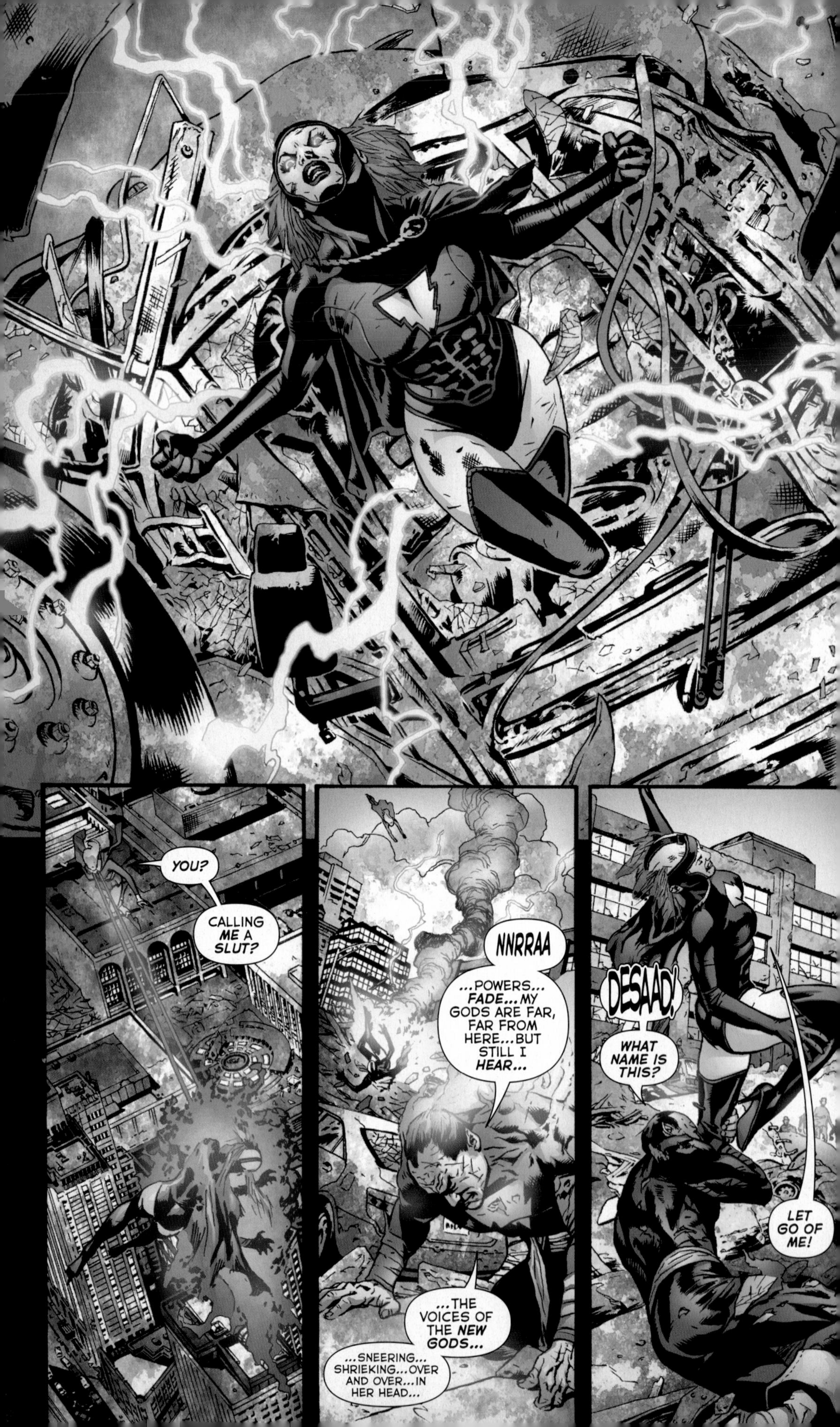

YOU?
CALLING *ME* A *SLUT?*
NNRRAA
...POWERS... *FADE*... MY GODS ARE FAR, FAR FROM HERE...BUT STILL I *HEAR*...
...THE VOICES OF THE *NEW GODS*...
...SNEERING... SHRIEKING...OVER AND OVER...IN HER HEAD...
DESAAD!
WHAT NAME IS THIS?
LET GO OF *ME!*

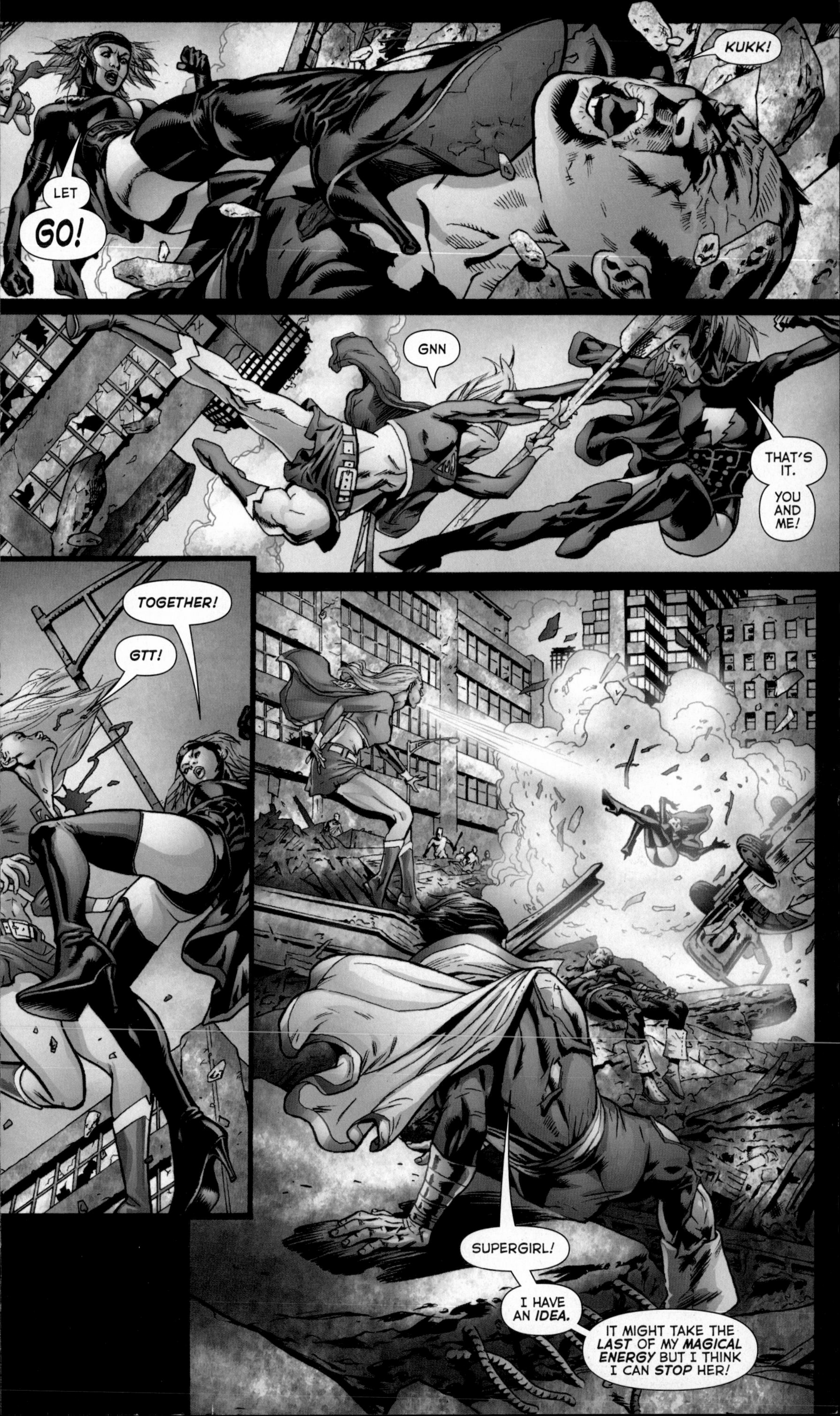
KUKK!
LET GO!
GNN
THAT'S IT.
YOU AND ME!
TOGETHER!
GTT!
SUPERGIRL!
I HAVE AN IDEA.
IT MIGHT TAKE THE LAST OF MY MAGICAL ENERGY BUT I THINK I CAN STOP HER!

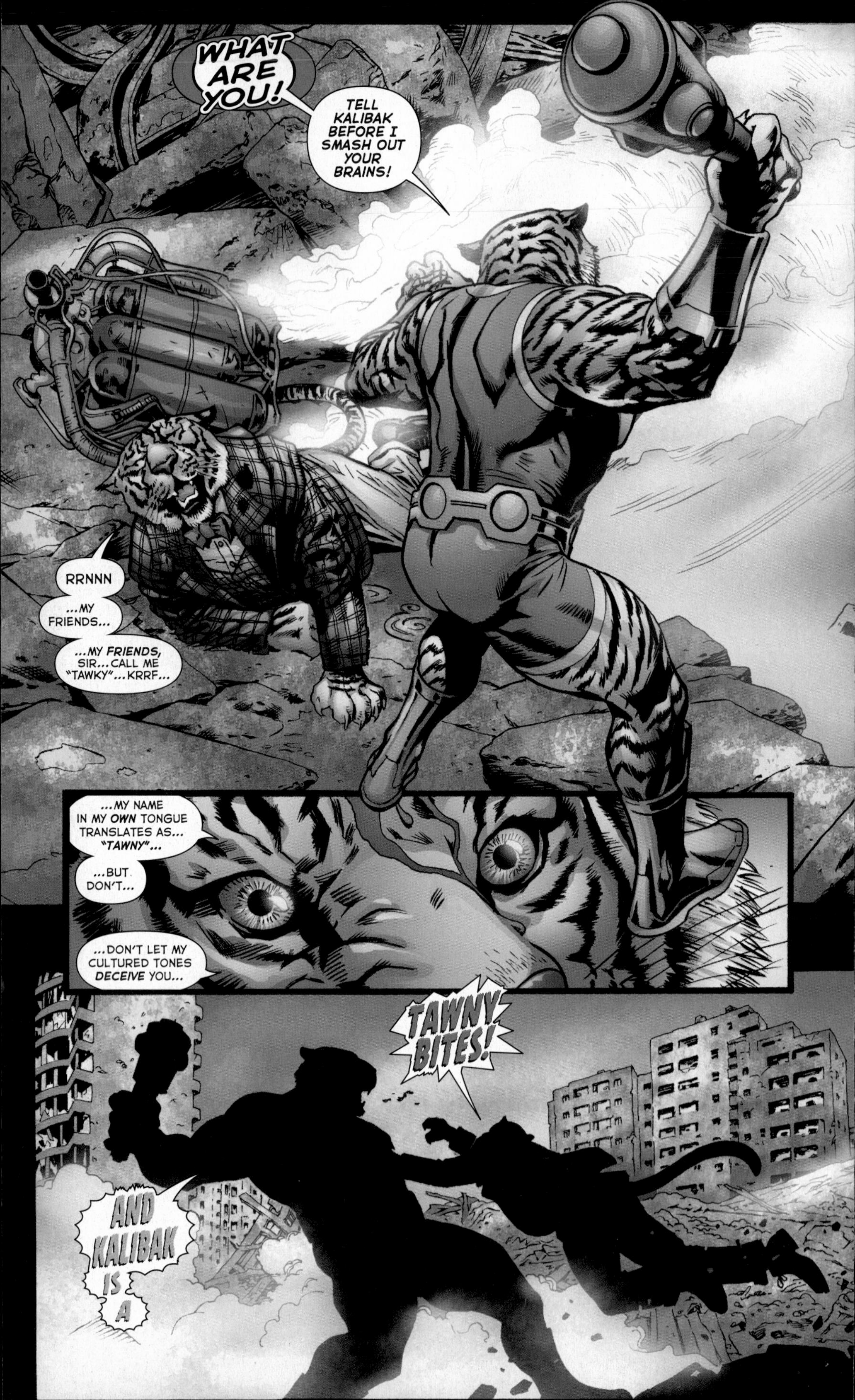
WHAT ARE YOU!
TELL KALIBAK BEFORE I SMASH OUT YOUR BRAINS!
RRNNN
...MY FRIENDS...
...MY FRIENDS, SIR...CALL ME "TAWKY"...KRRF...
...MY NAME IN MY OWN TONGUE TRANSLATES AS... "TAWNY"...
...BUT DON'T...
...DON'T LET MY CULTURED TONES DECEIVE YOU...
TAWNY BITES!
AND KALIBAK IS A

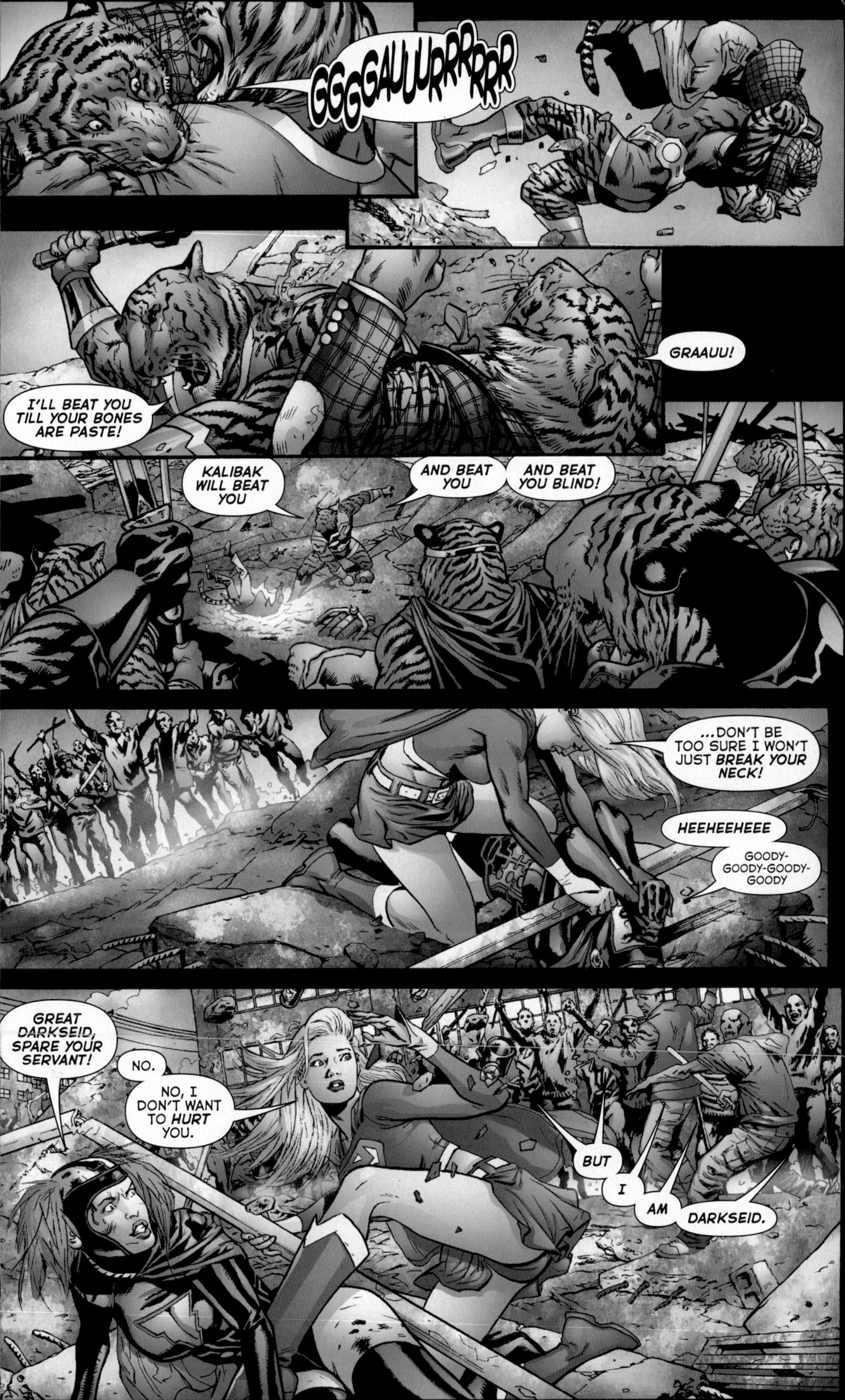
GGGGAUUURRRRRR
I'LL BEAT YOU TILL YOUR BONES ARE PASTE!
GRAAUU!
KALIBAK WILL BEAT YOU
AND BEAT YOU
AND BEAT YOU BLIND!
...DON'T BE TOO SURE I WON'T JUST BREAK YOUR NECK!
HEEHEEHEEE
GOODY-GOODY-GOODY-GOODY
GREAT DARKSEID, SPARE YOUR SERVANT!
NO.
NO, I DON'T WANT TO HURT YOU.
BUT
I
AM
DARKSEID.

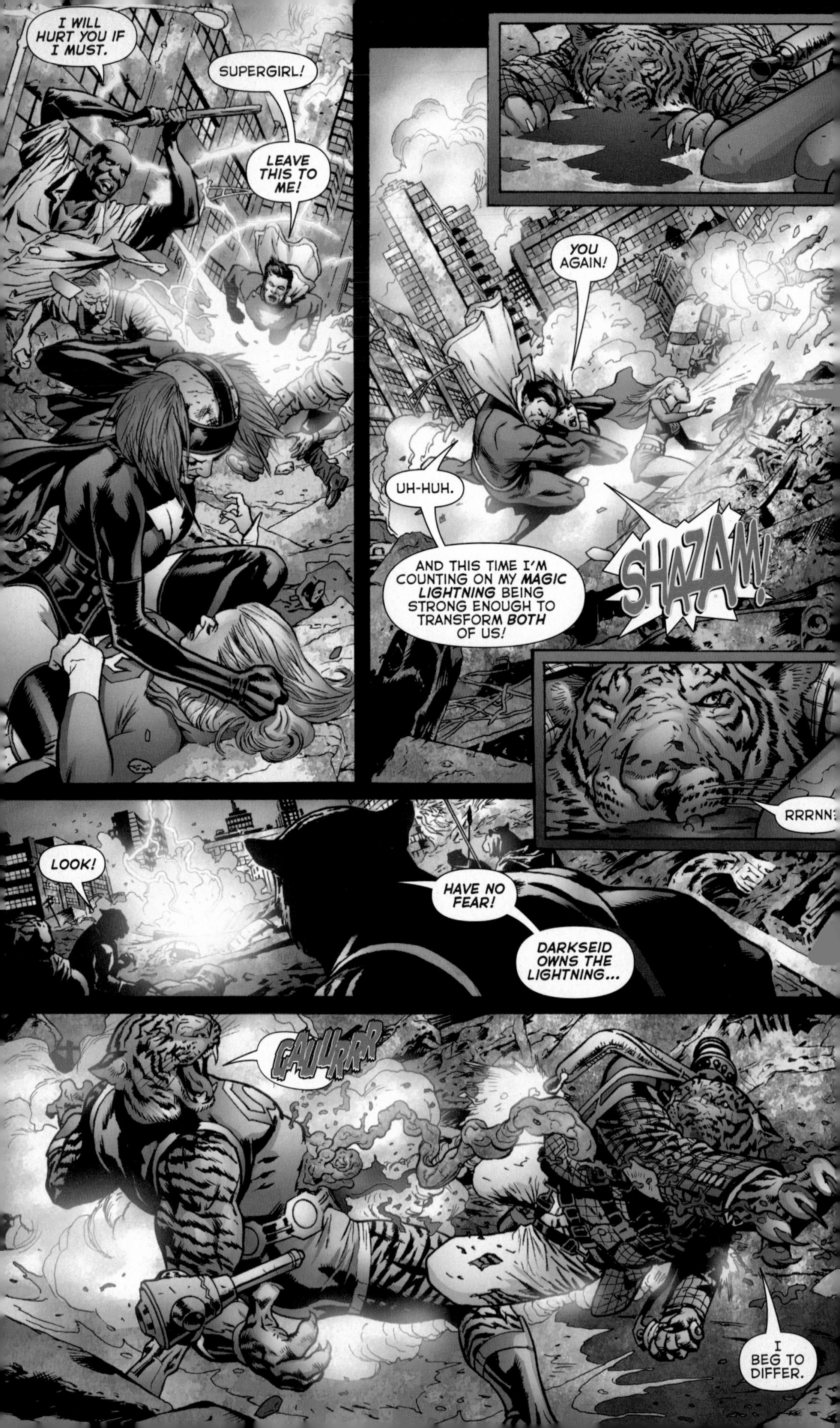
I WILL HURT YOU IF I MUST.
SUPERGIRL!
LEAVE THIS TO ME!
YOU AGAIN!
UH-HUH.
AND THIS TIME I'M COUNTING ON MY *MAGIC LIGHTNING* BEING STRONG ENOUGH TO TRANSFORM *BOTH* OF US!
SHAZAM!
RRRNN
LOOK!
HAVE NO FEAR!
DARKSEID OWNS THE LIGHTNING...
GAUURRR
I BEG TO DIFFER.

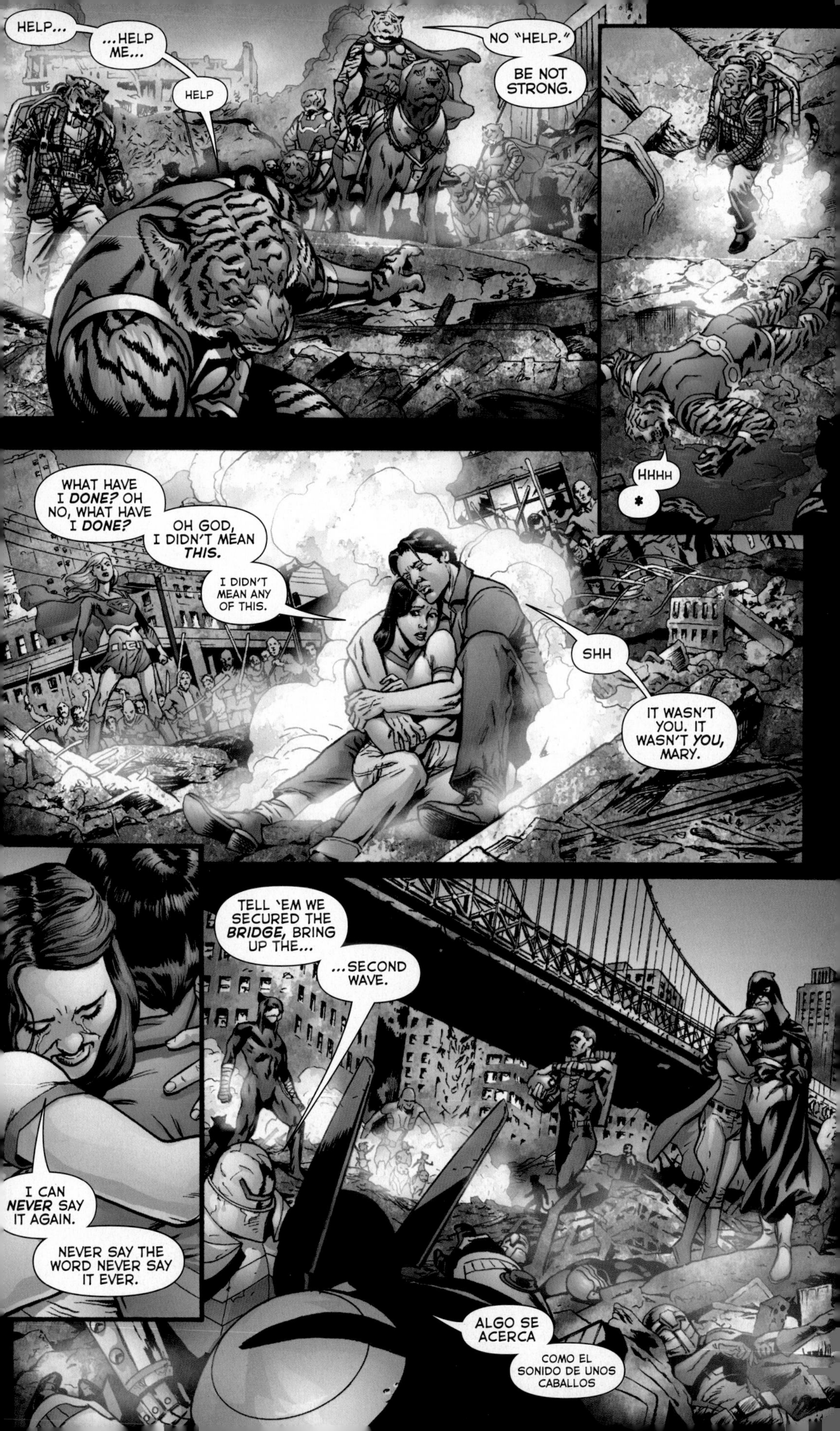
HELP...
...HELP ME...
HELP
NO "HELP."
BE NOT STRONG.
HHHH
*
WHAT HAVE I DONE? OH NO, WHAT HAVE I DONE?
OH GOD, I DIDN'T MEAN THIS.
I DIDN'T MEAN ANY OF THIS.
SHH
IT WASN'T YOU. IT WASN'T YOU, MARY.
I CAN NEVER SAY IT AGAIN.
NEVER SAY THE WORD NEVER SAY IT EVER.
TELL 'EM WE SECURED THE BRIDGE, BRING UP THE...
...SECOND WAVE.
ALGO SE ACERCA
COMO EL SONIDO DE UNOS CABALLOS

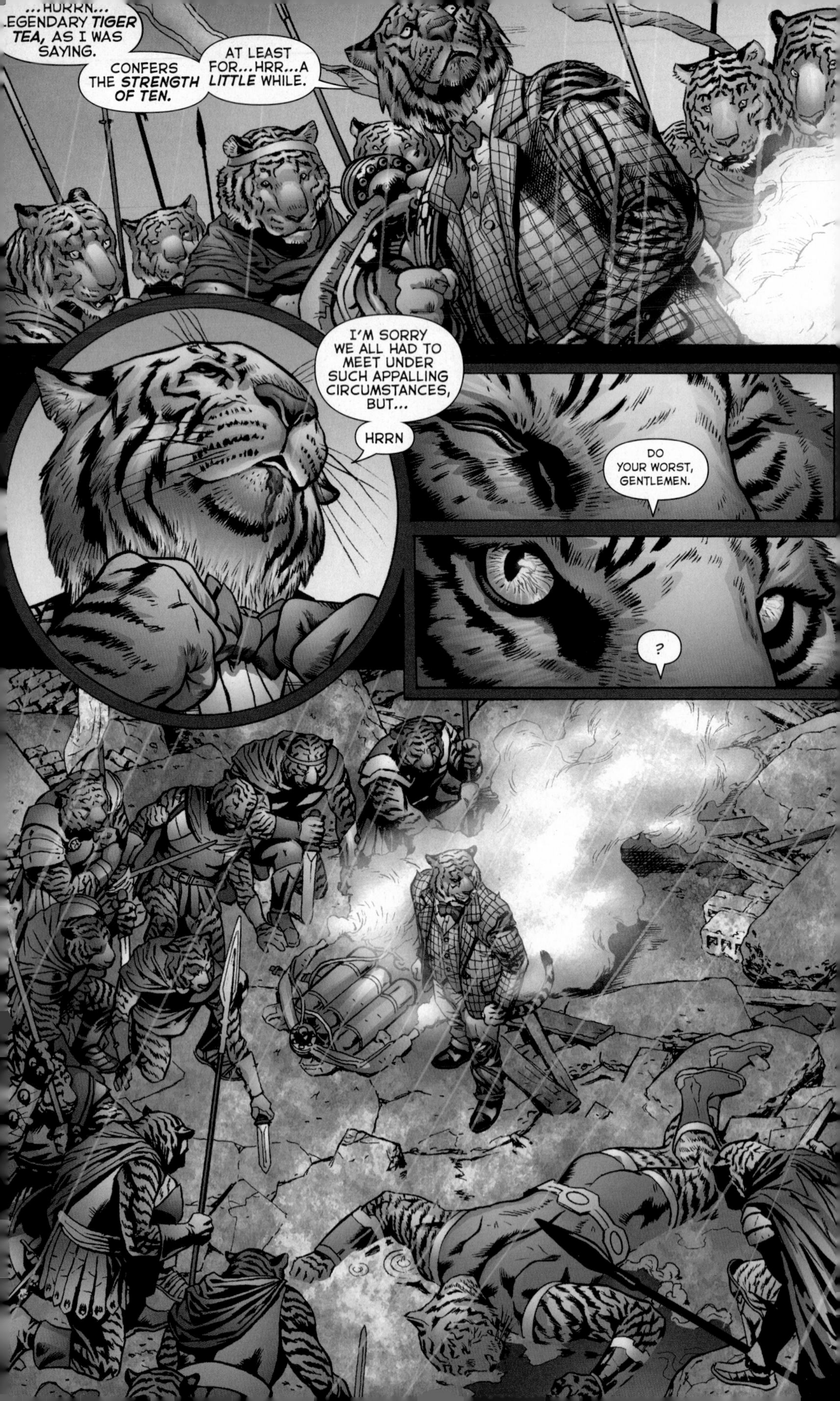
...HURRN... LEGENDARY TIGER TEA, AS I WAS SAYING.
CONFERS THE STRENGTH OF TEN.
AT LEAST FOR...HRR...A LITTLE WHILE.
I'M SORRY WE ALL HAD TO MEET UNDER SUCH APPALLING CIRCUMSTANCES, BUT...
HRRN
DO YOUR WORST, GENTLEMEN.
?

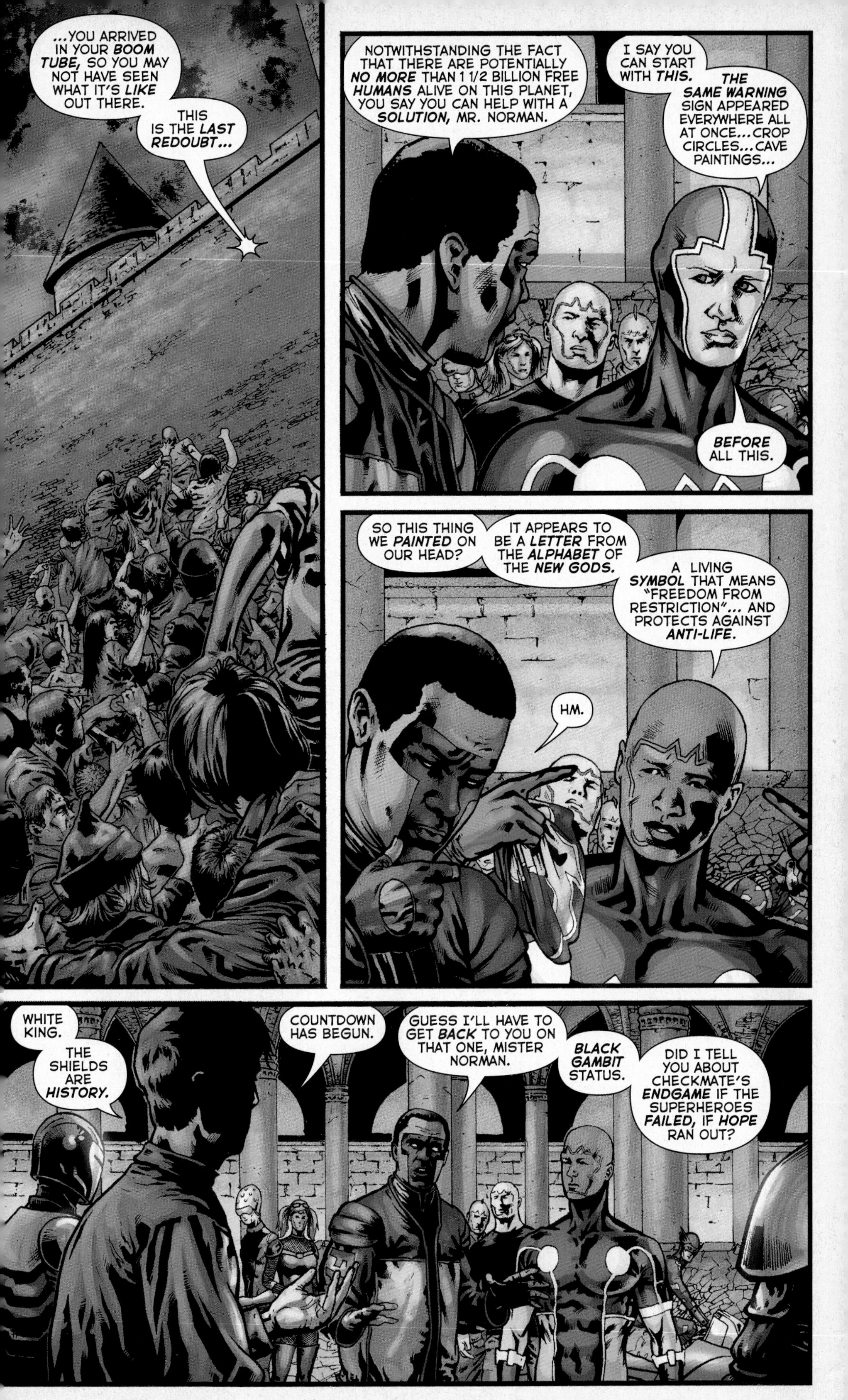
...YOU ARRIVED IN YOUR BOOM TUBE, SO YOU MAY NOT HAVE SEEN WHAT IT'S LIKE OUT THERE.
THIS IS THE LAST REDOUBT...
NOTWITHSTANDING THE FACT THAT THERE ARE POTENTIALLY NO MORE THAN 1 1/2 BILLION FREE HUMANS ALIVE ON THIS PLANET, YOU SAY YOU CAN HELP WITH A SOLUTION, MR. NORMAN.
I SAY YOU CAN START WITH THIS.
THE SAME WARNING SIGN APPEARED EVERYWHERE ALL AT ONCE...CROP CIRCLES...CAVE PAINTINGS...
BEFORE ALL THIS.
SO THIS THING WE PAINTED ON OUR HEAD?
IT APPEARS TO BE A LETTER FROM THE ALPHABET OF THE NEW GODS.
A LIVING SYMBOL THAT MEANS "FREEDOM FROM RESTRICTION"... AND PROTECTS AGAINST ANTI-LIFE.
HM.
WHITE KING.
THE SHIELDS ARE HISTORY.
COUNTDOWN HAS BEGUN.
GUESS I'LL HAVE TO GET BACK TO YOU ON THAT ONE, MISTER NORMAN.
BLACK GAMBIT STATUS.
DID I TELL YOU ABOUT CHECKMATE'S ENDGAME IF THE SUPERHEROES FAILED, IF HOPE RAN OUT?

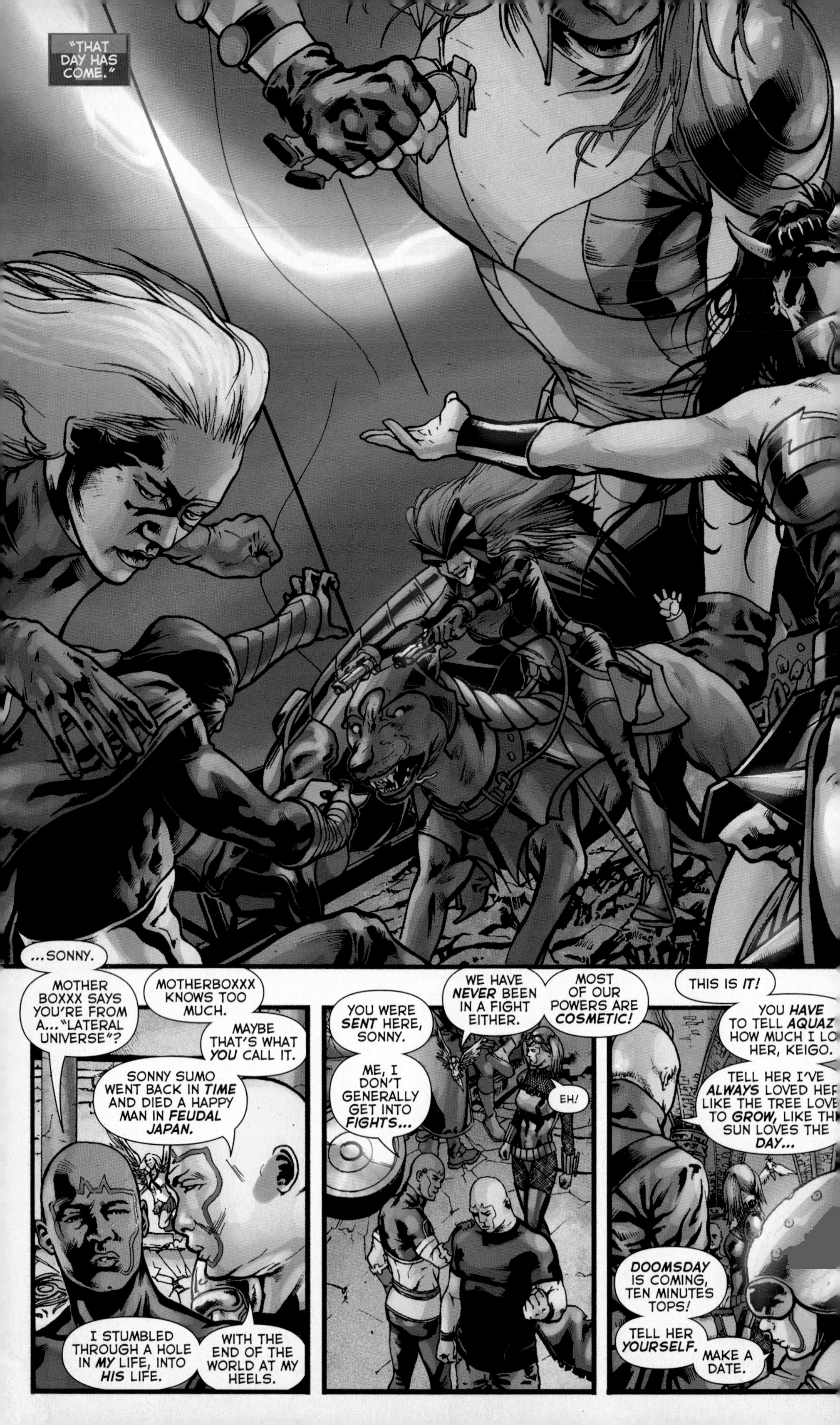
"THAT DAY HAS COME."
...SONNY.
MOTHER BOXXX SAYS YOU'RE FROM A... "LATERAL UNIVERSE"?
MOTHERBOXXX KNOWS TOO MUCH.
MAYBE THAT'S WHAT YOU CALL IT.
SONNY SUMO WENT BACK IN TIME AND DIED A HAPPY MAN IN FEUDAL JAPAN.
I STUMBLED THROUGH A HOLE IN MY LIFE, INTO HIS LIFE.
WITH THE END OF THE WORLD AT MY HEELS.
YOU WERE SENT HERE, SONNY.
ME, I DON'T GENERALLY GET INTO FIGHTS...
WE HAVE NEVER BEEN IN A FIGHT EITHER.
MOST OF OUR POWERS ARE COSMETIC!
EH!
THIS IS IT!
YOU HAVE TO TELL AQUAZ HOW MUCH I LO HER, KEIGO.
TELL HER I'VE ALWAYS LOVED HEF LIKE THE TREE LOVE TO GROW, LIKE TH SUN LOVES THE DAY...
DOOMSDAY IS COMING, TEN MINUTES TOPS!
TELL HER YOURSELF.
MAKE A DATE.

OH, THIS IS TERRIBLE.

I CAN'T SEEM TO TELL SONIC LIGHTNING FLASH HOW I FEEL ABOUT HIM.

I'M STILL TOO SHY!

WAIT UNTIL WE'VE SAVED THE WORLD!

THEN TELL HIM!

SO, TEAM...

LANTERN BOY, YOU GOT THAT RAY THING COMING OUT OF YOUR CHEST.

YOU CAN SCREAM YOURSELF RAW, YOU CAN SWIM LIKE A !**@¢#!

SUPERBAT, YOU NEVER TOLD ME WHAT YOUR POWER WAS....

I HAVE THE GREATEST POWER OF ALL, MISTER MIRACLE.

I AM SO RICH I CAN DO ANYTHING.

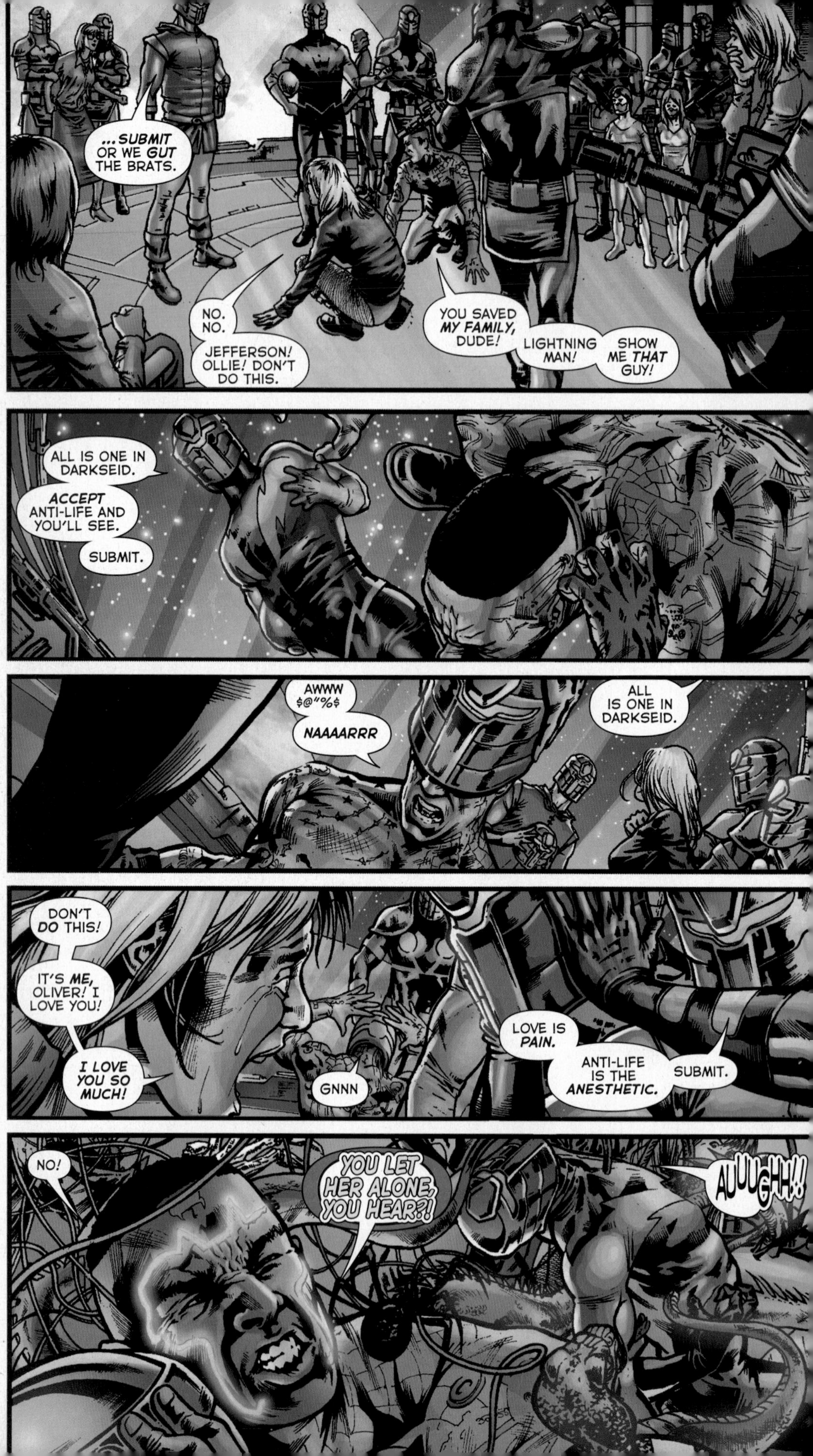

...SUBMIT OR WE GUT THE BRATS.
NO. NO.
JEFFERSON! OLLIE! DON'T DO THIS.
YOU SAVED MY FAMILY, DUDE!
LIGHTNING MAN!
SHOW ME THAT GUY!
ALL IS ONE IN DARKSEID.
ACCEPT ANTI-LIFE AND YOU'LL SEE.
SUBMIT.
AWWW $@"%$
NAAAARRR
ALL IS ONE IN DARKSEID.
DON'T DO THIS!
IT'S ME, OLIVER! I LOVE YOU!
I LOVE YOU SO MUCH!
GNNN
LOVE IS PAIN.
ANTI-LIFE IS THE ANESTHETIC.
SUBMIT.
NO!
YOU LET HER ALONE, YOU HEAR?!
AUUUGHH!!

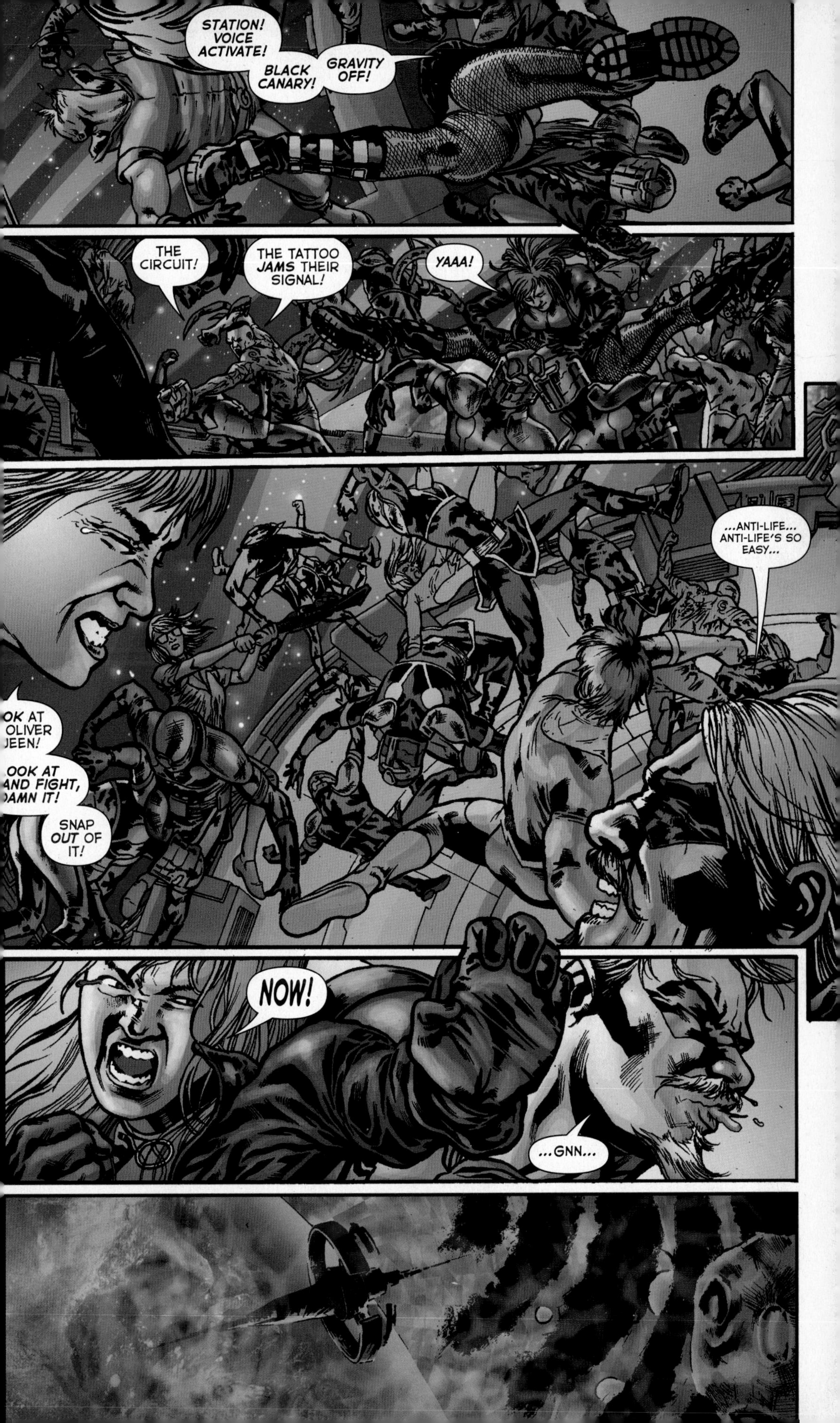
STATION! VOICE ACTIVATE!
BLACK CANARY!
GRAVITY OFF!
THE CIRCUIT!
THE TATTOO JAMS THEIR SIGNAL!
YAAA!
...ANTI-LIFE... ANTI-LIFE'S SO EASY...
OK AT OLIVER
OOK AT AND FIGHT,
SNAP OUT OF IT!
NOW!
...GNN...

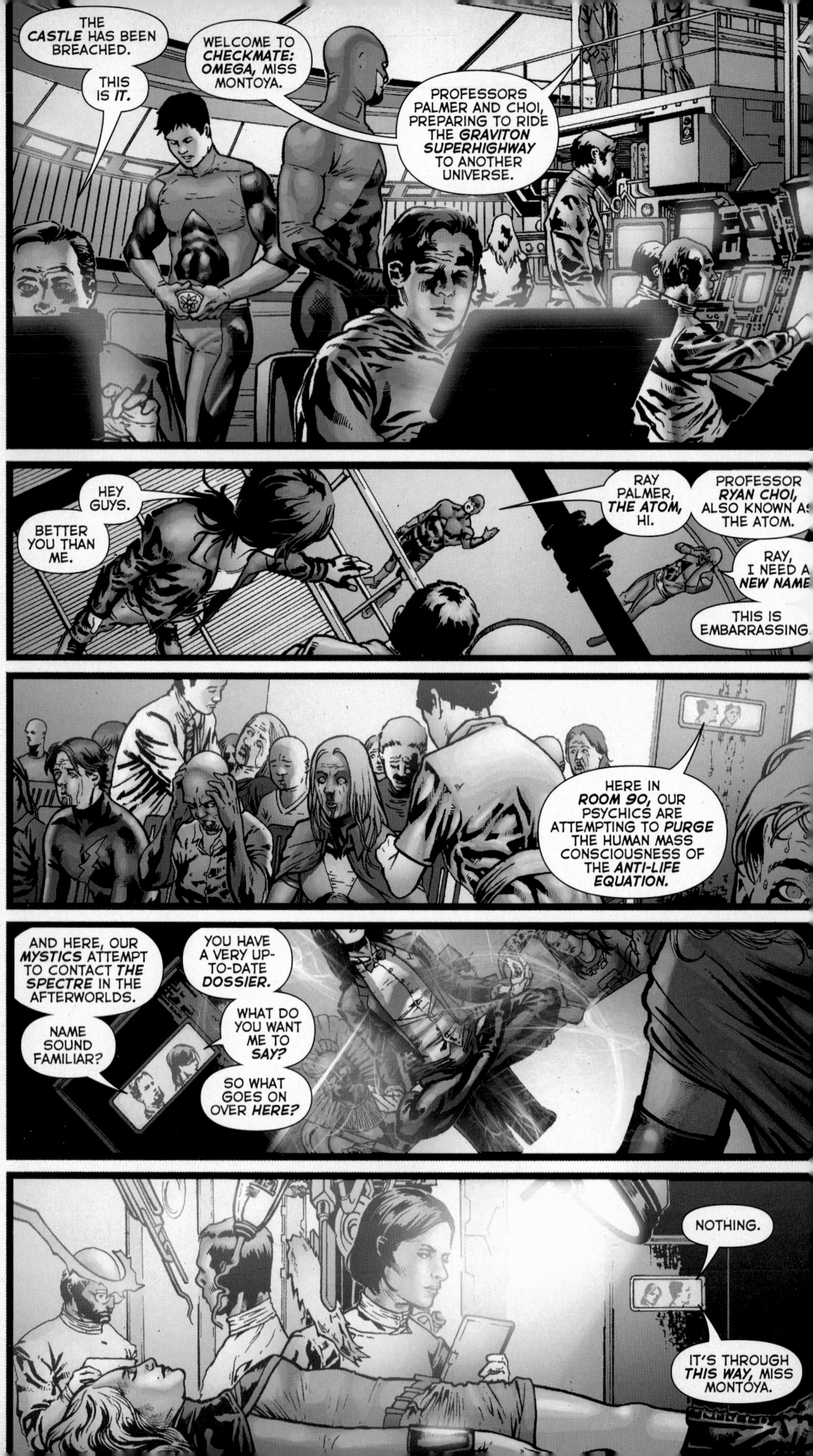
THE CASTLE HAS BEEN BREACHED.
THIS IS IT.
WELCOME TO CHECKMATE: OMEGA, MISS MONTOYA.
PROFESSORS PALMER AND CHOI, PREPARING TO RIDE THE GRAVITON SUPERHIGHWAY TO ANOTHER UNIVERSE.
HEY GUYS.
BETTER YOU THAN ME.
RAY PALMER, THE ATOM, HI.
PROFESSOR RYAN CHOI, ALSO KNOWN AS THE ATOM.
RAY, I NEED A NEW NAME.
THIS IS EMBARRASSING.
HERE IN ROOM 90, OUR PSYCHICS ARE ATTEMPTING TO PURGE THE HUMAN MASS CONSCIOUSNESS OF THE ANTI-LIFE EQUATION.
AND HERE, OUR MYSTICS ATTEMPT TO CONTACT THE SPECTRE IN THE AFTERWORLDS.
NAME SOUND FAMILIAR?
YOU HAVE A VERY UP-TO-DATE DOSSIER.
WHAT DO YOU WANT ME TO SAY?
SO WHAT GOES ON OVER HERE?
NOTHING.
IT'S THROUGH THIS WAY, MISS MONTOYA.

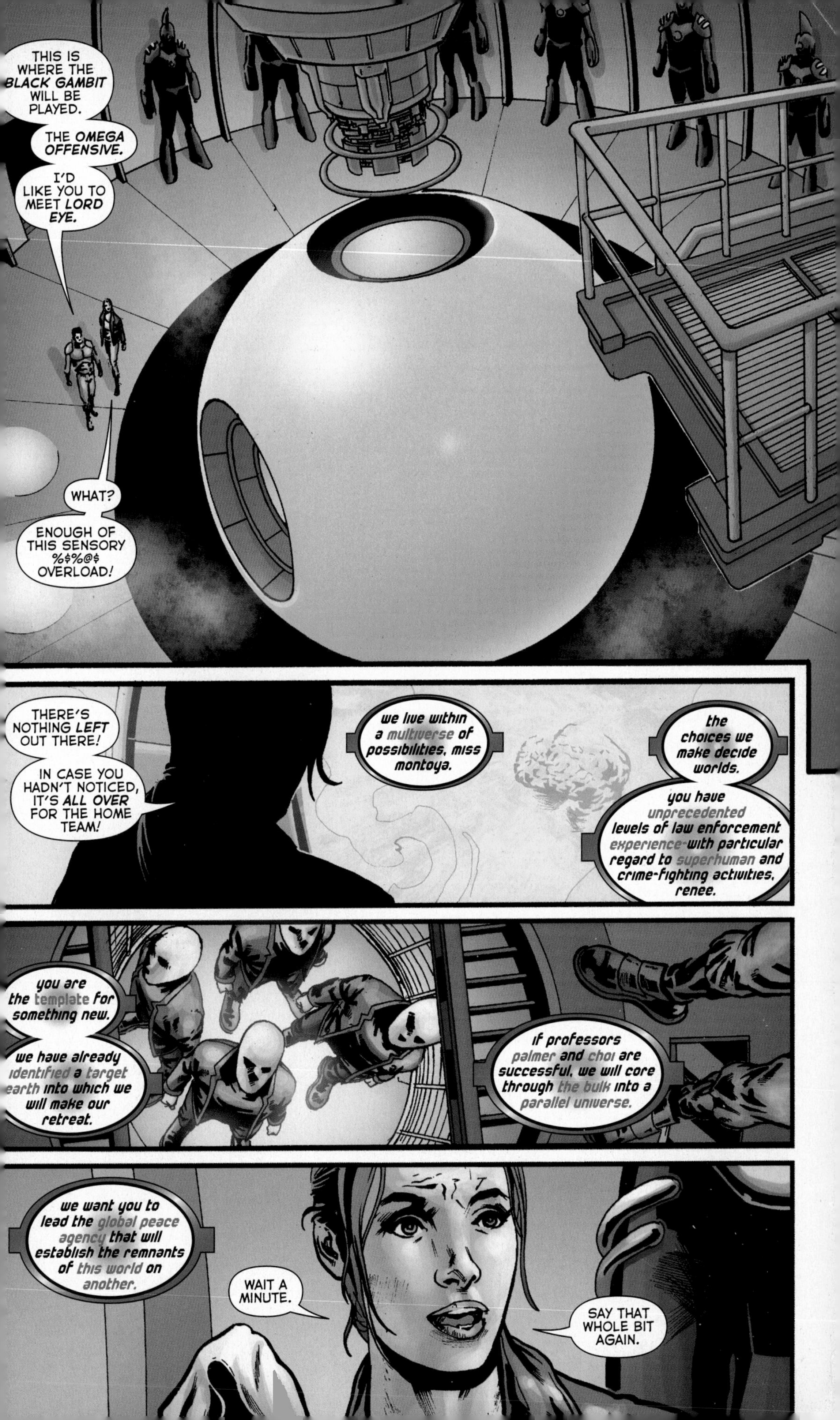
THIS IS WHERE THE BLACK GAMBIT WILL BE PLAYED.
THE OMEGA OFFENSIVE.
I'D LIKE YOU TO MEET LORD EYE.
WHAT?
ENOUGH OF THIS SENSORY %$%@$ OVERLOAD!
THERE'S NOTHING LEFT OUT THERE!
IN CASE YOU HADN'T NOTICED, IT'S ALL OVER FOR THE HOME TEAM!
we live within a multiverse of possibilities, miss montoya.
the choices we make decide worlds.
you have unprecedented levels of law enforcement experience--with particular regard to superhuman and crime-fighting activities, renee.
you are the template for something new.
we have already identified a target earth into which we will make our retreat.
if professors palmer and choi are successful, we will core through the bulk into a parallel universe.
we want you to lead the global peace agency that will establish the remnants of this world on another.
WAIT A MINUTE.
SAY THAT WHOLE BIT AGAIN.

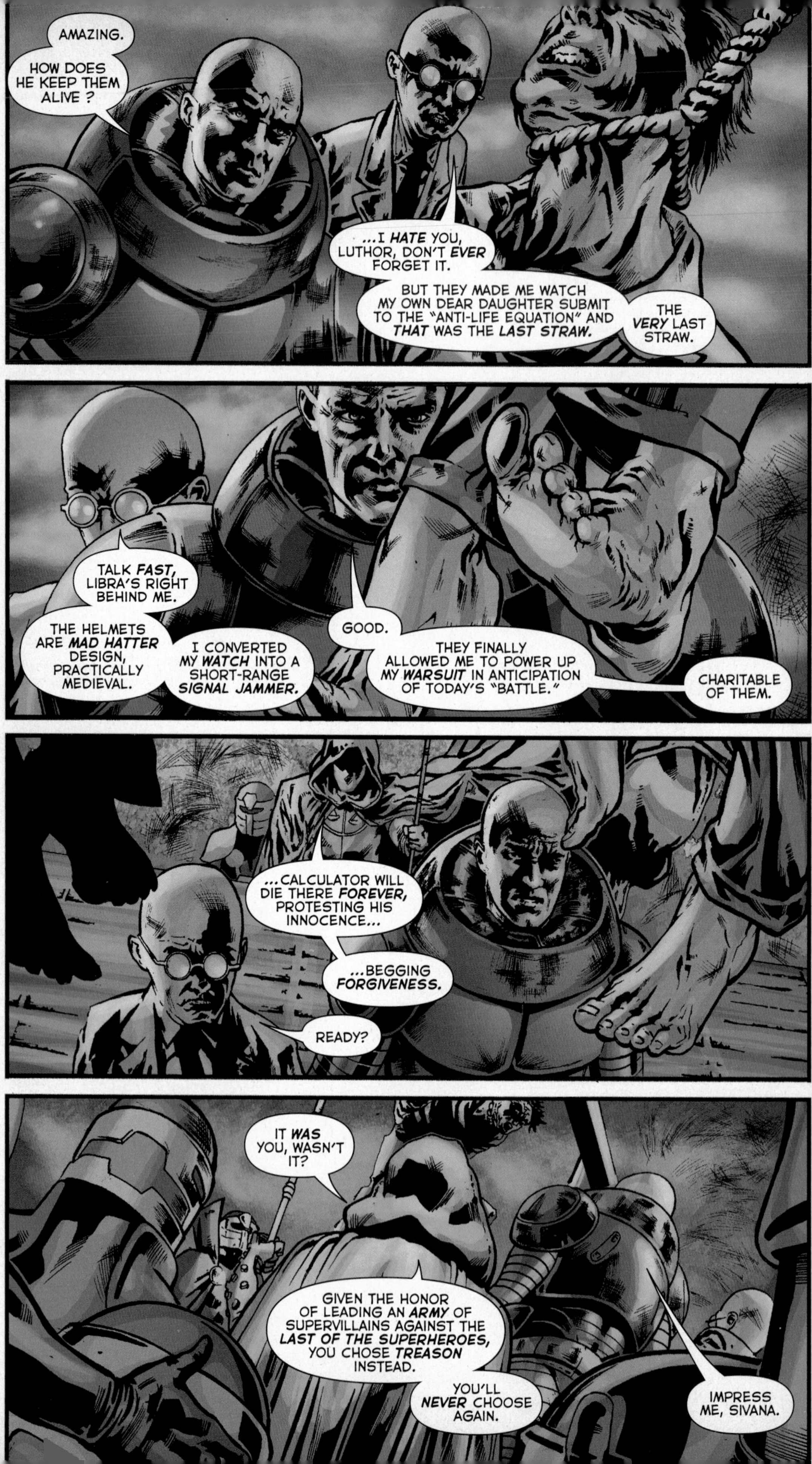
AMAZING.
HOW DOES HE KEEP THEM ALIVE ?
...I HATE YOU, LUTHOR, DON'T EVER FORGET IT.
BUT THEY MADE ME WATCH MY OWN DEAR DAUGHTER SUBMIT TO THE "ANTI-LIFE EQUATION" AND THAT WAS THE LAST STRAW.
THE VERY LAST STRAW.
TALK FAST, LIBRA'S RIGHT BEHIND ME.
THE HELMETS ARE MAD HATTER DESIGN, PRACTICALLY MEDIEVAL.
I CONVERTED MY WATCH INTO A SHORT-RANGE SIGNAL JAMMER.
GOOD.
THEY FINALLY ALLOWED ME TO POWER UP MY WARSUIT IN ANTICIPATION OF TODAY'S "BATTLE."
CHARITABLE OF THEM.
...CALCULATOR WILL DIE THERE FOREVER, PROTESTING HIS INNOCENCE...
...BEGGING FORGIVENESS.
READY?
IT WAS YOU, WASN'T IT?
GIVEN THE HONOR OF LEADING AN ARMY OF SUPERVILLAINS AGAINST THE LAST OF THE SUPERHEROES, YOU CHOSE TREASON INSTEAD.
YOU'LL NEVER CHOOSE AGAIN.
IMPRESS ME, SIVANA.

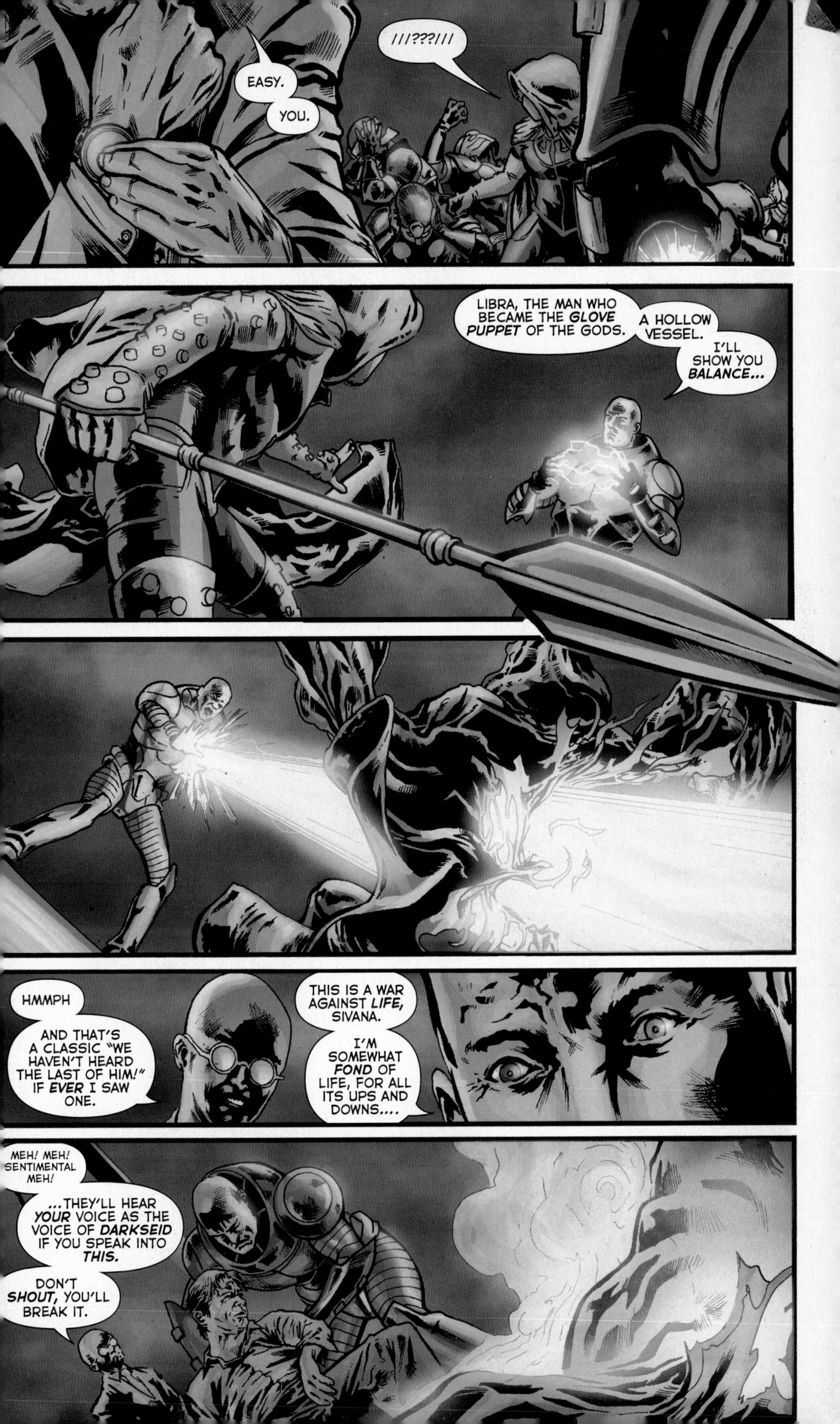
EASY.
YOU.
///???///
LIBRA, THE MAN WHO BECAME THE GLOVE PUPPET OF THE GODS.
A HOLLOW VESSEL.
I'LL SHOW YOU BALANCE...
HMMPH
AND THAT'S A CLASSIC "WE HAVEN'T HEARD THE LAST OF HIM!" IF EVER I SAW ONE.
THIS IS A WAR AGAINST LIFE, SIVANA.
I'M SOMEWHAT FOND OF LIFE, FOR ALL ITS UPS AND DOWNS....
MEH! MEH! SENTIMENTAL MEH!
...THEY'LL HEAR YOUR VOICE AS THE VOICE OF DARKSEID IF YOU SPEAK INTO THIS.
DON'T SHOUT, YOU'LL BREAK IT.

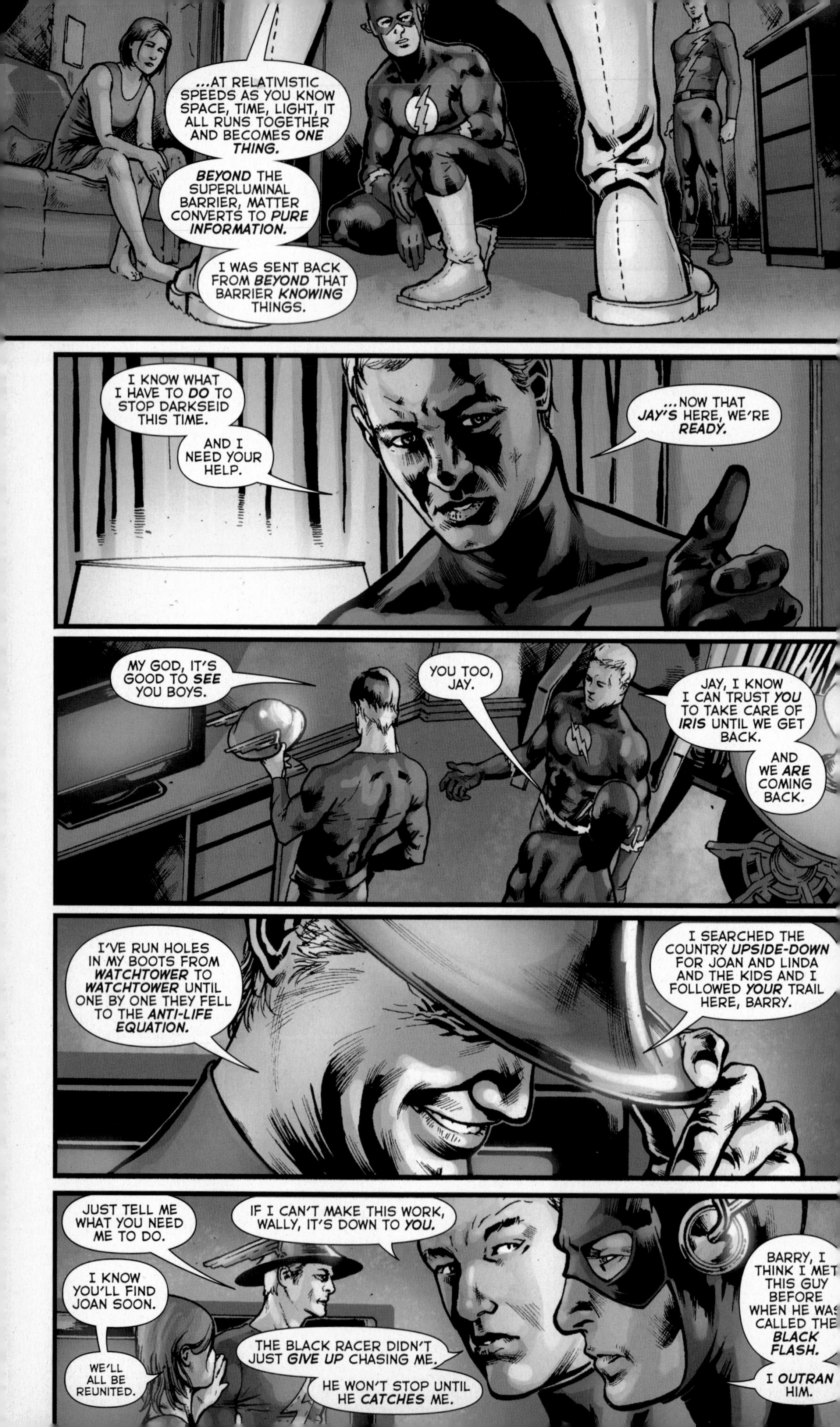
...AT RELATIVISTIC SPEEDS AS YOU KNOW SPACE, TIME, LIGHT, IT ALL RUNS TOGETHER AND BECOMES ONE THING.
BEYOND THE SUPERLUMINAL BARRIER, MATTER CONVERTS TO PURE INFORMATION.
I WAS SENT BACK FROM BEYOND THAT BARRIER KNOWING THINGS.
I KNOW WHAT I HAVE TO DO TO STOP DARKSEID THIS TIME.
AND I NEED YOUR HELP.
...NOW THAT JAY'S HERE, WE'RE READY.
MY GOD, IT'S GOOD TO SEE YOU BOYS.
YOU TOO, JAY.
JAY, I KNOW I CAN TRUST YOU TO TAKE CARE OF IRIS UNTIL WE GET BACK.
AND WE ARE COMING BACK.
I'VE RUN HOLES IN MY BOOTS FROM WATCHTOWER TO WATCHTOWER UNTIL ONE BY ONE THEY FELL TO THE ANTI-LIFE EQUATION.
I SEARCHED THE COUNTRY UPSIDE-DOWN FOR JOAN AND LINDA AND THE KIDS AND I FOLLOWED YOUR TRAIL HERE, BARRY.
JUST TELL ME WHAT YOU NEED ME TO DO.
IF I CAN'T MAKE THIS WORK, WALLY, IT'S DOWN TO YOU.
I KNOW YOU'LL FIND JOAN SOON.
WE'LL ALL BE REUNITED.
THE BLACK RACER DIDN'T JUST GIVE UP CHASING ME.
HE WON'T STOP UNTIL HE CATCHES ME.
BARRY, I THINK I MET THIS GUY BEFORE WHEN HE WAS CALLED THE BLACK FLASH.
I OUTRAN HIM.

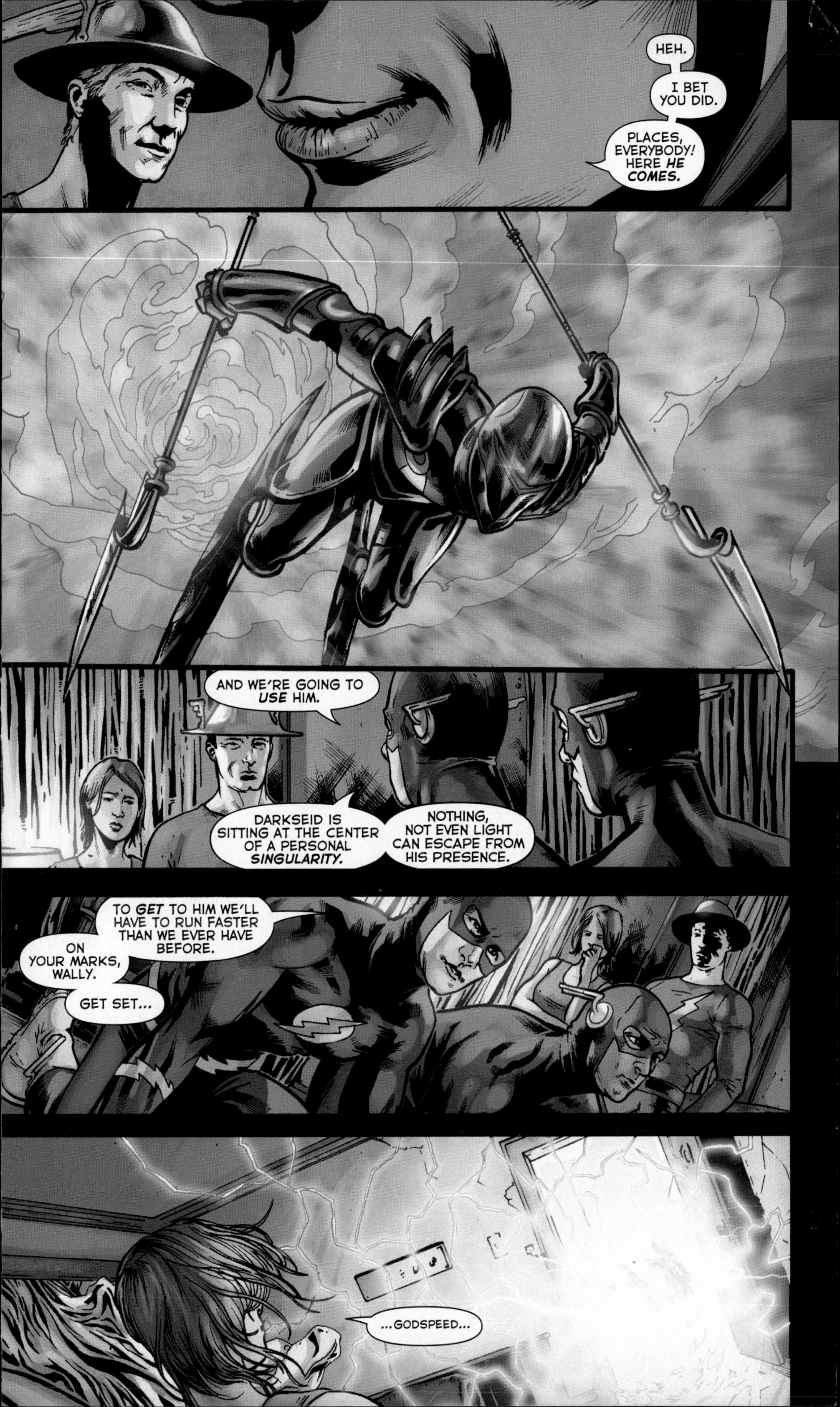
HEH.
I BET YOU DID.
PLACES, EVERYBODY! HERE *HE COMES.*
AND WE'RE GOING TO *USE* HIM.
DARKSEID IS SITTING AT THE CENTER OF A PERSONAL *SINGULARITY.*
NOTHING, NOT EVEN LIGHT CAN ESCAPE FROM HIS PRESENCE.
TO *GET* TO HIM WE'LL HAVE TO RUN FASTER THAN WE EVER HAVE BEFORE.
ON YOUR MARKS, WALLY.
GET SET...
...GODSPEED...

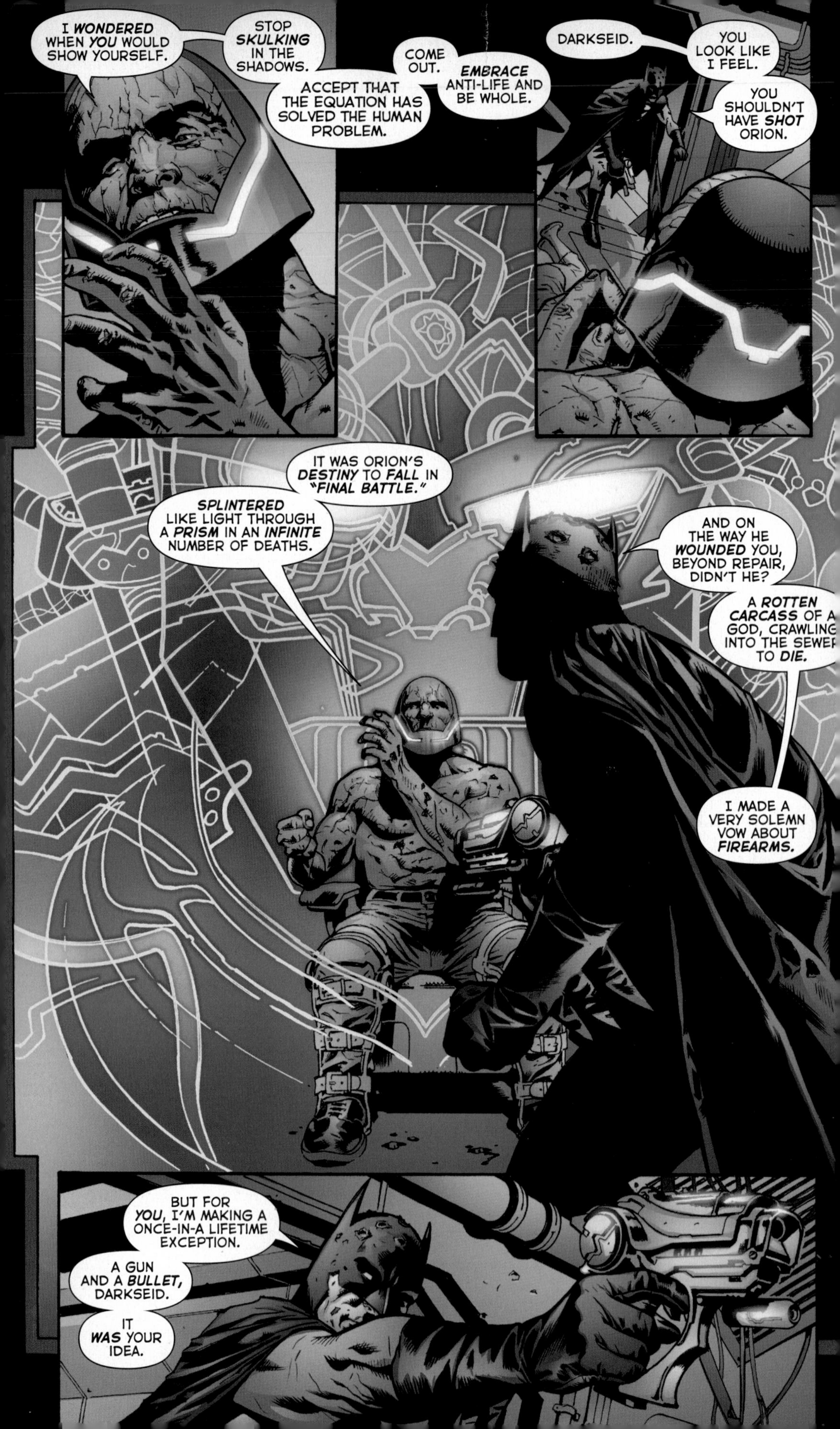
I WONDERED WHEN YOU WOULD SHOW YOURSELF.
STOP SKULKING IN THE SHADOWS.
ACCEPT THAT THE EQUATION HAS SOLVED THE HUMAN PROBLEM.
COME OUT.
EMBRACE ANTI-LIFE AND BE WHOLE.
DARKSEID.
YOU LOOK LIKE I FEEL.
YOU SHOULDN'T HAVE SHOT ORION.
IT WAS ORION'S DESTINY TO FALL IN "FINAL BATTLE."
SPLINTERED LIKE LIGHT THROUGH A PRISM IN AN INFINITE NUMBER OF DEATHS.
AND ON THE WAY HE WOUNDED YOU, BEYOND REPAIR, DIDN'T HE?
A ROTTEN CARCASS OF A GOD, CRAWLING INTO THE SEWER TO DIE.
I MADE A VERY SOLEMN VOW ABOUT FIREARMS.
BUT FOR YOU, I'M MAKING A ONCE-IN-A LIFETIME EXCEPTION.
A GUN AND A BULLET, DARKSEID.
IT WAS YOUR IDEA.

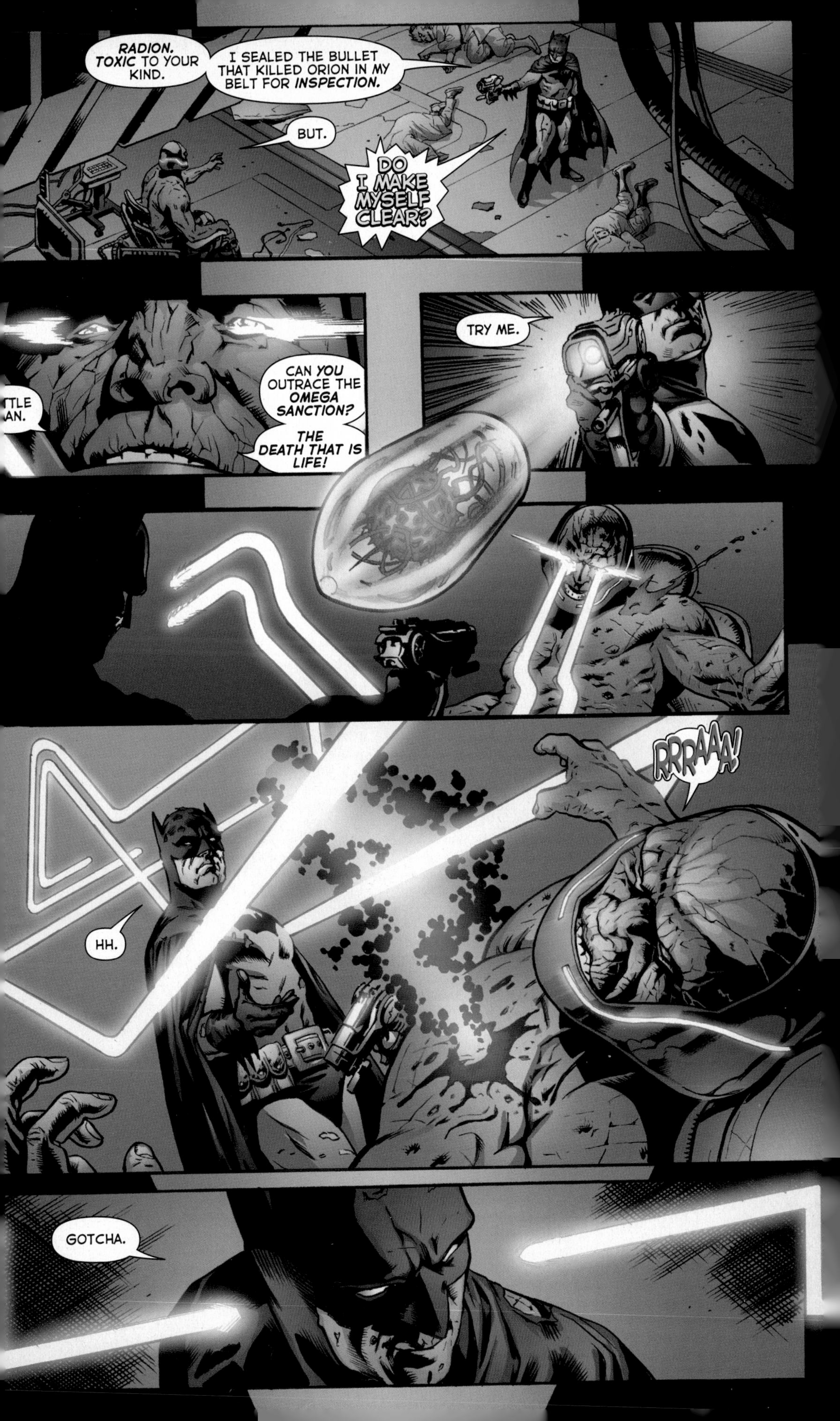

RADION. TOXIC TO YOUR KIND.
I SEALED THE BULLET THAT KILLED ORION IN MY BELT FOR INSPECTION.
BUT.
DO I MAKE MYSELF CLEAR?
TTLE AN.
CAN YOU OUTRACE THE OMEGA SANCTION?
THE DEATH THAT IS LIFE!
TRY ME.
RRRAAA!
HH.
GOTCHA.

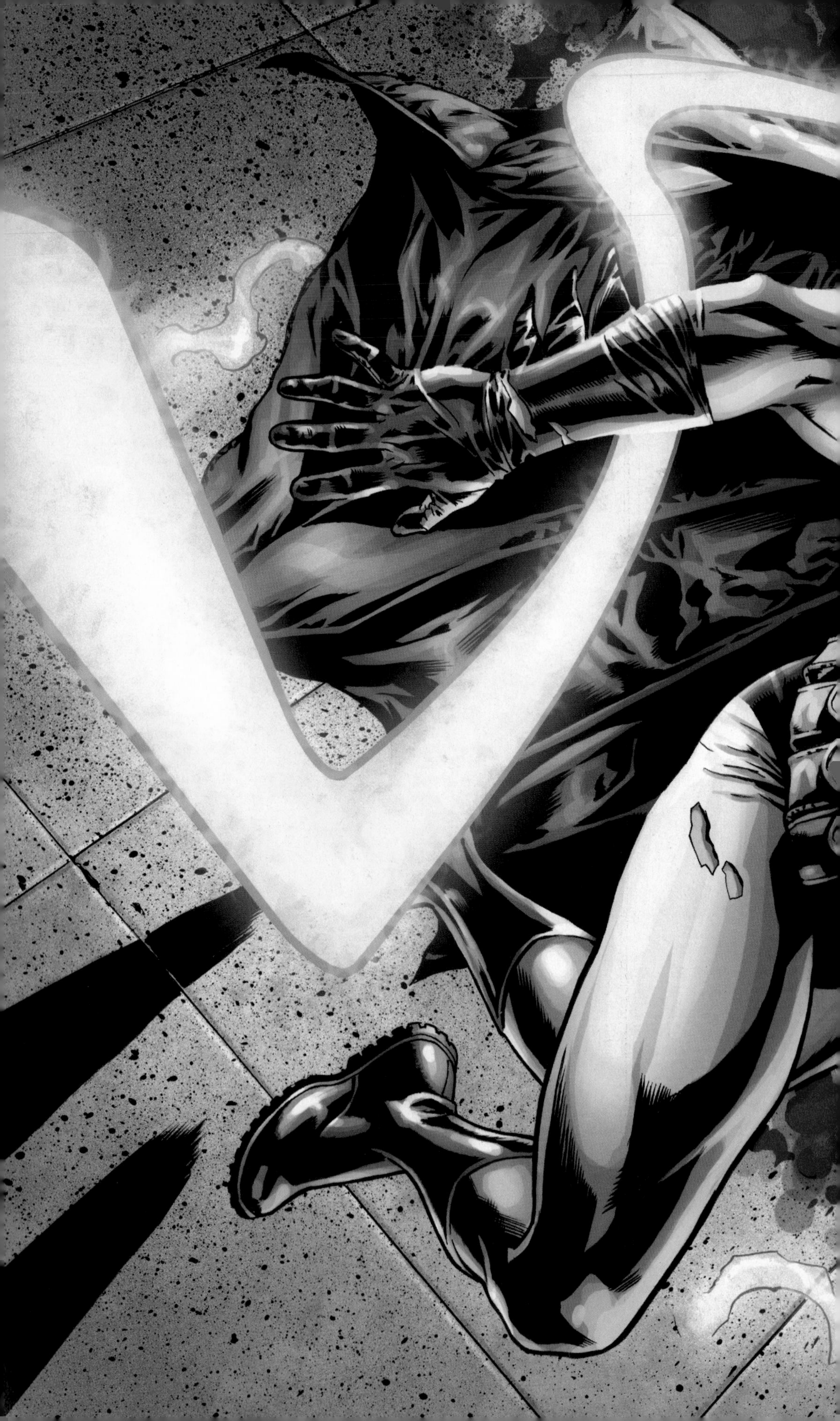

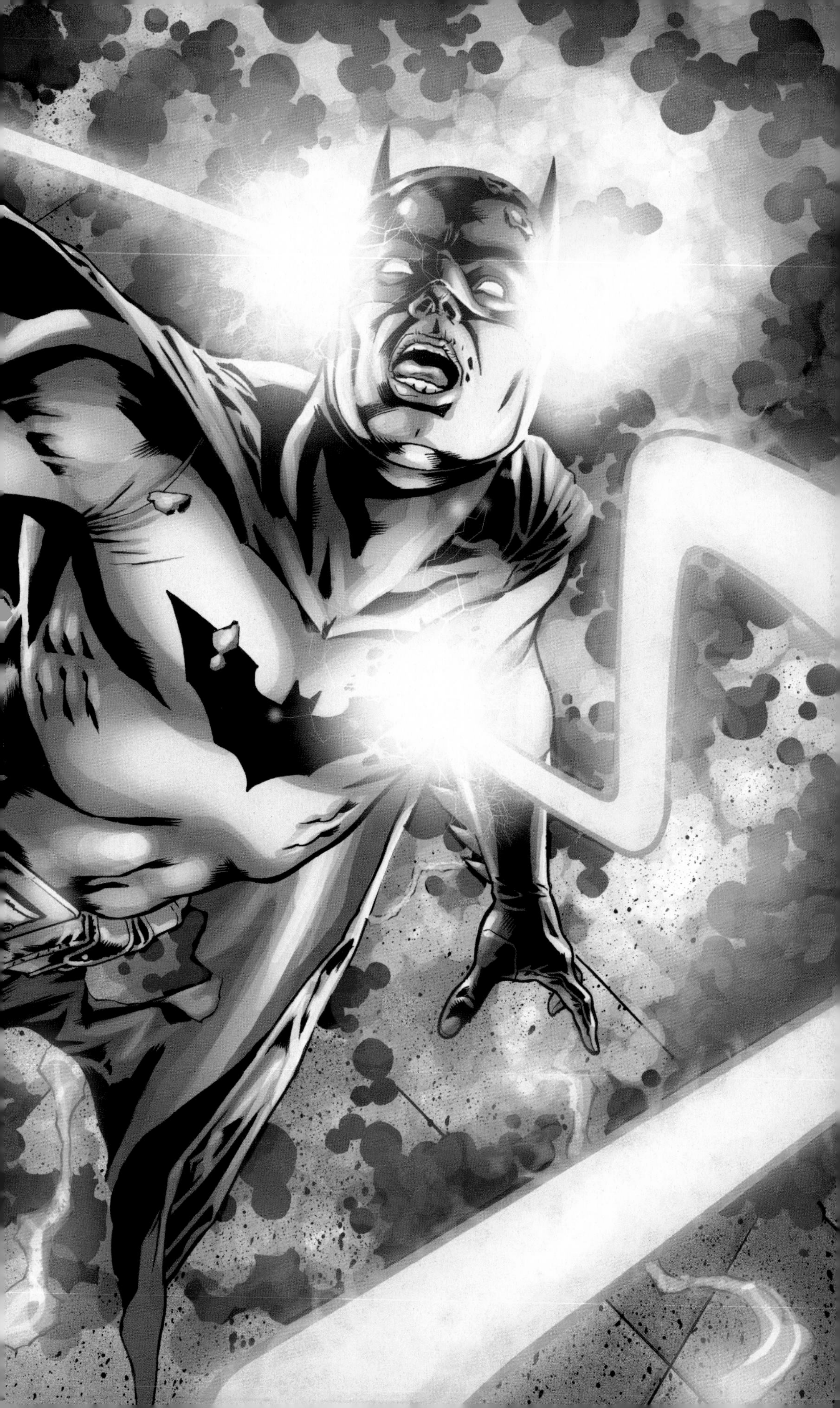

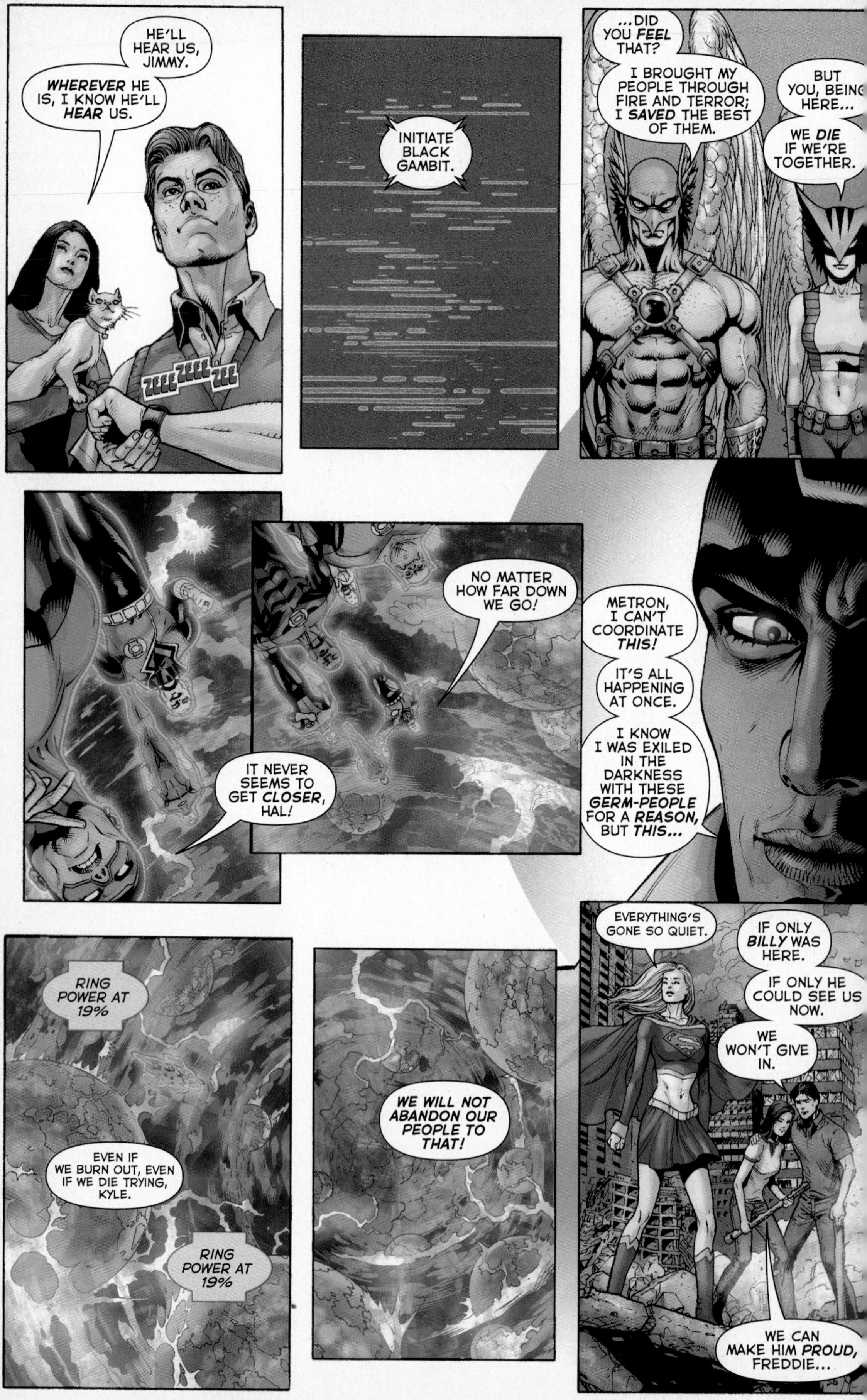
HE'LL HEAR US, JIMMY.
WHEREVER HE IS, I KNOW HE'LL HEAR US.
ZEEE ZEEE ZEE
INITIATE BLACK GAMBIT.
...DID YOU FEEL THAT?
I BROUGHT MY PEOPLE THROUGH FIRE AND TERROR; I SAVED THE BEST OF THEM.
BUT YOU, BEING HERE...
WE DIE IF WE'RE TOGETHER.
IT NEVER SEEMS TO GET CLOSER, HAL!
NO MATTER HOW FAR DOWN WE GO!
METRON, I CAN'T COORDINATE THIS!
IT'S ALL HAPPENING AT ONCE.
I KNOW I WAS EXILED IN THE DARKNESS WITH THESE GERM-PEOPLE FOR A REASON, BUT THIS...
RING POWER AT 19%
EVEN IF WE BURN OUT, EVEN IF WE DIE TRYING, KYLE.
RING POWER AT 19%
WE WILL NOT ABANDON OUR PEOPLE TO THAT!
EVERYTHING'S GONE SO QUIET.
IF ONLY BILLY WAS HERE.
IF ONLY HE COULD SEE US NOW.
WE WON'T GIVE IN.
WE CAN MAKE HIM PROUD, FREDDIE...

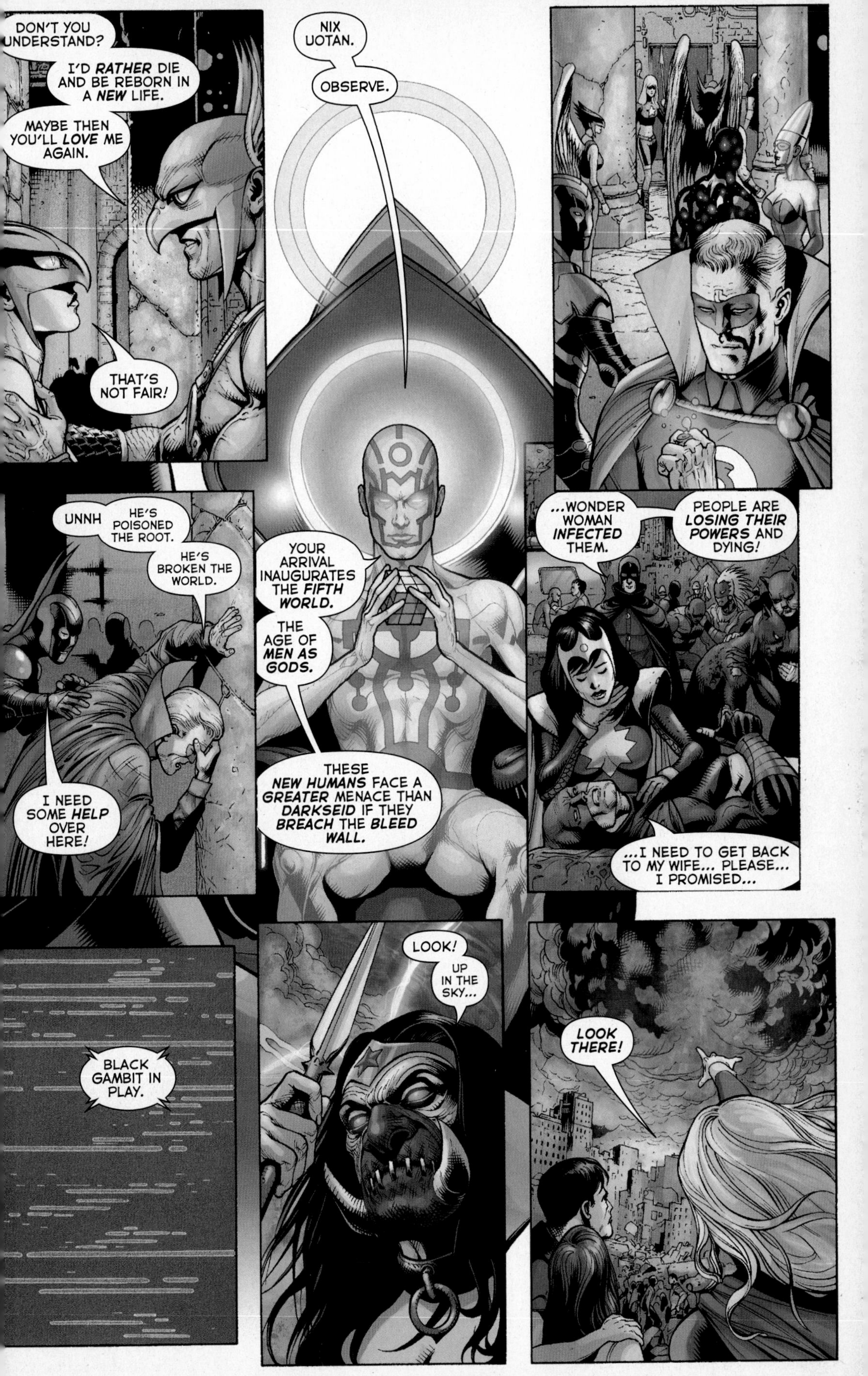
DON'T YOU UNDERSTAND?
I'D RATHER DIE AND BE REBORN IN A NEW LIFE.
MAYBE THEN YOU'LL LOVE ME AGAIN.
THAT'S NOT FAIR!
NIX UOTAN.
OBSERVE.
YOUR ARRIVAL INAUGURATES THE FIFTH WORLD.
THE AGE OF MEN AS GODS.
THESE NEW HUMANS FACE A GREATER MENACE THAN DARKSEID IF THEY BREACH THE BLEED WALL.
UNNH
HE'S POISONED THE ROOT.
HE'S BROKEN THE WORLD.
I NEED SOME HELP OVER HERE!
...WONDER WOMAN INFECTED THEM.
PEOPLE ARE LOSING THEIR POWERS AND DYING!
...I NEED TO GET BACK TO MY WIFE... PLEASE... I PROMISED...
BLACK GAMBIT IN PLAY.
LOOK!
UP IN THE SKY...
LOOK THERE!

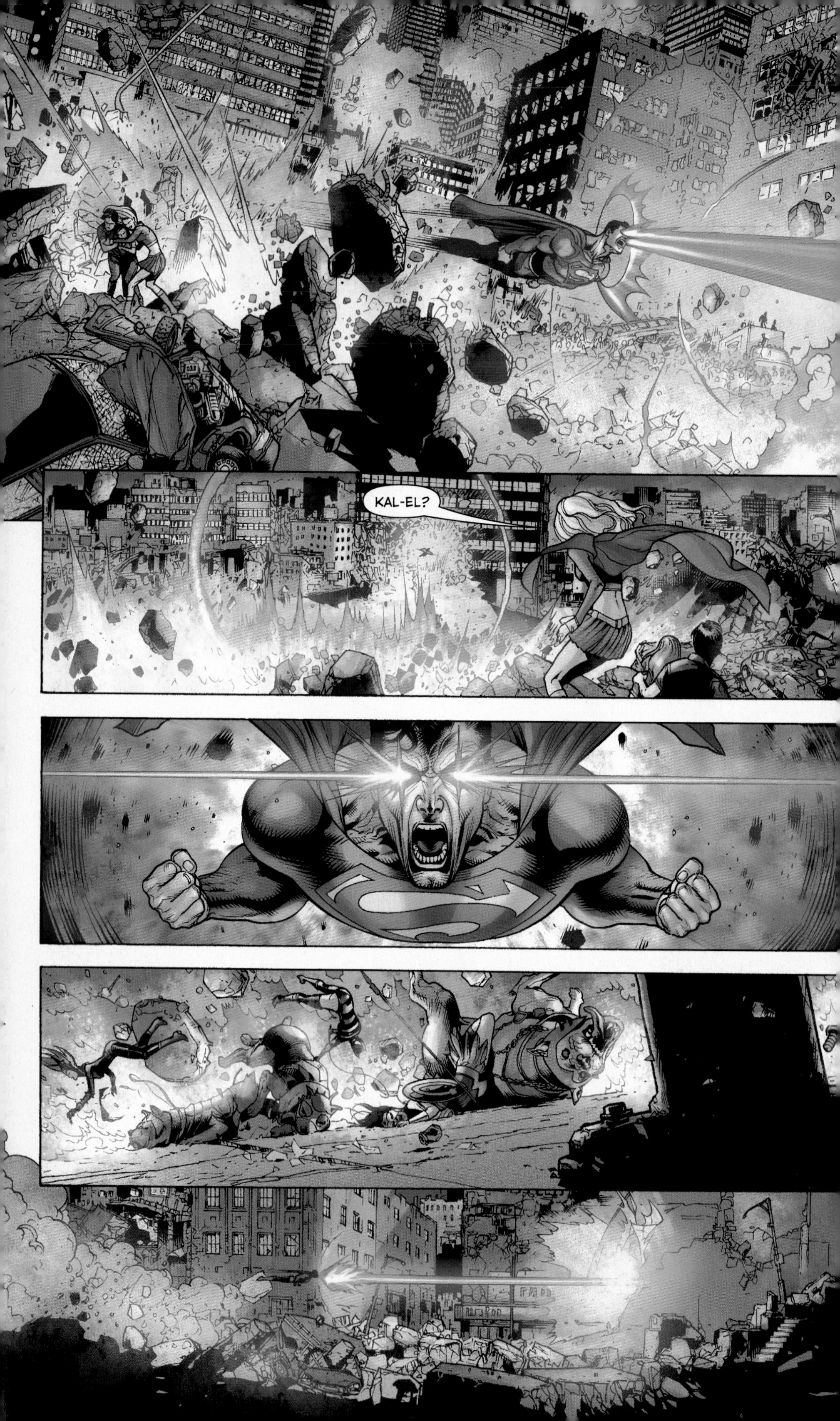
KAL-EL?

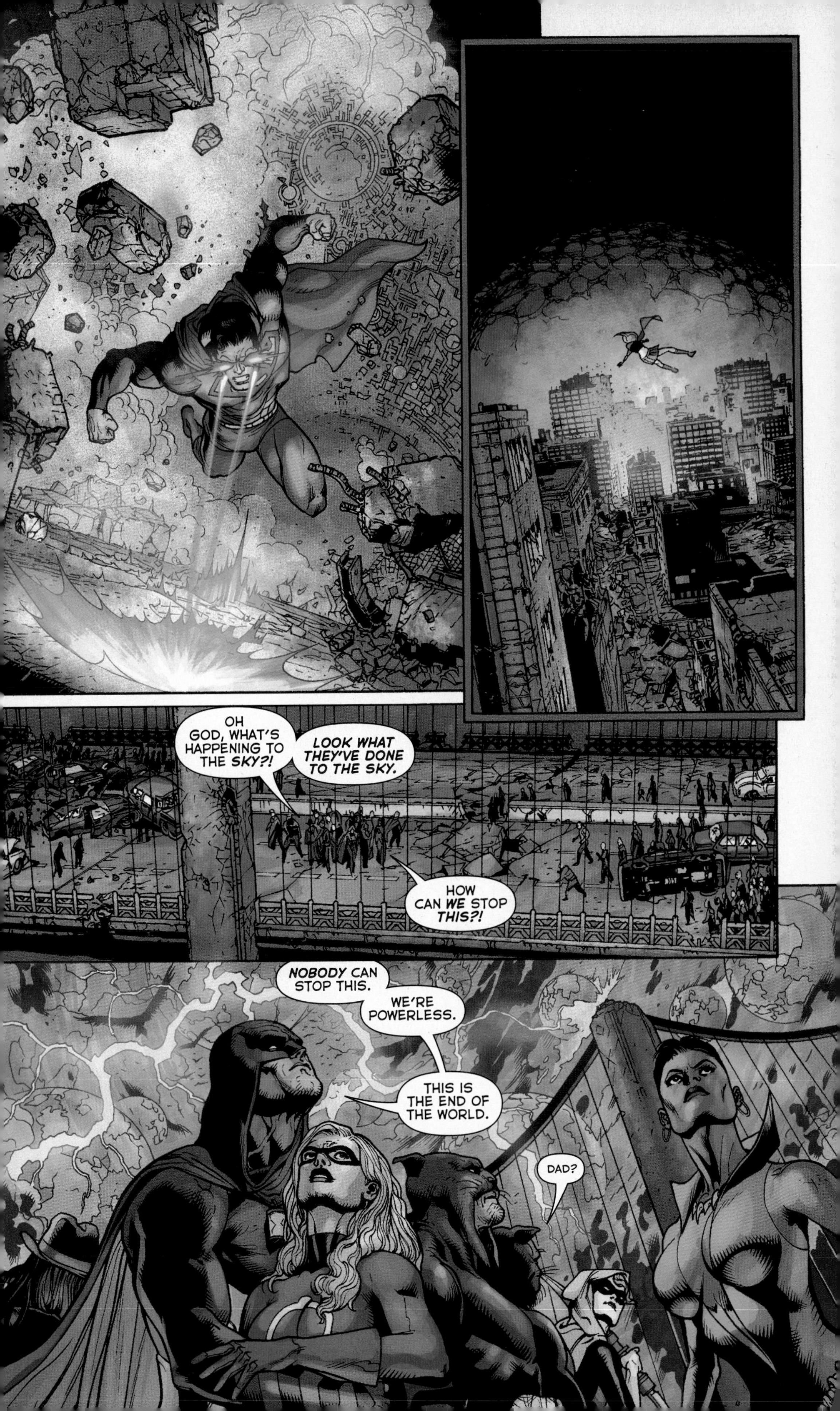
OH GOD, WHAT'S HAPPENING TO THE SKY?!
LOOK WHAT THEY'VE DONE TO THE SKY.
HOW CAN WE STOP THIS?!
NOBODY CAN STOP THIS.
WE'RE POWERLESS.
THIS IS THE END OF THE WORLD.
DAD?

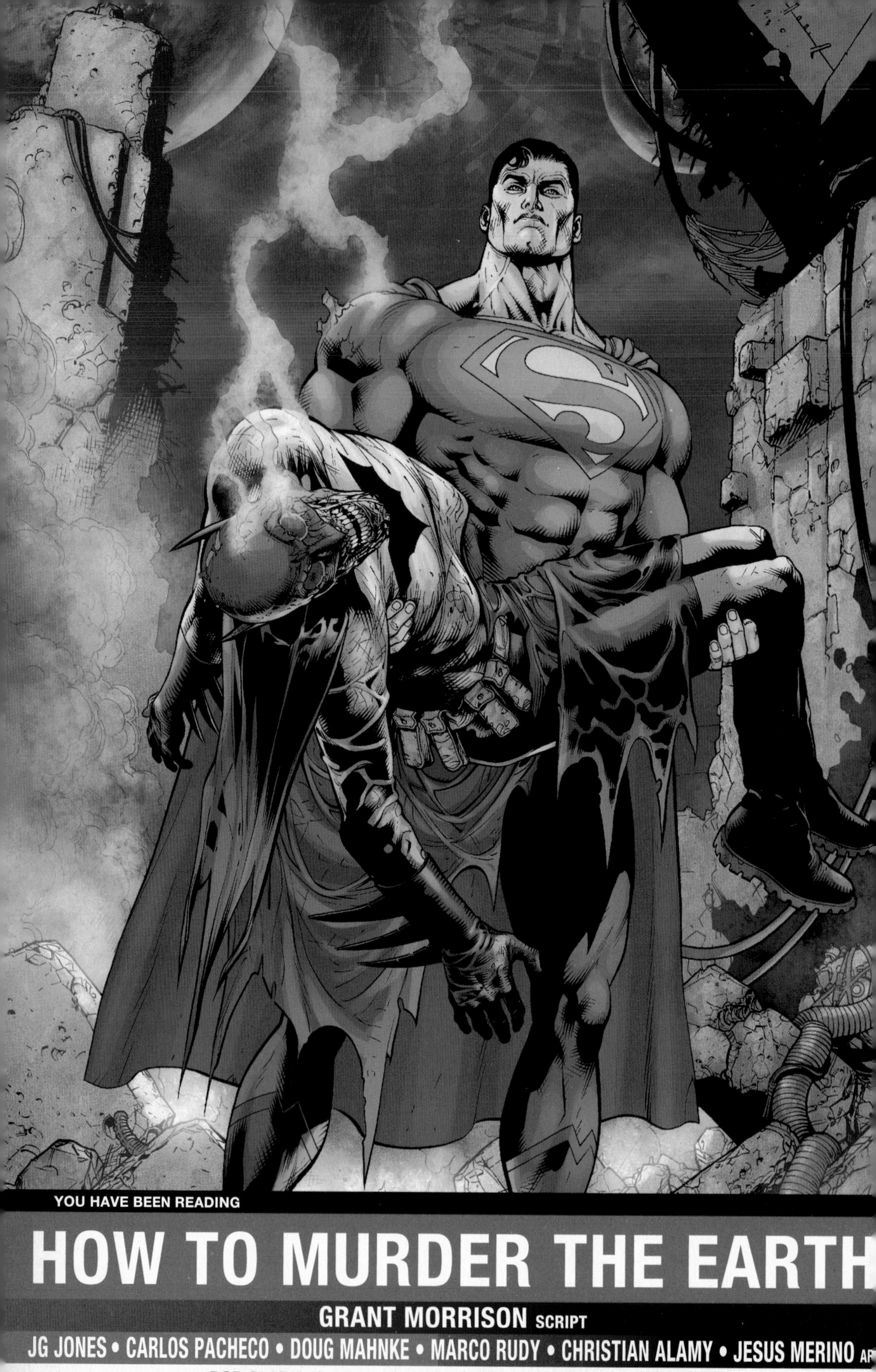

YOU HAVE BEEN READING

HOW TO MURDER THE EARTH

GRANT MORRISON SCRIPT

JG JONES • CARLOS PACHECO • DOUG MAHNKE • MARCO RUDY • CHRISTIAN ALAMY • JESUS MERINO AR

ROB CLARK JR. LETTERING **ALEX SINCLAIR & PETE PANTAZIS** COLORS

ver to FINAL CRISIS #7 JG Jones

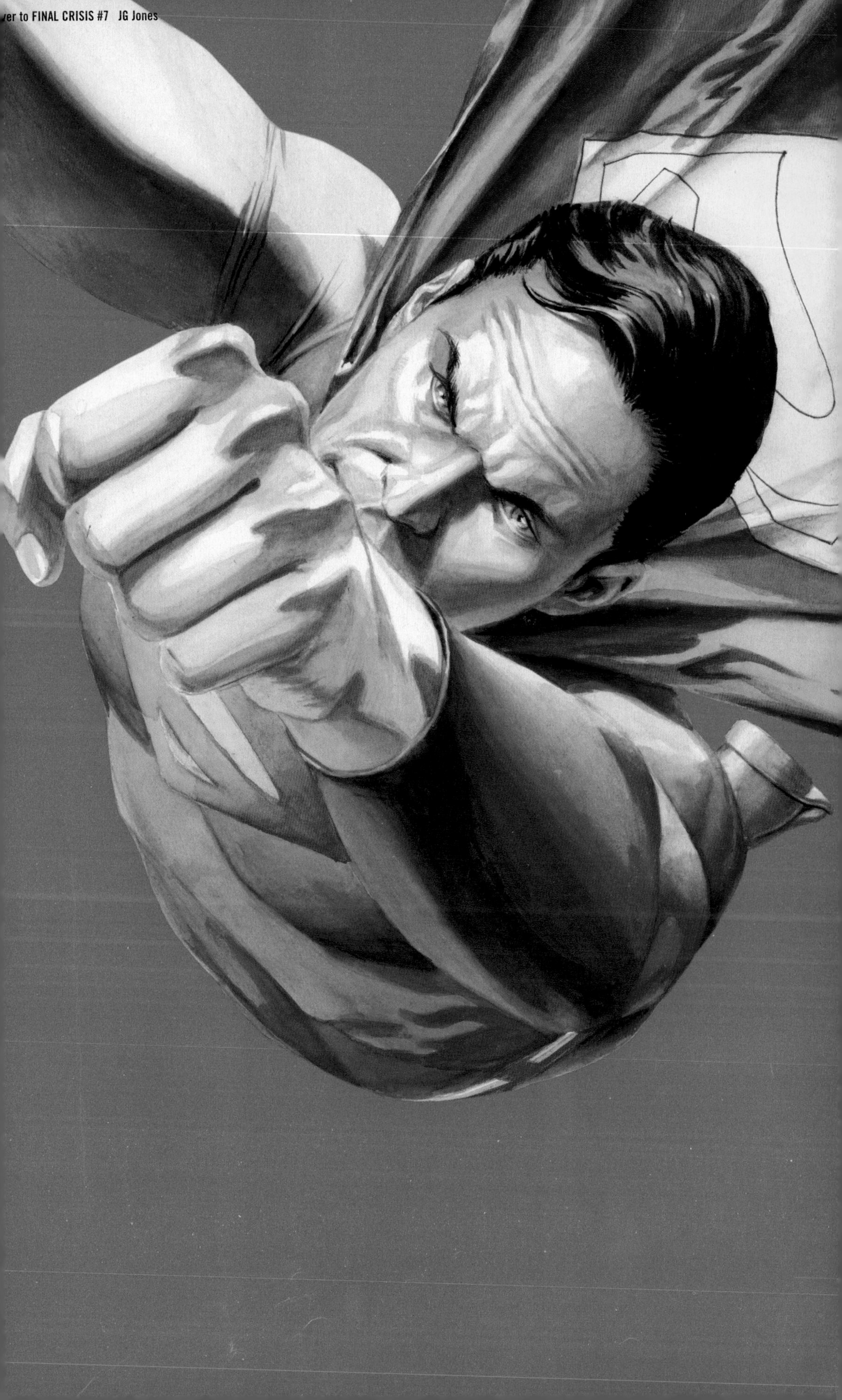

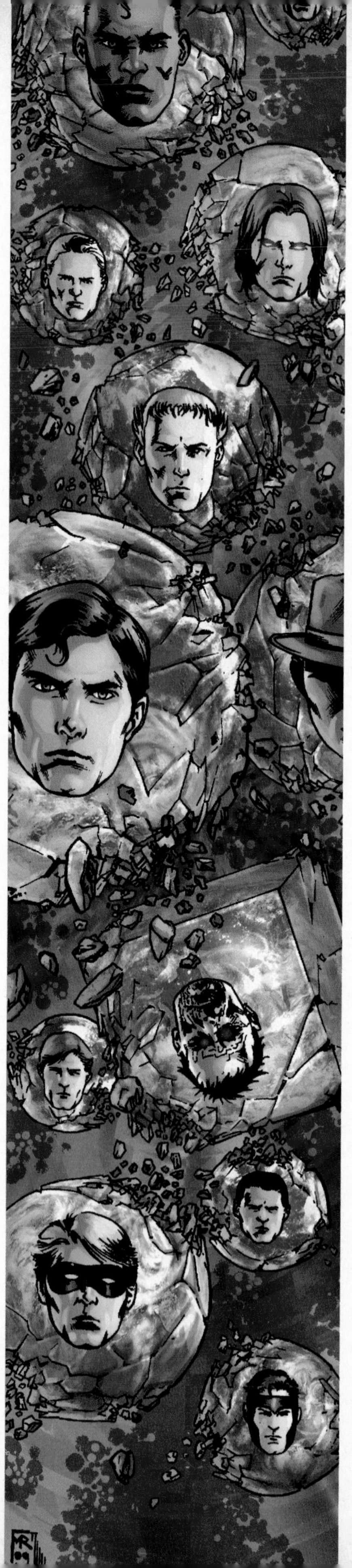

Marco Rudy with Alex Sinclair

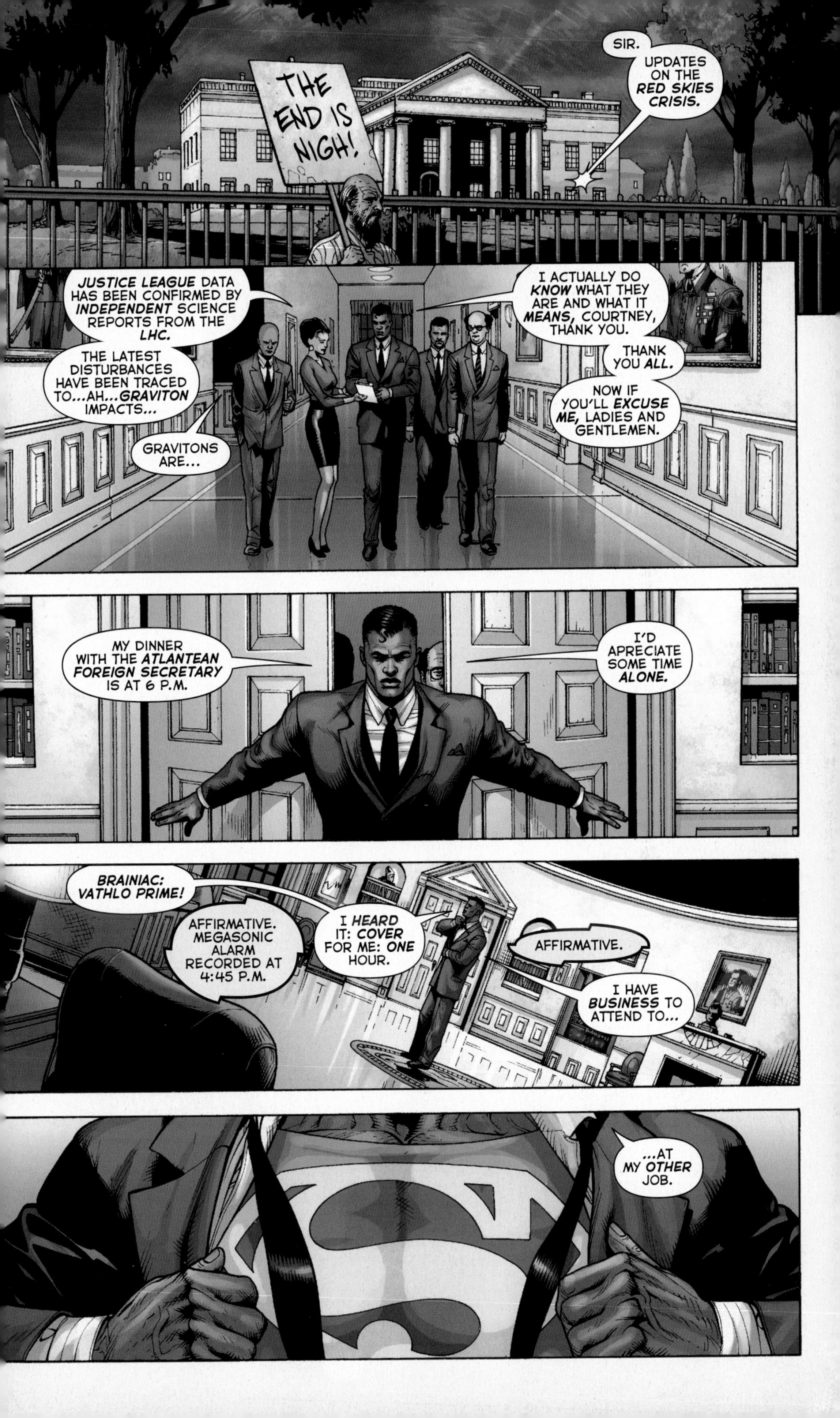
THE END IS NIGH!
SIR.
UPDATES ON THE RED SKIES CRISIS.
JUSTICE LEAGUE DATA HAS BEEN CONFIRMED BY INDEPENDENT SCIENCE REPORTS FROM THE LHC.
THE LATEST DISTURBANCES HAVE BEEN TRACED TO...AH...GRAVITON IMPACTS...
GRAVITONS ARE...
I ACTUALLY DO KNOW WHAT THEY ARE AND WHAT IT MEANS, COURTNEY, THANK YOU.
THANK YOU ALL.
NOW IF YOU'LL EXCUSE ME, LADIES AND GENTLEMEN.
MY DINNER WITH THE ATLANTEAN FOREIGN SECRETARY IS AT 6 P.M.
I'D APRECIATE SOME TIME ALONE.
BRAINIAC: VATHLO PRIME!
AFFIRMATIVE. MEGASONIC ALARM RECORDED AT 4:45 P.M.
I HEARD IT: COVER FOR ME: ONE HOUR.
AFFIRMATIVE.
I HAVE BUSINESS TO ATTEND TO...
...AT MY OTHER JOB.

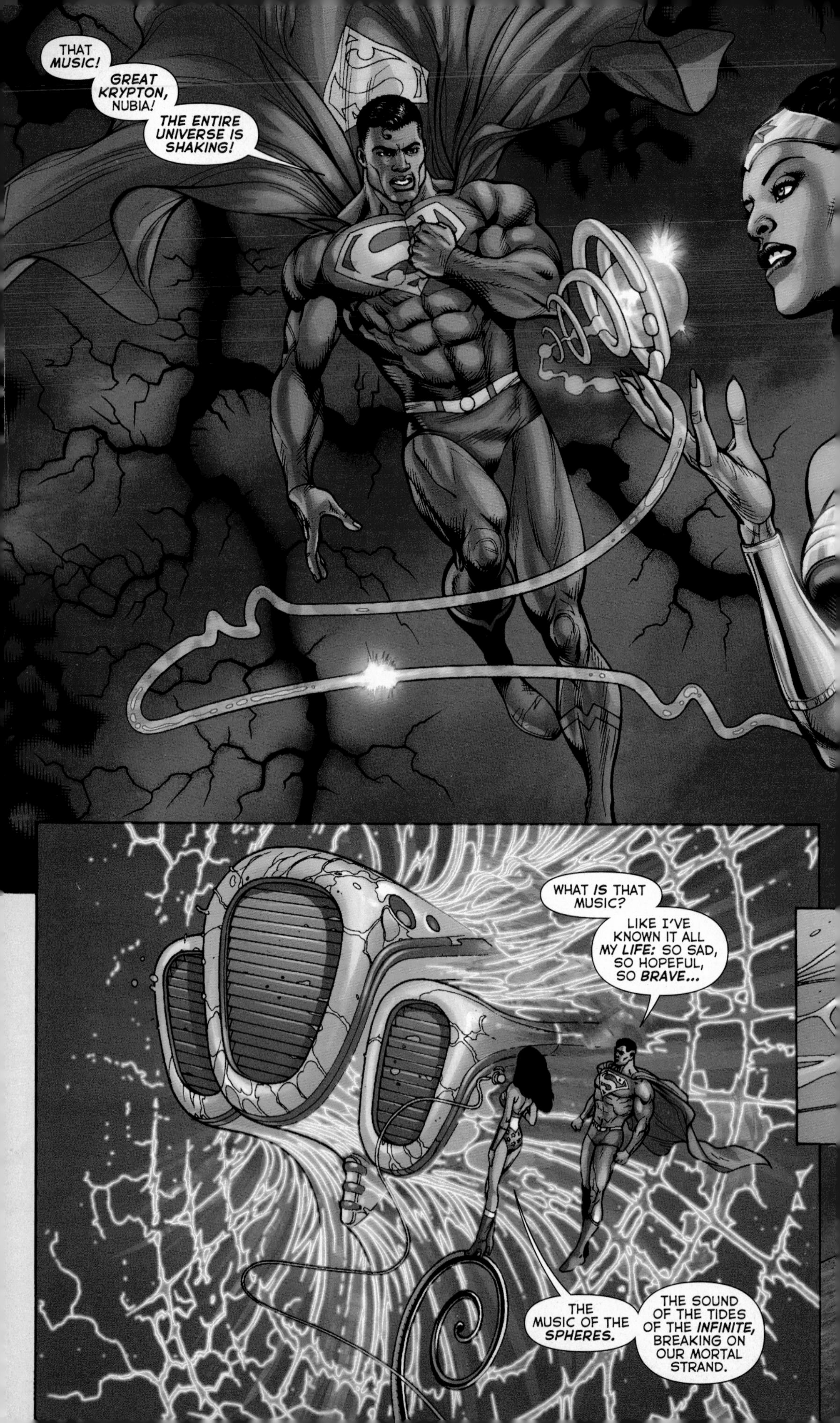
THAT MUSIC!
GREAT KRYPTON, NUBIA!
THE ENTIRE UNIVERSE IS SHAKING!
WHAT IS THAT MUSIC?
LIKE I'VE KNOWN IT ALL MY LIFE: SO SAD, SO HOPEFUL, SO BRAVE...
THE MUSIC OF THE SPHERES.
THE SOUND OF THE TIDES OF THE INFINITE, BREAKING ON OUR MORTAL STRAND.

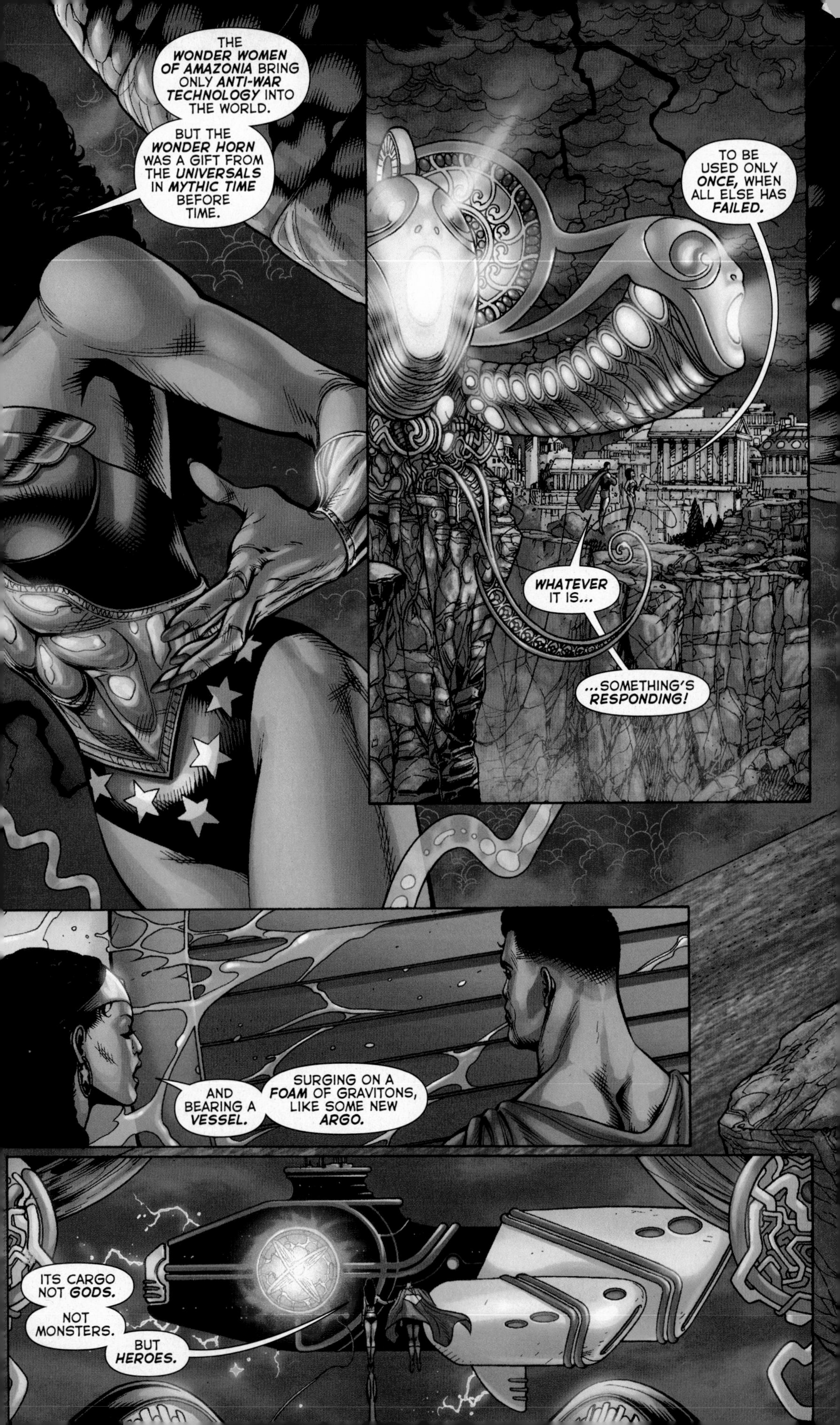
THE WONDER WOMEN OF AMAZONIA BRING ONLY ANTI-WAR TECHNOLOGY INTO THE WORLD.
BUT THE WONDER HORN WAS A GIFT FROM THE UNIVERSALS IN MYTHIC TIME BEFORE TIME.
TO BE USED ONLY ONCE, WHEN ALL ELSE HAS FAILED.
WHATEVER IT IS...
...SOMETHING'S RESPONDING!
AND BEARING A VESSEL.
SURGING ON A FOAM OF GRAVITONS, LIKE SOME NEW ARGO.
ITS CARGO NOT GODS.
NOT MONSTERS.
BUT HEROES.

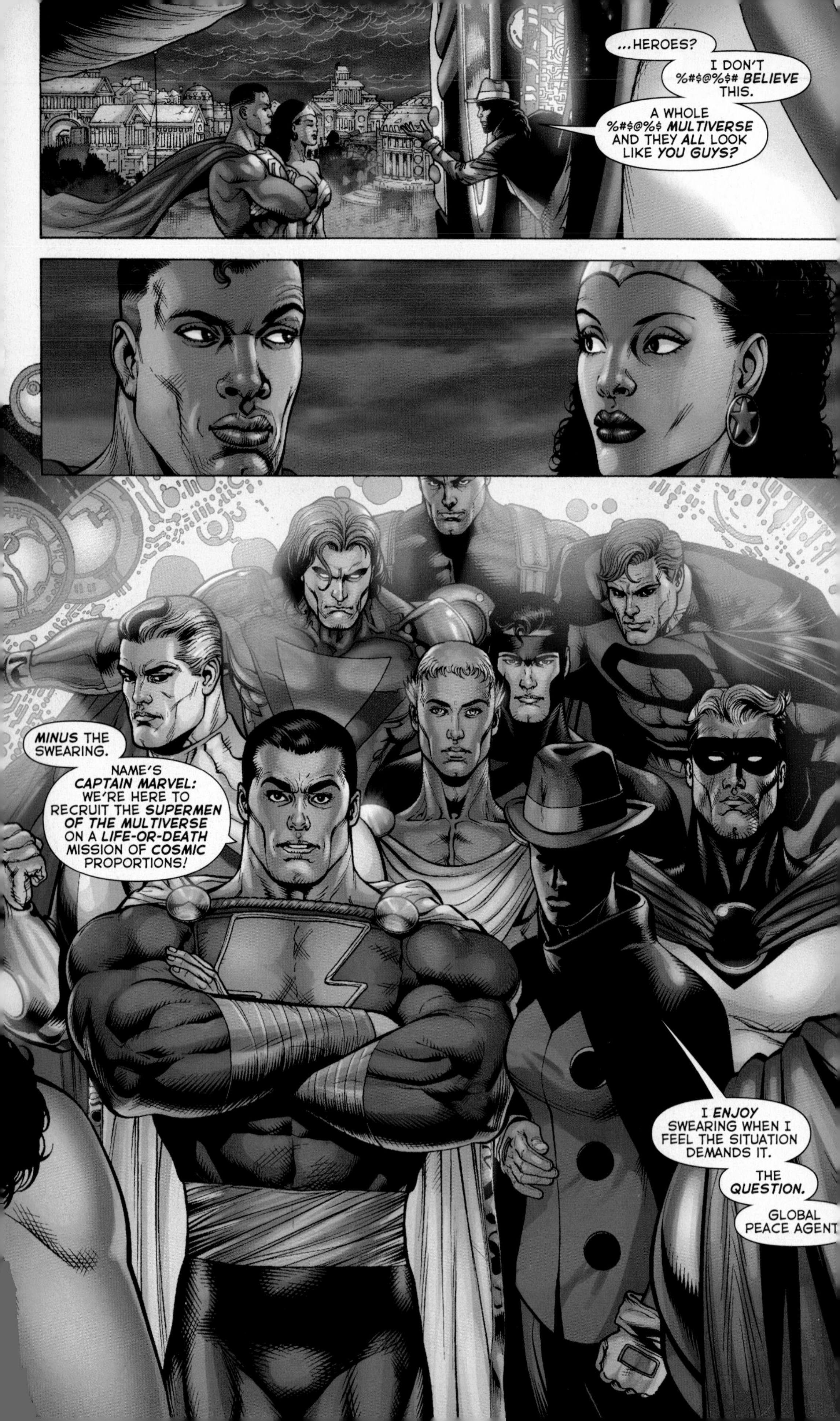
...HEROES?
I DON'T %#$@%$# BELIEVE THIS.
A WHOLE %#$@%$ MULTIVERSE AND THEY ALL LOOK LIKE YOU GUYS?
MINUS THE SWEARING.
NAME'S CAPTAIN MARVEL: WE'RE HERE TO RECRUIT THE SUPERMEN OF THE MULTIVERSE ON A LIFE-OR-DEATH MISSION OF COSMIC PROPORTIONS!
I ENJOY SWEARING WHEN I FEEL THE SITUATION DEMANDS IT.
THE QUESTION.
GLOBAL PEACE AGENT

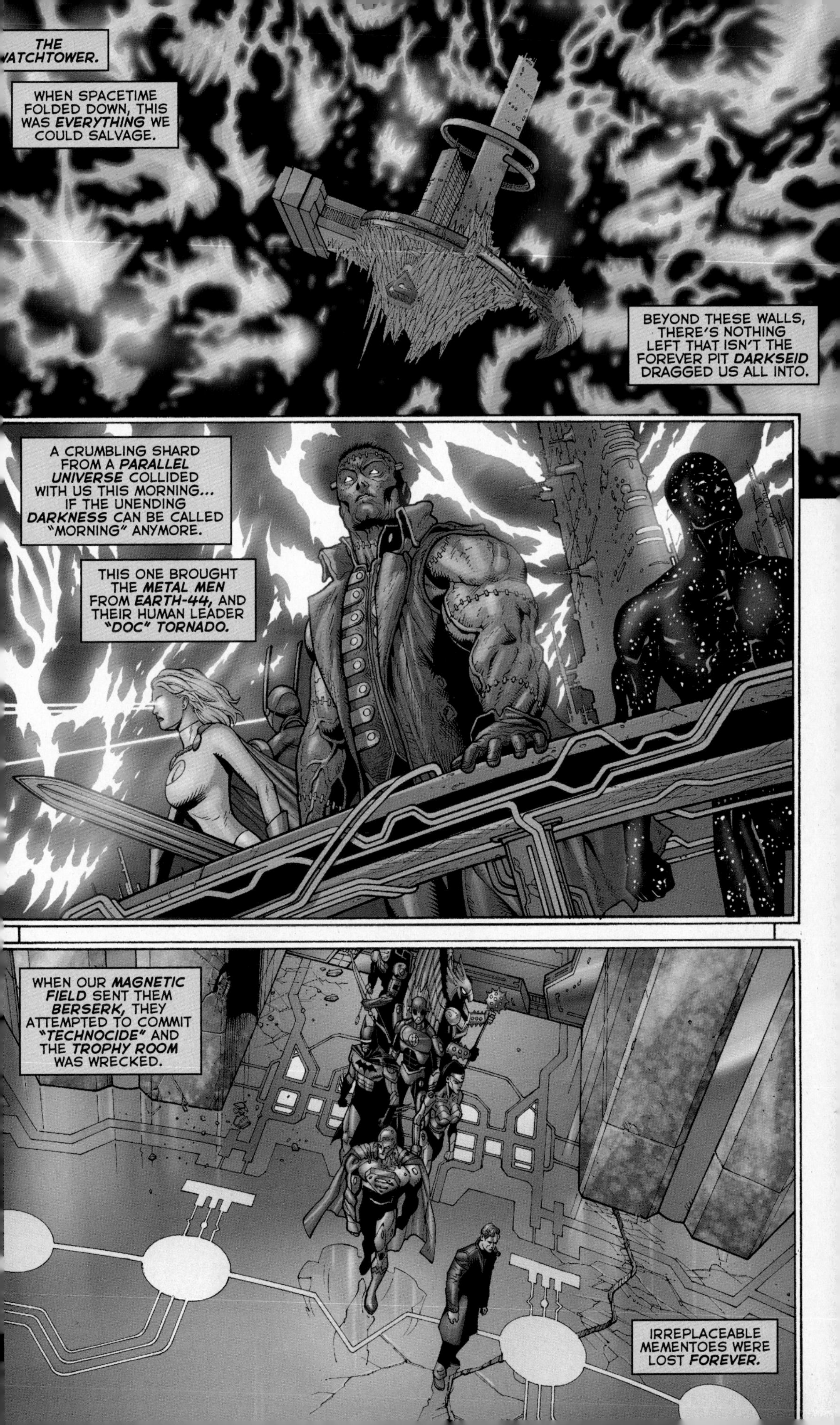
THE WATCHTOWER.
WHEN SPACETIME FOLDED DOWN, THIS WAS EVERYTHING WE COULD SALVAGE.
BEYOND THESE WALLS, THERE'S NOTHING LEFT THAT ISN'T THE FOREVER PIT DARKSEID DRAGGED US ALL INTO.
A CRUMBLING SHARD FROM A PARALLEL UNIVERSE COLLIDED WITH US THIS MORNING... IF THE UNENDING DARKNESS CAN BE CALLED "MORNING" ANYMORE.
THIS ONE BROUGHT THE METAL MEN FROM EARTH-44, AND THEIR HUMAN LEADER "DOC" TORNADO.
WHEN OUR MAGNETIC FIELD SENT THEM BERSERK, THEY ATTEMPTED TO COMMIT "TECHNOCIDE" AND THE TROPHY ROOM WAS WRECKED.
IRREPLACEABLE MEMENTOES WERE LOST FOREVER.

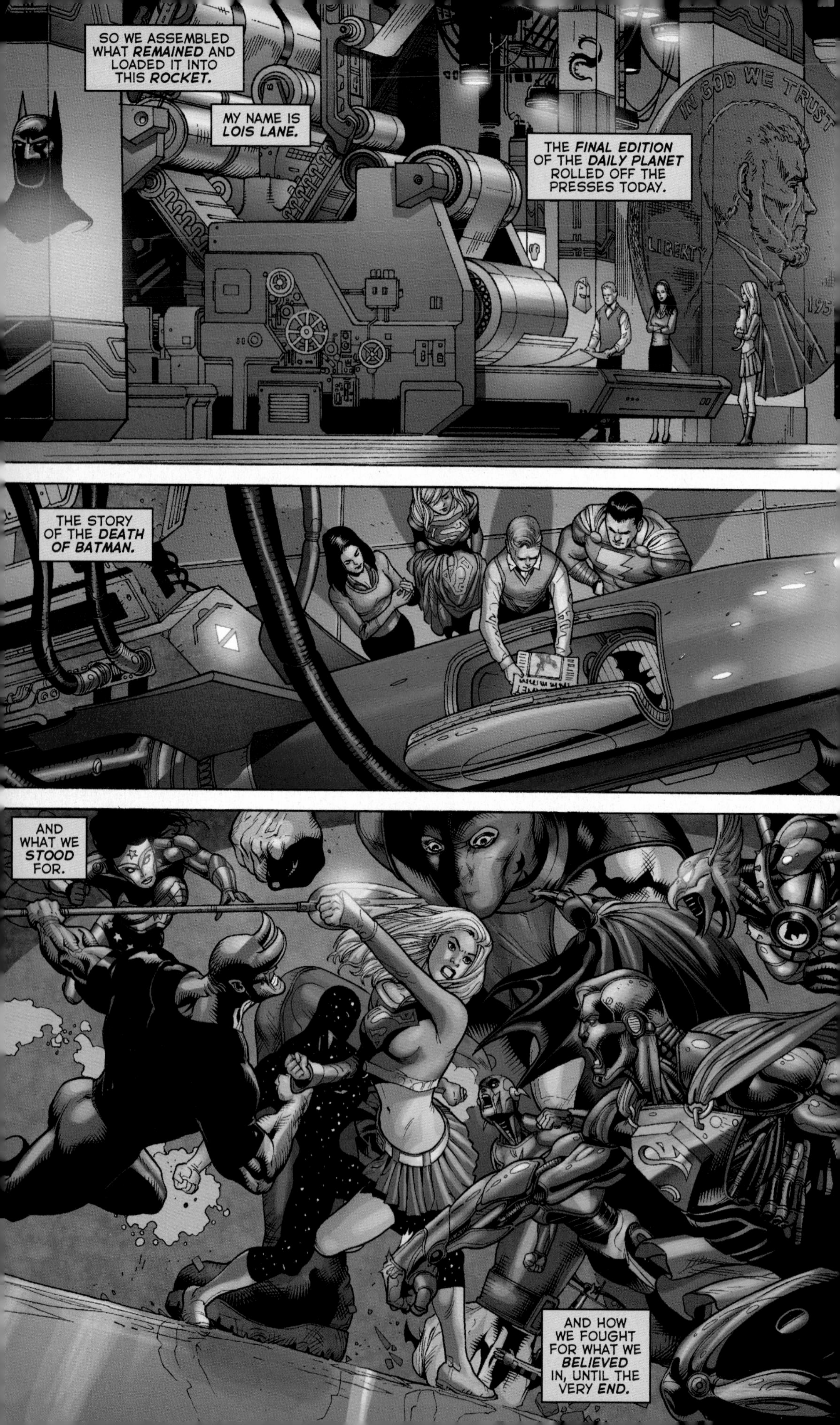
SO WE ASSEMBLED WHAT REMAINED AND LOADED IT INTO THIS ROCKET.
MY NAME IS LOIS LANE.
THE FINAL EDITION OF THE DAILY PLANET ROLLED OFF THE PRESSES TODAY.
IN GOD WE TRUST
LIBERTY
THE STORY OF THE DEATH OF BATMAN.
AND WHAT WE STOOD FOR.
AND HOW WE FOUGHT FOR WHAT WE BELIEVED IN, UNTIL THE VERY END.

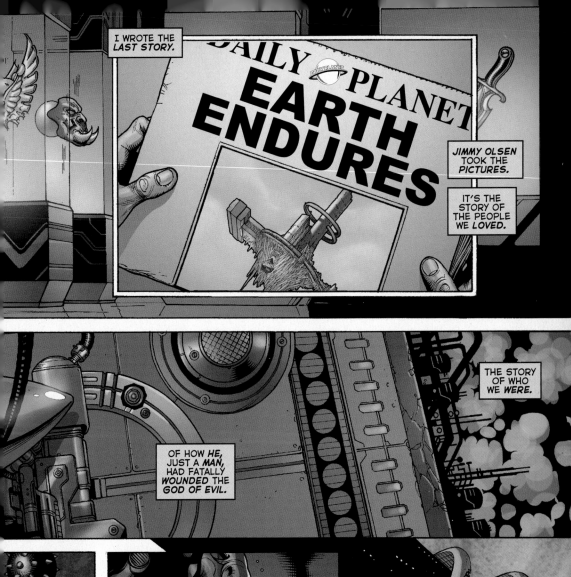

I WROTE THE *LAST STORY.*

DAILY PLANET
EARTH ENDURES

JIMMY OLSEN TOOK THE *PICTURES.*

IT'S THE STORY OF THE PEOPLE WE *LOVED.*

THE STORY OF WHO WE *WERE.*

OF HOW *HE,* JUST A *MAN,* HAD FATALLY *WOUNDED* THE GOD OF EVIL.

CALL IT A MESSAGE IN A BOTTLE.

MAYBE *SOMEONE,* SOMEWHERE, WILL *FIND* IT.

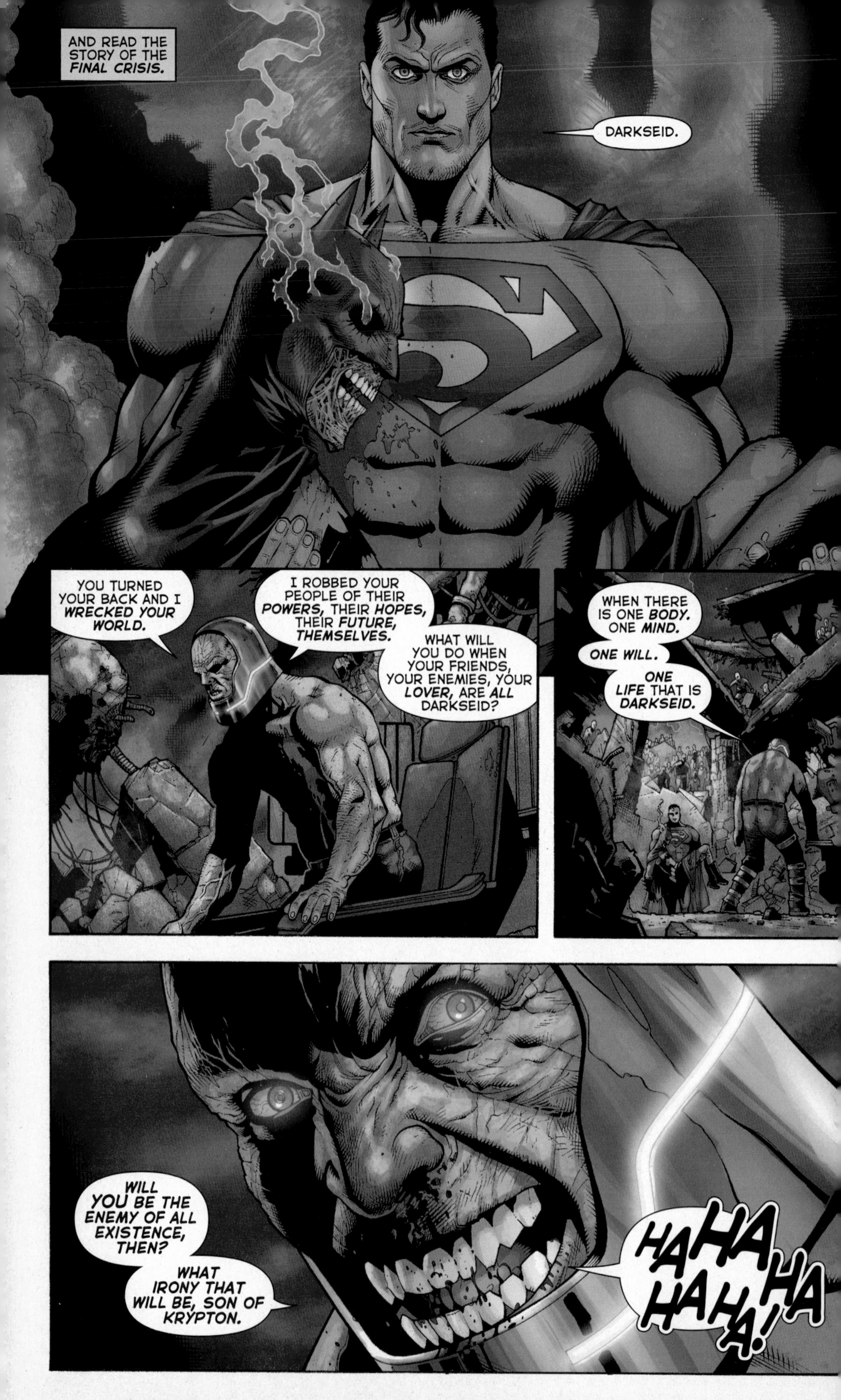
AND READ THE STORY OF THE *FINAL CRISIS.*
DARKSEID.
YOU TURNED YOUR BACK AND I *WRECKED YOUR WORLD.*
I ROBBED YOUR PEOPLE OF THEIR *POWERS,* THEIR *HOPES,* THEIR *FUTURE, THEMSELVES.*
WHAT WILL YOU DO WHEN YOUR FRIENDS, YOUR ENEMIES, YOUR *LOVER,* ARE *ALL* DARKSEID?
WHEN THERE IS ONE *BODY.* ONE *MIND.*
ONE WILL.
ONE LIFE THAT IS *DARKSEID.*
WILL YOU BE THE ENEMY OF ALL EXISTENCE, THEN?
WHAT IRONY THAT WILL BE, SON OF KRYPTON.
HAHAHA HAHAHA!

MONSTER! WHAT HAVE YOU DONE!

KILL ME, SUPERMAN.

KILL THE FRAIL OLD MAN UPON WHOSE SOUL DARKSEID FED AND FATTENED!

HOW CAN YOU HURT A FOE MADE OF PEOPLE?

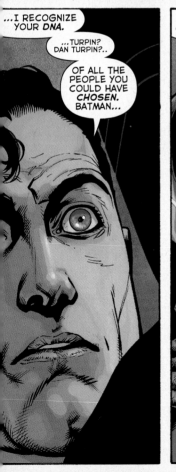

...I RECOGNIZE YOUR DNA.

...TURPIN? DAN TURPIN?..

OF ALL THE PEOPLE YOU COULD HAVE CHOSEN, BATMAN...

HE WOULD HAVE RESISTED LONGER THAN I WISHED!

TURPIN STRUGGLED JUST ENOUGH TO NURTURE ME BEFORE HIS SURRENDER!

KILL HIM.

AUUGH!

KILL ME AND YOU KILL EVERYTHING!

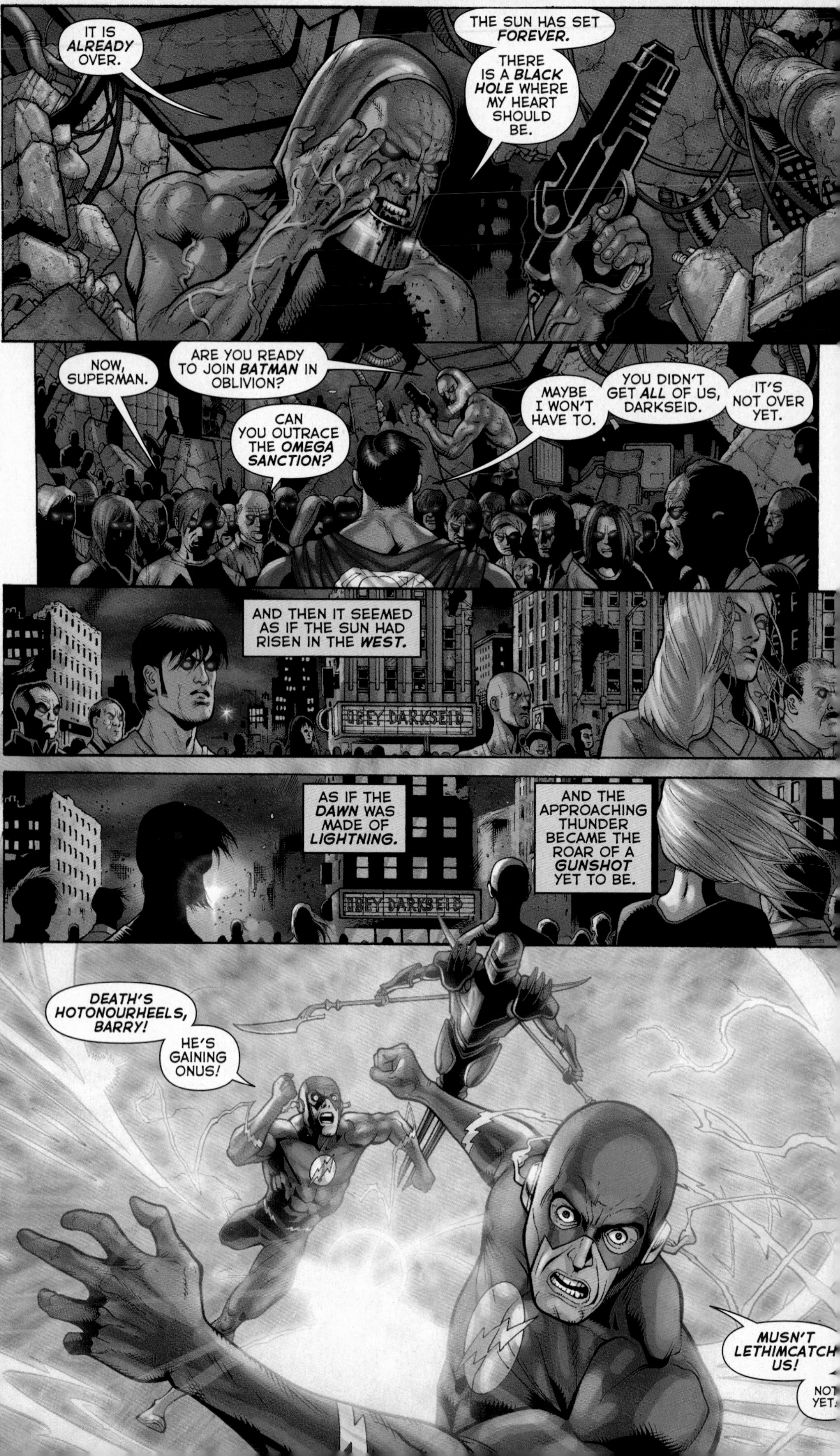

IT IS ALREADY OVER.
THE SUN HAS SET FOREVER.
THERE IS A BLACK HOLE WHERE MY HEART SHOULD BE.
NOW, SUPERMAN.
ARE YOU READY TO JOIN BATMAN IN OBLIVION?
CAN YOU OUTRACE THE OMEGA SANCTION?
MAYBE I WON'T HAVE TO.
YOU DIDN'T GET ALL OF US, DARKSEID.
IT'S NOT OVER YET.
AND THEN IT SEEMED AS IF THE SUN HAD RISEN IN THE WEST.
OBEY DARKSEID
AS IF THE DAWN WAS MADE OF LIGHTNING.
AND THE APPROACHING THUNDER BECAME THE ROAR OF A GUNSHOT YET TO BE.
OBEY DARKSEID
DEATH'S HOTONOURHEELS, BARRY!
HE'S GAINING ONUS!
MUSN'T LETHIMCATCH US!
NOT YET.

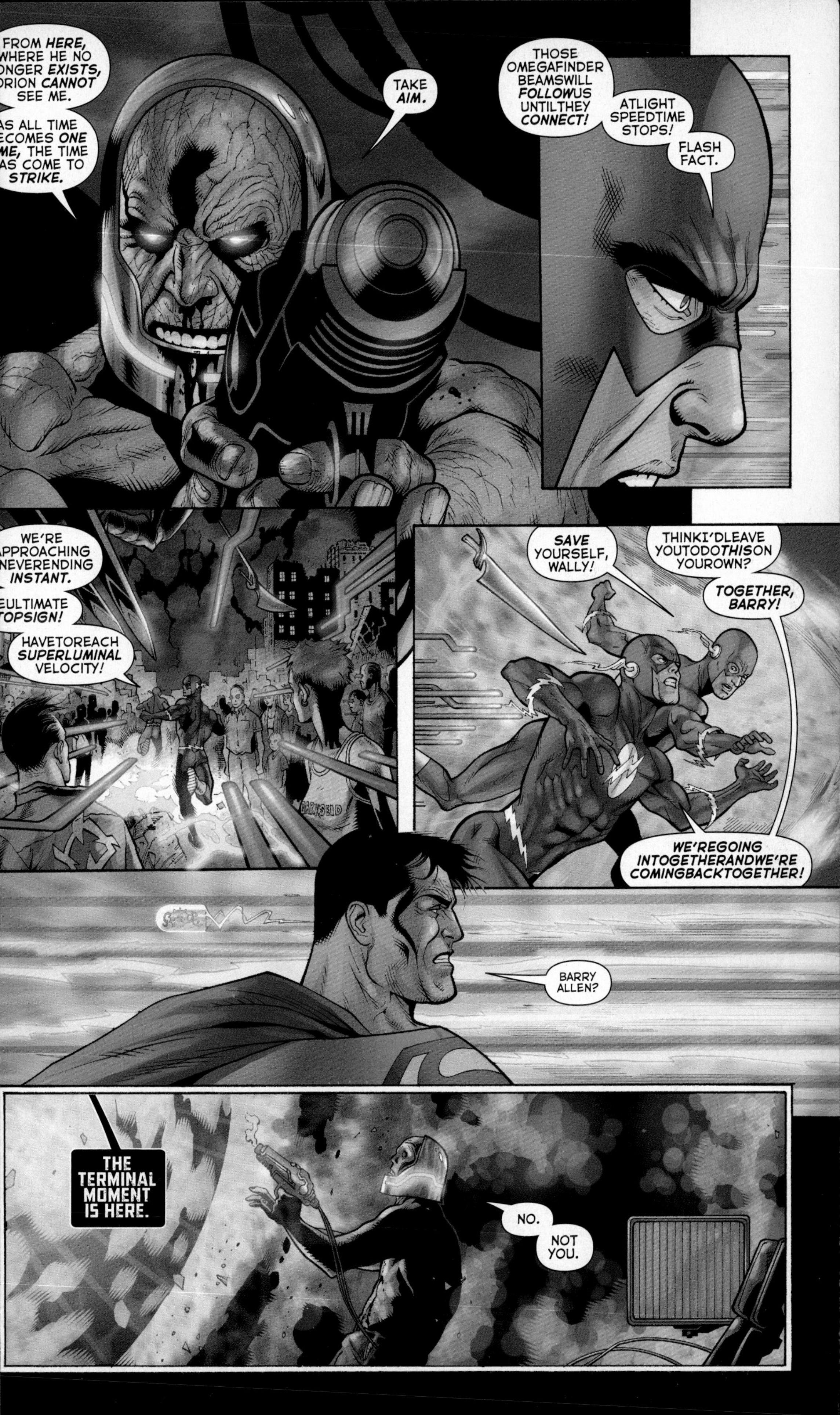
FROM HERE, WHERE HE NO LONGER EXISTS, ORION CANNOT SEE ME.
AS ALL TIME BECOMES ONE TIME, THE TIME HAS COME TO STRIKE.
TAKE AIM.
THOSE OMEGAFINDER BEAMSWILL FOLLOWUS UNTILTHEY CONNECT!
ATLIGHT SPEEDTIME STOPS!
FLASH FACT.
WE'RE APPROACHING NEVERENDING INSTANT.
EULTIMATE TOPSIGN!
HAVETOREACH SUPERLUMINAL VELOCITY!
SAVE YOURSELF, WALLY!
THINKI'DLEAVE YOUTODOTHISON YOUROWN?
TOGETHER, BARRY!
WE'REGOING INTOGETHERANDWE'RE COMINGBACKTOGETHER!
BARRY ALLEN?
THE TERMINAL MOMENT IS HERE.
NO.
NOT YOU.

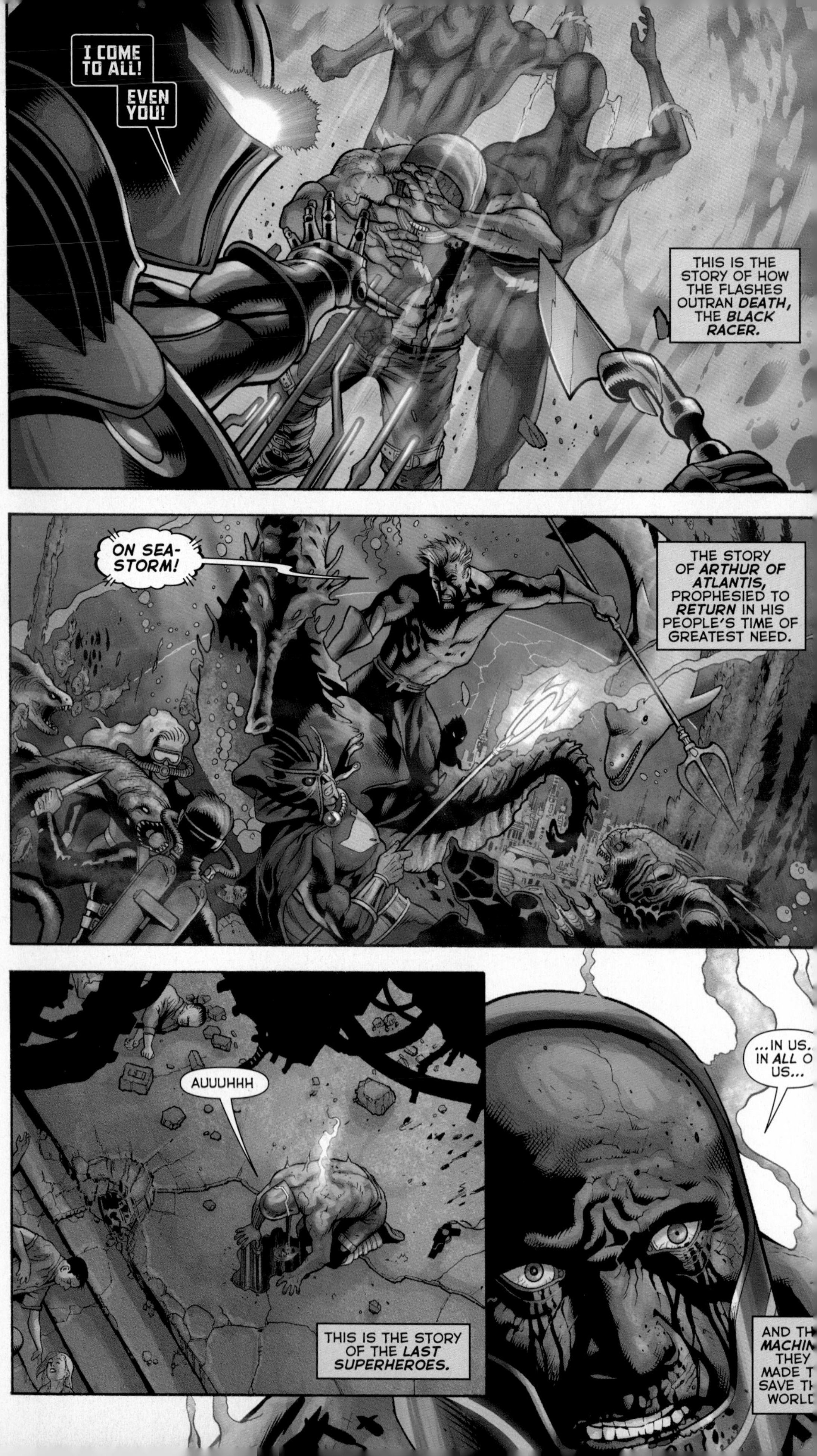
I COME TO ALL!
EVEN YOU!
THIS IS THE STORY OF HOW THE FLASHES OUTRAN *DEATH*, THE *BLACK RACER.*
ON SEA-STORM!
THE STORY OF *ARTHUR OF ATLANTIS,* PROPHESIED TO *RETURN* IN HIS PEOPLE'S TIME OF GREATEST NEED.
AUUUHHH
THIS IS THE STORY OF THE *LAST SUPERHEROES.*
...IN US. IN *ALL* O US...
AND TH *MACHIN* THEY MADE T SAVE TH WORLD

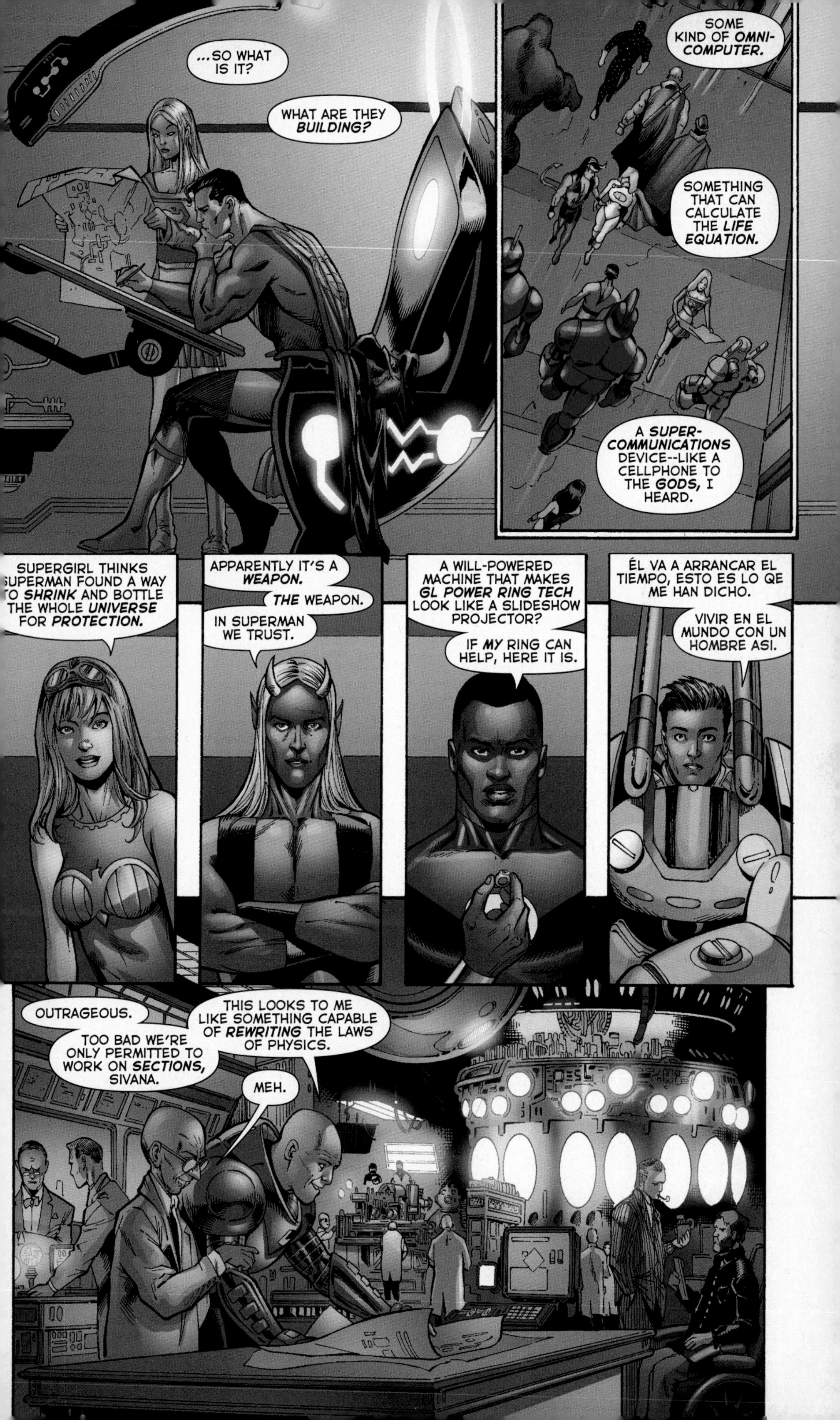

...SO WHAT IS IT?
WHAT ARE THEY BUILDING?
SOME KIND OF OMNI-COMPUTER.
SOMETHING THAT CAN CALCULATE THE LIFE EQUATION.
A SUPER-COMMUNICATIONS DEVICE--LIKE A CELLPHONE TO THE GODS, I HEARD.
SUPERGIRL THINKS SUPERMAN FOUND A WAY TO SHRINK AND BOTTLE THE WHOLE UNIVERSE FOR PROTECTION.
APPARENTLY IT'S A WEAPON.
THE WEAPON.
IN SUPERMAN WE TRUST.
A WILL-POWERED MACHINE THAT MAKES GL POWER RING TECH LOOK LIKE A SLIDESHOW PROJECTOR?
IF MY RING CAN HELP, HERE IT IS.
ÉL VA A ARRANCAR EL TIEMPO, ESTO ES LO QE ME HAN DICHO.
VIVIR EN EL MUNDO CON UN HOMBRE ASI.
OUTRAGEOUS.
TOO BAD WE'RE ONLY PERMITTED TO WORK ON SECTIONS, SIVANA.
THIS LOOKS TO ME LIKE SOMETHING CAPABLE OF REWRITING THE LAWS OF PHYSICS.
MEH.

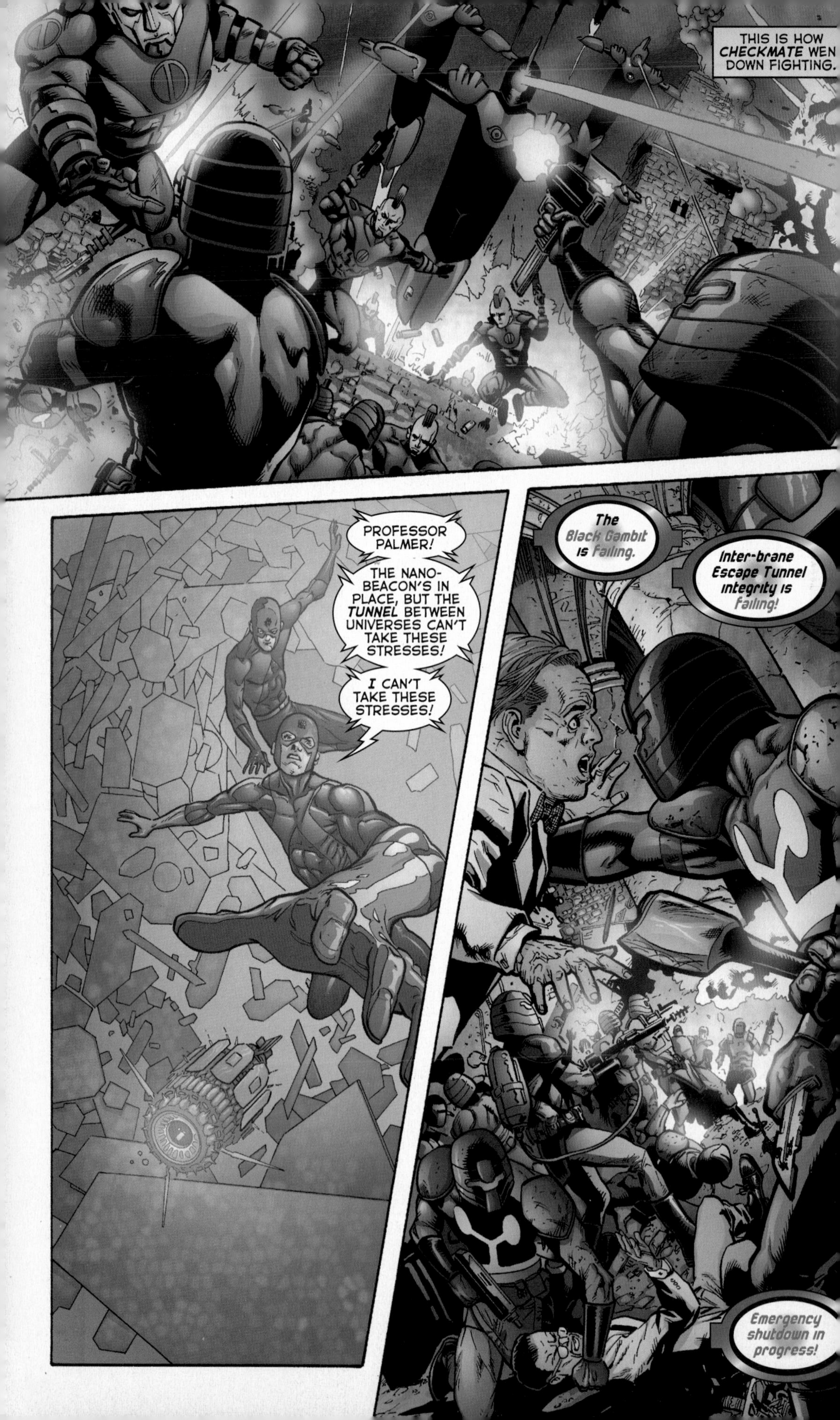
THIS IS HOW *CHECKMATE* WENT DOWN FIGHTING.
PROFESSOR PALMER!
THE NANO-BEACON'S IN PLACE, BUT THE *TUNNEL* BETWEEN UNIVERSES CAN'T TAKE THESE STRESSES!
I CAN'T TAKE THESE STRESSES!
The Black Gambit is failing.
Inter-brane Escape Tunnel integrity is failing!
Emergency shutdown in progress!

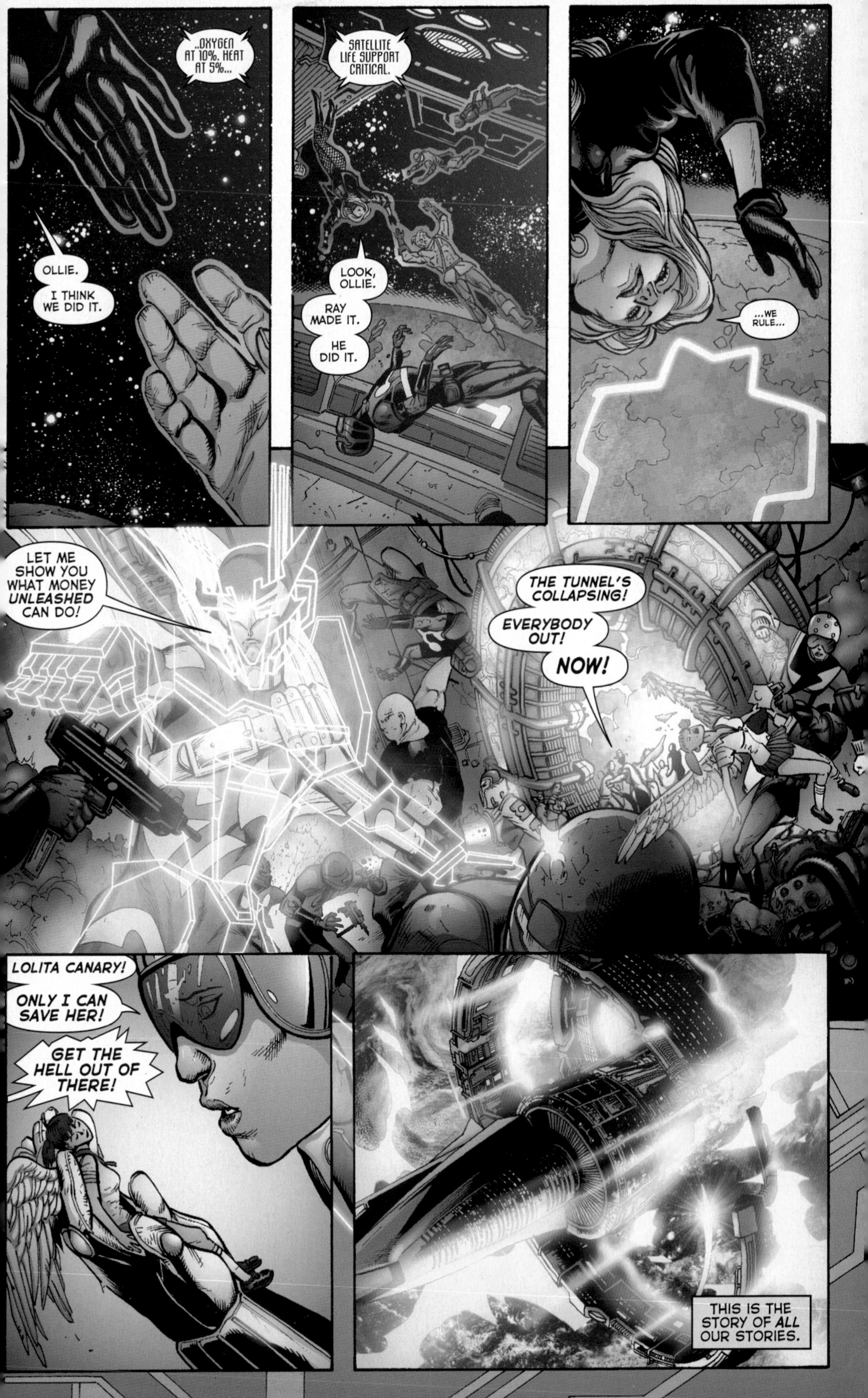
..OXYGEN AT 10%. HEAT AT 5%...
OLLIE.
I THINK WE DID IT.
SATELLITE LIFE SUPPORT CRITICAL.
LOOK, OLLIE.
RAY MADE IT.
HE DID IT.
...WE RULE...
LET ME SHOW YOU WHAT MONEY *UNLEASHED* CAN DO!
THE TUNNEL'S COLLAPSING!
EVERYBODY OUT!
NOW!
LOLITA CANARY!
ONLY I CAN SAVE HER!
GET THE HELL OUT OF THERE!
THIS IS THE STORY OF *ALL* OUR STORIES.

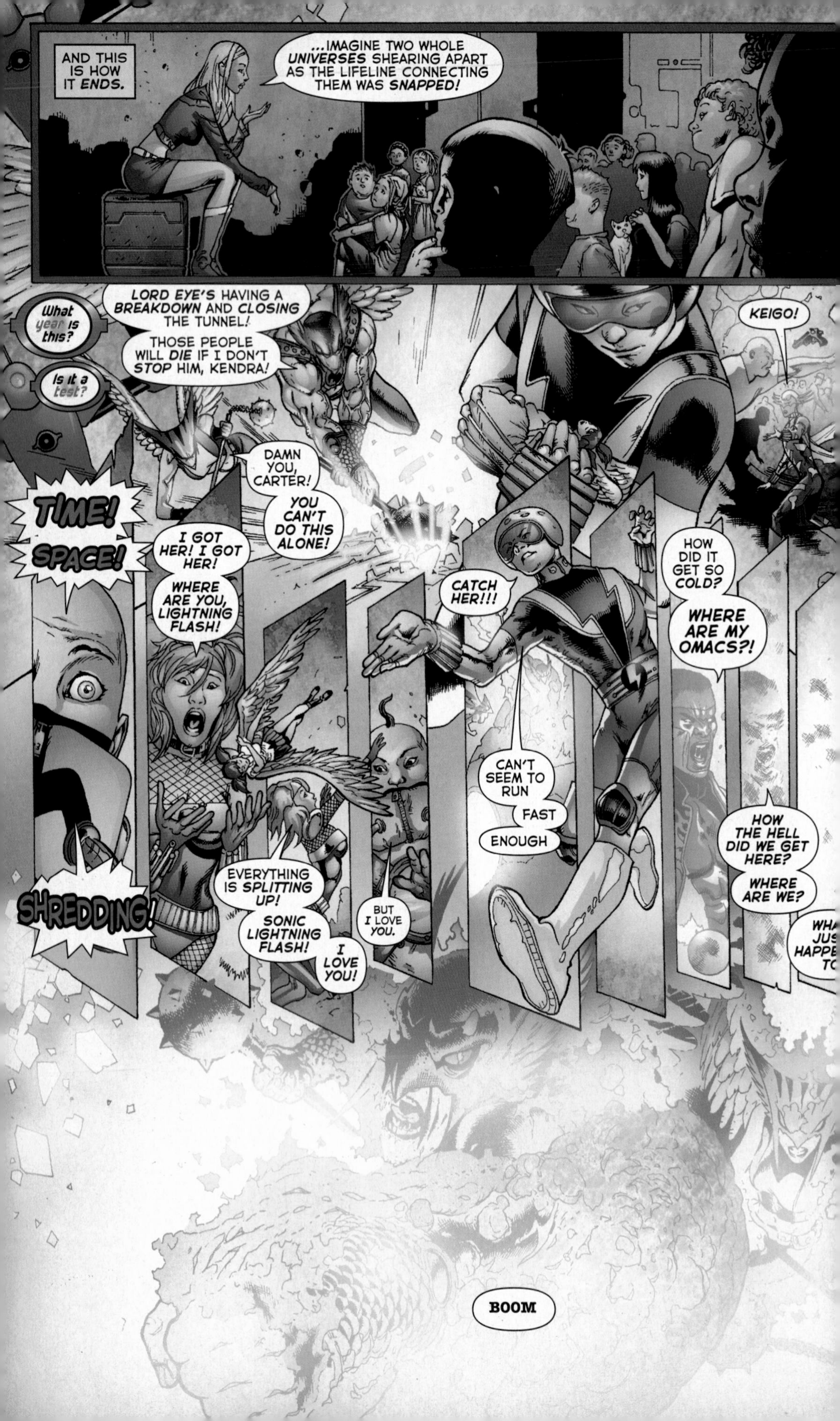
AND THIS IS HOW IT ENDS.
...IMAGINE TWO WHOLE UNIVERSES SHEARING APART AS THE LIFELINE CONNECTING THEM WAS SNAPPED!
What year is this?
Is it a test?
LORD EYE'S HAVING A BREAKDOWN AND CLOSING THE TUNNEL!
THOSE PEOPLE WILL DIE IF I DON'T STOP HIM, KENDRA!
KEIGO!
DAMN YOU, CARTER!
YOU CAN'T DO THIS ALONE!
TIME!
SPACE!
I GOT HER! I GOT HER!
WHERE ARE YOU, LIGHTNING FLASH!
CATCH HER!!!
HOW DID IT GET SO COLD?
WHERE ARE MY OMACS?!
CAN'T SEEM TO RUN
FAST
ENOUGH
HOW THE HELL DID WE GET HERE?
WHERE ARE WE?
SHREDDING!
EVERYTHING IS SPLITTING UP!
SONIC LIGHTNING FLASH!
BUT I LOVE YOU.
I LOVE YOU!
BOOM

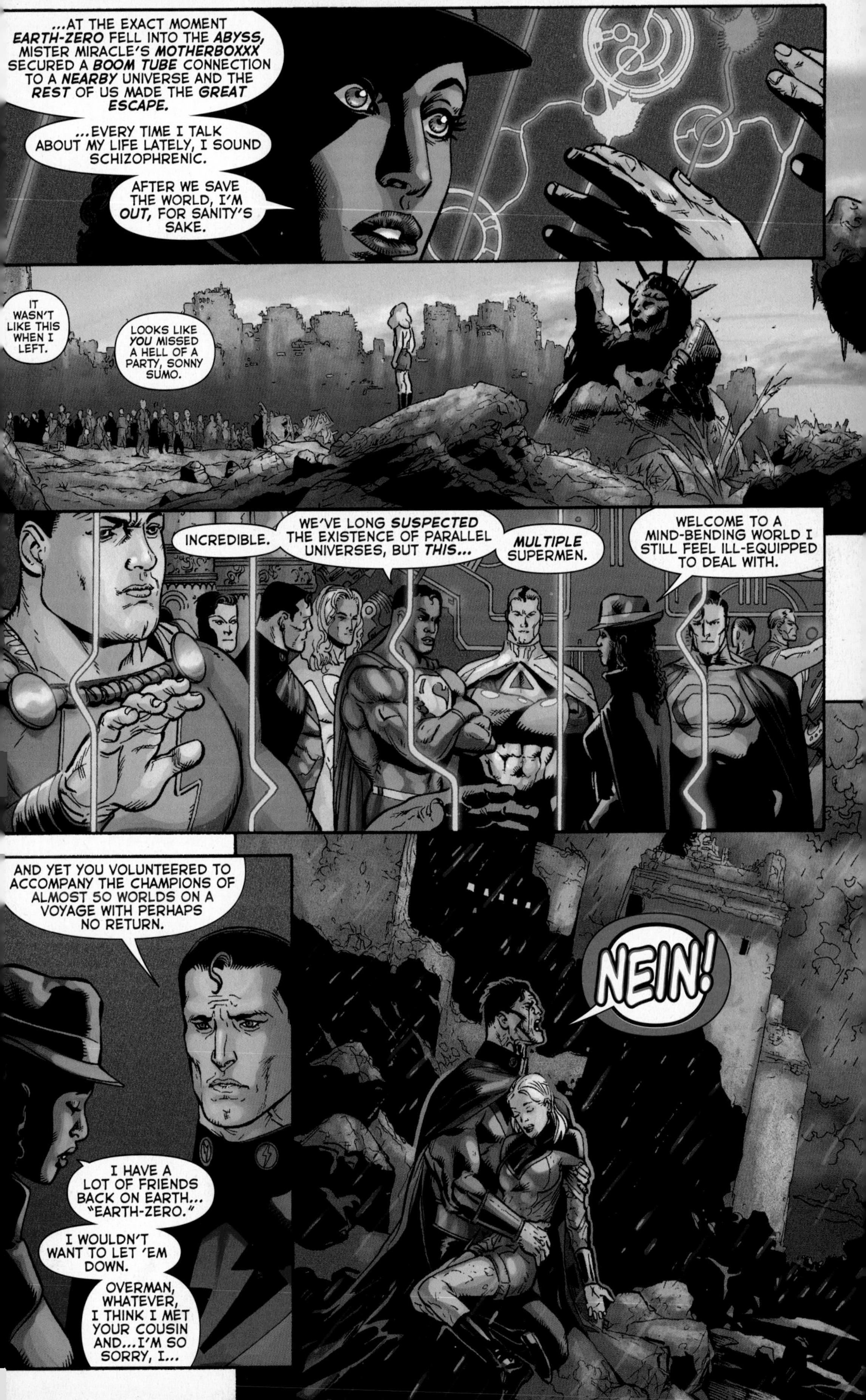

...AT THE EXACT MOMENT EARTH-ZERO FELL INTO THE ABYSS, MISTER MIRACLE'S MOTHERBOXXX SECURED A BOOM TUBE CONNECTION TO A NEARBY UNIVERSE AND THE REST OF US MADE THE GREAT ESCAPE.
...EVERY TIME I TALK ABOUT MY LIFE LATELY, I SOUND SCHIZOPHRENIC.
AFTER WE SAVE THE WORLD, I'M OUT, FOR SANITY'S SAKE.
IT WASN'T LIKE THIS WHEN I LEFT.
LOOKS LIKE YOU MISSED A HELL OF A PARTY, SONNY SUMO.
INCREDIBLE.
WE'VE LONG SUSPECTED THE EXISTENCE OF PARALLEL UNIVERSES, BUT THIS...
MULTIPLE SUPERMEN.
WELCOME TO A MIND-BENDING WORLD I STILL FEEL ILL-EQUIPPED TO DEAL WITH.
AND YET YOU VOLUNTEERED TO ACCOMPANY THE CHAMPIONS OF ALMOST 50 WORLDS ON A VOYAGE WITH PERHAPS NO RETURN.
I HAVE A LOT OF FRIENDS BACK ON EARTH... "EARTH-ZERO."
I WOULDN'T WANT TO LET 'EM DOWN.
OVERMAN, WHATEVER, I THINK I MET YOUR COUSIN AND...I'M SO SORRY, I...
NEIN!

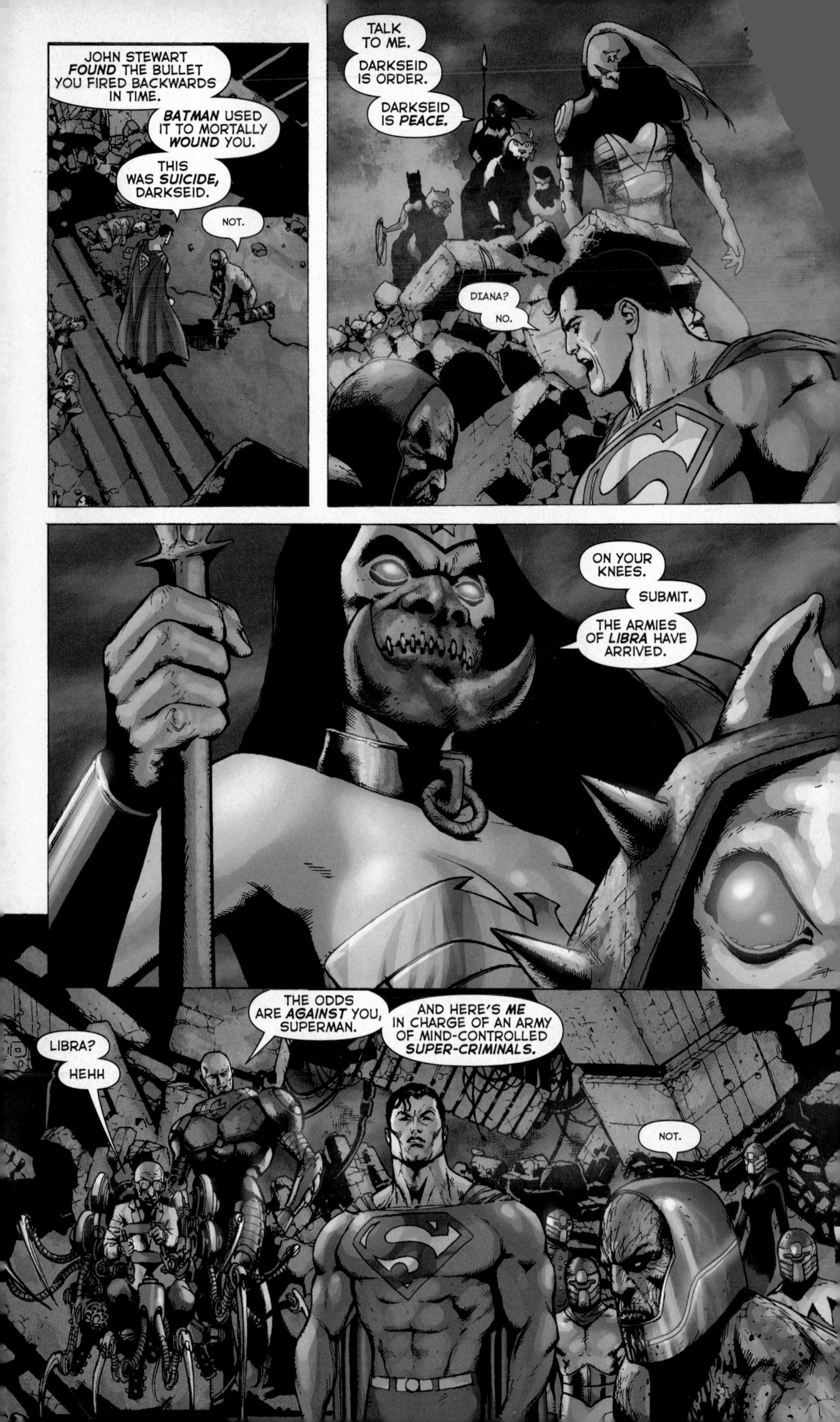
JOHN STEWART FOUND THE BULLET YOU FIRED BACKWARDS IN TIME.
BATMAN USED IT TO MORTALLY WOUND YOU.
THIS WAS SUICIDE, DARKSEID.
NOT.
TALK TO ME.
DARKSEID IS ORDER.
DARKSEID IS PEACE.
DIANA?
NO.
ON YOUR KNEES.
SUBMIT.
THE ARMIES OF LIBRA HAVE ARRIVED.
LIBRA?
HEHH
THE ODDS ARE AGAINST YOU, SUPERMAN.
AND HERE'S ME IN CHARGE OF AN ARMY OF MIND-CONTROLLED SUPER-CRIMINALS.
NOT.

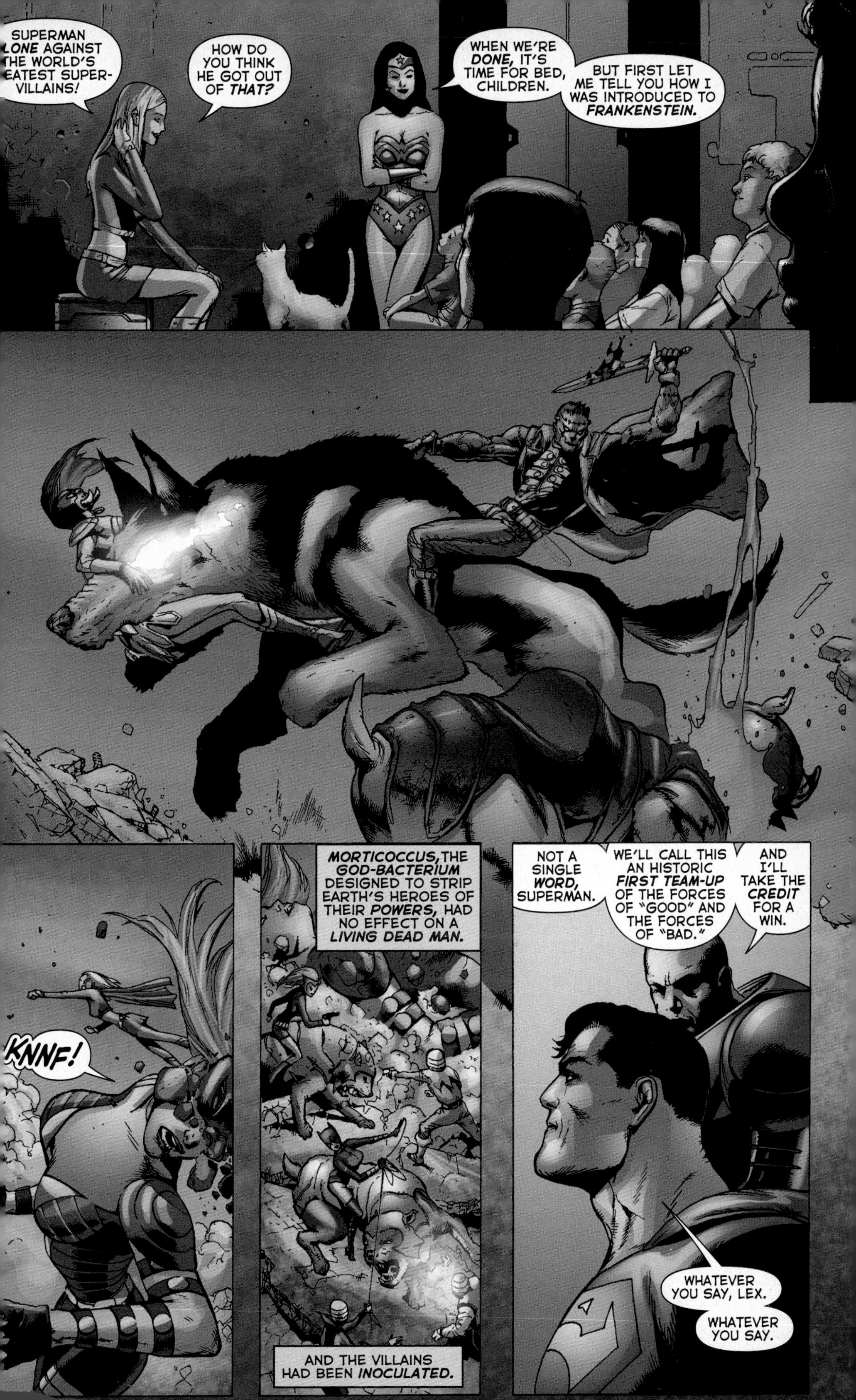

SUPERMAN LONE AGAINST THE WORLD'S EATEST SUPER-VILLAINS!
HOW DO YOU THINK HE GOT OUT OF THAT?
WHEN WE'RE DONE, IT'S TIME FOR BED, CHILDREN.
BUT FIRST LET ME TELL YOU HOW I WAS INTRODUCED TO FRANKENSTEIN.
KNNF!
MORTICOCCUS, THE GOD-BACTERIUM DESIGNED TO STRIP EARTH'S HEROES OF THEIR POWERS, HAD NO EFFECT ON A LIVING DEAD MAN.
AND THE VILLAINS HAD BEEN INOCULATED.
NOT A SINGLE WORD, SUPERMAN.
WE'LL CALL THIS AN HISTORIC FIRST TEAM-UP OF THE FORCES OF "GOOD" AND THE FORCES OF "BAD."
AND I'LL TAKE THE CREDIT FOR A WIN.
WHATEVER YOU SAY, LEX.
WHATEVER YOU SAY.

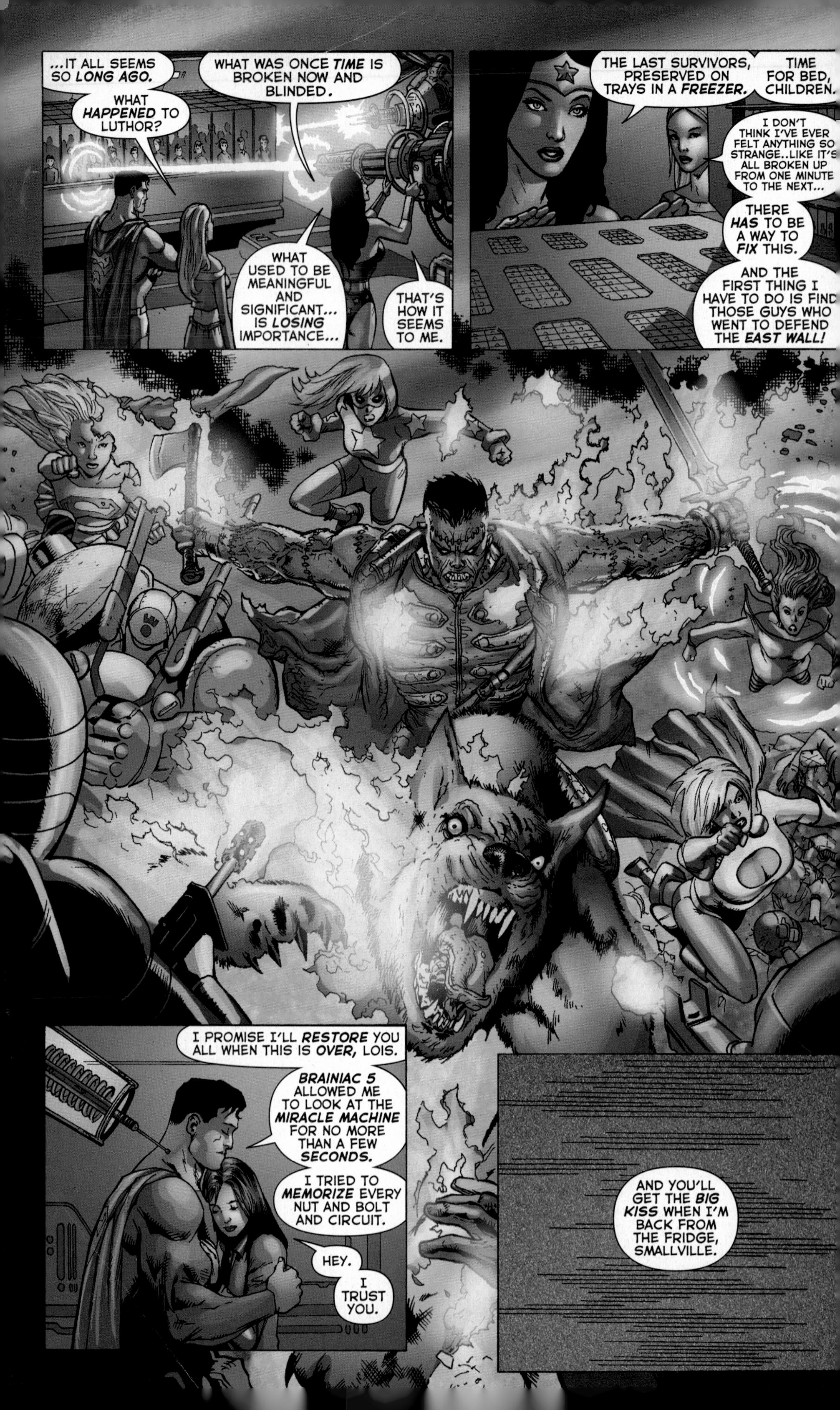
...IT ALL SEEMS SO LONG AGO.
WHAT HAPPENED TO LUTHOR?
WHAT WAS ONCE TIME IS BROKEN NOW AND BLINDED.
WHAT USED TO BE MEANINGFUL AND SIGNIFICANT... IS LOSING IMPORTANCE...
THAT'S HOW IT SEEMS TO ME.
THE LAST SURVIVORS, PRESERVED ON TRAYS IN A FREEZER.
TIME FOR BED, CHILDREN.
I DON'T THINK I'VE EVER FELT ANYTHING SO STRANGE..LIKE IT'S ALL BROKEN UP FROM ONE MINUTE TO THE NEXT...
THERE HAS TO BE A WAY TO FIX THIS.
AND THE FIRST THING I HAVE TO DO IS FIND THOSE GUYS WHO WENT TO DEFEND THE EAST WALL!
I PROMISE I'LL RESTORE YOU ALL WHEN THIS IS OVER, LOIS.
BRAINIAC 5 ALLOWED ME TO LOOK AT THE MIRACLE MACHINE FOR NO MORE THAN A FEW SECONDS.
I TRIED TO MEMORIZE EVERY NUT AND BOLT AND CIRCUIT.
HEY.
I TRUST YOU.
AND YOU'LL GET THE BIG KISS WHEN I'M BACK FROM THE FRIDGE, SMALLVILLE.

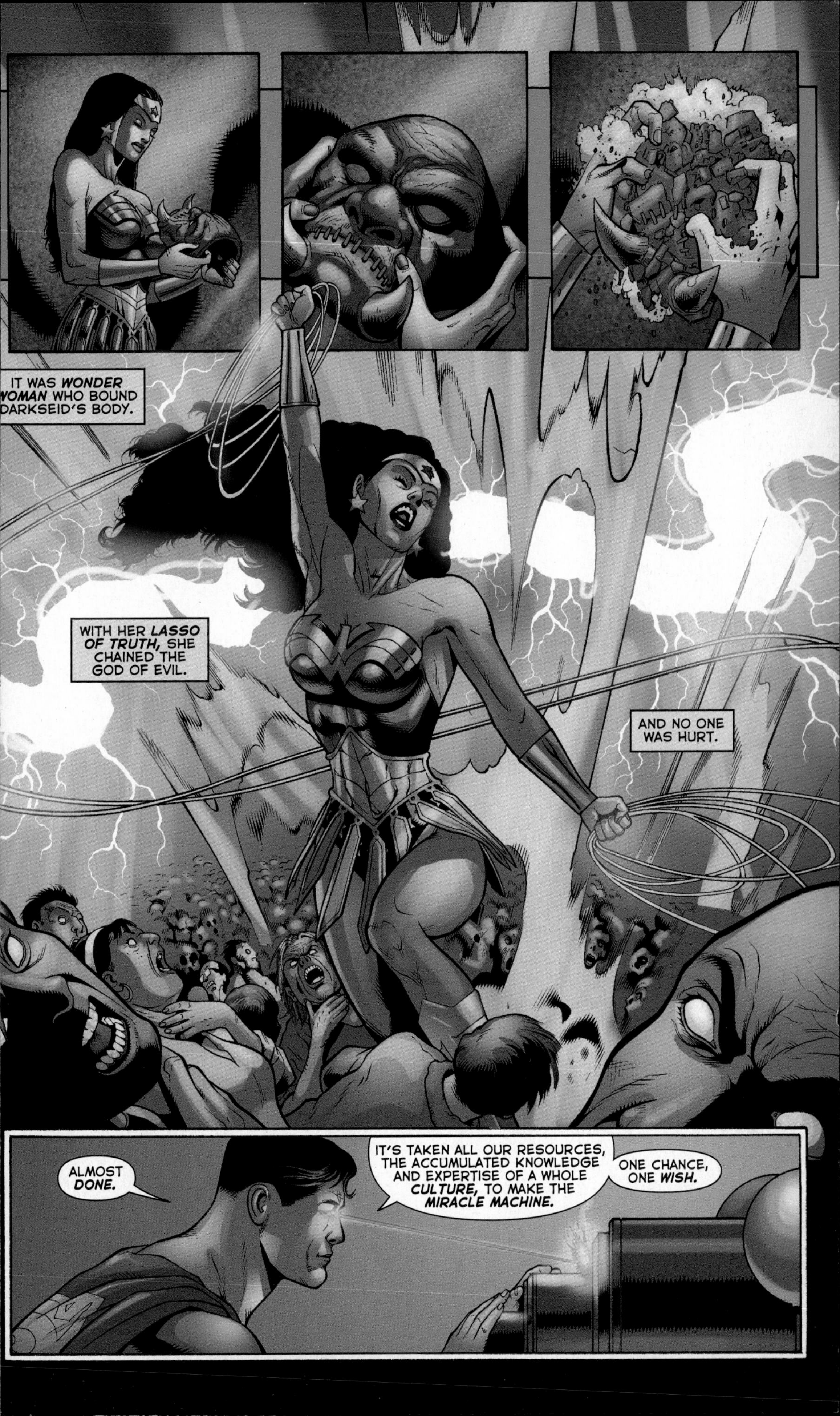
IT WAS *WONDER WOMAN* WHO BOUND DARKSEID'S BODY.
WITH HER *LASSO OF TRUTH,* SHE CHAINED THE GOD OF EVIL.
AND NO ONE WAS HURT.
ALMOST *DONE.*
IT'S TAKEN ALL OUR RESOURCES, THE ACCUMULATED KNOWLEDGE AND EXPERTISE OF A WHOLE *CULTURE,* TO MAKE THE *MIRACLE MACHINE.*
ONE CHANCE, ONE *WISH.*

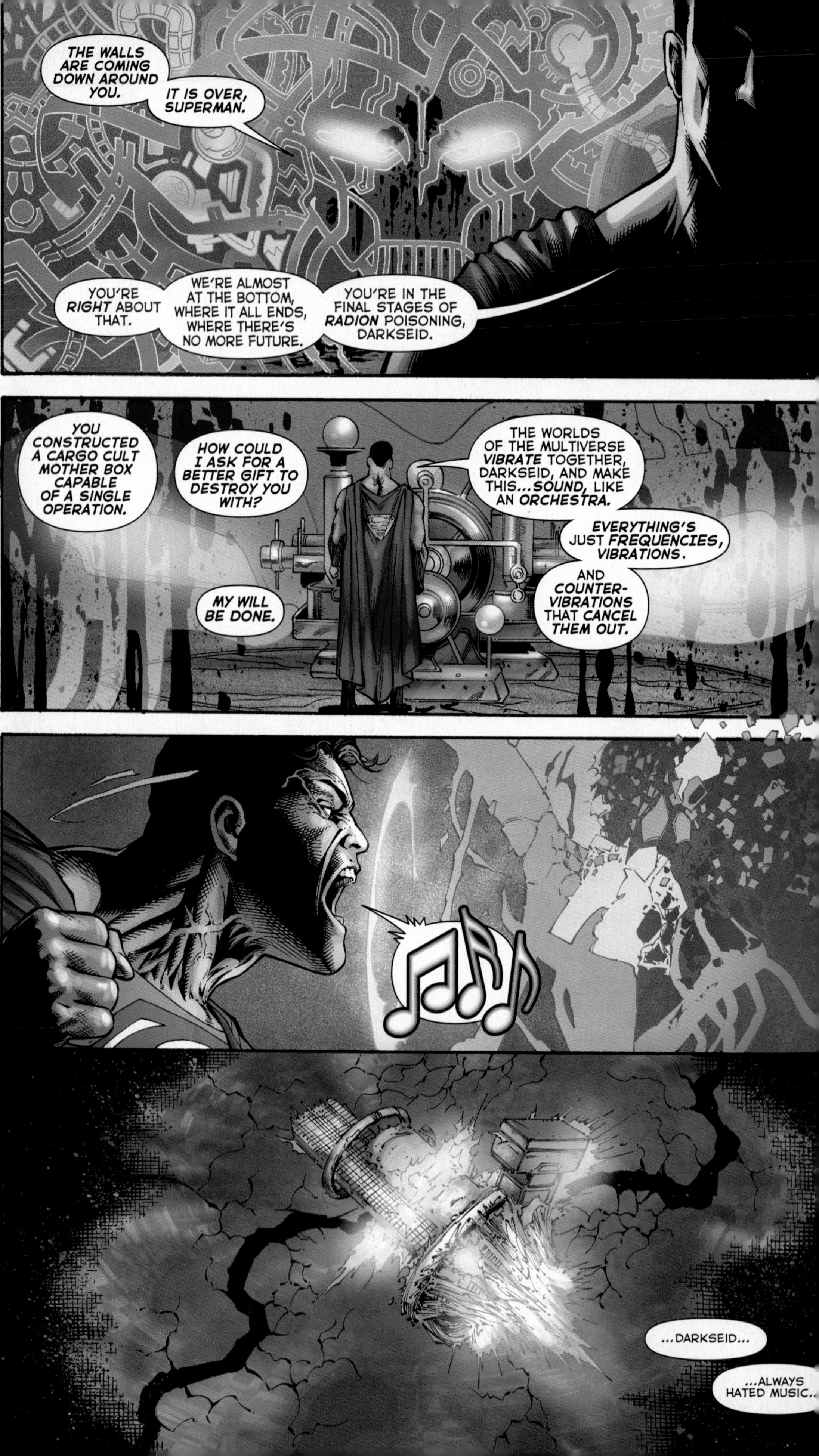
THE WALLS ARE COMING DOWN AROUND YOU.
IT IS OVER, SUPERMAN.
YOU'RE RIGHT ABOUT THAT.
WE'RE ALMOST AT THE BOTTOM, WHERE IT ALL ENDS, WHERE THERE'S NO MORE FUTURE.
YOU'RE IN THE FINAL STAGES OF RADION POISONING, DARKSEID.
YOU CONSTRUCTED A CARGO CULT MOTHER BOX CAPABLE OF A SINGLE OPERATION.
HOW COULD I ASK FOR A BETTER GIFT TO DESTROY YOU WITH?
MY WILL BE DONE.
THE WORLDS OF THE MULTIVERSE VIBRATE TOGETHER, DARKSEID, AND MAKE THIS...SOUND, LIKE AN ORCHESTRA.
EVERYTHING'S JUST FREQUENCIES, VIBRATIONS.
AND COUNTER-VIBRATIONS THAT CANCEL THEM OUT.
...DARKSEID...
...ALWAYS HATED MUSIC...

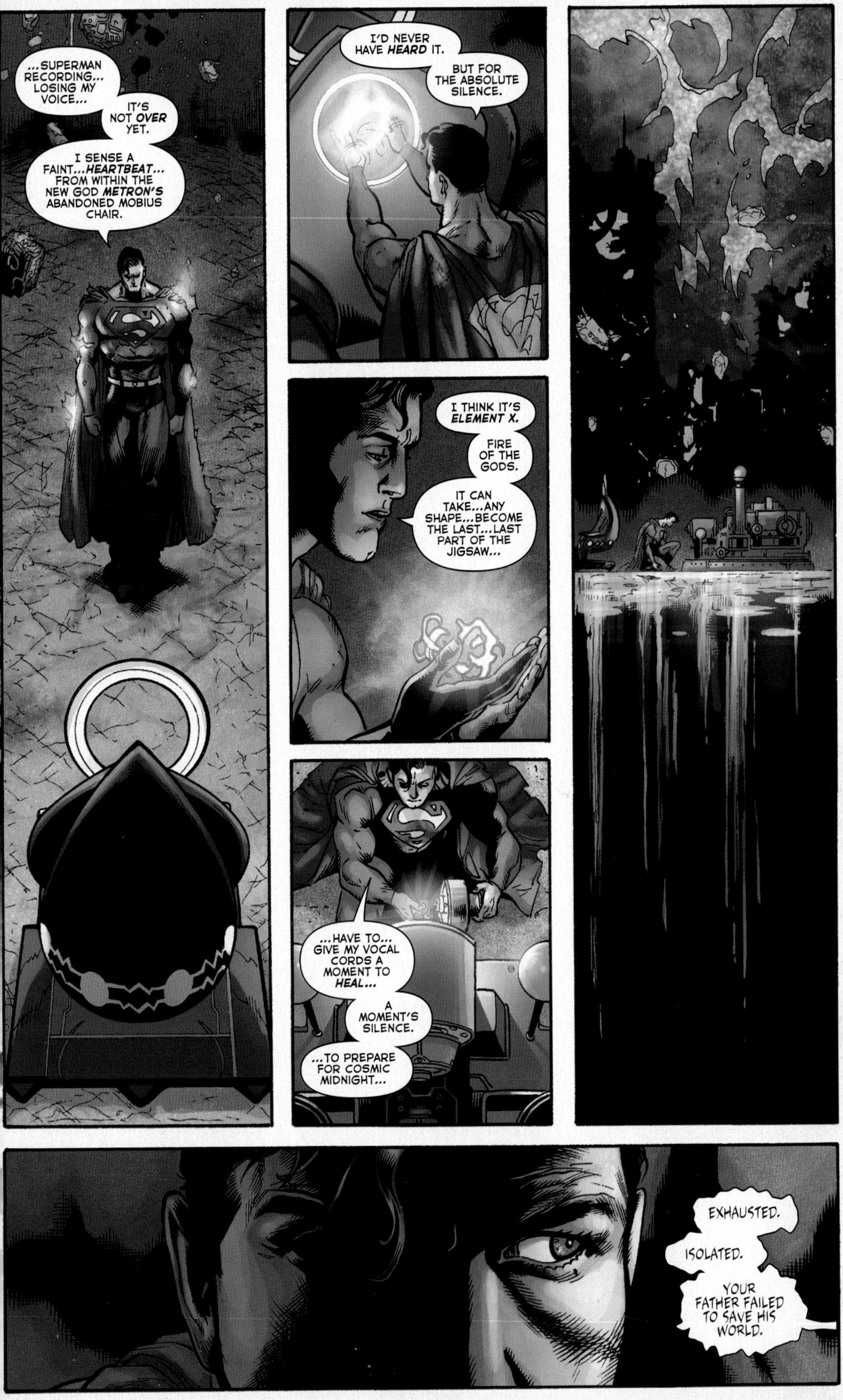
...SUPERMAN RECORDING... LOSING MY VOICE...
IT'S NOT OVER YET.
I SENSE A FAINT...HEARTBEAT... FROM WITHIN THE NEW GOD METRON'S ABANDONED MOBIUS CHAIR.
I'D NEVER HAVE HEARD IT.
BUT FOR THE ABSOLUTE SILENCE.
I THINK IT'S ELEMENT X.
FIRE OF THE GODS.
IT CAN TAKE...ANY SHAPE...BECOME THE LAST...LAST PART OF THE JIGSAW...
...HAVE TO... GIVE MY VOCAL CORDS A MOMENT TO HEAL...
A MOMENT'S SILENCE.
...TO PREPARE FOR COSMIC MIDNIGHT...
EXHAUSTED.
ISOLATED.
YOUR FATHER FAILED TO SAVE HIS WORLD.

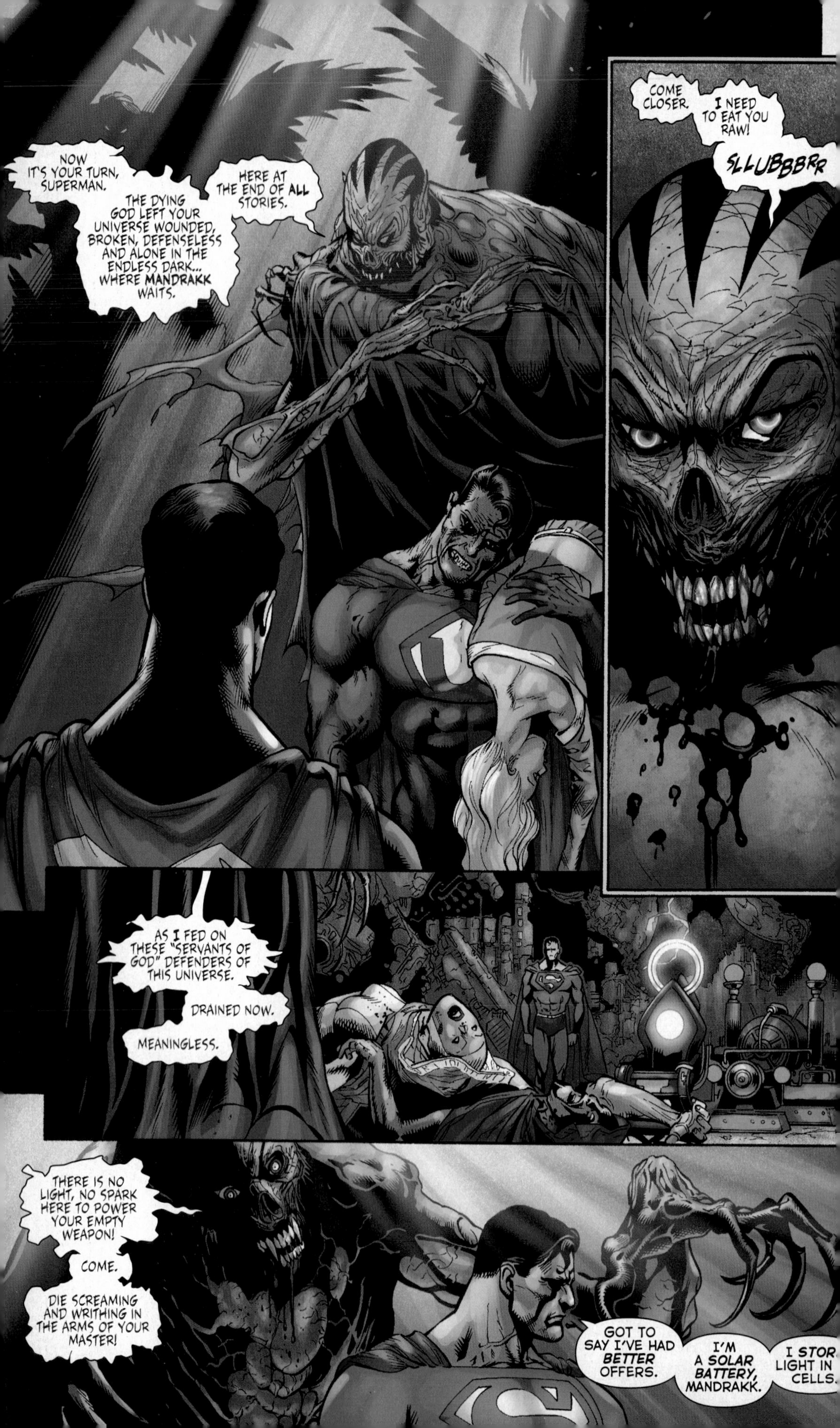
NOW IT'S YOUR TURN, SUPERMAN.
THE DYING GOD LEFT YOUR UNIVERSE WOUNDED, BROKEN, DEFENSELESS AND ALONE IN THE ENDLESS DARK... WHERE MANDRAKK WAITS.
HERE AT THE END OF ALL STORIES.
COME CLOSER.
I NEED TO EAT YOU RAW!
SLLUBBBRR
AS I FED ON THESE "SERVANTS OF GOD" DEFENDERS OF THIS UNIVERSE.
DRAINED NOW.
MEANINGLESS.
THERE IS NO LIGHT, NO SPARK HERE TO POWER YOUR EMPTY WEAPON!
COME.
DIE SCREAMING AND WRITHING IN THE ARMS OF YOUR MASTER!
GOT TO SAY I'VE HAD BETTER OFFERS.
I'M A SOLAR BATTERY, MANDRAKK.
I STOR LIGHT IN CELLS.

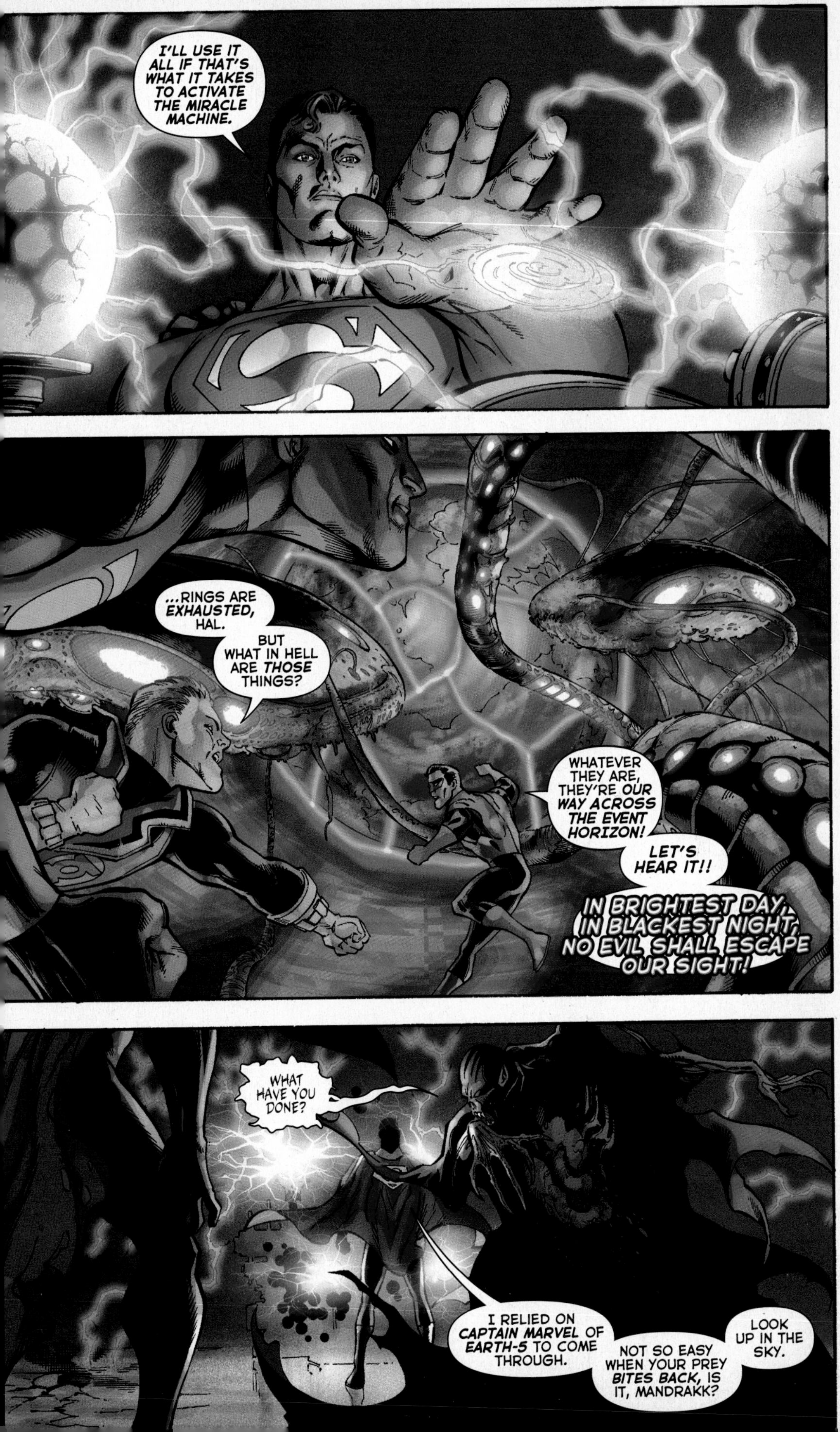
I'LL USE IT ALL IF THAT'S WHAT IT TAKES TO ACTIVATE THE MIRACLE MACHINE.
...RINGS ARE EXHAUSTED, HAL.
BUT WHAT IN HELL ARE THOSE THINGS?
WHATEVER THEY ARE, THEY'RE OUR WAY ACROSS THE EVENT HORIZON!
LET'S HEAR IT!!
IN BRIGHTEST DAY, IN BLACKEST NIGHT, NO EVIL SHALL ESCAPE OUR SIGHT!
WHAT HAVE YOU DONE?
I RELIED ON CAPTAIN MARVEL OF EARTH-5 TO COME THROUGH.
NOT SO EASY WHEN YOUR PREY BITES BACK, IS IT, MANDRAKK?
LOOK UP IN THE SKY.

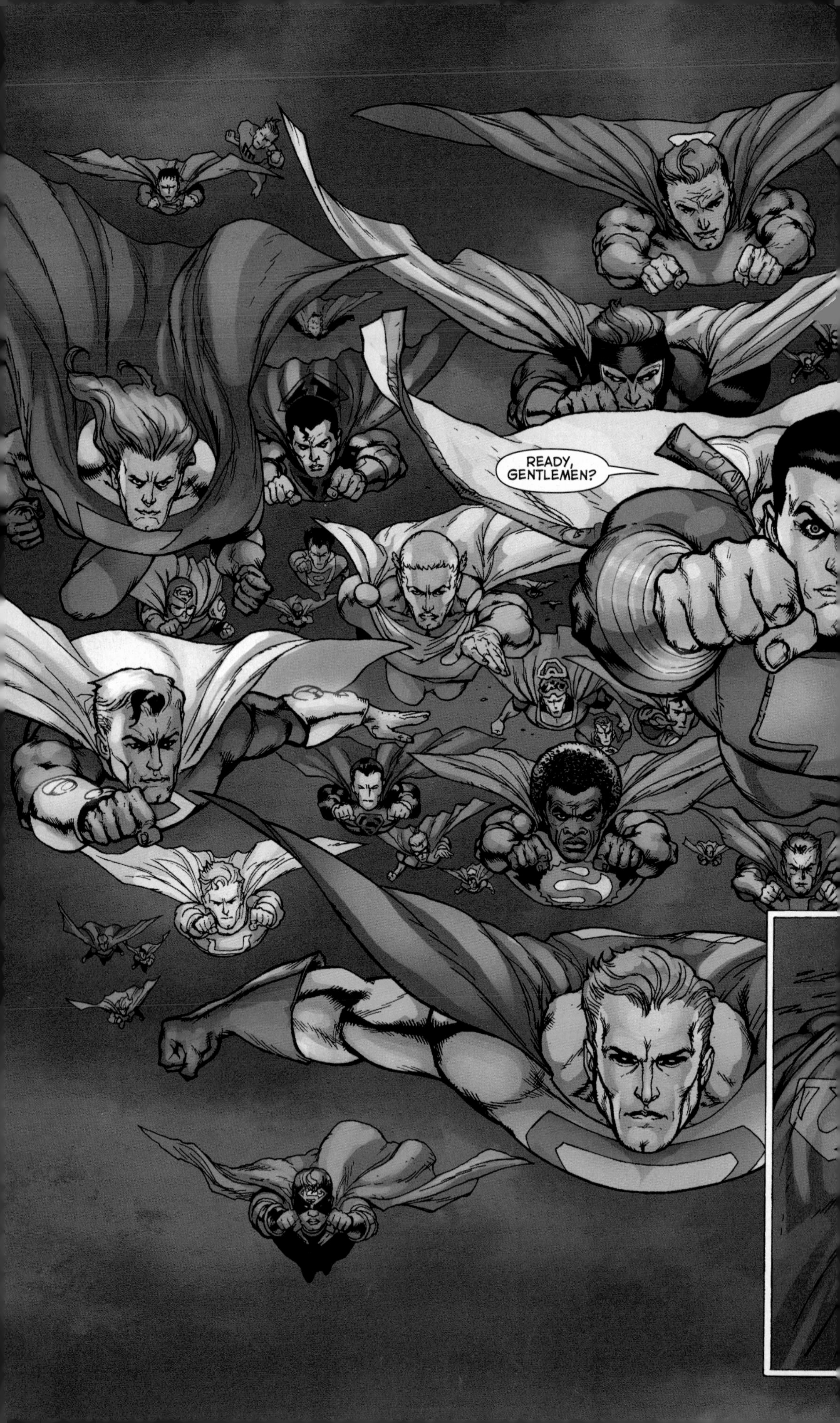
READY, GENTLEMEN?

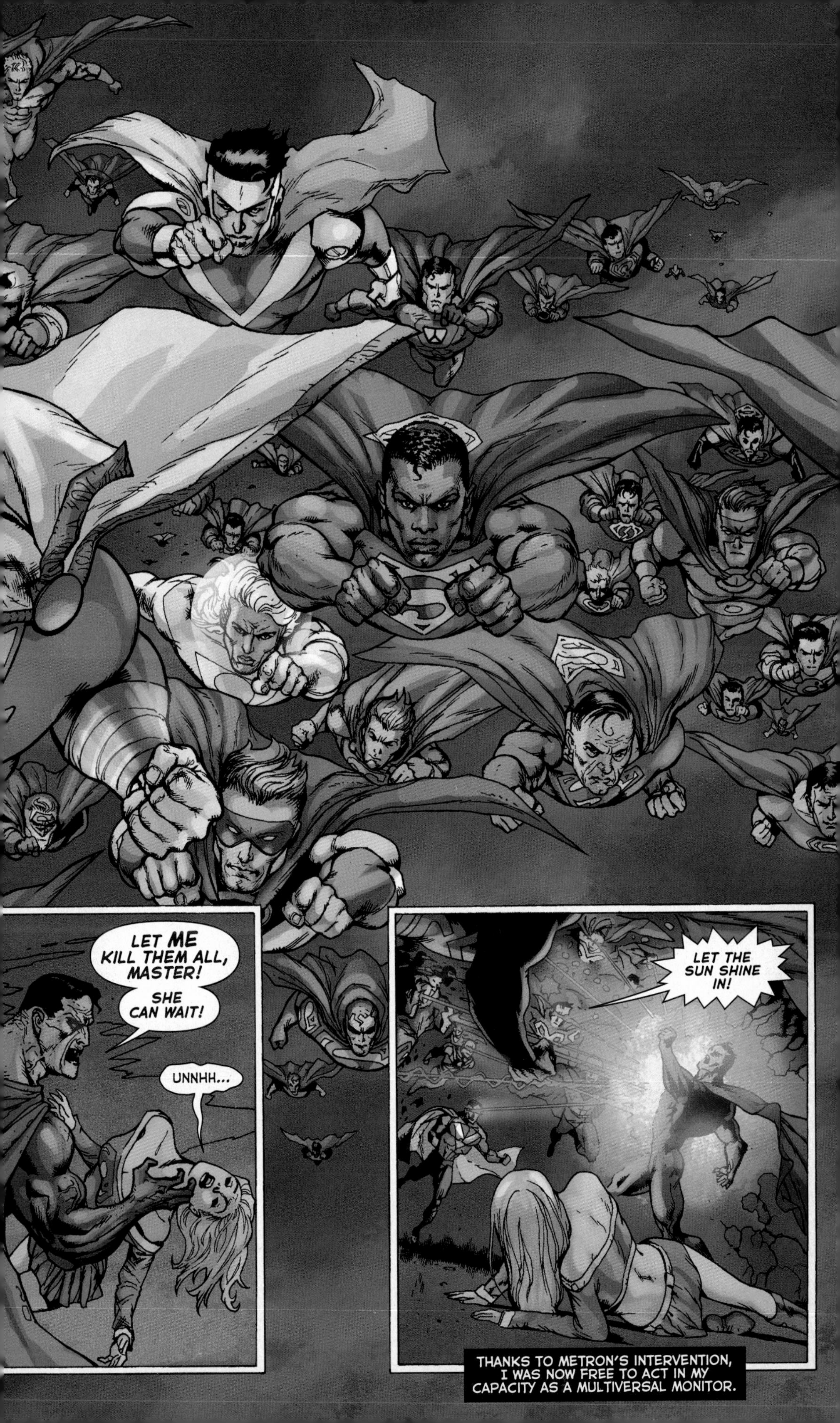
LET ME KILL THEM ALL, MASTER!
SHE CAN WAIT!
UNNHH...
LET THE SUN SHINE IN!
THANKS TO METRON'S INTERVENTION, I WAS NOW FREE TO ACT IN MY CAPACITY AS A MULTIVERSAL MONITOR.

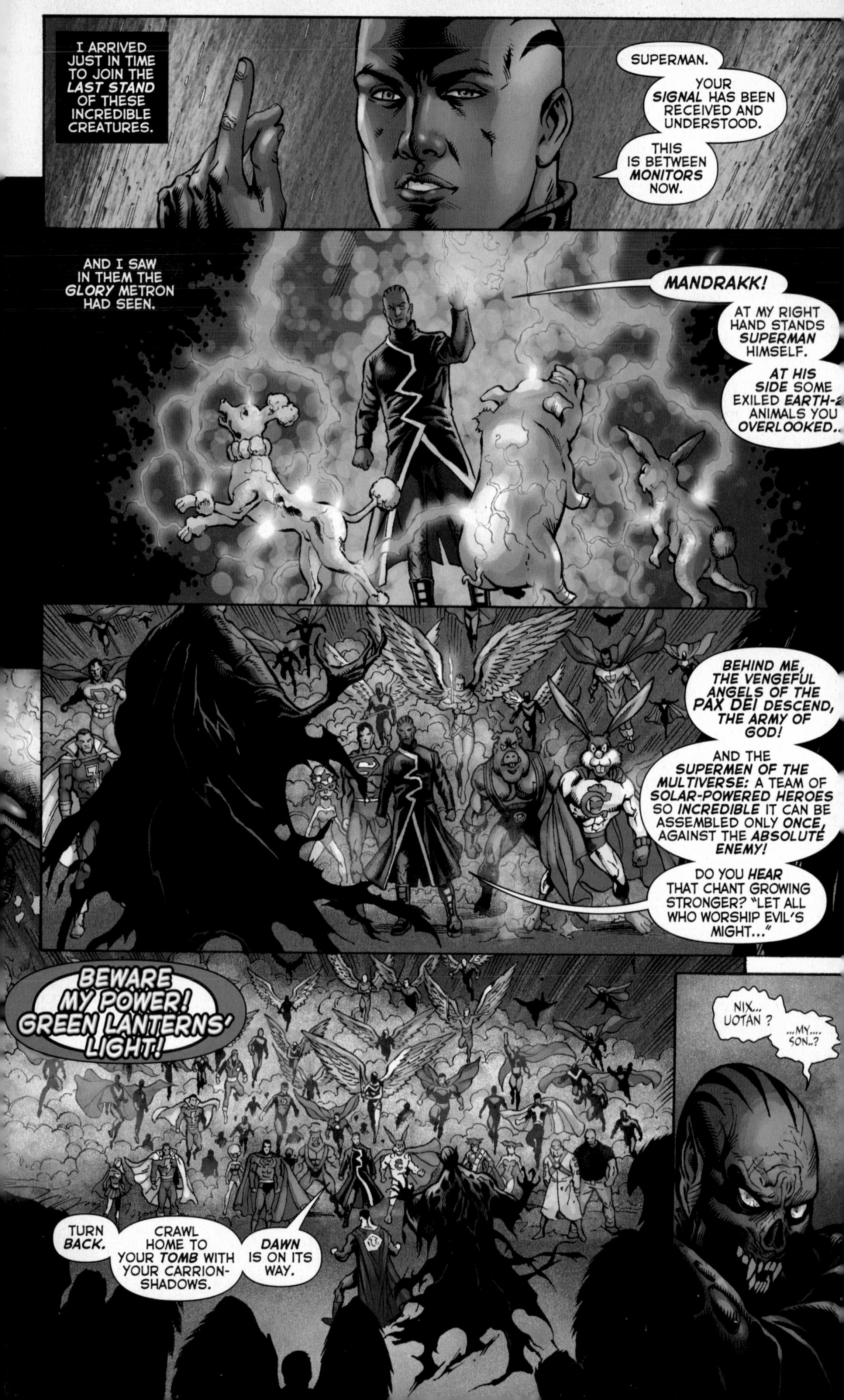

I ARRIVED JUST IN TIME TO JOIN THE LAST STAND OF THESE INCREDIBLE CREATURES.
SUPERMAN.
YOUR SIGNAL HAS BEEN RECEIVED AND UNDERSTOOD.
THIS IS BETWEEN MONITORS NOW.
AND I SAW IN THEM THE GLORY METRON HAD SEEN.
MANDRAKK!
AT MY RIGHT HAND STANDS SUPERMAN HIMSELF.
AT HIS SIDE SOME EXILED EARTH-2 ANIMALS YOU OVERLOOKED...
BEHIND ME, THE VENGEFUL ANGELS OF THE PAX DEI DESCEND, THE ARMY OF GOD!
AND THE SUPERMEN OF THE MULTIVERSE: A TEAM OF SOLAR-POWERED HEROES SO INCREDIBLE IT CAN BE ASSEMBLED ONLY ONCE, AGAINST THE ABSOLUTE ENEMY!
DO YOU HEAR THAT CHANT GROWING STRONGER? "LET ALL WHO WORSHIP EVIL'S MIGHT..."
BEWARE MY POWER! GREEN LANTERNS' LIGHT!
NIX... UOTAN ?
...MY.... SON..?
TURN BACK.
CRAWL HOME TO YOUR TOMB WITH YOUR CARRION-SHADOWS.
DAWN IS ON ITS WAY.

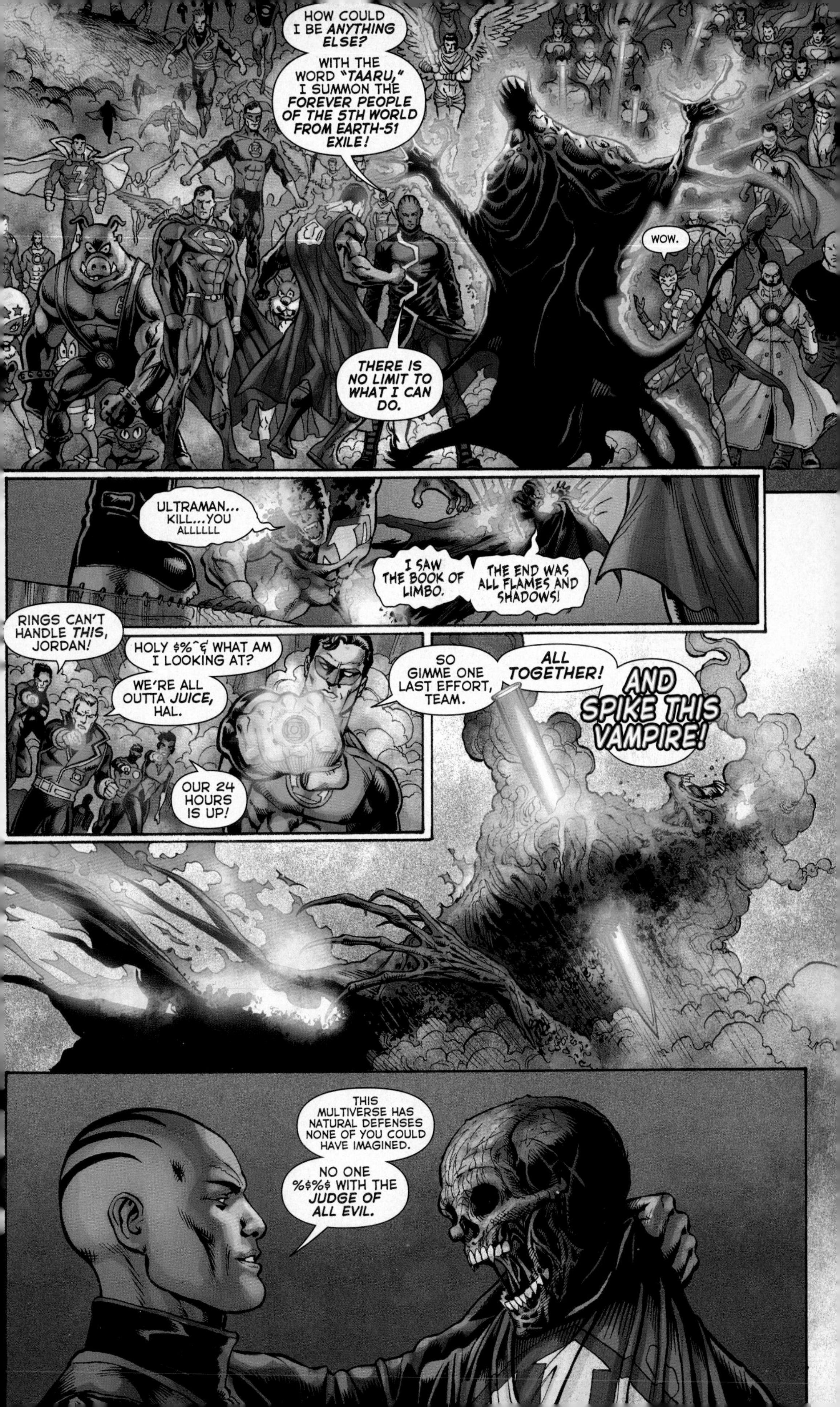

HOW COULD I BE ANYTHING ELSE?
WITH THE WORD "TAARU," I SUMMON THE FOREVER PEOPLE OF THE 5TH WORLD FROM EARTH-51 EXILE!
WOW.
THERE IS NO LIMIT TO WHAT I CAN DO.
ULTRAMAN... KILL...YOU ALLLLLL
I SAW THE BOOK OF LIMBO.
THE END WAS ALL FLAMES AND SHADOWS!
RINGS CAN'T HANDLE THIS, JORDAN!
HOLY $%^& WHAT AM I LOOKING AT?
WE'RE ALL OUTTA JUICE, HAL.
OUR 24 HOURS IS UP!
SO GIMME ONE LAST EFFORT, TEAM.
ALL TOGETHER!
AND SPIKE THIS VAMPIRE!
THIS MULTIVERSE HAS NATURAL DEFENSES NONE OF YOU COULD HAVE IMAGINED.
NO ONE %$%$ WITH THE JUDGE OF ALL EVIL.

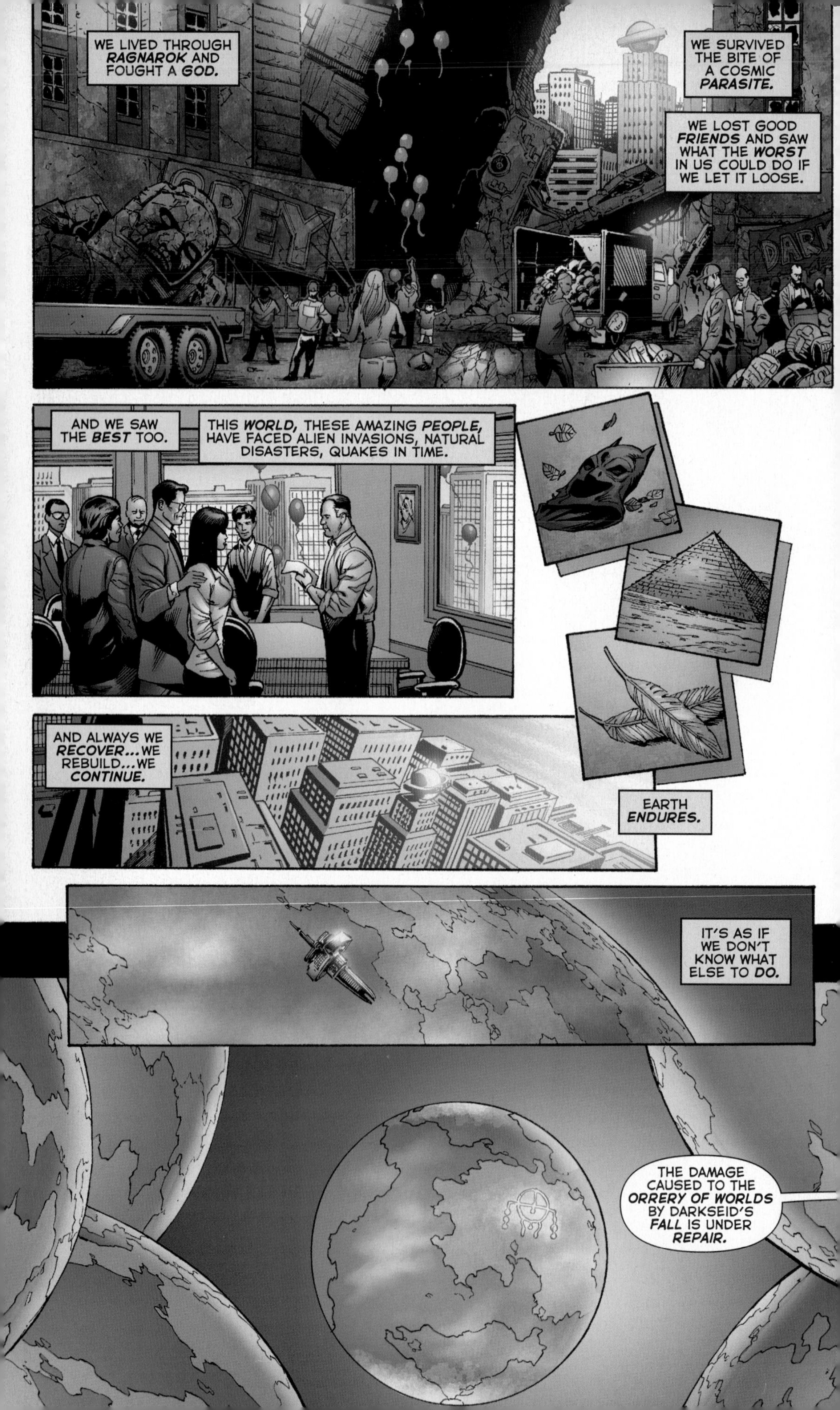
WE LIVED THROUGH RAGNAROK AND FOUGHT A GOD.
OBEY
WE SURVIVED THE BITE OF A COSMIC PARASITE.
WE LOST GOOD FRIENDS AND SAW WHAT THE WORST IN US COULD DO IF WE LET IT LOOSE.
AND WE SAW THE BEST TOO.
THIS WORLD, THESE AMAZING PEOPLE, HAVE FACED ALIEN INVASIONS, NATURAL DISASTERS, QUAKES IN TIME.
AND ALWAYS WE RECOVER...WE REBUILD...WE CONTINUE.
EARTH ENDURES.
IT'S AS IF WE DON'T KNOW WHAT ELSE TO DO.
THE DAMAGE CAUSED TO THE ORRERY OF WORLDS BY DARKSEID'S FALL IS UNDER REPAIR.

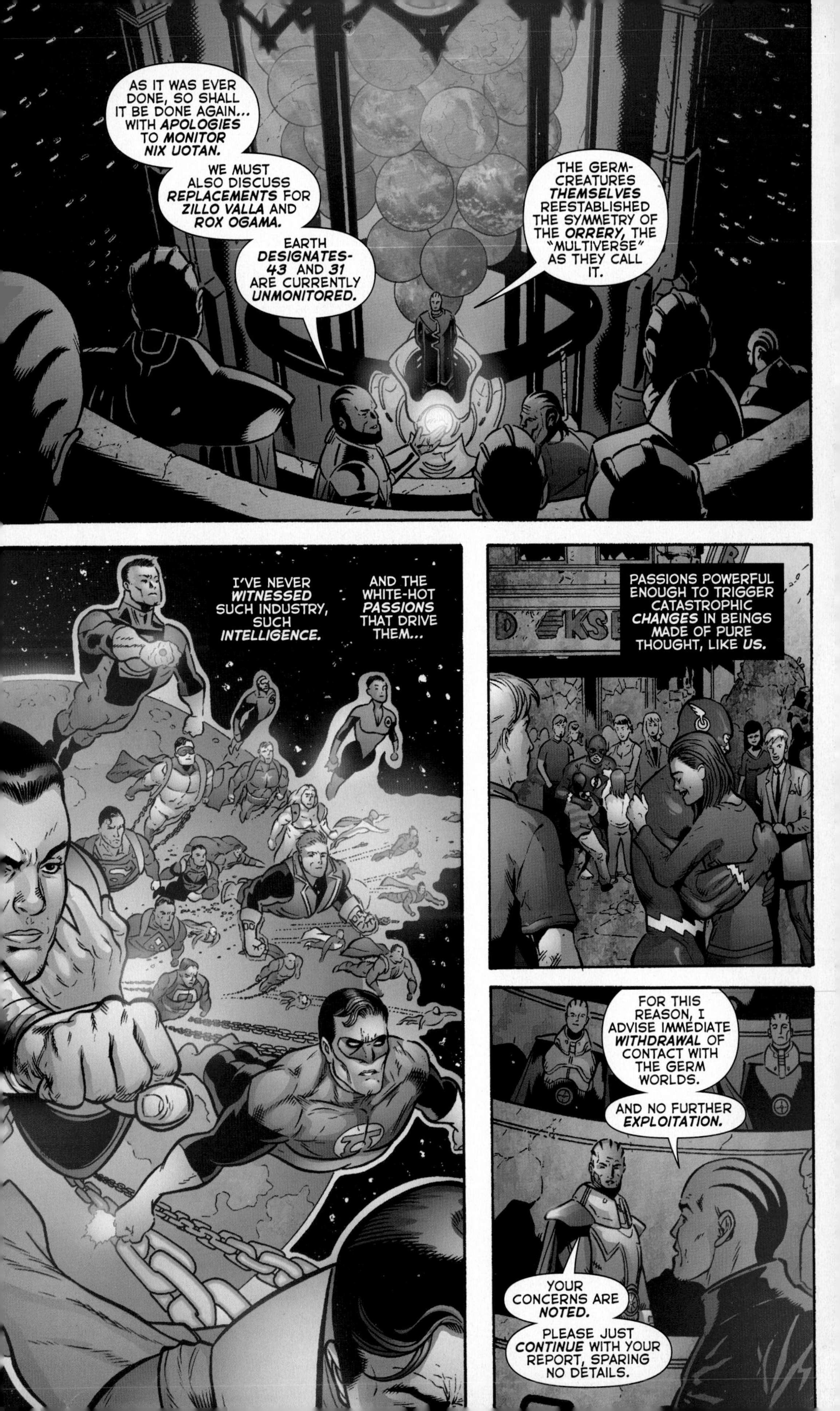

AS IT WAS EVER DONE, SO SHALL IT BE DONE AGAIN... WITH APOLOGIES TO MONITOR NIX UOTAN.
WE MUST ALSO DISCUSS REPLACEMENTS FOR ZILLO VALLA AND ROX OGAMA.
EARTH DESIGNATES-43 AND 31 ARE CURRENTLY UNMONITORED.
THE GERM-CREATURES THEMSELVES REESTABLISHED THE SYMMETRY OF THE ORRERY, THE "MULTIVERSE" AS THEY CALL IT.
I'VE NEVER WITNESSED SUCH INDUSTRY, SUCH INTELLIGENCE.
AND THE WHITE-HOT PASSIONS THAT DRIVE THEM...
PASSIONS POWERFUL ENOUGH TO TRIGGER CATASTROPHIC CHANGES IN BEINGS MADE OF PURE THOUGHT, LIKE US.
FOR THIS REASON, I ADVISE IMMEDIATE WITHDRAWAL OF CONTACT WITH THE GERM WORLDS.
AND NO FURTHER EXPLOITATION.
YOUR CONCERNS ARE NOTED.
PLEASE JUST CONTINUE WITH YOUR REPORT, SPARING NO DETAILS.

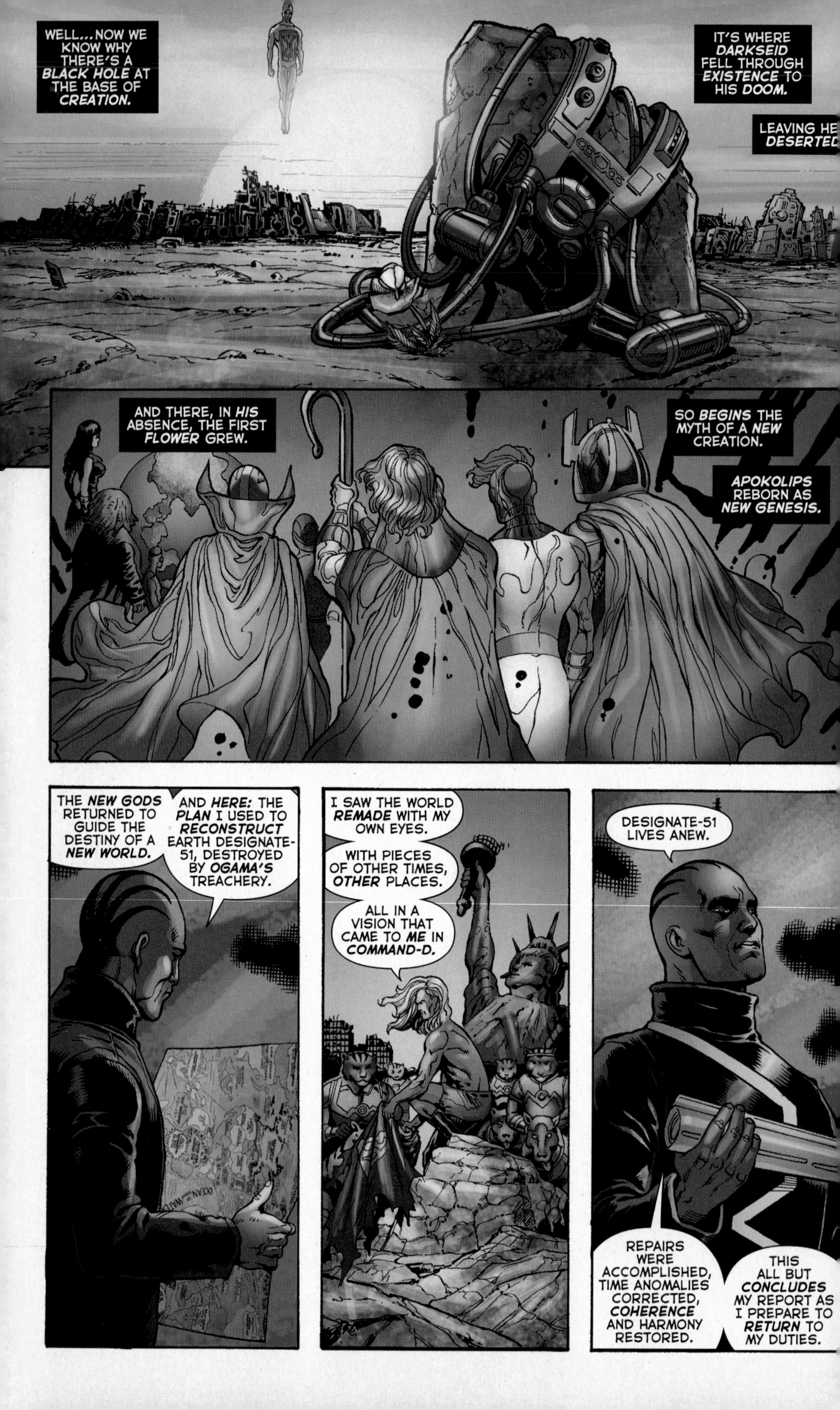
WELL...NOW WE KNOW WHY THERE'S A BLACK HOLE AT THE BASE OF CREATION.
IT'S WHERE DARKSEID FELL THROUGH EXISTENCE TO HIS DOOM.
LEAVING HE DESERTED
AND THERE, IN HIS ABSENCE, THE FIRST FLOWER GREW.
SO BEGINS THE MYTH OF A NEW CREATION.
APOKOLIPS REBORN AS NEW GENESIS.
THE NEW GODS RETURNED TO GUIDE THE DESTINY OF A NEW WORLD.
AND HERE: THE PLAN I USED TO RECONSTRUCT EARTH DESIGNATE-51, DESTROYED BY OGAMA'S TREACHERY.
I SAW THE WORLD REMADE WITH MY OWN EYES.
WITH PIECES OF OTHER TIMES, OTHER PLACES.
ALL IN A VISION THAT CAME TO ME IN COMMAND-D.
DESIGNATE-51 LIVES ANEW.
REPAIRS WERE ACCOMPLISHED, TIME ANOMALIES CORRECTED, COHERENCE AND HARMONY RESTORED.
THIS ALL BUT CONCLUDES MY REPORT AS I PREPARE TO RETURN TO MY DUTIES.

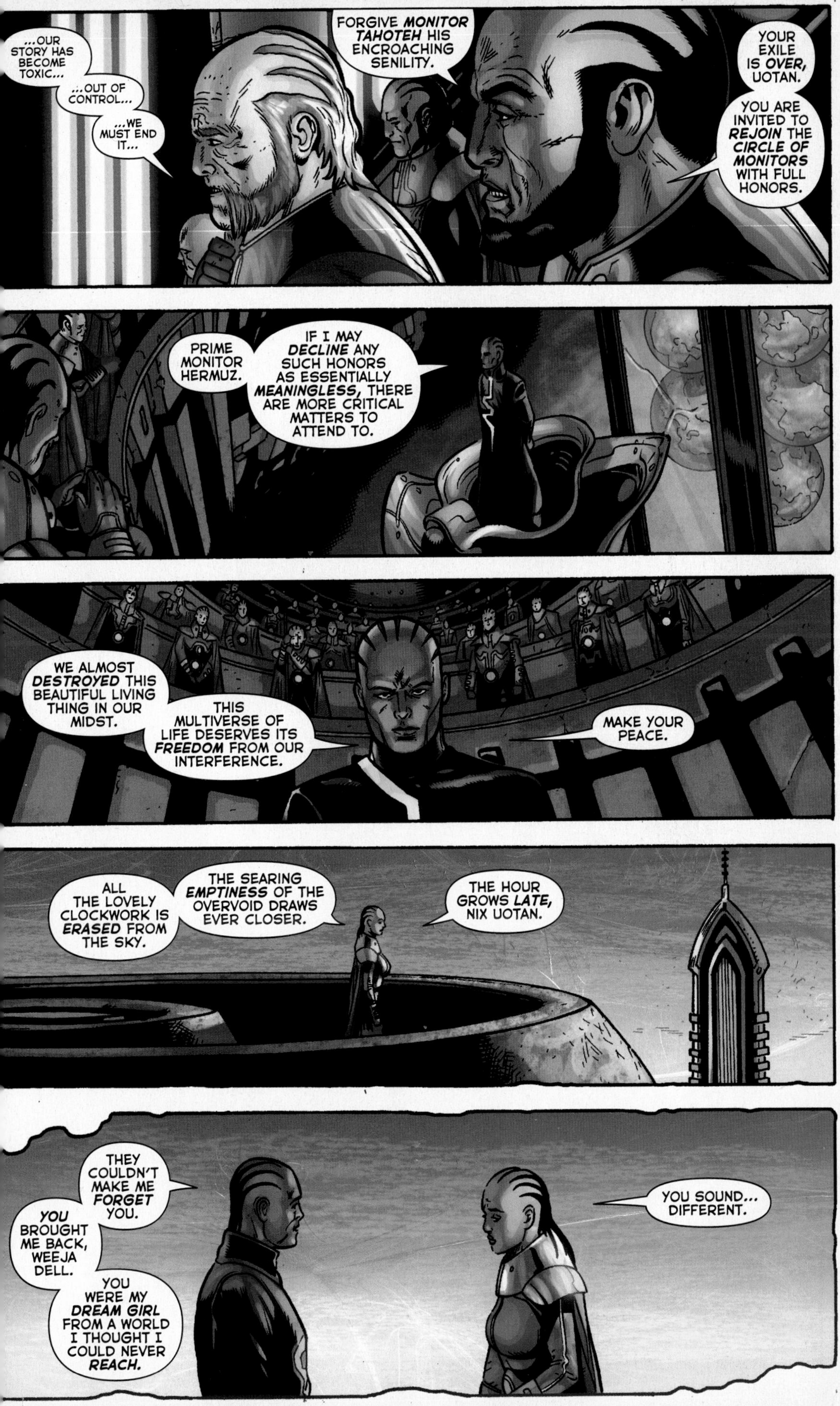
...OUR STORY HAS BECOME TOXIC...
...OUT OF CONTROL...
...WE MUST END IT...
FORGIVE MONITOR TAHOTEH HIS ENCROACHING SENILITY.
YOUR EXILE IS OVER, UOTAN.
YOU ARE INVITED TO REJOIN THE CIRCLE OF MONITORS WITH FULL HONORS.
PRIME MONITOR HERMUZ.
IF I MAY DECLINE ANY SUCH HONORS AS ESSENTIALLY MEANINGLESS, THERE ARE MORE CRITICAL MATTERS TO ATTEND TO.
WE ALMOST DESTROYED THIS BEAUTIFUL LIVING THING IN OUR MIDST.
THIS MULTIVERSE OF LIFE DESERVES ITS FREEDOM FROM OUR INTERFERENCE.
MAKE YOUR PEACE.
ALL THE LOVELY CLOCKWORK IS ERASED FROM THE SKY.
THE SEARING EMPTINESS OF THE OVERVOID DRAWS EVER CLOSER.
THE HOUR GROWS LATE, NIX UOTAN.
THEY COULDN'T MAKE ME FORGET YOU.
YOU BROUGHT ME BACK, WEEJA DELL.
YOU WERE MY DREAM GIRL FROM A WORLD I THOUGHT I COULD NEVER REACH.
YOU SOUND... DIFFERENT.

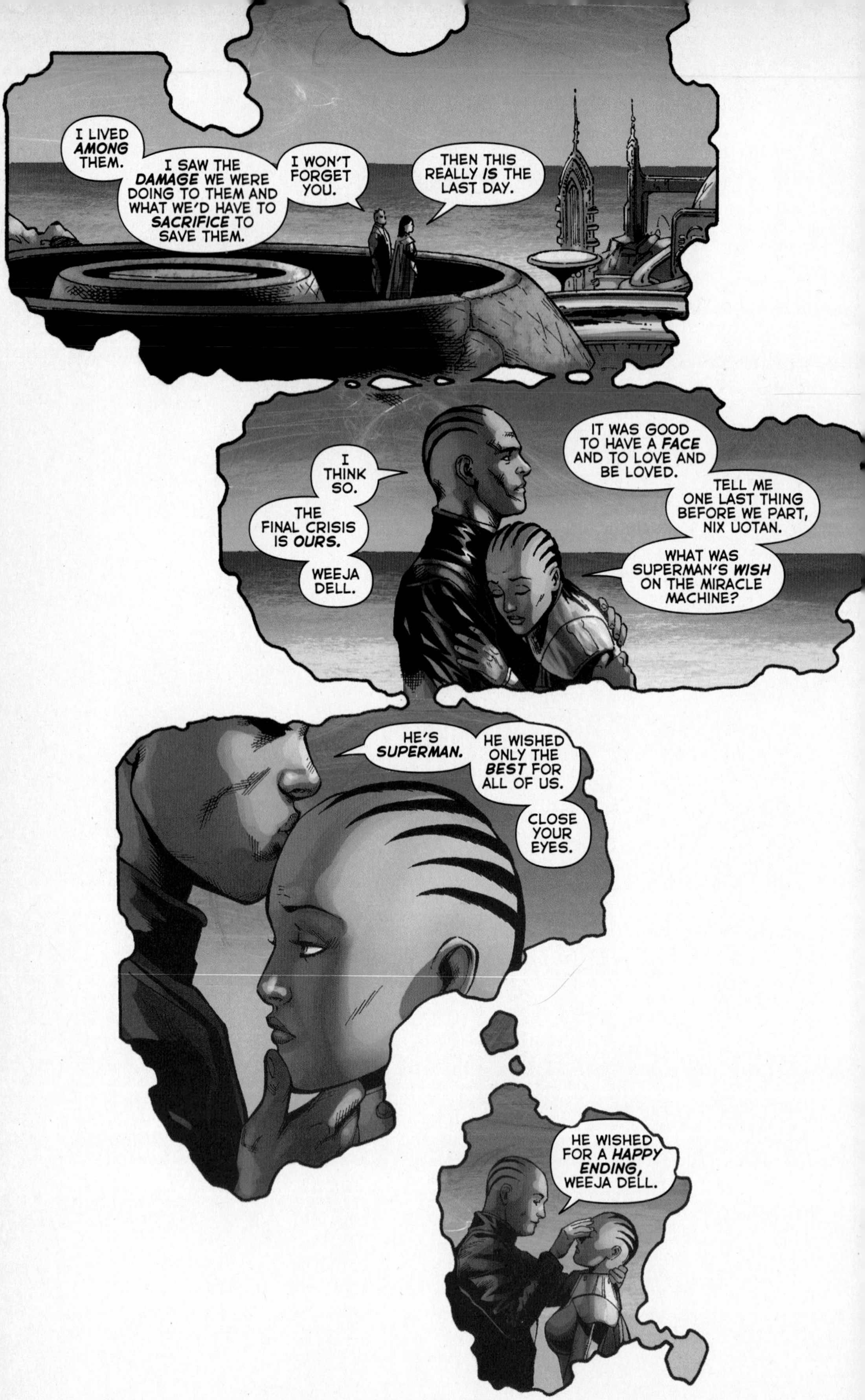
I LIVED AMONG THEM.
I SAW THE DAMAGE WE WERE DOING TO THEM AND WHAT WE'D HAVE TO SACRIFICE TO SAVE THEM.
I WON'T FORGET YOU.
THEN THIS REALLY IS THE LAST DAY.
I THINK SO.
THE FINAL CRISIS IS OURS.
WEEJA DELL.
IT WAS GOOD TO HAVE A FACE AND TO LOVE AND BE LOVED.
TELL ME ONE LAST THING BEFORE WE PART, NIX UOTAN.
WHAT WAS SUPERMAN'S WISH ON THE MIRACLE MACHINE?
HE'S SUPERMAN.
HE WISHED ONLY THE BEST FOR ALL OF US.
CLOSE YOUR EYES.
HE WISHED FOR A HAPPY ENDING, WEEJA DELL.

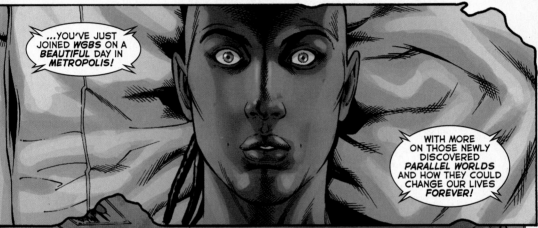

...YOU'VE JUST JOINED *WGBS* ON A *BEAUTIFUL* DAY IN *METROPOLIS!*

WITH MORE ON THOSE NEWLY DISCOVERED *PARALLEL WORLDS* AND HOW THEY COULD CHANGE OUR LIVES *FOREVER!*

THIS IS ONE STORY THAT'S ONLY JUST *BEGINNING.*

YOU HAVE BEEN READING

NEW HEAVEN, NEW EARTH

GRANT MORRISON • SCRIPT   **DOUG MAHNKE** • PENCILS

TOM NGUYEN, DREW GERACI, CHRISTIAN ALAMY, NORM RAPMUND, RODNEY RAMOS, DOUG MAHNKE & WALDEN WONG • INKS

TRAVIS LANHAM LETTERING   **ALEX SINCLAIR** w/TONY AVINA & PETE PANTAZIS COLORS

SOME TIME LATER, WHEN OLD MAN HAS FINISHED REFRESHING THE STORIES ONE FINAL TIME AT THE HOLY GROUND...

...HE COMES TO REST.

HE THINKS OF THE SHINING ONE AND THE BURNING BUSH IN THE LONG-AGO NOW.

OLD MAN HAS CARRIED THE STRONG FIRE FROM PLACE TO PLACE, LEARNING ALL ITS URGENT LESSONS.

HE HAS MADE WITH HIS HANDS THINGS FIRST SEEN IN ITS SWIFT AND SUBTLE HEART.

WHERE NEW THOUGHTS ARE BORN IN A FURNACE.

HIS SKULL IS FILLED ONE LAST TIME WITH BRILLIANT FLAME.

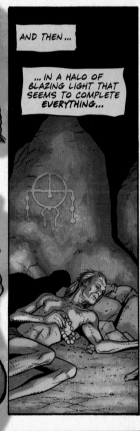

AND THEN...

... IN A HALO OF BLAZING LIGHT THAT SEEMS TO COMPLETE EVERYTHING...

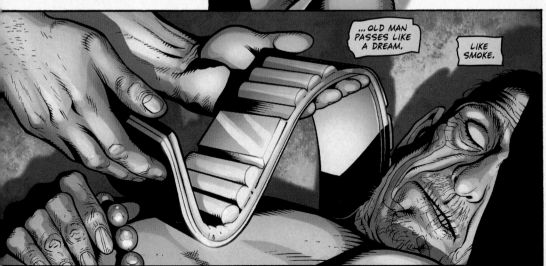

...OLD MAN PASSES LIKE A DREAM.

LIKE SMOKE.

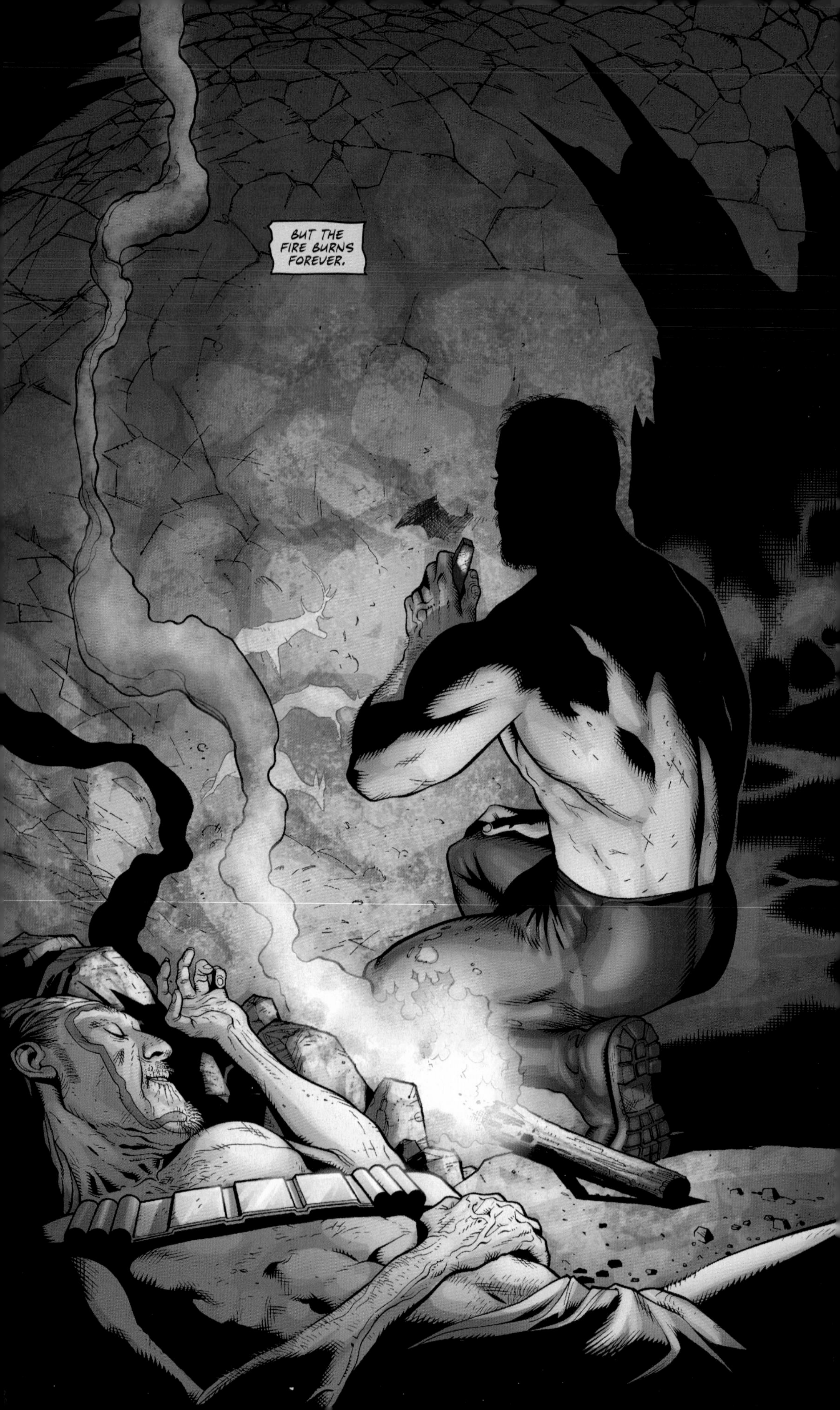
BUT THE FIRE BURNS FOREVER.

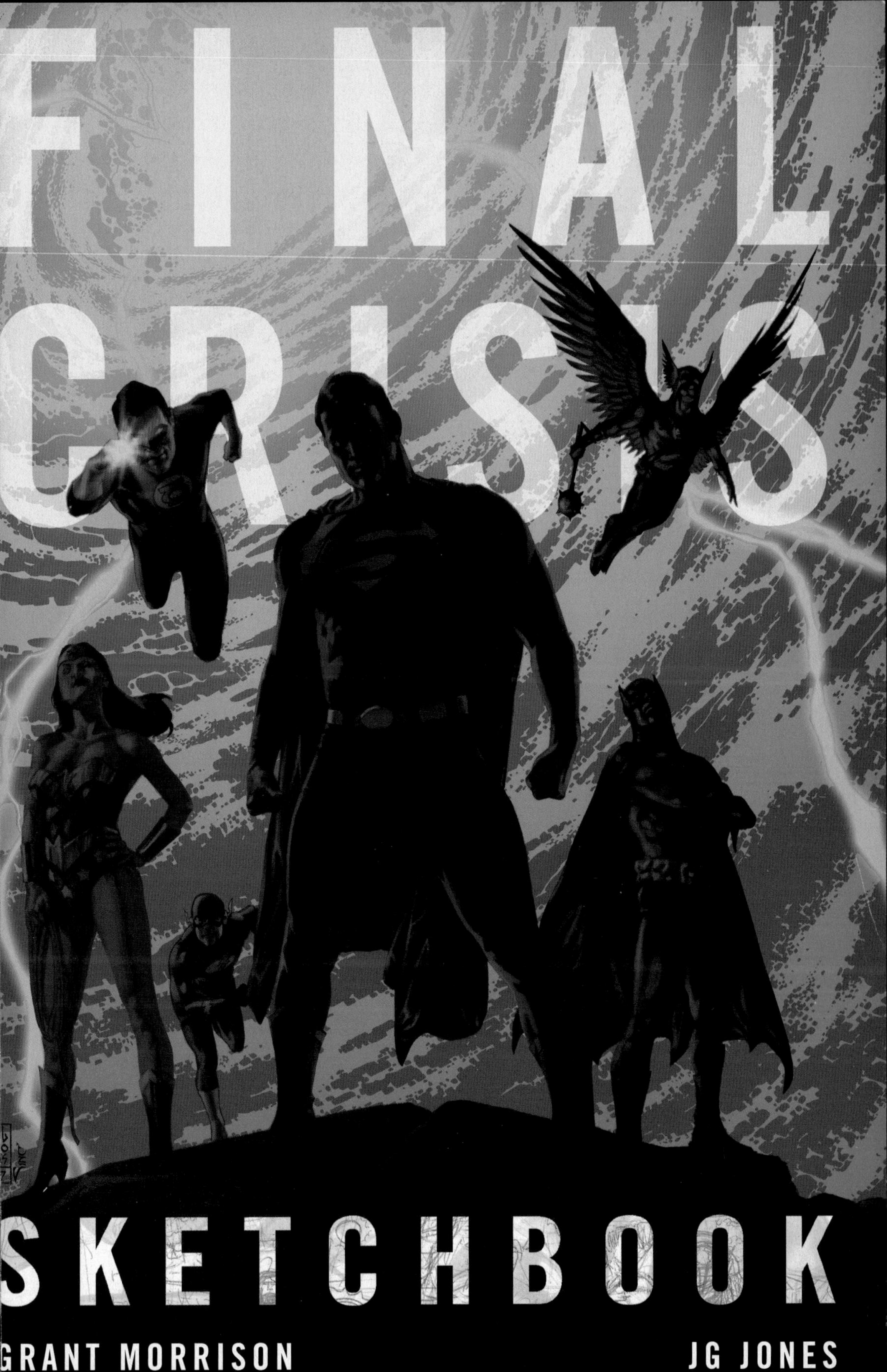
FINAL
CRISIS
SKETCHBOOK
GRANT MORRISON
JG JONES

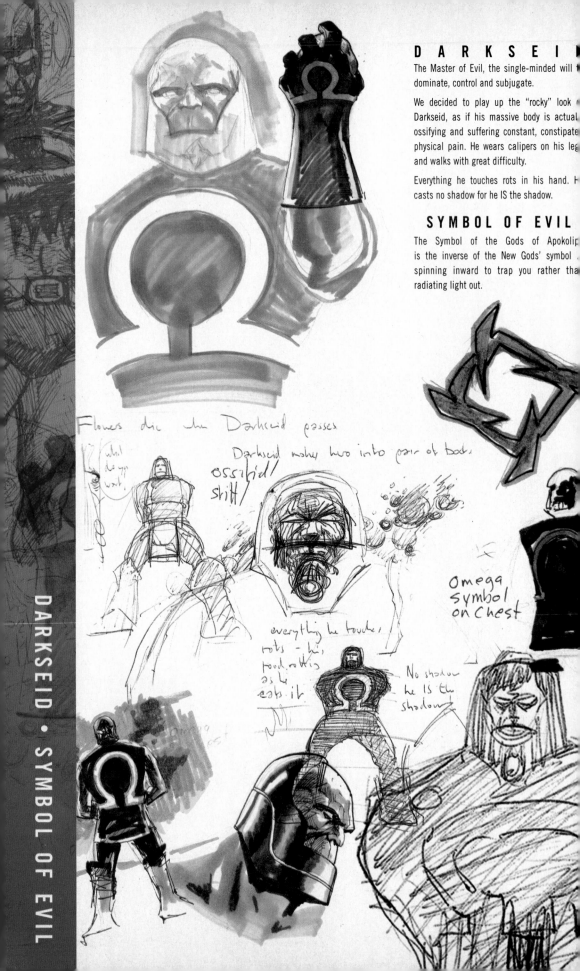

DARKSEI

The Master of Evil, the single-minded will
dominate, control and subjugate.

We decided to play up the "rocky" look
Darkseid, as if his massive body is actual
ossifying and suffering constant, constipate
physical pain. He wears calipers on his leg
and walks with great difficulty.

Everything he touches rots in his hand. H
casts no shadow for he IS the shadow.

SYMBOL OF EVIL

The Symbol of the Gods of Apokolip
is the inverse of the New Gods' symbol
spinning inward to trap you rather tha
radiating light out.

Flowers die when Darkseid passes

Darkseid makes two into pair of bod,

ossified
shift

everything he touches
rots - his
food rots
as he
eats it

Omega
symbol
on chest

No shadow
he IS the
shadow

GRANNY GOODNESS

Granny, the implacable rod of iron, who turns innocent children into brutalized soldiers for Darkseid. Here, Granny hides her wrinkled, evil face behind a doll-like mask of obedience, and corsets her ample middle-aged body into what she feels is a more appealing shape. She is every monstrous, slobbering auntie, every cruel schoolteacher, every vain matron at a dressing table mirror.

DESAAD

The sadistic torturer of the gods should be sleazy and perverse. I like the idea of him wearing high heels under his robe. The comb-over slick with grease, the furtive, twisted expression, the clammy, sweaty skin.

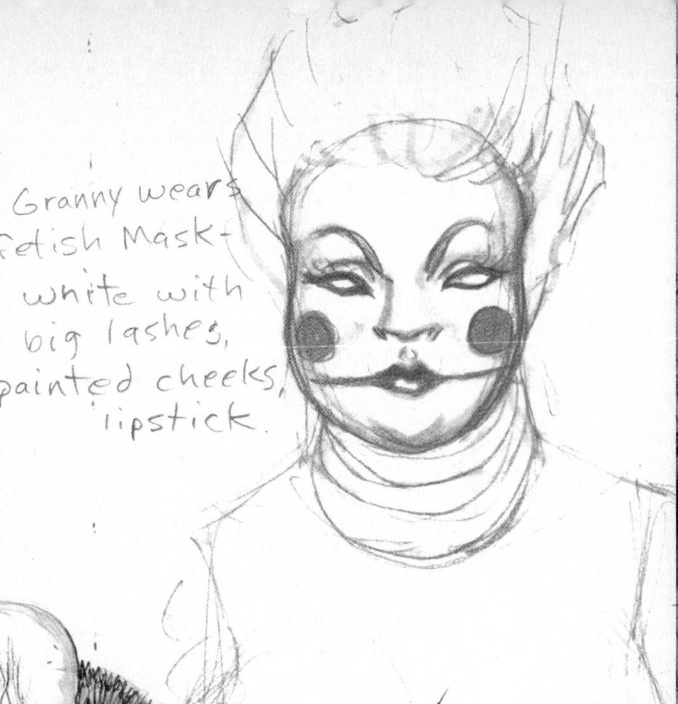
Granny wears Fetish Mask- white with big lashes, painted cheeks, lipstick.

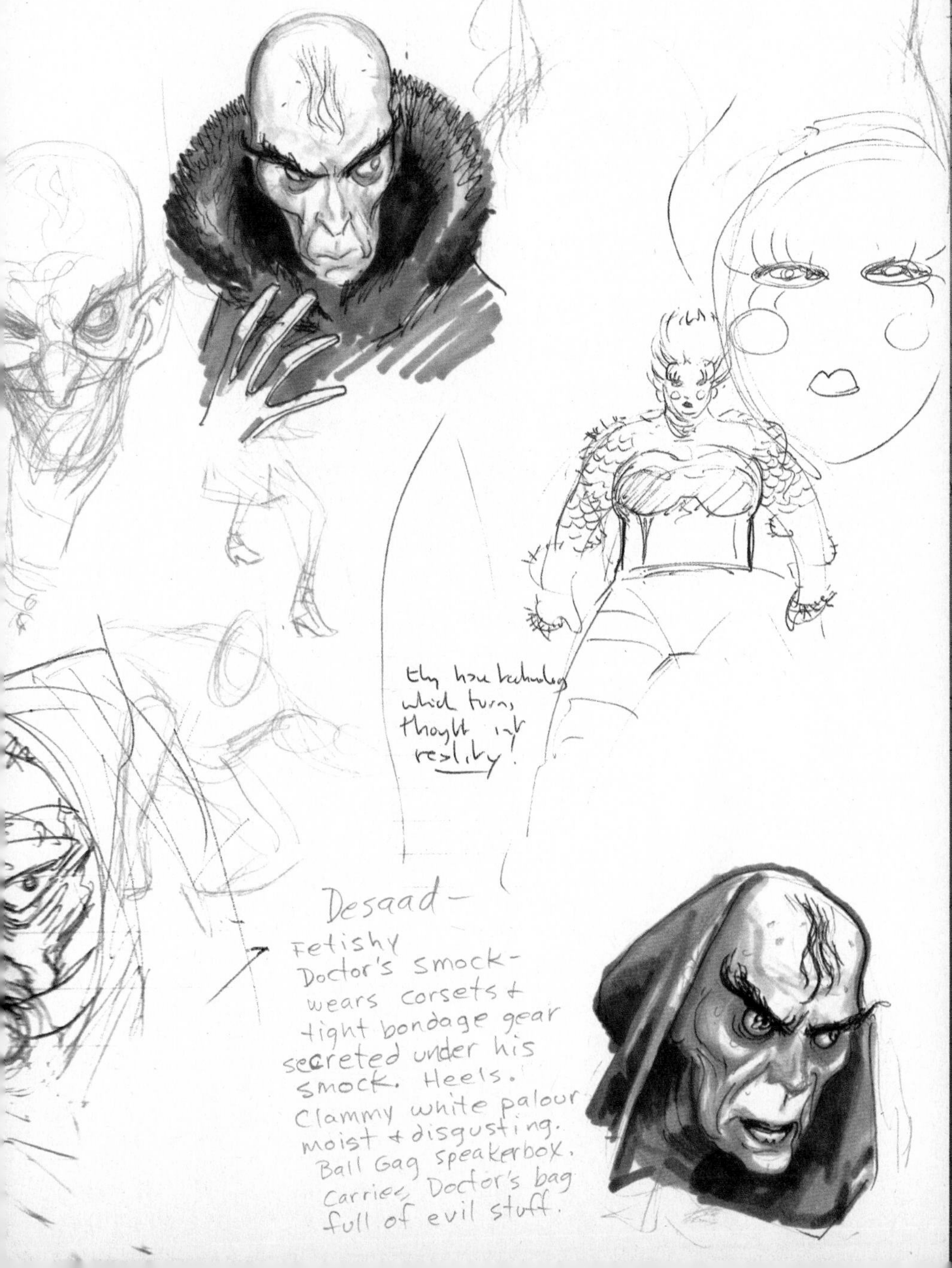
thy hve technology which turns thought int reality!
Desaad-
Fetishy Doctor's smock- wears corsets + tight bondage gear secreted under his smock. Heels. Clammy white palour moist + disgusting. Ball Gag speakerbox. Carries Doctor's bag full of evil stuff.

LIBRA

Libra appeared in a Justice League story back in the '70s, where he stole a bunch of superhero powers and abilities, only to find that the influx of raw power was too much for his physical body to contain. Growing larger and larger and ever more intangible, he disappeared into the cosmos, yelling wildly about becoming a god. He seemed too good to waste in a story like this one and has returned here as a kind of "John the Baptist" forerunner and recruiter for Darkseid and the religion of crime.

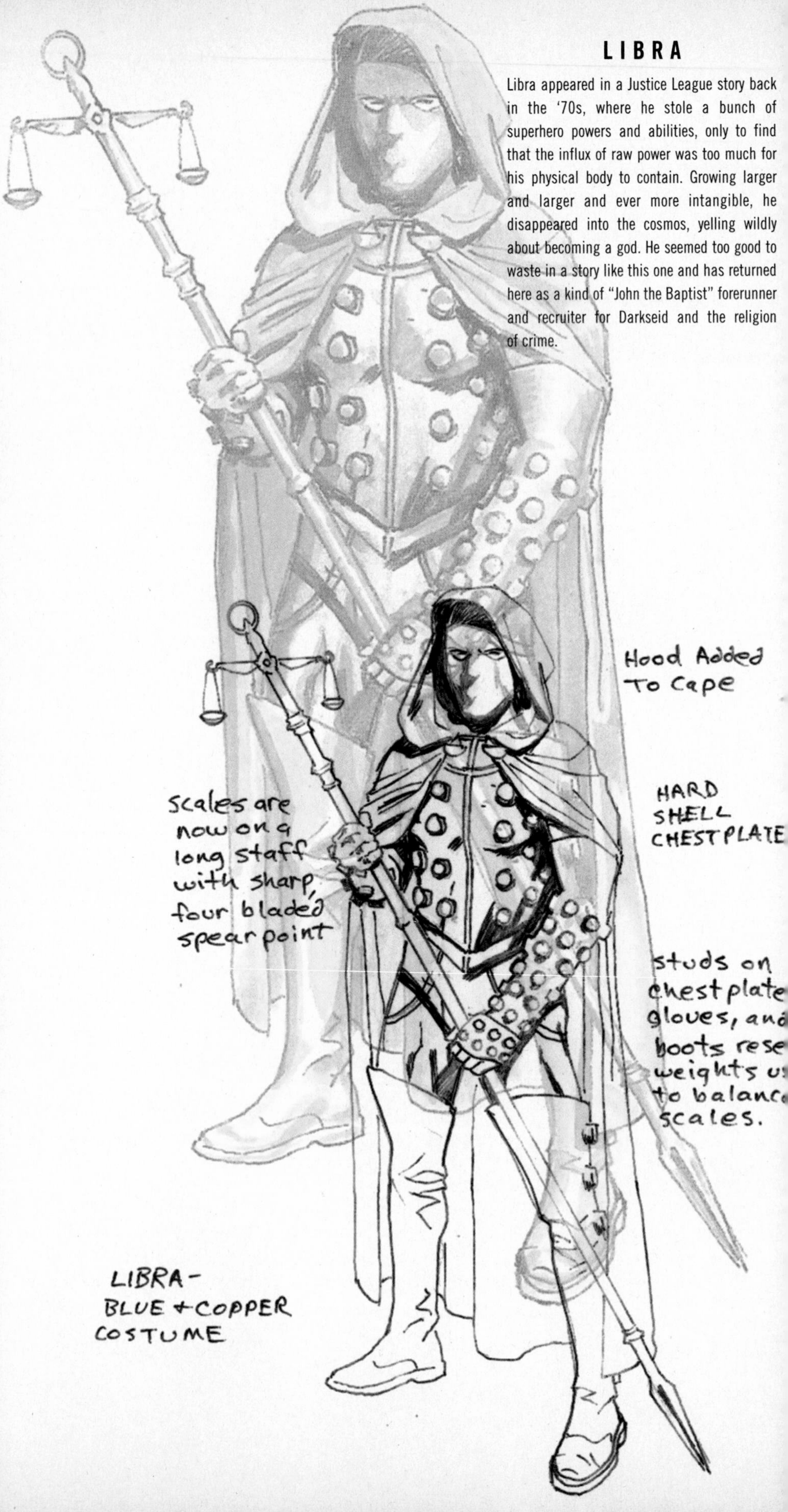
Hood Added To Cape
HARD SHELL CHESTPLATE
scales are now on a long staff with sharp, four bladed spearpoint
studs on chestplate gloves, an boots rese weights u to balanc scales.
LIBRA - BLUE + COPPER COSTUME

KAMANDI

Appears in the first issue and the last. Doesn't require a great deal of work — ripped jeans and tousled hair never go out of fashion!

MISTER MIRACLE

Shiloh Norman stays the same from the SEVEN SOLDIERS series — he is a showbiz celebrity super-escape artist who believes he has experienced direct contact with the New Gods. Mister Miracle is the only man who knows that Darkseid is active on Earth...he is also the only living human immune to the Anti-Life Equation of the Evil Gods and the possessor of a "Mother Box"; this sentient computer from New Genesis is the last functioning relic of that lost paradise.

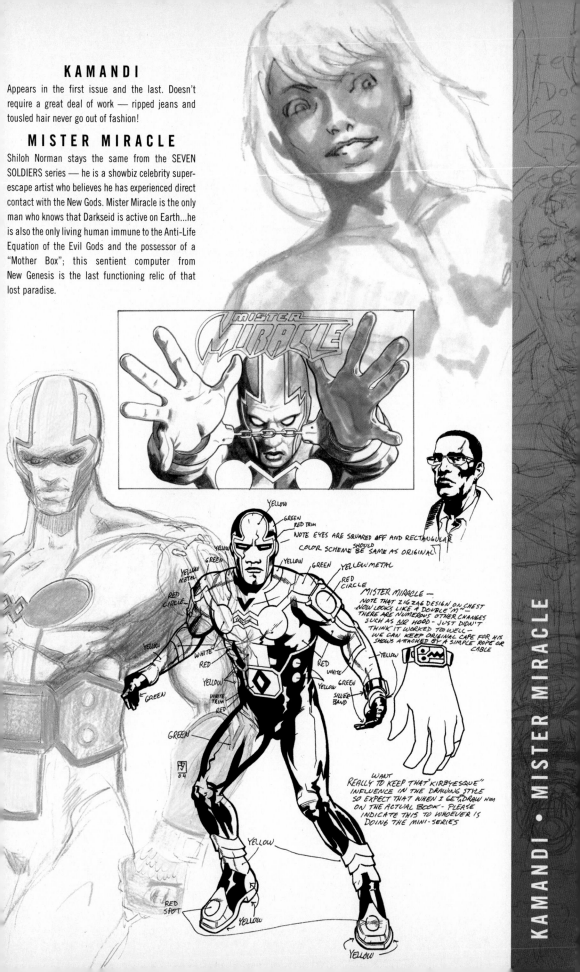

YELLOW

GREEN
RED TRIM
NOTE EYES ARE SQUARED OFF AND RECTANGULAR
COLOR SCHEME SHOULD BE SAME AS ORIGINAL

YELLOW
GREEN
YELLOW
GREEN
YELLOW METAL

RED CIRCLE

YELLOW METAL

RED CIRCLE

MISTER MIRACLE —
NOTE THAT ZIG ZAG DESIGN ON CHEST NOW LOOKS LIKE A DOUBLE "M" — THERE ARE NUMEROUS OTHER CHANGES SUCH AS NO HOOD - JUST DIDN'T THINK IT WORKED TO WELL — WE CAN KEEP ORIGINAL CAPE FOR HIS SHOWS ATTACHED BY A SIMPLE ROPE OR CABLE

YELLOW

YELLOW
WHITE
RED
YELLOW
RED
WHITE
YELLOW GREEN
SILVER BAND

GREEN

WHITE TRIM
RED

GREEN

I WANT REALLY TO KEEP THAT "KIRBYESQUE" INFLUENCE IN THE DRAWING STYLE SO EXPECT THAT WHEN I GET DRAW HIM ON THE ACTUAL BOOK - PLEASE INDICATE THIS TO WHOEVER IS DOING THE MINI-SERIES

YELLOW

RED SPOT

YELLOW

YELLOW

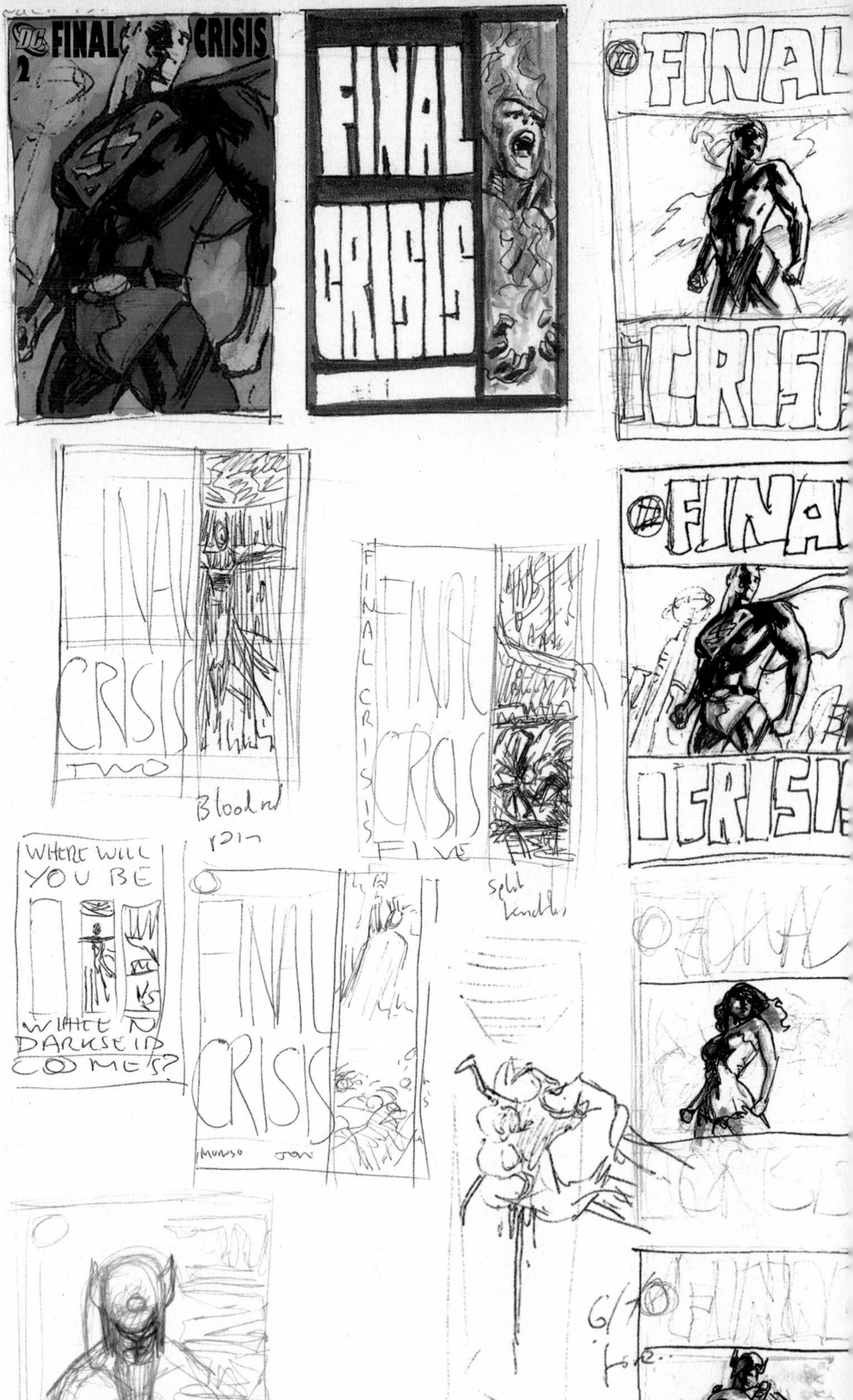
FINAL CRISIS
2
FINAL CRISIS
FINAL
CRISIS
FINAL
CRISIS
FINAL CRISIS
TWO
Blood red rain
FINAL CRISIS
FIVE
WHERE WILL YOU BE
WHEN DARKSEID COMES?
FINAL CRISIS

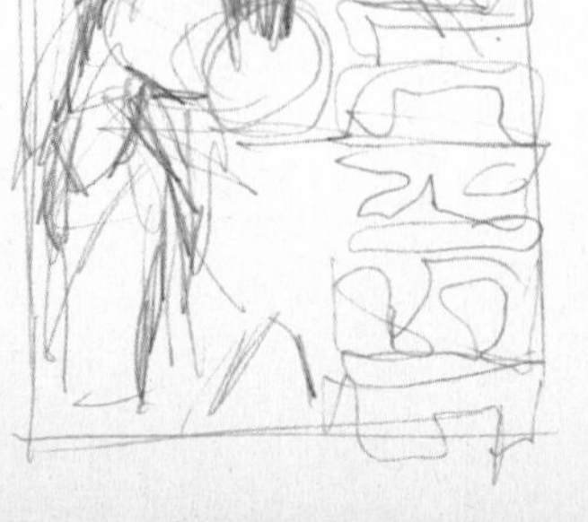

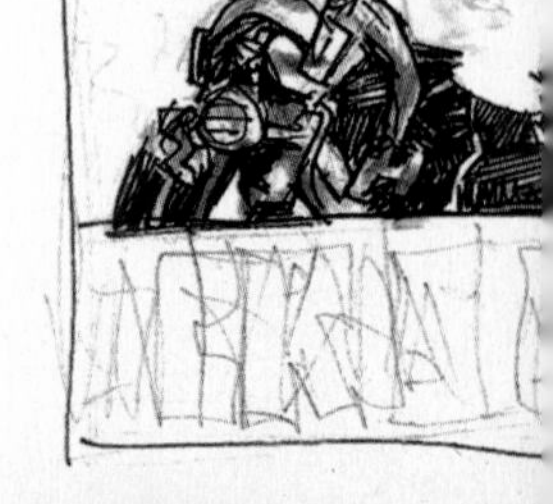
FINAL

Initial cover concepts by Grant and J.G. that later evolved into the final concepts of a full figure hero shot and a story-related sliver image.

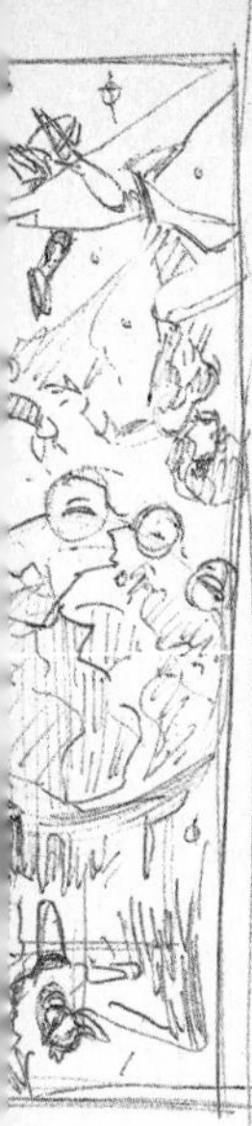
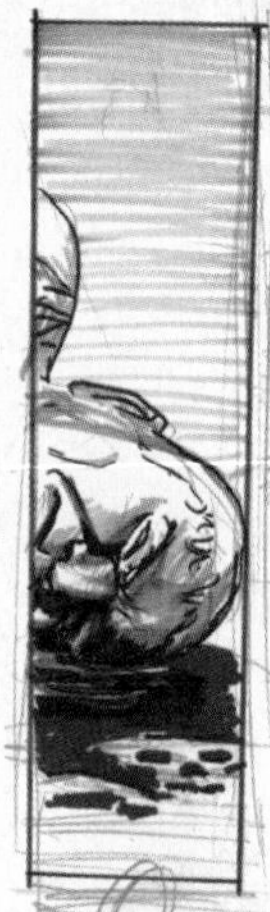
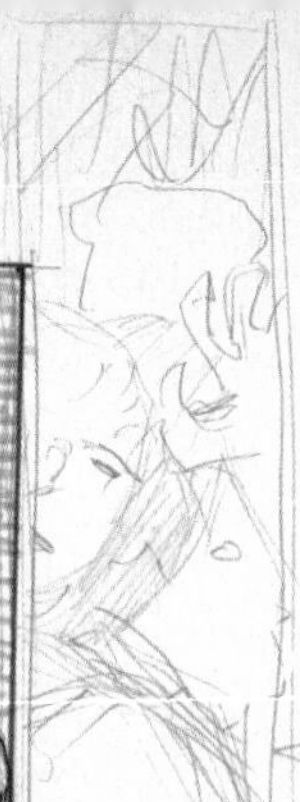
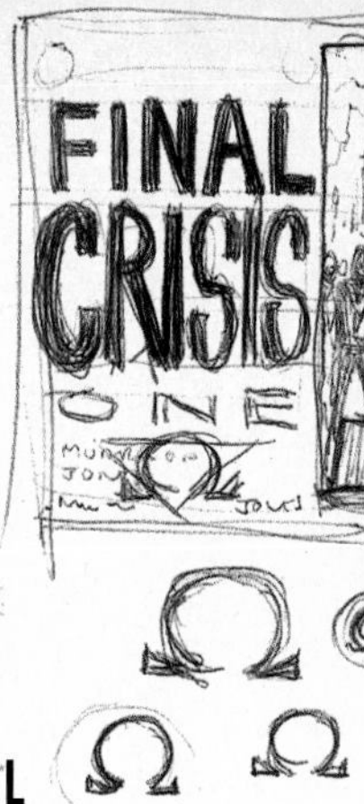
FINAL
CRISIS
ONE
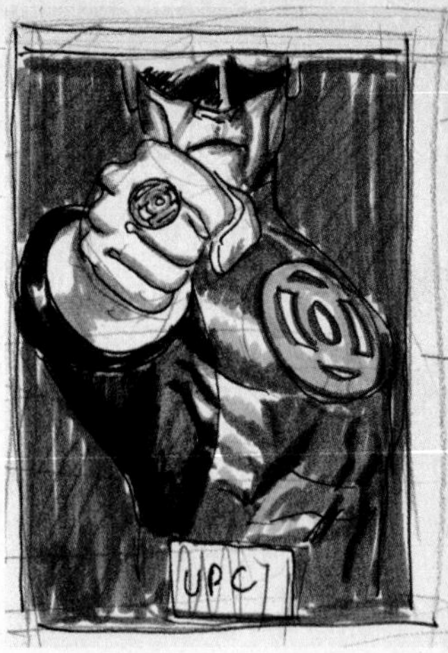
UPC

FINAL CRISIS #1

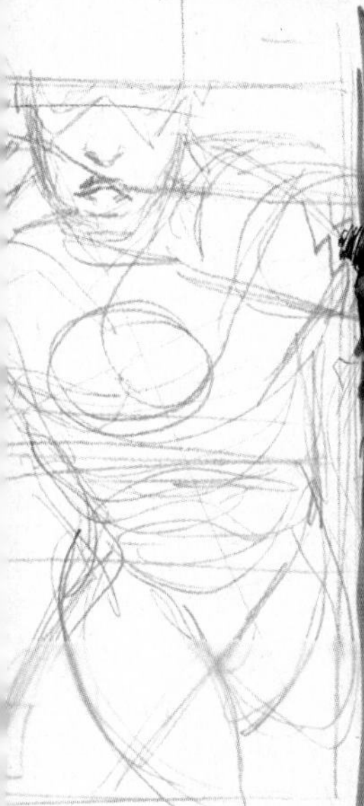
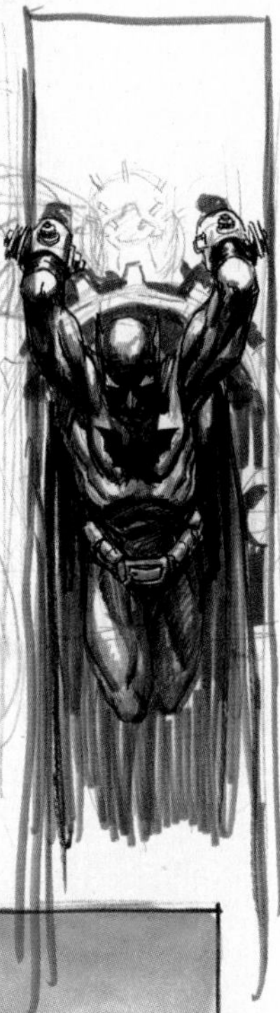
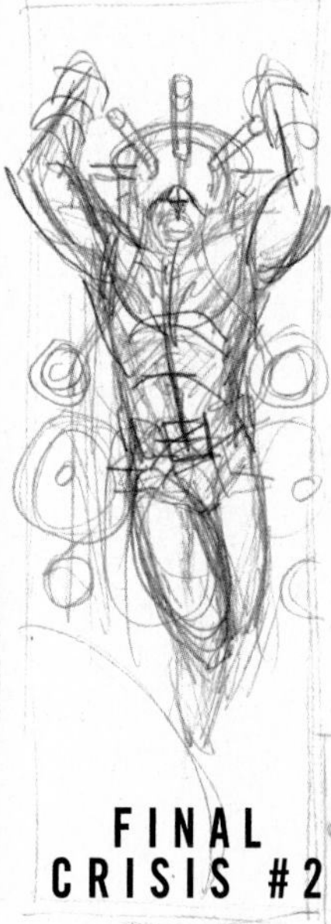
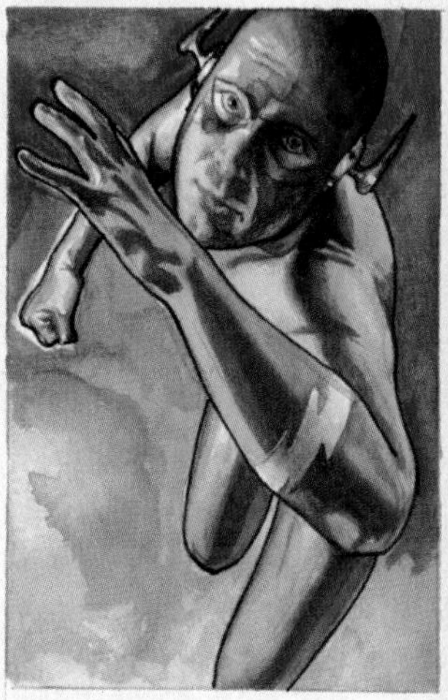
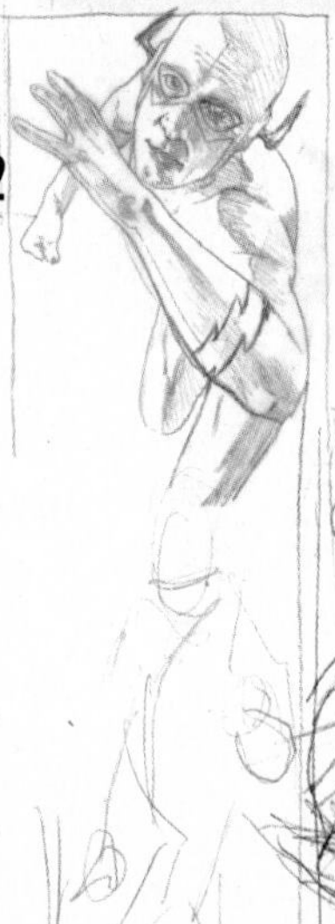

FINAL CRISIS #2

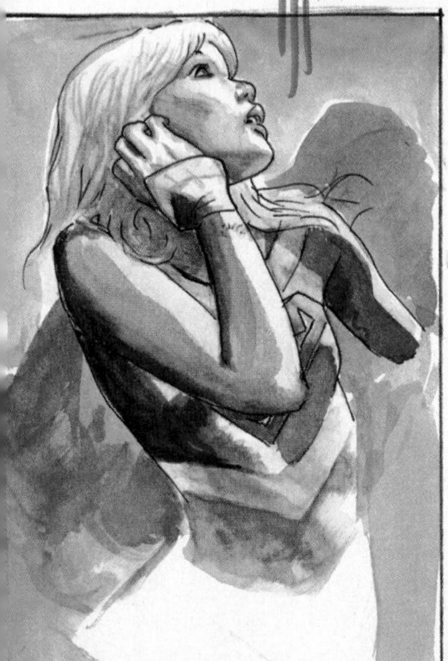
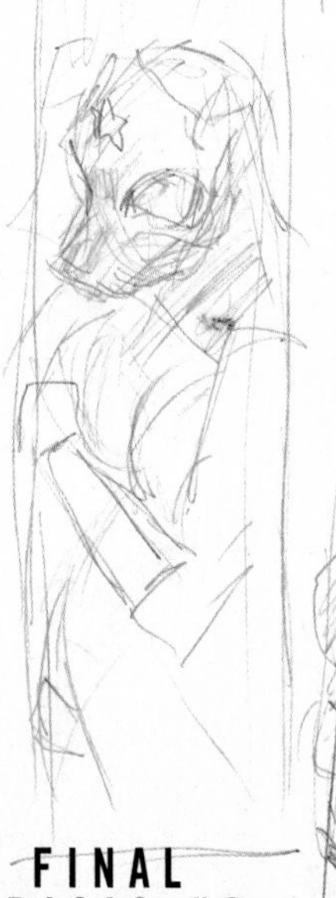
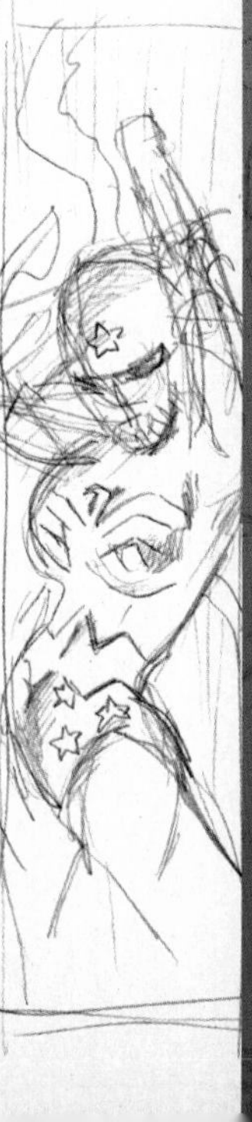

FINAL CRISIS #3

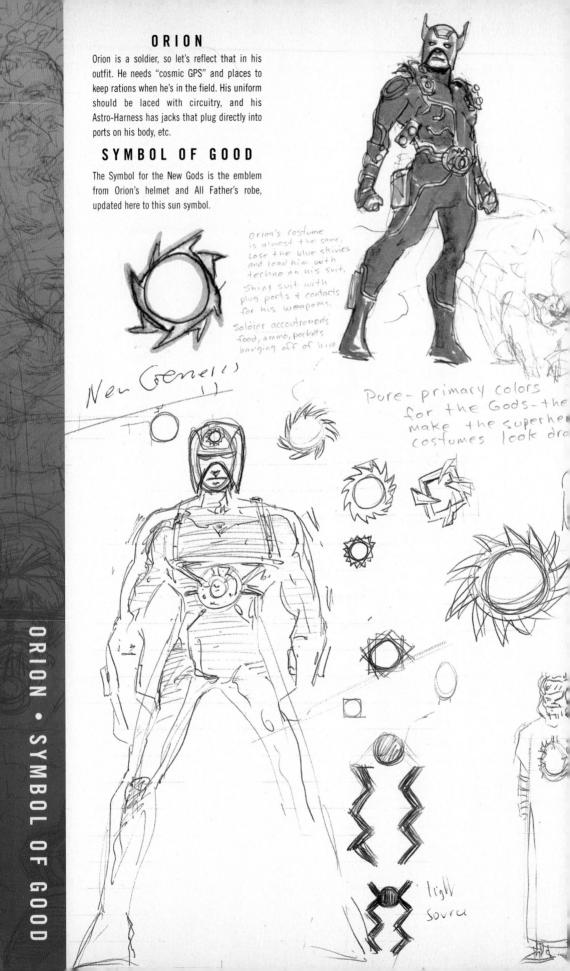

ORION

Orion is a soldier, so let's reflect that in his outfit. He needs "cosmic GPS" and places to keep rations when he's in the field. His uniform should be laced with circuitry, and his Astro-Harness has jacks that plug directly into ports on his body, etc.

SYMBOL OF GOOD

The Symbol for the New Gods is the emblem from Orion's helmet and All Father's robe, updated here to this sun symbol.

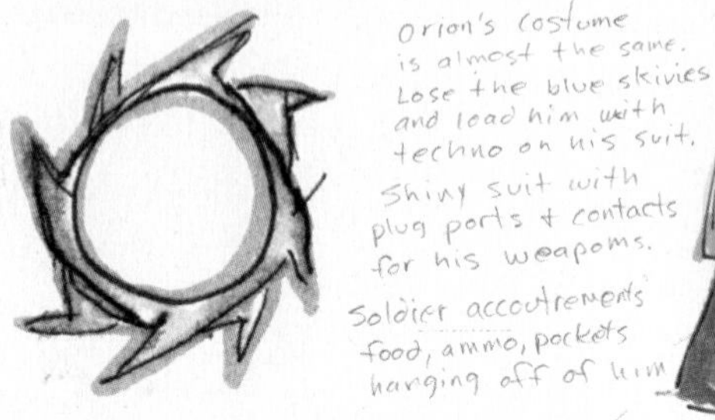
Orion's costume is almost the same. Lose the blue skivies and load him with techno on his suit.
Shiny suit with plug ports + contacts for his weapons.
Soldier accoutrements food, ammo, pockets hanging off of him

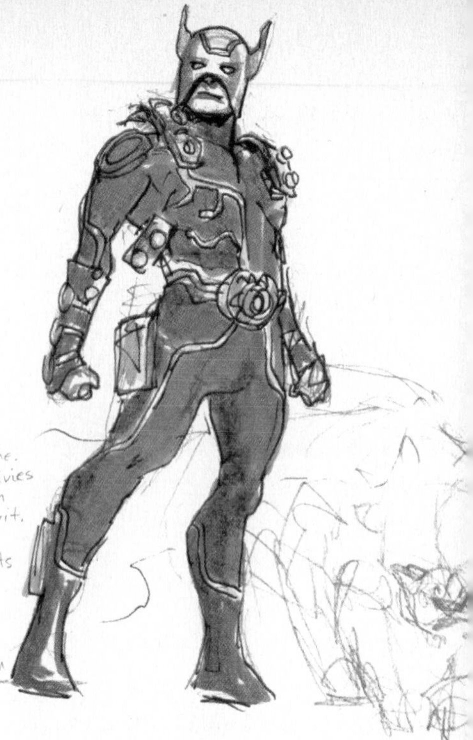

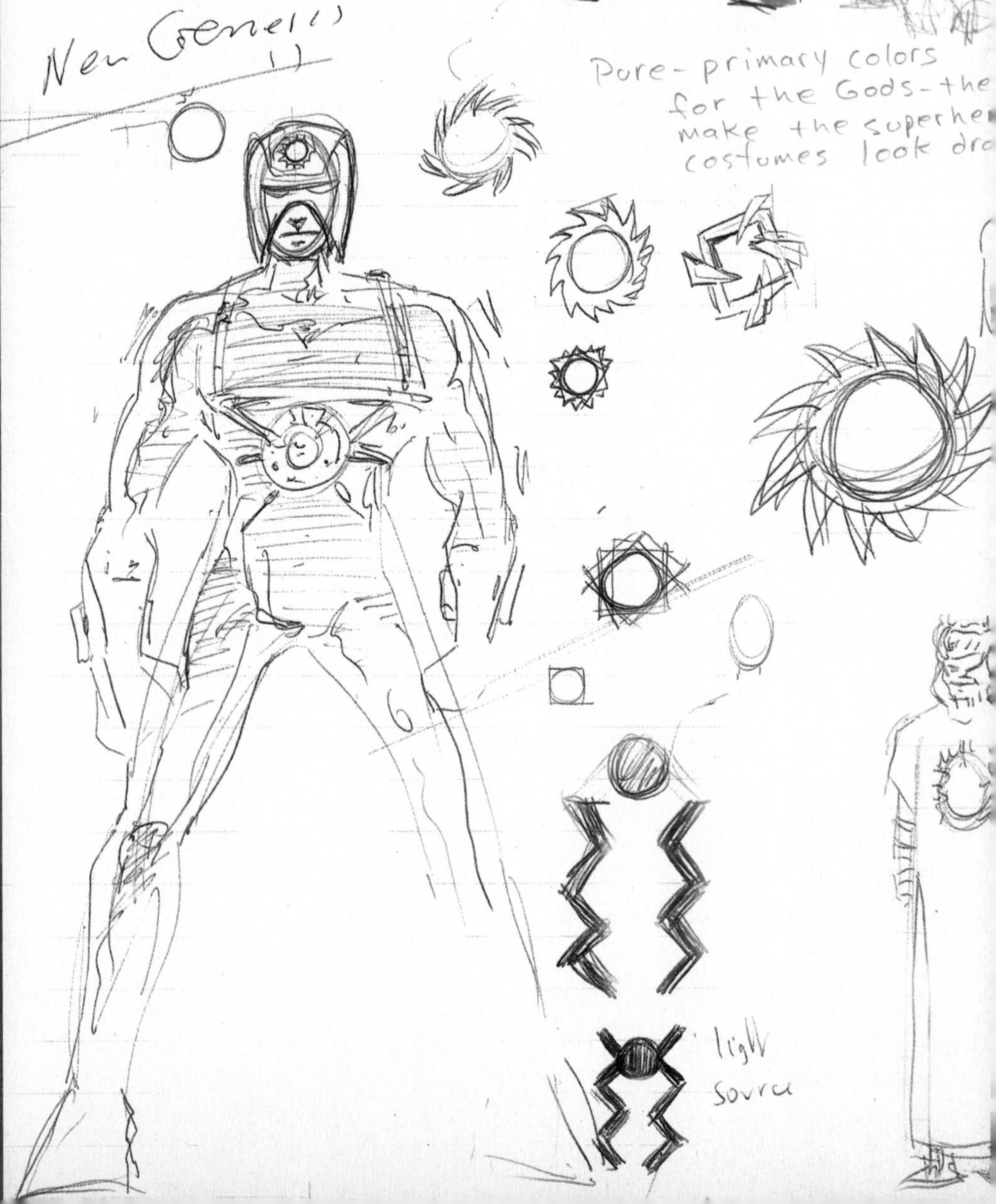
New Genesis
Pure-primary colors for the Gods-the make the superhe costumes look dra
light source